THE OPERATOR

THE
OPERATOR

David Geffen
Builds, Buys, and Sells
the New Hollywood

TOM KING

RANDOM HOUSE

NEW YORK

FOR MY MOTHER AND FATHER,

MY BROTHER, AND MY SISTER

FOREWORD

I met David Geffen at a birthday party at the home of Randal Kleiser, the director of *Grease* and *The Blue Lagoon*, in August 1992. My employer, *The Wall Street Journal*, had recently transferred me to the Los Angeles bureau to serve as an entertainment reporter. In the subsequent years, I developed a cordial relationship with Geffen, occasionally calling him for a quote or just to chat about the business.

I telephoned him at the start of 1996 and told him that I wanted to write a book about him. Geffen was aggressively opposed to the idea and quickly ended the conversation. A week or so later, I called him again. He softened somewhat as I explained that I envisioned a serious book, marketed by a first-rate publisher. He told me he had recently read *Buffett: The Making of an American Capitalist*, which had been published by Random House and written by a *Journal* colleague, Roger Lowenstein. Buffett was Geffen's hero, and he implied that he would be pleased if his life merited a similar treatment.

I made it clear that I wanted to write a biography that would examine his towering professional achievements as well as his compelling personal journey. After a couple of months of discussions, he agreed not to stand in my way. He said he would encourage his friends and family to talk to me, further adding that he himself would sit for a limited number of interviews, all with the understanding that he would have no control over what I chose to write. Thus, while this is not an authorized biography, it is important to note that it was written with Geffen's cooperation.

I had long been fascinated by his success story, which had recently taken another turn with the creation of DreamWorks SKG, the studio he had founded in the fall of 1994 with his friends Steven Spielberg and Jeffrey Katzenberg. Geffen was already known worldwide as the man who had discovered Jackson Browne and the Eagles and had been the inspiration for Joni Mitchell's song "Free Man in Paris." He had produced *Risky Business,* the movie that made Tom Cruise a star, and had been the money-man behind such Broadway musicals as *Cats* and *Dreamgirls.* Some people had their first glimpse of him in the supermarket tabloids of the mid-1970s as Cher's boyfriend; in 1992, he had garnered national headlines when he made public his homosexuality.

Geffen had come to be involved with nearly every medium in the entertainment world, and he had been almost invariably successful. From humble beginnings in Brooklyn, where he learned entrepreneurial skills from his mother, Geffen—with searing focus, unyielding drive, and outlandish nerve—had devised and implemented strategies to propel himself to the top of the heap of Hollywood powerbrokers. Now a billionaire, his influence stretched far beyond the corridors of Hollywood and into the worlds of Wall Street, real estate, art, and politics. He was a confidant of both Bill and Hillary Clinton and was an occasional visitor to the White House.

During the first year of this project, Geffen made himself quite accessible; in fact, he called me two or three times each week with brief stories or names of people he thought I should interview. He bravely authorized me to talk to the psychiatrist he had seen for a number of years as a child. He offered the telephone numbers of a couple of significant former boyfriends.

I was surprised to find, however, that many of Geffen's friends were reluctant to talk, even though he encouraged them to do so. Most, apparently, did not believe him when he told them, "I'm comfortable with everything—say whatever you want." When various other authors had set out to write books about him in the past, he had sent letters to nearly everyone he knew, imploring them not to cooperate.

"Nobody's going to tell you anything really nasty about him because they are afraid of him," Ahmet Ertegun, the head of Atlantic Records and one of Geffen's earliest mentors, told me.

Ertegun's prediction turned out to be wrong. Interestingly, though, a number of the people who did talk candidly—even if they had not said anything mean—almost instantly regretted what they had said. Carrie Fisher, one of Geffen's brightest and most articulate friends, tracked me down at Los Angeles International Airport the day after our first interview, telling me she was panicked about the stories she had told.

Marlo Thomas, who was briefly involved romantically with Geffen in the 1970s, was another frightened subject. At her request, I went to meet with her in Massachusetts, where she was appearing in summer stock. A seasoned interviewee, she was distraught when our talk ended, in a frenzy that she had said something that might upset Geffen. She also telephoned me a few weeks later, worrying again about one truly benign comment she had timidly made.

I often felt like a therapist whom many people had been waiting for years to see. "Can I lie down when we do this?" Michael Ovitz only half-jokingly asked, after finally agreeing to be interviewed. For many people, the process was downright agonizing: Sandy Gallin, one of Geffen's closest friends, grew teary in his Las Vegas office as he re-counted the story of his most painful blowout with Geffen.

Surprisingly, Geffen did not make any serious attempt to co-opt me or to otherwise try to steer me away from the more emotionally charged corners of his life. In fact, in my meetings with him, I was often astounded as he shared remarkable anecdotes. He himself turned out to be one of the best sources for this book.

But the good times between us were not meant to last. On the telephone one morning, he began screaming at me when I told him I would be interviewing his brother, Mitchell, later that day. David and Mitchell, who is ten years Geffen's senior, had at that point not spoken to each other for a couple of years.

"You can't interview my brother!" Geffen erupted. "Tom, you agreed not to talk to him! We can call this whole thing off—*right now!*"

"David, you have one sibling," I responded, reminding him that I had made no such agreement. "Do you think I would write this book and agree not to talk with him?" I also pointed out that just a week earlier he had said "ask my brother" when I had inquired about how their father had died.

While this heated interchange left me slightly flustered, I realized that Geffen had, perhaps unwittingly, given me a gift. Now I knew exactly what David Horowitz, a former top executive at Warner Communications, meant when he told me, "I used to have phone conversations with David that would leave me sweaty."

My relationship with Geffen, it seemed, mirrored all the others in his life. I considered myself fortunate that he was not treating me any differently, for I now could experience firsthand what it was like to interact with him.

On Halloween 1997, by which time I had interviewed Geffen eight times at his home in Malibu, he telephoned me and told me that he had decided to grant me no further interviews. As I was affixing a black beard to my face for a costume party to which I planned to go dressed as Abraham Lincoln, Geffen grew angry and charged that I had abandoned my stated plan to write a serious biography. He alleged that I was now compiling material for a salacious tell-all book. I told him that I had not changed course.

Although Geffen decided to stop providing me with information, he did not, to my knowledge, tell anyone about his change of heart until more than a year later. I interviewed another hundred or so people after that stormy conversation, and many of them asked Geffen if they should meet with me. As far as I know, never once did he tell anyone not to talk to me. In total, I interviewed close to three hundred people.

To be sure, many subjects did decline to be interviewed, although I suspect that in most cases these individuals do not care one way or another what Geffen thinks about their decision. I believe that some of the artists Geffen helped make famous—Don Henley, for example— resent the fact that Geffen is richer and arguably more in the spotlight than they are. I suspect that some prefer not even to acknowledge that Geffen's life, regardless of how it is portrayed in this book, warrants such attention.

I also learned that many people are simply not ready or willing to talk about the experiences they had with David Geffen. Courtney Ross, the widow of late Time Warner chairman Steven J. Ross, arguably the most important mentor Geffen ever had, was one such reluctant subject. Ross had done a great deal for Geffen, but Geffen did not see it that way; he had repaid him by making insensitive comments to the press as Ross lay dying from cancer. Upon receiving my query requesting an interview, Mrs. Ross faxed the letter to Geffen. His secretary confirmed that Geffen was cooperating with me and suggested that she should, too.

Mrs. Ross's assistant called me and said Mrs. Ross would be willing to do only a ten-minute telephone interview and informed me that she would tape it. When the appointed hour arrived, her assistant phoned. "Mrs. Ross will not be doing the interview today," the assistant said. "She needs some more time to think about what she wants to say to you."

I placed additional calls to Mrs. Ross and later sent her another letter, but I never heard from her again. Fortunately, Steve Ross's longtime attorney, Arthur Liman, did agree to be interviewed, and he provided me with invaluable insight into the Ross-Geffen relationship. Liman himself died from cancer not long after our interview took place.

The most disappointing rejection came from Joni Mitchell, whose relationship with Geffen, I believe, boosted his career as much as it did hers. The two had met in the late 1960s, were platonic housemates for a time, and had helped each other through numerous personal trials. She had been a star at both of the hugely successful record labels he founded, Asylum and Geffen.

David Crosby warned me that an interview with Mitchell would be "poisonous." Geffen had said many disparaging things about her to me and worried aloud about whom I would believe in depicting their story. "If I didn't talk to her for the rest of my life, I wouldn't miss her for a minute," Geffen told me without hesitation.

I wrote several letters and placed many telephone calls to Mitchell, all of which went unanswered. Finally, in December 1998, her manager called to say she would do a short telephone interview the next day. "There's at least one story she wants to make sure you include in your book," he told me.

The following day, however, the manager called back and said she had reconsidered. Joni Mitchell did not want to talk about David Geffen after all.

I wrote her yet another letter and—at the suggestion of a friend who had heard Mitchell mention in a National Public Radio interview that her cat Nietzsche had learned to dance—I sent a box of gourmet cat treats to her home in Bel-Air. She never responded.

"Why would you want to write a book about *him*?" Mitchell Geffen once asked me. "Why don't you write a book about somebody who's done some good for the world! Why don't you write a book about Jonas Salk?"

If I have done my job right, the answer will, I hope, be clear.

TOM KING
Los Angeles, California
December 1, 1999

CONTENTS

THE OPERATOR

Batya and Abe Geffen in a 1931 wedding photograph taken in Tel Aviv. She didn't find him particularly handsome, but believed he would make a good husband. (Courtesy Sonya Eichler)

CHAPTER 1

MADAM MISCHA

|||

Amazingly, when the stock market crashed in 1929, Abraham Geffen did not scrap his vacation plans. He had little money and a tenuous hold on his job as a Western Union telegrapher, but he was determined to get out of Brooklyn and see the world.

A year after the crash, the twenty-six-year-old bachelor, a slight five feet six inches tall, set out on an adventure through Africa and Europe. He had lived frugally for years and had saved his money precisely for this reason. He was fascinated by the sea and had read countless books in preparation for the journey. He also had a penchant for photography and purchased the best camera he could afford.

In France, he tried out the French he had taught himself by reading the newspaper. In Egypt, he rode camels and toured ancient pyramids. But it was in Tel Aviv that the course of Abe's life was forever changed. There, he stumbled into a restaurant and took notice of the owner's niece, a pretty seamstress from the Ukraine named Batya Volovskaya. She was twenty-two, had auburn hair, and stood just four foot ten. At 110 pounds, she was a firm, chunky woman. Her face was her main asset: She had a stark white complexion dotted by bright red cheeks and piercing blue eyes.

Unlike Abe, who was gentle and reserved, Batya was boisterous and aggressive, and she instantly sensed an opportunity. Separated from her parents since the age of thirteen, she felt alone in Palestine. She yearned to marry an American, move to the United States, and enjoy its freedom. Batya saw Abe as her ticket. A trifle vain and beginning to feel like an old maid, she told him she was just eighteen.

She proceeded to romance him and appointed herself his personal guide to Tel Aviv, then a world center of Jewish intellectual and artistic life. Batya showed Abe the communities in which poets, writers, actors, musicians, painters, and sculptors practiced their crafts. The population, just fifteen thousand in 1922, had jumped to almost one hundred thousand and showed no signs of slowing.

Batya could not speak English, but she and Abe were able to converse in Yiddish, and the two quickly developed a mutual admiration. Batya was impressed by what Abe told her about his life in New York City, where he had lived since leaving Russia at age two with his parents and younger brother. He showed her the tattoo of an anchor on his arm and told her about a cross-country motorcycle ride he had taken with a friend.

It was hardly a torrid romance, as evidenced by Batya's letters to her parents in the Ukraine. She wrote that she did not find Abe particularly handsome, but he treated her well, and she believed he would make a good husband.

Her aunt in Tel Aviv warned her to wait. She was about to visit relatives in Chicago and promised to stop in New York to make certain that Abe did not already have a wife there. Abe's vacation time, however, was running out. The two said good-bye, though Abe vowed to come back and marry Batya after the union had her relatives' blessing.

Family lore has it that Batya's aunt did indeed find her way to the Geffens' in Brooklyn and confirmed Abe's status as a bachelor. After her aunt returned to Tel Aviv with the good news, Batya was euphoric. Her dream might actually come true.

Back in the United States, Abe proved to be a master correspondent. He wrote to Batya often, keeping her advised of his plans for a second trip to Palestine. He saved every dime he could and a year later returned to Tel Aviv, where they were married on March 19, 1931.

The Geffens lived in Tel Aviv for a few months and then left for a honeymoon in France. They set sail for America from Le Havre on board the SS *Ile de France*. On November 12, they arrived at Ellis Island in New York. It was a day Batya never forgot.

Batya Volovskaya was born in 1907 in Yagorlik, a small village in a lush Ukraine valley, near the Dnestr River. Her mother, Sarah, was an educated woman who ran her own small pharmacy and cosmetology business. But the dominant parent in young Batya's life was her father, Israel Volovsky, a well-to-do Jewish landowner. He was a stern man with a violent temper. His remarkable explosions over such seemingly trivial incidents as the breaking of a dish created a steady fear in Batya and her five younger sisters and brothers.

Batya was inspired by her mother's entrepreneurial drive and eagerly helped her to make the creams and makeup that she sold on Sundays at the market. When young Batya said she wanted to make clothes for a doll, Sarah asked a friend to teach Batya to sew. It was clear even then that Batya had a gift for working a needle and thread, a talent she later put to use in America.

Because Yagorlik offered only four grades of school, Israel and Sarah decided in 1920 that Batya should continue her studies in Kishinev, some six hours away across the Romanian border, where she could live with relatives. She was only thirteen. It was a risky plan: Since the Russian Revolution in 1917, guards had been placed at the border, and there were reports that some Jews were killed as they attempted to cross the Dnestr.

Sarah gave young Batya a pair of white gloves she had worn at her wedding. After Batya crossed the river, she was to give one of the gloves to a man on the other side who knew the Volovskys; he would return to the Volovskys' home, knock on the second window from the west, and leave the glove. When the family was reunited, Batya was told, the two gloves would be hers. That night, the Volovskys waited nervously at the kitchen table. Finally, there was a knock: The glove had been returned.

Soon after Batya's arrival in Kishinev, the Bolsheviks solidified their power in Russia. All communication between Russia and Romania was broken off. In Yagorlik, uncertainty about Batya's fate left the Volovskys heartbroken. At the dinner table, Israel told the other children, "Mother can't eat because she thinks that Batya is hungry." Finally, in the summer of 1926, a letter arrived from Batya. The aunt she had gone to live with had died, leaving her, now nineteen, alone in a foreign land.

A family she had befriended had obtained a visa to go to Palestine, and Batya convinced them to allow her to masquerade as their daughter. Batya knew that her father had three sisters in Tel Aviv, and she miraculously found her way to the home of one of them.

Batya lived for a time with her relatives, but they were poor, and she felt like an outsider. Before long, she cobbled together enough money to rent a small apartment and eked out a living by sewing clothes and baby-sitting. She also learned to speak Hebrew and helped out in an uncle's restaurant.

Abraham Geffen had not known any other life than the one he had had in New York. He was just shy of three and his brother, Isidore, was about to turn two when their father and mother, Elias and Minnie Geffen, packed a few belongings and left their home in Vilna, Russia, to set sail for America. Vilna had been a place where Jewish learning and Yiddish culture flourished. In the late 1800s and early 1900s, however, Alexander III had limited Jewish residence to certain streets, and anti-Jewish riots increased.

It was a terrifying life that affected Elias and Minnie in an extraordinarily personal way: Military conscripts on an anti-Semitic rampage in the middle of a bitter winter nabbed their Isidore, then a newborn, and threw him into the snow. The Geffens revived their frozen infant by warming him in the oven. It was at that moment that Elias decided to seek a better life for his family in America.

The four Geffens made their way across Europe to Rotterdam, where they boarded the *Statendam* on March 18, 1906. When they arrived in New York thirteen days later, they were ill equipped for life in the United States. Neither Elias, a thirty-one-year-old bookbinder with just thirty-three dollars in his pocket, nor his twenty-nine-year-old wife spoke English. They were in good company, of course, as Ellis Island was flooded with Yiddish-speaking Jewish immigrants escaping persecution from all over Europe.

After passing through New York, Elias moved his family to Chicago, and it was there, on July 6, 1908, that Minnie gave birth to their third and final son, David. Within a few years, the family was back in New York, and they settled in Brooklyn. The Geffens lived in a small house made even more crowded by the boarders they took in. They had an icebox and a coin-operated gas meter.

Abe's childhood was not happy. He was frightened of his father, an absentminded ne'er-do-well who took his frustrations out on his eldest son, sometimes physically beating him. Elias had a weakness for gambling, and he once blew the family's savings on a game of pinochle. He had such an affinity for card playing that he sometimes lost track of the time, fell behind in his bookbinding work, and forced Abe and Isidore to help him meet his deadlines.

At fourteen, Abe confided to Isidore that he planned to run away to sea and become a merchant marine. He hung out on the docks of Manhattan and got a tattoo. But Isidore blabbed the plan to Elias and Minnie, and they forbade Abe to leave.

In 1916, tragedy struck when David, just eight years old, was taken ill with rheumatic fever. He was soon diagnosed with chronic rheumatic endocarditis, a painful disorder that was slowly destroying his heart. Minnie focused all her energy on her sickly child, loudly admonishing any who touched the milk she reserved for him.

Abe was jealous of the attention showered on David. His resentment toward his parents grew even more as it became clear that Isidore had significant musical ability. Elias and Minnie arranged for Isidore to study cello at the Institute of Musical Art (later the Juilliard School of

Music). Abe, who fashioned himself an intellectual, also wanted to go to college. But the family's precarious financial situation prevented him from doing so, forcing him instead to work to help make ends meet.

In music school, Isidore changed his name to Igor and had a life-changing experience that had a profound impact on the Geffen family for decades. Taken ill one day at school, Igor's roommate was visited by a Christian Science practitioner who miraculously proclaimed him "well" after reading him passages from *Science and Health,* the textbook written by church founder Mary Baker Eddy. A few months later, when Igor became sick himself, the practitioner was able to work the same magic on him; from that day forward, Igor considered himself a Christian Scientist and not a Jew.

Through Igor, Abe also became fascinated with Christian Science. It was a radical move for a Jew to suddenly align himself with a Christian church, but they were not alone. The brothers were among thousands of American Jews who were drawn to Christian Science churches at the time—a trend viewed as alarming by the Central Conference of American Rabbis, who dismissed Eddy's religion as both illogical and dangerous. Many Jews were drawn to the Christian Scientists' emphasis on healing the physical by means of the mental, Eddy's philosophy being that "disease is an error of mortal mind" and that prayer, not doctors, resolves all illness. Other Jews were simply ashamed or scared of being Jewish and were exercising their newfound freedom to choose their own religion.

Elias and Minnie became enraged when they discovered that Igor and Abe were quietly spreading the Christian Science message to their weakened younger brother, attempting to convince David that he ought to stop taking his medications and focus instead on the healing strength available in *Science and Health.* Although Elias and Minnie did not go to synagogue regularly, they did celebrate the Jewish holidays and were proud of their heritage.

Then, on February 1, 1926, at two-thirty in the morning, following nearly a ten-year battle with rheumatic fever, David, age seventeen, died in his mother's arms. Abe and Igor decided that they would each name a son after their younger brother.

The Geffens hosted a wedding party for Abe and Batya upon their arrival in New York in November 1931. Congratulations were sent from Saint Louis, where Igor and his wife, Julia, lived with their two-year-old son, David Henry. Igor had met the former Julia Seaman, a Brooklyn girl, while playing one summer in the orchestra at the Breezy Hill Hotel in the Catskill Mountains. They moved to the Midwest when Igor landed a job as a cellist in the Saint Louis Symphony.

Batya and Abe rented a one-room apartment at 504 Grand Street on Manhattan's Lower East Side. But the thrill of the honeymoon wore off quickly. With the Depression in full swing, Western Union had made significant job cuts, and Abe was unable to get his position back. He tried to line up other jobs but was unsuccessful in keeping any one for very long.

Batya gave birth to their first son, whom she gave the Russian name Mischa, on February 6, 1933. Living at the poverty line and lacking even the money to buy milk for their baby, the Geffens went on a relief program. Batya was a proud woman who felt a deep sense of shame when welfare workers visited their apartment. Abe was not happy to be on relief, either, but it seemed that he was more comfortable with the situation than she was.

She was still struggling to learn English, but there was one thing she now understood fully: the makeup of the man she had married two years earlier. Like his father, Abe was simply not ambitious. Batya had suspected this from the moment she met him in Tel Aviv, yet it had been precisely his passive nature that had appealed to her. Having grown up in an oppressive family environment where she had not had a voice, she had sought a husband who would allow her to be the boss.

One day, a neighbor, knowing of Batya's talent, asked for help fixing a fastener on her brassiere. Batya offered to make the woman a new bra.

The bra she made was a good one, and word of her talent spread quickly. Her world in New York was populated with scores of heavyset immigrant women, and Batya sensed there was a market for inexpensive, custom-made brassieres and corsets. Facing the most desperate financial situation of her life, she established a small home business, marketing herself as "Madam Mischa." Resigned to the notion that her husband might never be employed, Batya then taught him to sew, and the two sat side by side at sewing machines, making undergarments.

By law, Batya was required to wait one year after arriving in the United States before she could apply to be naturalized. When the time finally came, she hurried to the courthouse and filled out a petition, taking along a former coworker of Abe's from Western Union and a housewife friend to serve as witnesses. On the form, Batya fibbed and said that she had been born in 1909, not 1907. Several months later, she was informed that her petition had been approved. On August 31, 1933, she returned to the courthouse and took the oath of allegiance. Batya Geffen was officially an American citizen.

Before long, there was enough money coming in from Batya's bra business that the Geffens no longer had to accept government assistance. Still impossibly cramped in their tiny apartment, they decided to move to Brooklyn, which offered more space for the dollar and where Abe's parents already lived on New Lots Avenue.

Batya found them a one-bedroom, first-floor apartment in Borough Park, a lower-middle-class neighborhood. Shortly after they moved in, she also rented the tiny one-room studio apartment adjacent to theirs and used it as her workshop. There, she and Abe installed their sewing machines and set up a couple of makeshift fitting rooms. The corner of the workshop doubled as little Mischa's bedroom.

Home to many first- and second-generation Jewish immigrants, Borough Park was an urban enclave whose endless streets of dingy brick apartment buildings were made somewhat less dreary by the full green trees that lined them. It was a safe place where residents did not lock their doors. Neighbors sat outside their buildings on folding chairs on hot summer nights, swapping stories, supporting one another, and watching their kids play such games as stickball in the streets. The fathers worked hard and dreamed of saving enough money to one day buy a house on Long Island or in New Jersey.

The gossipy residents of 5609 Fifteenth Avenue had never before seen a couple quite like the Geffens. The wife was the breadwinner, a true original who wore pants, rode a bike, and refused to reveal her age. The husband was a henpecked man who went for long walks alone and sometimes read an entire book in a single evening.

Batya moved about the neighborhood with the force of a hurricane and subjected everyone to her amateur psychology. She was convinced she was put on the earth to tell people how things ought to be done—whether or not they asked for instructions. She told people how to raise their children. She told smokers to quit. She told her neighbors how to dress and criticized those who did not stand up straight. She had an opinion about everything, and she never once hesitated before speaking her mind.

Batya was incapable of seeing life through anyone's eyes other than her own. She had good intentions and often had good advice, but her assaults were frequently unpleasant, ineffective, and counterproductive. Many times, people were shaken and relieved when the attack was finally over.

Abe did his best to find humor in the situation. "Ah, Batya!" he said typically after one of her blistering verbal attacks decimated a neighbor. "One in a million!" But Batya had more advice for Abe than anyone else, and before long she began wearing him down with it.

The temper that Batya inherited from her father began to flare up as Abe's loafing developed into a chronic problem. She was providing for the family *and* raising their son, while he was sitting in his chair reading Christian Science literature, which she regarded as babble. She knew they were Jewish, and she was proud of it.

Unable to take much pride in making brassieres for his wife, Abe fell into a serious depression. He started taking long naps during the day, but Batya, sensing his depression, slapped him awake. She blasted him with a diatribe about how he could not escape reality by dreaming all day.

Batya's controlling style seemed to work in business, however, though the slogan at her store could well have been "the seller knows what's best for you." It soon seemed that every woman in the neighborhood bought bras from Batya. Thanks to her enterprise, the Geffens had, before long, saved enough money to buy a used baby-grand piano and to enjoy the luxury of a vacation. One August, Abe, Batya, and Mischa took a bus to Lake George in the Adirondacks for a camping trip. It was not a glamorous vacation, but it was an escape from the hot city. The trips became an annual tradition, and soon the Geffens purchased a small canoe with an outboard motor, which they kept near the lake at Bolton Landing.

The vacations represented the few happy moments in young Mischa's otherwise difficult childhood. Saddled with an embarrassing name, Mischa was teased by schoolchildren who called him Mischa Pisha. He was further humiliated by Abe, who, passing along the abuse he had weathered from his own father, hit him when he misbehaved. Abe showed little interest in his son's athletic activities, instead forcing him to take piano lessons, despite the fact that he demonstrated no interest or ability. Abe might have been using Mischa to get back at his brother and to prove to his parents that his child was as gifted as the two children Igor and Julia were now raising in Saint Louis.

Batya was thirty-five when she gave birth to her second son, David Lawrence, on February 21, 1943. Abe was asleep in a chair at their apartment when the hospital called in the middle of the night with the news.

"Momma had a boy," Abe yelled to Mischa, now ten, who woke up and began jumping up and down on his bed in excitement. Abe did not get up from his chair. He turned his head and fell back asleep. "He was that kind of guy," David's brother remembered years later.

At that time, it was unusual for a woman of Batya's age to have a baby. As a result, David was viewed as something of a miracle child. Little David had curls of blond hair and was his mother's pride and joy. It was clear from the start that she felt a different connection to David than she did to her first son, personified by the pet names she chose for

Abe with his elder son, Mischa, who found his name

embarrassing and later changed it to Mitchell.

(Courtesy Mitchell Geffen)

them, "Mischa, my son" and "King David." Batya loved Mischa, but David was now the baby of the family, and he came into the world at a more promising time, when life was somewhat easier for the Geffens. Batya held little David's hands and told him that everything they touched would turn to gold.

David was a precocious child who even uttered an occasional word of profanity at a very early age. The neighbors gasped at what came out of David's mouth, whether the words were vulgar or cute. But Batya and Abe never stifled his rambunctious behavior. When Rose Slutsky, who lived in the apartment next door, complained to Batya that David was biting her daughter, Joani, Batya refused to intervene.

"If you pay attention, he'll keep on biting her," Batya told her.

"So, Batya, what do I do? Wait until he bites Joani's arm off?" Rose asked.

Unlike as they had with Mischa, Batya and Abe gave David carte blanche to act as he wished. When he was unusually fresh, his mother giggled and rolled her eyes. "God bless you, David," she said. "You're so sweet."

Of all the relationships in the family, the symbiotic bond between Batya and David was the most powerful, far stronger than the link Batya had with her husband. She felt that David could do no wrong. She was hell-bent on giving David everything she had been denied.

Abe, meanwhile, had grown fed up with taking orders from his wife and finally did something rather dramatic about it. Putting to work the skills Batya had taught him, he took a job in Mount Airy, North Carolina, working as a production manager at a brassiere maker called Woltz Textile Products. He traveled to Mount Airy for a few stints that lasted a couple of months each.

Back in New York, he also managed to land a job at Todd Shipyards, building navy vessels for use in the war. With Abe off at work, Batya did double duty overseeing the children and her business. Up on the roof to hang the wash out to dry, Batya tied one end of a rope around her waist and the other end around David's. She frequently enlisted Mischa to care for David, telling him to make sure his younger brother got a certain amount of sun every day while she tended to her business.

The responsibilities of raising two children and running a business helped distract Batya from the war in Europe. The letters she had written to her parents in Tiraspol, Ukraine, where they had moved in 1938, had not been answered since 1940, and she feared for their safety. But one day in 1946, a telegram from one of Batya's younger sisters, Deena, arrived at the Geffens' apartment. Batya trembled as she held it. It was the first communication she had had from anyone in her family in Russia in six years. Deena, who was now living in Moscow, wrote, GIVE ME A CALL. WE WILL TALK. Batya was thrilled. She had had many sleepless nights in the last several years, fearing the worst as newspapers chronicled Hitler's devastation and its aftermath. She figured the telegram, giving Batya a telephone number and instructing her to call at an appointed hour, was a good sign.

Citizens in the Soviet Union were not free to call the United States, but Deena had charmed a Jewish postal worker. The woman told Deena she could use the phone there if her sister called the post office at an agreed-upon hour. Batya rang at the moment Deena had instructed, and she heard the voice of the sibling she had not seen since 1920.

"Deenishka!" Batya screamed. "How are you?"

"I am fine. I am married," Deena responded in a somber, businesslike tone. "But I am the only one alive. Everyone else is dead."

"What?" Batya said, incredulous.

"Father, mother, Rose, Shmulik, Clara, Mascia, everybody," Deena explained, listing the names of all their other siblings. "They are all dead." Deena said that most had perished in the September 1941 massacre at Babi Yar, a huge ravine outside of Kiev that served as a mass execution ground during the Nazi occupation. Along with thousands of other Jews, the Volovskys were duped into believing they were about to be moved to a labor camp. Once at Babi Yar, however, they were ordered to strip naked and were led, in groups of ten, to the edge of the ravine, where they were systematically machine-gunned from the opposite side. Their half-sister Rose and her husband and children, Deena told Batya, were shot at another site and thrown down a well by the Ukrainian militia.

Deena explained that she herself was not killed because she had been teaching school in Orenin, near the Polish border, and had escaped to the east in a car with other teachers before the militia or the Germans could get to them.

After hearing about the unthinkable fate her family had suffered, Batya began sobbing and begged Deena to pack up her things and come to America.

"I will never go anywhere! I love my country!" Deena said emphatically, fearing trouble from the guards who she believed were monitoring her conversation. "If you want, come and visit me here. I have everything you will ever need."

Batya did not tell her boys the devastating news about the grandparents they had never known. Instead, she tried to put it out of her head and focus on her family and her business.

Unfortunately, Batya's coping strategy of burying the catastrophic news did not work.

CHAPTER 2

LIKE MOTHER, LIKE SON

|||

The strain on Batya grew worse after Abe's father, Elias, died in the spring of 1947 at the age of seventy-three. He had spent the last month and seven days of his life in a room at Kings County Hospital in Brooklyn. He died a poor man, leaving an insignificant amount of money to Minnie, who still lived in the humble apartment on New Lots Avenue. When Elias died, she had her telephone disconnected because she could no longer afford it. The burden of caring for her fell mostly on Batya, the family breadwinner. She was a devoted daughter-in-law who saw to it that Minnie was comfortable.

Batya was feeling additional stress from raising her older son. By 1949, Mischa had grown into a belligerent sixteen-year-old who fought with his parents and was deeply jealous of the preferential treatment they gave David. Now in high school, Mischa was a hopeless truant who brought home poor report cards. After convincing a doctor to give him testosterone shots, he had grown four and a half inches to six foot one in three months. Fed up with the taunting from other boys and the sniggers he endured from girls he was interested in dating, he took it upon himself to change his name to Mitchell.

Batya contacted Dr. David Abrahamsen, a Manhattan psychiatrist she and Abe had heard speak at a Knights of Pythias meeting, and begged him to take Mitchell on as a patient. It was unusual in that era for a Brooklyn teenager to get psychiatric help, but Batya believed the benefits would outweigh any stigma her son might have to live with if other kids found out.

Meanwhile, Abe and the boys, as well as neighbors and friends, soon began to notice that Batya occasionally displayed odd behavior. One morning, for example, she burst into the next-door apartment of Nat and Rose Slutsky.

"Joani is dancing on my piano again!" Batya shrieked.

Mitchell, who had taken a summer job at a textile factory, stopped home one day to show his parents a roll of taffeta he was delivering. "This fabric has spells on it," Batya said, unraveling the fabric and throwing it around the room. "I'm going to take the spells off of this fabric."

Even David, who was now six, could tell that all was not right with his mother. At a candy store, she did not let him purchase a rubber ball that the shopkeeper bounced in front of them; she did not want one that had been "used." David wanted to fit in and be a normal kid like his pals Kenny Rosenblatt and Freddy Schulman. But his mother's behavior was proving to be an embarrassment, making him an outcast.

Mitchell finally asked his father what was going on. "Mom's crazy," Abe responded simply. One night, after Abe found Batya literally wandering the streets, he realized he could not care for her. The anxiety created by the fate of her family in Russia had boiled to the surface. The pressure on her had also been intensified as Abe's work dried up after the war, and she found herself the sole wage earner once again.

Batya was having a nervous breakdown, and she needed to be hospitalized. Abe returned with his wife to Kings County Hospital, where he had watched his father die just two years earlier. But this time, he was checking a patient into the psychiatric unit.

Never far apart: Batya and her favorite child, "King David."

(Courtesy Deena Volovskaya)

Abe took his sons to visit Batya at Kings County often. After she had been there a relatively short time, administrators at the hospital informed him that they no longer had room for her and that she would have to be moved to another hospital, out on Long Island. But Abe bribed a hospital official with fifty dollars, and Batya stayed in Brooklyn.

Grandma Minnie, now seventy-two, moved to the apartment on Fifteenth Avenue to clean and cook in Batya's absence. Batya's hospitalization, which was to last nearly six months, proved to have an injurious effect on David, who was forced to endure the sneers of the neighborhood kids, who knew that his mother had been sent away. The children also chided him about his out-of-work dad; when they asked what his father did for a living, David made up stories to save face. "I didn't know what he did," he later said.

Caring for David was an overwhelming challenge for Minnie, who spoke little English even after forty-three years in the United States. David's loud and hyperactive high jinks made her anxious, and she demanded that Abe get him out of her hair for a time each day so she could have some peace. Many times, Abe took David into Manhattan to see movies on Forty-second Street.

David was wearing out his teachers at the P.S. 180 elementary school as well. One teacher had conferences with the school nurse in which they discussed his "nervous" behavior. The nurse diagnosed him as having an "emotional problem." He talked constantly, craved attention, and was habitually late to school. The nurse also worried about David's slight frame, noting that he was "very thin" and "small," standing just forty-six inches high and weighing only forty-one pounds, well below the average for boys his age.

Others in Batya's condition could have been hospitalized for a year or more, but tough Batya willed herself out in short order. For the last month or so of her hospital stay, she was allowed to go home on weekends. The Geffens did not have a car, but the Slutskys did, and so Nat shuttled Abe and Batya back and forth.

Batya was back home at Christmastime 1949, but she was still vulnerable and insecure. It took her many more months to regain self-confidence, and it was clear that in subtle ways her life had changed forever. Rose Slutsky regretted that she had not recognized the signs of the deep trouble Batya had been in and now did her best to be a sympathetic friend. One day, Batya came in with a holiday card she had received and asked Rose what she saw on it. There was a picture of Santa Claus and a Christmas tree, but Batya also saw a man standing behind the tree. Rose told her gently that there was no man there.

Since returning home from the hospital, Batya had grown concerned about David and contacted Dr. Abrahamsen, the psychiatrist who had previously seen Mitchell, to see if he would treat both her and her younger son. To Batya, the doctor seemed like a perfect fit: In 1945, he had published a book entitled *Men, Mind, and Power,* which explored the psychological forces behind the Nazi movement.

Abrahamsen agreed to see them, and so David began his first relationship with a psychiatrist. It was the first in a lifetime of such associations, in which he searched for the secrets to a contented life. Of course, with this first psychiatrist, little David was not really conscious of the fact that he was seeing a shrink; to him, Abrahamsen was merely a kindly man who gave him stamps for his postage collection.

Their awful separation behind them, Batya and her special child were reunited and once again walked hand in hand wherever they went. They took the train into Manhattan, and Batya, who now dyed her graying red hair blond, waited as David met with Abrahamsen on Park Avenue. David loved being in Manhattan and frequently convinced his mother to take him to the movies after his appointments. One he never forgot was *Quo Vadis,* the 1951 MGM epic starring Robert Taylor and Deborah Kerr.

Soon after recovering from her breakdown, Batya decided to move the bra business out of the apartment. Her boys were getting older, and she belatedly concluded that it was not ideal for women to be traipsing around their home all day long, clad only in undergarments. She found a small shop, about three blocks from the apartment, on busy Thirteenth Avenue, near the Fifty-fifth Street station of the West End train, a perfect location for attracting customers. The site had previously been a mattress store and was in need of some sprucing up, but Batya saw the potential and signed the lease.

The four Geffens worked together cleaning out the store and preparing to move Madam Mischa's business in. With a new store, Batya felt a new name was in order. She decided to call it Chic Corsetry by Geffen. She had a sign made up that summed up her skill: "If you look buxom, try our bra that makes you look smaller and younger!" Over the next several years, the business grew enough to enable the Geffens to afford their first car, a green 1955 Chrysler. By 1956, Batya had stockpiled enough cash to be able to buy, for about forty thousand dollars, the building that housed her business.

David might not have realized it, but he was being educated by a master entrepreneur. Batya succeeded in teaching him the value of hard work and the possibilities of life under even the most difficult circumstances. She was a brilliant businesswoman who could account for every penny that went into and out of the enterprise. She kept her overhead low by driving hard bargains with her suppliers and by closely monitoring her expenses.

Most important, she taught her young son how not to get hustled. One day, she quoted a price on a corset she thought a customer was trying on, then realized she had quoted a less expensive garment. She told the client she would stick with the price, but only if the woman bought the item then and there. The customer left the store to do some comparison shopping and then returned, convinced Batya had offered her a genuine bargain. But it was too late.

"I told you I would live by that while you were here," Batya told the customer, "but not if you left." The woman began to shout, but Batya refused to budge.

The long hours Batya and Abe spent at the shop meant David was left unsupervised for an extraordinary amount of time. Many parents in Borough Park did not allow their children to cross the street alone, yet

Batya did not blink as David fearlessly hopped the train and headed to Manhattan by himself when he was only ten years old.

David often got off at the Times Square station and went to see many of the best musicals of Broadway's Golden Age. He paid $2.90, for instance, for a balcony seat at *My Fair Lady* at the Mark Hellinger Theatre. To David, Broadway was a magical wonderland that called to him, a world far away from the life he knew at home. He became obsessed with show business and soaked up every word of Walter Winchell's and Hedda Hopper's gossip columns.

The first time he went to see a movie at Radio City Music Hall, he went out to the concession stand to buy chocolate cigarettes. When he went back inside, the Rockettes had just finished a big production number and the audience was applauding wildly. David fantasized that the crowd was cheering for him. He walked down the center aisle slowly, dreaming that he was heading up to the stage to accept an Academy Award.

But while the entertainment world moved him emotionally, it also prompted his dark side. On the Great White Way, David became something of a ticket shark, ordering tickets to the opening nights of Broadway shows and then scalping them outside theaters. Though this was a business for grown-ups, David was unafraid and managed to build quite a successful venture. In the years to come, he sometimes even bribed schoolteachers with show tickets in order to get them off his back.

David also spent countless hours alone in Manhattan's movie theaters. Since children were not admitted alone, he conned adults into buying him tickets. Meanwhile, he apparently committed mail fraud from home by joining the CBS Record Club approximately fifty times, filling out membership forms with different names such as David Deffen and David Griffin. At no cost to him, he quickly assembled a comprehensive library of show-tune albums. A crafty hustler was emerging.

Apparently, Batya had failed to teach her young son one fundamental lesson: the difference between right and wrong. Although she herself was morally grounded and had learned the value of earning an honest dollar, David early on found that it was easy to cheat and sometimes simpler to get what you wanted if you lied. Batya did not reprimand him or explain why such behavior was dishonest and unacceptable. She figured her son was simply demonstrating a healthy sense of street smarts and chose to look the other way.

Only occasionally did one of David's shenanigans raise Batya's ire enough to prompt intervention. He once sat through so many showings of *Singin' in the Rain* that she called the police to report him missing. Another time, she put a lock on the family telephone when she realized David was making scores of expensive long-distance calls. Ironically, years later, the phone became David's primary tool in business, and he logged well over one hundred calls a day.

Perhaps feeling that her parenting strategy with Mitchell had failed, Batya did not want to come down too hard on David. Mitchell had graduated near the bottom of his high-school class and flunked out of a city college after only a few months. Frustrated, Abe and Batya arranged to send their eldest son away to military school in Georgia.

Mitchell's hostility toward his parents was painful to them. As a result, they did an about-face, showering David with extravagant praise rather than the tough discipline they had given their oldest son. When Mitchell asked his dad why he and Batya had spoiled David, Abe responded, "We don't want David to hate us the way you do."

Batya did force David to go to Hebrew school and insisted that there be an orthodox ceremony for his bar mitzvah. Despite the fact that the event was held on a Saturday, the Geffens broke the Sabbath and drove to the synagogue, parking a few blocks away so the rabbi would not know. Once there, Batya and Grandma Minnie sat upstairs along with the other women and watched as David read from the Torah and was welcomed into manhood. Batya made certain that the party afterward was a memorable affair. It was held in Manhattan, at Jack Silverman's Old Roumanian "restaurant-cabaret" on Allen Street.

Just thirteen years old, David displayed not only a blatant lust for money but a remarkable lack of self-control as well. Cash was the tra-

David is surrounded by relatives and family friends at his
bar mitzvah party, held in February 1956 at Jack Silverman's
Old Roumanian "restaurant-cabaret" in Manhattan. In the front
row, Abe is at the far left; Batya is on the far right.

(Courtesy Mitchell Geffen)

ditional gift at bar mitzvahs, and boys typically stuffed the sealed envelopes into their pockets or handed them to their parents, anxiously waiting for the party to end so they could go home and count the booty. But David was not interested in following conventions. Every time he collected an envelope that night, he raced to the bathroom to see how much cash was inside. At the end of the night, he had collected $250.

He told friends and family at the party that he was planning to become a dentist. Dentists, he figured, were rich, and that was his goal in life. "I want to earn a thousand dollars a week, have an apartment on Ocean Parkway, and drive a Cadillac convertible," he said. David's cousin Sonya, who attended the bar mitzvah, later wrote to her parents, "He's enterprising, thinks of nothing but money, but he will have it and I hope it will make him happy."

Unfortunately, though, the event was also tinged with sadness. David was still much shorter than most boys his age—he played the mayor of Munchkin City in *The Wizard of Oz* at Shallow Junior High—and he cringed as one of Batya's uncles from Chicago openly bemoaned his slight frame. "Well, Abe, he's no football player," the uncle exclaimed, slapping him on the back.

Aware that David's height bothered him, Batya determinedly drilled into him the same advice she often repeated to herself. "You may not be very tall, but you will stand head and shoulders above everyone," she declared. "You think of yourself as head and shoulders above everyone else, and you will be." Although she was tiny herself, Batya's booming voice and commanding presence did make her appear taller. David decided to follow suit.

The summer after David's bar mitzvah, the Geffens again vacationed at Lake George. One day, while out with Batya and David in the family's small boat, Abe suffered a stroke, fell into the water, and nearly drowned. Heroically, Batya jumped out of the boat and rescued Abe, hoisting him back into the canoe and navigating them quickly to shore. It was the last time they ever vacationed in the Adirondacks or that Abe ever enjoyed his favorite passion—a simple boat ride.

Batya ordered her husband to see a doctor, but he refused, clinging steadfastly but quietly to his Christian Science beliefs. Just fifty years old, Abe turned gray, started to lose weight, and began limping. He moved slowly and now appeared to be a man twenty years his senior. When Batya did finally bully him into seeing a doctor, Abe told the man that he felt fine.

As Abe began to crumble physically, so too did his relationship with his wife. Like most people in Batya's life, he had been overtaken by her and was now exhausted. The two increasingly complained about each other to others. Batya was angry with Abe for not taking care of himself. Abe was annoyed with Batya for not letting him worship his God the way he wanted. His spirit finally broken, he simply gave up. The truth was that there was no room in the family for anybody but Batya and David.

Abe loved his youngest son and sang songs such as "The Ballad of Davy Crockett" to him. But David, who had idolized his father prior to his mother's breakdown, was gaining a clearer understanding of the family dynamic and began to feel resentful of him. He recognized that Abe was not like fathers who supported their families. Additionally, both David and Mitchell saw that their mother did not respect Abe, so neither did they.

In his last year at Shallow Junior High, David's grades began to sink, and teachers complained that he was immature and "need[ed] improvement" in areas such as effort, courtesy, and self-control. Batya and Abe did not see many of his worst report cards, since David secretly forged their signatures on them. Few people thought he was a kid with potential.

Surprisingly, while David was struggling at school, Mitchell had seemingly turned a corner and achieved some success, making his parents proud. After military school, he served two years in the army in the Far East and then returned to New York, where he graduated with a B.S. in industrial management from New York University. He dreamed of becoming a lawyer and left for the University of Texas at Austin to begin law school. It looked as though the Geffens' eldest son would be the family's big success story after all.

In November 1957, Minnie died at the age of eighty. She had grown into a feisty old woman who complained that she could not walk, see, hear, or smell, but nonetheless she occasionally amazed family members by walking across a room to pick up a tiny speck of cellophane from the floor.

Igor came from Saint Louis for Minnie's funeral, and during his stay he and Abe drew together to help each other cope with the loss. Igor was astonished at Abe's frail physical condition following his stroke and prescribed Christian Science as the only sure remedy. Abe had never formally joined a Christian Science church, and in fact had told people he was an agnostic. Nonetheless, he believed his brother was right. Igor was an usher at the Christian Science church he and Julia attended, and he promised to help if Abe came to visit them.

D avid was now heading to a tough high school in Bensonhurst with the stigma that neither of his parents was quite well.

New Utrecht was an overcrowded public school with a sophomore class that alone numbered more than 1,800. Its student body was roughly half Jewish and half Italian Americans. The majority of its graduates went on to college. The school boasted fiercely competitive athletic teams and scores of other activities, including a mimeograph squad and math team. But there was another area in which a student at New Utrecht could make a name for himself. That was the theater department, and David headed straight there. As a sophomore, he joined the drama club, which managed the backstage activities of the school's plays and musicals.

By far, the most significant annual production at New Utrecht was *Sing,* a talent show of sorts in which the sophomore, junior, and senior classes competed against one another to produce the best musical revue. The revues featured skits and music written by the students and typically parodied some aspect of school life.

After two performances judges named one class the winner. When David was a sophomore, *Sing* was only in its third year of existence, but the seniors had won each year, and it seemed to many to be a rigged affair in which the graduating class was honored every time, despite the quality of the performances.

Students in each class elected chairs—one boy and one girl—to produce their class's entry. The chairs oversaw the work on the many committees that handled the writing, set design, and costume chores. As a sophomore, David worked backstage on his class's effort, *Noah's Ark*. It was a mammoth production, with four hundred sophomores onstage. The seniors won again, however, with a splashy revue entitled *Tribute to the Gods*.

David decided this was an arena in which he could excel. Next year, he vowed, he would be one of the chairs of the junior *Sing*. After getting off to an above-average start at the beginning of his sophomore year, David's marks in Hebrew, biology, and mathematics all dived in the spring. The year came to a close with frustrated teachers bemoaning his fractious behavior. But as his junior year got under way in September 1958, David had honed his political skills and was singularly focused on his campaign to become the male junior *Sing* chair.

When the votes were counted, David Geffen and Sue DeWild were named co-chairs of the junior *Sing*. Batya was so thrilled she decided to take out an ad for the corset shop in the *Sing* program. When a shortlist of show candidates was put to the class for a vote, *Juniors de Paris* emerged victorious.

Although she bought her bras at Batya's store, Sue DeWild did not like David. A pretty girl with auburn hair who at five foot eight hovered over him, Sue was popular but bossy and even a bit kooky. She viewed David as a lying cheat obsessed with taking credit. Her older brother had taken her to thirty-two Broadway plays and musicals to prepare her for this moment, and she did not need some annoying punk telling her what should go on when the juniors went to Paris.

But the production was an enormous undertaking, and there was room for both Sue and David. Unnoticed at New Utrecht until this moment, David finally found his place to shine. He was the biggest cheerleader of the whole production, even helping to inspire the stage crew as it painted a giant backdrop that showed the Eiffel Tower as well as "Chookies French Café," the Parisian version of a diner near New Utrecht.

Abe and Batya came to the Saturday night performance; the winner was to be announced shortly after the conclusion of the show, and David wanted them to be around to hear the results. After the senior *Sing* came to a close, the *Sing* commissioners asked the audience to remain in their seats, explaining that the results were being tabulated and that a winner would be announced shortly. The cast and crew of all three revues waited nervously in the wings and out in the halls for the big moment.

The judges adjourned to the assistant principal's office to tally the ballots. It was not even close. The three-year winning streak claimed by the seniors had come to an end. Pandemonium erupted in the auditorium as the *Sing* commissioners announced that *Juniors de Paris* had been selected as the best *Sing* of 1958.

Batya leapt up out of her seat and screamed with joy, pulling at Abe and telling him that they had to call Mitchell in Texas. This evening became the highlight of David's high-school career. If he did not know it before, he knew it now: He was going into show business.

D avid, now fifteen, was struggling with thoughts that he was different from other boys, who talked enthusiastically about having their first sexual experiences with girls. He, on the other hand, was attracted to other boys, but such thoughts confused him, and he did not know what they meant.

It was an era in which it was a near impossibility for a gay teenager to accept, much less proclaim, his or her homosexuality. It was not something that was talked about fondly in Borough Park, and there were certainly no positive gay role models with which a boy could identify.

Although most behavioral scientists agree that homosexuality is not genetic, both David and his brother maintained healthy suspicions that their father had homosexual tendencies, though they had only slight anecdotal evidence on which to base their belief. David, for example, learned much later that the area on Forty-second Street where Abe took him during Batya's hospitalization was a meeting place for gay men.

David was determined not to let his secret out. He had enough trouble at New Utrecht, where small boys who were not football stars were dubbed sissies. He did not wish to be even more the subject of jocks' torments. There was already a lot David did not find attractive about himself when he looked in the mirror. He was small framed and short, and he had a nose he thought of as big and ugly. He was also the son of broken-down, unbalanced parents. And now he detected indications that his sexual orientation was one that many people termed deviant. He grew more insecure and frightened that people would discover who he really was and judge him harshly.

Mitchell, who had spent the summer of 1959 waiting tables at a resort hotel in the Catskills, returned to Austin that fall, only to find a telegram telling him to call home. An ecstatic Batya told him a letter had arrived in Borough Park saying he had been admitted to law school at the University of California at Los Angeles, a far more prestigious institution than the University of Texas.

David did not have such positive developments in school. A joyous time for many students, David's senior year at New Utrecht was sad and anticlimactic. Not surprisingly, he and Sue DeWild were elected in a landslide to co-chair the senior *Sing,* but the two fought bitterly over the selection of a theme.

One day, Sue was cutting class and hanging out at Chookies when Mr. Hersh, the school principal, tracked her down and suspended her, nullifying her post as co-chair. Sue alleged that David, forcing a showdown, was the one who told Hersh where she could be found. Several days later, Sue's suspension was overturned when a group of kids who held committee posts on the senior *Sing* threatened to quit if Sue was not reinstated. Called a traitor and unable to coexist with Sue, David quietly resigned. Just a year earlier a hero of the drama department, David all but vanished from its corridors.

Like his mother, David had grown terrifically intense and was exhausting to those who spent time with him. He was branded a liar by one of his instructors. He also mouthed off and cut classes habitually. David charted especially poor grades in chemistry and mathematics and appeared to push Mr. Cherniss, his English teacher, to the brink. Filling out a character card on David, Mr. Cherniss wrote, "Rather talkative, self-centered, ignores teacher's orders and instructions. Is fresh, at times, and conceited, as well. Is not as good as he thinks he is."

David did not hang out with the best crowd and took to smoking cigarettes outside the school doors. It was there that he determined to get out of Brooklyn the minute school was over. Now that he was not involved in *Sing,* he took on various part-time jobs after school in order to finance his escape. He worked at Leslie's dress shop on Thirteenth Avenue and then landed a job in the mailroom at Remington Rand, the typewriter and adding-machine maker, in Manhattan. He boldly offered a suggestion to Dause Bibby, the president of the company, on how to improve business in the mailroom. Bibby replied by writing David a kindly letter praising his initiative.

Two months before David's graduation, Abe went to Saint Louis for a five-week visit with his brother, Igor. Since Batya was showing little understanding of his Christian Scientism, and his health was in a free fall, Abe decided to take Igor up on his offer to help.

Ever since Minnie's death a year earlier, the brothers had developed a steady correspondence, discovering they had more in common with each other than they had known. Like Batya, Igor's wife, Julia, had been hospitalized following a nervous breakdown. Like her husband, she, too, became a Christian Science zealot.

After Abe arrived in Saint Louis, Igor and Julia introduced him to a church practitioner who lived just a couple of blocks from their house in the suburb of Rock Hill. Abe went to see him several times each week. When he left on May 6 to return to Brooklyn, a deluded Julia wrote Mitchell that "your dad seems in excellent health" and noted that "the limp has gone down considerably." She also quoted some of Mary Baker Eddy's passages and suggested that Mitchell join the church.

Abe returned in time to see David finish school at New Utrecht. He had a final grade average of 73.59, placing him 529th out of 1,015 stu-

David's high school graduation photograph. It was
at New Utrecht High that David developed his
passion for show business.

dents (another eight hundred had graduated in January). The *Comet,* New Utrecht's yearbook, predicted Dave Geffen would one day run for president.

David could not wait to get out of Borough Park. He was eager to begin a new life where no one knew who he was or where he had come from. When Mitchell suggested he come to live with him in California, David began reading want ads, looking for a ride. Even though Mitchell resented the relatively privileged childhood Abe and Batya had lavished on David, he still felt protective of his younger brother and wanted to see him succeed. David found his ad and left, not even sticking around to pick up his diploma.

It was an inopportune moment to leave. Abe's condition was dreadful, and he had never looked worse. His weight loss now totaled forty pounds, and he was fading fast. A couple of weeks after David left town, a desperate Batya checked Abe into Kings County Hospital. But Abe's doctors told Batya that he had come to them too late. There was little chance they could save his life.

Meanwhile, arriving in Hollywood for the first time, David thought he had found paradise. The land of sunshine, Gidget, surfboards, convertibles, green lawns, and beautiful houses was even more intoxicating than he had imagined. His life's ambition was soon established after he read a new biography of MGM studio boss Louis B. Mayer; written by Bosley Crowther, it was called *Hollywood Rajah.* "I want this job," he thought to himself.

One day while walking around the UCLA campus near his brother's apartment, David was stopped by a casting director who was recruiting college kids to be extras in a low-budget movie called *The Explosive Generation.* The movie starred William Shatner as a teacher who causes an uproar when he has his students write essays on their attitudes about sex. It was David's first time on a movie set. More than ever, he knew that he was in the right town.

Mitchell became engaged to Sandra Getz, a young woman whose wealthy family was in the auto-supply business, and plans were made for a wedding in California that fall. Batya was heartbroken that Abe's hospitalization threatened to keep her from attending. One morning that August, she telephoned Igor and, sobbing, dropped hints that she wanted him to come to New York to care for his brother so that she could go to the wedding. Christian Science was killing her husband, and she was furious with Igor for having introduced him to it in the first place. Igor told Batya that he would not criticize her if she opted to go to the wedding and leave Abe in the care of the hospital staff. Igor told his family that Batya had sounded hysterical and was not making sense.

David was too preoccupied in his quest for fame and fortune to worry about his dying father or the other dramas that filled his family's lives. Thinking that UCLA had a nice ring to it, he began telling people he was enrolled there. It was a lie he peddled quite effectively for several years. In a letter to Igor and Julia at the end of the year, he wrote that he had been attending the school since September.

In truth, David was taking a single night class at Santa Monica City College. Using the letter the president of Remington Rand had sent him a year earlier, he landed a job working at the company's Univac division on Wilshire Boulevard. Since he did not have a car, he took the city bus to work, where he sorted punched cards for use with the Univac 120, one of the first electronic computers. It was mind-numbing work, but at least he was in California.

David had been in Los Angeles just seven months when Batya called and demanded that he return to Brooklyn to help her. She was going to the hospital twice a day to feed and bathe Abe, while continuing to work full-time at the corset shop, and she was worn out. Igor had disappointed her and Mitchell, now married and working full-time, was also unavailable.

Showing that at heart he was an obedient son who could not defy his mother, David returned to New York, though he was not happy about it. He was irritated at his mother for telling him that his dreams had to be deferred. He enrolled in night school at Brooklyn College—his grades were not good enough to entitle him to take day classes there—and went only rarely to visit his dad at Kings County.

After ten months in the hospital, Abe's doctors told his wife that the end was near. Soon after, Batya and David had a fight after David refused to go to the hospital with her, insisting he had other plans that day. Batya prevailed, and the two went off to see Abe.

After lapsing in and out of a coma-like state for weeks, on this day Abe lay still. Batya sat on the edge of the bed and stared plaintively at him. "David, go downstairs and get your father some ice cream," Batya said. "I want to feed him some ice cream."

David thought this exercise was a waste of time.

"Fuck you, get it yourself," he shouted. The rage that Batya had inherited from her father had now clearly been passed on to the next generation. Batya left the room and went to the hospital cafeteria to get the ice cream.

Abe turned his head slowly and focused disapprovingly on his son. "You shouldn't talk to your mother like that," he managed. "What would happen if she died? You'd never be able to say you're sorry."

Two days later, on March 29, 1961, David came home to the apartment to find a telegram, already opened by Batya, informing the family that fifty-seven-year-old Abe was dead.

The funeral was held at Sherman's Flatbush Memorial Chapel on Coney Island Avenue in the Midwood section of Brooklyn. As the small parade of mourners made its way to the cemetery, the teenage David Geffen sat ponderously in a limousine with his brother. But he was not thinking about his father's casket in the hearse up ahead. Instead, he was reveling in his first-ever ride in a limousine.

"You know, Mitch, nobody knows that we're not rich," David said with a smile. "We could be rich riding in this limousine."

CHAPTER 3

RUN, SAMMY, RUN

|||

A few months after Abe's death, David stole a Social Security death-benefit check that had arrived, addressed to his mother. The money was issued to Batya for David, who at eighteen was technically a minor and thus entitled to Social Security compensation separate from hers. David, reluctant to take the risk that Batya might not hand the money over, swiped the check without her knowing it had even arrived.

Given his con-artist talents, it was not hard for David to convince a bank teller to cash the check. The money, amounting to a couple thousand dollars, temporarily sated David's lust for cash. He earmarked it to finance another getaway from Batya and Borough Park.

More than anything else, Batya was relieved that Abe had been put out of his misery; now she turned her full attentions toward David. Batya still called her younger son "King David" but nonetheless was increasingly concerned that he was making poor decisions about his life. She harped at him for not taking his night classes at Brooklyn College seriously. David's talk about show business seemed rather silly to her, and she whined that he ought to go to college full-time and earn a degree, as his brother had.

Following his mother's orders, David decided to give college one more try. He applied to UCLA, but his application was denied. The only school he knew that accepted near dropouts like him was the University of Texas at Austin, where Mitchell had been accepted, despite his weak grades. His application was approved, and, at the end of the summer of 1961, he flew to Austin.

The social side of campus life appealed to David. He enjoyed the notion of playing the wild freshman. He also hoped that the environment might help to stir feelings of sexual attraction toward girls. He went through fraternity rush and pledged the Tau Delta Phi house.

But from the moment classes began, it was clear that college and David were not meant for each other. Plagued by the same issues that had beset him in high school, he simply did not have the attention span that college required. He was eager to get into the real world and seemed incapable of spending long hours studying in a library. He was also an awkward fit at the fraternity, and the experience succeeded only in subjecting him to a traumatic hazing.

When David complained to Mitchell about the schoolwork, life in Austin, and the hazing, Mitchell encouraged him to come back to California. Using the last of the Social Security money, he flew to Los Angeles without completing his first term or taking any final exams. There was to be no further formal education for David Geffen.

Since his marriage to Sandra Getz had fallen apart after less than a year, Mitchell learned that marrying for money was not necessarily a good thing. He had found a new girlfriend, Renee Merar, graduated from UCLA law school, and was studying for the state bar examination. He was preparing to start a small law firm, where his name would be on the door: Geffen and Mizrahi. Back in Brooklyn, Batya was very proud.

Renee picked up David at Los Angeles International Airport. He was surprised to discover that Renee's sister, Annette, was dating Phil Spector, the legendary music producer of such hot girl groups as the

"Madam Mischa": *Batya in front of her corset shop*

on Thirteenth Avenue in Borough Park.

(Courtesy Deena Volovskaya)

Ronettes and the Crystals. David was ecstatic to suddenly have a connection to show business. He determined to find a way to make it work for him.

Alone and lonely in New York, Batya decided to visit her sons. She closed up the store, packed two frozen chickens, and boarded a plane. Once in California, she confided to Mitchell that she was worried that David, who had just turned nineteen, was going nowhere with his life. She was unimpressed that he had caught a fleeting glimpse of himself on-screen in *The Explosive Generation* and continued to press her case that he ought to go to college.

After Batya's departure, Mitchell wrote her a letter apologizing for being a difficult child and thanking her for her financial assistance with his law-school expenses. "Please take care of yourself, and don't let Dave bother you," he wrote. "I think that he will do well also." To David, Mitchell apparently sang a different tune: "You're going to be a failure, just like our father," he snapped.

Before long, Annette Merar married Phil Spector, and she soon invited Mitchell and Renee to Spector's recording sessions at Gold Star Sound Studios on Vine Street in Hollywood. Mitchell and Renee then invited David to tag along. Now David had an introduction to Spector and a front-row seat watching music history being made. In the years to come, he used this connection in ways that Phil Spector never knew.

Spector was the first music mogul David saw in action, and he studied his every move. Spector was only a little more than two years older than David, but he was already a millionaire and a star. He was a renowned eccentric, and most people around him felt it was an understatement to call his behavior unbalanced. He was an egomaniac, a control freak, and a screamer. "They're all mine," he liked to say, referring to his stable of stars. "Without me, they're nothing."

Like David, Spector was from the boroughs of New York. He had formed his own record label, Philles Records, and was well on his way to becoming known as pop music's most distinctive record producer. He was almost single-handedly responsible for defining the girl-group genre, in which trios sporting heavy eye makeup and beehive hairdos sang about the travails of love among the bubblegum set.

Spector created a dense production technique that relied on lavish orchestration, layers of percussion, and waves of echo that one critic called "hormone-thrilling." Inside Gold Star Studio A, where Spector recorded many of his biggest hits, waves of sound ricocheted off the walls and low ceiling, bouncing out of two echo chambers before being captured on tape. In the years to come, Spector's technique became known as the "wall of sound," and many other record producers tried to imitate it.

There was so much activity at Gold Star that David, now twenty, was hardly able to take it all in. He attended many sessions in which Spector recorded such hits as the Ronettes' "Be My Baby" and "He's a Rebel," the number-one single by the Crystals. It was here that he met Sonny Bono, Spector's diminutive lackey, and his girlfriend, a tall and exotic-looking teenager named Cherilyn LaPiere. LaPiere, who was soon to shorten her name to Cher, sang backup on some of the Ronettes' records.

David was aware that the "wall of sound" had made Spector richer and more famous than most of the acts he recorded. He was wide-eyed as Annette told him about their penthouse apartment on East Sixty-second Street in New York, which had a magnificent view of the East River. He realized that Spector achieved his success without either movie-star looks or a terrific singing voice. "I could do this," David thought.

But Spector was hardly an admirable role model for David. Time and again, Spector demonstrated reckless disregard for others and engaged in irrational behavior that many people simply could not tolerate. It was during the time of the recording sessions that David attended that Spector began an affair with Ronnie Bennett, the lead singer of the Ronettes. Before long, he dumped Annette to marry her.

Spector was also downright rude to David, who, though he tried to sit quietly and soak in Spector's genius, could not control his enthusi-

Phil Spector, pop music's most distinctive record producer,
and the Ronettes at Gold Star Studios in Hollywood. It was at Gold
Star that Geffen met Cherilyn LaPiere, later known as Cher.
(Ray Avery/Michael Ochs Archives/Venice, CA)

asm and frequently approached Spector with questions. Instead of being flattered by young Geffen's fawning behavior, Spector regarded him as a pesty gnat, belittling him harshly in front of the others.

One night after a recording session, Spector took his troupe of stars out for a late-night junk-food fest at Kentucky Fried Chicken. "Would you like to go, kid?" Spector asked David as he was leaving the studio. "Yes . . . yes!" David replied eagerly. When they got in the limousine, Spector forced David to sit up in front with the chauffeur. At the restaurant, David pulled out a chair at the table where Spector and his singers sat. Spector raised a hand. "No, no, no," he snarled dismissively. "Go sit over there with the chauffeur."

David was both hurt and humiliated and never forgot the way Spector had treated him. But rather than reacting as most people would and running away in shame, David showed an uncommon persistence, electing instead to stay and learn. The incidents made him all the more determined to become a success in the business. "Mitch is wrong," David thought. "I am not going to be a loser like our dad."

Before long, Mitchell and Renee planned to get married. The wedding was held in September 1963 at a temple in Las Vegas. Afterward, a celebratory dinner was held at the Sultan's Table, a gourmet restaurant inside the Dunes Hotel. Unfortunately, Batya was unable to afford to close the store for another visit and so did not attend. Mitchell never forgot that David showed unusual emotion over the situation, actually crying at the ceremony because their mother was not there to share in the occasion. In that moment, David was able to see the tragedy of his mother's life and all the suffering she had endured for herself and her family. It tore him up.

David had been suffering tremendous misery in a clerical job he had landed at a bank. Inspired by Spector, he now began furiously applying for entry-level entertainment jobs. Finally, he received an offer to work as an usher at CBS Television City. His job was to help people to their seats for live tapings of CBS's shows. It was then the era of musical-variety shows, and many of Hollywood's biggest entertainers had shows on the Tiffany network.

David was so excited about the offer that he would have paid for the opportunity to work there. He also now could pay Mitchell and Renee back for their help in getting him into the Spector sessions. He arranged for them to have the best seats to *The Danny Kaye Show* and *The Red Skelton Hour.* David delighted in standing at the back of the studio when the lights came down and the stars came out. His bosses at CBS assigned him other tasks as well, such as baby-sitting Sid Luft and Judy Garland's children, Lorna and Joey, while their mother taped her program.

One of the few things that David did not like about California was that he became increasingly insecure around so many beautiful people. He could not do anything about his height, but he found out quickly that he could do something about his nose. Mitchell had gone to a Beverly Hills plastic surgeon named David White for a nose job, and David was impressed with his brother's transformation. He took out a loan from the CBS credit union to cover the $350 cost. The surgery succeeded in giving David a smaller nose, but he was never fully satisfied with the results.

After a few days off to recover from the operation, Geffen was back at CBS leading audience members to their seats. On November 22, 1963, during a taping of Art Linkletter's talk show *House Party,* word swept through the studio that President Kennedy had been assassinated in Dallas. Geffen, who identified strongly with the Democratic Party and was a fan of the Kennedy administration, was stricken with emotion.

Many people in the audience had begun to cry, yet, to Geffen's disgust, Linkletter brazenly warmed up the crowd as if it were business as usual. "Well, folks, the show must go on," Linkletter said in addressing the audience. When a man cheered inappropriately, Geffen's fury was unleashed. He lunged forward and took a swing at the man. He was fired immediately, his career at CBS over after just a few months. Out of money, Geffen headed home once again to Borough Park.

He was not happy to be at home with his mother. But he was even more determined than ever to get a job in show business, resolving to find his own place in Manhattan as soon as possible. Through a temporary employment agency, he was given a job as a receptionist at the production offices for *The Reporter,* a newspaper drama starring Harry Guardino that CBS had just ordered for the next fall season.

Eager to make an impression and be promoted, Geffen offered up unsolicited critiques of the show's scripts. His boss was not amused, and he was fired unceremoniously after just two weeks on the job. Geffen was devastated that he had blown yet another opportunity. As he packed up his few belongings, Alixe Gordin, the show's casting director, stopped by to offer her condolences. Gordin had grown fond of Geffen and gave him some advice.

"You should be an agent," she said. "You don't have to have any talent for that." She then told Geffen that some of the brightest lights in the entertainment business had gotten their start in the mailrooms of the major talent agencies. Although it was not a glamorous job, it was a way to get a foot in the door, Gordin said. The William Morris Agency mailroom, she explained, was the best place a young person could learn the business. But competition for jobs there was stiff, and it would be quite a coup to land one.

Calling in a favor at an agency she did business with, Gordin got Geffen an interview at the Ashley Famous Agency, a midsize firm that represented such stars as Ingrid Bergman and Yul Brynner. Geffen saw Al Ashley, the brother of agency chief Ted Ashley. Al raised his eyebrows when he reviewed Geffen's résumé. Having filled it out truthfully, Geffen declared that he had not graduated from college. The résumé also showed, of course, that he had bounced around from job to job since high school.

"My God, this wouldn't indicate that you'd succeed at *anything,*" Al Ashley said, kicking Geffen out of his office.

Refusing to accept defeat, Geffen developed a new strategy that was long on moxie. He would go straight to the top: He wanted a job at the William Morris Agency, the largest talent agency in the world.

This time, the truth was not going to get in his way. He crafted a story and a plan that showed he had incredible guts as well as a willingness to gamble. From Borough Park, Geffen made an impassioned phone call to the agency and was put through to Howard Portnoy, the man who hired the mailroom staff.

"I am Phil Spector's cousin," Geffen lied, twisting his family connection. Portnoy agreed to meet Geffen for an interview.

The next day, he put on a suit and tie and took the subway into Manhattan. The Morris office was located at 1740 Broadway, a little more than ten blocks north of Times Square. Once there, he headed for the twenty-first floor, where a receptionist asked Geffen to wait while she retrieved Portnoy.

As he entered the mailroom for the first time, Geffen was overwhelmed. The room was a hotbed of activity, punctuated by clacketing Teletypes and the noisy churn of a mimeograph machine. The actual working space was small and crowded, with young men almost falling over one another as they moved about.

Just inside the door was a small desk belonging to Jim Harkins, a tall Irishman in his late seventies who was known in the mailroom simply as Uncle Jim. Harkins had been radio comic Fred Allen's right-hand man but had fallen on hard times after Allen's death. He landed a job at the agency coordinating deliveries around the city. He was a bitter and crude old man whose language was peppered liberally with profanities. "Get out of here, you little cunt lappers!" he barked at the trainees after handing them a list of deliveries and pickups.

Portnoy ushered Geffen into his small office in the corner of the mailroom and handed him an application. A college education was not required for the job—only about half of the trainees had degrees—but Geffen lied anyway, writing that he had graduated with a degree in theater arts from UCLA.

Geffen made a powerful impression, despite the fact that Portnoy sensed his story about Spector was phony. He gave Geffen the drill: Being a mailroom trainee is not an easy job. You will work long hours and do whatever we tell you to do, he warned. You will sort and deliver the mail within the agency and run errands outside, such as delivering scripts to stars or picking up Broadway tickets for the agency chief's wife. The pay is low: fifty-five dollars a week. After a certain period of time, it is expected that you will move out of the mailroom and become a secretary to an agent. From there, it is your opportunity to lose. Many of the agency's top executives had started out in just this manner.

To Geffen, all this seemed like wonderful stuff, and his enthusiasm was evident to Portnoy. Typically, Neil Felton, the agency's head of personnel, personally approved each hire, even those in the mailroom. But Felton was busy that day, and he told Portnoy to make his own call. Portnoy hired Geffen on the spot: His first day would be June 22, 1964. He was told to show up in a suit and tie.

Now twenty-one, Geffen was determined not to screw up this opportunity. On his first day, he introduced himself to the other young men in the mailroom, querying each to find out how long they had been there and quizzing them as to how one might get promoted most quickly. He learned that it was up to every man to decide which department he aspired to work in: film, television, theater, or music. Being in the mailroom was something like an audition.

Geffen had been in his new job for only a week when the mailroom was buzzing with news that left him paralyzed with fear: A trainee hired a few weeks before him had been dismissed for lying on his application.

"Who would have thought that they would actually check this stuff?" a panicked Geffen thought. He did not consider the option of telling his supervisor that he, too, had fibbed. He could not take the chance that he would be fired.

Instead, he devised a plan. He came in an hour early every day for four months and rifled through every one of the bags of mail, hunting for the letter from UCLA that he was certain would arrive, informing the Morris office that the university had no idea who David Geffen was. Portnoy attributed his early arrivals to ambition, but in truth it was simply terror.

The letter eventually came. When it did, Geffen took the envelope and begged his brother Mitchell to help him with his plan. Mitchell agreed and drafted a letter saying that David had graduated from UCLA with an undergraduate degree in theater arts. He then mailed it from his law office in Los Angeles. In the surest sign yet that Geffen's moral compass was off-kilter, he did not believe that he had done anything wrong. He felt he had simply exercised his gift for resourcefulness. This was to become the most-repeated tale of his career, and he proudly boasted about it throughout his life.

Men at the Morris office could not help but see that young Geffen bore a striking resemblance to Sammy Glick, the disturbing antihero of *What Makes Sammy Run,* Budd Schulberg's 1941 novel. Demonstrating an arrogant disregard for the views and welfare of his fellow people, Sammy Glick was a backstabbing huckster who employed appalling tricks to run to the top in Hollywood, kicking others off the ladder as he rose higher and higher.

Having tossed aside all notions of right and wrong, young David Geffen simply lived by different rules than did the rest of society around him. Unconstrained by traditional ideas of acceptable social behavior, he was free to use all of the resources at his fingertips to achieve his lofty goals. If Geffen read the book Schulberg wrote as an angry attack on antisocial behavior, he likely viewed it as a valuable textbook. Nothing was going to stop him.

From the first day, Geffen read every memo he came in contact with and feverishly studied the Teletype that transmitted messages to and from the agency's West Coast office. Long-distance phone calls were expensive, and agents made them only in the case of emergencies; as a result, the majority of the company's business was done in full view of anyone who read the Teletype. Geffen loved delivering the mail and quickly trained himself to read memos that were upside down on people's desks. He chatted up the mailroom graduates who were now secretaries and joked about his "cousin" Phil Spector.

Employing the strong work ethic he had learned from his mother, Geffen simply worked harder than anyone else. He came in early and stayed late. Each weekend, four trainees were sent down the street to help out with small jobs on *The Ed Sullivan Show,* which the agency had "packaged"; Geffen volunteered frequently for the task. For once, Geffen had found a subject at which he could excel. The Morris office was his college; the mailroom was the library.

He also found a new best friend. David Krebs was a good-looking kid who also had just joined the mailroom. Although they were both from Brooklyn, Krebs and Geffen had had very different lives. Krebs was from Sheepshead Bay, a slightly more affluent neighborhood than Borough Park. He had also managed to achieve not one but three degrees from Columbia University.

Like all trainees, Geffen and Krebs were sent to three months of secretarial school at night to learn how to type and take dictation. There the two young men bonded.

After being less than popular in high school, Geffen was not about to do anything that might jeopardize his status among the in crowd at the Morris office. So, since most of the guys in the mailroom smoked marijuana, he did too. Although he was not a pothead like some of the others, he played along and was the one who gave Krebs his first joint.

At dinner once at Krebs's parents' home in Sheepshead Bay, Krebs's mother was charmed by her son's new coworker. She suggested Geffen would be a perfect match for Krebs's sister, Judy. Geffen carefully ignored hints that he ought to ask her out on a date.

Geffen and Krebs began going together on the daily "Broadway run," which entailed stopping at various theaters to pick up tickets for the agency's top executives and whichever clients were in town. The job could sometimes be accomplished in as little as thirty minutes, but the trainees were not expected back at the agency for an hour or so. Geffen and Krebs killed the extra time in a coffee shop, with Krebs listening intently as Geffen plotted their careers. Geffen told Krebs he intended to get rich fast and had been thinking of ways to leapfrog up the agency ladder. A man could spend a lifetime at the Morris office, building a career, and one day have enough money to buy a house in the suburbs. But Geffen did not have the patience to wait.

Geffen was entitled to a short Christmas vacation that first year, but, in an indication of his single-minded determination to succeed at the agency, he decided instead to spend the time working in the mailroom of the Los Angeles office. It was then that he met Barry Diller, a Jewish kid from Beverly Hills who years later became one of Geffen's best friends, when the two were among the most powerful moguls in all of Hollywood. Together they would inspire both awe and fear, and become the mailroom's most famous and successful graduates. But initially, Diller and Geffen did not make an immediate connection. They were both focused and driven young men, but they were from vastly different socioeconomic backgrounds and did not instantly see the traits in each other that later caused them to bond. Geffen did, however, make an impression on Diller. He thought Geffen was a rather odd duck for using his vacation time to work in the company's other office.

Back at work in the New York mailroom, Geffen convinced some of the established Morris agents to let him hang with them in the back of clubs in Greenwich Village, such as the Bitter End, the Gas Light Café, and the Café Au Go Go.

One night at the Gas Light Café, he struck up a conversation with Herb Gart, a manager who had recently come to New York with the comedian Bill Cosby. Geffen, dressed in his usual uniform of a dark suit, white shirt, and tie, told Gart his plan: He was only in the mailroom now, but he wanted to make a name for himself signing actors. He saw Broadway plays and musicals all the time, read scripts voraciously, and imagined which actors could break out in which parts. One day, he promised, he would represent movie stars and directors.

Gart was impressed and looked for an opportunity to help Geffen. When Marty Litke, an agent who had been at the Morris office for about eight years, wanted to sign one of Gart's clients, an oddball comedian and songwriter named Biff Rose, Gart offered an ultimatum: You can have him, but only if this kid Geffen from the mailroom is involved. "Who?" Litke asked. Biff Rose signed to the Morris office, and Geffen was one of the three agents assigned to represent him. He had his first client.

He next set his sights on romancing Nat Lefkowitz, the celebrated head of Morris's New York office. In an obvious reference to the diminutive stature of Lefkowitz, as well as other senior executives, the joke at the agency was that if you were short, you would go all the way to the top. Geffen, who had achieved his full height of five foot seven and a half, knew that at the very least he had that in his favor.

Trained as an accountant and a lawyer, Lefkowitz had joined the agency's financial department in 1927. A Brooklyn native, he was a conservative man with graying hair who did not say much and spoke quietly when he did. But he was respected widely at the agency and in the entertainment world at large and was credited with guiding the agency from what was primarily a vaudeville office to a full-service company representing talent in theater, movies, radio, and television. At his funeral in 1984, the officiating rabbi called him a man of "moral instincts with ethical imperatives."

After hearing that Lefkowitz, who was fifty-six, came to work on Saturdays, Geffen decided he would, too. For weeks, Geffen stalked Lefkowitz, whose office was on the twentieth floor, until one Saturday the two stood together waiting for the elevator. Geffen introduced himself and struck up a conversation. Lefkowitz, impressed with this display of unbridled ambition, asked him if he would join him for a sandwich at the Carnegie Deli, around the corner on Seventh Avenue. Geffen flattered the executive and begged him to regale him with stories about the entertainment business.

Lefkowitz liked Geffen and was impressed by both his doggedness and his appropriately reverential manner. He soon introduced him to his wife, Sally, and they sometimes invited David to join them for dinner at their apartment on Central Park West or for a night out at the theater. The other young men in the mailroom were stunned to find that Geffen was not lying when he said he had formed a friendship with the president.

Enlisting Lefkowitz's support was a brilliant move. Geffen had realized the value of having a "rabbi" in life, someone powerful to help him get what he wanted. He demonstrated an uncanny ability to understand the vulnerabilities of such men and was not intimidated by them. Unlike most trainees, who could not see beyond the immediate tasks at hand, Geffen saw a much bigger picture. Lefkowitz became the first in a long string of father figures that Geffen adopted as mentors. Clearly, Geffen benefited the most in these relationships, but in many cases those he enlisted for help also felt enriched by the experience.

He had insinuated himself in the business at the Morris office and made himself irresistible and unavoidable at the same time. Some of his peers saw his flattery act as nothing more than simple brownnosing and were turned off by his brash style. But others, including higher-ups such as Lefkowitz, found Geffen charming. Lefkowitz quickly developed a paternal feeling toward the young man, seeing in him what he saw in himself: Someone who was devoted to the craft twenty-four hours a day and who loved every minute of it.

Geffen worked in the mailroom for six months. He was delivering the mail one day when he was stopped by Scott Shukat, who offered him a job as a secretary to Ben Griefer, one of the office's most respected television agents. Shukat had been Griefer's secretary, responsible for answering the telephone and other clerical duties, but had now been promoted to Griefer's assistant, responsible for such things as budgeting talent costs and monitoring activity at the TV studios during tapings. Geffen was thrilled to be a part of the action.

Brooklyn-born and raised in Queens, Shukat had joined the mailroom near the end of 1962. Prior to that, he had pursued a career as an actor. His big chance had come in 1959, when he was cast in the Broadway production of *Fiorello!* Unfortunately, a telegram arrived the next day calling him into service in the army.

He, too, had lied on his employment application at the Morris office, listing his stage name, Scott Logan, Jr. But when he arrived at the office on the first day and saw the executives' names on the company directory in the lobby—Lefkowitz, Kalcheim, Griefer, Weiss, and so on—he hustled back to the personnel office and told them his given Jewish name.

It soon became clear that Geffen and Shukat were quite different. Shukat was a smart and hardworking Boy Scout, a patient guy who respected the rules. Geffen, on the other hand, was a fast-talking operator looking to beat the system. The fact that Shukat had been Griefer's secretary for nearly two years made Geffen think he was nothing more than a trained seal who was going nowhere fast. Geffen did not listen to his pal, David Krebs, who defended Shukat, a fraternity brother of his at Columbia.

Shukat and Geffen sat side by side just outside of Griefer's office. Although Shukat was essentially Geffen's supervisor, he felt threatened by Geffen and was envious of his drive. Shukat stopped into the office one night well after business hours and was stunned to find Geffen there, making deals on the telephone. "I saw this actor, he's great, and I'm going to try to get him to be seen for that show you were talking about," Shukat overheard Geffen say. Shukat himself had barely started to sign clients.

Much of the time, Geffen was on the telephone with John Hartmann, a young agent he had befriended on his Christmastime trip to the Los Angeles office. Like Geffen, Hartmann was something of a Sammy Glick type. When Geffen met him, Hartmann had just returned from a special assignment as a gofer for Colonel Tom Parker, the manager of Elvis Presley, one of the Morris office's most important clients.

To cover some of the long-distance phone calls, Geffen called the local switchboard at CBS and claimed to be Jerry Rubin, a CBS executive he had met. Disguising his voice, he told the operator that he was calling from out of town and needed to be transferred to an agent at the Morris office in Los Angeles. Geffen and Hartmann talked on the phone for an hour or more on CBS's dime.

Using the small pay increase that came with his promotion to secretary, Geffen moved eagerly out of his mother's apartment and into Manhattan for the first time. For $130 a month, he rented a tiny one-room apartment in the Wilshire House, a building on West Fifty-eighth Street that was an unofficial dormitory for young men at the Morris office. Batya did not understand David's new job, but she was proud that he was demonstrating responsible behavior for the first time in his life. He looked smart as he left for the office dressed in a suit and tie every morning, and she was sad when he moved his things out. Once again, she was alone in the apartment on Fifteenth Avenue.

Now twenty-two, Geffen began to mentor other secretaries and trainees. Jeff Wald, who supported his petty salary by peddling marijuana in the mailroom, immediately latched onto Geffen. Larry Kurzon was initially turned off by Geffen's refrain about Phil Spector, but he too soon found his charm intoxicating. Hal Ray was another college dropout who liked David's style; he also got an apartment in the Wilshire House.

But by far the most important alliance Geffen made was with Elliot Roberts, a dope-smoking clown who had grown up across the street from Wald. In the years to come, Roberts hitched his star to Geffen's and played a critically important role in David's life. Of all the friends Geffen made at the Morris office, Roberts was the one who saw Geffen's gift most clearly and who recognized that his own talent, matched with Geffen's, would make a potent combination.

Born Elliot Rabinowitz, Roberts had dropped out of two colleges after graduating from high school, changed his name, and decided to pursue a career as an actor. The big roles did not come, though, and his biggest audiences were the people who took the studio tours he led as a page at NBC. He eventually gave up acting and joined the William Morris mailroom at the suggestion of Hal Ray. Although he was not as swift as Geffen, he was nevertheless a hustler, and he had an outrageous sense of humor. David took Roberts under his wing, instructing him to meet him at the office at 6:30 A.M.

"David, no one's there," Roberts said.

Geffen responded with a knowing glance. "That's why we *will* be." He showed Roberts how he had taught himself the rudiments of deal making by studying memos and opening the mail.

Geffen was a rule breaker, and his new cronies believed in him and dreamed of being carried to the top on his coattails. One Saturday, Geffen and Kurzon were snooping around the office when Geffen came across an envelope marked "confidential." He opened it anyway and found a gold mine: a list of all the employees at the Morris office and their weekly salaries.

The top brass at the Morris office indeed encouraged the trainees to read the mail and study memos, but this type of investigation was not what they had in mind. Kurzon was abashed. "David, put that away," he said. "I'm scared. This is too heavy. But let me see just a couple of names!" The two studied the list.

Geffen hustled and made a copy for himself. "Once David had that information, he could play people against each other," Kurzon recalled, years later. "It gave him tremendous leverage because he could say to his boss, 'I understand that this guy is making this, so I have to make that.'"

At night, Geffen and his followers made the rounds in the Village with the older agents and then hiked back to the Wilshire House, where they smoked grass and played cards. Geffen, Wald, Ray, Roberts, and Kurzon delighted in telephoning Scott Shukat in the middle of the night to wake and annoy him.

"If you wake me up one more time, Geffen, I'm going to throw you out the window," Shukat screamed.

Ben Griefer had joined the Morris office in 1950, overseeing one of early television's most popular programs, Texaco Star Theater's *The Milton Berle Show*. A gentle straight shooter, Griefer supervised production of the New York–based TV programs the agency packaged. The era of variety shows was in its last days, but it was still quite a profitable business. Revenues from shows such as *Sing Along with Mitch* and *The Jimmy Dean Show* were keeping the lights on at the Morris office.

Griefer annoyed some of the agents at William Morris because he did not give preferential treatment to the agency's clients. A lot of them thought he should simply book his shows with Morris clients such as Shelley Winters, Danny Thomas, and Elizabeth Taylor. But Griefer believed his job was to make his shows successful and use the best talent, regardless of which agency represented them.

Unlike everyone else at the Morris office, Griefer spent time talking with agents at competitive shops, such as General Artists, Ashley Famous Agency, and Associated Booking. Every year or so, he compiled for Nat Lefkowitz every agency's client list, based on the information he had gathered from his talent scouting. It was not an easy task. Agencies guarded their client lists fiercely, fearful that the release of such a list would invite the competition to make raids. Thus, the job had to be performed covertly, and Griefer was especially good at it.

Calling General Artists one day, Griefer had the good fortune to encounter a new employee. "Look, if you just give me a list of your clients, I can make it easier for you to sell them and for me to know what you've got, who's available, that kind of thing," he told the young man. Anyone at the company with any experience at all would certainly not have agreed to such a request, but the inexperienced young man promised to send over the list right away.

When it arrived in the mail, however, Geffen intercepted it. He took the list and headed straight to Lefkowitz's office, anxious to please and eager for the opportunity to show how capable he was. Indeed, it made a great impression on Lefkowitz, who patted Geffen on the back and praised his good work.

On the lookout for the list, a puzzled Griefer called his new contact at General Artists and asked why he had not yet sent it. "I sent it to you a week ago," he was told.

Griefer, who rarely spoke above a whisper, hit the roof when he discovered the identity of the crook. "You're fired," he screamed at Geffen, who began to shake in fear. A big grin came across Shukat's face.

Geffen knew that this was the moment to use the relationship he had cultivated so carefully with the man at the top. He went directly to Lefkowitz's office and broke down, weeping and wailing about how much the job meant to him. According to his brother, Mitchell, David later bragged that he had saved his job by making up a story about how his mother had breast cancer and that he was paying the bills for an operation. Lefkowitz, already sympathetic toward Geffen, rehired him on the spot.

Griefer was irate when he heard that Lefkowitz had reversed the firing. He insisted that the agency should not tolerate such behavior. In his opinion, Geffen's actions were tantamount to stealing and should be considered unforgivable.

Lefkowitz listened patiently to Griefer's ranting but said, "We're not firing David Geffen."

Griefer continued to press his case, explaining that Geffen was also responsible for countless nighttime long-distance phone calls that were showing up on his telephone reports.

"I know everything that he's doing," Lefkowitz responded. "He's trying to learn the business."

Griefer was astonished to see that Lefkowitz was treating Geffen as if he were his own son. Geffen had a number of enemies at the agency, but he had the man at the top on his side, and that was the only person that mattered. It was onward and upward for David Geffen.

Up from the mailroom: Geffen (fourth from the left) with
fellow William Morris agent Scott Shukat (third from the left)
at the party to announce the signing of the Youngbloods.

(Courtesy Scott Shukat)

ROCK 'N' ROLL

|||

Nat Lefkowitz placated Ben Griefer by giving him a new secretary and then promoted Geffen to assistant to a crusty agent named Harry Kalcheim. Kalcheim was a bright but forgetful character who joined the agency in 1941 after booking big bands to play between films on the Paramount theater circuit during the 1930s.

Having gotten the rundown on Geffen from Lefkowitz, Kalcheim informed Geffen that he could sign clients or do whatever he wanted, as long as he took care of his typing and dictation. He soon took a liking to Geffen and encouraged him to listen in on his telephone conversations, employing the method many agents at the Morris office believed was the single best way for young comers to learn the ropes.

During this time, Geffen struck up a friendship with a young agent named Owen Laster and asked if he could help him sign clients. Laster was a conscientious young man who was both amazed and amused by Geffen's nerve. Laster was the kind of guy who, unlike Geffen, might well pay his dues contentedly and spend his entire career at the agency.

A play Laster had seen Off-Broadway a couple of years earlier, *The Days and Nights of Beebee Fenstermaker,* was to be telecast one evening, and he suggested that Geffen watch it. At the office the next day, Geffen raved about the show, and Laster suggested that the two attempt to sign its star, Rose Gregorio. They arranged to meet the actress for lunch. The pitch worked; before long, Gregorio signed to the Morris office.

More interested in Broadway than in anything else, Geffen chased and signed Jordan Christopher, a striking actor who had married Sybil Burton after Richard Burton left her for Elizabeth Taylor during the filming of *Cleopatra.* Geffen made the deal for Christopher to replace Michael Crawford, a British actor, in *Black Comedy* at the Barrymore Theatre. With her settlement money from Burton, Sybil opened Arthur's, billed as "America's first celebrity discotheque." It was here that she, her new husband, and Geffen hung out together.

With Marty Litke, also now a pal, Geffen signed Carmen Mathews, who had been cast to play Mrs. Hutto in *The Yearling,* a Broadway musical based on Marjorie Kinnan Rawlings's novel. Litke and Geffen also signed Steve Saunders, a thirteen-year-old from Centerville, Georgia, who had been cast to play the leading role.

Geffen was in heaven. He loved schmoozing his new clients. On weekends, he shuttled to New Haven, where *The Yearling* was in an out-of-town tryout. He was convinced there was a big career ahead for Steve Saunders. The critics, however, did not like the show. *The Yearling* opened at the Alvin Theatre on December 10, 1965, and was shut down after only three performances.

But Geffen's commitment to his clients proved so complete that Nat Lefkowitz soon promoted him to agent. He also rewarded Geffen with a whopping raise, sending his salary over the two-hundred-a-week mark. Bestowing upon him a plum assignment, Lefkowitz made Geffen an agent in the TV department.

Lefkowitz made it clear to everyone at the agency that he was giving Geffen an unprecedented amount of latitude, allowing him to keep his theater clients as well as Biff Rose. As a result, he enjoyed an enviable status among his peers—one that might have been called agent-at-large. Other young agents scratched their heads and tried to figure out just exactly how Geffen had become the boss's favorite son.

Geffen began holding court at the weekly TV department meetings, masterfully stroking the egos of veteran agents while at the same time pursuing his own agenda. Agents a few years older than Geffen who stood at the back of the room during meetings were left speechless as he strode fearlessly into the room and took a chair at the table next to Wally Jordan, the cigar-chomping department chief.

At the meetings, Geffen often prattled on about a fellow he had met at the University of Texas named Ronny Pearlman, who he claimed would be the hottest writer the TV business had ever seen. He also talked up a hippie named Lorne Michaels and soon got him a gig writing for a situation comedy starring Phyllis Diller called *The Pruitts of Southampton.*

Armed with his first expense account, Geffen now delighted in traveling to Los Angeles on business, where he spent time with his friend John Hartmann. The two came up with an ambitious scheme to sign clients and represent them as a team. Together they signed Steve Binder, a TV director who in 1965 had launched NBC's *Hullabaloo,* one of the first programs spotlighting rock-'n'-roll acts such as the Supremes, the Ronettes, and Sonny and Cher.

Hartmann had a couple of years on Geffen at the agency, and had just bought a splashy new ranch house in Woodland Hills. Geffen was awestruck when he saw the place, which boasted a pool, stables for eight horses, a barn, and a large circular driveway where Hartmann parked his spanking new convertible.

The house, he explained to Geffen, came thanks to a bonus he had received for signing some acts in the fledgling music department, home to the agency's rock-'n'-roll acts. He had met with Jerry Brandt, the department's slick new chief, and played a part in the signing of a Los Angeles rock group called Buffalo Springfield. That group, which featured

Stephen Stills, Neil Young, and Richie Furay, among others, brought a harder rock edge to the folk-rock and country leanings of earlier groups such as the Byrds. Their hit "For What It's Worth," about a clash between police and hippies on Sunset Boulevard, was to become a defining song of 1960s rock.

Geffen, whose musical tastes did not stretch much beyond Broadway show tunes, felt as if Hartmann was speaking a foreign language. He was surprised to discover that someone could get rich at the Morris office in any area other than the motion-picture or TV departments. He made a mental note to check out Jerry Brandt when he returned to New York.

Geffen and Hartmann sat out in Hartmann's barn atop bales of hay and talked for hours about show business, brainstorming strategies on how to beat the system at the Morris office. The two had become loyal allies, and Geffen felt comfortable with his new friend.

Geffen then took a courageous step and decided to share with Hartmann his deepest secret. "You know, I'm homosexual," he said quietly. It was a remarkable admission, given both the era and the fact that he worked in a conservative office environment dominated by skirt-chasing tough guys. Geffen quickly augmented his statement by adding that he was not entirely certain of it.

Hartmann, who was straight, was surprised. Another friend of his at the office had made the same admission to him earlier that year, which at the time had prompted Hartmann to cry. Though he was surprised, he was now getting used to such pronouncements, and he took Geffen's declaration somewhat in stride.

Back in New York, Geffen felt somewhat unburdened, having articulated his feelings. Warily, he began to be more open about them and also decided to share the news with Larry Kurzon. But Kurzon's reaction was not so blithe as Hartmann's.

"Oh, David, you don't want to be homosexual," he said, thinking he might be able to talk him out of it. "Don't be homosexual . . . please!"

At the same time Geffen was beginning to admit his homosexuality, the United States was becoming deeply involved in the Vietnam War. It was not long before a notice arrived in Geffen's mail from a draft board in Brooklyn, calling him to register for classification. His first reaction was to panic, but Robert Drivas, an actor friend who was represented by the Morris office, told him to simply check "yes" to the question, "Do you have any homosexual tendencies?"

Trembling, Geffen went to the draft board and covered up the form as he checked the box. The actor's advice was right on the money. After reviewing his paperwork, the draft board promptly classified him as "physically or mentally unable to serve." He was officially off the hook.

Jerry Brandt was not an easy guy to miss. He wore expensive suits and Ebel gold watches, rode around in a limousine, and took frequent vacations to Puerto Rico. He had put the Morris music department on the map by signing the Rolling Stones, who had just hit in the United States with their first single, "(I Can't Get No) Satisfaction."

Geffen began pursuing and pestering Brandt the same way he had pursued Nat Lefkowitz a few months earlier. Occasionally, Geffen even managed to edge his way into Brandt's limousine as he scouted his way through the clubs of Greenwich Village.

Brandt told Geffen that he, too, had begun his career at the Morris office mailroom. He had been fired after delivering an envelope two hours late—he had been in Central Park smoking a joint and did not realize that a roomful of executives were waiting for it. He then got a job in the booking department at General Artists, where he signed such early rock acts as Danny and the Juniors. But Brandt wound up quitting after clashing with the agency's chief, a stodgy old-timer who thought that rock 'n' roll was just a passing craze.

The Morris office, realizing that they had let a winner slip away, brought Brandt back in an executive post. But to his frustration, he quickly discovered that the top brass was not much more enlightened than that at General Artists. Despite the fact that they had represented Elvis Presley since 1955, the agency did not see the rock revolution coming. In 1964, Brandt told Geffen, he was stupefied as the agency refused to support the department's pursuit of the Beatles, who had formed a few years earlier in Liverpool.

When Lefkowitz and his lieutenants explained that rock 'n' roll was a business they did not want to be in, Brandt busied himself putting together the *Cavalcade of Stars,* a road show featuring a group of unknown music acts and a clean-cut kid from Philadelphia named Dick Clark as emcee. It was only after the Beatles' hit "I Want to Hold Your Hand" edged Bobby Vinton out of the top spot on the popular music charts that the Morris office realized rock 'n' roll was a moneymaking business it could not ignore.

After listening to Brandt, Geffen explained that the only records he owned were Broadway cast albums and that he planned to rocket to the agency's top echelon by signing movie stars and directors. Brandt looked at the scrawny kid and laughed as Geffen ticked off the names of the theater actors he now represented.

"Listen, jerk, you're twenty-two years old," Brandt told him. "Whaddya think, Norman Jewison is going to sign with you?" he asked, invoking the name of the famed movie director. The music department, he said, was the place where a young agent could make a name for himself.

Brandt's advice had a profound impact on Geffen. He at once rejiggered his career plans. He did not quit the TV department, but he did begin to spend a big chunk of his time hanging out with the music agents and sitting in on their meetings. At one of these meetings, Brandt told the agency's senior executives that they might get the chance to sign the Animals, one of the hot groups at the core of the so-called British Invasion.

"Animals? William Morris doesn't sign animal acts!" growled Harry Kalcheim's brother Nat, also an agent from the old school. "We could have had Zippy the Monkey!"

Geffen listened intently as Brandt complained that the dullards at the Morris office would have missed the boat on the rock revolution altogether if not for him. He told Geffen it was a miracle that they had allowed him to sign the Rolling Stones, given that the group's manager, a crafty entrepreneur named Allen Klein, demanded that the agency charge only a 7 percent commission. The Morris office charged its other clients 10 percent. Lefkowitz and his lieutenants relented only after Brandt ran the numbers and explained passionately how lucrative the act could be.

By clueing Geffen in on the terms of the deal, Brandt was essentially giving him his first lesson in the nuts and bolts of rock-'n'-roll concert booking. For every Stones concert he booked, Brandt told Geffen, the agency pocketed 7 percent of a $25,000 advance against 60 percent of the gross receipts. Clients in the agency's nightclub department such as Eartha Kitt and Maurice Chevalier had never earned an advance anywhere near that sum. What's more, the Stones' tour was packed with concerts for ten solid weeks, far longer than the average Las Vegas booking.

Geffen was not a whiz at mathematics, but this arithmetic was easy, and he figured that he, too, could make a lot of money in this arena. It was not an undying passion for music that made him decide to try to make his fortune in the business; he did it because he might get rich quickly. If the hot entertainment trend had been circus jugglers, David Geffen would undoubtedly have put on clown makeup and haunted the big tents, searching for clients. As it turns out, what was hot was rock 'n' roll.

Nat Lefkowitz was very pleased with Geffen and his success in signing clients. When the agency moved to new headquarters at 1350 Avenue of the Americas, Geffen was given his first secretary and a small corner office on the thirty-third floor, alongside the agency's most senior executives.

Now twenty-three, Geffen was also rewarded with a hundred-dollar-a-week raise, bringing his weekly salary by the end of 1966 to a little more than three hundred dollars. Though it was a serious strain on his budget, Geffen began buying custom-made suits at R. Meledandri on Fifty-sixth Street, the Italian tailor where Jerry Brandt bought his clothes. Meledandri was an elegant shop, located just across the street from the Drake Hotel, and men who wore the tailor's suits stood out on the streets of Manhattan. The reinvention of David Geffen was beginning.

Plunking down $450 for a suit and shopping at the boutique where only the most senior executives at the agency shopped was Geffen's way of signaling to his bosses that he was determined to enter their league. Although in just a few years he was to give up suits in favor of a wardrobe consisting almost solely of blue jeans and white T-shirts, for now he believed in dressing for success.

Following the tips he had picked up from Brandt, Geffen began buying scores of new pop records and listening to them endlessly. One night at his apartment in the Wilshire House, Geffen played an album by Buffy Sainte-Marie for Elliot Roberts, Hal Ray, and Jeff Wald. As Sainte-Marie warbled her touching ballad "Now That the Buffalo's Gone," Geffen began to weep. His buddies had never before seen anyone react to music in that way. Ray responded by putting his arm around Geffen.

At the office, Geffen discovered that his newfound interest in music unwittingly reunited him with his old nemesis Scott Shukat. Shukat had graduated from Ben Griefer's desk to being the newly formed one-man phonograph-record department. Until then, the Morris office did not make record deals for its clients. The only way the music department had made money was by booking its clients' tours and TV appearances.

Now that was about to change, and it meant Geffen was going to have to team with Shukat on any record deals for his acts. Geffen could find and sign the act, but Shukat, whose clients were the record companies, would close the deal.

Geffen first turned to Herb Gart, the manager who had helped him sign Biff Rose, who was now handling a group called the Youngbloods. Led by Jesse Colin Young, the Youngbloods was a Boston act that included Jerry Corbitt, Joe Bauer, and Lowell "Banana" Levinger. Gart felt the Youngbloods were ready to record their first album and got the Morris office to represent them, with Geffen the lead agent. Geffen and Shukat together made a recording deal at RCA, and, in a photograph taken at the signing, the two stood beaming alongside the group's members.

The Youngbloods' biggest hit was on their first album and was not even one they had written themselves: Chet Powers's "Get Together" captured the mood of the late 1960s rock scene with its lyrics extolling brotherhood and universal love.

Before long, it became clear that Geffen would do or say almost anything to wangle introductions, build relationships, and win clients in the music world. While hanging around with the music agents one day, Geffen lied and said that he had had a meeting with Paul Simon, one half of Columbia Records' hot new duo Simon and Garfunkel. Shukat was dumbfounded. He and Geffen had been at Columbia earlier in the day, and Shukat had witnessed Geffen telling Bill Gallagher, an executive at the label, that he would love to *meet* Simon. Geffen never wound up signing Simon, but he did, before long, finagle an introduction to him.

The legend went that Geffen signed the Association—a band that made it big with such songs as "Never My Love" and "Cherish"—after having heard that the band's manager had been intoxicated at a wild party one night. Geffen was not at the party, the story went, but he called the manager the morning after and referred to "conversations" they had had the night before. Geffen told the manager that he had, "as requested," drawn up the contracts to represent them at the agency. "Where does the chutzpah come from?" Owen Laster thought, upon hearing Geffen tell the story. Geffen remembered the story differently; he said he signed the group after being introduced to them by Joe Butler, the drummer in the Lovin' Spoonful.

One afternoon early in the summer of 1967, while closing a deal for another act at a lawyer's office, Geffen and Shukat received an unexpected bonus: a hot stock tip. Allen Klein, the manager of the Rolling Stones, was rumored to be interested in launching a takeover of Cameo-Parkway Records, the Philadelphia-based record label that was home to Chubby Checker. If the deal happened, Cameo-Parkway stock would shoot up.

Shukat did not pay attention to the tip, but Geffen did. He ran back to the office and called a broker, risking his savings on Cameo-Parkway Records. The stock was trading at three dollars a share. On July 28, Klein and Abbey Butler, a New York stockbroker, bought a controlling interest in Cameo-Parkway Records. The stock soared, closing that day at 8.625. In late August, the record label revealed it was considering a merger with Klein's company, and the stock before long topped sixty dollars a share. David Geffen was making a significant amount of money in the stock market for the very first time.

Meanwhile, in Los Angeles, Barry Diller had quit the Morris office to become assistant to Leonard Goldberg, the head of West Coast programming at ABC. Within a few short months, Goldberg was named head of network programming and moved to ABC's headquarters in New York, taking his protégé with him. Before long, Diller was running the department himself.

Geffen kept his eye on Diller and invited him to stop by his apartment. Diller, who had grown up in a sprawling house in Beverly Hills, was shocked at Geffen's tiny one-room apartment. It was immaculately neat, but Diller could remember closets in his California house that were larger. "I can't believe that a human person can live in such a small place," Diller thought.

By the end of the summer of 1967, Geffen had become known widely in the New York agency community as the Morris office's hottest new agent. In addition to signing many successful music acts, he was making a lot of noise in the TV department. He made a gainful deal for the writing team of Kenny Solms and Gail Parent to work on a new CBS variety program called *The Carol Burnett Show.*

Many young people in the business were awed by Geffen's meteoric rise and turned to him for advice. One such person was Joel Dean, who worked at Chartoff-Winkler, a personal-management company that was home to such comedians as Jackie Mason and the husband-and-wife team of Jerry Stiller and Anne Meara. The company's founding partners had gone off to Hollywood to make movies and left Dean in charge. Having signed Buffy Sainte-Marie, Dean felt there was an opportunity to expand the company's music roster and wanted a partner to help out.

Geffen first suggested his friend Jeff Wald, who had just married singer Helen Reddy. Wald was about to take the job when he got a rival offer to book acts at Mr. Kelly's, a club in Chicago. With Wald unavailable, Geffen then told Dean he could not go wrong if he hired Elliot Roberts, who was then suffering in a dead-end job as a secretary in the theater department at the Morris office. Roberts took the gig and saw his sixty-five-dollar-a-week salary almost double overnight. Little did Geffen know that by introducing Dean to Roberts he had unwittingly set into motion a chain of events that was to ultimately have a massive impact on his own professional career.

Roberts and Geffen were inseparable friends, and Roberts called Geffen constantly to ask him what to do. His first meeting with Stiller and Meara showed that he was in over his head.

"Well, what do you think, Elliot?" a dubious Stiller asked, curious to hear Roberts's plan for their careers. "What do you think we should be doing now?"

Roberts scratched his head. "I don't know. Did you *eat*? Maybe we should eat now."

Within a month, all of the comedians on the Chartoff-Winkler roster had rebelled and hired other managers.

Moments before it seemed that Roberts would be out of a job, Buffy Sainte-Marie encouraged him to go to Café Wha? in Greenwich Village one night to hear her friend Joni Mitchell, a folksinger from Canada, who was playing third on a bill after Richie Havens and a comedian. Like Joan Baez and Judy Collins, Mitchell was a fluttery kind of soprano who was able to slide effortlessly from middle register to piercing high notes midword. She was a tall, slender twenty-four-year-old whose long dishwater-blond hair and thick bangs framed beautiful green eyes.

Roberts was overwhelmed as Mitchell took her place on a stool on the small stage, plucked at her acoustic guitar, and sang her heart out on songs she had written herself. Mitchell's lyrics to tunes such as "Both Sides, Now" and "Chelsea Morning," intensely personal ballads about former loves and the world around her, were haunting, sophisticated, and poetic.

Roberta Joan Anderson, born in Saskatoon, Saskatchewan, in 1943, developed a love for guitar while in art school and dropped out to move to Toronto to become a folksinger. She married another folksinger named Chuck Mitchell, and they moved to Detroit, where they were a nightly folk act at a coffeehouse called the Chess Mate. But in early 1967, Joni left Chuck and moved to New York, booking herself into any club there that would take her, as well as performing in other cities along the East Coast. She soon became known as the singer who had created special "tunings" for each song she played.

Mitchell had only been in Manhattan a few months when Roberts caught her act at Café Wha? He approached her at the end of her set and was surprised to hear that she did not have a manager. "I really love your music," he said. "I'd love to work with you."

"I'm leaving tomorrow for Detroit," Mitchell told Roberts, explaining that she had booked herself on a three-and-a-half-week tour.

"Listen, I'll go with you," Roberts told Mitchell. "I've got nothing to hold me down. I'll meet you at the airport tomorrow, and I'll do the tour with you. After three weeks, let's see how you feel. If you want me to manage you, I will. If you don't, I won't."

A hunch told Mitchell that Roberts was a decent man. She did not want to go to Detroit alone, concerned that she might run into Chuck, who controlled 50 percent of her music-publishing rights and had been harassing her since they had broken up. It would be good to have someone looking after her on the road, she thought.

Out on the tour, Mitchell asked Roberts to become her full-time manager. She authorized him to negotiate what was essentially a divorce settlement, in which she got back the music-publishing rights she did not already control.

Back in New York, Roberts tried unsuccessfully to get a record deal for his new client. She auditioned at Columbia and at RCA, but the labels were not biting. He begged disinterested talent scouts to come hear her act at clubs in the Village. The era of folk groups such as the Kingston Trio had ended, Bob Dylan had turned electric, and rock bands such as Big Brother and the Holding Company were stealing the headlines. Leery record-company executives thought straight folk performers were a thing of the past.

Mitchell continued to travel and do club dates, including some in Coconut Grove, Florida, where she was spending time with her new boyfriend, David Crosby, formerly of the Byrds. Roberts, meanwhile, tried to drum up interest in California. He contacted Reprise Records, which liked Mitchell's songs; what really put a record deal on the fast track, however, was Crosby's promise that he personally would produce Mitchell's first album. The Byrds had been a successful act, and Crosby's involvement lent an air of credibility to the Mitchell project. Reprise made the deal and arranged to bring Mitchell, Crosby, and Roberts to California. Roberts said good-bye to Chartoff-Winkler.

Roberts took an office in the Clear Thoughts building on La Cienega Boulevard, which was filled with pot-smoking beatniks and bands looking for representation and record deals. Roberts was on the telephone almost daily to Geffen, looking for advice on how to most effectively book concerts for Mitchell.

He tried to explain to Geffen what was happening in Los Angeles, but even he could not fully comprehend it. "All these bands are happening out of nowhere," he told Geffen. He said that a new band called the Doors had been rehearsing downstairs. Geffen found Roberts's talk about the West Coast and its opportunities tantalizing.

Roberts's luck was just beginning. Buffalo Springfield was in the studio across the hall from where Mitchell was recording. She went over and said hello to Neil Young, who had been a friend of hers since they had been sixteen years old. They had also played on many bills together since. After an introduction by Mitchell, Roberts and Young quickly became good friends, and within a couple of days Roberts rented a room in Young's new house in Laurel Canyon. A week later, he was managing not just Joni Mitchell, but also Buffalo Springfield and David Crosby.

G effen's trips to California became more frequent, and he relished them. He still had the same enthusiasm for Los Angeles that he had had during his first trip there six years previously. And now that he was a player, he enjoyed the visits even more, staying at such ritzy locales as the Beverly Hills Hotel or the Beverly Wilshire.

He continued to work his West Coast clients constantly, including Steve Binder, the director. On one trip, Binder invited Geffen to dinner with him and his wife, Judy, at his house on San Ysidro Drive in Beverly Hills. After they had eaten, Steve and Judy's kids went to bed, and the three adults retreated to the living room.

The agency business was really a pain, Geffen complained to the Binders, and he had had enough. The men at the Morris office were fine guys, but it did not take a brain surgeon to realize that it would take forever to climb the corporate ladder there. Geffen wanted more, and he wanted it now. He told the Binders what he had been pondering since meeting Jerry Brandt: going out on his own. The management business would offer Geffen more control and richer, quicker rewards. But he needed a client to get started.

Binder shot up and began rummaging through a stack of 45s by the record player. "Listen to this," he said, putting on "Wedding Bell Blues," a song written and performed by a young girl from New York named Laura Nyro.

As Nyro's voice drifted through the speakers—"Marry me, Bill. . . . I love you so, I always will . . ."—Geffen was entranced. Who was she? Where did she come from?

That her name meant nothing to him showed how little Geffen knew about the music business. Nyro was by no means a star, but most people in the record world knew her as having been the laughingstock of the Monterey International Pop Festival, the summer concert that had ignited the careers of Jimi Hendrix, the Who, and Janis Joplin, among others. Even Binder had read about the egg Laura Nyro had laid at Monterey.

Laura Nigro was born in the Bronx in 1947, the daughter of a Jewish mother and a Italian-Catholic father who played the trumpet but made a living tuning pianos. Only nineteen years old when her first album, *More Than a New Discovery,* was released, the portly young woman had been wrangled into publishing and management contracts by Artie Mogull, a hustler who had once signed Bob Dylan to an early publishing deal.

Mogull could not relate much to Nigro or her music, yet something told him it was special. He did not interfere with her songs, but he did insist that she change her name, fearing people might pronounce it "Negro."

Nothing much happened when Verve-Folkways released her debut album in 1966. But when KHJ, a radio station in Los Angeles, began playing "Wedding Bell Blues," the song caught the attention of Ode Records chief Lou Adler, who was instrumental in organizing the Monterey concert.

An estimated two hundred thousand hippies showed up for the three-day love-in, themed "Music, Love, and Flowers." Nyro went onstage the second day, between the Butterfield Blues Band and Jefferson Airplane.

Her performance was nothing short of a disaster. Monterey Pop was a gathering of hard-core rock 'n' rollers, and Nyro delivered what amounted to a slick Las Vegas cabaret routine. Having blown her last hundred dollars on costumes and choreography, she came out in a floor-length ball gown, with backup singers named Delores and Juliette in tow.

As the audience of teenage potheads booed, Nyro bungled her way through a few songs, wrapping up the set with "Wedding Bell Blues." The pickup band could not follow her complex, sophisticated arrangements. Her performance lasted sixteen minutes, and by its end Laura Nyro was a camp legend.

Crushed, she ran from the stage in tears. "What did you think?" she asked Mogull.

"I'll tell you what I thought," Mogull steamed. "When I was a kid, my mother and father took me to the circus, and at one point three elephants came out and did dance steps. That's what you reminded me of."

Geffen could not believe the story. He thanked Binder for the tip and jumped on an airplane back to New York, where he found a broken-down Nyro, hiding out in a tiny apartment at 888 Eighth Avenue, in Hell's Kitchen. She was determined she would never sing in public again.

CHAPTER 5

TUNA FISH MUSIC

|||

Eight eighty-eight Eighth Avenue was a huge apartment building that filled an entire block in what was one of New York's filthiest crime-ridden neighborhoods. Residents who called Hell's Kitchen home faced a daily dodge of drug addicts, knife-wielding thugs, and prostitutes who packed the sidewalks.

Geffen had gotten Nyro's address and phone number out of Artie Mogull, the manager he hoped to displace. He was nervous as he rang Nyro's doorbell but calmed himself by thinking through the pitch he had rehearsed. As he entered the apartment, he looked around and stiffened. It was overrun by cats, to which he was allergic. Fortunately, he was able to convince Nyro to open a window.

Nyro was not an attractive girl, but there was something oddly sensuous about her. She was heavy, with very long black hair that fell to just below her waist. She wore big black dresses that looked as though they had spent years on dusty racks at secondhand stores. Even on the streets of New York, Nyro's dark plum lipstick and black nail polish made her stand out.

This was Geffen's opportunity to sign a star client who he thought could make him rich and famous. She had been mistreated, he told her, establishing himself as an ally. It was outrageous, he exclaimed, because it was clear she was a unique talent destined for stardom. Let me take charge of your career, Geffen pleaded, promising that such mistreatment would never happen again. Only she knew how the music should sound. If he represented her, he promised, she would be in control of the final product.

Nyro was obviously pleased, but she told him, "I will not sing in public."

Eventually, Geffen explained, she would, and he was going to make sure that that day was nothing less than spectacular. He proceeded to outline a grand vision in which he would find the best people to help her construct the most elegant act ever. Long after people had forgotten about Monterey, he said, a newly confident Laura Nyro would make a stunning debut at the finest performance space he knew: Carnegie Hall.

To Nyro, this sounded like quite a plan. Lighting an empty tampon tube she had stuffed with marijuana, she took a seat at her upright piano and played thirteen songs—including "Eli's Comin'," "Poverty Train," and "Stoned Soul Picnic." This was her story, she told him, an autobiographical collection of songs about a young girl's spiritual journey from childhood to maturity.

The music stunned Geffen. He was sure he had found the next Barbra Streisand. The two sat and talked about the future while eating tuna fish, Nyro's favorite food. For the first time since Monterey, Nyro was hopeful. She liked this little guy David Geffen. He seemed to be genuine, besides being cute and funny.

But what about Artie Mogull? Don't worry about him, Geffen told Nyro. She brought out her old contracts, and Geffen promised to get her a good lawyer and a speedy resolution. Next, he outlined their business relationship. He would be her agent, and she would become a client at William Morris. They would be fifty-fifty partners in a music-publishing company called Tuna Fish Music. Nyro was delighted.

Geffen pays homage to his star client, Laura Nyro,

at his apartment on Central Park South.

(Stephen Paley/Michael Ochs Archives/Venice, CA)

Early on, Geffen recognized that publishing was one of the areas in the music business where the real money was being made. Long after an artist's star has faded, publishers benefit financially for years to come, pocketing royalties whenever a group records a song or sheet music is sold.

But the publishing arrangement Geffen struck was improper. Regulations drawn up by the American Federation of Television and Radio Artists (AFTRA) to govern agents prohibited them from owning music-publishing companies. Talent agents were licensed only to arrange record deals and concerts. The guild's rationale was that an agent who could benefit financially from an artist's publishing might favor that artist over others on an agency's roster in booking concerts and the like.

Artists' personal managers, on the other hand, had no such restriction and often owned stakes in their clients' music-publishing operations. It was believed that a manager typically had a far more intimate relationship with an artist and therefore should rake in riches if he or she became a star. Geffen thus told people he was Nyro's agent, despite the fact that he was functioning as her agent and her manager.

David Geffen was not alone in trying to pull a fast one. A number of agents had struck similarly fishy deals, and some even went so far as to skim money off the top of cash transactions. Geffen saw the big advantages of breaking the AFTRA rule and gambled that the top brass at the Morris office would not find out about his dishonest little deal.

Geffen soon became Nyro's most passionate advocate, basically telling people she was the next coming of Christ and that it was just a matter of time before she arrived. Heads turned on the thirty-third floor of William Morris when the singer came to visit her new agent. Decked out in black velvet, wearing purple Christmas-tree balls as earrings, and adorned with other gaudy costume jewelry she had picked up at Woolworth's, Nyro looked, essentially, like a witch.

Little by little, Geffen won her trust. He treated her like royalty and loaned her money so she could live high until the stardom and riches he promised materialized. He also arranged for his accountant, Max Mensch, to begin handling her money as well.

Geffen made sure there were limousines to shuttle Nyro around town. Together with Beautybelle, Nyro's massive German shepherd, the three were whisked out of Manhattan to Nyro's favorite restaurant, the White Castle drive-in on Queens Boulevard.

Before long, however, the burger binges started to bother Geffen, and he fretted that Nyro's weight might work against her. Her latest publicity photos, showing her nearly 180-pound frame stuffed into a wedding dress, certainly were not helping. One night, as Nyro took second helpings at a Chinese restaurant in Times Square, he spoke up. "Don't be such a *chazzer,*" he reprimanded her, using the Yiddish word for a pig of a person.

Geffen and Nyro were becoming great friends, though, and within a few months she did not make a move without consulting him. To some, it appeared as though they had fallen in love, an image Geffen did little to dispel and even promoted in the years to come. But theirs was a platonic relationship; Geffen confided in Nyro early on that he was sexually attracted to men. And even though she dated men, there was an air of sexual ambivalence about her as well. Her song "Emmie" became known as pop's first lesbian love song.

Geffen's friendship with Nyro also led him to increase his drug use, and it was with her that he first experimented with acid. Yet he was not drawn to the drug scene as Laura was. Although he recognized that Nyro's LSD trips and other drug taking provided her with creative fire- power that influenced her songwriting, Geffen realized that, for him, such hallucinations got in the way of achieving his goals.

As Nyro polished her new songs, Geffen went about working to undo the management and publishing contracts she had signed with Artie Mogull. As it turns out, Mogull had made a critical mistake. Dick Barovick, a top music-industry lawyer whom Geffen had put on the case, told Geffen that Nyro had been a minor when she had signed the agreements. As such, Barovick said, the contracts required special court approval, which Mogull foolishly had not obtained. In addition, the agreements were scheduled to remain in effect for five years, at a time when, Barovick argued, the same law held that contracts lasting more than three years were unreasonable.

Geffen was delighted. Barovick fired off a telegram to Mogull and his attorneys informing them that the agreements were being terminated on those grounds. He demanded that Mogull make a full accounting and return to Nyro all of her commissions and copyrights.

Geffen next plotted to make a new label deal for his client. He went to see Jerry Schoenbaum, the head of Verve-Folkways, but found that he had lost interest in Nyro, claiming her first album had sold "almost nothing." Unfazed, Geffen decided to shoot for the stars. Columbia Records, home to Barbra Streisand and Miles Davis, was in his mind the classiest label of them all. That was where he felt Laura Nyro should be.

C BS Records head Clive Davis was one of the slickest and most intimidating figures in the business. A Harvard graduate who had been trained as a lawyer, Davis had risen through the CBS hierarchy swiftly, and in 1967 was installed as its president.

For years, the company's Columbia label had been known as the address of show-tune warblers such as Andy Williams and Robert Goulet, but Davis was changing that. He sensed that the emergent "underground" movement was more than just a fad, and he sought to rid Columbia of its conservative image by acquiring the best of these new acts. He spiced up the label's roster by overseeing the careers of Bob Dylan and Simon and Garfunkel.

What's more, Davis had been to the Monterey Pop Festival and had signed several acts, among them Blood, Sweat & Tears, the Electric Flag, and Big Brother and the Holding Company, whose lead vocalist was Janis Joplin. With the additional signings of the Chamber Brothers and Spirit, it was clear that Davis felt there was a revolution in the making.

Geffen, meanwhile, had gotten about all the use he could squeeze out of Nat Lefkowitz and was searching for a more powerful rabbi. Fearless, Geffen called Davis's office and snagged a tryout in which Nyro would audition for him personally. Davis, of course, had seen firsthand Nyro's sad performance at Monterey but nonetheless was taken with her writing.

Once Geffen and Nyro arrived at CBS's offices on West Fifty-second Street, they were escorted into a small room, where Davis was waiting for them. There was only a piano, a TV set, and a few pictures on the wall. Nyro immediately complained about the room's lighting. "Can we turn it down?" she asked. Davis agreed to shut off the lights, and Nyro began to play her songs by the glow of the television, giving a flawless performance that left Davis impressed.

"I've seen the kind of star Barbra Streisand is," Nyro told Davis, uttering a line that Geffen had coached her to deliver. "And I know I've got the goods to make me one as well." Davis offered Nyro a contract on the spot.

It was not long before Geffen helped Nyro leave her dumpy apartment in Hell's Kitchen. He found her a small nineteenth-floor penthouse on West Seventy-ninth Street, in the heart of the more fashionable Upper West Side.

He then introduced her to Stephen Paley, a photographer he had met at the Café Au Go Go. Nyro became so comfortable with Paley that she allowed him to be one of only a couple of people who could photograph her. Paley used clever angles to come up with shots that flattered Nyro's unusual profile. One day, in the small park behind the American Museum of Natural History, Paley snapped comical shots of Geffen and Nyro fooling around. Geffen slipped on a dog collar and crouched down as Nyro held the end of a leash and cracked up.

Geffen realized quickly that he had extraordinary access to Clive Davis and talked to him on the telephone daily. Besides orchestrating the day-to-day affairs of Laura Nyro's life and career, Geffen was also now in constant contact with Elliot Roberts, offering him advice on how to care for his clients in California. Roberts had weathered the nasty breakup of Buffalo Springfield and now represented only one of its founding members, Neil Young, as well as Joni Mitchell. Geffen coached Roberts as he went back to Reprise Records, the label that had made a deal with Mitchell, to secure a recording contract for Young. Geffen was building his own friendships with the two artists, having won Young over with his effusive praise of "On the Way Home," a song Young had written for Buffalo Springfield.

But it was Geffen's continuing work in the TV department that continued to earn him a higher salary and modest bonuses at the Morris office. At the end of 1967, Nat Lefkowitz handed him yet another hundred-dollar raise, taking his weekly salary above four hundred dollars. Geffen expanded his wardrobe from Meledandri and coached his secretary, a young man named Peter Lampack, on the virtues of fine dressing.

But Geffen's dislike for the TV business was growing. He resented the tiresome duties of his job and passed some of them along to the eager Lampack. More and more, Geffen felt he should quit the Morris office and form his own management company around Laura Nyro. That way he would not have to take guff from anyone and would have the freedom to call his own shots. Conveniently, he also would not have to hide his music-publishing role any longer.

He had become friendly with Steve Leber, who had succeeded Jerry Brandt as head of the music department. Geffen suggested that Leber quit, too, and go into business with him. Leber was an ambitious young man who had started a business booking bands on college campuses while attending Northeastern University in the early 1960s. Following up on Brandt's success, Leber signed such acts as the Beach Boys, Steppenwolf, Ray Charles, and Stevie Wonder to the Morris office.

Geffen took Leber to the rehearsal studio to watch Nyro in action. There he explained his dreams of what he thought he and Leber could accomplish as partners. He spent countless evenings with Leber and developed a deep admiration for his wife, Marian. He had dinner with them at their apartment on Twenty-eighth Street and sat with them at various music-industry events. Geffen's friendship with Marian foreshadowed a long string of powerful friendships with the wives of his colleagues. He would, in some cases, forge a tighter bond with the wives than with their husbands.

Leber seriously considered Geffen's offer, but it frightened him. He and Marian had just had a baby girl, and he thought it imprudent to bet his future on what seemed to be a risky entrepreneurial gig. He became the first of many people who years later kicked themselves for having passed up an opportunity to partner with David Geffen.

Recording of Nyro's *Eli and the Thirteenth Confession* began in January 1968 with the taping of "Eli's Comin'." After having dinner with the Lebers, Geffen dropped by the studio to check on Nyro. He wanted to make sure that she was happy and that she and Charlie Calello, the producer he had hired, were making progress. He brought many industry people by the studio to meet Nyro and tirelessly repeated his refrain about how big the album was going to be.

One day in the studio, Nyro and Calello were at loggerheads. Calello asked her bluntly how she wanted a song to sound. In earlier sessions, Nyro had told him she wanted a song to sound "blue" or "green," so he was expecting another color. Nyro stared into space and was silent for two full minutes. Finally, a smile came across her face and she pointed across the room.

"Like my chair," she said. It was a plain chair made out of wood. Calello understood that Nyro wanted the song and the arrangements to be simple.

Despite the fact that she had told Clive Davis she wanted to be a star, Nyro was uncomfortable in the spotlight and really wanted to just sit home alone and write her songs. It was nearly impossible for her to say the word *commercial.* She was an artist—and a perfectionist, at that. Her demands caused the original budget of fifteen thousand dollars to more than double to thirty-six thousand. Whereas normally three singers came in to do the background singing, Nyro insisted on doing all of the background vocals herself. So instead of completing three tracks in a single session, Nyro and Calello only finished one.

The recording process was made even more complicated by the fact that some days Nyro was so drugged that she could not work. One evening in the studio, she stopped playing in the middle of a take.

"Oh Charles, I feel the keys on the piano," she said woozily. "They feel so . . . oh, wow!" Calello left the booth and ran into the studio, only to find that she had a joint six inches long dangling from her lips.

It was Geffen's calculated coddling of Clive Davis that enabled Nyro to make the album the way she wanted. As the deadline passed and production costs swelled, a frustrated Calello told Geffen he needed more time and money.

"Whatever you want, tell me, and I will get it for you," Geffen told him. Calello, who at thirty was five years older than Geffen, was amazed at how he was able to get the CBS machinery, which for most was a bureaucratic maze of obstacles and dead ends, to work in his favor.

With the album nearly finished, Geffen headed to California to check up on his West Coast clients. He packed along a copy of Nyro's demo and loaned it to Bones Howe, a music producer he had met through his work with the Association. The phone in Geffen's room at the Beverly Hills Hotel rang early the next morning. On the other end was an ecstatic Howe.

"There are two songs on here that I guarantee you are hit records for the Fifth Dimension," Howe said. "One is 'Stoned Soul Picnic,' and the other is 'Sweet Blindness.' " Geffen was thrilled but warned Howe to slow down.

"You can't cut them," he said. "I've just made this deal with Clive, and I couldn't possibly have someone else record one of her songs just yet. Laura has to finish the record, and Clive has to choose the first single. After that, you can do whatever you want." Howe agreed to wait.

Back home in New York, Geffen was greeted by bad news on the legal front. Artie Mogull was taking the position that the management

*Geffen with his new mentor Clive Davis, the
legendary head of CBS Records and one of the most
intimidating figures in the business.*

(Courtesy Clive Davis)

and publishing contracts Nyro signed were valid and binding. The battle over Laura Nyro was going to get messy. Geffen instructed Barovick to file a lawsuit against Mogull.

Mogull's stance irritated Geffen no end, but he tried to ignore it and instead went about furiously promoting *Eli and the Thirteenth Confession.* He concocted a plan to invite members of the music press to a "playback session" in which Nyro would introduce her album and then play selected cuts for reporters. The idea was to create a stir even before the album arrived in stores.

Clive Davis, meanwhile, had developed an extraordinary affection for David Geffen. Davis, his wife, and their two children welcomed Geffen into their home on weekends and treated him like family. Geffen loved Davis and dreamed that if Davis—whose only interest in music as a kid had been in show tunes—could make it to the top of the business, so could he. Davis, for his part, was impressed by Geffen's quick mind and devotion to Nyro. Never in his long career did Davis find a manager who believed in a client more than David Geffen believed in Laura Nyro.

Geffen played Davis masterfully and engendered in him a feeling of loyalty, thanks in part to the gossipy tips from management circles that Geffen fed him. Geffen also helped steer huge moneymaking acts such as Chicago and Mac Davis to Columbia. He did not represent these acts, but other young managers valued his advice and listened as Geffen talked up Columbia and Clive Davis. Having David Geffen on his side proved to be a valuable connection for Clive Davis.

As a result, Davis eagerly met the various nutty demands Nyro made. When she determined that she wanted her first album for him to be fragrant, for example, Davis arranged for a perfume to be put into the vinyl. In the credits on the back of the album jacket, Nyro thanked "David L. Geffen: Agent and friend."

Eli and the Thirteenth Confession was released on March 13, 1968, to great critical acclaim. But it did not fly off record-store shelves. It sold steadily but slowly, selling only about 150,000 copies. But Nyro was becoming famous in spite of the lackluster sales, and Geffen deserved much of the credit.

Davis picked "Eli's Comin'" to be the album's first single, but few radio stations bit, concerned that Nyro's unusual voice would not appeal to listeners. As a result, the song did not make an appearance on any important pop charts.

If it was not clear before, it was certainly clear now that as a pop artist Nyro had one major thing going against her: her voice. She had a piercingly high warble that could have been smoothed out had she agreed to tone down a falsetto here or change a pace there. Her music also would have had a more commercial ring had she allowed others to orchestrate her songs with studio arrangements.

The minute Columbia chose "Eli's Comin'" as its first single, the way was cleared for Bones Howe to have the Fifth Dimension record Nyro's songs. Their slick, bouncy covers of "Stoned Soul Picnic" and "Sweet Blindness" jumped onto the charts almost overnight. "Sweet Blindness" peaked at number thirteen; "Stoned Soul Picnic" made it to number two.

This was great news for both Nyro and Geffen, the sole owners of Nyro's publishing company. When other groups recorded her songs, the publishing company banked about three cents per record sold. Tuna Fish Music suddenly looked to be a very valuable asset, and Laura Nyro and David Geffen were both getting rich.

Geffen's star was now shining brighter than ever, and in the spring of 1968, rivals of William Morris began to court him. The Ashley Famous Agency, which four years earlier had laughed him out the door, now badly wanted him to come build up their music and concert department.

Geffen, now twenty-five, was wowed by their offer to pay him one thousand dollars a week, the precise amount he had dreamed as a kid that rich people made. He went to Nat Lefkowitz, who informed him that the Morris office could not match the offer, which was a little more than twice what they were paying him. He wished Geffen well and sent him on his way. His last day was May 10, 1968, six weeks shy of four years after he had started there.

A smart man known for his ability to size up people, Lefkowitz probably knew that Geffen's ambitions were so huge that they were not likely to be fulfilled at the Morris office. Lefkowitz also may not have wanted to get in a bidding war with Ashley Famous in part because Ted Ashley was his nephew.

Ashley went to work at the Morris office in 1937, when he was just fifteen years old. Uncle Nat was an exacting boss who rode him hard but gave him an incomparable schooling in the ways of show business. Ashley rose quickly through the ranks and within a few years represented writers of commercial jingles. Eight years after joining the Morris office, he caused a rift in the family when he declared he was quitting to form his own agency.

The tension only increased when Ashley Famous took out full-page advertisements in the trade papers announcing it topped the Morris office in the number of hours of television programming it had packaged. While nowhere near as big as the Morris office, Ashley Famous had amassed a venerable client list that included John Wayne, William Holden, and Tennessee Williams.

In late 1967, Ashley sold his agency for thirteen million dollars to Kinney Service, which was in the parking-lot and funeral-home businesses. Kinney was run by the owner's son-in-law, a suave dealmaker named Steven J. Ross, a tall and handsome man who had grown up in the Flatbush section of Brooklyn. Years later, as chairman of Warner Communications, Ross was the man directly responsible for the transactions that were to make Geffen a billionaire.

Even as Geffen joined Ashley Famous, Ted Ashley was secretly helping Ross come up with a plan to make an even bigger move into Hollywood. Ross wanted to buy Warner Bros., and Ashley had the connections to help him meet the players there.

News of Geffen's departure from the Morris office sent shock waves through the agency. Scott Shukat, who had made Nyro's multirecord deal in tandem with Geffen, burned when he discovered that Lefkowitz had even allowed Geffen to take Nyro's record deal with him. Shukat had done much of the grunt work hammering out the deal's fine points and was rightly expecting that his bonus in the years to come would reflect the commissions earned on the remaining albums in the contract. But now there would be no more Laura Nyro albums commissioned at the Morris office.

The appointment at Ashley Famous was important for Geffen because it was the first time he had taken a job that was committed completely to the music business. He was based in the agency's New York office but spent time in California signing acts there as well.

Geffen wasted no time in building up the agency's concert division. Like the Morris office, Ashley Famous derived its income from booking the concert dates and tours of its clients. But Geffen, again violating talent-agency taboo, continued to administer Laura Nyro's publishing. Whereas he might have been concerned about the breach becoming public at the Morris office, at AFA he was in charge of the department. He considered himself AFA's policy setter and did not care about the nature of his arrangement with Nyro.

With his higher salary, Geffen left his studio apartment at the Wilshire House, sold the furniture to David Krebs, and moved a couple blocks to 230 Central Park South, where he rented a swank duplex owned by Helen Noga, the wealthy and matronly manager who had made a star out of Johnny Mathis. The apartment was furnished with a white Steinway grand piano in the living room and a sweeping view of the park. Geffen's standard of living had taken a serious turn for the better.

Once again displaying indomitable guts, Geffen set his sights on Albert Grossman, the biggest gun in the management business, whose clients included Bob Dylan, Janis Joplin, and Peter, Paul & Mary. With his small spectacles, potbelly, and long gray hair tied in a ponytail,

Grossman looked more than a little like a bedraggled Benjamin Franklin. He was only forty-four but looked much older and was viewed by many as more powerful than the record-label chiefs with whom he negotiated deals.

Like Colonel Tom Parker, Grossman was a pioneer in the business of artist management, an interesting thinker who came at the business with a revolutionary point of view. Demanding that his folksinging clients be treated with respect, he was a key architect of the shift in power from the record companies to the talent. He charged his clients steep fees and exercised a sometimes unhealthy dominance over them, but he defended them aggressively and allowed them to take as long as they needed to finish their albums. Alternately revered and despised, Grossman pushed label chiefs to the wall and threatened them if they did not agree to the terms he sought. "If the bird ain't happy," he liked to say, "the bird don't sing."

David Geffen admired Grossman's power and style and wanted to be in business with him. Geffen thought that if he could get Grossman to pull his clients from the Agency for Performing Arts (APA) he could, in one move, transform the music department at Ashley Famous.

In the summer of 1968, Geffen went to Grossman's office on East Fifty-fifth Street to make his pitch. Grossman did not really like agents much and was not interested in switching agencies. Geffen made many promises and argued that he could secure far better terms for his clients than those they were getting from APA. Grossman finally told him that he was not unhappy with the job APA was doing and in fact liked working with the young man, Todd Schiffman, who oversaw his accounts there.

That was all the tip Geffen needed. He got on the phone, found Schiffman at home in Los Angeles, and began selling him on the notion that he ought to quit APA and join Ashley Famous. The following week, Geffen flew to Los Angeles, where he and Ted Ashley did their best razzle-dazzle act for Schiffman. At APA, Schiffman, who was the same age as Geffen, had a staff of only three; Geffen said he would make him head of the West Coast concert division, giving him a staff of twenty-five. Ashley, a superb salesman, told Schiffman that Ashley Famous's strong TV and motion-picture operations would give his clients other opportunities not available at APA. Schiffman accepted the job.

It was becoming clear that one of Geffen's principal gifts was an ability to identify the industry's best talent scouts and convince them to work for him. He was somehow able to distinguish between those who had the instinct to find the next big act and those who did not. He learned early on that there was great value in listening to others with proven track records. Strong lieutenants, he was beginning to realize, had the power to make him look better.

His timing in contacting Schiffman could not have been better. Schiffman was recovering from a nervous breakdown and welcomed the help in booking concerts for Grossman's ever-ballooning stable of artists. There was something else about Geffen that Schiffman, who was openly gay, liked. Geffen told him that he, too, was gay, and Schiffman liked the idea of having a gay boss.

But the real clincher for Schiffman was that he, like Geffen, had a shady artist-management operation on the side, and Geffen told him that keeping it alive while working at Ashley Famous was fine by him. While at APA, Schiffman had discovered a band called Iron Butterfly and had used his brother-in-law as the front man in a management company that handled their affairs. Schiffman himself was collecting a manager's share of their sizable record and publishing revenues, just as Geffen was with Laura Nyro.

"I don't give a shit about that," Geffen said. "We look the other way." Iron Butterfly's second album featured a hit called "In-A-Gadda-Da-Vida" that set record charts on fire. Produced for just $7,000 in 1968, the album grossed $14 million and made Todd Schiffman a wealthy man.

Sure enough, shortly after Schiffman joined Geffen's team, Albert Grossman moved his clients to Ashley Famous. In no time, the music roster at Ashley Famous included such celebrated names as Janis Joplin, Paul Butterfield, Peter, Paul & Mary, Kris Kristofferson, the James Cotton Blues Band, Ian & Sylvia, and the Band. (Bob Dylan, Grossman's brightest light, was in hiding and not performing, having suffered a well-publicized motorcycle accident in 1966.) Suddenly, the agency that had not been a real player in the music business was one of the hottest shops in town. Ted Ashley felt he had bet on the right man.

Geffen went about signing other acts to the agency. Would-be clients found him devastatingly persuasive and were wowed by the attention he lavished on them during the chase. When he turned on the charm, Geffen was able to lead artists to believe they were the only act he had ever cared about. One of his signing secrets was that he would say anything, making outlandish promises that he never intended to keep.

Meeting with a psychedelic-rock sextet called the Strawberry Alarm Clock, Geffen promised to use his star acts and Ashley Famous's connections with popular TV shows to help them break out.

"We're going to get you six *Ed Sullivan* shows," Geffen promised the band, "and we're going to get you on Janis Joplin's next tour."

Schiffman, who was not in a position to be moralizing, was nonetheless shocked. "David, what are you doing?" he said after the meeting. "Six *Ed Sullivan* shows? Are you kidding? Janis Joplin wouldn't piss on these people! We're not going to give them *any* Janis Joplin dates."

"If they have another hit, we'll get them one *Ed Sullivan* show, and we'll get them a couple of dates on somebody else's tour. I don't care," Geffen responded calmly. "And if they don't have another hit, well, fuck 'em."

W alking along El Camino Drive in Beverly Hills one afternoon with his pal Joel Dean, Geffen met the man with whom he would develop a decades-long friendship, bonded in a love that many would term brotherly. Dean flagged down Sandy Gallin, a successful TV agent, and introduced him to Geffen. Gallin and Geffen quickly became inseparable, incorrigible gossips who traded bits of information like shares of stock on the Big Board.

Like Geffen, Gallin had had a take-charge mother and a flaky father who had also died from a stroke. Gallin, who had been born in Brooklyn and raised in Lawrence, on Long Island, had gone to Boston University, graduating in 1962. He shot to stardom after booking the Beatles for their legendary 1964 American debut on *The Ed Sullivan Show.* At twenty-eight, Gallin was made senior vice president of Creative Management Associates, the youngest one in the agency's history. When he met Geffen, Gallin's star client at CMA was Tiny Tim, a wacky ukulele player who sang goofy ditties such as "Tiptoe Through the Tulips with Me" in a breathy falsetto.

Gallin had known he was gay from an early age but had nonetheless married a woman on Christmas Day 1965. The marriage collapsed after only eight months.

Freed by his divorce, Gallin became one of West Hollywood's most notorious party throwers. He spent lavishly on his soirees and made certain they were populated with the most attractive gay men in town. One night at his big new house on Sierra Mar Drive above Sunset and Doheny, Gallin threw a bash at which Tiny Tim and Laura Nyro performed. Together, the two looked sort of like circus freaks, and the partyers were stunned. Dick and Tommy Smothers, who lived down the street, showed up with Janis Joplin, who hit on Geffen and begged him to take her home with him. He, of course, demurred.

Geffen's seemingly well-adjusted good spirits at such parties, however, masked another side that remained deeply troubled by his sexuality. He had had sex with many men but no relationships to speak of, and, unlike Todd Schiffman or Sandy Gallin, he was not comfortable calling himself a homosexual.

With most people, in fact, Geffen attempted to float the notion that he was straight. Even though he saw that being gay did not hurt the careers of men he knew in show business, he was concerned about being labeled "gay" and determined to make a serious attempt at living life as a heterosexual. But he was afraid of having sex with women, and he questioned his ability to do so.

Geffen's attempt to lead a straight life confounded some of his heterosexual friends and acquaintances, many of whom assumed he was gay. Bones Howe and his wife, Melody, for example, rolled their eyes when Geffen told them how he felt about Nyro.

"I think I'm going to marry Laura," he said.

"I don't know if that's a good idea," Howe replied.

His stated romantic interest in Nyro was clearly an act, evidenced by the fact that it did not bother him when Nyro began dating Jim Fielder, the bass player in Blood, Sweat & Tears. Geffen hung out with the couple frequently and looked to Nyro in particular as a trusted confidante with whom he could share his innermost feelings. During one night out with Fielder, Nyro, and a mutual friend named Ellen Sander, issues relating to his sexual identity became cloudier.

Sander was a music journalist who had helped to establish rock criticism in the mainstream press. Geffen had discovered the value of cultivating relationships with members of the press, and Sander became a beneficiary of tips that Geffen fed her off-the-record. Sander repaid the favor by calling him a wunderkind in columns she wrote for such publications as *The New York Times, Vogue,* and *Crawdaddy.*

Late that night, the four friends went to Sander's apartment at 533 Third Avenue on the East Side. They were on acid and listening to music, and Geffen, deep in a hallucination, read aloud poetry that Sander had written.

"I really understand what every word is doing here," Geffen said. "The way each word is affecting another word, it is just beautiful."

The conversation soon turned to sex, and Geffen, his guard down, made a proclamation: "I have never had sex with a woman."

"Well, you *are* going to have it tonight!" Sander declared.

Nyro and Fielder soon made their exit, leaving Geffen and Sander alone, and the two began necking. They had been friends for some time, and Sander, who had a broad smile and black hair that fell to her shoulders, was surprised Geffen was interested in her sexually. She did not think that he felt anything toward her other than a brotherly kind of admiration.

The two began to undress when Geffen suddenly burst into tears. "What's the matter?" Sander said, worried that she had done something to upset him.

"I'm afraid that I'm gay," Geffen said.

Geffen (extreme right) with (from left) photographer
Stephen Paley, rock journalist Ellen Sander, and Jerry Wexler,
the number-two man at Atlantic Records.

(Courtesy Stephen Paley)

"Why do you think that?"

Geffen started to ramble. "I feel like I'm falling in love with my secretary," he said, telling her about the young man who answered his telephone at work. "I don't know. I'm just really scared that I'm gay."

"I don't think you're gay, David," said Sander, who did not have any homosexual friends. "Don't worry," she said, continuing to kiss him. "We don't have to make love. It's all right." Geffen continued to weep. Tripping on the acid, the emotions were contagious, and Sander began crying, too.

In the end, the two did wind up having intercourse, with Sander talking Geffen through the entire adventure, reassuring him that he was a good lover. For Geffen, the night was a key experience, and he credited Sander with helping him to conquer his fear of having sex with women. He could do it after all, and, he determined, he *would* do it.

Though he did not intend to give up his sexual exploits with men, he was going to try to keep those encounters as quiet as possible. Most important, he could now envision himself actually leading a traditional life—marrying a woman, settling down, and raising a family. And that was what he intended to do.

MAGIC IN
LAUREL CANYON

|||

It was not long before Geffen grew bored, restless, and unhappy at the Ashley Famous Agency. Even though he was signing some of the biggest acts in the business, booking concerts was tedious and thankless work, and there was only so much money to be made.

At moments such as the night that he and Todd Schiffman signed the Doors, Geffen wondered where his career was heading. The band, which had hits such as "Light My Fire," had played hard to get. Schiffman and Geffen finally insisted that they sign contracts before leaving for a European tour in the summer of 1968. Without them, the agents said, they would not be able to book their fall tour in the United States. The band agreed to meet the agents backstage after a gig in Asbury Park, New Jersey, before leaving for Europe the next morning.

Schiffman flew to New York, but his flight was three hours late, and an ever-impatient Geffen steamed as he waited for him in a limousine at the airport. Finally on the ground, Schiffman and Geffen instructed the limo driver to step on the gas because the concert had already started. A mile from Asbury Park, the limo's electrical system conked out, and the car came to a screeching halt. Geffen and Schiffman, contracts in hand, ran down the side of the road toward the Steel Pier, where the band was playing. Sweaty and disheveled, the two arrived at the venue just as Jim Morrison and his cohorts were getting into their limousines to go to Manhattan. They signed the papers, but David Geffen was not interested in any more such chases.

Soon Geffen became obsessed with the brazen idea that he ought to quit the agency and form his own label and personal-management firm. Having studied Clive Davis, he decided that he, too, had the savvy to make it in the record industry. Recalling what his mother had drilled into him about his "golden hands," it was not much of a stretch for him to envision David Geffen, the music mogul.

Geffen tried to get his friend Sandy Gallin to quit Creative Management Associates and become his partner in a new label. But Gallin, who represented such clients as Richard Pryor, Cass Elliot, and the TV producer Chuck Barris, was nervous about leaving the comfortable confines of the agency that had been his only employer since he graduated from college.

"I really like it here," Gallin told Geffen. "Why don't you come work here, too? I'm having a helluva lot of fun. I think you would, too." Geffen was amazed that Gallin was turning him down and thought Gallin's idea that he return to the agency business was ludicrous.

"You are out of your mind," Geffen told him. Telling David Geffen "no" later became one of the biggest regrets in Sandy Gallin's life.

With Gallin passing on his offer, Geffen decided to ask a superstar to be his partner. He boldly told Clive Davis that he ought to leave his job as president of Columbia Records and become his partner in a new label that they would run as co-CEOs. Showing just how formidable a player Geffen had become, Davis showed some interest in the venture, and they even talked about making Laura Nyro the label's first artist.

Back in California, Elliot Roberts was busy trying to make a star of Joni Mitchell. Her eponymously titled debut album, released in

David Crosby, Stephen Stills, and Graham Nash
hit on a winning sound. Geffen performed his own song
and dance to charm the trio. (Henry Diltz)

May 1968, had not set any sales records but was a critical success, and a Los Angeles disc jockey named B. Mitchell Reed, whom Roberts had befriended, gave it prominent airtime.

Mitchell's career was helped along further as other, more established acts began to record her songs. Judy Collins, a folksinger from Seattle who was a rising star on Elektra Records, had a hit with "Both Sides, Now." Tom Rush, another singer-songwriter on Elektra, sang "The Circle Game." Mitchell was established as a promising female singer-songwriter and was making Roberts a player in the music business.

With the money from her new record deal, Mitchell had bought a rustic little house on Lookout Mountain Road in Laurel Canyon, a winding road that started at Sunset Boulevard and stretched to Mulholland Drive at the top of the Santa Monica Mountains. Her new house, which was built into the side of a hill, looked something like a tree house, and soon became a popular hangout for her musician pals. The romance between Mitchell and David Crosby was beginning to falter, but they remained friends, and he introduced her to his plump pal Cass Elliot, whose group, the Mamas and the Papas, was about to disband, following a spectacular run of such chart hits as "California Dreamin'."

One night, the Hollies, a British group that was also crumbling, played the Whisky on Sunset Boulevard, entertaining the crowd with their hits "Bus Stop" and "Carrie-Anne." Cass Elliot knew Graham Nash, the group's de facto leader, and she took him to Mitchell's house to introduce him to Crosby. The next day, Nash and Elliot were at Mitchell's house as Crosby and Stephen Stills were harmonizing on Stills's song "You Don't Have to Cry."

"Sing that again," Nash said. Crosby and Stills repeated the song. Nash asked them to repeat it once more. The next time they began, Nash let out a high cry that rose up over the top of the blend Crosby and Stills created. The sound, an explosive three-part harmony, caught them all by surprise and dazzled Elliot and Mitchell. The three, who were all looking for a new avenue, decided to form a group.

Both together and separately, the three musicians began writing songs to showcase their new sound. "Suite: Judy Blue Eyes" started out as a long poem Stills had written about his girlfriend, Judy Collins. David Crosby wrote "Long Time Gone" the night Bobby Kennedy was shot. "Marrakesh Express" was a song Graham Nash wrote based on a 1966 trip he had taken with his first wife, Rose.

Even though his heart was not in it, Graham Nash had to return home to the United Kingdom to make some dates for the Hollies and to break the news that he was quitting. But before he went, the three new friends went into a recording studio and belted out rough demos of "Helplessly Hoping," "You Don't Have to Cry," and "In the Morning When You Rise."

The men, still uncertain as to what they might call their band, asked Elliot Roberts to be their manager. But after a few months, when it came time to secure a recording contract for the group, Roberts realized that he was not up to the task. Although he had snared recording deals for Young and Mitchell at Reprise, Roberts did not know how to untangle the contractual commitments of the three singers and consolidate them onto a single label.

Nash, because of his role in the Hollies, was on CBS's Epic label and still owed the company one more album. Crosby had some old commitments to CBS's Columbia label because of the Byrds. And Stills had unfulfilled contract obligations to Atlantic stemming from Buffalo Springfield. Roberts did not have contacts at any of those labels, and he additionally feared that the inflated egos of the singers might be too much for him to handle on his own. There was only one person he knew who could pull off this kind of trick.

At that moment, David Geffen was in the Virgin Islands with Laura Nyro. He had planned the trip, booking them at the posh Morningstar Hotel on Saint Thomas, so that Nyro would relax and he could make another run at convincing her that she was ready to perform in public. But the trip backfired. When he finally broached the idea of her performing in front of an audience, Nyro lashed out at him.

"You're fired!" she said. Her outburst turned out to be more of a control issue. Later in the day, she rehired him, but it was a seminal moment for Geffen: He realized then that it was not smart to have all of his eggs in one basket. He was determined to hunt for another client when he got back to the States.

Elliot Roberts's timing could not have been better. He asked Geffen to co-manage the new group with him, subject, of course, to the band's approval. Roberts told Geffen he believed that they were special. Instead of the angry music many rock groups recorded to protest the war in Vietnam, this new group's music was different. They sang gentle and consoling ballads that also reflected feelings of loss and sorrow. Roberts said he would get him a copy of the demo the band had made as quickly as possible.

It was now clear that Geffen and Roberts had skills that were devastatingly complementary: Roberts knew the artists who had the talent to make it big; Geffen knew the executives who had the power to make it happen. Roberts also had the demeanor and the vocabulary to communicate with the rock artists who, for the first time, stood to make boatloads of money in the music business.

Geffen was ecstatic and determined to quit his job at Ashley Famous and form his own company that would include a management arm and perhaps even his own record label. Crosby had already met Geffen through Roberts and Mitchell, but for Stills and Nash this was their first encounter. Like a hyperactive leprechaun, Geffen did his best song-and-dance act for the three singers.

He first told them about many of his William Morris exploits, and then eagerly outlined his plan for the new band. He told them he was optimistic about their prospects for success and guaranteed that their combined superstar status would help him secure unheard-of terms from concert promoters. He also said that he was the one to help them make a record deal. It would be his recommendation, he said, that the band sign with CBS, given that Nash and Crosby were already under contract to its Epic and Columbia labels. Geffen told them he was tight with Clive Davis and suggested that Davis would surely be enthusiastic about signing them.

Geffen's sell job worked particularly well on Stephen Stills, an attractive, soft-featured young man from Texas. But it did not result in an instant deal, mostly because David Crosby did not trust Geffen. Stills, Nash, and Crosby left the city and retired to a house in Sag Harbor, on Long Island, to refine their songs and debate the management issue.

Stephen Stills had a great deal of pull with the band, and David Geffen knew it. From the beginning, Stills was responsible for most of the group's complex instrumental scores and he served as the group's unofficial leader. Nash was an acoustic guitarist, and Crosby was a solid rhythm guitarist, but neither of them had played much lead guitar. Dubbed "Captain Manyhands" by the other two, Stills created and executed most of the parts for the finger-picked acoustic and complex rhythm guitar, as well as all the parts for bass, lead guitar, and organ. His vote was worth a lot and he cast it for Geffen.

Graham Nash also liked Geffen. In hearing Geffen's stories about how he lied to get his job at the Morris office, Nash sensed a rebellious streak in Geffen with which he could identify.

But Crosby believed that Geffen was a ruthless businessman who was just out to get rich. He was also broke and deeply in debt. Nevertheless, that had not made him any less cocky; he seemed in no hurry to make a deal and instead suggested that the group meet with Simon and Garfunkel's manager to see what he could offer them.

Finally, Stills convinced Crosby that they should go with Geffen, pacifying him by reminding him that Elliot Roberts, with whom Crosby played basketball, would share the management duties. Stills hit on a particularly persuasive argument by telling Crosby that if they were going to win big, they needed a monster like Geffen on their side to look out for their interests. Before long, Stills had Crosby saying the same thing. "We're in a shark pool here," Crosby said. "We need a shark to look after us."

Stills telephoned Geffen and told him the good news. The band arranged to meet him to shake hands on the arrangement at his duplex on Central Park South. The moment they walked in, however, Crosby dropped a bombshell. "You know, we like you and we want you to be our manager," he said, "but we don't want to sign any contracts."

The idea that an artist and a manager would not have a contract spelling out the terms of their relationship was preposterous at the time. But Geffen wanted the band badly and reasoned wisely on the spot that such contracts had dubious value anyway. "I don't think I want to be involved in as intimate a relationship as a personal manager with anybody if they don't want to be with me," he said later. "The relationship is based on a certain amount of love and understanding and mutuality, and if those things don't exist, what's the point of having it?" He decided that one of his trademarks as a manager would be that he would not ask artists to sign agreements. Turning to Crosby, Geffen said, "Well, that's OK, I don't believe in contracts myself."

But just as the four men were about to shake hands, Crosby found himself flipping through the vast record collection belonging to Helen Noga, the dowager from whom Geffen was subleasing the apartment. Crosby wigged out as he saw that the entire wall was filled with syrupy albums by artists such as Johnny Mathis and Mantovani, the cheesy Italian orchestra conductor. "Is this what you listen to?" Crosby snapped. "Is this your taste in music?" Crosby would not listen as Geffen explained frantically that the albums were not his.

Geffen ran to the phone, dialed Laura Nyro, and begged her to come over immediately. For all her moods, Nyro nonetheless loved Geffen, and she could sense that this was a moment in which he really needed her. When she walked into the apartment, an ashen Geffen pointed to Noga's piano, a white baby grand, and ordered her to play. As Nyro began singing, Geffen did not even need to say the obvious: *This* was the kind of music he listened to. Crosby's heart melted as he watched Geffen hover over Nyro as she banged out tunes that she was soon to record for her second Columbia album, *New York Tendaberry.*

With Laura Nyro and another promising client to launch his personal-management company, Geffen went to see Ted Ashley and told him he planned to quit. Ashley and other senior officials at the agency were upset that Geffen was skipping out on them after less than a year, but he refused to stay on. He wanted out, and he wanted out now. In February 1969, Geffen left Ashley Famous and opened the doors of his own firm, which he immodestly called David Geffen Enterprises. Seeking to give more heft to the news, he lied and told *Cashbox,* a music-industry trade magazine, that he had also formed his own record label and that he had signed a distribution deal with "a major firm."

D espite the blowup that had taken place in the Virgin Islands, Geffen remained fiercely committed to making Nyro a star. Yet even though she was his closest friend, they often had enormous arguments that left Geffen hurt and disturbed. Elliot Roberts concluded that Geffen was in love with Nyro because he could not sleep or go on with life in a normal fashion as long as a spat remained unresolved.

Geffen was succeeding in rebuilding her sense of self-worth, however, and at last she agreed to play a single concert date. Geffen booked her at a college in Buffalo, far away from the harsh spotlight of the music scene in New York. Roberts was in New York and offered to come along and handle the lights and sound for the show. Geffen and Nyro were nervous in the car, and the three spoke little during the long trip. The concert, to the great pleasure of Geffen, Nyro, and the audience, was a big success.

As Nyro prepared to go into the studio to record *New York Tendaberry,* Geffen decided he could no longer resist the pull to move to California. Ever since Roberts had begun reporting from the West Coast, Geffen had felt that there was huge money to be made in Los Angeles and believed that he could dominate the scene if only he were there full-time.

His main tie to New York was Nyro, but now her confidence had rebounded, and she had agreed to play several more concerts, including ones at the Manhattan branch of the Pratt Institute and the Brooklyn Academy of Music. As a compromise, Geffen hired Lee Houskeeper, a twenty-year-old who was the gofer for Stills's group out in Sag Harbor, to keep watch over her. Paid by Geffen, Houskeeper served as road manager on some of Nyro's concerts.

Geffen's major task before he could move to California was to make a record deal for the as-yet-unnamed band featuring Stills, Crosby, and Nash. It was to take only a few days to accomplish, but pulling it off forced Geffen into a challenging game of three-dimensional chess. More than any previous deal, this one was to illustrate how Geffen's persistence and single-mindedness were to be the keys to his success over the next three decades.

He had already filled Clive Davis's ears with hyperbolic praise about the new act, and he now played the demo tape for him. Davis was indeed impressed; he had believed in the Byrds and the Hollies and was sorry they had broken up. He had further enjoyed the performance of Buffalo Springfield at Monterey and admired Stephen Stills. Geffen informed Davis that he was off to Atlantic Records to get a release for Stills; once he had that, he explained, he could make the deal at CBS.

The only person Geffen knew at Atlantic Records was Jerry Wexler, Atlantic's president, a renowned music man who just a year earlier had signed Aretha Franklin and shepherded her soul hits "Respect" and "I Never Loved a Man (the Way I Love You)." Geffen called Wexler's office at 1841 Broadway, made an appointment, and headed over. It was to be a rough morning.

A tall man with a graying beard, thick black eyebrows, and black-rimmed glasses, Wexler was twenty-five years Geffen's senior. He was a curmudgeon with a notoriously short fuse, and he despised agents. He bristled as Geffen hurried into his office and made his brash pitch about how he wanted to take Stephen Stills over to Columbia so he could be in a new band with David Crosby and Graham Nash. Buffalo Springfield was history anyway, Geffen exclaimed with a flourish, so this really was not all that big of a request.

Wexler, who cared deeply about music, and personally produced the recordings of many of Atlantic's star acts, thought Geffen's aggression went beyond the bounds of civilized behavior. Seeing Geffen as nothing more than a parasite looking to make a buck, Wexler lost his temper.

"Get the fuck outta here!" he barked. Geffen's eyes grew huge as Wexler picked him up and physically ejected him from his office.

Huffing and puffing, Geffen ran back to his apartment on Central Park South, where Stephen Stills was eagerly awaiting his report.

"My God, they're animals over there," he said. "We've got to get you out of there."

The next day, Atlantic Records chairman Ahmet Ertegun caught wind of what had gone down. Ertegun called Geffen and told him he was a big fan of Stills and that he had been the executive at Atlantic who had signed Buffalo Springfield. He was curious, he told Geffen, to learn about Stills's new group. On the telephone, at least, Geffen thought that Ertegun sounded quite unlike the hotheaded Wexler. He was excited that there seemed to be a rational person at the label with whom he could talk. Geffen hustled back to Atlantic and headed to Ertegun's office.

A hmet Ertegun was born in Turkey, was fluent in three languages, and had been driven around in chauffeured limousines since he was a child. His father had been a Turkish ambassador, as a result of which the Erteguns had spent time in Switzerland, France, England, and Washington, D.C. It was in England that ten-year-old Ahmet slipped away to the London Palladium to listen to the orchestras of Cab Calloway and Duke Ellington, the start of a lifelong obsession with black music. It was an art form to which he and his older brother, Nesuhi, dedicated their lives.

As a kid, Ahmet defied his mother's wishes and ventured out at night into New York's black neighborhoods, such as Harlem, to hear the best black musicians in America play jazz and the blues. Ertegun grew into an educated and cultured entrepreneur and formed, along with a for-mer dentist named Herb Abramson, Atlantic in 1947. He then turned the company into a record-industry powerhouse, making such stars as Ray Charles, Joe Turner, Wilson Pickett, and Otis Redding. Twenty years later, Ertegun and Wexler (Abramson had left in the late 1950s) sold Atlantic to Warner Bros., which in turn had become part of Steve Ross's Kinney Service. Ross soon changed the name of the company to Warner Communications.

Ertegun had style, panache, and a kind of old-world charm. He was a fabulous raconteur and was extremely rich. He liked to drink and smoke and boasted that he could stay up later than people half his age. He was everything that David Geffen wanted to be.

From the moment he scurried into Ertegun's office, Geffen was cap-tivated. Bald except for a thin stretch of hair above his ears and around the back of his head, Ertegun, forty-five, had a finely groomed goatee and heavy eyelids that closed slowly over his eyes. He wore the finest handmade suits and sported fashionable ties and stylish handkerchiefs that spilled out of his breast pocket. At the Morris office, Geffen's old mentor Jerry Brandt had worn fine suits, but he now saw that Brandt did not carry them the way Ertegun did. More important, Geffen could see that the two men were in different leagues: Jerry Brandt was a booker; Ahmet Ertegun was a *legend.*

Ertegun could see that David Geffen came from a very different world than the one he had known growing up. Geffen quickly rattled off his oft-told tales about Borough Park and William Morris. He also told Ertegun about how he had rescued Laura Nyro.

The two conversed easily for almost an hour, with Geffen master-fully flattering the fabled music titan. When Geffen asked him how to make it in the music business, Ertegun said, "Well, you walk very slow."

A perplexed Geffen asked him to explain.

"You walk very slow and maybe by chance you'll bump into a genius, and he'll make you rich."

Geffen instantly decided Ertegun was a man he wanted to get to know better and told him so. Geffen seemed particularly interested as Ertegun talked about his burgeoning modern-art collection and his aristocratic friends in Europe. Ertegun, for his part, could see that Geffen was a culturally undeveloped animal, lacking grace and sophistication. Yet he was an amusing young man, and, unlike Wexler, Ertegun found his boundless energy beguiling and hardly threatening. Ertegun decided he would take on the challenge of refining this raw apprentice.

Finally, Geffen made his pitch for Stephen Stills.

"We're not going to let go of Stephen Stills," Ertegun told Geffen gently. "That is out of the question."

He had few complimentary things to say about Nash and Crosby and suggested to Geffen that he still controlled the one musician who would be the new group's star. Stills had been the anchor of Buffalo Springfield, he told Geffen, ignoring the significant contributions of Neil Young and the others.

Ertegun laid out a new plan: Instead of releasing Stills to go join the others at Columbia, why didn't Geffen get releases from Columbia for Nash and Crosby and have the new group record for Atlantic? The idea had not even crossed Geffen's mind, but he thought Ertegun's pitch was brilliant. The group would then have an ally in the label's chairman, and Geffen himself would have a powerful new friend in the record business.

Geffen hurried down to Black Rock, the building at Sixth Avenue and Fifty-second Street that was home to CBS Records, and informed Clive Davis that he had changed his mind. Davis was upset that Geffen had reneged on his promise to bring this new act to CBS.

"Absolutely no," he said, when Geffen asked him to release Crosby and Nash. "We'll have to work out some kind of compromise. For instance, I'll take the first record, and they can have the subsequent records."

Geffen shot back up to Ertegun, who said he did not like Davis's proposal. He had seen Buffalo Springfield break up after only a handful of records and demanded that the deal be reversed. "Listen, I wouldn't guarantee that these guys will be together to finish even a first record," he told Geffen. "Tell Clive *I'll* take the first record, and he can have all the rest."

Davis, sensing correctly that Geffen was dumping him in favor of a new mentor, was not pleased. But Geffen's mind was made up; Ahmet Ertegun was his new pal, and there was nothing Davis was going to be able to do to change that. To put the whole messy situation behind him, Davis then offered his own solution: He wanted Poco, a new band just signed by Atlantic that featured some other ex–Buffalo Springfield members, Richie Furay and Jim Messina. If Geffen could get Ertegun to give up Poco, Davis bargained, Atlantic could then have David Crosby and Graham Nash. The whole deal would be a little like trading baseball cards.

Geffen once again returned to Ertegun's office. But the Atlantic chairman said he was reluctant to give up the new act. "That's pretty heavy," he told Geffen, who then begged him to play ball.

"Ahmet, you must do this for me," he pleaded.

Finally, Ertegun agreed to the trade, and the band signed to Atlantic Records. Soon afterward, the new act decided to use their own names for that of the band. Arranged so that the moniker rolled off the tongue, the order would be Crosby, Stills & Nash. Plans were made to record the group's first album in Los Angeles.

As he had been with Laura Nyro, Geffen was instantly CSN's most enthusiastic advocate. He loved the band's music and became teary the first time he heard "Suite: Judy Blue Eyes." "They're going to be huge! They're going to be huge!" he said upon playing the record for Ertegun in New York.

Ertegun was excited, too, but he had more measured expectations. "They're not going to be as big as the Association," he warned.

In Brooklyn, Batya, now sixty-one, had begun to worry about David's welfare after he had informed her that he had left his talent-agency job and was now working for himself as a personal manager. By being his own boss, he told her, he could wear blue jeans and T-shirts all day long.

"I don't understand," Batya told him. "What does a manager do? What does it mean to manage somebody?"

When David responded that managing meant advising people on their careers, she became even more baffled.

"You?" she asked.

Her youngest son had turned twenty-six in February 1969 but Batya could not help but continue to mother him as if he were still a child. When he told her he was battling the flu that winter, she telephoned Lee Houskeeper and told him she needed him to come to the corset shop in Borough Park at once.

There was a blinding blizzard as Houskeeper made his way west on the Long Island Expressway from Sag Harbor, taking various wrong turns and getting lost in Brooklyn before pulling up in front of Batya's shop on Thirteenth Avenue. Tiny Batya toddled out through the snow to the curb. In her hands was a jar filled with hot chicken soup, which she ordered Houskeeper to deliver immediately to David's apartment.

Before long, Batya telephoned David and shared with him the excellent news that she had met a man and planned to remarry. Samuel Sandler was a soft-spoken mailman she had met at a "senior dance" at the Flatbush Jewish Center, and the two had recently become engaged.

Sam, a sweet, fifty-four-year-old divorcé, adored Batya. Like Abe, however, he was a rather passive guy, and Batya no doubt chose him for the same reasons she had chosen Abe. It had been seven years since Abe died, and David was glad to see his mother happy once again. David and Mitchell went to Las Vegas, where Batya and Sam exchanged vows in the study of a local rabbi.

The CSN deal clinched, Geffen finally moved to Los Angeles. Although he continued to lease the Central Park South apartment in New York, he was ever afterward to call Los Angeles home.

Not interested in wasting time finding a place to live, Geffen called Wayne Weisbart, an agent friend who worked at the Morris office in Beverly Hills, and asked him if he could rent a room in his house in

Studio City. Geffen set up shop in the front bedroom of Weisbart's house, wiring it with multiple phone lines and hiring his own maid to clean and cook for him.

But just as soon as he arrived on the West Coast, problems were erupting back in New York. Clive Davis's anger with Geffen over the CSN situation had festered to the point where the two men now rarely even spoke to each other. One day, Lee Houskeeper, who was in the studio with Laura Nyro recording the *New York Tendaberry* album, received an alarming phone call from Davis just as a reporter and photographer from *Life* magazine arrived to interview her. Davis told Houskeeper that he was suspending Nyro's recording sessions effective immediately. The problem was that Roy Halee, Nyro's producer, was also producing Simon and Garfunkel's new album across the hall. Halee was burning out under the pressure, and Simon and Garfunkel, recording such songs as "Bridge over Troubled Water" and "The Boxer," demanded that Davis assign Halee to their sessions full-time.

Houskeeper did not tell Nyro, who he knew would not take the news well. Nyro was fragile and stressed out and halting the sessions would have destroyed the momentum she had worked for months to establish. She had even asked Houskeeper to arrange for a horse-drawn carriage to pick her up at her apartment and take her to the recording studio each night; the clackety-clack of the hooves seemed to put her in the precise frame of mind for recording.

Houskeeper phoned Geffen in California with the news. Geffen flew into a rage and instructed Houskeeper to phone Davis right back and deliver this speech: "Say that you just told Laura the news, and that she is throwing a fit and saying all kinds of nasty things about you, Clive," Geffen snarled. "Tell him that unfortunately there's a reporter and a photographer here from *Life* magazine who have heard the whole thing."

Davis was horrified when Houskeeper called back and gave the incendiary speech as Geffen had coached; he knew *Life* was working on a story on Nyro, and he certainly did not want to jeopardize that publicity. He frantically told Houskeeper not to do anything—he would get right back to him. Minutes later, Davis called Houskeeper to tell him he had cleared the time and that Nyro could finish her album as scheduled, with Roy Halee as producer.

Unfortunately, Geffen's problems with Nyro extended beyond the recording studio. Nyro's motion for summary judgment in the lawsuit against Artie Mogull was finally heard in New York state court early in 1969, but Judge Samuel H. Hofstadter's decision pleased neither Geffen nor Mogull.

The judge, citing Mogull's failure to seek approval from the court, nullified Mogull's management agreement with Nyro. However, he refused to negate Mogull's publishing agreement with her, stating that the law was limited to "performance contracts" and said nothing about publishing. The judge ruled that a full trial was needed to resolve the issue.

Geffen steamed. For more than a year now, he had repeated to himself that Mogull had had nothing to do with Nyro. Mogull, however, was also unhappy. Both parties appealed the judge's order.

Crosby, Stills & Nash, meanwhile, were busy recording their album in Hollywood, at Wally Heider's Studio III. The sessions went smoothly but sometimes ran long into the night, and each man bragged that he smoked a joint and snorted a line of cocaine before the start of every session.

The relationship between the three singers was the best it would ever be, and it seemed to onlookers as though they were linked psychically. Geffen, Roberts, Ertegun, and Joni Mitchell, who was now dating Graham Nash, stopped by the studio to watch as the guys banged out one song after another. Some of the tracks, such as "Lady of the Island," were recorded effortlessly on the first take.

As the June 1969 release date of CSN's debut album neared, Geffen was on the phone daily with Ertegun in New York, brainstorming ideas for promotion. Everyone agreed that "Marrakesh Express," a catchy, upbeat tune that showcased the group's harmonies, would be the perfect song to promote as the album's first single.

Next, Geffen turned his attentions to plans for the band's first tour. If the group was to break out quickly, it would need a large venue in which to kick the tour off, one that would generate enormous publicity and get the message out about their revolutionary new sound.

Geffen soon began hearing reports that a music festival was being organized to take place that August in Woodstock, New York, a two-and-a-half-hour drive northwest of New York City, and quickly made a deal for the band to play there. Geffen could not know that his new act's performance at the so-called Woodstock Music and Art Fair was to forever link each to the other.

MOGUL
IN TRAINING

|||

G effen wanted more than anything to form his own record label, and he fumed as Clive Davis dragged his feet on Geffen's offer to become partners in such a new venture. Trying to stir up more interest and press Davis to make a decision, Geffen went to the music press and announced once again that he would be launching a label operation shortly. On May 24, 1969, three months after *Cashbox* had reported the news, *Billboard* put the story at the top of its front page. It duly reported Geffen's exaggerated claims that he had been offered a label deal by "several major companies."

Geffen had recognized how easy it was for him to manipulate the press. The media were to become some of his most powerful tools to help him get what he wanted. *Billboard* quoted Geffen as saying that he had narrowed the offers down to two companies and would decide on one soon. He said his label would be a "cooperative venture" in which all the artists would participate in the company's profits.

He spoke too soon. His plan with Clive Davis soon imploded when the two men had a huge disagreement over how big a roster the new label would have. While Davis, used to running a music conglomerate, argued for a long list of clients, Geffen wanted the company to have only a few artists. Davis decided to stay at Columbia. The other offers Geffen claimed to have had apparently vaporized as well.

Davis Crosby, Graham Nash, and Stephen Stills were swimming in the pool behind the house where Geffen was living in Studio City the first time they heard "Marrakesh Express" on the radio. The song, and the album, released the third week of June 1969, were instant hits, and critical reaction was swift and effusive. At last, Geffen was managing an act that was both acclaimed critically and successful commercially.

The friendship between Geffen and Stephen Stills continued to grow. Geffen invited the musician to stay at his Central Park South duplex when Stills went to spend a few months in New York. Geffen spent considerable time there, too, and for a period the two were roommates who seemed to be straight out of *The Odd Couple.* While Geffen was a finicky creature obsessed with cleanliness, Stills was a slob who left clothes on the floor and open containers of food on the counter.

Their conversations sometimes turned to personal matters, yet Stills did not quiz Geffen on his sexual exploits. Stills figured that Geffen was gay, but he could sense that he was uncomfortable with his sexuality. To Stills, it was a nonissue; he had a number of close friends who were gay.

Geffen and Stills meticulously planned the details of Crosby, Stills & Nash's first set of live concerts. But Stills was concerned that the band's acoustic act would not be enough to fill big concert venues. He thought that the group should first play an acoustic set and then change gears, pulling out electric guitars and wowing crowds with some rock 'n' roll. Stills knew that they could not pull off such a feat on their own; they needed another instrumentalist to jack up the group's sound.

Stills first thought that a keyboard player was what the group needed. He went to England to try to convince Stevie Winwood, who was playing in Blind Faith with Eric Clapton, to join the group. But

Elliot Roberts contemplates Neil Young, Neil Young contemplates the camera, and Graham Nash chats with David Geffen at the offices of the Geffen Roberts Company on Sunset Boulevard in West Hollywood. (Henry Diltz)

Winwood was not interested, and neither was Stills's second choice, Mark Naftalin, who played keyboards for the Butterfield Blues Band.

Geffen and Stills were having dinner with Ahmet Ertegun at his townhouse on the Upper East Side when Ertegun offered the winning idea. Ertegun put on old Buffalo Springfield records, including "I Am a Child," a song written by Neil Young. "We ought to add Neil to CSN," Ertegun said. "There's something about Neil Young that goes with this."

"But, Ahmet," Stills protested, "he's already quit on me twice. What do you think's gonna happen this time?"

Stills reluctantly agreed to float the idea to his two partners. Crosby and Nash were resistant at first, concerned that the band needed a backup musician, not another star performer to share the spotlight. Even though Young's first solo album had not sold particularly well, he was highly regarded for his songwriting abilities and his talent on the guitar. He had just finished his second solo album, on which he used a trio of backup musicians he called Crazy Horse.

Geffen was also concerned about Young, having heard stories from Elliot Roberts of the strained relationship between Young and Stills. Buffalo Springfield, after all, had broken up largely because Stills and Young disliked each other so intensely that they sometimes refused to be in the studio together. Geffen also knew that Young and David Crosby had had some difficulties dating back to the festival at Monterey, at which Crosby had played in Neil Young's place.

But Stills valued Ertegun's advice and came slowly to the conclusion that he was right. Geffen told Roberts of the plan, but Roberts refused to be the one to approach Young about the potentially explosive combination. He insisted that Stills personally would have to invite Young to join the group.

Stills made the phone call and, to the dismay of the others, Young was receptive. Despite their past differences, Young nonetheless had fond memories of Buffalo Springfield and knew there was a special combustion of musical energy when he and Stills played together.

In a sign that other troubles would surely plague the group down the road, there was a sticking point: The three principals did not want to add Young's name to the marquee. The solo album that was to make Young a star, *Everybody Knows This Is Nowhere,* was not to be released until later that month. In the meantime, the three cocky superstars did not want to mess with their now-famous band's name.

For Young, it was a deal breaker. "If my name's involved, if I'm getting an equal share, I'll deal with Stephen," he told Roberts. "But it has to be equal, because he's going to overplay, he's going to step on me and do all the other things that he does." The three original partners reconsidered, finally voting unanimously to bring Young on board; at the beginning of August 1969, the group was rechristened Crosby, Stills, Nash & Young.

At this point, Geffen and Roberts decided to formally become business partners in a management enterprise. It made sense to do so, given that they were co-managing what looked to be a very big act. In addition, Roberts took on a small role in managing Laura Nyro, with whom he had once shared a brief but passionate bit of necking. Geffen, for his part, offered his advice on the career of Joni Mitchell, who greatly enjoyed the time she spent with Geffen. None of the clients signed management contracts, and Geffen told people that he thought of the company as "kind of like a family/love thing."

Meanwhile, the organizers of the music festival set to take place in Woodstock had begun looking for other locations since a suitable site could not be found. After investigating one site in Wallkill, about thirty miles south of Woodstock, they finally reached an agreement to hold the event on Max Yasgur's farm outside Bethel, New York. As Geffen finalized arrangements for CSNY to play there, he hit on an opportunity for the band to play the night before at the Auditorium Theatre in Chicago.

The city of Los Angeles was shaken on August 9 when a hit team led by a psychopath and aspiring songwriter named Charles Manson stormed the Beverly Hills home of movie director Roman Polanski, killing his pregnant wife, actress Sharon Tate, and four of her guests.

The next day, Geffen visited his friend Lou Adler, who had a house at the end of Carbon Beach, a fancy stretch of sandy property in Malibu. Geffen and Adler walked along the beach but stopped when they came upon Terry Melcher and his girlfriend, actress Candice Bergen. They were standing in front of an elegant beach house owned by Melcher and his mother, Doris Day.

Geffen and Adler listened as a frightened Melcher and Bergen told them that they suspected that they might have been the murderers' real targets. Melcher, who was an independent producer at the Beatles' Apple Records label, had auditioned Manson but opted not to record him; what's more, until just a few months earlier, he and Bergen had lived in the house where Tate and the others had been murdered.

Geffen's eyes, however, roamed up to the beach house. He was struck by its simple beauty and fell in love with it at once. Compared with some of the other homes along Carbon Beach, it was rather small, but it had large windows and a deck that faced the ocean. It did not have a large yard and in fact was situated right off the Pacific Coast Highway.

Like his father, Geffen had a fascination with water and boats, and he found the sound of the ocean calming. "One day," he thought, "I'll own this house."

Joni Mitchell, whose second album, *Clouds,* had furthered her reputation as one of music's premier singer-songwriters, was the opening act for the debut Crosby, Stills, Nash & Young concert in Chicago on August 16, 1969. After Mitchell performed, Crosby, Stills, and Nash took to the stage and played "Suite: Judy Blue Eyes" as well as a couple of other acoustic songs from their just-released album. They then introduced Neil Young, who joined them for an acoustic version of "On the Way Home," the old Buffalo Springfield tune. As Stills promised, the group then traded in their acoustic guitars for electric ones, and blasted the crowd with rock 'n' roll that shook the rafters. The concert ran nearly three hours and was an unqualified smash.

The next day, the band and its entourage flew to New York from Chicago. Geffen was anxious as he read in *The New York Times* about the mob, so far peaceful, that had descended on the Woodstock festival. More than three hundred thousand young people, double the estimated crowd, had gathered at the site for the three-day folk-rock concert featuring, among others, the Who, Janis Joplin, Jefferson Airplane, and the Band.

But the *Times* was reporting that the area had become paralyzed with traffic. Rainstorms had turned Yasgur's farm into a sea of mud, making it nearly impossible to get in or out. At the end of the first day, Short Line Bus, which had provided the only bus service to the site from New York City, canceled all future trips at the request of police.

The first night was scheduled to wrap up around four o'clock in the morning, but the torrential downpour prompted the organizers to call it quits around midnight. Joan Baez closed the night, leading the crowd in singing "We Shall Overcome."

After just one day, the organizers had run out of food and fresh water, hippies were sleeping on the rain-soaked ground, and doctors were being called from everywhere to come and treat those who were suffering from bad acid trips and other accidents. To Geffen, it sounded like a disaster, and one that he would like to avoid.

Stills arranged for a private plane to take the group to a small airport a few miles from the site; helicopters would then take them the rest of the way. Meanwhile, Geffen and Roberts huddled and made a plan. Roberts would go to the festival with the band, but Geffen would stay in Manhattan with Joni Mitchell, who had also planned to go to Woodstock but was scheduled to appear on *The Dick Cavett Show* the next night. Geffen feared that Mitchell would get stuck upstate and miss the valuable TV appearance.

Roberts, who had a fear of flying, was panicked as the helicopters hovered over the concert site. Rain pounded the side of the helicopters as they made an uneasy landing. The band was impatient as their shuttle ride to the stage was late, concerned that their equipment would get soaked. They stole a nearby pickup, hot-wired by Neil Young, and tore off toward the stage area with Stills's friend Jimi Hendrix clinging to the hood.

The band went on at about three o'clock in the morning on the final day of the festival; they performed their act as they had in Chicago, opening with the acoustic set. When they finished, the crowd erupted in applause.

"Thank you," Stills told the crowd. "We needed that."

"This is our second gig," Crosby chimed in.

"This is the second time we've ever played in front of people, man!" Stills continued. "And we're scared shitless!"

The stage crew brought out the band's amplifiers, and the musicians went to work delivering their powerful electric set.

For many who attended, it was this performance that they remembered as the highlight of Woodstock. The messages of free love, democracy, and idealism in Crosby, Stills, Nash & Young's songs perfectly embodied the mood and feeling of the festival.

Back in Geffen's apartment in New York, Mitchell was entranced by news coverage of the event. She was on a bit of a religious kick, having turned to God for guidance at a time when she and her newly famous friends found themselves being looked to for leadership by scores of young people. It was a role she took seriously. The festival impressed her as something of a modern miracle, "like a modern day fishes-and-loaves story," she remembered, reflecting on it as a huge mass of optimistic people demonstrating unusual cooperation. It was these feelings that inspired her to write a song entitled "Woodstock."

Geffen's fears that people would be trapped at the Woodstock festival proved to be unfounded. The four members of the band returned to New York the following day, in time to accompany Mitchell to the *Dick Cavett Show* and even join her on air for a moment. But there was little time to rest. The next day, CSNY and Mitchell were scheduled to open a five-night stand Geffen had booked at the Greek Theater in Los Angeles.

With CSNY's concerts proving to be huge successes, Geffen and Roberts pushed the newly augmented band to make an album. "Suite: Judy Blue Eyes," the second single on CSN's album, had reached number twenty-one, but fans liked the hard rock-'n'-roll element added by Neil Young, and the managers bet that an album featuring the four musicians would do even better.

The musicians eagerly went about writing songs for the new album. Graham Nash was now living with Joni Mitchell in her house on Lookout Mountain and sat at her piano looking at the two cats in the yard as he wrote a song called "Our House." Neil Young wrote a tune called "Helpless," Stephen Stills penned a song entitled "4+20," and David Crosby wrote the song that also became the name of the album, "Déjà Vu."

But there were just too many egos, and it soon became clear that Crosby, Stills, Nash & Young was to have a rather short life. The trouble began when, during a concert at the Fillmore East in New York attended by Bob Dylan, Stills went off the program and, hoping to impress Dylan, hogged the stage and sang three solos. At intermission, the four musicians were at one another's throats.

Then, tragedy struck: Just before they were to open a four-night stand at the Winterland Auditorium in Northern California, Christine Hinton, Crosby's girlfriend, was killed in a car crash. The concerts were canceled. Crosby was devastated, but in October he joined the group in the studio as scheduled to record their new album. The band was moved by Joni Mitchell's song "Woodstock," and asked her to teach it to them so they could include it on their record.

This time, the warm feelings that had been so much in evidence when Crosby, Stills & Nash had recorded their debut album were noticeably absent. The recording sessions went over budget as the four wasted time bickering and fighting over credits for the songs. After finishing a cut of "Woodstock" that satisfied three of the members, Stills continued to tinker with it, and petty arguments broke out as the others accused him of weakening it.

When the album was finished in mid-November, the band began a tour that Geffen and Roberts had coordinated. Called the "Carry On" tour, the event marked the first time a rock-'n'-roll act had played so many arena shows in such a short time. The tour lasted three months, a longer period than any of the musicians had ever performed on the road. In the first month alone, they played Honolulu, Denver, Salt Lake City, San Antonio, Phoenix, Los Angeles, Sacramento, Pittsburgh, Cleveland, Chicago, and Detroit.

Geffen hated touring with the band and ended up spending little time on the road with them. He was antsy and disliked dealing with boorish promoters. Roberts, on the other hand, was more relaxed about hanging out with the musicians on tour. He became the duo's point man on the road, ready to handle the problems that developed at each new venue.

Geffen and Roberts's management partnership was hotter than ever, but Laura Nyro, the client Geffen believed in most, was decidedly not hot. Despite generally positive reviews, *New York Tendaberry* sold only about two hundred thousand copies. Columbia's attempts to interest radio stations in playing her singles failed once again.

What's more, the strain of managing Nyro was beginning to wear Geffen down. After a small publication wrote a glowing profile of Nyro that misspelled her real last name, Nigro, as Negro, she flipped out. She demanded that Geffen drive through Manhattan, pick up every copy he could find, and bring them back to her apartment to burn in the fireplace. Geffen did as he was told but was quietly growing tired of Nyro's eccentric high-jinks.

He also began to fear that Nyro would never cross over, that her singing abilities would never match her unique songwriting talent. It stunned him that Nyro seemed content with the status she had achieved as a cult figure. He thought his job was to make her wealthy and famous, and it was now becoming clear that the two had different goals.

He soon realized that the best thing he could do would be to continue to get others to record her songs, thereby increasing her fame incrementally and, since they were equal partners in Tuna Fish Music, making them both rich. Geffen pushed the catalog of Nyro's songs aggressively. He made a deal with Blood, Sweat & Tears to record "And When I Die." The Fifth Dimension recorded "Wedding Bell Blues." Three Dog Night sang "Eli's Comin'." The three bands were terrifically successful at the time, and by November 1969 all three songs were in the top ten.

Laura Nyro's star was shining brighter than it ever had, and now the dream that Geffen had promised her came true: He secured a gig for her to give two concerts at Carnegie Hall. Nyro was both excited and nervous about it. At Geffen's request, Sandy Gallin cut short a vacation in Acapulco with their mutual friend Barry Diller to be at Geffen's side for the concert.

The concerts were held the weekend following Thanksgiving. When Nyro took to the stage, her fans greeted her with a standing ovation. The stage was empty save for a grand piano on which Geffen, at Nyro's direction, had placed a single rose in a tall, narrow vase. The concerts were simple affairs, with Nyro playing and singing unassumingly. One critic called the engagement one of the major events in popular music of the 1960s.

Days after the Carnegie Hall concerts, Geffen went to Clive Davis with an offer to sell Tuna Fish Music to CBS. He was praying for a windfall and wanted to strike while the iron was hot. Geffen felt that the songs Nyro was writing for the next album were not as good as the songs that were now in the top ten. "There will never be a moment like this again," he thought, seeing dollar signs amid his client's fine achievement.

Davis was interested, in part because he had recently committed to build up April-Blackwood, CBS's music publishing company. Tuna Fish Music had already earned over half a million dollars, and Davis knew it would automatically continue to earn substantial income as an annuity from past copyrights.

Davis and Geffen shook hands on a plan for CBS to acquire the company in a tax-free exchange of stock, as soon as the lawsuits with Artie Mogull were settled. Geffen and Nyro were to split the value of seventy-five thousand shares of CBS, which were trading at forty-five dollars each, making the deal worth more than three million dollars. At the same time, Nyro was to sign a new long-term recording contract at Columbia. It was a staggering amount of money, the likes of which had rarely before been applied to the value of any solo artist's catalog of songs. David Geffen and Laura Nyro would become millionaires.

Geffen succeeded in getting the trade papers to write major articles about the whopping publishing deal. The music business was abuzz with the news, stunning the crowd at the Troubadour on Santa Monica Boulevard in West Hollywood. Monday was "Hoot Night" at the Troubadour, when unknowns could get up and play, and Geffen was a regular who was now treated like royalty. Many people quizzed him on how he had secured the unheard-of terms; others sought his advice in negotiating their own deals or solving other business problems.

Johnny Rivers, a singer from Baton Rouge who had been the first act at the opening of the Whisky in 1964, turned to Geffen when negotiations to sell his Soul City label to Bell Records faltered. Discussions between the lawyers and accountants on both sides had reached a standstill, but Geffen stepped in and with seeming effortlessness negotiated a deal that both sides considered fair.

Instead of paying Geffen a fee, Rivers agreed to sell him his house just outside the city limits of Beverly Hills, high above Sunset Boulevard, for the bargain price of one hundred thousand dollars. As real estate in the so-called Beverly Hills Post Office neighborhood went, it was a rather modest-sized house, but it sat on a large piece of property. Situated on Alto Cedro Drive, just north of the fancy Trousdale Estates, the home had a gate at the driveway and a pool on the hillside. There would be no more renting rooms from friends for David Geffen.

Geffen was riding high. Yet he remained unsettled and plagued by feelings of insecurity and dissatisfaction. He was driven by a devil that constantly told him he needed to be bigger, more, and something else. He simply was not the kind of man who was going to stand in one place for very long.

He decided suddenly that now was the right moment to turn his attentions to fulfilling the fantasy he had had since reading *Hollywood Rajah,* Bosley Crowther's biography of Louis B. Mayer. While Geffen greatly enjoyed his newfound position as the music industry's boy wonder, he wanted, above all, to be a powerbroker in the movie business.

It was a high hurdle that few music executives had ever cleared. The titans of Hollywood were a clubby bunch who tended to look down on the record industry as the stepchild of the entertainment business. Even though the profits in the record business often dwarfed those made by even the most successful movies, the motion-picture business was the center of all glamour in Hollywood.

So when Sandy Gallin continued to press his case that Geffen ought to come be an agent at Creative Management Associates, Geffen sensed an opportunity. Freddie Fields, the chairman of the agency, was the most powerful motion-picture agent in the business. Geffen thought that he might be able to use a connection to Fields as a springboard to establishing himself as a power in movies as well as in music.

Fields, who was married to actress Polly Bergen, and his partner, David Begelman, oversaw the most envied client list of Hollywood's stars, including Henry Fonda, Natalie Wood, Steve McQueen, Paul Newman, and Barbra Streisand. (Their most famous client, Judy Garland, had died of a drug overdose that summer.)

Gallin arranged for Geffen to meet with Fields. The agency's rock-'n'-roll department was the weak link at the company, and Fields recognized instantly that Geffen might be able to do for CMA what he had done for Ted Ashley at Ashley Famous a year earlier.

Geffen told Fields that he would join the agency on one condition: that he be given the office directly adjacent to Fields's own. That would make him the only music agent on the motion-picture-department floor. The physical location of his office would send a signal to everyone in Hollywood about Geffen's import at the agency. Geffen, who did not want to be pigeonholed as "the music guy," hoped it would also give him influence over matters other than his specialty. Fields agreed to the terms and welcomed Geffen aboard.

By bringing all of his music-management clients to CMA, Geffen made an immediate impact. Suddenly, the agency represented CSNY, Joni Mitchell, and Laura Nyro—among the biggest names in the business. Elliot Roberts conveniently continued on as the stars' manager. The roles of Geffen and Roberts were not clearly defined, which was how Geffen liked it, and he boasted that they were "able to really control it from both ends." But technically Geffen was only the artists' agent, and as such he was once again breaking the guild regulation by continuing to share in Laura Nyro's publishing-company revenues until the deal with CBS went through.

Once at CMA, Geffen identified a number of singers he wanted to sign. But now his reputation was such that a number of artists came to him first. One was Jimmy Webb, a songwriter who had a year earlier won the Song of the Year Grammy Award for "Up, Up, and Away," a number-one hit for the Fifth Dimension. Webb was spending most of his time in Las Vegas, where he came out at the end of Connie Stevens's act to join her in a duet of his song "Didn't We?" He knew his career was on the skids. He had written and recorded an odd song called "MacArthur Park," but it had been Richard Harris's version that had climbed the charts. Webb's own solo albums were tanking.

Having heard about Geffen from the Monday-night crowd at the Troubadour, Webb arranged to meet with him. Geffen looked skeptically at Webb when he explained that he wanted to be a singer-songwriter like Joni Mitchell.

"You're really interested in a *career*?" Geffen said dismissively. "Wow, I just thought you were some guy who hung out in Las Vegas with Connie Stevens."

Webb, a preacher's son from Eld City, Oklahoma, was hurt and terrified by Geffen's frankness. But Geffen liked Webb's songs and felt he could help him get his career turned around. He made a new record deal for him at Warner Bros. Records and began looking for other places to showcase his talent.

At CMA, Geffen was in Fields's office every day, ushered in by Fields's assistant, a young man named Jeff Berg, who years later became the chairman of the agency (known then as ICM). Geffen was a loose cannon who had a point of view on everything and was not afraid to share his opinions with anyone, including Fields. He was aggressive and mercurial, and he often shocked people with his blistering assessments.

When Geffen first met David Begelman, who a few years later became known as one of Hollywood's most notorious felons, he looked him in the eye and said, "You know, what I admire most about you is your ability to lie with such grace." He once called Joel Dean, now a music agent at CMA, and said, "You are probably one of the worst music agents we have here."

But it was that same unbridled assertiveness that won him the attention of Hollywood's powerbrokers. His style was abrasive, yet some people found it irresistible. He finagled relationships with Robert Evans, the president of production at Paramount Pictures, and David Picker, the head of United Artists. Before long, there was not a single person in Hollywood who would not meet with him.

As Geffen busied himself developing the promotion plans for CSNY's first album, *Déjà Vu,* and lining up a producer for Laura Nyro's third, tapes from undiscovered bands filled Geffen's in-box. It was impossible for him to listen to them all, though, and many of them simply ended up, unopened, in the trash.

But Dodie Smith, Geffen's secretary, happened to put her fingers on one package in the trash that somehow felt special. It contained a photograph of the artist, a mustached young man with a pretty face and stringy brown hair. The photograph was different from other publicity stills because it had been printed in sepia tones and resembled an old-time photograph from the 1800s.

What really grabbed Smith, however, was the letter that accompanied the photograph and demo tape. Smith became dizzy when she read it. "Dear Mr. Geffen," it began, "I write to you out of respect for the artists you represent."

She bolted into Geffen's office and put the letter under his nose. "David, read the note this young man has put with his demo tape," she said excitedly. "The opening line was enough for me!" Geffen did not appreciate the letter the way Smith did, but he listened to the tape, a crude recording of a song called "Jamaica Say You Will." He liked what he heard and told Smith to make an appointment for the singer, whose name was Jackson Browne. It was to be another wise business decision.

CHAPTER 8

SEEKING ASYLUM

|||

Jackson Browne was a lanky kid who had been born in Germany but moved with his family to California when he was twelve. He started writing songs as a teenager, inspired by his sister and her guitar-playing friends, who played bluegrass music. Browne was moved by the story-telling folk songs of Bob Dylan, Joan Baez, and Woody Guthrie.

By the time he was in high school, Browne had found a manager, who booked him to play in such Orange County clubs as the Paradox and the Golden Bear. He spent nearly every weekend driving north to Los Angeles to hear folksingers play in Hollywood.

Browne went to the Troubadour and played many times on "Hoot Night." There, he attracted the attention of some influential figures, including David Crosby, who suggested David Geffen as someone who could help Browne's career take off. "He's an agent, but he's one of us," Crosby told Browne, promising to make an introduction. "He's the guy who can deal with all the executives in the business world."

But Crosby did not follow through. After the success of Crosby,

Stills & Nash, Crosby was an untouchable star again, and Browne was unable to reach him.

Figuring that he would have to make the move on his own, Browne set about making a demo and asked two new friends to be his backup musicians on the recording. The friends were Glenn Frey and John David "J. D." Souther, Los Angeles transplants who had been in a band called Longbranch Pennywhistle. After making a couple of albums for Amos Records, they, too, were looking for a new road.

Browne, who at twenty-one was five years younger than Geffen, brought his guitar to Geffen's office and played him a few of his songs. Geffen struck Browne as unlike the other managers he had met, and they had only a short conversation before Geffen agreed to take him on.

"OK, I'll manage you," he said, moved by Browne's movie-star good looks and promising songwriting skills. "This will be fun. I like your songs."

Geffen did not think that Browne was ready to audition for label chiefs, but he was willing to make a serious investment of time and money in the young man. For one thing, Browne did not yet have enough songs to fill an album. More important, Browne's voice was a little shaky, and he tended to mumble when he sang. Geffen thought that singing lessons would help build his confidence.

He sent Browne to a vocal coach named Warren Beregian, a onetime opera singer who taught singers to breathe by performing such outrageous acts as pushing vibrating Black & Decker tools against their diaphragms. Browne at first thought he was a bit of a quack, but he ended up seeing him for two years, and Beregian helped him break many bad habits.

As he did with Laura Nyro, Geffen stepped in and took control of Browne's life. Browne was out of money, so Geffen invited him to live, rent free, at his house on Alto Cedro Drive. He also gave him money to buy clothes, food, and other things. Browne brought his friends Frey and Souther up to Geffen's house, and the three went skinny-dipping in the pool. The only concern Browne had now was writing his songs and learning to sing.

Geffen and Jackson Browne in a men's room conference,
Santa Monica Civic Auditorium. Gerry Beckley, of the group
America, is at left. (Henry Diltz)

At the Grammy Awards on March 11, 1970, Crosby, Stills & Nash won the Grammy for Best New Artist. Their debut album, which reached number six on the charts, stayed on the charts for more than two years.

As they were being honored at the Grammys, Atlantic released *Déjà Vu,* the first album by Crosby, Stills, Nash & Young. It, too, was a smash and became the group's first album to reach number one. Geffen went about booking concerts to support the album but had cautious expectations about the viability of the group. The "Carry On" tour, which had ended in Copenhagen at the beginning of the year, had been a gigantic success but had left the group falling apart at the seams. The four musicians desperately needed a break from one another.

They joined forces again in late April and began rehearsals so that they could go out on the road for the second time as a foursome. The band gave a concert in Denver, but they seemed unrehearsed and ragged, and tension grew once again as Stephen Stills hogged the spotlight. Toward the end of the concert, Neil Young walked offstage in the middle of a song and refused to return for the encore. Relations among the four grew worse, and, owing to flaring egos, their engagement in Chicago was canceled just a few hours before it was to begin.

It took a national tragedy to get the band together again. On May 4, 1970, four students participating in an antiwar demonstration were killed by National Guardsmen at Kent State University in Ohio. News reports of the tragedy inspired Neil Young to write a song called "Ohio." The single was released on June 27, 1970, and leapt to number fourteen on the pop charts.

Still, as Neil Young warbled his haunting lyric, "How many more?" he might also have wondered how many more concerts he would have to do with Stephen Stills. The success of "Ohio" and "Our House," the band's next hit single, could not hold the group together for long. After their final concert in Minneapolis, the band split up, each of the members going off to pursue solo projects.

Geffen began telling people that managing the group had been the most unpleasant professional experience of his still young career. His friendship with Stephen Stills had disintegrated, and he now grew especially irritated by what he saw as Stills's childish behavior. He hated David Crosby, who he told people was "obnoxious, loud, demanding, thoughtless, and full of himself." Of the four, Geffen said, Crosby was "the least talented."

Geffen believed the group had had the potential to be the American version of the Beatles, but they had allowed petty jealousies to get in the way and were now throwing it all away. Atlantic Records was hungry for another album by the group, but Geffen knew it would be impossible to get them to recombine in the studio. He suggested that Atlantic put out an album of tracks recorded live at their various concerts that summer. The album was aptly titled *4 Way Street.*

A s CSNY collapsed, Geffen was busy building the music department at CMA into a rock-'n'-roll powerhouse. Freddie Fields was thrilled as Geffen lured such established stars as James Taylor and Van Morrison to the agency. Geffen also talked constantly about his as-yet-undiscovered new client, Jackson Browne, predicting he was on the brink of stardom.

But it was ensuring the sale of Tuna Fish Music to CBS that occupied Geffen most. It had been six months since Geffen and Clive Davis had shaken hands on their deal, but the lawsuit with Artie Mogull was still pending, and CBS would not close the deal until the matter was resolved.

"It's taking so long," Geffen told Davis on the phone. "I hope there's nothing to be concerned about."

"You have my word of honor," Davis told him.

Still, Geffen grew nervous as the songs Nyro had written fell out of the pop chart's top ten. Determined to keep the perception alive that she was the hottest songwriter in the business, he continued pushing other celebrities to record her songs.

Searching for a home run, Geffen set his sights on Barbra Streisand, the reigning queen of the music business. A year earlier, he had come to be friends with Richard Perry, who was then producing an album by Tiny Tim. Now Perry had been tapped to produce Streisand's new album, which in a departure from her previous show-tune records was to be a compilation of contemporary songs. Geffen knew that if Streisand recorded one of Nyro's songs, it would mean hundreds of thousands of dollars in royalty income. He was determined to make it happen.

Perry liked Geffen and agreed to help set up a meeting with Streisand. Just twenty-eight, Streisand was a giant in Hollywood, having won an Oscar, an Emmy, and several Grammy Awards. Nyro, who was in California for her own standing-room-only engagement at the Troubadour, was excited at the prospect of meeting Streisand. On the way to the meeting, however, Geffen told Nyro to tell Streisand that she had written "Wedding Bell Blues" with her in mind. Nyro was horrified by Geffen's suggestion that she lie.

At the meeting, when Nyro did not cough up the line, Geffen himself chimed in with it. Streisand was overwhelmed, but Nyro could not stand by such a falsity.

"I'm sorry," she said, "but that's not true."

Geffen was embarrassed and furious, and he scolded Nyro in the car after the meeting. In his mind, he had suggested the lie only in order to try to win her greater wealth and fame.

"I just asked her to support me in this one thing," Geffen complained to Ellen Sander. "It's not a big lie. She should have understood that I was just trying to sell the song to America's premier songstress."

As it turned out, a lie was not needed to interest Streisand in recording Nyro's songs. In an extraordinary endorsement of her work, Streisand agreed to include three songs on her new album, including "Time and Love," "Hands Off the Man (Flim Flam Man)," and "Stoney End," which she also elected to use as the album's title. It was an incredible sale, one that further solidified the powerful positions both Nyro and Geffen had assumed in the music business.

Complications in the sale of Tuna Fish Music, however, lay just ahead. Geffen read the stock pages in the newspapers every morning and was aghast as he watched the value of CBS's stock plummet. The stock had sunk from forty-five dollars a share when he and Clive Davis had shaken hands on the deal to twenty-five a share by the middle of August 1970. The deal was now worth only $1.875 million.

He called up Davis and vented his frustrations, losing control and blasting his full rage at him. "It's terribly unfair that we should have to suffer like this," Geffen yelled, demanding that Davis promise to pay the amount that Tuna Fish was valued at nine months earlier.

Worn out by Geffen's bristling attack, Davis gave in. Under a renegotiated deal, Davis promised that the stock would have a minimum value of thirty-five dollars a share. That would make the deal worth $2.6 million, less than the original agreement but still far above the current price.

Geffen had realized that his most powerful weapon was his voice. He was a gifted screamer, and he had learned quickly that he could scare people into giving him whatever he wanted. His rage was so formidable that it left some of his victims gasping for air.

The irony was that Geffen was most likely more frightened than his victims. While he saw himself most of the time as the smart, fast-rising star he had become, there seemed to be fleeting, dreadful moments when his confidence shattered and he was gripped with fear. In these moments of harsh self-criticism, perhaps he looked in the mirror and saw himself as a shadow of his father, the failure who had never gained respect.

Kicking and screaming until he got his way, Geffen built up an enormous wall around himself, most likely praying that others would not also see that shadow. He was quite successful at keeping it hidden, and few people could catch even a glimpse of the insecurity. All most people knew was that David Geffen could be a holy terror. It was wise, many people who dealt with him felt, not to get in his way.

The commissions from Crosby, Stills, Nash & Young were making Geffen a twenty-seven-year-old with a net worth approaching a million dollars. He used some of the cash to remodel the house on Alto Cedro Drive, installing glass doors and windows and replacing the dated furniture that Johnny Rivers had left behind. He also bought a Rolls-Royce Corniche, just like the one Ahmet Ertegun had.

Ertegun played a central role in Geffen's life, and very few hours went by in which the two did not speak on the telephone. Ertegun and his wife, Mica, an interior decorator, had grown greatly fond of Geffen, inviting him to the heady dinner parties they hosted at their townhouse on East Eighty-first Street in Manhattan. The Erteguns introduced Geffen to their glittering friends, such as Robert Stigwood, the producer of Broadway's *Jesus Christ Superstar.* Geffen was not an erudite fellow, but he was charming and amiable, and he told funny stories.

When the Erteguns invited Geffen to join them on the Warner corporate airplane for a trip to Europe, he did not hesitate. The Erteguns treated him to the same first-class accommodations to which they were accustomed.

In London, Ahmet had an appointment to visit an art dealer from whom he and his wife had bought several paintings, and he invited Geffen to come along. Once inside the gallery, the dealer began showing Ahmet some new works when Mica, a tall, slender, and dignified woman, took Geffen aside and offered a piece of advice: "You should buy a painting," she said.

Ahmet chimed in. "Paintings always go up in value," he said. "And a painting is the nicest thing you can have in your house. Pictures will give your place some charm and make it interesting." It was advice that Geffen took to heart, and in that gallery he began building a collection of modern art that became one of the most envied in the world.

Mica told the dealer about Geffen's success with Laura Nyro and CSNY. "Listen, this man is hugely successful, and you will make him a collector if you can give him a good price," she told him. "This will be

Ahmet Ertegun, the head of Atlantic Records, and his wife, Mica, attend an art opening in New York. Ertegun's formula for success: "You walk very slow and maybe by chance you'll bump into a genius, and he'll make you rich." (Ron Galella LTD)

the first picture that he has ever bought. Do you have a Miró, or a Matisse, or some kind of drawing?"

The dealer raised his eyebrows and smiled. "I happen to have a terrific Picasso that I bought very recently," he told her and disappeared into the back room. He returned with *Buste,* a small abstract painting that Picasso had completed in 1954, relatively late in his artistic career.

Ahmet guessed that the painting was worth seventy-five thousand dollars; the dealer offered it to Geffen for only thirty-six thousand. Geffen agreed to the terms and arranged to have the painting sent to his home in Los Angeles.

Geffen soon decided that Jackson Browne was ready to make his first album. He had in mind a handful of labels and began setting up meetings. Geffen and Browne boarded an airplane and headed to New York for the first audition, with Clive Davis at Columbia Records.

In Davis's office, Browne began playing one of his new songs, "Doctor My Eyes." In the middle of the song, however, Davis's secretary came into the office and whispered in Davis's ear.

"I'm really sorry," Davis apologized to Browne and Geffen, interrupting Browne's audition. "I'm sorry, but I have to interrupt. Would you excuse me, please? I hate to do this, but I have to take this call. There's only one person on earth that could make me interrupt your singing, and that's Goddard Lieberson, and he's on the line," Davis said, referring to his boss. Davis left the room.

Browne was familiar enough with the music business to know that Lieberson was a heavyweight at CBS, so the interruption did not faze him. Geffen, on the other hand, was incensed at what he thought was Davis's rude behavior.

"Pack up your guitar," Geffen instructed Browne calmly, as he stood up and moved toward the door.

"What?" Browne replied.

"Pack up your guitar, we're leaving."

"We don't have to leave, Dave," Browne said.

"Just do what I tell you."

Browne dutifully put his guitar away and followed Geffen out of the office and past the secretarial station where Davis was talking on the phone.

"Wait!" Davis shouted after them, but Geffen, with a reluctant Browne in tow, had already reached the elevator.

Geffen's next stop changed the course of his life. He turned to Ahmet Ertegun and asked him to sign Browne to a contract at Atlantic. Geffen's frustration only grew as Ertegun, too, showed little interest in signing the young singer.

"Ahmet, look, I'm trying to do you a favor by giving you Jackson Browne," Geffen said, delivering a passionate pitch. "You'll make a lot of money."

"You know what, David, I have a lot of money," Ertegun replied. "Why don't you start a record company and then you'll have a lot of money, too."

It was exactly what Geffen wanted to hear. His eyes lit up as Ertegun further offered to be his partner. In exchange for a 50 percent ownership interest in the new label, Ertegun volunteered, Atlantic would cover all of the expenses, as well as handle the manufacture, distribution, and promotion of Geffen's records. The costs would be charged against the joint venture and any profits would be split equally between Atlantic and Geffen.

It was an astonishing deal that would not cost Geffen a cent. He realized without hesitation that now was the moment to realize his dream. If no one else would sign Jackson Browne, he figured, he would do it himself. Yes, he told Ertegun, count me in.

Geffen's first thought was that a label would be an asset that he could one day sell for a fortune. His principal desire had nothing to do with noble ambitions to find, nurture, and protect the careers of deserving artists. The discussions to sell Tuna Fish Music to Clive Davis had whetted his appetite for more and bigger assets he could call his own. Now his hunger appeared to be insatiable. David Geffen wanted more than anything to get rich.

Ertegun was not offering to partner with Geffen as a gesture of goodwill. He recognized that Geffen was a shrewd businessman who had the potential to make Ertegun and Atlantic Records a lot of money. If Geffen's new label took off, Atlantic's share of the profits, as well as the distribution fees it would pocket, would further enhance Atlantic's own standing in the business.

Ertegun was particularly interested in ensuring Atlantic's growth at this juncture because the competition between it and the other two labels owned by Warner Communications—Warner Bros./Reprise and Elektra—was intensifying, and he figured having Geffen on his team would be advantageous. Warner chief Steve Ross encouraged the rivalry between the three labels, figuring correctly that the spirited competition led to better overall performance.

Ertegun introduced Geffen to Ross and explained that he wanted to structure a three-year agreement. Ross was impressed with Geffen, but he thought the deal was very generous. But Ertegun was high on his young protégé, and Ross rarely questioned deals that Ertegun wanted to make. He gave the alliance his blessing and welcomed Geffen into the Warner family.

Geffen hustled back to Los Angeles and told Freddie Fields that he was quitting his job, which he had held for less than a year, effective immediately. After stints at three of the biggest talent shops in the business, David Geffen's days working as an agent were over.

"Asking me to come work here is the dumbest idea you have ever had," Geffen yelled at Sandy Gallin, who was still enjoying his job at CMA. "It has been a waste of a year."

The two had become best friends, but Geffen was occasionally annoyed with Sandy, mostly over career issues. Gallin was a sharp guy, but Geffen's intelligence set him in a different place altogether.

Geffen figured that he would need a partner in his new enterprise, but he did not consider Gallin, as he was still upset that he had turned down his invitation to go into business with him several months earlier. Geffen offered the job to two others, but received two more rejections. David Krebs, Geffen's old friend from the Morris office, thought his offer of a 5 percent equity stake in the label was chintzy. (Years later, Krebs was shocked when Geffen asked him why he had turned down his offer of a 30 percent stake, clearly having a different recollection.) Dick Asher, the number-two man at Columbia Records under Clive Davis, had a wife and family to feed and feared that the venture was too risky.

It suddenly became clear that there was only one person for Geffen to have at his side as he launched his new business.

Elliot Roberts was still running the management company that represented the individuals in CSNY and Joni Mitchell when Geffen asked him to become his partner in a new record label. He told Roberts about the deal he had struck with Atlantic, explaining that he envisioned it as a small operation that would put out the albums of a handful of new artists.

The way Geffen saw it, there was a natural synergy in owning both a record company and a management company. As managers, he and Roberts were always browbeating record labels to give them more money to support tours and other promotions in order to help break their acts. Now Geffen and Roberts would be both manager and label. They could use the management company to book and promote the acts it was recording on the label and vice versa. Controlling both sides of the business, Geffen told Roberts, would offer them greater control over their artists' careers.

But the real advantage, Geffen explained, was that they could use the record deal, which came complete with Atlantic financing, to cover the overhead at the management company. By laying off the expenses of the management enterprise on the record label, Geffen told Roberts, they would net a larger percentage of the gross at the management company, where they were making all their money. It was a win-win proposition that would put more cash in each of their pockets.

Although they would share responsibility for running both companies, Geffen said his primary focus would be the record label and proposed that Roberts take the lead at the management company. Geffen offered Roberts a partnership in which Roberts would have a 25 percent stake in the combined assets.

Roberts was stunned. Geffen had kept his talks with Ertegun secret, and Roberts had no idea that he had been contemplating such a plan. He was content with his life as a manager and never would have dreamed of such a plan on his own.

At first, Roberts was a bit reluctant. "Gee, I don't know if I want to give up my whole management company and take it apart," he said.

Geffen sighed and rolled his eyes. "Don't be stupid. I'll make you more money than you've made alone."

"Yes, David," Roberts responded.

Roberts soon came to feel blessed to have such a generous friend as David Geffen. He accepted the terms that Geffen had laid out. Geffen did not yet have a name for the new record label, but he and Roberts decided to call their management enterprise the Geffen Roberts Company.

Geffen liked the small offices Roberts had rented at 9126 Sunset Boulevard, and Roberts suggested that Geffen move there too. Nine framed gold albums were soon hung in the hallway, a testament to the successes their artists had achieved. The office, at the western edge of West Hollywood's Sunset Strip, was among a block-long row of Tudor-style bungalows that once had been apartments that housed the stars of the silent-screen era. The thing that Geffen liked most about the offices was the reasonable rent. From the day he opened his new business, Geffen had his eye fixed on the bottom line. He had the foresight to avoid the pitfalls that had proved fatal to so many others who had launched record labels before him. He was overhead averse and did not feel the urge to redecorate or to hire a large staff.

The only person Geffen hired was a secretary, a woman named Linda Loddengaard, who had worked in the music business as an executive assistant for several years. For the next seventeen years, Loddengaard served as Geffen's secretary, yet she did much more than simply answer his phones and keep track of his appointments. The two were to forge a relationship that was closer than even the most trusting bonds between bosses and their secretaries. More than his mother, Loddengaard was the one Geffen turned to in times of crisis. She covered for him one time when depression left him bedridden; on another occasion, she held his head in her lap as he sobbed. She came to know virtually everything about his life and was fiercely protective of his lifestyle, refusing to utter even a word about him to anyone, including her close friends at the company.

An East Coast blonde who never married, Loddengaard became one of the most powerful figures in Geffen's life, and he eventually empowered her to make important decisions on his behalf. In her role as the gatekeeper, she could be curt and chilly, and many of Geffen's friends and colleagues made a concerted effort to stay on her good side. Other people enjoyed Loddengaard's softer side—the warm, motherly figure who had a sense of humor and sometimes delighted office workers by baking cookies for them.

She helped set up Geffen's office, which had chocolate-colored shag carpet on the floor, a pendulum clock, and a handsomely mounted set of vintage *Collier's* covers on the wall. For guests, there was a brown corduroy couch, a black leather recliner, and a stork-legged captain's chair. For himself, Geffen picked out a plump leather Eames chair and situated it in front of a glass and chrome coffee table on which was positioned the office's most important asset: a telephone console that Geffen used to make an average of eighty to one hundred phone calls each day. Outside, a sign was hung above the parking spot closest to the front door that read RESERVED PARKING: DAVID GEFFEN ONLY. His still unnamed record company was open for business.

For all his money, David Geffen was turning out to be rather frugal. Inspired by his mother, he well understood that the delicate balance between profit and loss can be upset if expenses are high.

Perhaps his most revolutionary idea was to pay only nominal advances to his artists. Most record labels gave artists contracts with hefty advances, money that was guaranteed to them for each album regardless of sales. Record companies would cross their fingers that the records would become hits so they could earn back the advance. Once the revenues of a given album exceeded the amount of the advance, the artist's royalties, typically a percentage of sales, kicked in and brought the artist even more money.

In reducing the size of his advances, Geffen showed that he was as concerned about the use of other people's money as he was about the use of his own. He was uncomfortable with the idea that Atlantic Records would suffer financially if artists he signed produced records that did not sell. "There's no winning in a deal in which artists get bigger advances than the deal is worth," he thought. "It's not a good idea for people to make money in failure."

Geffen gambled that artists would not mind forgoing large advances once they realized what they would get in return by signing with him. His pitch was that his label would be the artist-friendly one, a place where musicians were guaranteed artistic freedom and freedom from deadline pressures. The label's money was available to underwrite whatever production expenses were needed to make the best albums possible. There were to be almost no budget restrictions. It all sounded remarkably seductive; he kept it a secret from everyone, including Elliot Roberts, that he was simply planning to build an asset that he hoped to soon sell for his own profit.

Geffen knew, of course, that artists he signed would need money to live, and he offered to happily advance them cash on a month-to-month basis to cover expenses. The artists he was signing, he figured, would be mostly unknowns who would be thrilled just to have both a record deal and a patron looking out for their careers. That is what he had done with Jackson Browne, and it seemed to Browne to be fair. By the time Browne's first album was released, Geffen had fronted him more than one hundred thousand dollars in living expenses.

He would argue additionally that artists who signed to his label would also get higher-than-normal royalty rates. Geffen also planned to employ a standard split-publishing system in which the label and the artist each got 50 percent of the revenues. Artists would sign contracts with the record label outlining these terms.

Geffen and Roberts wanted to use the new label as a launching ground for new acts. The one exception from their old acts was Joni Mitchell, whose first contract at Reprise Records was soon to expire and who wanted very much to be on the new label. Mitchell's latest albums, *Ladies of the Canyon* and *Blue,* had confirmed her as one of the most important singer-songwriters of her generation.

Geffen and Roberts planned to continue their practice of not asking clients of the management company to sign contracts, an enticement that artists instantly viewed as appealing. To further differentiate Geffen Roberts and add an air of class to the enterprise, Geffen insisted that they were in the business of providing "direction" rather than "management."

Their offices quickly became a home away from home for the artists Roberts and Geffen now co-managed. The piano Neil Young had used on his solo album *After the Gold Rush* was in the office, as were two acoustic guitars. There was also always an ample supply of marijuana available, and artists often stopped by to play a new tune or sit down and write one from scratch.

Geffen and Roberts had adjoining offices, and, having removed the door between them, the two could see each other and talk back and forth as they went about conducting business on the phone. From the first day Geffen moved his things to 9126 Sunset, Roberts spent more time in Geffen's office than he did in his own, and he rarely made a move without consulting him.

Shortly after Geffen came on board, Roberts complained to him that he was having trouble negotiating a new contract for Neil Young at Reprise. Mo Ostin, the head of the combined Warner Bros./Reprise operation, was a brilliant dealmaker many years Geffen's senior who played hardball in contract negotiations. Given that *After the Gold Rush* had sold well, Roberts hoped to win big contract gains. But Ostin was proposing only a small increase in Young's royalty rate. Roberts turned to Geffen for advice.

The next morning, Geffen stormed into the office, chortling that he had devised a solution. "I got it," he said. "We gotta fire Mo!"

"Excuse me?" Roberts said.

"Yeah, we gotta get Neil to fire Mo," Geffen said, proposing that they should draft an incendiary telegram to Ostin and sign it "Neil Young." The telegram would blast Ostin with such loaded threats as "Who do you think you are?" and "I am never going to record for you again!" Neil Young, who had a great deal of respect for Ostin, did not have the slightest idea that such a scam was going down.

They sent the telegram and, precisely as Geffen predicted, a panicked Ostin called up the moment he received it.

"Yeah, he's livid," Geffen said to Ostin, lying. "I think Neil just wants out of Reprise."

Ostin, as if on cue, began to spin, instantly offering to improve the contract. But Geffen decided to squeeze him further. "I think Neil just wants out of there," he said calmly.

"No, he doesn't!" Roberts said in a loud whisper from across the room. Geffen quickly put his hand over the receiver and shot Roberts a look that said, "Hush up, moron!" Roberts, something of a flat-footed accomplice, sometimes required a couple of seconds to realize what Geffen was up to. Finally, a grin came over his face as he watched his crafty partner in action. Ostin soon offered to throw in other perks.

Playing fair, Geffen had learned, was difficult and time-consuming; lying, on the other hand, was easy and effective. The secret that Young had "sent" a telegram to Ostin was safe because Geffen and Roberts, like most managers, forbade label executives from contacting their artists directly. In the end, Young had a new, lucrative contract, and Geffen and Roberts also had more money in their pockets.

Meanwhile, Geffen struggled to come up with a name for the label. He liked the name Benchmark Records, but Jackson Browne, who was staying in a guest room at Geffen's house, found it uninspiring. He and Geffen had forged a tight friendship, with Browne becoming Geffen's unofficial muse, serving as a sounding board on creative issues and suggesting other artists Geffen ought to sign and record.

Browne had a better reaction when Geffen began toying with the name Shelter Records. Geffen liked the moniker because it suggested a place where artists would be protected. When he realized Denny Kordell had already taken that name, however, he opened a thesaurus and looked up *shelter.* He found *cover, protection, refuge, haven, asylum,* and *sanctuary.* In an instant, the name of his new company seemed obvious: Asylum Records.

G effen was delighted as CBS's stock reversed its slide, hitting forty-eight dollars a share in the summer of 1971. He anticipated that he and Nyro would now get an even better deal. This was not how the top brass at CBS saw it, however, and Clive Davis had the unpleasant task of relaying this development to Geffen.

"David, I have some terrible news for you," Davis said. He explained that CBS chairman William S. Paley and president Frank Stanton wanted an adjustment to the terms of the deal.

Geffen was outraged. "What kind of dealmaking is this?" he demanded, refusing to budge. "You could get Paley to change his mind if you wanted to!"

Davis insisted that he could not and told Geffen he felt he was being unreasonable. When Geffen had demanded a renegotiation after the stock fell substantially, CBS had capitulated. But now that the shoe was on the other foot, Geffen would not entertain the notion of an alteration. "All we want is the same kind of flexibility that we granted you," Davis told him.

Davis made the situation as clear as he could: The board of directors would not allow him to make a deal without an adjustment. Nyro's third album for CBS, *Christmas and the Beads of Sweat,* had fared poorly, and now the deal was not looking as good to the corporation as it had more than a year earlier. Barbra Streisand's version of "Stoney End" had spent four weeks in the top ten at the start of 1971, peaking at number six, but there had been no other Laura Nyro successes since.

It was the rare occasion on which Geffen's bullying act did not work. He called Nyro, who was in Philadelphia working with hot soul producers Kenny Gamble and Leon Huff on her new album. Nyro was having fun with LaBelle, the trio of singers who were her backup on the album, but Gamble and Huff, not surprisingly, were having a rough time trying to get Nyro to do much of anything their way. Geffen relayed to her what had gone down between him and Davis and convinced her that they had been treated dishonorably.

"If this is the way we're going to be treated, let's fuck the money," he told her. "You can record for Asylum. We've always done well without money, and we'll do well without it in the future."

Nyro agreed. She had grown uncomfortable about Geffen's obsession with the sale of her publishing company anyway and was happy to see that he once again seemed focused first and foremost on her recording career.

At the end of July 1971, Geffen gave his first interview to outline his plans for Asylum Records, boasting to *Record World* that Joni Mitchell and Laura Nyro were to be among the label's star acts. Geffen announced that Nyro's contract with Columbia was "over." He said her first album for Asylum would be called *Gonna Take a Miracle*. He was half right: Nyro's next album *was* entitled *Gonna Take a Miracle,* but it was *not* released by Asylum.

CHAPTER 9

HEARTBREAK

|||

A hmet Ertegun pulled off a major coup, signing the Rolling Stones, thereby securing Atlantic Records' position as the most powerful record label in America. To herald the signing, Atlantic threw a blowout of a celebration in the south of France, where Mick Jagger and the other Stones had outlandish homes. Ertegun invited Geffen to join his entourage on the Warner corporate jet to Cannes.

Though Geffen was busy signing his own acts, he wanted to be at Ertegun's side in his hour of glory. Geffen, who now sported a beard and a mustache, wore an Atlantic Records T-shirt almost daily and was Ertegun's biggest cheerleader. But he also saw the trip as an opportunity to gain some business for himself. He knew the Stones would soon embark on a tour in the United States, and Geffen wanted the Geffen Roberts Company to book and manage it.

At the Hotel Majestic in Cannes, David cozied up to Prince Rupert Loewenstein, a stuffy merchant banker whom the Stones had hired recently as their business manager. Ertegun had negotiated the new recording deal with Prince Rupert, and the two had become good friends.

Seeking to ingratiate himself with the prince, Geffen told him that Cat Stevens, who had already struck it big with his hit "Morning Has Broken," was looking for a business manager. He knew Stevens, he said, and would see to it that he hire the prince.

Stephen Stills, who was now living in England and making a solo album, flew to Cannes to be close to Ertegun and Geffen, and sat next to Geffen as he romanced Prince Rupert. He was depressed to discover, though, that neither Geffen nor Ertegun paid him much attention. Geffen suggested that Stills hire Prince Rupert as his business manager; when Stills disregarded the advice, Geffen's contempt for the singer only increased.

Geffen told the prince why the Stones ought to engage him to book their U.S. tour. "Their last tour was a joke," he told Prince Rupert. "Tell me. Stephen Stills got one hundred thousand dollars for one night at the L.A. Forum. The Stones only got seventy-five thousand. Think about that."

If he had not already, Stills clearly got the point: Geffen was more interested in the Stones than he was in him.

Prince Rupert thought it unlikely that Mick Jagger would take to the cocky young manager and declined to support the idea. Although Prince Rupert soon developed a fondness for Geffen, his first reaction was that he behaved a bit like an unhousebroken puppy. "You're not quite sure whether he's going to sniff your balls or pee at your feet or bark," he thought.

Although he did not have Prince Rupert's blessing, Geffen found Mick Jagger at the hotel, nervously introduced himself, and told him he would like to book the Stones' upcoming tour.

"What is it that you really want?" Geffen asked.

"Well, we want to play smaller places for more money," Jagger told Geffen.

"Oh, terrific," Geffen said, rolling his eyes. "How do you propose to do that?"

Jagger told Geffen that they thought they could find a corporate sponsor such as Coca-Cola to underwrite the tour. In exchange, the

The Eagles pose in Topanga Canyon: Bernie Leadon, Randy Meisner, Don Henley, and Glenn Frey. (Henry Diltz)

Stones would give Coke a plug from the stage during their concerts. "We'd love to sing 'Things go better with Coke' every night." When Geffen told him he did not think that Coke would agree to sponsor a controversial act such as the Stones, Jagger brushed him aside. "That's the trouble with you, Geffen—you're so negative!"

Despite their squabble, Geffen and Jagger talked further. They did not work up a final agreement, but Jagger was impressed with the big numbers Geffen promised he could secure.

Back in Los Angeles, Geffen made some phone calls to concert venues to find out just how much he could get them to pay for the Stones. Robert Hilburn, a reporter who covered the rock business for the *Los Angeles Times,* called Geffen when he picked up reports that he might be involved with the hot group. Hilburn rushed a story into print when Geffen told him he had been hired to manage the Stones' U.S. tour.

When Jagger saw the article three days later, he was outraged at what he saw as Geffen's grandstanding. "You are an egomaniac!" Jagger screamed. "I want you to cut it out."

"Listen—forget it!" Geffen hissed. He told Jagger he did not want to have anything to do with his tour.

"The trouble with you, Geffen, is that you think we're another of your CSNYs or Joni Mitchells."

"No, I've never confused you," Geffen retorted. "I've never liked your music nearly as much." He hung up.

To counter the embarrassment that came with having to tell friends and colleagues that the deal had fallen apart, Geffen bad-mouthed Jagger and his group. "I wouldn't care to be involved with the Rolling Stones," he told Grover Lewis, a music-industry journalist. "It's all sycophantic, the whole Rolling Stones scene—the greater-than-anything, omnipotent, king-like crap." He added, "I find it very offensive, particularly those people who get next to it and then take on its importance. Who gives a shit?"

His comments were a direct slap at Ahmet Ertegun, who had worked so hard to sign the Stones to Atlantic. He was hurt by the remarks and upset that Geffen had used the trip to Cannes as a way to get business for himself. It was the first crack in the friendship between the two men, and it showed that Geffen was capable of mistreating anyone, even his mentor. Though Ertegun still admired him, he began to view Geffen as a greedy young man who too often tried to squeeze the juice out of every situation.

Clive Davis was furious when he read in the trade papers that Laura Nyro had signed to Asylum Records. Nyro's contract at Columbia was indeed expiring, but she had never given Davis any indication that she was unhappy. What's more, he could not believe that Geffen was going to walk away from the multimillion-dollar sale of Tuna Fish Music. CBS had made it clear that they would not acquire Tuna Fish unless Nyro signed a new long-term recording agreement at Columbia.

Davis was surprised when he received a letter from Nyro saying that she "couldn't believe" that he had not gotten in touch with her. He was in Los Angeles at a company sales retreat when he phoned Nyro at Sigma Sound in Philadelphia, where she was recording *Gonna Take a Miracle*. Nyro took that call, and a few subsequent others Davis made to her at her apartment in Manhattan on the weekends. "We love you here at Columbia," Clive told her emphatically, imploring her not to leave.

Geffen flew into a rage when he discovered that Davis had begun courting Nyro directly. He said that Nyro had not written Davis any letter, insisting that Davis had gone behind his back and filled Nyro with stories seeking to undermine her confidence in Asylum. Although label chiefs typically do not contact artists directly, Davis reasoned that this was not a typical situation, as Geffen, the Asylum boss, was his competition as well as Nyro's manager.

Caught in the middle, Nyro began to spin. She was uncomfortable about the conversations with Davis, but she began to question her decision to move to Asylum. The difference in values between her and Geffen had now become too great of an obstacle. Nyro faced the fact that the relationship, much like a love affair, must end before she was dragged down a road she had no interest in traveling.

Frightened and upset, Nyro told Richard Chiaro, who had succeeded Lee Houskeeper as Geffen's link to her in New York, that she was thinking about signing to a completely new label, dumping both Davis and Geffen. Finally, however, she decided to stay at Columbia and begin a new life without David Geffen. She timidly called Geffen and told him her decision.

"I want to stay with Columbia," she said.

Her words had a deadening effect.

"Well, h-h-how can you do this, Laura?"

"I feel safer there than with Asylum."

"It's your choice," Geffen said, scrambling to maintain his composure. "I'll do whatever you want."

After a pause, Laura changed her mind again. "No, I really want to be with Asylum, because you've done so much for me, and I love you and trust you and everything," she waffled. "But . . . uh . . . I don't like the name Asylum, and I want you to change it."

"Laura, I don't tell you what to call your songs," Geffen pleaded. "I think it's wrong of you to tell me what to call my record company. Asylum is *my* song."

Nearing a breakdown, Nyro flew off to Portofino, Italy, begging Richard Chiaro to keep her escape a secret. Chiaro kept silent, even though he was getting his paycheck from Geffen.

Devastated, Geffen called Davis and told him of Nyro's decision to stay at Columbia. Davis and Geffen promptly agreed on a final adjustment to the terms of the Tuna Fish Music sale: CBS would give Geffen and Nyro their seventy-five thousand shares valued at forty dollars each, for a total of three million dollars. The papers were drawn up.

There was only one catch, Davis told Geffen. The lawsuit with Artie Mogull, which had been dragging on for more than two years, had to be settled before CBS would write any checks. The Appellate Division of the New York Supreme Court had just handed Nyro and Geffen a resounding defeat, affirming the lower court's order that a trial was needed to determine whether or not Mogull's right to Nyro's publishing was still valid.

Rather than go through the costly process of a full trial, Geffen conceded defeat and agreed to settle with Mogull and his associates for $470,000. It put a dent in the big CBS payoff, but Nyro and Geffen still cleared more than a million dollars each in the deal.

Geffen gave the papers to Richard Chiaro and told him to find Nyro and make her sign them. Chiaro headed for Portofino and convinced her to sign the papers, including a new long-term contract with Columbia Records. He returned to New York with the papers and met an anxious Geffen at his lawyer's office on Sixth Avenue. Geffen breathed a giant sigh of relief. He had lost his star client, but he was, for the first time, a millionaire. He was only twenty-eight.

The victory proved to be shallow and not terribly satisfying. Geffen was crushed by what he saw as Nyro's betrayal, and he was embarrassed that he had to retract the announcement that she had signed with his new company.

Soon after the sale was finalized, Geffen and Elliot Roberts went to the Beresford, the apartment building on Central Park West to which Nyro had moved recently. Nyro and Geffen's professional partnership was over, but Geffen held out hope that they could salvage some kind of friendship. Geffen asked the doorman to ring her apartment. Nyro sent down word that as long as he was in New York she was out of town.

Geffen and Roberts walked quietly back to the Park Lane Hotel, where they were staying. Sitting on the edge of his bed there, Roberts held Geffen—a newly minted millionaire—as he began to sob inconsolably.

Trying to get his mind off Nyro, Geffen immersed himself in the business of assembling a roster of artists for his new label. Inspired by the success of both Nyro and Joni Mitchell, Geffen wanted to make Asylum the premier label for singer-songwriters. More so than vocalists who simply recorded other people's music, singer-songwriters, he figured, were better financial bets because they could make money performing their own tunes as well as selling them to others to record.

Geffen found most of the artists for his new label through Jackson Browne. Browne talked up his friend J. D. Souther, who seemed to write a song every day, and Geffen agreed to sign him as a solo act. Browne also convinced Geffen to sign his pal Ned Doheny, a scion of the wealthy family that first found oil in Los Angeles.

Browne also steered Geffen toward the band that was to make him more money than any single group or artist had before. Browne talked constantly about Glenn Frey, whom he had met shortly after Frey moved to Los Angeles from Detroit. Frey and Souther, who together formed Longbranch Pennywhistle, had been renting a cheap apartment in the same building where Browne lived in Echo Park, a blue-collar neighborhood east of Hollywood. Frey, twenty-three, spent a lot of time swimming at Geffen's house, and Browne convinced Geffen that Frey had what it took to become a rock star.

It was not a hard sell. Geffen was taken by Frey's rugged good looks and saw easily how he could make a whole generation of teenage girls swoon. Frey had started calling himself the "Teen King," a nod to the adolescent girls who swarmed around him, and Geffen endeared himself to Frey by calling him "T.K."

Upset that Longbranch Pennywhistle had been a bust, Frey now yearned to make it on his own as a solo act. But Geffen convinced him that he should try working with a group one more time, arguing that Longbranch Pennywhistle had flopped because the players were not right and the material was all wrong.

"David Crosby is in a band," Geffen told him. "You should be in a band." Geffen was determined to find a group of male singers who could repeat the success he had had with CSNY, and he thought that Frey could be the linchpin of the group.

Struggling to make ends meet, Frey accepted a gig singing backup to Linda Ronstadt, a black-haired torch singer from Tucson whom he had met at the Troubadour. Ronstadt, twenty-five, had been in a group called the Stone Poneys, but struck out on her own and began making a name for herself as a solo artist.

Preparing for a tour in the summer of 1971, Ronstadt asked Frey and three other guys in their early twenties to be her backup musicians. The others were Bernie Leadon, a banjo player from Minnesota who had played with the Flying Burrito Brothers; Randy Meisner, a bass player from Nebraska who had played briefly with Poco; and Don Henley, a drummer from Texas who had been in a band called Shiloh. With Ronstadt out front, the men played together for the first time that July, in a performance at Disneyland.

Geffen, meanwhile, set his sights on Ronstadt and went about trying to sign her to Asylum. Jackson Browne, who had been introduced to Ronstadt by Frey, helped with the effort and weighed in with his typically effusive endorsement of Geffen. Ronstadt and Browne became friends, and he was excited when she decided to record a song he had written called "Rock Me on the Water."

Ronstadt told Geffen that she wanted to be with Asylum but feared that she would not be able to get out of her contract at Capitol Records. After the Stone Poneys broke up, the label forced Ronstadt to make her solo albums there because the group contractually still owed Capitol a few records.

But her album *Silk Purse,* the cover of which featured a picture of her sitting in a pigsty, had not done well, and Capitol did not seem to know how to promote her. Geffen told her she ought to finish her current album at Capitol and that he would work out the details so that she could come to Asylum for the following one.

Linda Ronstadt was something of an odd fit with the other artists Geffen had signed, principally because she did not write her own songs. But Geffen was impressed with her versatility and dazzled by her ability to merge styles such as country, rhythm and blues, rock, and reggae. He believed she had the makings of a very big star.

By the time Ronstadt's tour was over that summer, the four men in her backup band had decided to form a group. Frey took his three new friends to meet with Geffen, and they were all captivated by his sales job. Henley and Frey were still under contract to Amos Records, but Geffen offered to pay the $15,000 and $12,500, respectively, to buy out the Longbranch Pennywhistle and Shiloh contracts. He told them he thought they would not be ready to record for several months and offered to front them cash to cover their living expenses in the interim. He sent them to his dentist to get their teeth fixed and arranged for his business manager, Jerry Rubinstein, to begin handling their financial affairs as well.

For Frey and Henley, the deal was clinched at Geffen's house as they sat naked in the sauna with Geffen, Jackson Browne, J. D. Souther, and Ned Doheny.

"I want to keep Asylum Records very small," Geffen told them. "I'll never have more artists that I can fit in this sauna."

In September 1971, the four men signed contracts for publishing and recording. Whereas Amos Records had controlled 100 percent of its artists' publishing rights, Geffen kept only half for himself. Indeed, it was his standard deal for the time: Geffen argued that any money the group made from their music publishing ought to be cross-collateralized against their recording advance as insurance for the label against a poorly selling record. The four artists, none of whom was represented by a lawyer, willingly signed the new deals and viewed them as fair.

Geffen decided to send his new group off to Aspen, Colorado, to write music and rehearse. He arranged for them to play under the name Teen King and the Emergencies; "the Emergencies" was a backhanded reference to Henley, a difficult guy who seemed to have a different crisis every day. Geffen lined up gigs for the group at such clubs as the Galley and Tulagi, where they wound up drawing big crowds.

The group next set about trying to decide on a real name. They wanted something short that had some imagery or perhaps some mythological connotations. Frey wanted a name that could have been the moniker of a Detroit street gang. Henley wanted something that had an Indian vibe. They finally agreed to call themselves the Eagles. Geffen liked it, he said, because it sounded like "the Beatles."

The publicity surrounding Asylum's impending launch attracted the attention of everyone in the music business and even the attention of some in far-flung places. Irving Azoff, a native of Danville, Illinois, was a student at the University of Illinois at Champaign-Urbana when he first learned about Geffen in *Rolling Stone* magazine. Azoff, a dynamo who stood just five foot four, was to play a major role in Geffen's life, mostly as a lifelong adversary whose Machiavellian ways almost matched Geffen's own.

Azoff was putting himself through college by serving as a manager to a couple of aspiring singers. He had found a young singer from Peoria named Dan Fogelberg, and Asylum Records seemed like a good fit. Azoff sent Geffen a demo tape Fogelberg had made.

When he did not hear from him, Azoff boldly picked up the phone and called.

"I heard the tape and I liked it," Geffen told him. "I played the tape for Jackson Browne, and he liked it, too. If you wait a year or so for us to get up and running, then I will sign him."

Eager to meet Geffen and check out the music scene on the West Coast, Azoff took a vacation to Los Angeles and looked up Geffen, who reiterated his enthusiasm for Fogelberg. "I can't sign him right now, but I like the tape," Geffen told him. "Let's stay in touch." Azoff was getting frustrated, though, and he told Geffen he was going to pursue deals with other labels. Azoff soon moved to Los Angeles and went to work doing just that.

When he not long after secured a deal for Fogelberg with Clive Davis at Columbia Records, Geffen called Azoff and ranted. "That's my artist! You have to give him to me!"

While the artists he signed to Asylum were singing Geffen's praises, others in the music business spent considerable time cursing his name. Charges flew that Geffen's word was not good, that he did not play fair, and that he was driven foremost by a desire to do what was best for David Geffen.

Even the mere sight of him sometimes prompted violent reactions. *Record World* noted that someone driving by the Troubadour pelted Geffen with eggs. Another time, Geffen had a tussle over a publishing deal in the alley behind the club with Albert Grossman, the once-influential manager whose career was on a downward trajectory. Friends pulled the two apart just before it looked likely to escalate into a fistfight.

An agent named Jerry Heller got into a screaming match with Geffen after Geffen reneged on a promise to give him the assignment to book a Joni Mitchell tour. Heller's office was directly across the street from Asylum's headquarters, and Heller angrily dropped boxes of Mitchell's albums and promotional materials out of his second-story window. The two shouted obscenities at each other from their respective windows as cars whizzed past below them on Sunset Boulevard.

It was part of the music business that the players engaged in a certain kind of competition with one another. Yet Geffen was different. He took everything personally and simply did not accept losing.

Throughout his career, there were countless murky situations in which Geffen himself was at least partly to blame for his contentious relations with people in the business. In these cloudy situations, however, Geffen routinely charged that he alone had been the one who was wronged.

Geffen's conscience always remained clear. "I don't have the burden of bullshit and lies and deceit and cheating. None of that plagues me because I don't do any of it," he told a journalist at the time. "Elliot and I have made as much money as anybody's ever made in the music business, and we've done that without cheating anybody, without fucking anybody, without taking advantage of anybody." He added, "Listen, it may sound conceited, but I think I'm unique in this business. I can sleep at night."

Crosby, Stills, Nash & Young's live double album *4 Way Street* was another huge seller, becoming the group's second record to reach number one. The group was the principal factor in allowing Geffen to crow that in 1971 the artists he managed sold a total of twelve million records. The group's members, however, continued to give him no end of aggravation. One of the major problems was that David Crosby in particular was struggling with a serious drug addiction that impaired greatly the band's ability to set priorities or make decisions. Unlike Elliot Roberts, Geffen was not a big drug user, and as a result he was frustrated in dealing with a group of people who seemed to be constantly high or stoned.

Stephen Stills was now the most irritating of all to him, and Geffen finally did something that was nearly unheard-of in the business: He fired him. "Since you're not going to listen to us, save the fifteen percent and get another manager," Geffen told Stills. "I'm not going to be involved where I see you fucking up time and time again. I don't need the money and I certainly don't need the frustration." Stills printed up bumper stickers to vent his frustration. Parodying a recent windy movie title, the stickers asked, "Who is David Geffen and why is he saying those terrible things about me?"

David Crosby was also giving Geffen heartache. Their relationship fell apart when Crosby and Nash were in New York for a concert at Carnegie Hall on Yom Kippur. Crosby ran out of marijuana and telephoned Geffen, insisting he bring him a supply at once.

"I'm not going to carry dope for you," Geffen told him. "I'm not going to take a chance like that."

Crosby yelled and screamed and threatened not to go on the next night if Geffen did not come through. Geffen finally relented. Crosby instructed him that Reine Stewart, a woman known as the band's "ecstasy coordinator," had the pot he desired. It was arranged that Stewart, who was flying into Los Angeles just before Geffen's flight to New York, would meet Geffen in the terminal for the drop-off. The meeting came off as planned, and Stewart handed Geffen a manila envelope. He placed it in his briefcase and headed for his gate.

Security at Los Angeles International Airport was a rather low-tech operation in 1971, mostly limited to small teams of airport personnel who occasionally asked fliers for a peek inside their baggage. As Geffen approached the desk, however, guards were searching everyone's belongings. Before he could turn back, a security officer opened his briefcase, picked up the manila envelope, and gave it a shake. Seeds rolled out.

"What's in this envelope?" the officer asked Geffen.

"I never saw this envelope before in my life," he lied.

Geffen was handcuffed and taken to jail. Feeling certain it would be nearly impossible to get a lawyer on the phone on Yom Kippur, he reluctantly decided to call his brother for help.

David's relationship with Mitchell had worsened since David had found success in the music business. It was David, not Mitchell, who had become the family's big success story. Mitchell seemed to have grown jealous of David's good fortune; David, for his part, still recalled how Mitchell had predicted he was going to be a failure like their father. The two had little to do with each other, and David dreaded the idea that he would owe his brother something if he called him for help. But he did not have a choice.

Mitchell was angry at having been disturbed on the holiday, but he nevertheless posted bail for his brother; it is not clear what if any charges were later brought against David. David rushed back to LAX and got on the next plane to New York. When the plane touched down, there was only an hour before the concert was set to begin. Geffen instructed the cabdriver to make a beeline for the Warwick Hotel, where Crosby and Nash were staying.

"Where's my grass?" Crosby snapped when he saw Geffen.

"I was arrested and put in jail," Geffen replied. "I don't have it."

"I'm going to fucking kill you!" Crosby snarled.

Geffen was continuing to lead a double life after he left work at the end of the day. He wanted to get married and have a family; to that end, he dated a number of women, including Freddie Fields's daughter, Kathy. Chuck Barris, the game-show producer and a friend of Geffen's, arranged for him to be a contestant on his TV show *The Dating Game*.

The bachelorette quizzing Geffen and two other men, unfortunately, selected one of Geffen's competitors.

But most of his friends knew that he was gay and were sad to see him so tormented by his sexuality. Most of his sexual partners were men, and there was even an occasional guy whom Geffen deemed important enough to introduce to friends such as Joni Mitchell and Graham Nash. Although he thought he was being discreet in balancing his two lives, in fact the signs that he was gay were all around.

The most obvious of these was the roster at his record label, which he clearly had stocked with male artists who, as a group, were attractive, somewhat androgynous-looking men. If their record covers were set out and viewed side by side, it did not take much of an imagination to see the makings of a beefcake calendar.

Geffen was unhappy, lonely, and sentimental, and he told his male artists, all of whom were straight, that he was afraid he would never find anyone to love. "I don't think I'll ever be happy," he told Ned Doheny. But rather than face his own sexuality, he instead took an unusual interest in his artists' relationships with others.

Even though he knew that he was attracted far more to men than to women, Geffen had not grown any more comfortable with the idea of calling himself a gay man. Although the gay-rights movement had burst into the public consciousness with the Stonewall riots in Greenwich Village in 1969, even people in Los Angeles still tended to talk about homosexuals under their breath.

He still hung out with Todd Schiffman. He also became friendly with another gay agent, David Forest. The three went to gay bars and restaurants along Santa Monica Boulevard in West Hollywood, just a couple of blocks east of the Troubadour.

In November 1971, the three dined at Por Favor, a Mexican restaurant that eventually became the site of a gay bar called the Mother Lode. They were joined by Christopher Cornett, a teenager whom Forest had recently begun dating. During their dinner, Schiffman sensed that Geffen was attracted to Cornett.

When they were finished with dinner, Geffen made a suggestion to the other three. "Why don't we all go up to my house," he said. "I want to show you something."

The four made their way to Geffen's house. It was dark as they entered, but the three gasped when Geffen flipped on a spotlight in the main room that shone directly on his Picasso. Forest and Schiffman, like Geffen, were newly wealthy people, but it was still an unusual occurrence to see an original painting of this stature in a private home.

The following night, Geffen went with Ahmet Ertegun to a concert at the Forum by the J. Geils Band, a hot Atlantic Records act. Todd Schiffman never forgot what Geffen told him transpired next: Christopher Cornett apparently spent the night at Geffen's house, and at dawn, Geffen awoke to realize that his Picasso was gone.

Panicked, Geffen telephoned Todd Schiffman. "Where can I get in touch with Chris Cornett?" he yelled frantically.

"Well, David, you know he lives with David Forest," Schiffman said. "You know David Forest's home number. Call him. What's going on?"

"I had Chris Cornett up here last night, and he stole my Picasso!" Geffen shrieked. "I woke up this morning, and it's gone!" He called the police and reported the painting stolen. It later became clear that Geffen had likely told the police the identity of the main suspect in the case.

Meanwhile, Geffen was telling his friends an elaborate story. Recalling how he had often complained to Ertegun that he feared the painting would be stolen, he telephoned Ertegun at the Beverly Hills Hotel and accused him of stealing the painting as a practical joke. Geffen maintained that he contacted the police only after realizing that Ertegun was not the thief. His story never included the name Christopher Cornett.

Geffen next confided a secret to Schiffman: "I don't really give a shit about the Picasso. I'd rather have the insurance money."

When the insurance company issued him a check for seventy-five thousand dollars, Geffen told Ertegun that he was glad the painting had been stolen. "Not only do I not have to worry about the picture any more, but I made almost forty thousand!" he cheered.

BIG DEAL

|||

A hmet Ertegun hosted a party at the St. Moritz Hotel in New York to celebrate the launch of Asylum Records. Geffen, Roberts, and their artists began the evening at Carnegie Hall, where Jackson Browne was the opening act for a sold-out concert headlined by Joni Mitchell, who was now dating Browne. After the concert, the Asylum entourage moved to the Sky Garden Roof restaurant atop the St. Moritz for a midnight supper overlooking Central Park. The hot-and-cold relationship between Geffen and Ertegun was hot once again, and Geffen told his mentor how grateful he was for what he had done for him. "We're going to be partners in everything forever," he told Ertegun.

Before returning to Los Angeles, Geffen accepted an invitation from Jerry Greenberg, one of Ertegun's top lieutenants at Atlantic, to spend a weekend at his house in New Haven, Connecticut.

"I want to take you to my favorite restaurant up here," Greenberg told Geffen. "You'll love the guy who runs it. He's a great friend of mine."

Greenberg took Geffen to Tivoli's and introduced him to the owner, a flashy gay man named Steve Rubell. Rubell, who within a few years was to open and preside over the most famous discotheque in the history of New York nightlife, had read the stories about Geffen's fast rise in the music business and was thrilled to meet him, especially since Neil Young was his favorite artist.

"Listen," said Geffen, "Neil's next album is called *Harvest,* and it's gonna be huge. I'll send you a copy of it when I get home."

Back in Los Angeles, Geffen bopped in and out of the studio as Jackson Browne recorded his first album at Crystal Sound. Following through on his promise, Geffen never flinched as Browne labored over his first effort for four months.

Browne embraced Geffen's idea that David Crosby sing harmony on "Doctor My Eyes," a ploy Geffen hoped might win the album quick acceptance among fickle radio stations. Browne liked the idea because Crosby had been the one who had told him about Geffen in the first place. Browne also liked Crosby because he had predicted stardom for Browne in *Rolling Stone.*

Browne reacted far less favorably to Geffen's next suggestion, causing a clash between their different objectives: artistry and commercialism. Geffen's friendship with Ode Records chief Lou Adler had given him a connection to Carole King, Ode's newest star, and Geffen implored Browne to record a song with her. King's debut album, *Tapestry,* released less than a year earlier, had won her the Grammy Award for Album of the Year. Geffen thought that with a cut with David Crosby and a cut with Carole King, Browne's album could not help but get noticed.

"I don't *know* Carole King," Browne said.

"That's OK," Geffen said. "Just invite her to play on a record with you. She'll do it."

"But I don't know her!" the young singer replied. "You want me to invite her to sing on my album because now *she's* got a big record? That's not music. That's commerce. It's bullshit."

Browne and Geffen did not speak for a couple of days after the argument. They made up when Geffen conceded that only Browne could

The young mogul, in his trademark blue jeans,

poses with his gold albums. Geffen felt compelled to succeed,

so he did. (Joel Bernstein)

decide who would sing on his album. "Look, we can't fight like that again," Geffen said.

Browne got in his truck and took a two-week driving trip through small towns in Arizona and Utah. It was on the road that inspiration struck for a song, which he titled "Take It Easy." Browne was amazed by the sight of sexy women in the Southwest who lived on ranches and drove pickup trucks, something he had never seen in Los Angeles. He was standing on a corner when a beautiful woman drove by in a Toyota, and he knew instantly that she should be the subject of the song's second verse. Browne was not a fast writer, though, and he wrestled unsuccessfully with the rhyme of the phrase for weeks.

Back in Los Angeles, Browne told Glenn Frey about the song he was working on and sang him the first verse.

"That's cool. Is it done?" Frey asked.

"No, it's not," Browne responded.

"Let me know when it's done," he said. "We'd like to record it." The Eagles, back from their rehearsal stint in Colorado, were finalizing the list of songs they planned to record on their first album.

Frey continued to pester Browne about the song, but Browne had grown so frustrated with it that he put it aside. "Do you mind if I finish it?" Frey finally asked. Browne, who was back in the studio trying to finish his own album, agreed to let his friend take a whack at it.

Frey sat down and came up with a verse about the woman Browne had told him about. He also did a major overhaul of the song's choruses, improving them without derailing Browne's original intentions. The Eagles began practicing the song and it quickly became one of their favorites; Frey and Browne agreed to share the songwriting credit.

The first two releases on Asylum Records, in October 1971, were duds. One was by a former prostitute and reformed junkie named Judee Sill; the other was by David Blue, a depressive crooner Geffen had signed after the singer came to his rescue when someone attacked him one night in front of the Troubadour.

Although Geffen and Roberts were not enjoying instant success with Asylum, they were making lots of money at their management company. All their clients maintained aggressive performance and touring schedules. They cleverly gained exposure for their lesser-known acts by having them open for their established stars.

Geffen later claimed that in 1972 Geffen Roberts was the largest music-management firm in the world, netting three million dollars that year. Certainly everyone knew about the company: A photograph of Geffen and Roberts stepping off an airplane even graced the cover of *Melody Maker,* an influential trade magazine in England.

At the end of January 1972, Reprise Records put out Neil Young's *Harvest* album, the follow-up record to *After the Gold Rush.* The album shot to the number-one spot on *Billboard*'s album charts. It was propelled by the success of the single "Heart of Gold," which reached number one on the singles charts. The album and the single were the biggest selling hits Young had.

Before long, Asylum Records had its own hits to crow about. Geffen sent the Eagles off to London to make their first record with a producer named Glyn Johns; it took only two weeks and $125,000 to record. Back in Los Angeles, Johns played the songs for Geffen and Roberts, who, while excited about the sound, felt that the album did not showcase Don Henley's vocal talents enough. They sent the band and Johns into a local studio to record Jackson Browne's song "Nightingale," featuring solos by Henley, whom Geffen had begun calling "the man with the golden throat."

When Browne finally finished his own album, meanwhile, Geffen pored over every detail of the marketing campaign. The album was entitled *Jackson Browne* and the cover featured a shot of a cloth water bag with the words "saturate before using" on it. Geffen purchased ads in all the trade magazines, as well as a giant billboard on Sunset Boulevard in West Hollywood, to herald the album's release. It was to become Asylum Records' first big success.

"Doctor My Eyes," the first single from Browne's album, was a major hit. The song rose to number eight on the pop-music charts, a stunning debut for a new artist. Geffen had a hit record and a new star on his hands. His instincts about the singer, whose talent had been underappreciated by Ahmet Ertegun and Clive Davis, had been right all along. On the album cover, Browne gave credit where credit was due: "Thanks to David Geffen," he wrote.

But it was the label's next release that sent the hysteria surrounding Asylum Records over the top. Geffen tirelessly plugged the Eagles as he had Laura Nyro years before, telling everyone he encountered that the group was going to be bigger than CSNY. The promotion men at Atlantic Records rolled their eyes in disbelief.

After Ahmet Ertegun heard "Take It Easy," however, a directive was sent down from the top that the promotion department should indeed work every contact to make the single a hit. "It will be number one in six weeks," Ertegun predicted boldly. His forecast proved to be somewhat optimistic, but he was not far off. The song, released June 3, 1972, reached number twelve by the middle of the summer. Anyone listening to a radio knew that there was a new band called the Eagles.

David Geffen found himself in the middle of the music industry's hottest new movement. The British Invasion had grabbed all the headlines in the late 1960s, but now in the early 1970s it was the "California Sound" that was getting the attention, and Asylum Records was becoming known as the movement's headquarters. There had been a California Sound beginning with the Beach Boys in the 1960s, but that group's tunes seemed slight compared with the serious warbling of the singer-songwriters who were now making their homes in Los Angeles.

Along with the airplay the Eagles got with "Take It Easy," the band's popularity grew in tandem with an aggressive performance schedule. Geffen and Roberts arranged for the Eagles to be the opening act for a number of big tours in the summer of 1972, including those of such diverse groups as the J. Geils Band, Jethro Tull, and Yes.

The Eagles' album had a couple of other songs Geffen believed could be chartbusters. Atlantic put out "Witchy Woman," which fared even better than "Take It Easy," rising to number nine on *Billboard*'s charts. Geffen had found the hot-selling group he had been looking for.

D avid Geffen was being very close mouthed last week. All he'll say is he's signing some very big acts," reporter John Gibson wrote in his column, "The Coast," in *Record World*. "Hold on to your acts, men, there's a gust coming."

The news soon broke that Geffen had signed Linda Ronstadt to Asylum, although Capitol Records demanded the rights to one of her next two albums in exchange for an early release from her contract. Jimmy Webb left Warner Bros. Records and joined the Asylum roster. The Byrds soon reunited for an album that was to be put out on Geffen's label.

Geffen Roberts was also red-hot. In addition to representing most of the acts on Asylum, they picked up clients recording for rival labels. One such act was America, a trio formed in London in 1969 that became famous with such hits as "Horse with No Name" and "Sister Golden Hair." The headlines just seemed to keep coming.

The management company was so successful, in fact, that Geffen and Roberts decided they needed help running it. Geffen convinced John Hartmann, his old William Morris buddy, to join the firm. Hartmann had been fired from the Morris office and had retreated to his home in Topanga Canyon. Geffen recognized that Hartmann had a rapport with artists, and he convinced him to return to work, luring him with the promise of an equity stake in the company.

Asylum Records and Geffen Roberts had become the most successful start-up record label and management enterprise, respectively, that people in the music business could remember. Geffen had succeeded because of an innate ability to strategize and understand the path to big success. Whereas most people could not see beyond the immediate tasks at hand, Geffen had a vision of what the brass ring looked like and was able to figure out when to make his grab in order to get it. Almost everything he did was part of a carefully plotted strategic plan, parts of which were extremely complicated.

But it was also his remarkable energy level, unfathomable work ethic, and an ironclad determination to win that catapulted him to the top. Perhaps frightened of failing at life, David Geffen simply had to succeed, and he was not going to let anything or anyone stand in his way. He was going to use every resource at his disposal, including his often badgering interpersonal style, in order to score. It was a combination that made him unstoppable almost every time out.

He still did not have the "ears" that his old mentors Clive Davis and Ahmet Ertegun had that helped them discover talent. But his success rate was higher than most, and the winners that he had proved to be so huge that few people even noticed the duds. What Geffen did have was Jackson Browne, a young man with many talented friends, and the smarts to sign them and leave them alone to make their music.

"It's easy in music to tell what's good," Geffen began telling people. "It's hard to tell what's bad."

Ever since his Picasso had been stolen, Geffen wanted to sell the house on Alto Cedro Drive and move. He had only been there a little more than two years and had given the house a major renovation, but he did not feel safe there. He began showing the house to prospective buyers. One of the first to see it was Warren Beatty and his girlfriend, Julie Christie, who together had starred in the movie *McCabe & Mrs. Miller* a year earlier.

Beatty was an enormous movie star, having appeared in such hits as *Splendor in the Grass* and *Bonnie and Clyde*. They struck up a congenial chat, and although Beatty was not interested in buying Geffen's house, he took a liking to its owner. He thought Geffen was a bright guy, and he found his ability to cut to the essence of an issue refreshing.

Beatty was a leader of Hollywood's liberal political movement, and he was just now marshaling the town's forces and money to support the presidential campaign of Senator George McGovern, the Democrat who would face President Nixon on the ballot later that year. Geffen was a man with money and clout, and he offered to help Beatty out in any way he could.

Beatty introduced Geffen to his pal Jack Nicholson, who had recently appeared in *Five Easy Pieces.* Geffen in turn introduced his new friends to Joni Mitchell, and the four went together to a celebrity-studded benefit for McGovern that raised more than three hundred thousand dollars for his campaign. Among others, the concert featured Carole King, James Taylor, and Quincy Jones. The star of the event, though, was undeniably Barbra Streisand, who stole the show with her rendition of "Happy Days Are Here Again."

The political involvement of stars and executives in Hollywood was reaching dizzying new heights, and the McGovern benefit foreshadowed a big role in Democratic politics in Geffen's future.

In August 1972, Los Angeles police arrested Christopher Cornett and two other men and booked them on suspicion of burglary in the case of Geffen's stolen Picasso. Cornett, age eighteen, and the other two were busted after they were observed moving the painting from a residence to an automobile in the Silverlake neighborhood. It is not clear if charges were ever brought against the three men.

Geffen's insurance company offered to give the picture back to him, on the condition, of course, that he return the seventy-five thousand dollars he had collected after it had been stolen.

"Take the picture back," Ahmet Ertegun told him unequivocally when Geffen called for advice.

"Oh no," David told him. "I'm rid of it. I made this money, I don't want to give *that* back."

The insurance company then put the painting up for auction, and Picasso's *Buste,* which Geffen had acquired only a couple of years earlier for $36,000, sold for $130,000.

Geffen making a poor business decision was a rare occasion. He was stunned that the painting had brought such a high price. He became irrational and shouted ludicrous statements at his friends.

"I lost all this money because of *you!*" he screamed at Ertegun. "*You* made me lose all this money!"

A sylum Records was not yet a year old when Warner Communications chief Steve Ross called Geffen and told him Warner would like to buy the 50 percent of the label it did not already own. Ross was the only salesman that Geffen knew who was more seductive than he was, and he basked in Ross's praise. Ross told him they should meet the next time Geffen was in New York.

Although Geffen's goal from the beginning was to one day sell Asylum and reap a cash windfall, he was taken off guard by Ross's offer. He was not surprised that Warner Communications was interested in buying him out, but he was shocked that Ross wanted to buy it so soon. Geffen did not contemplate for one second declining Ross's offer; he had an insatiable hunger for money, and this seemed to be the opportunity of a lifetime.

He was also motivated by the fear that Asylum's fast rise had been a fluke and that it could all fall apart at any moment. Although the Eagles were continuing to have success with their first album—its third single, "Peaceful Easy Feeling," was now rising up the pop charts—both Geffen and Roberts were terrified that the band was going to break up at any minute. There was a constant and growing tension between the four performers, and an explosion like the ones that had rocked CSNY might be imminent. It never occurred to them that within just a couple of years the band would release an album that became the best-selling record of all time.

Attempting to pump up Ross's enthusiasm and in turn increase his leverage in the negotiations, Geffen began cultivating the media, who responded with fawning articles about him. At the beginning of September, the *Los Angeles Times*'s rock columnist Robert Hilburn weighed in with a lengthy feature headlined A RISE FROM MAILROOM TO RECORD ASYLUM. Hilburn noted that of Asylum's first five records, three had gone gold, meaning they had shipped at least five hundred thousand copies to record stores. Year number two, Hilburn reported, would see the release of albums by such "sure sellers" as Joni Mitchell, Linda Ronstadt, and the Byrds. *Record World,* in a story headlined IT'S THE ARTIST, NOT THE COMPANY, had Geffen explaining that it was his "artist-oriented" strategy that had caused Asylum to succeed.

Geffen had had limited contact with Steve Ross, but he was in awe of him, having watched from the sidelines as he developed the Warner film and music empire into one of Hollywood's most successful companies in just a few years. Of all the people Geffen had come in contact with in the entertainment business, Steve Ross impressed him the most. The power Ross exerted seemed nearly immeasurable, and Geffen fantasized that he might be able to catapult through Warner's ranks and one day succeed him as chairman.

Once in Ross's office, Geffen fell victim to his charisma, an act so polished that it made even a slick charmer such as Ahmet Ertegun seem like an amateur. Ross took Geffen into his private conference room and told him how pleased Warner Communications had been with the success of Asylum. When Geffen reached for a cigarette, Ross dashed to his side, lifted a lighter off the table, and lit it for him.

Getting down to the business at hand, Ross asked him to name his price. Simultaneously flustered by Ross's directness and bowled over by his charm, Geffen made an enormous negotiating mistake: He was the first to name a number.

"You can have it for seven million," Geffen blurted, uttering the biggest number he could imagine Ross would agree to pay. He figured it was a huge stretch, given that Ross knew that the label was going to post earnings of only about $150,000 in its first year.

Without blinking, Ross agreed to Geffen's price, on two conditions: First, Geffen had to quit the management business. Warner saw a conflict of interest in Geffen's ownership of both a label and a management company, and it was concerned about its liability under the California Labor Code. Second, Geffen had to agree to sign a seven-year employment contract with Warner Communications. Geffen eagerly shook Ross's hand. It was agreed that Geffen would be paid roughly two million dollars in cash and five million dollars in Warner Communications stock, which at the time was trading at about forty-five dollars a share. The deal made Geffen one of the fifteen largest individual shareholders in the company. He would also be paid an annual salary of $150,000.

Geffen focused on the millions of dollars he was getting for selling his label, but Ross cared mostly about the employment contract. Ross believed that his company's most valuable assets were the executives who ran its businesses. Even though Asylum had released just a few hit albums, it was clear that Geffen was a winner of extraordinary proportions, and Ross wanted to have him on his team for the long run. Within just a couple of months, it became clear that the deal was as incredible for Steve Ross as it was terrible for David Geffen.

But for now, Geffen was ecstatic, and he concluded that the sale meant that he would never again have to worry about money. A week before the acquisition was announced, *Newsweek* weighed in with an article on Geffen and his success. Headlined GOLDEN BOY, the feature called him "the fastest rising young man" in the music business. Included in the piece was a tale Geffen had fabricated: He said that Ahmet Ertegun had given him fifty thousand dollars a few years earlier when he was down on his luck.

"I thought I'd be a success even back in the mailroom at William Morris," Geffen told the magazine. "It was just inconceivable to me I couldn't win it all."

The article was most noteworthy, though, because Geffen was solely credited as the one who "took four washed-up musicians out of three failed bands and made them Crosby, Stills, Nash & Young." Apparently, he had made no mention of Elliot Roberts or his role in helping to build Geffen's management and record empire.

Just as when he made the initial deal to establish Asylum Records, Geffen did not tell Roberts about Steve Ross's offer to buy the company until he had already accepted it. When Roberts finally found out, he told Geffen he thought the sale was premature.

"This is a huge mistake," he said. "We'll live to regret it."

Roberts had known for months that Geffen was growing bored with Asylum Records, and he was not surprised that he had accepted Ross's offer. Even as the label bathed in the glowing publicity that Geffen had engineered, Geffen talked constantly about wanting to get into the movie business. He spent most of his free time with his new Hollywood pals. Steve Ross was his new hero, and Geffen had told Roberts that he wanted one day soon to run the Warner Bros. movie studio. He was simply getting his power cards and credentials in order.

Roberts, to be sure, did not put up too much of a struggle. Although Roberts was technically Geffen's partner in Asylum, Geffen was the majority owner and was free to do with it whatever he pleased. Roberts's protests were also not all that pronounced, in part because the sale made him rich. Geffen gave Roberts roughly 25 percent of the sale price and additionally gave him his 75 percent interest in Geffen Roberts. Roberts saw his net worth climb, on paper at least, into the seven figures.

The acquisition was announced just before Thanksgiving 1972, with Warner crowing that Geffen was to continue as president of the label. Atlantic Records was to continue to distribute Asylum's albums, and Warner's newly founded international-distribution unit was to get the rights to release Asylum's records overseas once a series of licensing deals Geffen had made with EMI and other record companies expired. Warner also picked up the 50 percent of the artists' publishing rights that Asylum had controlled.

The sale brought cries of outrage from the Asylum artists. The loudest complaints came from the Eagles, especially Don Henley, who viewed the sale as a breach of the promises Geffen had made to them a year earlier as they sat in his sauna. Geffen had now turned Asylum

Batya (left) with her second husband, Sam Sandler,

and her sister, Deena Volovskaya, shortly after Deena emigrated

from Russia to the United States. The sisters had not

seen each other in fifty-five years.

(Courtesy Deena Volovskaya)

over to a huge entertainment conglomerate. Worse, Henley figured, Asylum's one major asset was the Eagles, and they were getting nothing from the sale.

Henley's biggest gripe was that half their music-publishing rights was now in the hands of a burgeoning corporation. An idealistic young man, he was repulsed by the idea. Don Henley began to call David Geffen a liar.

Linda Ronstadt and others were also surprised by the sale, confused about Geffen's intentions, and concerned about the validity of other promises he had made to his artists. Asylum Records now seemed less like a sanctuary and more like a place for the insane.

Geffen had a mutiny on his hands, and he scrambled to patch things up with his artists. His main defense was to insist that despite the sale Asylum would continue to be the same company. "Nothing is going to change," Geffen promised. "Elliot and I are here, and we're going to continue to run the company as we always have." The artists were soon to find out that Geffen was not going to keep that promise either.

His bank account newly enlarged, Geffen telephoned his mother in Borough Park and told her that she should close up the corset shop and move to California. Wanting her to enjoy some of the money he had accumulated, he said he would buy her and Sam a house of their choosing in Los Angeles.

Batya, now sixty-five, was thrilled with David's offer. She was exhausted from years of working long hours at her business, and she was eager to live closer to her two sons. She also wanted to be nearer to Mitchell and Renee's two daughters, Vivian and Elaine, so she could be a proper grandmother. She put the corset shop up for sale and soon accepted an offer of about eighty thousand dollars, double the price she and Abe had paid when they bought the building in 1956.

Sam helped Batya pack up her favorite sewing machine, as well as some old rolls of fabric, and the two moved west. Batya spent only one day with a realtor before finding a small house on Gilcrest Drive, high above Sunset Boulevard in Beverly Hills, that she wanted. Sam, who had retired after thirty years as a mailman, toddled down the hill toward Sunset and landed a part-time job as a doorman at the Beverly Hills Hotel.

Within a few years, Batya's world brightened further when her only surviving sibling, Deena Volovskaya, came to California from Russia. The sisters, who had not seen each other in fifty-five years, had a sparkling reunion. Deena, a widowed schoolteacher who was fifty-six when she came to the United States, had planned to stay for only two weeks, but Batya insisted she stay in Los Angeles forever.

Deena did not speak English, and was confused and uncomfortable when Batya first took her to meet David in Malibu; she declined his generous offer to buy her a car. But she learned English and got a job, and in the years to come developed extraordinary affection for her nephew. Both Batya and Deena were grateful for the sense of security David extended them.

VACATION IN
FRANCE

|||

To Geffen's chagrin, Warner Communications' stock fell steadily in the months following his deal to sell Asylum Records. Just after the start of 1973, the shares fell to thirty-one dollars, and suddenly Geffen's great deal did not seem so great after all.

Still, his payout was a lot of money, and the sale catapulted him into the ranks of California's really rich. Just thirty, he claimed that his net worth was about twelve million dollars. In addition to the house he had bought for his mother in Beverly Hills, Geffen used some of his newly found wealth to buy some things for himself. He bought a piece of residential property on Carbon Beach, near Doris Day's house, and he hired Charles Gwathmey, a renowned New York architect, to design a house for him there.

He also added a Mercedes-Benz to his collection of cars, which now also included a Porsche Targa and the Rolls-Royce. He still wore his customary blue jeans every day, but now he purchased expensive pairs that were expertly faded and tailored. He began wearing Italian loafers and started getting forty-five-dollar haircuts in which his stylist trimmed his whirly curls close to his skull.

On the shrewd advice of Gil Segel, who along with Jerry Rubinstein served as his business manager, Geffen also invested a chunk of the money in Southern California real estate. Among the properties he purchased were a number of small office buildings along Wilshire Boulevard near a new commercial development known as Century City.

But he was surprised to realize that the millions of dollars he had just banked and the trappings he had been able to acquire with it did not make him happy. It hit him when he was in London on a business trip, lying on a bed in a posh hotel, smoking a joint, and staring at the ceiling. All his life he had dreamed of being a multimillionaire, thinking that money would solve his problems. It had not, and he fell into a deep depression. At his office, he had the look of a person who was constantly nervous. He restlessly rattled a pair of balls in his hand like Captain Queeg in *The Caine Mutiny*.

"I'm not happy," he thought. "I'm alone. My life is my work."

Warren Beatty grew concerned about Geffen's emotional state and suggested he consider seeing a psychiatrist. Beatty was particularly high on his own therapist, Dr. Martin Grotjahn, and encouraged Geffen to give him a call. He did, and before long he began five-day-a-week analysis.

He found that he had plenty to talk about with Dr. Grotjahn. Much of psychoanalysis is based on an examination of one's family history, and Geffen had a wealth of territory to cover. His few conversations with his brother were brief and almost always ended in arguments. His relationship with his mother, who now lived less than a mile away, was not much better. The fights he had with Batya bothered him greatly, and he decided to avoid her. To some extent, Geffen had succeeded in reinventing himself, but his interactions with his brother and his mother were painful reminders of his childhood and the life he was trying to forget.

Geffen found analysis valuable in attempting to understand why he was always quarreling with the important people in his life. He found

Geffen stands in the shadows as his friend, roommate, and star artist, Joni Mitchell, performs. Mitchell would immortalize Geffen as her "Free Man in Paris." (Joel Bernstein)

in therapy a way to acknowledge the feelings that arose from some of the nasty confrontations in which he engaged. "The one thing I despise doing is to make decisions based on how other people will view or judge me. I've found that there's no escape from that kind of judgment, anyway," he said at the time. "If I'm nice to people they say 'I wonder what he wants.' If I'm not nice to them, I'm a snob. I have no right to be *me,* you know. And I intend to be me. Whatever that is."

It was in analysis that Geffen decided he wanted to be straight. For a time, he dated Janet Margolin, a movie actress who had starred in *David and Lisa.* He told friends that it had been difficult to have a personal life because his business had been all consuming. "It's something I'm working on hard, to try and have that balance," he said.

His sessions with the analyst also helped him recognize that there was comfort to be had in patching up the differences he had had with some of his foes. With Clive Davis, he made the first move. "My emotion is spent. I haven't been happy since we fought," he told Davis over the phone. "We were such good friends before, let's be that way again." Davis agreed, not wanting to carry the feud any further.

There always seemed, however, to be another war to wage. The latest brouhaha that required Geffen's energies was a dispute with Doug Weston, the tyrannical, six-foot-six owner of the Troubadour. Weston's power stemmed from the fact that he had a monopoly: The Troubadour was the only club influential enough to launch a new act; if managers wanted their acts to play there, they had to play by his rules. He often extracted unreasonable demands that artists commit to years of dates at prearranged terms that were bargains for him if an artist went on to become a star.

Geffen and Roberts bickered with Weston over the engagements of many of their artists, and they grew particularly enraged when Weston refused to book David Blue, whose albums were not selling well. Geffen threatened that if Weston did not book Blue, he would start a club to rival the Troubadour. Weston laughed and refused.

True to his word, Geffen went about making plans to open his own club. In addition to Geffen and Roberts, many others were also fed up with Weston's bullying, and a number of their peers eagerly accepted the invitation to join in the venture. The group eventually included Lou Adler and Bill Graham, the impresario behind the famed Fillmore clubs in San Francisco and New York.

A suitable location was found on the north side of Sunset Boulevard, just a couple of short blocks east of Asylum's offices. Geffen suggested they name the club the Roxy after a theater of the same name in New York where he used to go to movies as a kid. Adler suggested they open a smaller room upstairs from the main space that would be called On the Rocks. Plans were drawn up for a September opening.

In March 1973, Linda Loddengaard arranged to have painters come in and give the offices of Asylum and Geffen Roberts a fresh coat. When they were finished, she kept watch as they hung up sixteen framed gold records in the hallway.

Following the sale of Asylum to Warner Communications, Roberts assumed control of the management business. In a further bid to demonstrate to Warner and the community that the record company and the management enterprise were now separate, Geffen moved his office to the first floor, while Roberts stayed on the second floor.

In fact, Geffen continued to play a big role in the management company. This was in part because Roberts was breaking under the strain of trying to run the company alone. For a time, he disappeared to a newly purchased ranch outside San Francisco to recuperate. Nevertheless, the company continued to thrive, having recently picked up Poco, the country-rock band that CBS had gotten from Atlantic in the CSN trade in 1969.

Looking for an additional manager to help John Hartmann, Geffen hired Harlan Goodman, a handsome young guy from Chicago whom he and Roberts had met years earlier at CSNY's performance the night before Woodstock. Geffen was sold on Goodman when he learned that he had worked at the Chicago office of the William Morris Agency.

"Let me tell you what's happening here," Geffen told Goodman. "Elliot hasn't been in the best of health, and he's going to be hopefully spending more time up at the ranch. But you and John are going to run this place." Goodman and Hartmann became buddies and connected with the artists, especially Graham Nash and David Crosby.

Unbeknownst to Hartmann and Goodman, there was a big problem brewing. The anger the Eagles felt toward Geffen as a result of the sale of Asylum was so intense that it began to influence their songwriting. Don Henley and Glenn Frey began to pen tunes that included indirect references to the merger. Henley and Frey had cowritten a ballad called "Desperado" and decided to expand its theme into a cycle of songs that reflected their cynicism about the music business and fame in general.

In England, where the band went again with producer Glyn Johns to record their second album, Frey grew even more upset with Geffen. He realized that EMI, which Geffen had hired to handle Asylum's U.K. releases, was not promoting the group's first album very aggressively there. Frey soon concluded that the sale of Asylum to Warner had removed any incentive EMI might have had to break the label's acts, since EMI knew that when its contract expired, Warner would assume overseas distribution responsibility.

Released in May 1973, the Eagles' second album, entitled *Desperado,* was a commercial failure. Although the album had a couple of pleasant-sounding tracks, there was no obvious hit single. "Tequila Sunrise," which was also cowritten by Henley and Frey, died at number sixty-four on the pop charts. While the Eagles' first album had risen to number twenty-two, the follow-up album stalled at number forty-one.

It should not have been a surprise that the Eagles' second album failed. Many bands have disappointing follow-up albums, often because their label pressures them to turn out another record quickly. Where a first album is worked on for as long as ten years or more, the second album frequently gets put together in a few short months. Routinely, a band's third album showcases the style with which a group has grown comfortable.

Disappointed with the performance of *Desperado* and tired of listening to the Eagles' constant griping, David Geffen turned his attentions away from the group and decided to go after the next great thing. He began plotting to sign an established star who could win him even bigger headlines than the Asylum sale had.

People in the music business had for years predicted that if Bob Dylan reteamed with the Band, whose members had served as the backup musicians on his 1966 world tour, they would break box-office records. But no one seriously thought a reunion was possible.

For one thing, Dylan had grown reclusive following his motorcycle accident after the world tour. Moreover, the Band had started turning out their own hits, such as "The Weight" and "The Night They Drove Old Dixie Down." David Geffen decided he would pull off the reunion others called impossible.

Geffen knew Jonathan Taplin, a movie producer who had been the Band's first road manager, and asked him to introduce him to Robbie Robertson, the group's de facto leader. His plan was to get Robertson in his corner and then convince him to help get Dylan on board. Then, Geffen hoped, he could even sign Dylan to Asylum Records. That would be nothing short of amazing, Geffen knew, because Dylan had made all his albums for Columbia. But Geffen was determined to make it happen.

On a trip out to Los Angeles from his home in Woodstock, Robertson agreed to meet Geffen at his office. A street-smart kid from Canada, Robertson had never met anyone quite like David Geffen. Geffen shocked him by disclosing frank details of his personal life in the opening moments of their first meeting. He told him he had just returned from an appointment with his therapist and revealed details of his recent sexual exploits with men. The frank admissions actually put Robertson at ease and he felt open to talk about almost anything. Geffen used the strategy throughout his life to great effect.

Geffen impressed Robertson with the articulate way in which he spoke about the Band's music and how it had affected him. He told him what was going on at Asylum. It was a brilliant soft sell: He did not mention a word about the Band's contract, Bob Dylan, or a possible tour. Robertson was not naive, however, and he had an idea of what Geffen was after. Besides, his deal at Capitol was up soon.

Robertson returned to Woodstock, and Geffen started a telephone campaign to solidify the bond. Soon, he had some business in New York and told Robertson that he wanted to come up to Woodstock to visit. There, Geffen made a direct pitch. He proposed an extraordinary record deal for the Band in which he offered simply to split the profits fifty-fifty. Robertson had been used to complicated contracts in which the artist got a small percentage of the royalties, minus the overhead and other items.

Robertson told the other members of the Band about Geffen's proposal. Levon Helm, Rick Danko, Richard Manuel, and Garth Hudson listened as Robertson laid out the terms. "This guy, he's like quite the guy," Robertson told them. "There's something about him. . . . He's thought things out in an innovative way." Robertson arranged for Geffen to meet the other members of the group the next day.

Robertson's compatriots were not as a whole suspicious people, but they were essentially country boys, and Geffen's presentation was a tad flashy for their tastes. Robertson was rooting for Geffen, but he could tell that Geffen did not understand the other members of the Band. They were a motley group of odd characters who made strangely abstract comments to which Geffen did not know how to respond. The Band did not agree to sign with Geffen on the spot, but they did conclude that he had a pitch that merited further discussion.

Joni Mitchell's romance with Jackson Browne was short-lived and had an ugly ending. Unlike her previous relationships with Graham Nash and David Crosby, she was not the one to end this one. Browne broke it off and soon after began seeing a woman named Phyllis Major.

The disintegration of the relationship devastated Mitchell, and she turned bitterly on Browne. Geffen delicately tried to balance his relationships with the two big stars, both of whom he counted among his closest friends. Mitchell was living alone in an apartment on Crescent Heights Boulevard, just south of Sunset Boulevard, when she descended into a deep depression.

Geffen, meanwhile, found a buyer for his house on Alto Cedro Drive and began hunting for a new place. He settled on a lease on a mansion on Copley Drive in Beverly Hills. Blake Edwards, the movie director, and his wife, Julie Andrews, owned it, but they were now renting it out. Geffen invited Mitchell to move in with him as his roommate. She could have an entire wing of the house to herself, a comfortable environment in which to write her music. He would hire a couple of servants to clean and cook for them. Mitchell, who was apparently at the breaking point, said yes. The incident signaled how Geffen now and in the future would be a strong supporter of his friends during times of crisis.

His friendship with Mitchell had intensified in the year since he and Laura Nyro had ceased communication. Sensing Nyro's competitiveness, Geffen had not felt comfortable spending much time with Mitchell while Nyro was around. But now Geffen and Mitchell were each other's best friend, and he invested the same kind of energy into making her an even bigger star that he had used with Nyro. Mitchell's debut album on Asylum, called *For the Roses,* featured a single that was the biggest hit she had recorded to date. Called "You Turn Me On, I'm a Radio," it was on the charts for sixteen weeks, peaking at number twenty-five.

After Geffen and Mitchell moved into the house, some gossip columnists questioned whether they were a new twosome. Their friends knew better: He liked her because he could talk openly with her about his relationships with men; she found him to be a sensitive man who listened intently and helped with *her* love problems. He even proved to be something of a matchmaker, introducing her to Warren Beatty.

Sensing that Mitchell needed a vacation, Geffen proposed that they go to Paris. She was thrilled with the idea and also endorsed Geffen's thought that they include Robbie Robertson and his wife, Dominique. Geffen bet that some social time with Robertson would help him get closer to clinching a record deal with the Band.

Robertson and the Band were working on their album *Moondog Matinee* when Geffen called with the invitation for the following week.

"Let's do it," Robertson said. "Let's go." Dominique, who was French, was especially excited.

The four flew first-class and stayed at the Ritz Hotel. They walked along the Champs-Élysées, stopping in small cabarets and cafés on side streets, where Geffen ordered expensive bottles of wine for the group. Mitchell grew to like the Robertsons and asked Robbie if he would be interested in playing guitar on a song she planned to record called "Raised on Robbery." He was flattered and said he would be happy to.

On this trip, Mitchell drew inspiration for another song, one about David Geffen. She was amazed at how comfortable Geffen was while on vacation, and she began to appreciate the difficulty and stresses of his job. Each day, she pulled out her guitar and began strumming away, struggling to find a way to mesh chords with a lyric she had devised about an overburdened music mogul seeking solace and peace in Paris.

Mitchell was convinced that she had found the perfect way to honor her friend and roommate. The song had a rather melancholy feel to it as it seemed to directly address Geffen's loneliness and ongoing search for a man with whom he could share his life.

Mitchell was obsessed with the song, which she called "Free Man in Paris," and seemed to work on it throughout the trip. Her strumming eventually started to annoy Dominique, who began bristling when Mitchell reached for her guitar.

"Would you please not play the guitar?" an exasperated Dominique finally said one afternoon while the other three were having a chat at a café. "Would you stop singing . . . please?"

Robbie was embarrassed, recognizing that there were many fans who would gladly pay a lot of money to be the audience at such a private mini-concert. Mitchell, though, took the criticism in stride. After a few moments, she and Dominique burst into gales of laughter.

"Oh jeez, I'm sorry," Mitchell said. "I was starting up again, just as you guys were trying to have a conversation."

In a move that again demonstrated that he had moved spiritually and psychologically into the category of the super-rich, Geffen made a magnanimous gesture. "I'm going to go down and take care of the bill," he said to the group. "I'm not going to embarrass you, just let me do it. I had such a great time, I just want it to be my treat."

Geffen went downstairs but returned after several minutes, red faced.

"It must have been a lot of money," Robertson thought.

"They won't take my check," Geffen said worriedly. "I don't know what we're going to do."

"David, what we've spent here, we're going to have to do a lot of dishes," Robertson quipped.

Geffen brainstormed a bit. "I'm going to call Prince Rupert [Loewenstein]," he said at last, "and ask him to call the hotel and tell them I'm good for it. Or maybe he can pay the bill and then I'll pay him back or something."

Prince Rupert vouched for Geffen's credit, and the hotel agreed to accept Geffen's check. For all of them, it had been a magical trip. The medicine that Geffen felt Mitchell needed had worked, and in addition they now had forged relationships with two new friends—both of whom, importantly, were close to Bob Dylan.

After the trip, Geffen began the next phase of his campaign. Dylan and his wife, Sara, had just rented a house in Malibu. Geffen thought it could only help make his dream come true if Robertson and Dylan lived near each other.

"I think you should move to California," Geffen told Robertson. "Malibu is paradise. You can always change your mind." Then Geffen made an offer. "Why don't you just let me put this together?" he asked. "I'll get you a house in the Malibu Colony."

The Robertsons and their two daughters decided to take the plunge.

They packed up their things and moved sight unseen to a house that Geffen had found for them. Upon their arrival, Robertson called Geffen and told him they had arrived safely and loved the house.

Geffen picked up Robertson and took him over to his own house. He chose this moment to make his pitch a bit more aggressive.

"Why don't Bob and the Band do a tour together?" he asked.

Robertson explained that they had not done so because it was exactly what people expected them to do. "I know, but it's not expected anymore," Geffen said. "It's been a long time. It would be amazing, and I'll help put the whole thing together." Robertson began to think that Geffen's plans for the Band made sense.

But as Geffen drove Robertson back to Malibu, Robertson was overcome with a feeling that perhaps this was not such a good idea after all. "David, these guys. . . . They're from a very different school, and so is Bob," Robertson started. "You might have gotten a little sense of that when you met with them in Woodstock. I worry about you throwing yourself in the middle of all this."

Reaching Robertson's house, Geffen turned off his Porsche Targa and looked at Robbie. "Please, I'm a big boy, I can handle this, whatever it is," Geffen said. "Don't worry about me."

"I just want you to be sure and hear what I'm saying," Robertson continued. "There is a real possibility that you could get burned."

Because Geffen was so insistent, however, Robertson agreed to broach the subject with Dylan. While initially skeptical, Dylan thought that the idea merited consideration, and he agreed to meet Geffen.

The first meeting between Geffen and Dylan went well. Geffen hit the right tone, showering Dylan with compliments while careful not to appear sycophantic. It was an unlikely chemistry that seemed to work: Geffen made Dylan laugh, and Dylan made Geffen laugh, too.

Geffen engineered a succession of informal meetings with Dylan in which the two walked on the beach in Malibu and talked about matters both personal and professional. Dylan was interested in learning French, so Geffen arranged for them to take a course together.

Geffen soon outlined his idea for a tour. "Let me just put the right people in the right place, and you don't have to do anything," Geffen told Dylan. "All you have to do is make some amazing music, and I'll take care of the rest."

Geffen told Dylan he would hire Bill Graham, his partner in the Roxy, to serve as the tour's promoter. He told him he envisioned the tour beginning after the first of the year and hitting just about every major city in the United States. He said he had an idea to make tickets available only through mail order, an unheard-of ploy that he predicted would create a firestorm of publicity for the shows.

Dylan was impressed with Geffen's plan. Geffen clinched the deal when he told the star his fee: He did not want a cent. Geffen did not let on that he was playing a much bigger chess game in which he eventually sought to sign Dylan to Asylum Records. The tour was just his opening move.

A bear market on Wall Street, coupled with analysts' confusion over Steve Ross's strategy concerning the fledgling cable-television business, prompted Warner Communications' stock to continue to drop through the summer of 1973. By August, it had dipped as low as ten dollars a share. Geffen was aghast that his seven-million-dollar deal to sell Asylum, which he realized now had been way too low a price in the first place, was now worth less than half that amount.

Geffen whined about the stock to everyone in the Warner Communications family and especially lambasted Steve Ross and Alan Cohen, Ross's lieutenant who had responsibility for the company's music operations. Other executives with major stock holdings, notably Ahmet Ertegun, also griped about the stock, but no one fussed louder than David Geffen.

Finally Ross could take Geffen's screaming no more, and he devised a solution that he believed could also help solve another problem at the company. Elektra Records was a trouble spot, and Ross decided he would be willing to rejigger Geffen's stock deal if he would take the job as Elektra's chairman.

Jac Holzman started Elektra while attending Saint John's College in 1950. The son of a physician, Holzman grew up on New York's Upper East Side and, like Geffen, was a champion of the singer-songwriters of the folk era. Ross acquired Elektra in 1970, when Holzman was turning out hit records from such acts as the Doors, Judy Collins, Harry Chapin, Bread, and Carly Simon.

But in 1973, Elektra was still the smallest of Warner's three main record units, and Holzman was showing signs of burnout. The artist roster had grown too big, and the hit-to-miss ratio was not impressive. Holzman, whose interests had drifted to such technical issues as the development of quadraphonic sound, wanted out. Ross determined he needed a fireball to revitalize the label. Geffen, the rising star of the Warner music family, was the obvious choice.

The offer to run Elektra, a big record label with its own marketing and distribution operation, represented an extraordinary promotion for Geffen. But he feigned disinterest and loudly protested that he had no desire to run it. Craftily, however, he let Mo Ostin, the head of Warner Bros./Reprise Records and an ally of Steve Ross, know that he was open to the job if the terms were right.

Ross implored Geffen to take the job, proposing to combine Elektra with Asylum and have Geffen preside over the merged labels. To make Geffen happy, Ross offered to raise his salary to one million dollars and renegotiate his stock deal. For the remaining six years of Geffen's contract, Ross promised to pay Geffen in cash the difference between the average Warner stock price that year and the amount for which it was selling when Warner bought Asylum. In that time, the stock never did top the initial price, and Geffen as a result got makeup checks every year.

Geffen accepted Ross's offer. At the end of August 1973, Warner announced the merger and Geffen's promotion to chairman of the company now known as Elektra/Asylum Records. Holzman was moved to a corporate post as senior vice president of the parent company; among his responsibilities was the investigation of new technologies. Mel Posner, Holzman's longtime number-two man, stayed at Elektra/Asylum as president and reported to Geffen. Elektra, like Atlantic, was a New York–based label, but Geffen began exploring plans to move it to the West Coast.

Linda Loddengaard packed up Geffen's office and moved everything down to Elektra's West Coast office at 962 North La Cienega Boulevard, just south of Santa Monica Boulevard. The office switch actually meant little to Geffen, who had begun working more and more from home. Loddengaard knew that Geffen disliked coming into an office, and she made it possible for him to work wherever he pleased.

On the eve of his departure, Holzman prepared for Geffen a detailed seventy-page report on the state of affairs at Elektra. It included "fitness reports" on every employee at the label, in which Holzman candidly assessed each person's strengths and weaknesses. As a condition for preparing the report, Holzman made Geffen promise that the material would be kept confidential.

It was a promise Geffen did not keep. He shared the results of Holzman's report cards with several employees. In some cases, he used the reports to turn the employees against Holzman and make them loyal to him. Geffen told CFO Jack Reinstein, for example, that Holzman had recommended that he fire him. Geffen instead gave Reinstein a raise and stock options and thus made him a Geffen loyalist.

He wasted no time in putting his mark on the newly merged company: He dropped twenty-five of the thirty-five artists, fired the art director and the entire publicity, promotion, and production staffs. A new man was in charge, and everyone knew it.

The Eagles grew more and more uncomfortable with the notion that Geffen was their record label as well as their manager and publisher. Geffen supposedly no longer played any role in the management company, but the band knew that he was still pulling strings behind the scenes. To them, it was an obvious conflict of interest that benefited only David Geffen: How could their manager obtain rich contract gains from the head of their record company if the two were one and the same?

Geffen maintained that he had only the artists' best interests at heart and that he did not foresee such a conflict when he had begun the record company. In the beginning, after all, no artist had complained when Geffen asked for contracts assigning him rights to their music publishing. The conflict had become apparent only after the acts had found success.

The situation was complicated by the fact that the Eagles' business manager and lawyer also represented Geffen. Glenn Frey and Don Henley began to wonder how Geffen's business manager was able to look after their interests *and* Geffen's.

John Hartmann sat with the Eagles at Dan Tana's, the restaurant next door to the Troubadour, and listened as they complained about the situation. Frey and Henley asked Hartmann to leave Geffen and be their manager. "Yeah, OK," he said. The Eagles had grown to like Hartmann and knew that he, too, was on the outs with Geffen; Hartmann groaned constantly about how Geffen had reneged on his promise to give him a piece of the company.

The next morning, Henley and Frey telephoned Geffen to tell him they were leaving the management company and that Hartmann was going to represent them. His blood boiling, Geffen summoned Hartmann to his office and fired him before he could quit.

Geffen next went to the band and promised revenge if they left with Hartmann. "If you go with him, I'll bury you," Geffen told them. "And I own your records and your publishing." The band opted to stay. But they would not be there for long.

Irving Azoff, meanwhile, had opened his own firm to manage Dan Fogelberg, REO Speedwagon, and Joe Walsh. Roberts and Geffen contacted Azoff and convinced him to bring his clients and work for Roberts. The management company Geffen and Roberts had built was imploding and they needed help to hold it together. Beyond the ongoing drama with the Eagles, Poco had just fired the company.

Geffen, still steaming from what he felt was a betrayal when Azoff took Fogelberg to Clive Davis, got a bad vibe from Azoff. "This guy is going to be trouble," he thought. But he felt he did not have a choice; with Hartmann gone and Roberts out of commission, no one was manning the shop.

As Azoff walked in the door, Harlan Goodman, the other young manager at the company, decided to quit and join Hartmann in a new management venture. The two men hastily called a meeting with Poco and volunteered to represent them. The band eagerly agreed to become their first client, and the group was to have a significant amount of success with them in the mid-1970s. Whatever success Hartmann and Goodman found away from Geffen and Roberts, however, was nothing compared with what Irving Azoff was about to strip away.

Geffen greets Elton John at the sold-out opening of the Roxy, Geffen's club on Sunset Boulevard. "I made more enemies today than in my whole life," Geffen told the Los Angeles Times. *(Joel Bernstein)*

CHAPTER 12

"I GOT YOU BABE"

|||

The Roxy had its grand opening on September 20, 1973. It was to be a major success and broke Doug Weston's monopolistic hold on the Los Angeles club scene. It was quite an achievement for a man who was only thirty years old.

But on that night, something happened to Geffen that was far more important than any business deal he had ever consummated. He found true love, but one that would eventually almost crush him.

The Roxy's partners were besieged with requests for tickets to the sold-out opening with headliner Neil Young. "I made more enemies today than in my whole life," Geffen told the *Los Angeles Times*. Geffen's own group that night included Bob and Sara Dylan and Robbie and Dominique Robertson.

Although Neil Young had demanded that the majority of the tickets be made available to the general public, the crowd gathered that night included some of the biggest stars in the record business. Geffen stood outside and greeted Elton John and Carole King as they arrived amid a flurry of flashbulbs.

One glitch sent the Roxy partners into a momentary panic that after-noon: Nils Lofgren, the opening act, developed laryngitis. Lou Adler hooked his clients Cheech & Chong, and Geffen pulled in Graham Nash to open the show instead.

Geffen, with the Dylans and the Robertsons, had an early dinner be-fore heading to the Roxy, well in advance of the nine o'clock curtain. The club had a capacity of only a few hundred, and it was indeed the kind of place where the performers were nearly on top of the audience. Geffen and his group took their seats at a table right in front of the stage. As the club filled up and the last few people squeezed inside, the temperature in the room rose to an uncomfortable level.

Just after Neil Young started his set, something magical happened to Geffen. Cher, wearing a straw cowboy hat with a big feather in it, stepped into the club. Seeing an empty seat at Geffen's table, she asked the group if she could join them. Geffen looked up and stared into her eyes. To him, it seemed as though violins, not electric guitars, had started to play. Suddenly, he could not concentrate on Young's perfor-mance.

Geffen had met Cher more than ten years previously at Phil Spec-tor's studio, where she was a backup performer. As her star ascended, he had once tried unsuccessfully to convince her to record a Jackson Browne song. But tonight he was seeing her in a different light, and love was in the air.

Sonny Bono and Cher were at that moment the most popular TV couple in America, thanks to the success of their CBS variety series, *The Sonny and Cher Comedy Hour.* Now in its third season, the show was a ratings powerhouse, and the couple was wowing viewers with silly sketches and rollicking renditions of their saccharine hit "I Got You Babe." They broke box-office records when they played Las Vegas and had earlier that year appeared on the Academy Awards. Cher's sultry solo hit "Half-Breed" was leaping up the pop-music charts, and tonight she was out on the town without Bono.

At a break in the set, Dylan pointed to Cher's hat.

"Can you get me one of those?" he asked dryly.

A man who worked backstage approached the table and addressed Dylan and Robertson. "Hey, Neil's backstage, if you guys want to come back and hang out, you'd be welcome," he said.

In fairly standard fashion, Dylan, expressionless, offered up a non sequitur that he thought was funny: "No thanks, we just ate," he said. Geffen howled with laughter. A look of confusion fell over the man's face as he backed uncomfortably away from the table.

The break was soon over, and Geffen and Cher did not have much of an opportunity to talk. But he scribbled down his address and asked her to join him for dinner the next night. David Geffen was going to have a date with Cher.

Geffen had not previously made much of an impression on Cher, twenty-seven. She did not know who he was or what he did for a living. She did not even know that he was one of the owners of the Roxy.

Cher drove a white Porsche Daytona that had been customized with her name in large red script on the driver's door. The next evening, as she pulled out the slip of paper with Geffen's address on it, she was surprised to see that his house was just a couple of blocks from where she and Bono lived.

"How can he live around the corner from me?" Cher thought to herself. "I live in the richest section of Los Angeles. What's he doing here?" Sonny and Cher lived in a gated mansion at the end of Carolwood Drive in Holmby Hills, a swank enclave of Los Angeles that borders Beverly Hills. The couple had bought the fifty-four-room estate, a fixture on maps of the stars' homes, from actor Tony Curtis a few years earlier.

After Cher rang the bell, Geffen opened the door with a telephone in hand.

"Oh, hi," he said. "Oh, God, I didn't get a chance to take a shower. I'm on the phone. . . . Come in."

After a moment, Lou Adler arrived, and soon joined Cher and Geffen in the dining room. Geffen was funny, Cher thought, and she laughed at his jokes. Adler soon excused himself to check on things at the Roxy.

After dinner, Geffen and Cher retired to the living room. There,

America's beloved TV comedienne opened up her heart and spilled a host of painful secrets she had been keeping for months. Her marriage to Sonny Bono, she said, was in tatters. On television, Sonny and Cher appeared to be the perfect couple. Off camera, however, they were barely civil to each other. They had moved into separate wings of the Carolwood house and now exchanged few words.

Cher told Geffen that Bono was a dictator who had made her life a living hell. He had destabilized her to the point that she could hardly eat or sleep. She was anemic and had been driven so hard by the grind of TV tapings, Las Vegas engagements, and recording sessions that she frequently fell ill. From time to time, the exhaustion forced her to be hospitalized.

It had all gone sour starting with a blowup at the Flamingo Hotel in Las Vegas ten months earlier. One night after their act, Cher told Bono that she was in love with their guitar player, Bill Hamm. Bono freaked out as Cher informed him she wanted out of their marriage. He convinced her that the two were bonded inextricably in a highly profitable business. It made sense, he told her, to keep up the facade of a happy marriage if only for the sake of their bank accounts.

Cher's only escape was to shop, and it was an art she had perfected. It was the only time, she told Geffen, that Bono allowed her to go out unsupervised. She had now grown fed up with the charade and wanted a divorce.

Cher told Geffen about the treasure of her life, her four-year-old daughter, Chastity. Sonny and Cher now took Chas, as they called her, onstage each week during the closing moments of their TV program to sing "I Got You Babe." Cher told Geffen she worried about the impact the split would have on the little girl.

That Cher showed Geffen her most vulnerable side made him comfortable in sharing his deepest secrets with her, too. He told her about the sexual encounters he had had with men and how he was struggling with his sexual identity. He hastily added that his relationships with men had been about sex and nothing more. He was afraid of the opposite sex, he told Cher, but said that he believed a relationship with a woman would offer him the best chance to find true love. Cher had been surrounded by gay men her entire professional life, and Geffen's confessions left her unfazed.

"What is it that you *do*?" Cher finally asked Geffen.

"I am the chairman of Elektra/Asylum Records," he told her.

"Oh, well, you don't look like it," she said. "You just look like a little schlepper."

Geffen was charming, offsetting his usual braggadocio with vulnerability. The two stayed up well into the night, talking and laughing and exchanging the stories of their lives. Geffen told her he had become a millionaire more than five years earlier. He told her that he thought he had accomplished everything he had wanted to achieve, but that somehow the money and the fame was unfulfilling.

"I'm not alone anymore," Cher thought to herself. She had never known anyone in her life who made her feel so comfortable.

As Cher was about to say good night, Joni Mitchell walked in. Geffen had not told Cher that he had a roommate, so the appearance of another music-industry superstar surprised her. Mitchell and Cher worked at near-opposite ends of the music industry, but for each it was kind of a thrill to meet the other. They chatted a while longer, and then Cher returned home.

During his therapy session the next day, Geffen made a startling admission to Dr. Grotjahn. "I think I am in love with Cher," he said.

That night, Geffen asked Cher to go with him to Robbie Robertson's house in Malibu. Geffen was still trying to sign Bob Dylan and the Band to Elektra/Asylum, and he thought having her along might be an asset.

Cher left her car at Geffen's house, and he did the driving. On the way, they stopped for gas. As they sat in the car, Geffen said, "I told my therapist today that I think I am in love with you."

Cher was quiet. "Oh," was all she could manage, thinking to herself, "All right. This is a different wrinkle."

At the Robertsons' house, Robbie was puzzled as Geffen pulled him aside and enthusiastically told him that he was infatuated with Cher. Geffen had been candid with Robertson about his liaisons with men. In fact, when he had come to visit him and Dominique in Woodstock, Geffen had dragged them to a gay bar. "This is very interesting," Robertson told his wife, "that at this stage in his life he is taking this position."

Despite her attraction to him, Cher was not ready to consummate her relationship with Geffen. As they pulled into the driveway at Geffen's house, they each fumbled about, trying to figure out what to do next. Cher did not want to go inside, concerned that Geffen might make a pass at her. But she had left a jacket in the house and had to fetch it. She bolted inside, grabbed her coat, ran back out to her car, gave Geffen a peck on the cheek, and drove home.

Within a couple of days, Geffen and Cher were seeing each other every night, and soon the relationship extended into the bedroom. The two began what was Geffen's first fully functional heterosexual relationship. Years later, after he became Hollywood's most famous openly gay executive, many doubted whether the stories of his sexual relationship with Cher were true.

"I fucked her countless times," he has said. Cher has commented, "I was the first person to share his bed *and* to share his life. People don't believe that, or they don't want to believe it, or they don't understand how it could be. But we were really crazy about each other."

Sonny Bono, who was having an affair with a woman named Connie Foreman, became incensed when he learned that Cher had taken a new lover. He forbade her to return to the house on Carolwood Drive. Cher charged that Bono, along with their lawyer, Irwin Spiegel, worked to keep her hands off any of the couple's money. Their company, Cher Enterprises, had a bank account with millions of dollars in it. But soon the woman for whom the venture was named could not withdraw a single penny.

"You need a lawyer," Geffen told Cher.

"I have a lawyer," Cher said. "Irwin Spiegel."

"No, no, no," he said. "He's *Sonny's* lawyer. You need your own lawyer. I'm going to set all this stuff up for you. You need to be taken care of."

Geffen found Cher's total helplessness irresistible. As he had with Laura Nyro years before, Geffen quickly got lost in Cher's problems and set about trying to solve them. He eagerly assumed a role he was comfortable playing and expertly qualified to perform: manager.

Geffen began managing all things, big and small, in her life. He rented an odd little house for her, where she could begin a life apart from Bono, at the north end of Carbon Beach, just a few houses north of where he planned to build his own house. He even made sure her car was always filled with gas, despite the gas-shortage crisis. (Linda Loddengaard knew which gas stations had the shortest lines, and she sent the mailroom boy to fill up Cher's Porsche.) To help Cher cope with the many changes in her personal life, Geffen even arranged for her to begin seeing Dr. Grotjahn.

Geffen flew into a rage as he looked over Sonny and Cher's performance contracts. He learned that Cher Enterprises was controlled by Bono and Spiegel; Cher did not even have a vote in the affairs of the company. In truth, Cher had not shown much interest in such matters and had instead focused her attentions on the costumes and wigs she wore on their TV show.

But now that Cher wanted out of the contracts, the agreements merited attention. Bono and Spiegel had broad powers to set the schedule and force Cher to perform. The contracts also gave Bono the right to require Cher to work for Cher Enterprises exclusively. "You can't work under this contract!" Geffen screamed. "It's like slave labor!"

Cher told Geffen that performing on the TV show was fun and that she would like to continue doing it. It was not the best situation to work with Bono, she said, but it was tolerable. She was just relieved not to sleep with him anymore.

Geffen told Cher that she had to demand that Bono tear down Cher

Enterprises. There could be no deal, Geffen said, unless Bono agreed to start anew with contracts that gave Sonny and Cher equal votes in setting the agenda and freedom to do outside projects.

Just that month, Bono and Spiegel had boxed Cher into a slew of new entertainment commitments. They set Las Vegas dates at the Sahara in January and February and at Caesars Palace in June. She also was committed to play Harrah's in Lake Tahoe in March and on the Music Fair Theaters circuit in April, May, and September.

Geffen hired Milton A. "Mickey" Rudin, a fierce Hollywood attorney known for the work he had done for Frank Sinatra and Lucille Ball. He told Rudin that Cher never meaningfully assented to the terms of the contract. He also maintained there was an obvious conflict of interest with Spiegel representing both Bonos, now that their marriage was collapsing.

Rudin fired off a letter to Spiegel informing him that he was now representing Cher and that Spiegel's legal services would no longer be required. But Bono refused to acknowledge Rudin's demands. He did not believe Cher would walk away from the show-business empire he felt he had created for her.

With Bono balking at a restructuring, Geffen told Cher she did not have a choice: She had no money and had to begin legal proceedings against Bono in order to win back her fair share. Rudin contacted Cher's agents at the William Morris Agency and instructed them that no further Sonny and Cher commitments were to be made. Geffen also told Rudin to cancel the performance engagements that had been set up by Spiegel and Bono.

Geffen thought Cher's record contracts were also a disaster. Given that it was Cher's solo hits that were making the most money ("Gypsies, Tramps & Thieves" was the biggest-selling single in the history of MCA Records), Geffen could not believe that the receipts were being shared equally by Sonny and Cher.

Cher told Geffen that she had just begun work on a new solo album, *Dark Lady,* for MCA. To produce it, Bono had hired Snuff Garrett, an old neighbor of the Bonos who had produced many of their biggest hits. The first number Cher recorded was the album's title track, a trashy tune about a jilted dame whose fortune-teller is fooling around with her man.

Geffen cringed as he listened to a tape of the song Cher brought to his house one night. "Oh, sweetheart, this is just awful," he said.

"Dave, I know. I'm really embarrassed," Cher responded. "But I think it's going to be a big hit. What can I tell you?"

Hit or flop, Geffen thought it was the wrong material. He suggested she refuse to finish the other songs on the album. Geffen envisioned making Cher a classier act, singing the songs of the singer-songwriters he represented, such as Jackson Browne and Joni Mitchell.

Cher's eyes grew wide as Geffen explained that changing her act in turn would burnish her image and prepare her for a segue into the movies. From his days at the William Morris Agency, he knew Tony Fantozzi, the agent who now headed the Sonny and Cher account there. He said he would talk to Fantozzi and ask him to begin developing some film ideas.

Geffen advised Cher to finish the current season of *The Sonny and Cher Comedy Hour* at CBS. If she could make it through the final episodes, he told her, he would arrange to get her a solo TV show. Cher was excited about Geffen's plans. To celebrate her split from Bono, Cher got a tattoo of a butterfly on her behind. She was ready for a future without Bono and with Geffen.

The stock price of Warner Communications remained abysmally low. Wall Street analysts were skeptical of the music group's earning potential and were still confused by the company's strategy of acquiring cable-TV operators.

Steve Ross thought he had the answer. He believed Wall Street would turn bullish if it saw the company's diverse operating units working together to promote one another's products. It was a new concept that Ross and some others in Hollywood were calling "synergy."

Ross put together plans for a companywide meeting to discuss the plan. It was set to take place at a hotel in the wealthy suburb of Rye, just north of New York City. Many of the participants never forgot it, and not simply because they were often all huddled around TV sets to watch coverage of the unfolding Saturday Night Massacre in the ongoing Watergate scandal in Washington. They remembered it because of David Geffen's ugly performance.

Ross directed each Warner division to prepare a presentation of the products they were developing. This in turn, Ross hoped, would spark discussions of how the divisions could cross-promote one another's products. Separately marketed movie soundtracks were a relatively new phenomenon, for example, and Ross thought that his music executives ought to have ongoing discussions with their counterparts at the movie studio to identify potential hits.

The music group, though, did not have an impressive presentation prepared for the meeting. Ertegun and Geffen rousted Mo Ostin's number-two man, Joe Smith, from a deep sleep and recruited him to be the group's spokesperson. Smith, regarded as the division's best speaker, was jet-lagged from a business trip to Europe. Geffen told Smith that he should tell the group about *Don't Cry Now*, the first album Linda Ronstadt had made for Asylum, and *For Everyman*, the second album by Jackson Browne. He was especially excited about Browne's new song "Red Neck Friend," which, in a deal orchestrated by Geffen, featured Elton John on piano. Because of complications with his work visa, however, John was billed on the record cover as "Rockaday Johnnie." Smith dutifully scribbled the information down on the back of an envelope.

Even though it was a weekend retreat, most of the Warner executives wore ties. Geffen, however, showed up as usual in his jeans and white T-shirt. Steve Ross brought the meeting to order and then began calling on the various department chiefs to make their presentations. Ted Ashley, Frank Wells, and John Calley, the troika of executives that ran the Warner Bros. movie studio, had the slickest presentation of all. They wowed the group with splashy clips from their upcoming films

The Exorcist and *Magnum Force,* both of which were set to be released that December.

Similar presentations were made by the executives heading Warner's television, book-publishing, and cable-holdings operations. Even though he did not have music clips or a multimedia presentation to impress the others, Joe Smith survived by waxing on about the progress charted by the Atlantic, Warner Bros./Reprise, and Elektra/Asylum music groups.

When the presentations were done, Ross encouraged discussion among the division heads. It quickly spiraled out of control, however, when Geffen began shouting at other executives. He first chastised Jerry Leider, who worked in the company's television group, one of the company's lagging operations. "You're a failure! You should quit!" he screamed. "You're blowing all the money that we're making!"

Then Geffen turned his fury on Steve Ross. In front of everyone, he began scolding Ross about the Warner stock price, reviving an all-too-familiar gripe. That week, the stock had fallen to about twelve dollars, down from fifteen earlier in the month.

Ross listened politely as Geffen played out his temper tantrum. David Horowitz, who had been general counsel at Columbia Pictures Industries, had just joined the company and was appalled at Geffen's demonstration. "Who would have the effrontery to treat the chairman in this way?" Horowitz thought.

It was the first and last time in the Steve Ross era at Warner Communications that all the executives would gather for a synergy meeting.

B ob Dylan and David Geffen were becoming friends, but Geffen obviously wanted more from the bond. He knew that Dylan's contract at CBS's Columbia Records was up for renewal, and he wanted more than anything to get him to sign with Elektra/Asylum.

Dylan was no longer the giant star he had been in the 1960s. As music was splintering well beyond the standard two factions of blues-based music and folk-based music, there seemed to be no role for him in the new era. But Geffen knew that he was still revered, and he believed that Dylan could once again reach or even surpass the superstardom he had charted in the preceding decade.

Few thought Dylan was seriously considering leaving Columbia. He had been there since the start of his career, and the label had left him alone, protected him, and allowed him to make the kind of music he wanted.

But Geffen's timing was perfect: A couple of months earlier, CBS had been rocked by a scandal in which Clive Davis had been fired amid charges that he used company funds improperly. Also, for the first time in his career, Dylan did not have a manager, having split with longtime representative Albert Grossman following a dispute over finances.

Soon Geffen was not alone in pursuing Dylan. Others in the industry, including some within Warner Communications' music group, heard that Dylan might entertain other offers and started pursuing him. For example, Geffen's longtime nemesis Jerry Wexler, Ahmet Ertegun's number-two man at Atlantic Records, badly wanted to sign Dylan. Wexler thought he had it in the bag, in part because he and Dylan had just co-produced an album at Muscle Shoals Sound Studio by Atlantic artist Barry Goldberg.

But Geffen worked his star-courting act, by now a perfectly rehearsed pitch that rarely failed, on Dylan to devastating effect. He simply told him that if there was to be a tour, there naturally should be a new album in stores for fans to purchase at the same time. Who better to release it than Geffen, who was also masterminding the tour?

What convinced Dylan was an astonishing prediction Geffen made: He said that Elektra/Asylum could sell a million units per Dylan record, hundreds of thousands higher than the average charted at Columbia. "Columbia doesn't appreciate you anymore," Geffen told Dylan. "Come with me. I'll show you what you can really do. I'll sell records you never dreamed you could sell."

Then Geffen sweetened the deal by telling Dylan he would create a new record label that he could run. Elektra/Asylum would distribute the label's albums, of course, but Dylan would have the freedom to sign and record other artists to his label in addition to recording for it himself. Dylan liked the idea very much and told Geffen he would leave Columbia and sign to Elektra/Asylum. Finally, Geffen had won the headlines for which he had so desperately fought. DYLAN FORMS LABEL; ELEKTRA/ASYLUM TO DISTRIBUTE, one of the music trade papers announced.

But there was a caveat to the signing. Having been locked up in long-term contracts at Columbia and cautious about the match with Geffen, Dylan told Geffen he would make two albums for Elektra/Asylum. But in a sign that he was hedging his bets even further, he instructed his attorney, David Braun, to write up the contract for only one album. After that, he would reevaluate the situation. Geffen announced that Dylan's new Ashes and Sands Records would release one album to coincide with the tour and a second Dylan album that would be a recording of a concert on the tour. Despite the short-term deal, Geffen was convinced the marriage would prove to be a long-term proposition.

Dylan and the Band went into the Village Recorders studio in West Los Angeles on November 5 and banged out one of the quickest rock albums ever made. They finished the record, *Planet Waves,* in just three days. Ironically, it was Geffen's elaborate tour plans that boxed them into an impossibly short recording schedule, which resulted in an album that most critics and fans found disappointing. Dylan was still writing material in the sessions, and neither he nor the Band had the time to do their best work.

Geffen was too sidetracked by details of the tour to even notice that *Planet Waves* was cobbled together rather haphazardly. He finalized plans for Dylan and the Band to visit 21 cities, doing 40 shows in a 42-day period beginning January 3, 1974, in Chicago and closing February 14 in Los Angeles. If the dates sold out, the tour looked to be the most lucrative ever, topping other recent hot tours by Elton John, Led Zeppelin, and the Rolling Stones.

Just as he had predicted, Geffen's gimmicky mail-order ticket plan created a feeding frenzy the likes of which had never been seen before for a rock tour. Crowds materialized at post offices around the country waiting for 12:01 A.M. on December 2, the earliest postmark acceptable on ticket applications. The response was staggering: While the capacity for all shows on the tour was about 651,000, an estimated five million envelopes were received.

Geffen's ego swelled substantially in the wake of the Bob Dylan signing. No one bristled more at his strutting than Atlantic's Jerry Wexler, who boiled with envy when Dylan announced his decision to sign with Geffen. Wexler had despised Geffen ever since their first encounter five years earlier and had done his best to minimize contact with him since. It was not an easy task, given the tight bond that Geffen had forged with Ahmet Ertegun.

The first time the two saw each other after Dylan's choice became public was at a meeting in which Steve Ross and all the top executives at Warner's music operations convened at the lavish Beverly Hills home of Joe Smith to discuss business goals. Smith's wife, Donnie, had fretted over the menu for days, finally deciding to make cheese soufflés. She told her husband to get the finest wine for the occasion. The Smiths and their household staff worked for days preparing their Roxbury Drive home for the occasion.

The executives began the day with a photo shoot. Warner's music empire was the envy of the industry and a magazine wanted a photo of the titans who made the operation click. The photograph was taken by the Smiths' pool, with some of the executives perched on the diving board as others posed along the side. Besides Ross, Geffen, and Wexler, the others in attendance included Ahmet Ertegun and Mo Ostin.

At the pool, Geffen baited Wexler by bragging about how he had won Dylan. "OK, David, you've got Dylan. Now let's just forget the whole thing," Wexler huffed.

The executives adjourned to Smith's giant screening room, off the garage. Ross opened the meeting with a review of policy regarding intracompany competition. The policy had held that while it was fine for two or more of the company's labels to compete for an artist, it was not acceptable for one to offer more money than the others. The financial terms of any offer had to be identical, leaving the individual label chiefs to differentiate their offers only by non-monetary attributes.

To Wexler, it was a hot button he had been dying to push. "Well, if we're going to follow some kind of rules, let's talk about who's fucking up the rules here," he fumed, pointing at Geffen. "You stole an artist that we had!"

"You're an old washed-up music man, what the fuck do you know?" uttered Geffen, trying to appear cool but clearly concerned about Wexler's outburst.

Wexler rose from his chair, his face red, the veins beginning to become visible in his neck. Wexler lunged at Geffen, who was sitting on the couch.

"You *agent!*" Wexler screamed. "You'd jump into a pool of pus to come up with a nickel between your teeth!"

Smith, who had been sitting next to Wexler, bounded from his seat and grabbed Wexler from behind, nabbing him just before he threw a punch at Geffen. The room erupted into hysteria.

"We can't have this! We can't have this!" Steve Ross yelled to the warring men.

"I'm outta here," Mo Ostin exclaimed. "I won't sit through this."

Smith was able to calm down the participants, suggesting they move on to the next issue. Ross began talking about some technology issues, but the group was so shaken and distracted that Ross felt as though he was talking to a lamp.

Smith decided a break and a change of venue might help everyone cool down. "Time out here," he said. "We're not getting anywhere, I think we're still recovering from what we just saw here. Why don't we have lunch now?"

The group adjourned to the dining room of the main house. It was a lovely room with multiple chandeliers and a Braque on one wall. Once inside and seated according to the name cards that Donnie

Smith had made, however, the group was silent. Donnie peered in through the swinging door and motioned for her husband to join her in the kitchen.

"They hate the cheese soufflé, right?" she worried, perplexed at the silence. "I told you we shouldn't have had the cheese soufflé."

I n one of the few instances in which Geffen's instincts were proved wrong, Geffen believed that the Eagles' popularity had peaked with their first album. *Desperado* had been a commercial bust, and now it seemed to him to be a question whether they would even finish a third. After the group had gone to London with Glyn Johns, infighting had forced them to return after only six of a planned twelve-week recording stand. They had recorded only two songs.

It was just before Christmas 1973 when the band's feelings toward Geffen grew even more adversarial. Their business manager informed them that they had not made any money on their recently completed *Desperado* tour, as the profits had gone back to the management company, which he said was owed the money from back commissions. Frey, Henley, and the others were irate as they realized they did not have money to buy Christmas presents.

One day, after calling the management office to ask for a limousine to take the group to the airport for a concert date, Glenn Frey decided he could take no more. Irving Azoff, who had booked the concert, put his hand over the receiver and asked Elliot Roberts what he should tell Frey.

"Tell Glenn he doesn't get a limo," Roberts snapped. "Tell him to get a hippie in a cab and go to the fuckin' airport!"

Frey was steamed and let Azoff have it. "Yeah, that's good. America records for Warners. They get limos. We record for Asylum; we get hippies in taxis." Azoff listened as Frey complained for fifteen minutes about how Geffen and Roberts cared more about America than they did about the Eagles. Frey and Henley felt that Geffen, in his undying search for bigger and better, had written them off.

Azoff sensed an opportunity. He wanted the Eagles for himself and began working to get them. Ironically, he employed techniques and used arguments that he had learned from David Geffen.

On the telephone with Frey, Azoff assured the rocker that everything would be taken care of, and he arranged for a limo to take the band to the airport. Before long, Azoff also helped get the group back in the recording studio. After listening to the members of the band gripe, he realized that they could no longer work with Glyn Johns. Azoff suggested they hire Bill Szymczyk, who had produced Joe Walsh's first solo album, which the group liked. They went into the studio with Szymczyk to begin work again on the third album.

The Eagles had found what they believed to be a loyal ally in Azoff, and they soon asked him to leave and become their manager. Azoff orchestrated a meeting in which the band met with Geffen and Roberts and called them again on the conflict-of-interest issue. Geffen had grown nervous about his potential liability over this issue and did not put up a fight as the group announced it was leaving. But he nonetheless was outraged about the way in which the split was coming down. Geffen felt betrayed that Azoff, whom he had given a job, had schemed to leave with the group that he and Roberts had worked so hard to create. He grew even angrier as Azoff charged Geffen with reneging on a compensation agreement to give him a piece of the management company. Finally, someone was doing to Geffen what he had done to so many others, and Geffen did not like it.

Roberts was losing a hugely lucrative management client, but he had been breaking down under the strain and found the group unmanageable, anyway. Geffen, for his part, would continue to benefit from whatever success the Eagles charted; he was running their record company, and his salary and bonuses were certain to be affected by their performance going forward. As a result, further dramas between him and Azoff were certain to unfold.

"I'm not going to have a problem dealing with Irving," Geffen told others at the time, "because I'm just not going to talk to him or let him in the building."

Sonny Bono recognized that Cher's behavior had changed dramatically from the moment she had connected with David Geffen. By January 1974, relations between Sonny and Cher on the set at CBS reached an all-time low.

The rehearsals were painful for everyone. A skit in one of their final shows had Cher playing Mother Nature standing atop a mountain. Sonny played a seeker of truth, struggling to climb to the peak. "Mother Nature, what is the secret of life?" Sonny asked.

"Go fuck yourself," Cher snarled, not missing a beat.

Nobody laughed. "Can we try it again?" the director asked.

"Not without lawyers," Bono muttered.

Geffen coached Cher on the speech that would destroy Bono. She delivered it in Sonny's dressing room one night after a taping. Cher walked in and told her husband that she no longer wanted to do *The Sonny and Cher Comedy Hour.* He had wanted her to sign a new contract with Cher Enterprises, but she had refused, and now she was walking out.

"What?" Bono gagged.

"I already gave notice to CBS," she said.

"We've got contracts," Bono said desperately. "I mean, you can't. We are signed to record deals, nightclubs."

"I've already given notice to everybody—the record companies, the clubs." Cher left Sonny's dressing room and headed down the hall toward the door. He chased after her and cornered her. Fixing his eyes on hers, he begged her to reconsider.

"Well, I want you and David to get in a room and talk," Cher said, looking away. "Whoever wins, wins."

"No," Bono said defiantly. "No way. I'm not going to do that."

Bono began to spin. In his mind, he had created the act, written the songs, and choreographed the numbers. He was also the financial brain behind the duo, having carefully structured contractual commitments that would generate multimillion-dollar annuities for them over ten and fifteen years. But if he could not deliver Cher, then the contracts would be breached, freeing Geffen to negotiate new ones. New contracts, Bono knew, would involve only one half of the act.

Bono took the first step, filing for a legal separation from Cher the week rehearsals began for the final episode of *The Sonny and Cher Comedy Hour.* The show was taped on a Friday night that February. It featured the duo singing such songs as "Beautiful Sunday" and "I Got You Babe." When the taping was over, the two boarded separate airplanes and flew to Houston for their final concerts together.

Neither Sonny nor Cher wanted to do the concerts, but the Houston Astrodome was the largest indoor venue in America, they were the country's hottest act, and a fee of $150,000 awaited them. It was the shortest live performance of their careers, and yet it seemed to each to last an eternity. They managed not to look at each other during the shows.

During costume changes offstage, Cher was overheard complaining to crew members. "I can't wait till this fucking show is over," she said. "Goddammit, how much longer? I hate this. I hate it."

Back in Los Angeles, Mickey Rudin drew up divorce papers charging Bono with causing "involuntary servitude." Cher held that Bono "unlawfully dominated and controlled my business interests and career."

Bono was shocked at Cher's accusations and believed that she and Geffen had manufactured the notion of him as a slave master simply as a public-relations ploy. He countersued Cher for fourteen million dollars, demanding damages for the projected earnings that he would lose as a result of a split. Bono next dropped a thirteen-million-dollar lawsuit on Geffen, charging him with interfering with his contractual relationship with his wife and seeking a temporary restraining order.

As the legal wrangling was going on, Geffen was talking to CBS, promising that if the network would release Cher from her contractual obligations, he would return to negotiate a new solo show the minute she was ready to work again. CBS had no choice: Without Cher, there was no TV program. They decided to pull the plug on the show, avoid a costly legal fight, and cross their fingers that Geffen would keep his word.

News of the separation made the front pages of many papers across the nation. Sonny Bono's life with Cher was coming to an end. But his battles with David Geffen were just beginning.

"THE TIMES THEY ARE A-CHANGIN'"

|||

I t was not long before Geffen and Cher decided to get married. They would have to wait until Cher could get a divorce from Sonny Bono, of course, but they talked about the plan constantly.

Geffen's friends were more than a little surprised at his obsession with Cher. "Will you stop jerking off? This is embarrassing," his friend Sue Mengers, the brassy superagent, barked. "You're not going to marry her!"

"Sue, you don't get it," he said. "I *love* her."

Geffen wasted no time in giving Cher many extravagant gifts, including a Rolls-Royce. When she told him she hated it, he gave the car to his brother and instead gave her a diamond necklace he purchased at Van Cleef & Arpels on Rodeo Drive. He also gave her a diamond ring as an extra gift that he wanted her to think of as an incentive to quit smoking. Geffen himself smoked Marlboros, but he knew that smoking was not good for her voice.

He got a kick out of having a famous girlfriend, and he delighted in showing her off at such events as the Grammy Awards, where they were photographed standing arm in arm. For Cher, the social circle into which Geffen introduced her was new and fun as well. When she lived with Sonny, the Bonos did not have parties or socialize much.

Together, Cher and Geffen went to Aspen, which was beginning to become a popular weekend destination for Hollywood celebrities. Geffen obtained Warner Communications' corporate jet for the trip and loaded it up with his best pals: Warren Beatty, Jack Nicholson, and Lou Adler, as well as their girlfriends, Michelle Phillips, Anjelica Huston, and Britt Ekland, respectively.

It was quite a scene, and Geffen, who had started growing a beard at Cher's request, was finally at the popular table. The group took skiing lessons, partied at Jill St. John's house, and generally gaped in amazement as Cher made almost hourly changes of clothing. Some of her outfits were so cumbersome, the others wondered how she would ski in them.

Cher and Geffen went shopping for real estate. She wanted an Aspen retreat, and he thought that would be the perfect wedding present. Cher found a condominium she liked for $212,000; Geffen was not about to say no.

Back in Los Angeles, Geffen brought Cher along to a meeting he had scheduled with Charles Gwathmey, the architect he had hired for his property in Malibu. Geffen was a difficult client, but Gwathmey enjoyed working with him. He was not prepared, however, for the nightmarish turn the project took once Cher became a part of the equation. The designs for the house, a modern structure featuring a dramatic overhead ramp, had been finished before Cher weighed in with her review.

"You know, I have a huge amount of clothes," Cher told Gwathmey. "Can't you take this ramp and make that my closet?" she asked.

Gwathmey was flabbergasted and offended. In his mind, the ramp was the one sacred and organizing element in the whole building. "I don't think so," he managed. "It doesn't work that way." Even if it did not work that way for Gwathmey, some other arrangement would have to be worked out; Cher was priority number one in Geffen's life, and he typically granted her wishes.

Bob Dylan seeks David Geffen's advice on
board the plane chartered for Dylan's Geffen-orchestrated tour.
Their relationship was punctuated by hurt feelings,
crying jags, and screaming—all from Geffen. Dylan's chess
opponent is his friend Louie Kemp. (Barry Feinstein)

As Geffen's relationship with Cher was blossoming, he was becoming increasingly dissatisfied with the relationship he had with the most important woman in his life, his mother. Geffen had not spoken to his mother for several months when he began dating Cher, having feuded with her about matters small and large.

Geffen did not like his mother because she was strange and poor and not refined and rich. He tried to clean her up by hiring a chauffeur to take her shopping for new clothes; he fumed, however, when he discovered that she had directed the driver to the thrift-shop district on Western Avenue. How much easier life would be, he thought, if he had been born into a family of privilege. No matter how much success he achieved, it seemed he could not get beyond the handicapped self-image of a tortured and tiny poor Jewish boy with the eccentric mother and hopeless father.

Geffen was so ashamed of his humble background that he rarely talked about his family and actively sought to fashion a new one that was more to his liking. He developed a relationship with Preston Robert Tisch, the wealthy president of Loews and Lorillard Tobacco, his wife, Joan, and their son Steve. "I wish I had been born a Tisch," he told Steve. "I would have liked to have been your older brother." He said it as a joke, but he repeated it countless times. It clearly spoke to a tragic and unrelenting unhappiness with his own roots.

But one day while Geffen and Cher were driving around Beverly Hills, Geffen blurted out the first positive thing Cher had ever heard him say about Batya. "I want to go see my mom," he said.

"OK, cool," Cher said, curious to meet the woman that Geffen had told her he did not see.

Geffen headed toward the small house on Gilcrest Drive. Batya answered the door and, seeing only her son, let out a shout of joy. Seeing Cher, whom she and Sam watched on television, was a bit overwhelming. She welcomed her son and his TV-star girlfriend into the house and at once went about preparing tea and cake.

Cher looked about the two-bedroom, one-story house and gazed out the window at the spectacular view of downtown Los Angeles.

Batya, thrilled at meeting the woman whom David introduced as her future daughter-in-law, proudly showed Cher a marijuana plant she had grown.

Cher grew quiet as David and Batya slipped into their familiar bickering about Mitchell and other old family issues. Still, David was thrilled to have his mother meet Cher. She had suspected that he was gay, but they did not talk about it. This was a hopeful moment for her and her son, as he seemed to have found the woman of his dreams.

Cher was eager to help David come to terms with the ups and downs of his relationship with his mother and tried to be encouraging. "Mothers annoy you," Cher told Geffen in the car after they left. "That's their job. But she doesn't seem so bad."

Bob Dylan's tour with the Band was set to close in Los Angeles with a sold-out concert at the Forum on February 14, 1974. It was a smashing concert, and the record-business elite turned out for it. Geffen sat up front with Cher to accept congratulations from his peers, but it turned out to be one of the most humiliating evenings of his life.

At the end of the show, the crowd refused to stop cheering. Then the unimaginable took place: Dylan, who rarely spoke at his concerts, stepped up to the microphone. The crowd of Dylan junkies, the diehards who clung to any words the master poet expressed, quieted.

"We want to thank a legendary guy who put this whole tour together," Dylan started. "Without him, this thing just would not have happened." Geffen stood up, expecting to hear his name called out. "Can you help me give a warm round of applause, please," Dylan continued, "to . . . Bill Graham!"

Geffen slumped into his chair. He had been embarrassed in front of his peers. Graham, the club promoter who had traveled with the band to every site and made certain that the details were attended to, stepped out from backstage and shook Dylan's hand. The houselights came up, and the crowd headed out to the parking lot.

While everyone else was joyously celebrating the close of the historic tour, Geffen began to cry. Tears were still running down his face when he found Robbie Robertson backstage. "I can't tell you how much this hurts me," Geffen said.

Robertson tried unsuccessfully to make up for the oversight. "David, you misunderstood what Bob was saying," he said. "Bob was thinking about the road crew, and that's why he thanked Bill. Bob thinks of you as the main guy behind the scenes, not as a roadie putting up the lights."

Distraught, Geffen would not listen to Robertson's interpretation. As the other members of the Band rolled their eyes at Geffen's emotional outburst, Robertson reminded Geffen that he had cautioned him that trying to have a personal relationship with Dylan could be a painful thing.

"I told you this was going to happen," he said. "You start making people into who you think they are, and that's not really the way it works."

The next day, Robertson scrambled to patch things up. He telephoned Dylan and suggested they go together to Geffen's office and make an apology.

"He should have been thanked," Robertson said. "I mean, he was how we started this whole thing. Whether or not he was on the road putting up lights and carrying equipment, he played a big part in this." Dylan was silent. "We should go and thank him," Robertson continued. "It's the decent thing to do."

"Oh, Jesus," Dylan mumbled. "OK, OK. Let's do it."

Dylan and Robertson went to Elektra/Asylum's offices and apologized to Geffen. They also took out full-page ads in the trade papers, trumpeting "An immeasurable thanks to David Geffen who made possible Tour '74." But Geffen had been hurt irreparably.

Robertson and Dylan contacted Cher to see if she had a suggestion about something they might be able to do to make it up to Geffen. She told them Geffen's thirty-first birthday was only a week away and suggested that they plan a surprise party for him. Dylan's friend Louie Kemp arranged to rent the Grand Trianon Room at the Beverly Wilshire Hotel for the affair.

Mo Ostin, who was given the job of bringing the birthday boy to the hotel that night, asked Geffen to join him for a business meeting with Barbra Streisand at ten o'clock. Because they had been at a testimonial dinner for another record executive earlier in the evening, the two men were dressed in tuxedos when they arrived at the hotel.

Geffen began getting suspicious as Ostin led him toward the doors of the ballroom. As Ostin opened the door, seventy-five friends and associates let out a rousing cheer. In addition to Cher, Dylan, and Robertson, the crowd included Ahmet Ertegun, who had flown in from New York for the occasion, and Warren Beatty, Jack Nicholson, and Ringo Starr, among others. The room was decorated to resemble a carnival; there was a knife thrower, a cyclist, two mimes, a fire-eater, two wrestlers, a fortune-teller, and strolling musicians. A big cake had been decorated to read, "For the Man That's Responsible."

When the initial cheers died down, Cher began a short musical program by singing "Happy Birthday to You." She then sang "All I Really Want to Do," with Dylan singing harmony and the Band playing backup. After Cher and Rick Danko sang "Mockingbird," the program ended with Dylan singing "Mr. Tambourine Man."

At the end of the mini-concert, Artie Mogull ran over to pay his respects. Mogull was now head of MCA Records, the label that counted Cher among its acts. "I just recorded the songs," Mogull quipped. "You can have the single if I can have the album."

Before leaving the party with Cher, Geffen stopped by the fortune-teller's booth. "There is a lot of success in store for you," the fortune-teller told him.

The forecast was right. The next month, in an astonishing feat, the top three records on *Billboard*'s album charts had all been released by Elektra/Asylum. Dylan's *Planet Waves* had the top spot, followed by Joni Mitchell's *Court and Spark,* and Carly Simon's *Hotcakes.* It was an achievement few label bosses would ever accomplish and one that Geffen never again matched in his career. The news was heralded in *Time* magazine, where, under the headline GEFFEN'S GOLDEN TOUCH, he was hailed as "the financial superstar of the $2 billion pop music industry."

Still, not everyone was cheering. Joni Mitchell's affection for Geffen had been seriously diminished from the moment Bob Dylan had come into Geffen's life. She had grown jealous of and angry at the attention Geffen lavished on his newest signing. A year earlier, Geffen had told people that Mitchell was the best concert performer in America. But now, as she was out on tour promoting *Court and Spark,* the album that contained "Free Man in Paris," she stewed as Geffen seemed to care only about Dylan's live performances. Before long, she bought her own Spanish-style home in the ritzy Los Angeles neighborhood of Bel-Air and moved out of the house on Copley Drive.

Other people were angry with Geffen as well. Carly Simon, who had been at Elektra several years before the label had merged with Asylum, was upset over the lack of attention she was getting, too. Simon, her manager, and her producer, Richard Perry, were outraged because they heard from Geffen only when he complained that *Hotcakes* went over budget.

Perry was further hurt by reports that Geffen was bad-mouthing him all over town. He felt the criticism was unwarranted: Simon's last album, *No Secrets,* which he had also produced, had rocketed to number one in six weeks, thanks to the single "You're So Vain." Simon was Elektra's biggest female moneymaker, Perry knew, and he felt her star status entitled her to spend like a star.

In the wake of Geffen's crying episode backstage at the Forum, Bob Dylan, Robbie Robertson, and their compatriots in the Band began to rethink their plan to release their concert album, *Before the Flood,* on Elektra/Asylum. One reason for Dylan's change of heart was the sales performance of *Planet Waves.* Although the record hit number one on the album charts and sold about seven hundred thousand copies, it fell short of the million that Geffen had promised to sell. Since the tour had broken all records and left scores of ticketless fanatics out in the cold, Dylan felt, why couldn't Geffen deliver the record sales he predicted?

The truth was that *Planet Waves* was an unspectacular record. Dylan fans, deprived of seeing him in concert for so long, had indeed flocked to see him and the Band play live. But they were interested in hearing Dylan's standards and not necessarily interested in buying *Planet Waves.*

Robertson felt a moral obligation to give Geffen the album they had promised. "We said we would do this, let's do it," he told Dylan and the other members of the Band. "After this, if we don't want to record with him any more, then we won't. But let's just do what we said we would do."

Dylan, however, felt that he had the right to change his mind. The partnership with Geffen just did not feel right to him. Robertson, for his part, decided that if it came to it, his loyalties were to Dylan and the Band, the guys he had grown up with, not to Geffen.

Unbeknownst to Geffen, Dylan asked his attorney, David Braun, to quietly examine alternate distribution possibilities for *Before the Flood.* Dylan liked the idea of a TV ad blitz that would sell the album to consumers through a toll-free telephone number. If there was no record company involved, they figured, they would net a much larger percentage of the income.

Braun contacted Clive Davis, still out of work after losing his job at CBS, and asked him to draw up a proposal. Davis was amazed to get the call, having inferred from Geffen's bragging that he had locked Dylan up in a multi-record contract. Not so, Braun told him, adding that Dylan had missed Davis's careful guidance in the handling of *Planet Waves.*

Braun scheduled a meeting at the Beverly Hills Hotel for Dylan and Robertson to hear Davis's pitch. Davis argued against the order-by-TV idea, saying that it would cheapen Dylan's image. Instead, he suggested they set up their own distribution system and sell the album directly to rack jobbers who could get the album into record stores. About six such distributors controlled the majority of the business, he said, and he would be willing to personally negotiate deals with each of them. Davis would get a cut, of course, but Dylan and the Band would get a significantly higher return on each album sold than they would through a record company.

Dylan picked up the phone and called Geffen, asking him to come to the hotel at once. Geffen was stunned as he walked into the suite and saw Dylan standing with Davis, with whom he had only recently reconciled. "David, we're not going to put the concert album through Elektra/Asylum," Dylan said. "I'm going to do it myself."

"What do you mean?" Geffen shrieked. "You can't do this! We have an arrangement! We have a contract!" In fact, the contract was only for *Planet Waves;* Dylan's agreement to let Geffen have *Before the Flood* had been just a handshake.

"No, I'm not going to do it," Dylan said calmly. "Besides, it's not *your* money, David. It's Warner Communications' money."

Geffen began screaming at Dylan. "What happened to the guy who wrote 'The Times They Are A-Changin' '?" He stomped out of the hotel, livid that Dylan would betray him.

The next day, Cher fussed over her fingernails as Geffen shouted at David Braun on the phone, trying to bully him into getting Dylan to change his mind. "You have to force your client to honor the contract," Geffen shouted, turning beet red. Braun told Geffen he would do no such thing. "If you want the album, you're going to have to bid on it like everyone else," Braun told him.

That Dylan's attorney was now claiming not to remember the terms of the deal, whether it was a handshake or in writing, infuriated Geffen even more. He hollered at Braun a little more and then finally hung up. "OK, sweetheart. Where are we going?" Geffen purred to Cher, as though nothing unusual had transpired. "We're going to Mr. Chow's for lunch, right? Let's go to Mr. Chow's."

A few days later, Dylan, Robertson, and the other members of the Band met at Rick Danko's house in Malibu to review the album dilemma. Geffen waited in the living room for the verdict as the musicians and David Braun went into a bedroom to confer privately.

By now, the situation was reaching melodramatic proportions. One by one, Dylan and the members of the Band restated their positions.

With the exception of Robertson, no one wanted to give the album to David Geffen.

"You can't change your mind," Robertson implored. "You guys said you would give him this album, and now you're saying you don't want to." Dylan and the other men made it clear that they were pissed off at Robertson and were tired of his cheerleading for Geffen.

"OK, fuck him! Don't give him anything!" Robertson shot back, loud enough to be heard in the other room. "I don't give a shit. Everybody feels he doesn't deserve this, don't give it to him. We won't do it. Do whatever you want." The musicians emerged from the bedroom, and Braun explained the bad news to Geffen. Geffen, stung by Robertson's words, left quietly.

The next day, the phone rang at the Robertsons' house. It was Geffen. "I feel like the brother in *The Godfather*," he said. "You broke my heart."

"I didn't break your heart," an exasperated Robertson said. "What are you talking about? I'm the only one who's been sticking up for you. And to the detriment of these people who I grew up with I might add."

"You just broke my heart," Geffen reiterated. "I had such tremendous affection for you, and I have given as much of myself as I possibly can to you, and you just turned around and broke my heart."

After that conversation, Geffen refused to talk to Robertson, but he continued to call their house, asking to speak to Dominique whenever Robbie answered. As it turned out, the entire drama was about money and little else. Before long, Braun told Geffen that he could still get the rights to distribute *Before the Flood* if he could match the highest offer. The bidding was further intensified by the reemergence of Columbia Records, which regretted having let Dylan slip away. Braun let them into the bidding, using the specter of Davis's approach to throw Elektra/Asylum and Columbia into a spirited bidding contest from which only Dylan could benefit.

Geffen got the album, but he was forced to pay far more for it than he had wanted. He would not, however, have to endure the humiliation that he would have felt if he had had to explain why he had lost it.

In May, Geffen announced that Elektra/Asylum would release the two-record set on June 3, backed by "the largest advertising and promotional campaign in the company's history."

Before the Flood sold very well and turned out to be a moneymaker for Elektra/Asylum Records. But Geffen's relationship with Robertson had been dealt a serious blow. *Before the Flood* was Geffen's final collaboration with Dylan. Columbia soon announced that Dylan had returned to the label under a new long-term contract.

D espite his record company's enormous success, Geffen was not happy. He talked constantly about missing the Asylum days when he could count the number of employees and artists on two hands. The job had shifted: Instead of being a creative person, now he was managing managers, and he hated it.

He soon got the idea that he could free himself of many bureaucratic headaches if he could convince Ahmet Ertegun to merge Atlantic with Elektra/Asylum, forming a record colossus they could run jointly. Geffen would get a fancy new title on a par with Ertegun's, but at the same time he could pass on the mundane details of such things as marketing and distribution to Ertegun's staff.

Geffen floated the idea to Ertegun, who was surprisingly receptive. Ertegun had felt betrayed by Geffen when he had accepted the job as head of Elektra/Asylum in the first place, since Geffen had once told him they would be partners "forever in everything." Geffen pushed him relentlessly and, in a weak moment, Ertegun agreed to back his plan.

Steve Ross did not think it was a smart idea. He appreciated the financial benefits of maintaining three separate record companies, betting that chances were good that at any given moment one could offset losses in the others. He liked having three different companies and three different staffs running them, their different tastes helping to ensure that Warner Communications covered all the musical bases. But with Ertegun supporting Geffen's plan, Ross went along with it.

Geffen insisted that a press release be drawn up on the spot. On July 6, 1974, news of the merger was the lead story in all the trade papers. The new company, called Atlantic/Elektra/Asylum Records, was to be headed by Ertegun and Geffen as co-chairmen, with Jerry Wexler as vice chairman.

"We have contemplated merging our two divisions for some time now," the press release quoted Ertegun and Geffen, "in order to achieve more efficient operations for both companies. We believe that the combined Atlantic, Elektra and Asylum labels now have the best line-up of talent of any firm in our industry."

With Cher as his girlfriend, Bob Dylan his star artist, at least for the time being, and an impressive new title as co-chairman of Atlantic/Elektra/Asylum Records, Geffen was beginning to attract some extraordinary attention. *Esquire* magazine was interested in a cover story on the young mogul, and a writer named Julie Baumgold was assigned to handle the piece.

Geffen was delirious. He welcomed Baumgold into his life, offering her wide access to follow him and Cher around as they went about their extravagant lives in New York and Los Angeles. Geffen invited Baumgold to join him and Cher, as well as Diana Ross and her husband Robert Silberstein, for a shoe-shopping expedition. On the trip, Baumgold noted that Geffen had picked up one of Cher's favorite expressions: "I'll take one in every color." He told her about his relationship with Cher and how he was masterminding a plan to rebuild her career. "It's not that I want to do it. I'm not looking to be a personal manager," Geffen told the reporter. "I gave that up a long time ago, but this is the woman I love. . . . She needs help right now."

What Geffen did not realize was that his merger plan needed even more help. Mutiny was declared at Atlantic Records the day plans of the merger made the papers. Geffen's press release had been rushed out before Ertegun had explained it to his staff. Ertegun, in fact, had been frightened to share news of it with Jerry Wexler and his other lieutenants.

Ertegun was now in Europe on a business trip, but Wexler tracked him down. He and other top members of Ertegun's executive team refused to be a part of the merger. Wexler declared he would not report to Geffen. Jerry Greenberg, Ertegun's promotion man, and Sheldon Vogel, Atlantic's finance chief, both threatened to quit. They did not like David Geffen, having suffered unending abuse from him when he was their joint-venture partner in Asylum Records.

The merger was undone just as quickly as it had been announced. Ertegun was not a man who liked confrontation, and he told Geffen he could not stand to lose his most trusted employees over the matter. He quickly backpedaled, and a retraction was issued. The merger plan was off.

Geffen was mortified and outraged. He accused Ertegun of abandoning the plan because his friends told him it would be a demotion for him. "How can you do this to me?" he yelled.

Ertegun tried unsuccessfully to calm Geffen down. "Now come on, David," he said, "I'm sorry it is not going to work, but you need to understand. I'm trying to hold this company together, and I have to protect Jerry and everybody else."

Geffen refused to listen, and his temper continued to rise. "This is between *us!*" he bellowed. "You know this is the best thing for the company."

C her missed living in the mansion on Carolwood Drive and resented that Sonny Bono had strong-armed her into moving out. Geffen's legal arsenal did some research and discovered that all Cher had to do to live in the house was to move back in. Geffen decided to give up the Copley Drive house and move in with Cher.

And so, one night in July 1974, Bono's girlfriend Connie Foreman was in the Carolwood house alone when she heard a ruckus outside. Looking out the window, she saw that the giant gates at the foot of the drive were open. She saw two private-security-company sedans parked near the front door.

As Foreman raced down the stairs to assess the situation, the front door burst open. Geffen, Cher, and two security guards stormed in and staged what Bono's lawyers later termed a "guerrilla raid."

Hysterical, Foreman ran to her bedroom and telephoned Bono, who was at a recording session. Trying to reach Cher, Bono called the house's main line. When Cher answered, Bono demanded to know if she had a court order to be in the house. He later testified that he had sold his half of the mansion to Cher but stayed on at the house when she failed to pay him.

Geffen picked up an extension and began shouting at Bono. "There's a policeman here and he's got a gun," Geffen threatened. Bono thought that meant he was going to get shot if he tried to walk into the house. Chastity Bono had not long before warned him to be careful. "Mommy says she is going to get the police and they're going to throw you out," she had told him.

The security guards gathered up Bono's clothes and other belongings and kicked out Foreman. But nothing could prepare Sonny Bono for what came next in his fight with his wife's new lover. A court battle was looming for custody of Chastity, one pitting Bono against Geffen.

Geffen and Cher dressed up for a night on the town in 1974.
When Cher accepted a date from Gregg Allman,
Geffen threatened to sue. (Peter Borsari)

CHAPTER 14

HAMMER
AND NAILS

|||

It did not look as though Sonny Bono stood a chance in his plea for joint custody of Chastity. He and his lawyers simply could not compete with the arguments cooked up by the lethal combination of Geffen and Cher's attorney, Mickey Rudin.

Bono said that Cher refused to deal with him about when he could and could not see Chastity, choosing instead to make Geffen her representative. The situation reached a low point one weekend when Bono called to alert Cher that he would be late in returning Chastity after spending a weekend with her in Palm Springs.

"Son, I don't want to discuss it," Cher said. "Since you set it up with David, let me put him on the phone."

Geffen got on the phone and castigated Bono as if he had legal authority over Chastity.

"I am her father and Chas will be home when I can get her there," Bono told Geffen. "End of discussion."

Photographs of Geffen and Cher began cropping up in the *National Enquirer* and the other tabloids that were covering the sensational custody battle in Santa Monica Superior Court. Up at the house on Gilcrest, Batya read the tabloids and clipped reports that featured photos of Cher with David, keeping them with other stories trumpeting her son's successes.

Cher had been receiving $7,500 a month support but now sought monthly alimony of $32,000, plus $1,500 support for Chastity. On the stand, Cher revealed that she saw a $75-an-hour psychiatrist three times a week, spent $6,000 a month on her wardrobe, and paid more than $600 in one month to her manicurist.

When it was Bono's turn, he unleashed his hatred for Geffen, telling the court that he was upset that Geffen and Chastity were sleeping under the same roof. One of Bono's lawyers argued that Geffen was a nuisance and a bad influence on the child.

Finally, though, the judge found in Cher's favor, awarding her temporary legal custody of Chastity, $25,000 monthly alimony, and $1,500 monthly child support. Bono was granted custody every second weekend and for five consecutive days every second month. The judge said he would reevaluate the ruling in six months.

The court victory energized Geffen as he turned his attention to winning new solo record and TV contracts for his girlfriend. He marched into MCA Records, the label that Sonny and Cher were signed to, and presented a take-it-or-leave-it offer: Cher would finish the *Dark Lady* album if MCA would release her from any further joint commitments. MCA decided not to fight and accepted Geffen's offer.

Geffen thought the best label for Cher was Mo Ostin's Warner Bros. Records. Ostin had just signed a deal with Phil Spector that included the formation of a Warner-Spector label, and Ostin thought Cher would be an ideal fit in that venture. Spector, who had produced the first post-Beatles works of John Lennon, had known Cher since she was a teenager backing up the Ronettes on such songs as "Da Doo Ron Ron" and "Be My Baby."

But Geffen was skeptical and still bruised by the way Spector had treated him in the early 1960s. From Geffen's perspective, Spector was a nut and a has-been. Reciprocally, Spector still saw Geffen as an annoying twerp, and it set him off when he learned that he would have to interact with him to make the Cher album.

The years had not been kind to Spector, once the most famous producer in the business. Despite the prize assignment of working with Lennon, over the past decade Spector had become known more for his erratic behavior than for his records. In fact, he had become so unstable that he had taken to bringing armed guards into his studio to protect him from the forces he claimed were threatening to ruin him.

Geffen told Cher that he doubted Spector was the right man to produce her new album. But Cher had some fond memories of working with Philip, as she called him, and told Geffen she wanted to give it a try.

Geffen and Cher went to see Spector, but the producer was so crazed at the sight of Geffen that he canceled the session. It was an unexpected by-product of the night that John Lennon and his friend Harry Nilsson had been in the studio when Geffen and Cher had stopped in. Lennon and Nilsson left with them, and the group went to Hugh Hefner's Playboy Mansion to soak in the hot tub.

Before Geffen would assign Spector the job of producing the album, he insisted Spector and Cher test their relationship by producing two singles that would be marketed on a 45. Spector was incensed that Geffen was forcing him to audition for the job.

Geffen was a regular guest in the studio as Cher began recording the two songs, but Spector was never happy to have him there. For the A side, Spector selected a ballad called "A Woman's Story"; the B side, he decided, would be a slowed-down version of the Ronettes' 1963 smash, "Baby, I Love You." The hope was that "A Woman's Story" would be a breakthrough hit for Cher. Spector employed his old "wall of sound" technique, by now a dated style, on "A Woman's Story." He backed Cher with an overwhelming and ethereal chorus of voices, making it sound to one critic "like Cher was delivering a message from heaven above."

Geffen thought that Spector's choices were all wrong. He demanded that Spector turn down the "wall of sound" so that Cher's voice could be heard over the roar. Spector grew so irritated with Geffen's meddling in the booth that at one point he turned around and punched him. Geffen was startled, but he told Cher, who was standing out in the studio, that it was like being hit by a baby.

Geffen thought that Spector's choice for the flip side of the record was even worse. "Baby, I Love You" had been a hit in the early 1960s, but this was a completely different musical era, and Geffen believed that Cher's fans would not like it.

After Geffen criticized the choice, Spector pulled out a gun he kept in the studio and pointed it at Geffen. "Don't you come near me!" Spector screamed. "I am in charge here, not you!"

"That man's a maniac!" Geffen told Cher. "Sweetheart, he's a maniac!"

"Yes, Dave," Cher responded nonchalantly. "We all know that, but he's not going to do anything with that thing." Spector did not fire the gun, but Geffen implored Cher to let him find another producer. It was not a hard sell, especially after "A Woman's Story" flopped.

As troubles mounted in the recording studio, Geffen was also working on deals to rekindle Cher's TV celebrity. After Geffen told CBS that Cher was ready to star in her own TV series, CBS tapped George Schlatter to be the show's executive producer. Schlatter was a burly veteran of the TV business who had met Cher when she did a guest stint on *Rowan and Martin's Laugh-In,* which Schlatter had created and produced.

Plans were drawn up to launch *Cher* with a Wednesday-night special in January 1975. The show would then move to its new regular time slot the following Sunday night, where it would compete against NBC's *Wonderful World of Disney* and enjoy the coveted lead-in position to CBS's powerhouse drama *Kojak.*

Geffen met with Schlatter and set about securing hot music stars to make guest appearances on *Cher.* Schlatter recognized that Geffen had access to the music community that he did not and gladly allowed Geffen to take charge. Music people tended to stay away from TV appearances, but Geffen was able to persuade two superstars to appear with Cher on the initial special: Elton John and Bette Midler. Schlatter, believing it was critical to have a strong TV personality to balance out the singers, hired Flip Wilson, who he figured would be a perfect foil to Cher in the comedy skits.

With the custody battle behind them and divorce proceedings winding up as well, Cher and Geffen decided they would get married over the holidays in 1974. As Cher was about to begin rehearsals for her new TV show and also pursuing plans to go back into the recording studio, the wedding planning would have to be done in the spare time she really did not have. Geffen could see that Cher was overwhelmed and insisted she take a break. He arranged to send her, her sister, and a few other friends to Europe on a vacation.

The night before Cher left on her trip, she and Geffen went to hear the Average White Band play at the Troubadour. At the club, two *National Enquirer* reporters convinced Cher to give them an interview. She told them she could not "hold out much longer" from marrying Geffen, saying that he was "the only man in the world I'd ever marry."

But it was a lie. Inside, Cher was beginning to be plagued by gnawing thoughts that marrying David Geffen would be a mistake. In fact, she had been having an affair with the bass player from the Average White Band. When Geffen discovered that Cher was cheating on him, he was destroyed, and he became scared and paranoid. But Geffen's obsession with Cher continued, and he was relieved when the affair ended after only a short time. He still wanted to marry her.

Throughout her four-week vacation in Europe, however, all Cher could think of was how Geffen's incessant focus on marriage had made her uncomfortable. Although she was grateful for the assistance he had lent in putting her finances in order and getting her career back on track, she was increasingly concerned that Geffen was not all that unlike Sonny Bono. Like Bono, he could be controlling, and Cher was frightened of marrying another man who threatened to quash her independence. Geffen's sexual attraction to men also was no small issue. "This isn't going to work," she thought.

Geffen and Cher talked every day while she was away, mostly bickering about wedding plans. Most days Cher believed she should end the relationship. But then there was an occasional day when she thought that marrying Geffen would not be so bad.

From the moment Cher returned from Europe, Geffen recognized a change in her and sensed that she was slipping away from him emotionally. But it seemed as though he felt he could reinvigorate the relationship if he could work some more magic with her career. He knew what his powers were and, always more comfortable in a business arena than in a personal one, thought Cher would marry him if he could wow her with his business dynamism.

His latest idea involved goosing her recording career by hiring Jimmy Webb to produce her first album for Warner Bros. Records. The album, which was to be called *Stars,* featured songs by many of the singer-songwriters Geffen represented or admired. It included a Neil Young song called "Mr. Soul," a Jackson Browne song entitled "These Days," and a song by Webb called "Just This One Time." The album's title track was written by another folkie, Janis Ian.

It was a terrific stretch for Cher to pull off such material and harder still because she was attempting to record it at the same time rehearsals for her new TV show were beginning at CBS. The show, meanwhile, had its own set of problems. From the start, Cher battled with George Schlatter over her image. Cher was embarrassed by her silly TV persona. Schlatter felt that the image she projected on her earlier show—that of a sweet, funny girl—was perfect for TV and that she was not qualified to play the tough rock-'n'-roll queen she believed she was. In short order, she came to call Schlatter "Hammer"; he called her "Nails."

On the first day of rehearsal, Cher balked at Schlatter's suggestion that the special open with a spotlight on a newly vulnerable Cher, singing a poignant version of "Let Me Entertain You" from the musical

Gypsy. "OK, Hammer," she mocked, feeling that his suggestion would make her look square. "Then what do I do?"

"Well, then you come down the runway, and you welcome the audience. You'll say 'Hello' and 'Good evening.' "

"Oh, no," she refused, dismissing the idea. "I'm not into that shit."

"This is going to be a long season," Schlatter whispered to Digby Wolfe, the show's head writer. Then he give it another try: "Cher, you are now the star of the show," he said. "You have to come down and acknowledge the people."

"It's old-fashioned!" she screamed.

"You're right, it's old-fashioned," he said. "That's what the audience wants to see."

Schlatter wisely deciphered that the only way he could get Cher to do as he wanted was to get David Geffen on his side. "David, she has to come out and overcome all of this stuff," Schlatter said. "They split up, people want to know why they split up, what's going to happen to Chastity, et cetera. Here we've got this woman who's only been seen hurling sharp brittle retorts at Sonny. She's never really been seen talking sincerely to the audience."

"You're right," Geffen told him. "Don't worry. I'll talk to Cher."

David Geffen's wealth was impossible to hide, and many people came to him asking for money. He was generous, not forgetting those who had helped him along the way. One who came to him with an outstretched hand was Jerry Brandt, his old mentor from the Morris office. Since leaving the Morris office himself, Brandt had had a rough go of it, losing money in clubs such as the Electric Circus and the Paradise Ballroom, where he sought to revive the dance marathon.

Brandt came to Geffen asking him to sign an artist named Jobriath, who he was betting would be the next David Bowie. Geffen agreed to sign him, even though he was dubious of the singer's talent. Brandt grew desperate when, after spending fifty thousand dollars to team his artist with the London Symphony Orchestra, Jobriath came up with only one song, improbably entitled "Scumbag." Geffen agreed to advance him enough money to finish an album, on the condition that he sign a letter promising never to come to him asking for money again. "That's it?" Brandt said gleefully, agreeing to the terms. The album was a bust. It was not the last time Brandt came to Geffen for money, however, and Geffen did not turn him away.

Loser acts such as Jobriath did not even make a dent in the success story Geffen had created at Elektra/Asylum Records, which continued to be the most successful label in the business. The Eagles' third album, *On the Border,* turned out to be their biggest album yet. After the disappointing sales of their second album, the band rebounded with a record that featured its first number one hit, "Best of My Love," a song composed by Don Henley, Glenn Frey, and J. D. Souther, a frequent collaborator with the band.

Jackson Browne's career was also on an upward trajectory. His third album, *Late for the Sky,* did not have any hit singles on it, but it rose to number fourteen on the album charts, performing better than either of his first two albums. Joni Mitchell, too, had another hit album, this one called *Miles of Aisles,* a record produced from her live concerts. Like *Court and Spark,* it also reached number two on the charts and had a hit single.

But Geffen was disinterested in the music business and focused only on his next goal: He wanted more than anything to fulfill his dream of running the Warner Bros. movie studio. When word slipped out that Ted Ashley, chairman of the studio, was retiring, Geffen began a campaign for the job.

Ashley, who had overseen the rise of the studio since Steve Ross had purchased it five years earlier, was tired. His exhaustion had become apparent one day when he was given a copy of Marvin Kalb and Bernard Kalb's biography, *Kissinger.* He told people, "I want to read this book and not have to worry whether or not Steve McQueen is going to be available to play the lead."

Geffen called up Steve Ross and told him he wanted the job. Although Ross believed strongly in Geffen's many talents and abilities, he did not think he was the right man for the job. Geffen decided the best response was to pout. He settled back into a familiar refrain, whining loudly about the tanking stock price and questioning Ross's leadership skills. By the end of 1974, the stock had fallen to a low of six dollars per share.

Geffen then demanded that Ross release him from his contract. But Geffen's impassioned phone calls to the Warner chief were futile. He was only two years into the seven-year contract he had signed when he sold Asylum. Ross was not about to let him go.

Like a spoiled child, Geffen simply refused to go to work. Because he worked mostly from home and rarely went to the office anyway, most people at Elektra/Asylum's headquarters did not know about the stand-off. But it slowly began to make an impact, as his approval was needed on routine business matters.

Mel Posner, Elektra/Asylum's president, was preparing for an important meeting of the officers who oversaw operation of the Warner/Elektra/Atlantic distribution company known as WEA. Posner quickly realized that Geffen had no intention of offering any help. "David, I'm going to the WEA committee meeting," Posner started. "We have to make some decisions about price and policy issues."

"I'm not interested!" Geffen brayed. "I don't want to hear about it! If you want a decision, if you want an answer, you go see Steve Ross! I'm not interested!"

I t soon became clear how important Sonny Bono had been to the success of *The Sonny and Cher Comedy Hour.* Besides serving as the butt of Cher's jokes, his responsibilities, it turned out, included getting Cher out of bed and to the studio on time for rehearsal. Now, Schlatter fumed as the crew sometimes waited hours for her to show up. Schlatter again turned to Geffen, pleading for help.

Once she did get to rehearsal, she was usually a pro. But an entire day could be ruined if she broke a fingernail. Desperately insecure, Cher was obsessed with her makeup and nails and somehow believed that the magic combusted on-screen because of her beauty, not because of any inner gifts such as her ability to sing or make people laugh.

"Cher, you are not about a fingernail," a frustrated Schlatter said. "You are about communicating with a camera and opening up so that people are allowed to get to know you, to feel comfortable with you. They love you, but let's worry about the medley!"

The guest stars for the show's premiere had gathered in Los Angeles. Schlatter and his team passed out the scripts and began staging the episode. The first skit had two friends meeting at their ten-year high-school reunion. Flip Wilson played his famous Geraldine Jones character to Cher's hammy character Laverne, a tacky gum-smacking housewife who wore leopard-skin print dresses and oversized pink glasses.

The skits were interspersed with musical bits, some of which Cher did on her own. In others, she partnered with her famous guests. Elton John, wearing star-shaped eyeglasses, sat at the piano while he and Cher sang his hit "Bennie and the Jets."

The final rehearsal dragged on into the wee hours of the morning before the guest stars at last were sent home. Exhausted, Geffen and Cher stayed as Schlatter and the rest of his production staff talked about changes they planned to institute the next night. Schlatter also explained that the guest lineup for the next episode—Raquel Welch, Tatum O'Neal, and Wayne Rogers of the TV series *M*A*S*H*—had been finalized.

Geffen and Cher were still playing at being lovebirds, but theirs was increasingly a relationship of convenience, not a red-hot love affair. Indeed, there appeared to be no romantic connection. Geffen and Cher were simply lonely friends who were helping each other get through tough times.

"I have to go," Geffen whispered sadly to Digby Wolfe as Schlatter dismissed Geffen and Cher and the remaining production personnel. "I have to find a companion for Elton."

Wolfe's heart sank as he saw the loneliness in Geffen's eyes. "It's the companion for *you* that you're really looking for," Wolfe thought.

Geffen tried to soothe Cher's nerves as the studio audience assembled for the taping of the special that was to launch her solo TV career. The show opened as Schlatter had desired, with "vulnerable Cher" as the star. After she sang "Let Me Entertain You," Cher stood at the end of a runway and addressed the audience.

"For those of you who haven't noticed, I've been gone," Cher said nervously. "And for those of you who have noticed . . . I'm back!" The audience cheered. After asking for "a little commotion" for her dress, she turned serious. "My name is Cher and I'm twenty-eight, I have black hair and brown eyes. I'm five foot seven and a half. I weigh one hundred and four pounds when I'm happy, and I weigh one hundred and eight pounds when I'm miserable," she said. "Right now, I weigh one hundred and six, and my future is in your hands."

At the end of the show, Cher stepped out and dutifully closed the show per Schlatter's direction. "That's our show for tonight," she said, addressing the camera. "And I hope you liked it. If you did like it, tell your friends and come back. 'Cause I like seeing you, and I really love ya. So God bless you and good night and take it easy."

Behind the scenes, things were not going well in Geffen and Cher's relationship. Geffen was doing his best to ignore signs that Cher did not want to marry him. He continued to negotiate details of the purchase of his wedding gift to her, the condominium in Aspen. Cher, however, did not want it to go any further.

"You know what, Dave," she said. "I don't want the condo. I changed my mind." The truth, she finally told him, was that she did not want to marry him.

Geffen was devastated. He left the house on Carolwood Drive and moved into Bungalow Twelve at the Beverly Hills Hotel. He tried to transform the relationship into a friendship, but it was agonizing. He continually found himself moping around Cher's door.

"Let's just hang out tonight as friends," Geffen told her one night.

"OK," Cher said, willing to give it a shot. "We're going to go to the

Troubadour." Cher said that her sister, Paulette, and Tatum O'Neal, with whom she had become friendly during rehearsal, would also join them.

The group went to West Hollywood to see a program that included Etta James and Gregg Allman, who was doing a solo gig. He had just started making solo albums, in addition to those with his sibling Duane and the rest of the Allman Brothers Band.

Before going onstage, Allman spotted Cher in the crowd and sent over a hastily scribbled love note. Geffen grew suspicious when Cher excused herself to go to the bathroom at the break and did not return for fifteen minutes. On their way out of the club, Allman met them at the door and addressed Cher. "I'll speak to you later," he said.

Geffen was crazy. "What was that all about?"

Cher told Geffen that she had gone backstage to see Allman and accepted his invitation for a date. The party made their way back to the Beverly Hills Hotel, but Geffen was angry and blew up again. The relationship was over, but he now wanted revenge.

"If you see me walking down the street, you better cross over to the other side," Geffen told Cher. "And I want all my presents back."

"You know, you can have some, but there are certain ones that I'm not giving back," Cher said defiantly. "They were presents, and they're mine, and they don't have anything to do with this."

"I'll sue you!" he screamed.

"Go ahead!" Cher yelled back.

Geffen turned and flung open the door of the bungalow, slamming it into the head of an eavesdropping Tatum O'Neal.

"Come on, Tatum," Cher told her. "Let's go home."

CHAPTER 15

GETTING "IT"

|||

G effen was so paralyzed with his post-Cher depression that on some days he could not get out of bed. It was one of the rare times he sought the help and comfort of his brother, Mitchell, and Mitchell's wife, Renee, who was a marriage and family counselor. Renee and Mitchell grew terribly concerned when they realized that David was not eating. "I think he's going to die," Mitchell told his wife.

Linda Loddengaard covered for Geffen at the office and arranged for Dr. Grotjahn to make house calls to the Beverly Hills Hotel, where Geffen was living. His depression grew even worse after he read a report in *Time* magazine in which Cher said of him and Sonny, "I've traded one short, ugly man for another."

The sessions with Dr. Grotjahn were not offering much relief because the doctor still counted Cher as a patient, too. Geffen was at the breaking point, and yet he felt that he did not even have an objective psychiatrist. He sobbed to Warren Beatty that it had been inappropriate for the doctor to take on Cher in the first place, given that he was seeing him. But it had been Geffen himself who had insisted on it, and Dr.

Grotjahn, like most people worn down by Geffen's arguments, had given in to his wishes. After a time, Geffen left the hotel and convalesced at Beatty's house on Mulholland Drive. Finally, sensing the severity of Geffen's desperation, Dr. Grotjahn asked Cher to find another shrink.

As sympathetic as Beatty was, Geffen's friend Sandy Gallin was heartless and unmerciful. At the moment that Geffen and Cher broke up, Gallin got it into his head that he wanted to be Cher's manager. Geffen begged him not to pursue her, fearing that it would make it even more difficult for him to get her out of his system. But Gallin continued his pursuit and eventually succeeded. Geffen, incredulous, cursed Gallin.

Business was brisk at Elektra/Asylum, but Geffen could not bring himself to go to the office. The Eagles were in the studio recording their fourth album, including promising new songs called "One of These Nights" and "Lyin' Eyes." But Geffen could focus only on his broken heart.

When it seemed like things could not get any worse, the *Esquire* cover story hit newsstands, just in time for Geffen's thirty-second birthday. He had told Ahmet Ertegun and other friends that the profile was going to be glowing. But the monthly magazine's deadline had passed by the time Geffen and Cher had split up. Now, the story, trumpeting the two as a happy couple, was mortifying.

The story was headlined THE WINNING OF CHER . . . AND SOME OTHER MAJOR ACHIEVEMENTS OF DAVID GEFFEN. It was a profile of Geffen, but Cher was the celebrity, so she alone graced the cover. The copy on the front asked, WHO'S MAN ENOUGH FOR THIS WOMAN? Geffen spiraled deeper into despair as he read Julie Baumgold's article, which portrayed him as a materialistic egomaniac and an obnoxious braggart. Baumgold had recorded Cher and Geffen's banter out on their shopping sprees, and now it made him sick. Baumgold called him "insignificant" and "classless."

As he had been the first time he met Robbie Robertson and countless others, Geffen had been painfully indiscreet in sharing personal

Geffen strolls down Sunset Boulevard with his pal
Warren Beatty and Beatty's then girlfriend, Michelle
Phillips, late of the Mamas & the Papas.
(Frank Edwards/Archive Photos)

matters with Baumgold. He told her he had been in daily analysis for two years. He served up figures outlining his net worth and spending habits. The only story he seemed to tell her off-the-record resulted in a thinly veiled anecdote in which he complained about "the biggest artist of them all, a legend . . . who turned out to be so mean, so jealous, so cheap, ego-ridden and petty, such an ingrate." Clearly, he was talking about Bob Dylan.

Geffen and Cher, each clad in bell-bottom jeans, had allowed the *Esquire* photographer to snap pictures of them making out, and Baumgold described that situation, too. "Cher's tongue is deep inside Geffen's mouth," she wrote. She recorded many playful interchanges between the two. "Feel my ass," Cher had said to Geffen in front of the reporter. "Hard as a rock."

The story included all of Geffen's fake history of himself, including the lie that Ahmet Ertegun had floated him fifty thousand dollars when he was managing Laura Nyro. He was also dishonest when Baumgold asked him about reports that Nyro had once walked him through the park on a leash. He said it never happened, but photographer Stephen Paley had the pictures to prove it.

Baumgold also printed a slew of tacky and cocky quotes Geffen had given her: "The apartment (in Borough Park) was always filled with women with big tits"; "Sure I wouldn't mind signing Paul McCartney or Elton John, but I'm not very hungry." Further, a trip Baumgold had taken with Geffen to Tower Records on Sunset Boulevard—he pointed at various records, shouting "That's mine! That's mine! That's mine!"—was painstakingly re-created.

The article was horrifying, and it left Geffen even more depressed than he had been before.

As big a splash as Geffen had made in the music business, Barry Diller had made an equally impressive mark in the TV world. From the mailroom at the William Morris Agency, Diller had risen through the ranks at ABC Television, where he became vice president by age thirty-two, gaining fame as one of the architects of the movie-of-the-week and miniseries formats. As Geffen and Diller became superstars in business, they developed a friendship in which they did everything from exchange Hollywood gossip to listen to each other's personal trials.

They had a deep mutual admiration, but there was a sense of competitiveness as well, and each monitored the other's every move. The two bachelors, both ruthless alpha males, sometimes gossiped about each other.

Geffen and Diller's interest in each other stretched beyond respect for their individual professional achievements. They were both struggling with the notion of being gay, and both sought out women as partners. But along with their mutual friend Sandy Gallin, they held court at parties populated with the most handsome gay men in Hollywood, and sometimes they fought over the spoils.

Diller and Geffen had so many feuds and spats that sometimes they could not even remember what they were about. They were in the midst of one such spat when Diller was named chairman and chief executive of Paramount Pictures.

In early 1975, shortly after Diller took charge of Paramount, Robert Evans, the studio's production chief, told Diller that he was exhausted and eager to leave his job. He recommended that Diller hire Geffen to replace him.

"David Geffen?" Diller responded. "I don't even *speak* to David Geffen!"

"That's ridiculous," Evans told Diller, beginning a laundry list of Geffen's strengths. Evans persuaded Diller that he at least ought to meet with Geffen about the matter. Evans arranged a breakfast during which Geffen and Diller met face-to-face for the first time in more than a year.

Diller had just purchased a house on Coldwater Canyon in Beverly Hills, and Geffen met him there before they drove down to the San

Fernando Valley for breakfast. Neither Diller nor Geffen considered for long the notion that they could successfully coexist at Paramount, but the meeting did serve to reunite them.

That summer, Geffen at long last realized his dream of owning a beach home in Malibu. He abandoned plans to build the Charles Gwathmey–designed house when Doris Day's house, which he dreamed of owning since 1969, went up for sale. He bought it for $425,000, and it became his primary residence.

Diller quickly became one of Geffen's most trusted confidants, and Geffen shared with him his ambitions to run the Warner Bros. movie studio. Diller feared that Geffen would be unsuited to corporate life, with all its rules and regulations. Diller was careful, however, not to hurt Geffen's feelings.

By September 1975, Diller and Geffen had grown so tight that false reports began to circulate that the two were lovers. The rumors gained momentum when Diller invited Geffen to join him on an exotic boating vacation in Europe. The friends sailed for five days, traveling from London to Nice. They also went to Amsterdam and ended the vacation by flying back to New York.

At the airport in New York, Geffen and Diller were met at customs by Jeffrey Katzenberg, a twenty-four-year-old New Yorker who that year had been hired as Diller's assistant at Paramount. Among his jobs was expediting the chairman's customs checks at airports. Geffen, who had wasted many an hour in customs, was flabbergasted as Katzenberg's oiling of the customs workers enabled him and Diller to breeze through the process.

"That was the quickest ride through customs I've ever had," Geffen told Katzenberg, who was eight years his junior. Geffen saw immediately that Katzenberg had the hustler-like qualities that he himself had displayed at that age.

When they reached Manhattan, Diller and Geffen discovered that the ridiculous reports of a romantic liaison between the two had reached a fevered pitch. The two had been invited to a dinner party the evening of their arrival, but Geffen refused to accompany Diller, on account, Diller believed, of the rumors.

Diller went alone to the party, which was hosted by Diane von Furstenberg, the fashion designer who was becoming famous for her design of the wrap dress. Diller did not know von Furstenberg previously, but at the party the two experienced a magical connection, and they began a whirlwind romantic relationship in which they shared, for the next few years, residences in New York and Connecticut. Von Furstenberg had two children, and Diller became something of a surrogate father to them.

Peter Guber, the production chief at Columbia Pictures, told Geffen he knew just what would help him conquer his depression: est. He bragged that he did not need to be in therapy because of it.

Geffen asked what est was.

Guber told Geffen enthusiastically that est was a miracle therapy course that had helped thousands of people overcome anxiety, insecurity, and a sense of failure. The cure came after attending two weekends of seminars, at a cost of just $250.

The acronym *est* stood for Erhard Seminars Training, named for its founder, Werner Erhard. Erhard, born Jack Rosenberg, was a former encyclopedia salesman who had cooked up est in 1971, using bits and pieces of various disciplines ranging from Zen and Scientology to Gestalt psychology, Dale Carnegie courses, and yoga. The concoction had made him a media star—he appeared on *The Tonight Show*—and a very wealthy man. By 1975, more than one hundred thousand people had taken part in the training.

The course, however, was often run by drill sergeants who belittled the participants with humiliating exercises that sometimes left people vomiting and crying. Students could not wear watches and were refused bathroom breaks. At the bottom line, est left its students with one simple message: You and only you are responsible for your life. The program was full of gimmicky catchphrases such as "getting *it.*" Many people never figured out what *it* was and were left flustered by confusing explanations that *it* was "the process of experiencing oneself without any concept."

Geffen initially scoffed at the idea that a course lasting two weekends could solve the problems that more than two years of therapy had not. But Guber swore by it, repeated est phrases like a parrot, and succeeded in selling Geffen on it. He was in so much pain still that he was willing to try almost anything. He sent in his $250 and registered to take the course at the convention center in downtown Los Angeles.

The first session began at 9:00 A.M. on a Saturday. Geffen quickly spotted some familiar faces among the two hundred or so students. He sat with Bob Silberstein, Diana Ross's husband, and Richard Perry, the music producer who had cut Barbra Streisand's version of Laura Nyro's "Stoney End."

Perry and Silberstein found the seminars valuable, but for Geffen it was life changing. He surrendered to the process and eagerly volunteered to participate in the dramatic "sharing" exercises. He sobbed uncontrollably as he stood before the group with a microphone and gave a testimonial about the problems in his life. The exercise also included an instructor screaming at Geffen whenever he sensed he was saying anything phony.

For once, Geffen was not doing the shouting. Participants in est were told that passing blame gets you nowhere. One of the central messages of est—that a strong moral character is essential to a happy life—shook Geffen deeply. From that moment forward, he determined to live out the principles of est.

Because each day's session lasted until around midnight, Geffen and Perry had each decided to stay overnight at a hotel downtown. At the end of the first day, Perry discovered that the hotel had lost his reservation and was full. Geffen told him that his room had two beds and invited Perry to bunk with him.

Perry was a little concerned about sharing quarters with Geffen because the two had not spoken since their bitter feud two years earlier over Carly Simon's album. Armed with new lingo learned that day, Geffen astonished Perry by offering an apology. Perry told Geffen how hurtful his attack had been, and Geffen conceded that it had been unnecessary. He explained that at the time he had been feeling pressure from Joni Mitchell to make her album a hit. He had also been trying desperately to make his first Bob Dylan release a success. The est weekend proved to be a perfect setting to make amends.

Est was so exhilarating for Geffen that it succeeded in lifting him out of the depression he had been in. In the interim, Cher had married Gregg Allman. Geffen called her to tell her that he was at last moving on with his life. He encouraged her to enroll in est as well.

"Everything is fine now," he told her. "I still love you, but we don't have to be together, everything is great, and we can be friends." Cher was pleased and happy that Geffen was able to put the relationship in perspective.

But then he hit her with one of his typical bombshells. "I still want my jewelry back," Geffen said firmly.

"Dave, go fuck yourself," Cher snapped. "I'm not doing it."

In the year since Ted Ashley had retired as chairman of Warner Bros., the studio had put few movies into production. While Geffen did not get the job, many people in Hollywood felt that the man who had, Frank Wells, was miscast as Warners' new top man.

Geffen seized the opportunity and again began pestering Steve Ross to give him a shot at running the studio. Ross, tired of Geffen's advances, finally told him that he would try to make it happen. Geffen was thrilled. At last, he was going to get the opportunity to play movie mogul.

Ross insisted that as part of Geffen's transfer to the studio, he had to find his own replacement at Elektra/Asylum. But Geffen's first move was not to hire anybody but to fire his chief lieutenant, Mel Posner, telling him that the new chairman ought to have the right to bring in his own team of executives. Posner was numbed by the firing, especially as it had come just months after Geffen had promoted him to vice chairman and given him a raise above that outlined in his contract.

"It's nothing that you did, Mel," Geffen told him. "I need to find a successor for myself in order to get out of here!" Posner's firing simply confirmed that Geffen made decisions about people based upon what *his* needs were. Geffen did offer to help Posner get another job, but that issue was clearly secondary to his own. "There are times when I think David is the devil," Posner thought to himself. On his lawyer's advice, Posner continued coming to work every day, as though nothing had happened.

Geffen hardly noticed. The only thing on his mind now was the studio job, and he wanted to get out of town, get some space from Elektra/Asylum, and plot his next moves.

He called Paula Weinstein, a spunky young ICM agent whom he had met at Sandy Gallin's house, and made her an offer. "I need a vacation," Geffen told her. "I'm going to Brazil. Come with me." Weinstein had never been to Brazil and jumped at the chance to visit a new country.

Weinstein, who represented such actors and actresses as Jane Fonda, Louise Fletcher, and Donald Sutherland, was attractive, outspoken, and politically liberal. Her mother, Hannah, was a producer who had recently finished making the Diahann Carroll movie *Claudine*.

But almost from the moment their airplane touched down in Brazil, things started going wrong. Though it had come highly recommended, the hotel they had booked turned out to be a dump. The situation was made worse when both Geffen and Weinstein came down with dysentery after only a day of sight-seeing.

Geffen called Sergio Mendes, the piano-playing leader of the group Sergio Mendes and Brasil, whom he had just signed to Elektra/Asylum. Geffen arranged for him and Weinstein to move into Mendes's apartment. Mendes was happy to offer more comfortable accommodations in his homeland. Geffen then let Weinstein in on his next career move.

The two bonded in Brazil, a process facilitated in part by the dysentery. They somehow found humor in it and wept with laughter one afternoon as a doctor attempting to treat them insisted on measuring their heights. Geffen also continued to work the phones, calling Ross and other Warner executives in New York to see if his job switch could be speeded up.

To Weinstein, it was clear that Geffen would be a winner at the studio, and she wanted to ride on his coattails. "If you get that job, I want to go with you," she told him. "I don't want to be an agent much longer."

"Don't worry," he promised. "You're coming with me."

S teve Ross did not know exactly how to engineer Geffen's transfer. It was clear that a new leader was needed at Warner Bros., but Ross did not think that tapping an inexperienced, albeit energetic and smart, executive such as Geffen was necessarily the best fix. Geffen would need a seasoned partner who could show him the ropes but who would be willing to let Geffen sit in the driver's seat.

Ross knew of only one person who fit the bill: Ted Ashley. He decided to see if he could lure the retired chairman back to work with Geffen as his deputy. His pitch would be that Ashley would not have to work full-time but simply be in evidence as an elder statesman, training Geffen to soon take over.

There was only one problem with Ross's plan: Ted Ashley was less than enamored of David Geffen. He still nursed the wounds from when Geffen had deserted him at the Ashley Famous Agency after less than a year on the job. Realizing that this might be the only way that he could get a job at the studio, Geffen made up his mind to repair his relationship with Ashley.

He discovered that he and Ashley had something in common: They both were graduates of the est course. Ashley and his girlfriend, Joyce Easton, an actress who had played Janet Banning on *Days of Our Lives,* had seen their worlds transformed by it. Werner Erhard had even asked Ashley to sit on est's board of directors.

Even the toughest and coldest people were put in a sentimental mood by est. Ashley was one of them. Before retiring, he was a feared

Ted Ashley, the powerful chairman and chief executive
of the Warner Bros. movie studio. After Ashley retired, Geffen
campaigned passionately for the job. (Peter Borsari)

studio boss and nobody spoke too quickly or too loudly to him. But after est, Ashley was, at least for the moment, a softer, more approachable man. Geffen swooped in and worked his charm to great effect. Within a short period of time, whatever bad blood lingered between them seemed to disappear. Geffen's new house on Carbon Beach in Malibu was not far from Ashley's beach house, making it convenient for Geffen to drop by and court the retired studio chief.

Ashley began to think Steve Ross's plan sounded intriguing. He was no longer interested in spending every night out wining and dining stars, but he knew that Geffen would be. Geffen had told him that his pal Warren Beatty had told him about some movie projects that could be hits for Warners. Ashley's mind was made up: He was ready to lead, with Geffen at his side, another revival at Warner Bros.

Frank Wells was relieved when he heard the news. He had been crying out for help, overwhelmed by the workload. Wells, who had been chairman and chief executive since Ashley's retirement, agreed to relinquish the title of chairman and give it to Ashley; the two would share the chief-executive title.

Even as Geffen was making his move toward movies, there were a few loose ends he wanted to tie up in the music business. As part of his new employment agreement, Geffen asked Steve Ross to return to Jackson Browne the 50 percent of his music-publishing rights that Warner Communications had picked up when Geffen sold Asylum in 1972. Geffen felt a tremendous debt to Browne, who had brought him so many of Elektra/Asylum's most lucrative artists, and now Geffen wanted to return the favor. Ross granted the wish, and Jackson Browne controlled 100 percent of his music publishing.

But Geffen soon found out the truth in the old saying "no good deed goes unpunished." The members of the Eagles were furious that Geffen did not demand the return of their publishing rights, too, and they soon mounted an attack that threatened to drag Geffen into court.

The movie studio, meanwhile, put out a press release announcing Ted Ashley's return to the studio as chairman and the hiring of David Geffen as vice chairman. The story was front-page news on December

10, 1975. *Daily Variety* heralded the story as Ashley anointing Geffen as his "crown prince." With Geffen as the clear heir apparent, Warners at last had a viable succession plan in place.

In the meantime, Steve Ross had taken care of the staffing dilemma at Elektra/Asylum. Joe Smith, Mo Ostin's deputy at Warner Bros. Records, was named to succeed Geffen as chairman. Mel Posner was welcomed by Smith to continue in his post as the label's vice chairman. Posner stayed on for another nine years before going to work for Geffen again. His days of clashing with him were not over.

Geffen, though, was uninterested in the goings-on at the record label he had run so masterfully for the past two years. All he cared about was that his childhood dream of becoming a movie mogul was finally coming true.

THE PICTURE
BUSINESS

|||

M arlo Thomas was living in New York when she broke up with
her boyfriend, Herb Gardner, the writer of such plays as *A
Thousand Clowns.* The previous year, she had starred on Broadway in
Gardner's comedy *Thieves* and then filmed the movie version of the
play, but the five-year relationship had come unraveled. She wanted to
move back to Los Angeles, her home, where her mother and celebrated
father, Danny, still lived.

The only problem was that Thomas had no place to live; a tenant
was renting the Beverly Hills mansion on Angelo Drive that she had
bought with the money she made from *That Girl,* the late 1960s and
early 1970s sitcom in which she had starred. Barry Diller, whom
Thomas had known since she was seven, invited her to move into his
house on Coldwater Canyon, and she accepted.

Diller hosted Sunday-night movie screenings, and Thomas joined in
the fun, along with other regulars such as Geffen, Sue Mengers, and
Sandy Gallin. As the chairman at Paramount Pictures, Diller had access
to new movies that most people could see only in theaters. At the touch

of a button, a screen that filled an entire wall descended from the ceiling and transformed his living room into a theater. A projection room was hidden behind the bar at the other end of the room.

It was here that Geffen first met Thomas. She was beautiful and smart, but she could be feisty and foulmouthed, too, and he instantly developed a crush on her.

Thomas chuckled as Geffen regaled the group with stories about his experience in est. "Werner Erhard told us at the beginning that he was going to tell us everything we needed to know about sex," Geffen told the group. "I was so disappointed when the end of the first day came, and he had not said anything about it. Finally the last day comes, and there's only ten minutes left in the session when he says, 'By the way, I told you I'd tell you everything you ever needed to know about sex. Here it is: When you're hot, you're hot, and when you're not, you're not.' " Geffen howled with laughter.

Geffen knew that his friend Wendy Goldberg, the wife of ABC programming chief Leonard Goldberg, was friendly with Thomas, and he asked her to set them up on a date. Given the crowd in which she was introduced to him, Thomas had assumed that Geffen was gay and thought the request was a bit strange, but she agreed anyway. On their first date, Geffen, now wearing the badge of studio vice chairman, took her to the December 1975 premiere of Warners' new Stanley Kubrick movie, *Barry Lyndon.* He delighted in being photographed with her on the red carpet.

As the weeks went on, Thomas was surprised to see that Geffen was dead serious in his pursuit. He became fixated on her and smothered her with a lover's attention. When she went to Acapulco for a fashion shoot, Geffen followed her on the next plane.

The aggressive nature of Geffen's chase stupefied Warren Beatty. "You're going to Acapulco after her?" Beatty asked. "You don't even know her. Are you sure you want to do this?"

Geffen was sure, and his pursuit was blunt. "Marlo, you are the most inviting woman I have ever known," he said to her on the trip.

"What is he doing?" she wondered.

Marlo Thomas leads an entourage including talent agent Sue Mengers (left), Paramount chairman Barry Diller (obscured), and Thomas's new boyfriend, David Geffen. (Peter Borsari)

Thomas was not interested in a serious relationship, but Geffen somehow convinced her to be his girlfriend. For a time, it was a full-fledged relationship. Geffen was still clinging to the idea that life would be easier as a straight man. Moreover, he had not yet found a male companion with whom he could make the same emotional connections he had had with women.

When her tenant's lease expired, Thomas moved back into her house on Angelo Drive, and she and Geffen spent nights there as well as at his house on Carbon Beach. She hosted a dinner party at her house for Geffen, Ted Ashley, and others from the studio. All of the other top executives from Warner Bros. were married or dating women, and Geffen enjoyed having a girlfriend like the others.

W ith Ted Ashley's return to Warner Bros., the suite of offices on the second floor of the executive building at the Burbank studio was so crowded that there was no office available for Geffen. Unlike other executives who hungered to get behind the giant, solid doors that marked the entrance to the executive suite, Geffen did not seem to care that his office was not next to Ashley's. He was given an office down the hall, on the other side of the reception area, and he and his faithful secretary, Linda Loddengaard, set up shop there.

Geffen, now thirty-three, wanted to hit the ground running by quickly putting high-quality films into production. The studio was enjoying strong reviews for *Dog Day Afternoon,* Al Pacino's follow-up picture to his success in *The Godfather,* and was excited about another movie that would be released soon, *All the President's Men.*

Geffen's strategy was simple: Bring in the biggest names he could find and couple them with bright, young, undiscovered talent. Just as he had courted the most gifted singers, Geffen set out to bring the most talented actors, writers, and directors to Warners. And, as Geffen Roberts had for the top music acts of the late 1960s and early 1970s, Geffen's office now became a hangout for many of the brightest creative lights in the movie business. Geffen struck up friendships with

Elaine May, a sought-after screenwriter and the former comedy partner of director Mike Nichols, and Robert Towne, the Oscar-winning screenwriter of *Chinatown*.

Geffen reached back into his past for a raw talent as well. Albert Brooks had made a comedy album for Elektra/Asylum called *A Star Is Bought,* and Geffen thought he was ready for the movies. He signed him to a five-picture deal, the first of which was to be a comedy called *Real Life.* It told the story of a self-centered filmmaker who moves in with a family to make a documentary about them.

Meanwhile, Warren Beatty told Geffen there were two old movies he wanted to remake. One was *An Affair to Remember,* the 1957 weeper starring Cary Grant and Deborah Kerr, which itself was a remake of 1939's *Love Affair.* He also wanted to put a new spin on *Here Comes Mr. Jordan,* the 1941 fantasy about a prizefighter and amateur saxophonist who goes to heaven by mistake when he crashes in his private plane. Beatty convinced Elaine May to be his partner in writing the script; they called it *Heaven Can Wait.*

Beatty had become friends with Muhammad Ali and wanted him to play the prizefighter. In the movie, the fighter is returned to Earth but must live out his life in the body of a wealthy industrialist. Beatty thought it would be hilarious to bring a black boxer back in the body of a white man. Beatty and his friend Buck Henry planned to co-direct the picture.

From the very beginning of his tenure at Warner Bros., however, Geffen seemed to be an odd fit at the studio. After seeing a rough cut of *The Outlaw Josey Wales,* he went to deliver his notes to Clint Eastwood, one of Warners' most important and reliable stars.

"Clint, this is the best picture you've ever done," Geffen said. "I only want to suggest one thing: I think it would be better if it was twenty minutes shorter."

"I'm glad you took the time to see the picture, and I appreciate your comments," Eastwood said calmly. "Why don't you study the picture some more and see if you have any more thoughts. When you do, give me a call over at Paramount."

"Why over at Paramount?" Geffen asked.

"Because that's where I'll be making my *next* movie," Eastwood threatened.

Realizing he had put his foot in his mouth, Geffen quickly recanted. "Clint, the picture is perfect," he said quickly. "I wouldn't change one frame. Thank you very much." He dashed back to his office.

The exchange was an ominous sign because it showed that Geffen was not versed in the old studio games where producers and executives alike lie to one another about how much they love each other's movies. While in another venue Geffen's curt style might have been refreshing, in Hollywood it played poorly.

Paula Weinstein quit her job at ICM and joined Geffen at Warner Bros. in May 1976. One of the first movies Geffen "greenlit" was *Greased Lightning,* a Richard Pryor movie that was brought to him by Paula's mother, Hannah.

The movie, which told the life of black race-car champion Wendell Scott, was to be written and directed by Melvin Van Peebles, the director and star of a 1971 X-rated cult hit called *Sweet Sweetback's Baadasssss Song.* Shooting was set to begin July 15 in Georgia, and a supporting cast including Pam Grier, Beau Bridges, and Cleavon Little was secured.

But Geffen and everyone else at Warners knew they had a disaster on their hands the day the first dailies were shown at the executive screening room. Melvin Van Peebles seemed to be making an art film; the studio wanted a testosterone-charged commercial race-car movie.

When the lights came up, Ted Ashley and Frank Wells did not know what to say.

Guy McElwaine, the studio's production chief, decided he would break the ice. "Where are the fucking race cars, David?" he asked flatly.

Geffen, embarrassed that his movie seemed to be a train wreck, started pointing fingers. "I brought the movie in, *you're* the head of production!" he yelled. "That's *your* fucking job!"

Next, Geffen turned and blamed the situation on Paula Weinstein. "You didn't tell me this was happening!" he screamed in front of the others. "Why don't you talk to your mother? It's your responsibility!"

Geffen had indeed assigned responsibility for the movie to Weinstein, but she had refused to take it on, telling him that she thought it was inappropriate for her to be the studio's representative on this picture. "Well, I really didn't know about this, and I'm sorry," she said.

When Weinstein got back to her office, the phone was ringing. It was Ted Ashley, wanting her to come to his office at once. "This is not right, you have no responsibility for your mother's movie," he told her. "What did David ask you to do? Did he ask you to be responsible?"

After she met with Ashley, there was another message, this one telling her to report to Frank Wells's office. "Look, I want to make you feel better," Wells told her. "Neither Ted nor I expect you to be involved with this picture."

Weinstein felt relieved that the studio's top executives were telling her not to worry. But instinctively she felt that something was wrong. Feeling compromised, she soon concluded that Ashley and Wells were cross-examining her, trying to gather ammunition that they might one day use against Geffen.

McElwaine, for his part, flew to the set and fired Van Peebles. The studio then hired a director named Michael Schultz, who gave the studio the race-car scenes it wanted. Still, the movie was a flop and disappeared quickly.

Geffen complained to Marlo Thomas that he was not being given the authority to run the studio that Steve Ross and Ted Ashley had promised him. When Thomas and Geffen spent a weekend with Ross at his house in East Hampton, New York, Thomas told Ross he was making a mistake by not letting Geffen run the studio himself.

"How can you not give this to David?" she asked him. "He's a genius! Let him have it all."

"Well, it's more complicated than that, honey," Ross responded.

Geffen, who had succeeded stellarly at everything he had taken on so far in his professional life, now found himself failing for the first time. He was just beginning to realize that he had critically misjudged the cultural differences between the music industry and Hollywood, and that those differences were causing him to stumble badly.

Used to the relatively quick turnaround of record production, the slow-moving nature of the movie business made him agitated, nervous, and bored. Key to his recipe of success had been his ability to move quickly; but in the movie business, that same pacing proved to be a detriment, and it began to drive him crazy.

Despite the frustrations, Geffen demonstrated that he had solid instincts for casting. When the studio failed to convince Johnny Carson to accept the title role in a low-budget comedy called *Oh, God!,* Geffen suggested they hire George Burns. He then secured John Denver to play Burns's foil.

Geffen also showed that he was capable of making unpopular decisions. One involved *A Star Is Born,* which was set for release that Christmas and starred Barbra Streisand and Kris Kristofferson. Streisand's boyfriend, Jon Peters, who had just quit his job as a hairdresser and was producing the movie, was a volatile rookie who yelled when Geffen refused to allow him and his girlfriend to direct the picture. Geffen oversaw the hiring of director Frank Pierson.

Meanwhile, Geffen was networking frantically. He forged a relationship with Ray Stark, the sixty-year-old veteran producer of such films as *Funny Girl,* the Oscar-winning movie based on the life of Fanny Brice, Stark's mother-in-law. Geffen also picked up the phone and called Steven Spielberg to compliment him on his box-office blockbuster *Jaws,* which had been the biggest movie of 1975. *Jaws* had been made at Universal Pictures, but Geffen wanted to set alliances with all of the powerbrokers in town, not just those at Warner Bros.

The raid on Entebbe Airport in July 1976 did not help Geffen's career at Warner Bros. Ted Ashley thought the story of the raid, in which Israeli commandos rescued passengers from a plane that had been hijacked by Palestinian terrorists, would make the ultimate action picture. He signed Franklin Schaffner, who had directed *Patton,* and convinced Steve McQueen to star as Israeli Brigadier General Dan Shomron.

Ashley spent several weeks in Israel attempting to solidify the cooperation of its government and military. In his absence, Frank Wells ran the studio. Eyebrows were raised around the lot, however, when Joyce Easton, Ashley's girlfriend, began showing up at his office, even though she was not an employee of Warner Bros. She was there ostensibly to relay to the others updates from Ashley.

It became too much for Geffen one day when Easton, who was bright, attractive, and opinionated, called a meeting of the studio's top executives and began holding court. Geffen blew his stack, incensed that Easton felt that she was next in command after Ashley. "How dare she call a meeting and expect us to come!" Geffen shrieked.

Frank Wells and Terry Semel, the studio's distribution chief, were not big fans of Easton, either, but their style was more to roll with the punches and ignore her grandstanding. Geffen, though, was incapable of toeing the line. He was the only one to speak up and express his outrage about Easton's power play.

It was a strategic blunder. Ashley was devoted to Easton, and he would not tolerate anyone treating her rudely. For Easton, the love fest over David Geffen ended that day. Although she denied it, others were convinced she worked hard to make sure that Geffen's career at Warner Bros. would be shortened.

Ashley's plans for a feature about the Entebbe incident soon collapsed. But for Geffen, things were never the same once Ashley returned from Israel. For one thing, Ashley began inviting John Calley, the studio's former production chief, back to meetings at the studio, and seemed increasingly to ask for his opinion on various matters.

Worse, Ashley and Wells began to lose interest in *Heaven Can Wait* and were dismissive of Geffen after a poorly received screening of *The Late Show,* a movie starring Lily Tomlin and Art Carney that Geffen had shepherded.

But there was no scene in any of the movies Geffen presided over at Warners that could compare with the drama of the one that played out next in real life. It was a blowup that completely deflated Geffen's bid to take over as studio chairman.

Tom Laughlin was a Hollywood outsider who had hit it big writing and directing *Billy Jack,* a radical drama about a Vietnam veteran and the runaway teenager he protects in the Arizona desert. After Laughlin and Warners became embroiled in a lawsuit over the TV rights to *Billy Jack,* a proposal was floated that the studio could settle the lawsuit if it agreed to release the third Billy Jack movie, *Billy Jack Goes to Washington* (the second movie, *The Trial of Billy Jack,* had been far less successful than the original).

One evening, Ashley, Wells, Calley, McElwaine, Semel, and Geffen met to view the film at the executive screening room. The film ended at ten-thirty, and the executives went back to McElwaine's office to discuss whether or not they should make a deal to release the picture.

"I want everyone to write down on a piece of paper what you think the domestic box-office gross on this movie can be, and I'll do it, too," Ashley told the others. "Don't write your name on the paper."

The executives each scribbled a number, folded their slips of paper, and tossed the slips into a box on McElwaine's desk. Ashley took out the slips one by one and read them aloud. "Ten-point-five million . . . twelve million . . . fourteen million . . . fifteen million . . . thirteen-point-five million . . . *one million!* Which asshole said one million?" Ashley growled.

Geffen stood up. "This asshole said one million," he said.

"How come we have all these experts in this room, they all think the gross would be somewhere between ten and twelve or fifteen million, and you say one million?" Ashley asked.

"I didn't like it," Geffen replied.

"That's not fucking relevant to whether anybody will go see it," Ashley blasted back.

"I don't think anybody will go see it!"

"What did you think of the first two movies?" Ashley asked Geffen.

"I never saw the first two," Geffen explained.

At that, Ashley leapt onto the table and reached out as though to strangle Geffen. Geffen jumped onto the other side of the table, and the two men went for each other's throats.

Production chief Guy McElwaine pulled Geffen back off the table and sat him down on the couch, whispering in his ear, "Calm down. . . . It isn't worth it."

Ashley stepped down from the table and brushed himself off. He straightened his jacket and moved toward the door. Turning to look at the group, he stopped and shot one final look at Geffen. "I don't have to take this shit from anybody," he said, and stormed out of the office.

Irving Azoff (right) in a post-concert chat with
Eagles Don Henley and Glenn Frey. Azoff called David "she";
Geffen wished Azoff dead. (Henry Diltz)

CHAPTER 17

HEALTH SCARE

|||

The morning after the *Billy Jack* brawl, Ted Ashley telephoned Steve Ross in New York and demanded that he fire Geffen. "It's either me or him," he said. "If he's staying, I'm gone." Ross believed in Geffen, but he could not rule against Ted Ashley, the man who was most responsible for the revival at Warner Bros. since Ross's parking-lot company had bought the studio.

Within a day, Geffen's reign at Warner Bros. was over, after only eleven months. A press release had not yet been drawn up when someone leaked the news to gossip reporter Rona Barrett, who broke the story on local television in Los Angeles. Geffen had not yet had time to emotionally process the firing himself when he heard Barrett's report. He was stunned, hurt, and appalled, facing major defeat for the first time in his life.

Warner Communications put out a short news release on November 10, 1976, stating that Geffen had "resigned" and accepted a post to become "executive assistant" to Steve Ross. It was a bogus job, and one Geffen had no intention of doing. But he had three years left on his contract, and Ross refused to release him from his employment agreement. Typically, studios excuse fired executives from their contractual obligations and give them some kind of financial settlement, freeing them to find work elsewhere. But Ross was not about to allow Geffen, one of the most talented executives he had ever known, to leave and make money for one of Warner's competitors.

Although it seemed harsh and unfair to Geffen and some of his friends at the time, Ross was betting that Geffen's anger would subside and that someday he would return to the Warner fold and make a lot of money for himself and the company. Geffen became one of the few executives in the history of the entertainment business forced to sit on the sidelines, collect a weekly paycheck, and wait out a contract.

After Geffen left the studio, the movie projects that he had nurtured languished. Albert Brooks had to pitch his *Real Life* script all over again, this time to Ashley, who was decidedly uninterested. Brooks found a backer in Chicago and got the movie made on his own. The picture failed to make a splash when it was released a year later.

Ashley and Frank Wells continued to drag their feet on *Heaven Can Wait*. When Wells denied Warren Beatty's request for a watercooler in his office, a furious Beatty asked if he could have one day to see if he could interest another studio in the movie. In a single telephone call, Beatty got Barry Diller to agree to make the film at Paramount Pictures. It became a huge commercial success and was nominated for nine Academy Awards, including Best Picture.

Many people would rejoice if their employer paid them full salary for three years to do absolutely nothing. But sitting at home with nothing to do was torture for Geffen, a workaholic who for so long had defined himself by his career.

His telephones stopped ringing almost immediately, a sign that Hollywood would treat him just as poorly as it had treated countless other top executives who had been fired before him. He learned the lesson that in Hollywood it does not matter who you are, only how much power you have. Geffen began taking mental note of the many people who had deserted him in the wake of his firing. With so much time on his hands, his vindictive side began to churn.

Geffen was angry about the way he had been treated by Steve Ross, and the pain he felt as a result was excruciating. As 1976 turned into 1977, Geffen himself could not see the bright future that Ross had envisioned, the time in which the two would be reunited to celebrate more financial successes together. Although the nearly thirty-four-year-old Geffen told people he had "retired," he did assume he would one day return to work somewhere. He continued to pay Linda Loddengaard in the hopes that her full-time services would be needed before long.

Appearing at public events was traumatic, and Geffen ventured out only rarely, ashamed to face the town that had branded him a failure. For nearly a decade he had been a superstar in Hollywood's power game; now he had lost. If there was such a thing as a silver lining to his brief tenure at the Warner Bros. studio, it was that he now had an even better handle on how the Hollywood power game was played. Never again would he be beaten at it in such a degrading fashion.

The lesson he had learned proved to be little consolation in February 1977, when he left the house to attend Clive Davis's popular post–Grammy Awards breakfast at the Beverly Hills Hotel with Paul Simon and Sue Mengers. The event turned ugly when Brian Rohan, a music lawyer from San Francisco, noticed Geffen, got up from his seat, and moved toward his table. He was mad, believing Geffen had once gone behind his back to negotiate directly with one of his clients on a deal.

Rohan gave a swift kick to Geffen's chair, turning it upside down, tossing Geffen onto the floor and throwing the room into an uproar. Rohan next put his hands around Geffen's neck. Sue Mengers let out a scream. Paul Simon raised a giant saltshaker above his head to use as a weapon. Clive Davis started running across the room.

"Brian, what are you doing?" shouted Paul Simon.

"It's the only way I could hurt this guy. He won't return my phone calls!" Rohan steamed. "This is the only way that I could think to properly humiliate him!"

Simon and David Braun, Bob Dylan's lawyer, pulled the two men apart. Geffen, who said he did not return Rohan's calls because he had once made an anti-Semitic remark, was not hurt. The next day, Geffen got a call from Frank Sinatra, offering condolences and help if he wanted it.

Even while Geffen's professional life was falling apart, his personal life was also in disarray. The romantic sparks between him and Marlo Thomas disappeared, despite a valiant attempt on his part to keep the relationship alive. He took her to Barbados, where they went to a party at the house of Claudette Colbert. Marlo invited Batya and Sam to join her and David for dinner at her father's house in Beverly Hills; Batya watched in amazement as Danny Thomas put his arm around her son.

But Marlo Thomas was not interested in carrying on a relationship with a man she knew was more interested in men than in women. They slept together, but Geffen had made it clear that he considered himself bisexual and that his sexual encounters with men were important to him. She just as firmly made it clear to him that this was something she could not tolerate.

During his relationship with Thomas, Geffen had a fling with a twenty-one-year-old sandy-haired adult-film star named Gavin Dillard. Dillard, whose stage name was Gavin Geoffrey, had made his debut in a gay erotic film called *Track Meet*. The film was advertised with a billboard on La Cienega Boulevard, and Geffen arranged an introduction through some acquaintances he knew from the West Hollywood bar scene.

While Thomas was out of town doing publicity for the movie version of *Thieves*, Geffen invited Dillard over to her big house on Angelo Drive. Dillard, who had grown up in Asheville, North Carolina, felt intimidated by the house, but became more comfortable when Geffen suggested they go to his beach house.

Dillard wanted to be a singer, and Geffen briefly indulged his dreams, hooking him up with Warren Beregian, the vocal therapist. Geffen paid for twelve sessions at one hundred dollars a pop. Geffen kept a low profile when he was with Dillard and introduced him to few of his friends. During a trip to New York, Geffen became ill and lonely and bought a ticket for Dillard to fly to Manhattan to keep him company.

By February, when Geffen accompanied Thomas and her parents to the Los Angeles premiere of *Thieves,* the romantic relationship between Geffen and his actress girlfriend was over. They were better friends than lovers, they both realized. They maintained a friendship that lasted for years; sometimes, Geffen still confided his deepest fears to her.

"I'm afraid that if you love somebody and then they go away they'll leave a hole," he told her.

"David, you're very brave to love in spite of that," she said.

In the wake of the breakup, Geffen actively looked for opportunities to get out of town. Warren Beatty introduced him to Martin Peretz, the editor in chief of *The New Republic,* and he asked Geffen to join him on a vacation to Israel. Geffen accepted Peretz's invitation, hoping that some time away would help lift his spirits.

Like his mother, Geffen was not a religious Jew, but he was interested in seeing for himself the place where Batya had met his father so many years earlier. Peretz's role as chairman of the Jerusalem Foundation enabled him to secure meetings with the Israeli elite, including Golda Meir, Yitzhak Rabin, and Menachem Begin. He brought Geffen along to each meeting.

For Geffen, the dramatic highlight of the trip was a tour through the Yad Vashem, the Holocaust memorial in Jerusalem. He had not been overwhelmed by meeting the prime minister, but he found the memorial an emotionally shattering experience.

Elektra/Asylum Records had had another sensational year after Geffen had left for Warner Bros. Jackson Browne released *The Pretender,* his biggest album to date. Joni Mitchell released two more well-received albums, *The Hissing of Summer Lawns* and *Hejira,* the latter of which was one of Geffen's favorites.

The biggest success of all by far was charted by the Eagles, who released two monster albums in 1976. The first, a collection of the band's greatest hits, was certified platinum in its first week in stores that March. Its staying power was awesome, and for many years it was the best-selling album of all time. The second album, *Hotel California,* was another blockbuster and became known as the band's masterpiece.

But there was an old deal that kept Don Henley and Glenn Frey from savoring their phenomenal success. Both men still seethed over Warner's control of the music-publishing rights that had once been Geffen's. They put Irving Azoff on the case to get them back.

Their anger allowed Azoff to revel in his hatred for Geffen. "Don't ever let him say he's your friend, Don," Azoff told Henley. "He's Jackson's friend. David gave him back his publishing. If he's your friend, let him give you back your publishing."

Azoff apparently delighted in taking pokes at Geffen that some might term homophobic slurs; for example, he many times referred to him as a "she." Geffen, for his part, cringed whenever Azoff's name was mentioned. "I hope he dies!" Geffen yelped.

Azoff had gotten nowhere with Warner Communications despite two years of threats that the band would leave Elektra/Asylum if the company did not return the copyrights. Finally, in the spring of 1977, Azoff filed suit on the band's behalf, seeking the return of the rights and ten million dollars in damages. Warner Communications and Geffen were named as defendants.

In the suit, the Eagles argued that Geffen had acquired the copyrights through an illegal conflict of interest when he was their manager, publisher, and label boss. The Eagles held that they could not have gotten the record deal if they had not made the publishing deal as well. Under antitrust laws, they asserted, that was an illegal tying of interests.

Having sold the rights years earlier as part of the Asylum sale, Geffen himself was not on the hook for the money. But with nothing else to do, he stewed endlessly about the lawsuit, his enmity for Henley and Azoff mounting by the moment. He traded vitriolic phone calls with Azoff, convinced that he was the driving force behind the effort to squeeze the money out of Warner. He was on the phone constantly, attempting to marshal whatever sympathy and anti-Azoff sentiment he could find.

The lawsuit attracted a great deal of negative publicity for Geffen, whose reputation was already under attack in the wake of his studio failure. Warner, for its part, had been put between a rock and a hard place; if it fought the suit, it was likely to lose its hottest-selling band. The company soon agreed to settle and gave the Eagles the other half of their publishing rights. Azoff won, and Geffen slipped deeper into his depression.

It got worse. Gavin Dillard awoke one morning in August at the Malibu beach house to the sound of piercing screams coming from the bathroom. Geffen had urinated blood. His first thought was that Dillard had passed along the clap.

"I'm pretty certain that I'm clean," Dillard said.

"Under the circumstances," Geffen said, "how could you know?"

Geffen went to a urologist in Beverly Hills, who took X rays and then informed him he was concerned about something he saw in his bladder. To check him out further, the urologist told Geffen he wanted to conduct a cystoscopy, a bladder examination that required hospitalization. Geffen began crying hysterically. His first instinct was to run not to his mother but to Linda Loddengaard. She held his head in her lap as he cried, and she promised to be at his side the next day at the hospital.

Geffen checked into Cedars-Sinai Medical Center on August 15, 1977. Batya, Sam, Mitchell, and Linda paced in the waiting room during the surgery. Geffen was put under anesthesia for the procedure. When he awoke, he was alarmed to discover a catheter coming out of his penis. The urologist explained that the cystoscopy had shown a mushroom-shaped tumor in his bladder. The doctor had decided to operate and remove it immediately. The hospital's pathologists were busy conducting biopsies, and in twenty-four hours they would know if the tumor was malignant or benign. Geffen was panicked.

Linda Loddengaard alerted his closest friends of the developments. Marlo Thomas, who was on vacation in Anguilla with her new boyfriend, Phil Donahue, immediately flew back to Los Angeles. On the plane, however, she suffered an attack of appendicitis and had to be hospitalized herself. On his way to Cedars-Sinai, Sandy Gallin heard on the radio that Elvis Presley had died. Hoping to get Geffen to think about other matters, Gallin shared the big news with his friend.

"The future is an illusion," Geffen thought to himself. "I might have cancer. I could be dying."

The next morning, Geffen's doctor delivered the news: The pathologist's report indicated that the removed tumor was malignant. But the report also showed that the cancer was confined to the tumor itself and had not spread to the sensitive walls of the bladder. The doctor told Geffen he was not dying.

So-called transitional-cell carcinoma rarely strikes men as young as Geffen, who was just thirty-four. Such cancers typically occur in men in their fifties and sixties who had been either lifelong heavy smokers or print-shop workers who had been exposed to aniline dyes. Geffen soon quit smoking for good.

The experience left him crippled with anxiety. He cringed as the urologist explained that he would have to be hospitalized every six months for checkups. In roughly 70 percent of the cases, such polyp-like cancers in the bladder recur. In the worst-case scenario, the doctor told him, he would lose his bladder. Geffen was mortified as he concluded that having to wear an ileostomy bag would surely destroy his sex life.

Even though the doctor had made it clear that Geffen was not dying, the experience left Geffen petrified, and he began making out his will from his hospital bed. He planned to leave money to his mother and his brother. He assigned specific assets to friends such as Sue Mengers, Sandy Gallin, and Paula Weinstein.

"Don't worry, you'll be taken care of," he generously told a number of friends. "You'll never have to work again."

Then, seeking forgiveness from the many people with whom he had tangled so bitterly, he began calling some of his foes.

"I wanted to call you and apologize for any pain I have caused you," he told Guy McElwaine.

"David, you never caused me any pain," McElwaine assured him, baffled by Geffen's repentant tone. "You and I never had a problem."

Warren Beatty and Robert Towne stopped by to visit him at Cedars-Sinai, but Joni Mitchell did not. Geffen was hurt by the slight, which he called an act of disloyalty. Despite their recent falling-out, Steve Ross was among the well-wishers, telephoning Geffen in the hospital and asking what he could do.

"Let me out of my contract!" Geffen bellowed.

"Anything but that, David," Ross responded.

Out of the hospital, his suppliant attitude apparently forgotten, Geffen cursed Ross and Ted Ashley and expended extraordinary energy bad-mouthing the Warner Bros. movie studio. He got up early in the morning and worked the telephones furiously, calling everyone he knew and telling them that the studio was "poison." He saved his most fervent pitches for the people who still worked at Warner Bros. and advised them that they should leave, too.

Soon he was mad at Paula Weinstein, angry that she did not quit her job at Warners in protest. But Weinstein did not have another job lined up and was not independently wealthy like Geffen. She liked Geffen, was grateful for having had the opportunity to work for him, and tried to transform her boss-subordinate relationship into a friendship.

But it was difficult. When she attempted to gain goodwill with him by feeding him gossipy tips from the industry grapevine, it sometimes

backfired. She once confided in him that she was struggling in a negotiation with Sue Mengers. When Geffen tattled to Mengers that Weinstein had been complaining about her, Mengers went into a rage of her
own, calling Weinstein and asking her if she knew how to keep anything confidential.

After countless sessions with her analyst in which Weinstein lamented
the problems she was having in her relationship with Geffen, the analyst,
a heavyset German woman who rarely said much of anything, slowly uttered four words of advice: "No . . . more . . . David . . . Geffen!"

Weinstein decided to heed her analyst's advice and stopped returning
Geffen's phone calls. Geffen concluded that she was dumping him because he was now no longer in a position to help her career. He bitterly
turned on her and added her to his list of those he was trashing around
town. They did not speak for ten years.

D avid Geffen's investments in Southern California real estate were
now showing huge returns. The five million dollars he had invested from the Asylum sale had now turned into about twenty million.
He began every day with a phone call to Gil Segel, his business manager, who kept him apprised of his wealth. On Segel's advice, Geffen
had bought a shopping center in Sylmar, a two-hundred-unit apartment complex in Palm Springs, and a six-story office building along
Santa Monica Boulevard in Beverly Hills. Geffen bragged that he had
made more money in real estate than he had in the record business. He
spent hour upon hour singing the praises of Gil Segel, in the process
helping him win a slew of celebrity clients.

With these plentiful profits, Geffen purchased a two-bedroom apartment in New York City, on Fifth Avenue just across the street from the
Plaza Hotel. The building was only twenty years old and rather undis-
tinguished from the outside; but the apartment had an extraordinary
address and the potential to be a fabulous New York pied-à-terre. He
asked Charles Gwathmey to redesign the space and went about expanding his art collection to fill its walls. He spent lavishly on paintings

by René Magritte, David Hockney, Morris Louis, and Edward Hopper. He also became enamored with Tiffany lamps and began a buying spree.

But the money and the trappings it afforded him were of little comfort, given that he believed his days were numbered. He felt isolated and recognized that he did not have anyone with whom he could share his wealth. Most important, he was terrified of death and more frightened still at the notion of facing it alone. He envied Marlo Thomas's relationship with Phil Donahue and saw how he stayed by her side and comforted her when she was in the hospital. Who would comfort David Geffen?

He determined that if he was ever going to face his homosexuality, now was the time to do it. But in his quest for a boyfriend, Geffen did not look for a soul mate his own age with similar accomplishments. To be sure, there were few people with such credentials, but Geffen did not even try. He began hosting small parties at his beach house in Malibu, filling the guest lists with attractive men in their twenties.

At one such party he met Curt Sanburn, a college student at Yale University who had stopped in Los Angeles before heading back for his senior year. Sanburn did not know who Geffen was when his friend John Deason, a model featured in ads for L&M cigarettes, suggested that Sanburn come to the party. Sanburn was dazzled by the paintings of Ellsworth Kelly and other contemporary artists that lined Geffen's walls. He spent only a few moments talking with Geffen, and only afterward learned from Deason that Geffen had dated Cher and been the force behind Joni Mitchell, one of Sanburn's favorite artists.

Geffen was smitten with Sanburn and obtained his phone number from Deason. A few weeks later, Geffen telephoned Sanburn at his apartment at Yale. The two had many hours-long phone conversations in which a curious Geffen quizzed Sanburn about his life and background. Geffen was so obsessed that he went to New Haven and found the place Sanburn lived. Reports circulated in Los Angeles that David Geffen's new boyfriend was an Ivy League college student.

Geffen told Sanburn about being the subject of Joni Mitchell's "Free

Man in Paris" and soon confided that the young man was, as far as Geffen was concerned, the embodiment of the protagonist's long-sought, elusive "friend." Sanburn did not have a tape player, so Geffen bought him one. Geffen turned him on to Barbra Streisand's album *People,* as well as to the music of Jimmy Webb. He gave him a David Hockney print from the *Blue Guitar* series and a drawing Joni Mitchell had done while working on her album *For the Roses.*

Sanburn enjoyed Geffen's company and found it entertaining to talk with him about music and art, but that was the extent of his affection.

"I don't get it," Geffen told him. "Why aren't you attracted to me?" Geffen spent hours trying to analyze why Sanburn did not want to have sex with him.

Sanburn did not want to hurt Geffen's feelings with the truth: "He was short," he said later. "He didn't appeal to me at all. My boyfriends have always been tall, handsome guys." The romance stalled, but the two remained friends for a time. In a certain conflict of interest, Sanburn later wrote a flattering profile of Geffen for *GQ* magazine, failing to disclose that he once dated him.

For Geffen, many future relationships followed a sad pattern. He was able to easily lure the most handsome young men he desired, but most of them were attracted not to him but to his money or power. Beyond getting a fleeting sexual thrill, Geffen got no further along in his battle to come to terms with the boy from Borough Park he still occasionally saw in the mirror.

In January 1978, Geffen was admitted again to Cedars-Sinai for a follow-up cystoscopy. He spent two nights in the hospital and awoke to good news: The examination had not turned up signs of any tumors. He was free and clear for another six months.

Soon, Charles Gwathmey finished Geffen's new apartment in Manhattan. Geffen decided to move to New York, though he would have to return to California for the periodic cystoscopies. He rented the beach house in Malibu to MGM owner Kirk Kerkorian and moved to the East Coast.

Geffen delighted in showing off his new apartment and bragged nonstop about his architect. He invited a journalist and photographers in from *Architectural Digest,* and they served up a nine-page spread detailing his new home. Gwathmey had designed a new floor plan that contained a large entrance gallery, an open living room, dining room, study area, and a single large bedroom with an elaborate dressing room and bath suite. There was perfectly detailed cabinetry of natural oak in every room, and dark marble was used for the floors everywhere except the bedroom. Gwathmey and his partner, Robert Siegel, had combined the oak and the marble in two specially designed tables, one in the living room and one in the study.

The walls were lined with such paintings as Hockney's *Splash,* Magritte's *Le Seize Septembre,* and Fernand Léger's *La Gare.* There were also a number of Tiffany lamps. The place was decorated exquisitely, and Geffen himself deserved a great deal of the credit for how it looked. If anyone doubted that David Geffen had taste, the apartment on Fifth Avenue surely put those doubts to rest.

Among his first guests was Alan Cohen, the former Warner executive who had structured the Asylum Records joint venture and buyout. Cohen had left Warner to become head of Madison Square Garden, but he and his wife, Joan, had remained close friends with Geffen. They had many late-night bicoastal phone calls when Geffen lived in Los Angeles. Despite having been screamed at by Geffen regarding Warner's tanking stock price, Cohen admired him and fantasized about going into business with him.

The Cohens were impressed as Geffen took them on a tour of the apartment, which had spectacular views of Central Park and the midtown skyline. "David, this is the most magnificent lamp I have ever seen," Alan said, admiring a Tiffany floor lamp. "It really is, in the truest sense, a great work of art."

"I'm glad you like it," Geffen said nonchalantly, leading the Cohens into another room of the apartment, "because it's being sold at Sotheby's in their next auction."

Cohen stopped dead in his tracks, unable to believe what he had just heard. "He's not capable of loving anything," he thought to himself.

Remaining eager to be distracted from thinking about the cancer scare, Geffen decided to look up Steve Rubell, whom he had met in New Haven in 1971. Rubell was now in the gossip columns every day with his new Manhattan disco, Studio 54. Rubell was to take him into a world of celebrity, sex, and drugs.

THE MISTAKE

|||

After fashion designer Calvin Klein rocketed to stardom, David Geffen decided he had to meet him. Klein had quickly achieved remarkable prominence in 1977, in part because of his designer blue jeans, but also on account of the dramatic and high-profile abduction of his eleven-year-old daughter, Marci. By the time Marci had been rescued safely, Klein's national name recognition had soared, and two hundred thousand pairs of his jeans were sold in just one week.

Geffen was electrified by what he knew of Klein. He was always drawn to people with power and was curious to discover how they got it and how they hung on to it. Geffen's friend Ali MacGraw offered to introduce them.

Geffen, the son of Jewish working-class parents, had a background similar to Klein's. Klein grew up in the Bronx, where his parents owned and managed a grocery store. Klein also had a relative who knew how to sew: His grandmother was a seamstress who had had her own shop.

Klein was the ideal tour guide for Geffen. His marriage to Jayne having ended on a relatively amicable note, he was a single guy who was also interested in partying and staying out late. It was an era in which trendy types experimented with sex and drugs, and Geffen and Klein got their fill of both. Geffen liked many of Klein's friends, especially Fran Lebowitz, a dry-witted humorist and writer who shared Geffen's interest in talking.

This group was part of a generation that was rebelling against unhappy times brought on by such things as the Vietnam War, Watergate, and, most recently, the anti-gay-rights effort spearheaded by singer and orange-juice queen Anita Bryant. In this context, the thoughtful musical era of singer-songwriters faded in favor of a mindless time when disco was the rage. The movement took off with a hit song, "Love to Love You Baby," sung by a black Catholic girl named Donna Summer. When *Saturday Night Fever* hit movie theaters, the disco craze was launched with a vengeance.

Steve Rubell was the self-appointed master of ceremonies of this new movement, having presided over the opening of Studio 54 in Manhattan. Rubell owned the club along with Ian Schrager, a friend he had met while attending Syracuse University. Rubell was gay, and Schrager was straight, but together they formed a business partnership that seemed to be unbeatable. Their club,which opened in the spring of 1977, was located at 254 West Fifty-fourth Street, the site of an old CBS soundstage. After Studio opened, the word spread quickly that it was a haven for debauchery. Its reputation was solidified when photographs circulated around the world of an early party at which Mick Jagger's sultry wife, Bianca, surrounded by naked men, rode in on a white horse.

Rubell made no secret of the fact that Studio celebrated drug use; it was a highlight of every night when, from high above the dance floor, a huge moon with eyes, mouth, and nose descended. When the so-called Man in the Moon was lowered, a big coke spoon was thrust under the moon's nose. The crowd went wild.

The cover charge was fifteen dollars, but admittance was not based on who could afford it; people had to have a certain look that appealed to Rubell and his doormen. "Just make sure you don't let in anyone like

*Diana Vreeland (facing away from the camera) greets
Steve Rubell (left), Cher, Geffen, and Halston at a
New York party. (Ron Galella LTD)*

me," he once told one of his men. Like Geffen, Rubell was not that pleased with the looks with which he had been born.

Geffen and Calvin Klein, who was one of Rubell's closest friends, were of course ushered in past the throngs outside. Once inside, they sometimes went straight to the VIP room in the basement, reachable through a discreet door on the main floor that few non-VIPs even noticed. This was an amazing space where such diverse luminaries as Elizabeth Taylor and Mikhail Baryshnikov could be seen sitting on leather banquettes chatting with the likes of Betty Ford or Jimmy Carter's elderly mother, Lillian. Stars retreated downstairs to briefly escape the craziness of the main floor and do drugs or have conversations with other celebrities.

Geffen met a host of new friends, including Halston, the Iowa-born designer who had been made famous when discovered by Babe Paley, the wife of CBS chief William S. Paley. After one night of partying at Studio, Geffen segued to a party at Halston's townhouse on the East Side, where he was introduced to Donna Summer, whose hits "Heaven Knows" and "Last Dance" had become staples at Studio.

As Geffen's friendships with Klein and other new pals blossomed, his relations with various other longtime allies derailed. In the VIP room at Studio, Geffen saw Ahmet Ertegun, but Geffen felt snubbed and ignored by him. Ertegun, for his part, had felt rejected by Geffen ever since he had left the Atlantic fold to head up Elektra/Asylum, effectively disavowing his promise that they would be "partners forever."

By Geffen's calculations, Ahmet and his wife, Mica, were at the top of the list of those whom he believed had forgotten about him. Now Geffen began spreading mean-spirited rumors about Ertegun. "Did you know Ahmet is anti-Semitic?" he asked people. The reports of Geffen's rumormongering got back to Ertegun, who did not want to believe it; Geffen's accusations could hurt Ertegun's business, and he tried to convince himself that Geffen was above that kind of behavior.

But the relationship took a disastrous turn in May 1978. Paging through *The New York Times* one morning, Geffen came across a full-page ad promoting the new issue of *The New Yorker* magazine and its profile of Ertegun. In the making for seven years, the two-part article was finally being published, and Geffen knew that he would be in it. He had spent considerable time with George Trow, the author.

Geffen raced out to a newsstand to pick up the issue. He was dumbfounded as he returned to his apartment and began to read. "There was a brief vogue for David Geffen," Trow said in one section. The writer also recorded an incident in which Ertegun had overheard Geffen sucking up to Joni Mitchell on the telephone. "He must be talking to an artist," said Ertegun. "He's got his soulful look on. He is trying to purge at this moment all traces of his eager greed."

Geffen ran to the bathroom and vomited. He was hurt by the article and blamed it on Ertegun, who he felt shared the opinions expressed by Trow. He telephoned Ertegun and began ranting. "You're responsible for this outrage!" Geffen yelled. "George wrote these things about me because you told him to!"

"Don't be ridiculous, David," Ertegun said. "I don't have any control over what this man writes." Geffen decided he would never work with Ertegun again.

E ven as he was deep into the most sexually promiscuous period of his life, having sex with countless young men, Geffen still felt uncomfortable about being gay. He periodically dated women and still looked for someone to marry. His friend Paul Simon introduced him to his neighbor Lorne Michaels, the producer of NBC's *Saturday Night Live,* and together the three men went out on the town pursuing women. One of their targets was Carrie Fisher, the daughter of Debbie Reynolds and Eddie Fisher whose new movie *Star Wars* was breaking all box-office records.

Fisher was just twenty years old and uncertain what to make of the attention the men, each of whom was about fifteen years her senior, were lavishing on her. In the course of one week, she went on dates with each of them. Geffen took Fisher out for dinner, and then they spent the night back at the small apartment near the corner of Ninetieth Street and Central Park West that she shared with actress Teri Garr. "I'm going to sleep under the covers, but you have to sleep on top of them," Fisher told Geffen as they undressed.

Geffen and the others liked Fisher because she had enormous energy and was devastatingly clever. She told outrageous stories about her mother and father, as well as gut-busting tales about Harry Karl, the eccentric stepfather who had raised her. Geffen rapidly made her an offer: "You could be Mrs. Geffen."

Fisher liked Geffen, but his tempo frightened her, and she chose instead to date Paul Simon, whom within a few years she married. Fisher nonetheless took a place in Geffen's tight inner circle, and they were to help each other through serious personal dramas in the years to come.

Bored with the dating scene and eager to find a way to fill his days, Geffen hunted for a freelance job that would not put him in conflict with his still-active Warner contract, which had only one year left. Having enjoyed his visits to Curt Sanburn at Yale, Geffen got it into his mind that he would be a good university professor. Even though he himself had not graduated from college, he was able to arrange, partly through Martin Peretz, to teach a noncredit seminar at Yale in the fall of 1978 and spring of 1979. His course on the music industry and arts management proved to be popular among students. He frequently wowed his students with celebrity guests such as Jackson Browne and Paul Simon. Geffen and Joni Mitchell had reconnected despite the trials of their tumultuous relationship, and she, too, agreed to speak to the class. On campus, students reported that Geffen was squiring around young men from the water-polo team and snickered that he was there only for the boys.

College was something Geffen had missed, but now he was getting the opportunity to experience some of it. The best part for him was that he still lived in Manhattan and shuttled via limousine to New Haven only once a week. When he came back to town, he had his fun there, too. His friendship with Steve Rubell had intensified, and the two, along with men they had met at Studio, took vacations in Barbados together.

But soon Rubell's party at Studio was over for good. On December 14, 1978, federal agents stormed Studio 54 and found garbage bags filled with nearly a million dollars stuffed in the walls and behind pipes. Rubell was nailed in his Mercedes, where another hundred thousand was found in the trunk. The IRS began a sweeping inquiry into allegations that Rubell and Schrager had skimmed millions of dollars off the top of their business and were cheating on their taxes.

In the months that followed, Studio 54 was hotter than it had ever been, and Geffen was on hand many nights, as Rubell continued gleefully to run his club as though it were business as usual. Geffen disapproved of Rubell's actions but, unlike many, did not desert him, even when Rubell and Schrager were indicted on federal income-tax charges and sent to prison.

The follow-up cystoscopy examinations that Geffen underwent at Cedars-Sinai in Los Angeles, meanwhile, eventually forced Geffen to face his own reality. He was shocked when an examination in August 1979 did not yield the same free and clear results of the three previous ones. This time, Geffen's urologist told him that he had spotted what he called an "atypia" on his bladder. The doctor told him it was nothing to be alarmed about but added that he wanted Geffen to start coming in every three months for examinations, instead of every six.

Geffen panicked, got in his car, and drove to Sandy Gallin's office on Sunset Boulevard to tell him what the doctor had said. Sitting on Gallin's couch, Geffen cried as he told Gallin he was convinced he would soon lose his bladder and have to wear a bag.

"I don't like the way this doctor is talking to you," Gallin said sharply. "You need to get another doctor. I want you to go see my doctor right away."

Gallin phoned Dr. Elsie Giorgi, whom he thought of as one of the city's best diagnosticians. Geffen went straight to Giorgi's office. "With your money and your connections, you can get to the best doctor in the world," Dr. Giorgi told Geffen. She suggested that he ought to go to Memorial Sloan-Kettering Cancer Center in New York, where cutting-edge cancer research was being conducted.

Geffen called Marlo Thomas, thinking that her father, who founded Saint Jude's Children's Hospital in Memphis, might have a recommendation for a specific doctor he should contact at Sloan-Kettering. As it turned out, Marlo herself had a connection there. She had a friend who suggested that Geffen see Willet F. Whitmore.

Some of Geffen's friends were surprised that he had waited so long to get a second opinion. "I don't understand: One person tells you you have cancer, then you say OK and don't ever go to ask another person?" Fran Lebowitz asked him. "That's the kind of thing a Gentile would do. Would a Jew take *one* opinion from a doctor? I wouldn't."

Whitmore was a giant in the field, a charismatic man recognized as the father of urologic oncology. He admitted Geffen to Sloan-Kettering and performed the same kind of cystoscopy that the doctor in Beverly Hills had. The next day, with the biopsies completed, Whitmore called Geffen and told him he was cancer free and that he would like to see him in a year. Whitmore did not spot the "atypia" that had alarmed the doctor in Beverly Hills. Geffen found some consolation in the fact that he would have the examinations less frequently.

Resting at his apartment on Fifth Avenue, Geffen's heart began to pound a day later when he picked up the phone. But this time, Whitmore had surprising news. "You know, I've looked at the slides from your initial operation in California," he said. "I can't find cancer on any of the slides."

"You must be looking at the wrong slides," Geffen said.

"No, I'm looking at the right slides," Whitmore assured him. "I can't find cancer on them. There's no reason for you to come back here at all." The tumor that the urologist in Beverly Hills removed, Whitmore said, had not been malignant.

Geffen and his friends and family were relieved at Whitmore's news. They were angry at the doctor in Beverly Hills, but their anger was likely misdirected: The mistake was almost certainly made by the pathologists at Cedars-Sinai. Misdiagnoses of cancer *are* made, and in such cases pathologists are routinely at fault, especially at large hospitals such as Cedars-Sinai where they biopsy all kinds of diseases, not just cancer. But at Sloan-Kettering, the pathologists not only examine cancer exclusively but further specialize in specific malignancies. Diagnoses frequently get overturned there.

In the whisper circuit of Hollywood, even the news of Geffen's health engendered skepticism. Some of his enemies speculated that he had fabricated the whole drama as a way to draw sympathy in the wake of his embarrassing failure at Warner Bros. His friends and family knew the truth, but even those closest to him suspected that the depression from which he was suffering was as serious as any possible cancer. "I never really felt that David was in a serious critical physical danger," Sandy Gallin said. Perhaps, Gallin and other friends thought, the health scare was a blessing. It forced Geffen to take stock of his life, evaluate the state of his relationships, and recognize the good fortune with which he had been blessed.

Geffen himself was not particularly angry at the urologist. "I'm just glad it's over," he told Marlo Thomas. "I don't want to spend two or three years being angry about it. I'm just going to take this as a gift and get on with my life."

One of the first items Geffen wanted to take care of was to tell his mother that he was gay.

"We'd known," she said nonchalantly.

"How come you never mentioned it?" David asked.

"Well, you never mentioned it and we didn't want to upset you."

With the expiration, at last, of the seven-year Warner employment contract he had signed in 1972, Geffen decided it was time to go back to work. But as the 1970s, a decade in which he had experienced enormous highs and suffered depressing lows, came to a close, a question remained unanswered: What was he going to do?

To many people, it seemed clear that Geffen ought to return to the record business. Mo Ostin, the longtime head of Warner Bros. Records, had kept in contact with him during his retirement, and he continually urged him to return to the business. But Geffen was reluctant to revisit ground already covered. He questioned whether he had anything more to contribute to the music industry.

Hoping a vacation might help clear his head, Geffen accepted an invitation from Paul Simon and Lorne Michaels to go with them to Barbados. Geffen considered Simon and Michaels to be among his most trusted advisers, and he quizzed them both for career advice.

"Begin with what you know: the record business," Simon said firmly. "You don't know where it will lead you."

The music business was in one of its periodic times of consolidation in which labels made drastic cutbacks and put many people out on the street. Disco was peaking, and it was unclear what new kind of music would fuel the industry's next wave. Geffen began to think that his friends were right.

Soon, a proposal came along that piqued his interest. His friend Alan Cohen asked him to join him on a bid to acquire EMI Records. Cohen had valuable confidential information that the label might be for sale, and he had retained Bear Stearns in London to begin formulating a bid. But shortly into the process, Geffen apparently changed his mind and asked his friend Alan Hirschfield, who was just being installed as vice chairman at Twentieth Century Fox, to join him in making his own offer for the label. A few years earlier, Geffen had supported Hirschfield, then the number-two executive at Columbia Pictures, in a horrendous dispute with his then boss, David Begelman. Hirschfield had greatly appreciated Geffen's friendship and wanted to return the favor.

Cohen was astonished after he returned from a meeting with Bear Stearns to find that Geffen had turned on him. "I spoke to Alan Hirschfield about EMI," Geffen told Cohen baldly on the phone, "and he thinks that's a good deal that Twentieth will do with me." Cohen was so flabbergasted at Geffen's betrayal that he never spoke to him again.

Hirschfield and Geffen went to London to explore a deal, but the talks quickly fell apart. The music business, however, kept calling. Geffen was astounded when Jerry Greenberg obtained an enormously lucrative deal from Warner Communications to start a new label. Geffen began to salivate and dream about the terms *he* could secure in this market.

"What do you think I would get if I went back into the record business?" Geffen asked his old nemesis David Braun.

"Well, nowhere near as much as Jerry because Jerry is the president of Atlantic and you have been out of the business for four, five years," Braun predicted naively. Braun and Geffen had in the ensuing years patched up their differences, but this comment put him on Geffen's bad side for good.

Mo Ostin kept coming back to Geffen, though, and he soon offered a concrete proposal. "David, why don't you start another record company, and we'll finance it?" Ostin asked, offering to set up a joint-venture company like Asylum had been initially. "I know you could achieve the success you had with Asylum again and this time be even bigger."

Geffen's eyes grew huge. Mo Ostin had said the magic words, and Geffen decided he had found the partner for whom he had been looking. After a nearly five-year absence, David Geffen was ready to return to the music business.

Robert Towne on the set of the troubled
Personal Best *with actresses Mariel Hemingway (left)*
and Patrice Donnelly. (Warner Bros./Photofest)

1980: BACK TO
WORK

|||

I t was perhaps only in Hollywood that an executive like David Geffen would choose to go back to work for the same company he had spent three years cursing. The reality was that despite Geffen's moaning, there were not many options, and he recognized that Warner Communications was arguably the best-managed entertainment conglomerate in the world. He knew the players, had a grudging respect for Steve Ross, and usually knew how to get what he wanted from him. Moreover, Geffen was flattered by Mo Ostin's pursuit and believed that Warner Bros. Records was the best record company in America.

Though Ostin and Ahmet Ertegun both worked for Warner Communications, that was where their similarities ended. While Ertegun enjoyed jetting around the world and attending elegant parties, Ostin was a family man who went home to his wife and sons. While Ertegun courted the press and enjoyed seeing his name in celebrity columns, Ostin kept his head down, preferring for his artists to get the headlines.

Their reputations as music men, however, were equally strong. Ostin got his break in 1961, when Frank Sinatra formed Reprise

Records and hired Ostin to run it. Sinatra signed such friends as Dinah Shore, Dean Martin, and Sammy Davis, Jr. Ostin, who wore conservative suits and ties and thick-rimmed glasses, was the administrative guy. After Sinatra sold Reprise in 1963, Ostin got involved with the creative side of the business and signed the label's first rock band, the Kinks. The new owner, Steve Ross, admired Ostin and put him in charge of Warner Bros. Records as well as Reprise. Under Ostin's leadership, the label was a giant success through the 1970s, signing acts such as Fleetwood Mac, George Harrison, Rod Stewart, and James Taylor.

In his attempt to close a deal with Geffen, Ostin offered Neil Young, still signed to Reprise, as a star artist to get his new label started. Young was still managed by Elliot Roberts, and the three were excited about working together again.

Although Mo Ostin was hot on teaming with Geffen, other people at Warner Communications had qualms about once again dealing with Mr. Volatile. Some executives thought Geffen had been lucky the first time around with Asylum. Others saw him as a petulant child and were not eager to see him running around the halls again.

But Ostin had the power to make a deal no matter what anyone else thought. He felt that Geffen's ability to talk to artists was a unique skill, and he believed that Geffen had a sensitivity and a persuasiveness with artists that was unparalleled.

Geffen liked the proposal and especially liked the idea of going into business with Ostin instead of Ahmet Ertegun, whom he no longer considered a friend. Geffen envisioned a label that, like Asylum Records a decade earlier, was quite small. He wanted to keep overhead low, hire a skeleton staff, and sign just a small group of artists.

But Geffen told Ostin that he would not be content to simply run a label. In part because of his failure at Warner Bros., he wanted more than ever to prove himself a worthy producer of motion pictures. He also wanted to invest in Broadway shows. Marlo Thomas had introduced him to Bernard Jacobs, the head of the Shubert Organization, and the two had informally discussed the possibility of co-producing shows. Geffen had also become friendly with Michael Bennett, the creator of *A Chorus Line,* who had told him he would love to work with him in some way.

Geffen told Ostin he would make the record deal if Warner also agreed to bankroll him in movie and theater ventures. Geffen had had three years to stew about his first crack at the entertainment business, analyzing what he did well and figuring out the areas where he still wanted to succeed. Now, in a brilliant piece of handiwork, he cut himself one of the broadest deals in Hollywood.

Gil Segel and Geffen's lawyers drew up a contract outlining the terms he desired for the label: a straightforward joint-venture agreement in which Warner Bros. Records, for five years, would cover all of the new label's expenses, including artist signings and staff salaries. Warner Bros. would also provide services such as marketing and promotion as well as backroom functions. The profits would be split equally between the two partners. They each would own 50 percent of the venture's assets.

Just when it looked like Geffen had secured an incredible deal unlike any other, he extracted yet another exceptionally valuable bonus: absolute control of his label's manufacturing and distribution rights. He offered to sell those rights in perpetuity to Warner Communications, but, in a decision it came to regret painfully, the company passed.

Geffen would have the freedom to sell those rights to another company, even though any buyer would, under the current deal, have to remit half of the profits back to Warner Bros. Records. This extraordinary deal became even more so, in fact preposterously so, just four years later when Geffen negotiated an extension of the agreement. The new deal set up the pieces that eventually led to a cash windfall that made Geffen one of the richest men in America.

Steve Ross signed off on the terms and also promised that Warner Communications would one day buy the half of the record label it did not own. Ross further gave his approval to the theater deal Geffen requested, which worked just as the record-company joint venture did: Warner put up all of the money but split any profits fifty-fifty with Geffen. For Geffen, who said his own net worth had now grown to thirty million dollars, there was zero downside; if the plays and musicals he picked were losers, Warner would shoulder 100 percent of the losses.

The movie-production deal, however, was not as easy a sell. Ever a believer in Geffen's talent, Ross supported the proposal, but Ted Ashley and Frank Wells were still the top executives at the Warner Bros. movie studio, and they were against it, even though Geffen would be simply an independent producer whose films they would distribute. They had not forgotten how they had been treated by Geffen four years previously. Steve Ross asked Geffen to be patient and assured him that a deal would be made in due course.

Even though Geffen was not given a movie deal, Ostin recognized that overall Geffen was getting a tremendous package. At the last minute, Ostin reneged on his earlier offer to give him Neil Young. But Geffen instantly began working behind the scenes to steal Young away anyway; Elliot Roberts told Geffen that Young's contract was to expire before long, and Geffen convinced him that he should bring Young to his new label then.

The news of Geffen's return to the music business created a small stir when it broke in the trade papers in April 1980. Geffen, newly emboldened, was soon back out on the cocktail-party circuit, meeting and greeting music-industry executives and explaining the plans for his new company.

At one such fete at the Manhattan townhouse of Jann Wenner, the publisher of *Rolling Stone,* Geffen ran into Ahmet Ertegun for the first time since forging his new alliance with Mo Ostin. To Ertegun, the snub was obvious, and he laid that out in no uncertain terms.

"David, why didn't you come back to Atlantic when you started this thing?" he asked. "We could have worked together again."

"Are you kidding?" Geffen responded. "You're out of it. Without Jerry Greenberg, Atlantic is nothing! Atlantic is finished!"

G effen was ready to move back to Los Angeles to build his new empire. But before he packed up his things, he told his household
staff to be prepared for him to make many business trips to the East
Coast. He also made a rather snap decision to buy a $800,000 home at
40 James Lane in East Hampton. He had visited Steve Ross's house
there many times, and now he wanted East Hampton to be his weekend home when he was in New York.

In Los Angeles, the first thing he did was to call Linda Loddengaard
back into full-time duty. Then, in a bid to reignite the luck he had had on
Sunset Boulevard a decade earlier, Geffen returned to the same row of
offices and found that there was space to lease. Next, he went about finding a residence that was close to the office. Kirk Kerkorian had moved out
of Geffen's beach house in Malibu, but Geffen now wanted a second residence in town. He polled his friends and was delighted when Marlo
Thomas agreed to rent him her house at the top of Angelo Drive in
Beverly Hills. Within a year, after she and Phil Donahue got married
and settled in New York, Thomas sold the house to Geffen. Geffen and
Loddengaard set up an office in the house as well as one on Sunset.

Shortly after the new label was announced, one of Mo Ostin's top
lieutenants telephoned Geffen. Eddie Rosenblatt, Warner Bros. senior
vice president, director of sales and marketing, had known Geffen since
1971, the year Rosenblatt had come to work at the label. Rosenblatt and
Geffen had joked that one day they might go into business together.

For years, Rosenblatt had dreamed of being president of Warner
Bros. Records. Rosenblatt and Ostin were close, and their wives were
best friends. But the prospect of partnering with David Geffen was also
an exciting challenge.

"I would really like to work with you," Rosenblatt told Geffen. "I
want to be your guy. I want to run your company."

"Oh, Eddie, no, you don't," Geffen said. "Don't give up your job at
Warner Brothers. Who knows what this will be? You're used to Warner

Brothers and two hundred acts. We're only going to have four or five acts."

"It's going to be very successful," Rosenblatt said. "I really believe in you and your new company, and I want to work for you."

Geffen suddenly feared that Ostin might catch wind of the conversation and wrongly conclude that Geffen was trying to steal one of his top men. He did not want to make a misstep so soon after the deal had been drawn up. "I can't talk to you until Mo tells me it's OK," Geffen said. "I have to go."

Rosenblatt told Ostin of his thoughts. He articulated his desire to be president of Warner Bros. Records and asked Ostin if that was in the cards. If not, he said, he wanted to be allowed to leave to work with Geffen. Ostin told him he had already decided that Lenny Waronker was in line to become president. "If David will have you," Ostin told Rosenblatt, "you should go do this."

Rosenblatt drove out to Geffen's beach house, and Geffen hired him on the spot. Although Geffen had decided that executives at his new company would not have titles, he decided there would be one exception. He wanted Rosenblatt to be known as the label's president, sending the message that he was the number-two man, with responsibility for handling all the label's operations. Like Elliot Roberts in the 1970s, Eddie Rosenblatt was Geffen's loyal partner in this new decade. Like Roberts, Rosenblatt worked hard behind the scenes and played a major role in the company's success, but he allowed Geffen to bask in the limelight. In return, Geffen rewarded him richly.

Geffen was flooded with phone calls and résumés from people eager to work for him. Although he had contacts with many big stars, he recognized from the start that he needed to hire talent scouts to discover new acts. Now thirty-seven, he did not kid himself that he was in touch with the musical tastes of America's youth. He set out to find experienced young pros who were.

The first A&R (artists and repertoire) executive he hired was an eccentric redhead named Carole Childs, a single mother from Great Neck, on Long Island, whom he had met through lyricist Carole Bayer

Sager. Geffen became close to Childs for a time, but she ultimately proved to be a not particularly effective A&R executive. She was gone by the time the label made its mark.

Geffen's second hire, however, was among the best he ever made. John David Kalodner was a thirty-year-old talent scout who had made a name for himself at Atlantic Records by discovering the group Foreigner. Kalodner, who wore only white, was a chubby man with a long brown beard and a nasal voice. He had gotten his start in the music business in the early 1970s writing biographical press sheets for the artists on Atlantic. In that job, he had become an admirer of David Geffen and Asylum, and he counted the Eagles, Jackson Browne, Laura Nyro, and Joni Mitchell among his favorite artists. Kalodner was to become one third of a troika of A&R executives who supplied Geffen's label with its biggest acts.

The block-long building on Sunset Boulevard had been divided up into many different offices, and there was not enough contiguous space to house the entire staff. Geffen rented two offices, one for Kalodner and Childs and another, with a separate entrance, for himself and Rosenblatt. Keeping a close eye on expenses, Geffen decorated the offices, including his own, with used furniture.

G effen did not know what to call his new label and asked everyone he knew for suggestions. Stan Cornyn, who worked for Mo Ostin, thought that, as a light self-satire, Geffen ought to call it Titanic Records. He asked an art director at the label to sketch a logo in which the name was inscribed on a ship's life buoy.

Geffen did not like it and complained about his dilemma to Calvin Klein on his next trip to New York. "Why don't you call it Geffen Records?" Klein asked. Klein, of course, had named his company after himself, and it had seemed to work well.

"People in the record business just don't do that," Geffen responded. "They come up with names like Asylum, Capricorn, or Island."

Klein persisted and finally hit on a compelling reason Geffen ought to put his own name on the door: "You'll get laid more." Geffen smiled and decided to take Klein's advice.

Geffen hired Saul Bass, a Hollywood title designer who was renowned for the opening-credit sequences to such Alfred Hitchcock thrillers as *Psycho* and *North by Northwest*. He did not blink when Bass announced his hefty fee; he approved the very first logo Bass presented to him. It was a sphere with a giant G emblazoned onto it.

Geffen wanted to send a signal to the record industry that he was back as a serious force. The best way to do that, he figured, was to sign a handful of major established stars. The strategy required a significant financial investment, but Geffen reasoned that this would immediately launch the label into the big leagues and give it credibility.

By poaching established talent, Geffen was reversing the strategy that had worked so well for him in the 1970s, when he made stars out of unknowns such as Jackson Browne and the Eagles. What's more, signing established stars, as evidenced by the Bob Dylan nightmare, had not worked particularly well for him then.

He started by checking in with those stars with whom he had the strongest personal connections. Jackson Browne still owed Elektra/Asylum a number of albums under his existing contract and was not free to move. Joni Mitchell, however, was nearing the end of her contract at that label, and Geffen suggested that she come to his label when her deal expired. Despite the complicated ups and downs she had weathered with Geffen at Asylum, Mitchell still looked upon him with fondness and told him she was interested. She fell for his pitch promising her artistic freedom and distribution for life. She said she would join the label when her current contract expired.

To garner the immediate headlines he wanted, Geffen determined that he would have to go outside his immediate circle to find the superstars he needed. Tommy Mottola, a manager who represented Daryl Hall and John Oates, called Geffen and said the duo was hunting for a new label. Hall & Oates owed a couple of albums to RCA but were ready for a switch. Geffen was thrilled about the idea and agreed to meet with Mottola and his lawyer, Allen Grubman, when the men next visited Los Angeles.

Geffen then heard that Donna Summer, who had made her biggest album, *Bad Girls,* the year before, was also interested in switching labels. The so-called queen of disco had made all her records at Casablanca Records but now was disgruntled and wanted out. She fired Neil Bogart, her manager and the head of Casablanca, and filed lawsuits against both him and his label, claiming various indignities.

Having met Summer a couple of years earlier, Geffen found her receptive when he contacted her about coming to his new company. He eagerly anted up a costly long-term deal that guaranteed Summer advances of $1.5 million for each album. The signing brought Geffen splashy headlines. The record wunderkind was back.

But many people in the music industry were surprised by the signing of Donna Summer, in part because she was a far different kind of artist than the pensive singer-songwriters that had been Geffen's forte. The trades were filled with headlines asserting that disco had collapsed, and some questioned the wisdom of such an expensive deal for a star who symbolized a fallen era. But Geffen believed in Summer and was convinced that he could keep her star shining brightly.

News of the signing angered Casablanca, which promptly slapped Summer with a countersuit, charging that she was two albums short of fulfilling her contract. Summer argued that her contract was with Bogart, not the label, and further contended that a "greatest hits" collection as well as her appearance on the *Thank God It's Friday* movie soundtrack completed her obligations. Casablanca sought a restraining order prohibiting her from recording for Geffen Records, but the motion was denied. Geffen had his first big star.

Geffen continued to hound Steve Ross to make good on his promise to give him a movie deal. He was excited about making his mark in the music industry again, but more than anything he wanted to prove himself a player in the movie business. He still wanted to be Louis B. Mayer.

He had never produced a movie before, but he nonetheless boldly demanded that in the deal he have the authority to make whatever pictures he wanted, a power that was not granted to even such proven Warner stars as Clint Eastwood or Steven Spielberg. Soon Ted Ashley announced his plans to retire again, a move that Steve Ross knew would make it easier to set up Geffen's deal.

Meanwhile, Geffen immersed himself in Hollywood again, schmoozing with actors, writers, and directors and hunting for a project he could produce. Before long, one came along. His friend Robert Towne was struggling in his effort to make a movie called *Personal Best*, about two female runners who have a love affair.

The movie had been developed by Warner Bros., but on July 20, 1980, production had been shuttered after only a month, when the seventy thousand members of the Screen Actors Guild (SAG) and the American Federation of Television and Radio Artists (AFTRA) went on strike. Warner Bros. agreed to let Towne make the movie independently, which allowed him to continue filming during the strike. His cast included many college athletes, and he argued that any delays would limit the athletes' ability to return to college and compete on the winter indoor circuit.

Warner Bros., for its part, was happy to be free of the project; after just one week of production, Towne was apparently already one month behind schedule. There were no complete scenes, just endless slow-motion closeups of sweat running off the brow of actress Mariel Hemingway. Warner Bros. doubted that Towne would ever complete the picture.

Towne's new problem was that he did not have the money to finish it on his own. David Geffen agreed to be the Good Samaritan and save Towne's movie. It was a gesture of exceptional generosity that carried a big risk; there was no commitment yet from a major distributor, and Geffen would be on the hook personally for the money until he got one.

He began plotting to secure a distribution deal, talking up the project first to Barry Diller at Paramount Pictures. Diller and Towne were also close, having been friends since childhood. Geffen and Diller made a secret pact that Paramount would announce plans to distribute the picture once the strike was over.

Geffen stumbled upon another huge pop star who was looking to make a label switch. He had known Elton John since the early 1970s. John and Geffen were both sexually attracted to men, and they bonded when John and his manager, John Reid, were sharing a house in Los Angeles.

In the late 1970s, Elton John had fallen into a creative slump and was blaming MCA, which had released his extraordinary run of hit albums over that decade. His last album, *21 at 33,* had one hit, "Little Jeannie," but it had failed to sell the huge number of albums to which he had become accustomed. What's more, he felt that MCA was not doing enough to promote his records. Geffen ran into him at a party at Rod Stewart's house and convinced him to sign to his label.

The music industry, meanwhile, was abuzz with reports that John Lennon was back in the studio and recording his first album in five years. He had been enjoying a long hiatus in which he and his wife, Yoko Ono, raised a son, Sean. Record executives circled like vultures: He was a free agent, no longer represented by Apple Records, the home of the Beatles and many of Lennon's solo albums. The report was that the new album would feature songs by both Lennon and Ono.

Music-industry executives began banging on the Lennons' door, begging to make their pitches. Lennon, though, was upset that his wife had not won the respect of fans, rock critics, and label chiefs, and he wanted this album to correct that situation. He insisted that Ono answer the many phone calls that came in. One by one, the executives dismissed her rudely and demanded to speak with Lennon. Each time, Lennon directed Ono to hang up.

Geffen was hot to sign John Lennon. He had met him that bizarre night in 1975 when he, Lennon, Cher, and Harry Nilsson had ended up in Hugh Hefner's hot tub after Phil Spector had waved a gun at Geffen.

Geffen had never met Yoko Ono, but he shrewdly figured out that she was the decision maker in the process. He sent her a telegram and asked for a meeting in which he could discuss with her the couple's recording future.

When the telegram arrived at the Dakota, the historic and enormous apartment building at the corner of Central Park West and Seventy-second Street where the Lennons lived, Ono read it and then showed it to her husband, who focused immediately on the fact that the telegram was addressed to her.

"Well, he's it, isn't he?" Lennon said. "He's the one we'll go with."

TRAGEDY OUTSIDE
THE DAKOTA

|||

Geffen was in New York to attend a concert Elton John was to give in Central Park when he received a message that Yoko Ono had telephoned. He did not believe it was actually her until he dialed the number the next morning and realized it was indeed the Hit Factory, the studio in midtown Manhattan where Lennon and Ono had been rumored to be recording.

"We want to talk to you about our record," Ono told Geffen on the telephone. "Can you come to meet with me?" She asked him to come to her office at the Dakota. Geffen was nervous about the meeting and, for one of the few times in his life, fretted about what to wear. He did some research and found that Ono had an affinity for white and that everything in her office was white. With that in mind, Geffen decided he would wear all white. Ono, dressed in black, stifled a laugh when her assistant ushered Geffen in, unsure if his getup was silly or sweet.

Regardless of what John Lennon thought, his wife's talent as a singer was questionable, and everybody knew she was also an odd duck. She asked Geffen for a slew of figures, including his phone number, address, and birthday. On the spot, she began analyzing them. She believed in signs, and Geffen had heard that if Ono determined that your numbers did not add up or were otherwise unlucky, you were finished. Luckily, Geffen's data pleased Ono, who said, "Yes, you have very good numbers."

Ono got down to business. "What do you know about us?" she quizzed Geffen.

Geffen responded truthfully that he knew only some of Lennon's records.

"What about my music?" she asked.

"Well, I've never heard any of your records."

"Really," Ono said. "That doesn't sound like a very good reason for me to make a deal with you."

"I'm a big fan of John's, and I have a great deal of respect for the two of you, and we do a very good job. We're a good record company."

"What do you mean you're a good record company?" Ono fired back. "You haven't put out a record yet!"

"Well, we're gonna be great," Geffen said.

" 'Gonna be,' 'gonna be,' who knows about 'gonna be'?"

When Ono next asked Geffen what he planned to pay them, he reverted to one of his tried-and-true dealmaking tricks, refusing to be the first to state a figure. He had learned his lesson since 1972. When Ono insisted that Geffen throw out a number, Geffen calmly declined. "You have to tell me what you want," he said, "and if I can give it to you, I will, and if I can't, I won't."

Ono relented and told Geffen she and Lennon were hunting for at least a million dollars per album. Geffen had already promised similar terms to Donna Summer and Elton John, so he did not hesitate before agreeing. "OK, we've got a deal," Geffen replied.

"Oh no, we haven't," she said. "That's just what I want. I don't know that I want it from you. I'll think about it. I'll call you later."

The next morning, Ono called Geffen and asked him to come to the office at the Dakota again. When he arrived, Ono spelled out a few more of the details that she wanted in the contract. Geffen quickly accepted.

"He's the one we'll go with": Geffen poses with his star signings,
John Lennon and Yoko Ono. (Michel Senecal)

"Don't you want to hear the music first?" she asked.

"No, I'll wait until whenever you want to play it for me."

Unknowingly, Geffen had passed that test, too. "If you wanted to hear the music before you made the deal, we wouldn't have gone with you," Ono said. She shook Geffen's hand.

It was only then that Ono called for John Lennon to come join them in her white office. It was the first time Geffen had seen Lennon since 1975.

Lennon and Ono took Geffen to the Hit Factory and played the record they planned to call *Double Fantasy.* It had fourteen songs, split equally between Lennon and Ono. Geffen sensed that two of Lennon's songs, "(Just Like) Starting Over" and "Woman," had the makings of big hits.

He told Lennon he thought the album would be a major success. But Lennon was unsettled about the whole process and fretted about the effects of his self-imposed layoff. Indeed, even the feel of the instruments had become unfamiliar to him.

"You must remember," Lennon told Geffen, "I haven't picked up a guitar in six years. I forgot how heavy they are. The last time I was in the studio, they didn't have all this equipment."

On the way out of the Hit Factory, Lennon pulled Geffen aside. "You know, we have to take care of Yoko," he said. "You and I have what we set out to get, but Yoko never got [the respect] she deserves. And that has to be our goal with this record."

Now armed with his superstar lineup, Geffen soon came across another image-burnishing opportunity. He used his friendship with Linda Ronstadt, who was now dating California governor Jerry Brown, to obtain a seat on the University of California board of regents. It was ironic indeed that the uneducated boy who had built a career starting with a lie that he had graduated from UCLA now became part of the body that governed the state's higher-education system. Geffen got the headlines he wanted: Breaking the news of his appointment, the Los Angeles *Herald Examiner* ran his picture on the front page.

He was convinced his three star signings would guarantee his new label a launch the likes of which the record industry had never before seen. But Geffen soon discovered that there were unpredictable elements in the mix that he never expected. Although the fawning press and publicity generated by the signings was impressive, there was trouble behind the scenes almost from the day the deals were announced.

Donna Summer, for example, had undergone a major personal transformation. Burned out from the grind of exhausting tours, Summer had been hospitalized for depression. Terrified and suicidal, she cried out to God—and he answered. Suddenly, her depressive behavior changed, and she stopped taking the medication that doctors had prescribed. Summer believed it was her prayers that had done the job. She became a born-again Christian.

From a commercial point of view, it was not a good thing that the woman who had made a fortune essentially climaxing on record tracks had found Jesus. Having pocketed Geffen's seven-figure advance, she finally told him about her reorganized life's priorities. She was no longer interested in making her old kind of albums, she said. The artist, one of the few disco stars to write her own material, now wanted to dabble in more standard rock 'n' roll.

Summer also got married that year, and before long she was pregnant. The pregnancy unleashed hormonal havoc, and she also developed a serious case of writer's block. Geffen was horrified at the developments but staunchly supported her, crossing his fingers that her creativity would return and that her fans, too, might be interested in a change in style.

Geffen and Summer became fast friends, and she spent hours at the house on Angelo Drive. She found it difficult to work at home and was more comfortable working on her music at the piano in Geffen's house. Geffen got a big charge as she composed her song "Sometimes like Butterflies" in his living room.

But when the album, called *The Wanderer,* was finished, it was clear that it was not going to tear up the charts the way *Bad Girls* or any of the other Casablanca records had. Warner Bros. and Geffen nonetheless worked up a massive promotional push, and some in the record industry predicted it would be a big hit.

But it was not. Although the title track became Summer's ninth gold single in a row, the album peaked at number thirteen on *Billboard*'s chart and fell out of the top fifty after just two months.

Geffen lashed out at the rock stations, charging them with racism. "The problem with Donna's album," Geffen told the *Los Angeles Times,* "is that it's a rock record, but rock stations aren't playing it because of a prejudice against black artists and female artists. When you look at a rock station playlist and can't find a single black act, I think there's something radically wrong, and it has nothing to do with Donna Summer." One of the ironies in the situation was that Summer was one of the very few nonwhite artists Geffen ever signed. The truth was that Donna Summer's fans did not like what they heard.

If Geffen was disappointed with Donna Summer, that disappointment turned to dismay when Elton John turned in his first album, *The Fox.* Geffen did not like the songs, and stunned John by giving him a blisteringly candid review. John, arguably the biggest pop star of the 1970s, was not used to having his work judged harshly by music executives.

Years earlier, John had had a falling-out with his longtime collaborator, lyricist Bernie Taupin, and was now writing songs only sporadically with him. Geffen thought the songs John was writing with others were not very good and thought that more hits would come if John would simply agree to reteam with Taupin.

Geffen told John flatly that he would not release the album until he went back into the studio and improved it. John agreed to work with Taupin, and Geffen engineered a vacation in which they all went to Hawaii to give the album another try. They stayed with Allan Carr, the flamboyant producer of *Grease,* and got to work.

John Lennon and Yoko Ono's *Double Fantasy* was released at the end of November 1980. Critically, it received only lukewarm notices, with reviewers dismissing it as slight. John Rockwell, a critic at *The New York Times,* wrote that the songs "represent a tired recycling of his youthful idioms." But hard-core Beatles fans rushed to buy it anyway, and the album charted modest sales at record outlets.

Allen Grubman kept the Hall & Oates talks alive with Geffen, and the two men finally met one day for lunch at the Beverly Hills Hotel. Grubman had become a star lawyer in the music business in the late 1970s during Geffen's retirement, and the two did not know each other. They enjoyed each other's company and chatted about growing up in Brooklyn and landmarks there such as Nathan's Famous hot dogs at Coney Island. They cut a deal within twenty minutes.

But with *The Wanderer* a bust, reviews for *Double Fantasy* unimpressive, and prospects for a hit Elton John record slim, Geffen began to get nervous. Warner Bros. Records was apprehensive about the huge amount of money Geffen had committed to the star acts and questioned whether a Hall & Oates deal would be a prudent move. He had three tired acts, and it looked like he was about to flush more money down the drain on a fourth.

Geffen telephoned Allen Grubman and gingerly felt him out on the possibility of getting out of the deal. "Allen, I have a problem," he started. "The people at Warners have a real concern about whether we should do this deal. If there were any way that you could help me out, by making a deal somewhere else, I would appreciate it. If not, we have a deal. We shook hands, and I will honor it." Grubman and Geffen were sort of simpatico in their outlooks on life, and they shared the belief that rules were made as guidelines and not as hard-and-fast laws. If one needed to bend a rule here or there to achieve a goal or make a deal, Geffen and Grubman both believed, then so be it.

Grubman offered to try to off-load the deal onto another label. Clive Davis, now heading Arista Records, had long been interested in Hall &

Oates, so Grubman called him. "We're about to close a deal with Hall and Oates with David Geffen on the West Coast," Grubman told Davis. He then got creative about the circumstances surrounding the deal: "The guys, though, really are not that crazy about the West Coast," he said. "If you're willing to come to the table, I might be able to do something."

Davis fell for it and made the deal. By the time the deal with Arista took effect, Hall & Oates's popularity had waned, and Davis had a money loser on his hands. Geffen, for his part, had been spared what could have been another embarrassment, and for that he had Allen Grubman to thank.

G effen was back in New York on Monday, December 8, when Yoko Ono called and said she and Lennon wanted him to come to the Record Plant in midtown Manhattan. When Geffen entered the studio, Lennon was jumping up and down and dancing around the room. Ono was sitting in a chair in the corner with a serious expression on her face.

"Wait'll you hear Yoko's record. It's a smash!" Lennon said. He put on a song called "Walking on Thin Ice." "This is better than anything we did on *Double Fantasy*."

"Oh, John, it's not that great," Ono said, embarrassed.

"Oh yes it is," he said. "It's better than anything the B-52's ever did. And we want you to put it out before Christmas."

"Let's put it out *after* Christmas and really do the thing right," Geffen told Lennon and Ono. "Take out an ad."

"An ad!" Lennon exclaimed to Yoko. "Listen to this, Mother, you're gonna get an *ad*!"

Lennon then told Geffen that Annie Leibovitz had photographed them that morning for an upcoming *Rolling Stone* cover story. Jann Wenner wanted a photo of Lennon alone for the cover, but Lennon convinced Leibovitz that the photo should include Ono, too.

"Oh, it was really great," Lennon told Geffen. "I got undressed and wrapped myself around Yoko."

"You got *undressed*?" Geffen asked.

"It's gonna be great!" he said.

The Lennons had few friends, and soon Geffen had become one of their most trusted and dependable confidants. He asked the Lennons if they wanted to go with him to see David Bowie in *The Elephant Man* on Broadway. They said that they would indeed like to see the play. They also talked to Geffen about a record they wanted to do that would be called *Yoko Only*.

Geffen had to go. "Maybe we'll have dinner tomorrow," he told them.

"Great," Lennon said. "Where do you want to eat?"

"We don't have to make that decision right now," Geffen said.

"Yeah, that's right," Lennon said.

Geffen returned home to his apartment on Fifth Avenue, turned off the telephone ringer, and got into bed. As had been the case on many previous nights, lying next to him was a male prostitute. A little after 11:00 P.M., Geffen turned over in bed and noticed that the light was flashing on his phone. He picked it up and heard a woman screaming on the other end of the line.

"I'm a friend of Yoko's. John's just been shot," the woman said. "They're at Roosevelt Hospital. Run right over."

Geffen thought it was a crank call and hung up. A moment later, however, he picked up the phone and called the Record Plant just to make sure. It was not possible, the security guard at the studio told him. Lennon and Ono had just left in a limousine ten minutes earlier. It *was* a crank call, Geffen decided.

The phone rang again. It was the same woman. "Why haven't you left?" she said. "He's shot! She needs you!"

Another line rang. It was Eddie Rosenblatt, who was in town, staying at the Sherry Netherland Hotel, next door to Geffen's apartment. Rosenblatt told him he had been watching *Monday Night Football* on TV when Howard Cosell broke the news that Lennon had been shot.

"Meet me downstairs," Geffen told Rosenblatt. "We're going over to the hospital."

Lennon and Ono had left the Record Plant at about ten-thirty, picked up dinner, and then headed home. When Lennon got out of the limousine in the driveway at the Dakota, Mark David Chapman, a deranged twenty-five-year-old who had lived in New York for less than a week, stepped out of an alcove and fired several shots into Lennon's back with a .38-caliber revolver.

Chapman was a disturbed fan who had talked of killing Lennon for some time. He came to New York to do just that and had stalked the singer outside the Dakota for a few days. At 5:00 P.M. on the day of the murder, Lennon had even obliged Chapman with an autograph after Chapman had thrust a copy of *Double Fantasy* in front of him as he and Ono left their home en route to the Record Plant.

News of Lennon's shooting spread quickly, and crowds of fans caused pandemonium outside Roosevelt Hospital. Geffen struggled through the throngs of people to the doors to the emergency room, but he could not get past the police. "I'm David Geffen!" he yelled frantically. "I'm expected! Yoko's expecting me!"

Geffen pushed his way past the cops and slipped into the hospital, finding a hysterical Ono in a small room. "Someone's shot John," she told him as he held her in his arms. "Can you believe it? Someone shot him."

A policeman motioned Geffen outside and told him the shattering news that had already reached Ono. "He's dead. He died on arrival at the hospital."

Geffen and Rosenblatt accompanied Ono back to the Dakota shortly after midnight. Rosenblatt went back to his hotel, but Geffen stayed with Ono for a few hours as she made a handful of telephone calls, including one to Julian, Lennon's son from his first marriage. Five-year-old Sean Lennon was asleep in the apartment.

Hundreds of fans had congregated outside the Dakota by midnight, and the vigil grew to more than one thousand by one o'clock. The crowd began chanting lyrics to Lennon's songs. Some raised peace signs. Others lit matches and lighters and held them solemnly in the air.

The next morning, Lennon's assassination was the lead story on the front page of *The New York Times,* complete with a photograph of a stricken Ono being escorted out of the hospital by Geffen. The newspaper accounts said that Chapman was safely in jail.

Ono was paralyzed by the loss. She complained of weak knees and rarely left her bed. In part because the vigil outside continued for days, it was not a quiet time for the mourning Lennon family. Ono's bedroom faced the front of the Dakota, so it was impossible to escape the noise from outside. Some days, as many as two thousand mourners gathered. Many cried and screamed uncontrollably. At other times, Lennon's music was played on a loudspeaker and the crowd listened in silence.

After a few days, Geffen grew concerned that Ono had grown dangerously despondent. He enlisted the help of Calvin Klein to try to cheer her up. He was also worried that she had not eaten anything, so he and Klein orchestrated an escape out the back of the Dakota. They took her to an out-of-the-way restaurant called the Blue Book on East 116th Street.

Wary of appearing exploitative, Geffen directed his marketing team to halt all advertising for *Double Fantasy.* News of this only added to the sales frenzy. The album jumped ten spots in one week to number one on *Billboard*'s album chart, while the single "(Just Like) Starting Over" jumped to the top as well. Record stores across the country rationed copies of the album. Geffen Records was only a few months old, but it had an enormous hit on its hands.

Double Fantasy became Lennon's best-selling post-Beatles album, eclipsing the formidable sales charted by *Imagine* and *Walls and Bridges.* The publicity surrounding his death was extraordinary and prompted excessive debate. The *Rolling Stone* cover with Leibovitz's shot of a naked Lennon crawling like a white mouse up a clothed Ono prompted cries of shock. Ono was naturally sensitive to anything written about her late husband and was especially outraged over an article in *Billboard* that was headlined LENNON'S EGO AND INTRANSIGENCE IRRITATED

THOSE WHO KNEW HIM. The article called Lennon an "unthinkably rude" person.

Taking his cue from Ono, Geffen announced his company would not advertise in *Billboard* for a month. Geffen called its coverage "unforgivably insensitive" and said it could not be ignored. "To allow it to go unnoticed would be to say that nobody gives a shit," Geffen said. "I do give a shit." The next week, *Billboard* apologized for the article, stating, "This publication . . . had no intention of offending anyone." Despite the apology, Geffen kept to his boycott.

He now had a major hit at his record company, but *Personal Best* suddenly threatened to ruin him. Barry Diller had promised that Paramount Pictures would release the movie after the SAG/AFTRA strike was over, but as the picture's budget spiraled out of control, Diller changed his mind. Geffen lost his temper, disbelieving that his friend would renege. Geffen and Diller had another of their legendary screaming fights, but Diller stood firm, and Geffen found himself once again without a distributor.

He next phoned his friend Alan Hirschfield, now the chairman of Twentieth Century Fox, and begged him to give him a movie deal there. But Sherry Lansing, whom Hirschfield had recently installed as the studio's head of production, refused to make the deal.

"Are you kidding?" Lansing told Hirschfield. "David Geffen is the laughingstock of Hollywood. Do you know what kind of signal this will send to the business if the first big deal I announce is with *him*?" Geffen did not know where to turn next.

Two days before Christmas, a desperate Geffen shut down production on *Personal Best*. He said that Robert Towne had lied to him about what had already been shot and what was left to shoot. "Towne had spent five million and there wasn't a coherent scene in the entire movie," Geffen told friends. Though he denied he used coke, Towne was considered a notorious drug abuser in Hollywood at the time, and Geffen alleged that his addictions had incapacitated him. He told

Towne that they should regroup over the holidays and assess what exactly was left to shoot. Towne suspected something was up, however, when Geffen barred him from doing any editing on the picture during the hiatus.

The reality was that Geffen's next move was far more vindictive than anything Towne imagined. In a move so boldly Machiavellian that it could have fit into a scene in Towne's script for *Chinatown,* Geffen threatened to back out of the picture altogether unless Towne agreed to sign a contract committing him to write and direct his next two movies for Geffen's new film company. Given that Towne and Geffen could not possibly ever work in harmony again, it was a twisted demand that Geffen almost certainly knew would cripple Towne's career. Geffen telephoned Towne's wife, Julie, and predicted financial ruin if Bob did not sign the papers.

Geffen's friends and colleagues were amazed at the rage and vitriol he exercised in his attack against Towne. To many, it was astounding to see how delighted and animated he became in describing his plan to destroy the director. Many simply could not recall or imagine Geffen ever being equally enthusiastic when discussing a creative issue or anything that was otherwise good. It was not enough for him to win; his foe had to lose.

The *Personal Best* drama also pitted Geffen against two other players in Hollywood, Michael Ovitz and Bert Fields, Towne's agent and lawyer, respectively. Geffen was furious at both when they voiced staunch opposition to his demand. They recognized that Geffen and Towne were ill suited to work together and argued that such an agreement would tie up the next six to seven years of Towne's life.

After the drama finally ended, Geffen was so impressed with Fields that he hired him to handle his non-music-industry legal affairs. But Mike Ovitz, who six years earlier had founded Creative Artists Agency, the talent shop that was fast becoming Hollywood's hottest, was another matter. Geffen took Ovitz's advice to Towne as a personal attack and never understood that Ovitz was simply representing the best interests of his client. Geffen's hatred for Ovitz grew exponentially as

Ovitz, like Geffen a former agent at William Morris, within a few years was referred to routinely as "the most powerful man in Hollywood." Geffen determined to make his life a living hell.

After refusing to sign the agreements, Towne suspected that Geffen might steal the film he had already shot, so he took it first. One night, from his office on the Warner Bros. lot, he took about 40 percent of the film and the accompanying soundtrack home. The next day, security guards at Warner Bros. kicked him out, along with his furniture, and slapped new locks on his bungalow.

Geffen thought that Towne would fold, but he did not. Towne began hunting for other money and scheduled twelve days of wrap-up lensing in March after Allen Klein, the Rolling Stones' former manager, offered to cover the costs. When Geffen found out about Towne's plans, he threatened to sue everyone involved. Fearful of exposing his cast and crew to the monstrous litigation he knew Geffen was capable of, Towne scrapped the shooting plans.

Geffen moaned constantly to his psychiatrist, Martin Grotjahn, whom he had begun seeing again after moving back to Los Angeles, about the *Personal Best* debacle. He had tried to do someone a favor and ended up getting killed. He called himself an "idiot" for giving Towne the money without a signed contract. "I am fighting with people in negotiations, and I don't want to fight," Geffen told Grotjahn. "I am too emotionally involved in this. It's bad for me and bad for business."

Dr. Grotjahn suggested Geffen ought to hire a lawyer for whom he was the only client, an idea Geffen thought was inspired. He figured that a lawyer could do all his negotiations and that in turn might help him stop tangling with so many people.

Geffen returned to the office on Sunset Boulevard and told Carole Childs about his shrink's advice. Childs's eyes lit up as she told him that he should hire an attorney named Eric Eisner.

"I've never heard of him," Geffen replied. "Where does he work?"

Childs explained that Eisner worked in the music department at Ziffren, Brittenham, Gullen, and Ingber.

"Why would you think he'd be the right person for me?"

"Because Eric has a heart of stone," she said.

A devilish smile played across Geffen's face. He agreed that a cold-hearted shark was precisely what he needed. Geffen wanted an advocate to negotiate his deals, fiercely protect his interests, and hammer out the fine points after he approved the broad strokes.

Geffen arranged to meet Eisner and was instantly smitten with him. Born in New York City, Eisner was a dashing thirty-three-year-old bachelor who had gone into entertainment law after graduating from Columbia Law School in 1973. No relation to Michael Eisner, then at Paramount Pictures, Eric Eisner had risen to partner at the respected Hollywood law firm.

He was tall, straight, college educated, and athletic—in many ways, the perfect heterosexual Geffen never got to be. In Eisner, Geffen saw his straight idol, found him irresistible, and wooed him with promises of a large salary and a large role at the company.

Eisner wanted to have the title of president; since Eddie Rosenblatt was already president of Geffen Records, Geffen offered Eisner the presidency of a newly formed David Geffen Company. In addition to handling Geffen's legal and business affairs, he would also head up the movie unit, even though he had no experience in the film business. It was quite a package for someone who was essentially the company's business-affairs man.

Instead of treating him as his employee, Geffen treated him as a friend and began including him in his social plans. He invited Eisner to spend time with him at his house and encouraged him and his friends to swim in the pool and enjoy meals prepared by Geffen's cook, Alice.

Just as Batya back in Borough Park went about "fixing" people who did not necessarily ask or need to be fixed, David began repackaging Eisner. He tried to make him into the perfect heterosexual Hollywood power player he himself wanted to be.

Geffen told Eisner he needed to get a nose job and suggested a plastic surgeon for the task. Similarly, Geffen told Carole Childs she needed an eye lift. Both had the operations and recuperated at the Angelo Drive house afterward. It seemed to be a classic case of projection, arising from Geffen's insecurities about his own looks. Indeed, he himself had become an ardent supporter of a Beverly Hills dermatologist named Arnold Klein, who gave him collagen injections designed to smooth out the wrinkles that were beginning to form on his face.

"I'm just a boy from Brooklyn who wishes he were six feet tall, with blond hair and blue eyes," Geffen told *Vanity Fair* years later. "That's who I really am."

I n the spring of 1981, Geffen became a proponent of a much hoped-for reunion concert by Paul Simon and Art Garfunkel. A proposal was floated that the two, who had split up in 1971, reunite for a tour that would include a concert in Central Park.

Geffen was friendly with both men, and, as he had with Bob Dylan and the Band in 1974, elected himself matchmaker. At best, Simon was ambivalent about a reunion with Garfunkel. He was enjoying the fruits of his successful solo career and did not wish to revisit his past partnership.

But Geffen saw it as a slam-dunk moneymaker for both and pressed Simon to put aside any problems he had with Garfunkel, do the concert, and record it for a live album. Partly swayed by Geffen's appeals, Simon agreed to the deal, and a September 19 concert date was set for Central Park. News of the alliance created a firestorm of publicity, and a deal to televise the concert was set.

At first glance, it seemed that Geffen had nothing to gain in encouraging the reunion, given that Garfunkel was under contract to CBS's Columbia label and Simon was a Warner Bros. artist. Warners was to handle the album's domestic distribution; CBS got international rights. But Geffen was to insinuate himself into the project and share in the publicity and profits from the concert recording. But it would happen at a terrible cost to him.

BIG DREAMS

|||

G effen's friend Michael Bennett, the creator of *A Chorus Line,* told him about the new Broadway musical he had been developing. Set mostly in the 1960s, it told the story of three young black women and their almost-overnight rise to the top of the pop-music world as a group called the Dreamettes. Bennett denied reports in the theater community that the musical was a thinly veiled history of the Supremes.

Bennett invited Geffen to attend a workshop production of the show, which was called *Big Dreams,* at the cavernous rehearsal studios he owned at 890 Broadway. His idea was to snare Geffen as a backer. Bennett was wowed by the story of how Geffen had snagged John Lennon's last album. Plus, the show was about the music business.

But *Big Dreams* sustained a major setback two days before Bennett and his company of actors were scheduled to perform the show for Geffen and other prospective investors. Jennifer Holliday, a heavy twenty-one-year-old from Houston whom Bennett had cast in the pivotal role of Effie Melody White, blew up and quit when Bennett decided to drop one of the character's songs, "Faith in Myself."

Although the cast was made up of unknowns and designed to have an ensemble feel, the creators recognized from the moment they discovered Holliday that she had the potential to break out as a star. This was in large part due to the show's first-act finale in which a despairing Holliday reached deep into her soul and belted a roof-shattering ballad called "And I Am Telling You I'm Not Going."

Holliday was gifted, but she was also fragile and moody, and Bennett had tired of sparring with her. Tom Eyen, who wrote the musical's book and lyrics, begged Bennett to pursue her. But Bennett refused to be manipulated by such grandstanding and found another actress to sing the role.

Geffen attended the workshop with Bernard Jacobs, head of the Shubert Organization. Jacobs was a brilliant, hard-driving, but grandfatherly mogul who had long served as Michael Bennett's leading patron. He and his wife, Betty, were like surrogate parents to him.

Jacobs and Geffen loved the workshop of *Big Dreams,* even though the actress with the most powerful performance was not there. It was now time for the two of them to talk money with Bennett. Thanks to a high-tech set dominated by revolving light towers and elaborate costumes, *Big Dreams* was positioned to be the most expensive musical ever mounted on Broadway, costing $3.5 million. Geffen did not flinch at the price tag, eyeing instead the opportunity to return to his roots on a grand scale.

It had been twenty-eight years since ten-year-old David had taken the subway to Times Square from Brooklyn to see musicals. Now he was about to enter the ranks of the biggest and most important producers along the Great White Way, bankrolling the man who at the moment was unquestionably musical theater's biggest star. The Shubert Organization and Geffen Records, along with ABC and Metromedia, offered to put up the money to finance the show. It was Geffen's first Broadway investment.

In return, Geffen obtained the rights to release the show's original-cast album. He also purchased, for one million dollars, the right to turn the musical into a movie. Radio stations typically dismissed Broadway

*"Broadway history . . . a show that strikes with
the speed and heat of lightning": co-producer Bob Avian,
Geffen, actress Deborah Burrell, director Michael
Bennett, and Bernard Jacobs of the Shubert Organization
at the opening of* Dreamgirls. (Peter Borsari)

cast albums as stodgy, but Geffen believed there were possible hit singles in the show. He argued successfully that the cast album should be put together by a hot record producer and be compiled as a pop album.

Within several weeks, Bennett concluded that Tom Eyen and others who said that no one could play Effie except Jennifer Holliday were right. He tracked her down and convinced her to return to the show. Geffen soon heard Holliday sing the role and was captivated by her shattering performance; he offered her a solo recording contract at Geffen Records.

Geffen was a hands-off producer who stayed in the background. But Bennett and his longtime producing partner, Bob Avian, welcomed Geffen's advice and comments. Geffen spoke up after one workshop production, objecting to a feminist anthem called "I Am Somebody" that the character of Deena Jones sang; he said that female R&B singers did not sing such songs in the early 1960s. "You're in the wrong period," Geffen said. The song was cut.

Some opinions he offered had nothing to do with the production. Geffen shocked Bob Avian, for example, by telling him that he ought to see a plastic surgeon and get an eye lift.

Geffen also offered one other crucial piece of advice. He did not like the musical's title and suggested *Dreamgirls*. Bennett and the other producers thought he was right, and the new title was adopted. Plans were drawn up for a nine-week out-of-town tryout in Boston, and the cast went into rehearsal.

G effen and Robert Towne were still at odds in June 1981, and weekly interest payments of sixty thousand dollars had caused the budget of *Personal Best,* on which nary a frame had been shot since before Christmas, to double, to fifteen million dollars. Geffen's troubles intensified when the bankers at Boston Ventures, the firm that had loaned Geffen the money to make the movie, called in the loan. They were nervous that he had not found a distributor and even more concerned that he would not be able to pay the money back. Geffen had collateralized the loan by putting up his homes and other personal assets. Now he feared he would lose everything. Geffen began to tell people that this was the single worst thing that had ever happened to him.

Geffen and Barry Diller, meanwhile, had not spoken for several months after their blowup when Diller chose not to distribute the movie. But the storm eventually passed, and the two resumed their friendship. Diller even offered to take another look at *Personal Best.* He said Paramount would distribute the movie subject to a screening of the footage that was available. Towne and Geffen were not on speaking terms, but they arranged through their lawyers to meet at Diller's house with all the film that existed.

Diller told Michael Eisner, his top lieutenant, that he wanted to release the picture as a favor to Geffen. Geffen, Towne, Diller, and Eisner began to watch the film in Diller's living room. Minutes after it started, Diller and Eisner exchanged dubious glances as they realized that the movie was a terrific mess. Releasing it, they knew, would surely mean saying good-bye to whatever money they paid for it.

When the lights came up, Diller and Eisner looked uneasily at each other and then at Geffen and Towne, who were counting on a simple agreement. Instead, Diller looked at the two and said, "Excuse us. We're going to have to go talk about this." Geffen and Towne were utterly nonplussed.

Diller and Eisner went upstairs to a guest room and burst out into gales of laughter. "What the hell are we going to do now?" Eisner said.

"What's worse?" Diller asked. "Going back in that room and telling them we're not going to distribute the picture, or distributing it even though we don't want to?"

The tension in the living room, meanwhile, was so palpable as to be unbearable. Geffen and Towne, who despised each other, did not speak a single word. They paced in opposite corners.

After about twenty minutes, Diller returned to the living room to tell Geffen and Towne that they had not yet reached a decision. "We just have to talk this through," Diller told them. "Don't misunderstand or anything, we know we have to make a decision, it's like yes or no. Just give us some more time."

Geffen was stupefied. His anxiety level, already elevated, shot up several more notches. Towne also feared the outcome of the debate. Seeking relief, he helped himself to the scotch in Diller's bar.

Back in the guest room, Diller and Eisner were distraught. They tried to devise scenarios for releasing the movie that would minimize any financial loss. They knew that as top executives of a publicly traded company the responsible thing was to pass. But that raised an uncomfortable question: "Are you going to tell them or am I?" Diller asked Eisner.

Diller darted into the living room about every fifteen minutes for the next two hours to apologize to Geffen and Towne, saying that he and Eisner had not yet reached a verdict. Towne threw back a number of glasses of scotch. Geffen had the doomed expression of a parent learning that an operation on a child had gone horribly wrong.

"I promise we'll give you an answer just as soon as possible," Diller said, disappearing again.

At one o'clock in the morning, Eisner finally made the decision that both he and Diller knew had to be made. "Look, we're not going to release this movie," Eisner said. "But I'm so exhausted I have to leave."

"You're not leaving!" Diller said, looking at his watch. "You can't leave until we give them our decision!" Diller reluctantly agreed to deliver the bad news but insisted that Eisner stand at his side as he did so.

In the living room, Towne swilled another drink and then stumbled to the couch, where he fell onto the cushions in a heap and passed out. Geffen grumbled as Towne began snoring loudly. He looked up hopefully as Diller and Eisner emerged together for the first time all night.

"David, we're not going to distribute the movie," Diller said.

"Fine, fuck it!" Geffen said, his eager expression turning at once to anger. He began heading for the front door.

"Wait!" Diller yelled. "Take Bob Towne out of here!"

"Bob Towne?" Geffen exclaimed standing in the doorway. "I hope he dies!" He left the house, slamming the door behind him. Watching

Geffen peel out of the driveway, Eisner said good night to Diller and left him alone with Towne.

"Bob!" Diller yelled in Towne's ear. Towne did not stir. Diller let out a frustrated sigh, threw a blanket over the director, and went upstairs to bed, locking his bedroom door behind him.

The next morning, Diller was happy to find that Towne was gone. He had gotten up in the middle of the night and struggled home.

Geffen was panicked and decided that there was only one person left who could bail him out: Steve Ross. Geffen had some leverage to demand help, he figured, because the John Lennon/Yoko Ono album was the biggest hit that any of Warner's record labels had had that year. Geffen found the home phone number for Jay Emmett, Ross's chief associate with responsibility for the company's movie operations, and begged him to pick up the cost of *Personal Best*.

"Jay, you gotta help me," an agitated Geffen implored. "I put up all my real estate. I'm into Bill Thompson at Boston Ventures for eight million."

"Take it easy, David," Emmett said. "We might be able to work something out."

Ross did not contemplate the situation for long before deciding to rescue Geffen. While Ross thought that it represented a bad misstep on Geffen's part, he also knew that Geffen's batting average was strong. He bet that Geffen would later hit home runs that would more than make up for the loss the company would take on this one picture. He reasoned that Geffen would be thankful for the help and would probably rededicate himself to succeeding for the company in the years ahead.

Ross instructed Bob Daly, who had succeeded Ted Ashley as chairman of Warner Bros., to strike a deal in which the movie studio would create a production company for Geffen to run. *Personal Best* would be its first release. Frank Wells continued to oppose the idea, but he was overruled by Ross and Daly. Within a year, Wells left the company, anxious to pursue a personal dream of climbing the world's highest peaks.

Geffen's film deal was extraordinary: It gave him the right to use Warners' money to make whatever movies he chose, up to a certain budget level, with no approval necessary from Daly or Terry Semel, who had been promoted to be Daly's number-two man. It was an authority that was never granted any other filmmaker at Warner Bros. But at his own insistence, Geffen would not be paid any money on any film he made that did not post a profit. When a movie crossed into the black, however, Geffen would be paid a whopping 10 percent of the gross. "I don't want to get paid if a movie doesn't succeed," Geffen told Daly.

As it turned out, Bob Towne was the big loser in the deal. As a condition to finance the completion of *Personal Best,* Warner Bros. forced him to give up his dream of directing "Greystoke," a Tarzan script on which he had worked for more than eight years. They paid him one million dollars for the rights, but they put part of the fee in escrow against any additional overbudgeting offenses on *Personal Best.* Towne went to Terry Semel's house in the middle of the night and shouted up at his bedroom window, begging him not to take "Greystoke" away from him.

Filming of *Personal Best* finally wrapped in July 1981, a full year after it had begun at the Olympic trials in the summer of 1980. But the fight between Geffen and Towne still had one final, ugly chapter before the *Personal Best* drama ended.

Geffen was an information junkie who stumped his friends by frequently learning news before it appeared in the papers. He was in the car with Eddie Rosenblatt, driving to a barbecue restaurant in 1981, when he told Rosenblatt about a mysterious illness that was striking and killing gay men in alarming numbers. The Centers for Disease Control had slowly identified the disease; soon it would be given the name AIDS. Geffen was troubled that he himself might contract it; after a test was developed, he took it and tested negative. He was among the lucky ones to dodge the AIDS bullet—especially lucky given his promiscuity.

Geffen, who frequently told Rosenblatt more about his sex life than Rosenblatt cared to hear, then turned the talk to business. Geffen told Rosenblatt that Warner Communications' international record-distribution company had just offered him one million dollars a year for three years in exchange for foreign rights to Geffen Records. Geffen said he thought the offer was chintzy.

Betting he could make more money if he sold the foreign rights to his records to another company, Geffen called his attorney friend Allen Grubman and asked him to test the marketplace. "What could you get me for the foreign rights to my label?" Geffen asked him.

"Fifteen million to seventeen million," Grubman responded.

"You get me fifteen million to seventeen million and you're my lawyer!" Geffen said gleefully.

Grubman knew which of Warner Communications' competitors to call first: Walter Yetnikoff, the foulmouthed chairman of CBS Records. CBS was Warner's biggest rival, and Yetnikoff delighted in besting Warner in any kind of deal.

"Walter, this is an opportunity of a lifetime," Grubman started, with his trademark salesmanship. "How would you like to be in business with Geffen Records?" Yetnikoff liked Geffen and believed he was a talented record man. But as Grubman predicted, he was most excited about the opportunity to strike at Warner. Grubman and Yetnikoff flew to California to meet with Geffen, who sold Yetnikoff on the deal after predicting he would soon release big hits, including his first record by Elton John and his second with Donna Summer. Yetnikoff signed a foreign-distribution deal worth fifteen million dollars a year for three years. And David Geffen had a new lawyer.

The deal irritated many people at Warner Communications, who claimed it said much about the depth of Geffen's loyalty. Mo Ostin, though, was one person who was happy about it; he knew that the annual foreign advance would come through the joint venture and cover much of the label's heavy start-up costs. It meant there was now little downside to the joint-venture deal with Geffen Records.

For Yetnikoff and CBS, however, the deal looked to be an almost instant loser. Despite Elton John's reteaming with Bernie Taupin, his album *The Fox* was a flop. Geffen reeled as the gigantic financial bet he had placed on the star soured and the comeback he had hoped to mastermind failed to materialize. Released in June 1981, *The Fox* featured Taupin/John collaborations on four of the eleven tracks, but critics said they were not even the best cuts on the record.

Geffen's other big-money star was not doing much better. Exasperated at the failure of *The Wanderer,* Geffen prayed that Donna Summer and her producer, Giorgio Moroder, would come up with a big winner the second time around. But in the summer of 1981, Summer and Moroder invited Geffen to New York to hear a new batch of songs. He was unimpressed. In an effort to rev Summer up, Geffen fired Moroder and hired the celebrated producer Quincy Jones.

The only bonafide hit the label had all year was a band called Quarterflash that Carole Childs had found in Portland, Oregon. Originally named Seafood Mama, the group was anchored by the husband-and-wife team of Marv and Rindy Ross; it was interesting only because Rindy was a rare female saxophone player. Their self-titled debut album went platinum and contained a hit called "Harden My Heart."

Warner Communications, in partnership with American Express, launched MTV in August 1981. It was the first twenty-four-hour cable music channel, and Geffen was among the first to recognize its potential power. He saw clearly what others did not: Music videos are record advertisements. He ordered up videos for many of his groups, including Quarterflash and Asia, a new group featuring former members of Yes that was preparing its first album. He even saw that MTV's strength would be to take a group like Quarterflash, a not particularly unique band, and put them before music fans in a new venue.

Meanwhile, Geffen hoped that Joni Mitchell and Neil Young would help make his new enterprise a winner. He gave both artists rich deals equal to the multimillion-dollar contracts he had extended to Elton John, Donna Summer, and John Lennon and Yoko Ono.

Afterter a successful tryout in Boston, *Dreamgirls* was preparing for its December 20 opening at the Imperial Theatre on West Forty-fifth Street. The day of the opening, Geffen was so excited that he wrapped up a David Hockney painting and sent it over to Michael Bennett as an opening-night gift.

Geffen put on his tuxedo and attended the opening night with Bernie and Betty Jacobs. They sat in orchestra seats and thrilled at the groundbreaking production Bennett had created. The crowd had a wildly positive reaction to the show, and many people stood up and cheered throughout such winning numbers as Jennifer Holliday's Act 1 finale.

At the opening-night party, Geffen and his fellow producers waited anxiously for the early edition of the next day's *New York Times* to be delivered by messenger. Frank Rich, the *Times*'s theater critic, was Broadway's most important reviewer. His critique had the power to determine whether *Dreamgirls* would have a short or long run.

As the producers feverishly scanned the review, they realized it was indeed the rave they had prayed for: "When Broadway history is being made, you can feel it," Rich wrote. "What you feel is a seismic emotional jolt that sends the audience, as one, right out of its wits. While such moments are uncommonly rare these days, I'm here to report that one popped up at the Imperial last night." Rich described the extraordinary star turn by Jennifer Holliday, and praised Michael Bennett too, reporting that he "has fashioned a show that strikes with the speed and heat of lightning."

Other critics, as it turned out, were not as enthusiastic in their assessments of the show. And in the coming months, *Dreamgirls* encountered other problems and obstacles that kept it from achieving megahit status. But David Geffen's fortunes on Broadway were soon to take an enormous leap to the top anyway. The long-dormant London theater scene had suddenly roused itself with a musical called *Cats,* and the

Shubert Organization had the rights to produce the show in America. Geffen eagerly assented when Bernie Jacobs asked him to be their partner once again.

Paul Simon said that CBS boss Walter Yetnikoff declared war on him when he left CBS's Columbia label, and that Yetnikoff had told people he planned to ruin Simon's career. Now, with the release date of the Central Park reunion-concert album nearing, Geffen contacted Simon with some jarring news. Yetnikoff was so angry, Geffen said, that he was refusing to release the album that CBS had contracted to distribute internationally.

Simon told Geffen not to worry and rejected Geffen's offer to "fix" the situation. "You don't have to fix it, David," Simon told Geffen. "He's going to put the record out because it is going to sell a lot of copies, and he's in a publicly owned company and he can't decide because he has a grudge that he's not going to distribute a record."

"You don't know Walter. He won't do it," Geffen said.

"Yeah, I do know Walter, David, and he will put out the record," Simon responded.

Geffen insinuated himself into the problem anyway and finagled a deal with Yetnikoff to release the album internationally with a Geffen Records logo. Geffen delighted in the idea that he could now tell people that he had Simon and Garfunkel on his label.

Simon did not think about the situation again until a few weeks later when Geffen called him with an unsolicited update. "I have great news," he told Simon cheerfully. "It's all set. The album is going to come out, and it's going to come out on Geffen Records."

Simon was livid. He did not like being informed by Geffen that his album was going to be on a label other than the one he expected it to be on. He still believed that Yetnikoff would have released the album on CBS's Columbia label and now suspected that Geffen had deceitfully used their friendship to wangle the deal to his liking.

"What's going on here, David?" Simon quizzed.

"Look, I did you a favor," Geffen replied. "And by the way, it's not going to harm you in any way that the album comes out on my label instead of Columbia."

"That's not my point. Walter is a very nasty guy, but he would have released this album!"

"You're wrong, Paul!" Geffen snapped.

"No I think *you're* wrong, David," Simon retorted and hung up.

CBS released the album internationally with a Geffen Records logo, and it greatly helped CBS justify its otherwise improvident deal with Geffen. Geffen, meanwhile, crowed to the press that he had snared the rights to the album, stopping only occasionally to explain that he had only the international rights.

An icy chill, meanwhile, descended on the friendship between Geffen and Simon, a connection Geffen had cultivated and treasured for years. Despite the fact that Simon married Geffen's pal Carrie Fisher, relations between the two men were never again the same.

Geffen poses underneath the Winter Garden marquee a few days

before the opening of Cats. *(Chester Higgins, Jr./NYT Pictures)*

CHAPTER 22

NOW
AND FOREVER

|||

Warner Bros. set a February 5, 1982, opening for *Personal Best.* Geffen and Robert Towne continued to battle up to the very last minute, arguing about such matters as the placement of the movie's credits. Towne wanted the credits to run at the end of the movie and instructed his editor to put them there. But Geffen was insistent that they run at the start of the film, right after his newly designed Geffen Company film logo; he forced the editor to snip the credits off the end and place them at the start. Towne charged that Geffen's maneuver was a violation of his "final cut" authority. He further alleged that Geffen had placed armed guards at theaters in Los Angeles and New York to keep Towne away from the film.

To no one's surprise, *Personal Best* received mixed reviews. While *Newsweek* called it "original and compelling," others slammed it as dull and superficial. "For what seems like two hours," wrote Joy Gould Boyum in *The Wall Street Journal,* "[the stars] do nothing but run, jump and lace their track shoes."

Geffen liked the film even though he detested Towne. *Personal Best—*

as well as *Making Love,* a movie, coincidentally released the following week, about a man who leaves his wife for another man—were ground-breaking in their sensitive on-screen portrayals of homosexual ro-mances, and Geffen was proud to be associated with the movement. *Personal Best* was one of only three movies that Geffen's film unit made in which he himself took an on-screen credit: "Executive Producer—David Geffen." There was only one other credit—Robert Towne, writer, producer, and director—before the film started.

Warner Bros. carefully opened *Personal Best* in just a handful of the-aters and it virtually sold out in those few engagements. But once the movie expanded out of major cities, it collapsed and suffered from poor word of mouth. The studio quickly gave up on it. Its total box-office gross was a paltry $4.5 million.

Two months after the movie's opening, Towne filed a $110 million lawsuit against Geffen, Steve Ross, and Warner Bros., alleging fraud, coercion, defamation, and breach of contract. Geffen, dismissing Towne's charges as "nonsense," told *The New York Times* that he had "never ever" been sued before (apparently forgetting about the suit the Eagles had filed against him four years earlier). Warner Bros. settled out of court.

In one of their final conversations, Geffen told Towne why he thought their partnership had failed. "You just didn't love me enough, Robert," he said, seeming to suggest that Towne should have behaved as had Laura Nyro and the others who had allowed Geffen to control their lives and careers. For years to come, Geffen blew a fuse whenever Towne's name was mentioned. To anyone who would listen, he de-lighted in unleashing charges that Towne was a scumbag and a drug ad-dict.

Geffen's ugly split with Bob Towne was nothing compared to the horrendous falling-out he had with the person he felt betrayed him next. Gil Segel had been Geffen's business manager since the late 1960s and had orchestrated his hugely successful series of real-estate investments. Geffen, in turn, had been Segel's biggest cheerleader. He relished the role he played in transforming him from a small-business operator to the chief of one of the most powerful business-manager outfits in the music industry.

But by 1982, the California real-estate market had cooled, and Geffen's investment portfolio suddenly did not look as stellar as it once had. Geffen took a closer look at the records and, with the assistance of his new henchman, Eric Eisner, figured that Segel was cheating him. Geffen got himself into a lather over Segel's fee structure and became convinced that Segel was charging him double when he sold some of the buildings Geffen owned. Segel insisted that his fee structure had never changed, but Geffen decided that it was unethical and scandalous. If anything, he felt Segel should give him a discount to reward him for all the clients he had led to him.

There are different stories about what happened next. Geffen said he fired Segel. But Segel, who had in the meantime sustained a head injury in a bicycling accident, claimed that he decided to retire. "This is not fun anymore," he concluded while in the hospital. "I don't like any of my clients. They're all assholes."

Either way, Segel soon found his client roster decimated, and for that he had David Geffen to thank. Geffen flexed his most vindictive muscles and mounted a campaign to ruin Segel that surprised even Geffen's worst enemies. With all the spirit and vigor he had employed to build Segel up, he now set forth to tear him down. He called many people that he had led to Segel and told them to fire him. He said that his statements that Segel had made him more money in the 1970s than he had made himself were false. Geffen handed his business to Gerald Breslauer, Segel's only major competitor.

Geffen's campaign was remarkably successful. Many of Segel's clients, including Joni Mitchell and Jackson Browne, walked out the door. "A lot of people did not leave," Geffen said, offering that in his view this was "to their detriment." Within a couple of years, Segel began a career as an extra in TV shows and movies. He was never the same after tangling with David Geffen.

Despite the disastrous experience of *Personal Best,* Geffen, now thirty-nine, forged ahead in his search for a movie that would establish him as a force in Hollywood. His next film came to him through Steve Tisch, son of Geffen's friends Bob and Joan Tisch. Steve, now a movie producer, hoped that Geffen would finance a movie he and his partner, Jon Avnet, were championing. It was a bittersweet satire about an industrious high-school senior and his encounters with sexuality and free enterprise.

In the picture, which was written by an idealistic young screenwriter named Paul Brickman, the high schooler explores a bit of his dark side when his parents go away on vacation. He is supposed to be studying for the Scholastic Aptitude Test, but instead he makes a date with a three-hundred-dollar-a-night prostitute. Before long, the two become business partners and turn his parents' suburban Chicago home into a brothel. The film, which Tisch and Avnet rather immodestly saw as *The Graduate* for the 1980s, was called *Risky Business.*

Ironically enough, the script had previously been in development at Warner Bros. But Warners had killed it after Brickman refused to make the picture into a teen sex romp like *Porky's,* the tasteless blockbuster that had just been released. For Warners, the gamble was made even more prohibitive because Brickman, who had never directed a movie, insisted on doing so. He figured that was the only way to ensure that his story made it to the screen in one piece. Steve Tisch knew that if Geffen elected to make the picture, Warners would have no choice but to distribute it.

Geffen agreed to read *Risky Business.* But the subject matter made him uncomfortable, and he told Tisch he would not finance it. He did not have any interest in making pictures that were in any way raunchy or violent; he was interested in making quality films that pushed the creative envelope. Geffen's idol was Sam Spiegel, the maverick producer of *Lawrence of Arabia,* and he dreamed of winning legitimacy and distinction by making pictures like the ones Spiegel had. Of course, Geffen also wanted to make pictures that would make money.

Turned down by Geffen, Tisch and Avnet took the picture to every major studio in town, only to have doors close at each stop. Those that expressed interest echoed the sentiments heard at Warner Bros., asking for a rewrite or demanding a seasoned director. Tisch and Avnet stuck by Brickman. Tisch decided to call Geffen again and plead with him to read the script a second time.

"I'm going to New York in a couple of days. I'll read it again on the plane," Geffen told him. "By the time I get to my apartment in the city I'll give you an answer." Tisch did not hold out much hope; he knew that Geffen went with his first instincts and rarely changed his mind.

But on the trip to New York, Geffen became engrossed in *Risky Business*. He howled with laughter when he reached a line in which the hooker, lamenting the perils of her chosen line of work, complains, "My pussy's so sore it feels like Hamburger Helper." When he got to the city, he telephoned Tisch with the news. "I don't know if my frame of mind was different this time or what, but the bottom line is I love it and I want to make the movie," Geffen said. The only change he demanded was that Brickman make the prostitute at least twenty years old. Brickman agreed to the switch. *Risky Business* at long last had a green light.

From the start, Geffen seemed to be the dream producer. He promised to leave Brickman alone to make the movie as he desired. There was only one matter over which Geffen demanded to have veto power: the casting of the two lead characters.

Geffen's relationship with Brickman was reflective of the relationships he had forged with his recording artists. His strategy all along had been to grant young smart talents free rein up until when the product was almost finished; he then stepped in to shape the all-important marketing. Geffen knew his strength: He could gauge the market as no one else could.

But sometimes Geffen was not able to keep his hands off the creative product itself, and this was the case with *Risky Business*. It was a ferocious battle Geffen fought with himself; while he did not want to squelch artists' creativity, he at the same time understood what the public wanted, and sometimes the two impulses collided.

Interestingly, Geffen diverged the most from his ideals with established stars, such as Donna Summer and Elton John. Despite their fame, he was much more critical of the choices they made. Geffen was unusual in his willingness to take on stars and tell them news they did not want to hear. But, like his assessments of the work of newcomers, Geffen's creative instincts here too were often dead-on. In making promises he could not keep, however, he dramatically eroded his carefully crafted reputation as an artists' advocate.

Brickman and Avnet and Tisch, working out of the casting office on the lot at Warner Bros., pored over stacks of pictures and résumés in their hunt for two actors to play the lead roles of Joel Goodsen, the high-school senior, and Lana, the prostitute. They saw many actors before deciding to give screen tests to the four people they believed were best qualified for the parts. The actors—Kevin Anderson, Brian Backer, Talia Balsam, and Megan Mullally—went to a soundstage in the San Fernando Valley, where Brickman filmed them in pairs doing a short scene. In the movie, Joel and Lana become lovers, and it was crucial that the two actors have a certain chemistry on-screen.

The filmmakers invited Geffen to view the screen tests. Brickman thought the four actors gave fine performances. But after the lights came up, Geffen told his director that he had not yet found the right actors.

"I won't make the movie with these actors," Geffen said. He argued that the movie would not work unless the actor playing the male lead was a sexy hunk. "I want you to cast someone in the role of Joel that I would want to fuck!" Geffen shrieked. "You have not come up with that person yet."

Brickman went back to the drawing board. Nancy Klopper, the film's casting director, soon told Brickman that they should call in Tom Cruise, a nineteen-year-old actor who had played a supporting role in

Taps and was currently filming Francis Ford Coppola's *The Outsiders*. Klopper thought that Cruise had a look. She was right.

Everyone noticed Tom Cruise when he came into the Warner Bros. casting office. Indeed, they could not miss him. He had just come from the set of *The Outsiders,* in which he played a punk in a gang and had greased, slicked-back hair and a chipped tooth. "This guy is completely wrong," Avnet whispered to Brickman.

Despite their initial doubts, Brickman handed Cruise a page from the script and asked him to read. Cruise read a few lines but then stopped.

"Do you mind if I try this another way?" Cruise boldly asked Brickman. The actor started again but interrupted himself seven or eight more times, suggesting small changes in the dialogue. He took control of the meeting and gave a mesmerizing performance that flabbergasted the filmmakers.

Since Cruise had plans to leave Los Angeles the next morning, Brickman and his producers asked him if he would do an impromptu screen test that night. Brickman decided to test Cruise against Rebecca DeMornay, an actress they had earlier considered but rejected. They had liked her, but she had stumbled over some of the lines in a reading, and they were unsure if she was up to playing a starring role. Now, however, Brickman thought the chemistry between her and Cruise might be just what they were looking for.

Because the producers had already spent the money they had allotted for screen tests, Tisch suggested they shoot the test at his home and on videotape. Avnet offered to shoot the test himself with his own video camera. The filmmakers quickly lined up costume and makeup people and told them to clean Cruise up. They got the grease out of his hair, removed the makeup that made his tooth appear broken, and put him in a preppy button-down shirt.

At Tisch's house, Brickman gave Cruise and DeMornay six short scenes, staging each one before Avnet's video camera rolled. It was five o'clock in the morning before they finished. When they were done, Brickman and his producers knew they had found the actors to head their cast.

Brickman rushed the videocassette over to Geffen, who screamed with delight when he saw it. He recalled seeing Cruise in *Taps* and thought he was a perfect choice. Geffen found Cruise so arrestingly handsome in the screen test that he had a copy of the videocassette made for himself and proudly displayed it in his office. Unsure of how to spell his name, Geffen scribbled "Tom Cruz" on the side of the tape.

Soon the team had set a modest budget of $6.3 million and scheduled shooting to begin in Chicago that summer.

The Thirty-sixth Annual Tony Awards were presented at the Imperial Theatre, the home of *Dreamgirls,* on June 6, 1982. Geffen went with the Jacobses, and all three crossed their fingers that *Dreamgirls,* which had been nominated for thirteen Tonys, would take home the big prize, certain that a Best Musical win would guarantee a long run on Broadway.

It was a disappointing night. While Bennett and his associate Michael Peters won the award for Best Choreography and Jennifer Holliday snagged the prize for Best Actress, the Best Musical award went to *Nine,* and its director, Tommy Tune, beat Bennett. *Dreamgirls* was eventually honored in other ways, though. The original-cast album, the biggest-selling cast album since *Hair,* later won two Grammy Awards.

Plans to bring *Cats* to the Winter Garden Theatre on Broadway in October, meanwhile, were well under way. Based on T. S. Eliot's volume of light verse, *Old Possum's Book of Practical Cats,* and set to music by Andrew Lloyd Webber, the show featured thirty-six actors in colorful makeup and feline costumes. In London, it had received only tepid critical notices, but it had captivated audiences. Crowds left the theater humming a haunting ballad called "Memory."

Geffen smartly recognized that the show's success in London would likely be replicated on the Great White Way. Bernie Jacobs licensed the show from Andrew Lloyd Webber and his producing partner, Cameron

Mackintosh, and budgeted the production at three million dollars. The same team of producers from *Dreamgirls* was lined up, and Geffen was asked to contribute one million dollars.

The theatrical wing of Geffen's company was up and running. Bernie Jacobs soon asked Geffen to partner with the Shubert Organization on a few other theatrical ventures, including two Broadway plays, *"Master Harold"* . . . *and the Boys* and *Good.* They also asked him to join them in producing a low-budget Off-Broadway musical called *Little Shop of Horrors.*

This show, the most inexpensive of all of Geffen's theater ventures, most captured his imagination. With book and lyrics by Howard Ashman and music by Alan Menken, the musical was based on an old Roger Corman movie about a dim flower-shop assistant who nurtures a people-eating plant.

Geffen thought it was enormously clever and believed there was a hit cast album in the show, as well as a winning Hollywood movie. He offered to be the show's majority backer, investing two hundred thousand dollars, as it moved from the tiny Off-Off-Broadway WPA Theater to the Orpheum, an Off-Broadway house on Second Avenue.

Little Shop of Horrors won enthusiastic reviews and was named Best Musical by the New York Drama Critics Circle. It became the highest grossing musical in Off-Broadway history, running five years, with more than 2,200 performances. And though Geffen did indeed make a movie out of it, the process was ultimately more painful even than the experience he had had with *Personal Best.*

*R*isky *Business* began shooting in Chicago on July 7, 1982, and first-time director Paul Brickman quickly fell behind schedule. Brickman and Jon Avnet nonetheless felt unquestioning support from Geffen. Because the picture was modestly budgeted, he did not flinch as the costs increased somewhat due to the longer-than-anticipated shooting schedule.

Geffen beams as Steve and Courtney Ross (left) and Steven Spielberg wait for the curtain to go up on opening night of Geffen's off-Broadway musical Little Shop of Horrors. *(Ron Galella LTD)*

Geffen was an extremely unobtrusive force throughout the production, visiting the set in Chicago only once. The night of his visit, Geffen had dinner with Brickman and Avnet at Leslie's, a small restaurant in the suburb of Evanston, and suggested that they fire the actor they had cast as Guido the Killer Pimp and reshoot his scenes with someone else.

"He's no pimp," Geffen said authoritatively. "Pimps are big, rough, threatening guys. There are no pimps like this scrawny guy."

Brickman disagreed. "I've always seen that character as something of a weasel, which to me is always more dangerous than some beefy thug." Avnet chimed in to support Brickman. "It's perfect casting."

Then Geffen, the self-proclaimed artists' champion, repeated the vow he had made to Brickman. "It's your movie. I can't tell you how to make it," he said. "I'm not going to interfere."

The words were etched in Brickman's brain. "I am so lucky," he thought. "This guy is terrific." The disagreement over the casting choice was never again mentioned, but another, far more important dispute loomed. And once again, Geffen would not be able to keep his word.

Before long, it became clear that the three-million-dollar budget estimate for the U.S. production of *Cats* had been far too conservative. The Winter Garden Theatre on Broadway at Fiftieth Street required extensive renovations to make way for the show and its sprawling junkyard set, which had been designed by John Napier. Bernie Jacobs authorized an increase in the budget to $3.9 million, surpassing *Dreamgirls* as the most expensive musical in Broadway history. The cost overruns made Jacobs jittery about the show's prospects, and he asked Geffen if he would be willing to increase his stake to one half from one third.

Geffen agreed, but Jacobs almost immediately retracted his request, nervous that Geffen would control too large a share. When Jacobs later opted to bring in a fourth major investor so that each party would kick in 25 percent of the budget, Geffen refused to take anything less than one third.

"Not on your life!" he screeched. "I have a third. That's what I want! I'm not giving up a penny!" The truth was that, even as the budget and accompanying risks were escalating, David Geffen believed in the show more than any of the other investors did.

Since he would not budge, the final capitalization broke down to Geffen controlling one third of the show, with the Shubert Organization, Metromedia, and ABC each taking one third of the remaining two-thirds stake. The investment was officially made under the name of Geffen Records, but this time Geffen put his name and not the name of the record label on advertising materials and in the program.

Thanks to sales of *Double Fantasy* and the extraordinary buzz surrounding *Cats,* it appeared that David Geffen had mounted an impressive comeback. A few days before *Cats* opened, *The New York Times* featured Geffen in a glowing profile, complete with a photograph of him grinning under the show's marquee.

"The record business is a disaster, Broadway is a disaster. Things are bad but I'm doing well," he told the *Times.* "I'm Billy the Kid, the fastest draw. It's not arrogance. It's the truth. I'm good at deciding what people like. I'm gifted at knowing what will be a success before it is a success." Perhaps anticipating a question, he said: "I'm not Sammy Glick. I've never killed anyone. I don't have to. I'm too talented."

Geffen glossed over the fact that his first movie had been a debacle. Nor did he indicate that the success of Geffen Records was in fact rather shaky. The *Times*'s reporter did contact Geffen's off-again, on-again friend Clive Davis, who was not afraid to call it as it was. "He's losing money on Elton John and Donna Summer," Davis said. "They were very overpaid, which is what is really hurting the record industry these days."

Geffen fired back, "Clive Davis is wrong and he's jealous."

By the time *Cats* opened on October 7, 1982, the show's budget had ballooned to more than five million dollars. But it was clear that *Cats* was going to be a gigantic hit; it had a record six million dollars in advance ticket sales, and orders were pouring in. Geffen packaged up a Tiffany lamp and sent it to Bernie and Betty Jacobs as an opening-night gift. He took Calvin Klein and Bianca Jagger to the opening. As a birthday gift, he also invited Klein's teenaged daughter, Marci, who considered Geffen something of a second father figure, and arranged to have Timothy Hutton, who was in New York filming the movie *Daniel,* escort her.

The group went to the opening-night party and waited until the first edition of *The New York Times,* containing Frank Rich's review, was brought in. Rich offered a rather mixed criticism, scalding it for a plot that could be missed in a blink. But he did acknowledge that there was something enchanting about it: "Whatever the other failings and excesses, even banalities, of 'Cats,' it believes in purely theatrical magic, and on that faith it unquestionably delivers." Despite other mixed and negative notices, crowds lined up in record numbers. The show's marketing line—"Now and Forever"—did not seem to be hype. Geffen had made what came to be regarded as the single best investment ever made in a Broadway show.

Geffen snuggles with boyfriend Steve Antin and Cher
at Area, a New York club, in 1983. For a time, Antin's good
looks compensated for his "inappropriate" behavior.

(Doug Vann/Globe Photos, Inc.)

THE ELEKTRA/ASYLUM FIASCO

‖

G ee, you've made a few hit movies," Geffen said to Steven Spielberg, who in addition to *Jaws* had also directed *Close Encounters of
the Third Kind* and *E.T.* "How much money do you have?"

Spielberg, who was only briefly acquainted with Geffen, was astonished by the question. He stammered nervously. His girlfriend, Kathy
Kerry, worked for Geffen's music-publishing company, but Geffen was
essentially a stranger to him.

"It's OK, Jerry Breslauer is my business manager, too," Geffen said.
"It will go no further than this."

Spielberg reluctantly told Geffen a ballpark figure of his net worth.
It was a big number, of course. Geffen had just one more question. "Do
you like art?"

Spielberg said he did and told Geffen which artists he most admired.

"Do you own any of those paintings?" Geffen asked.

"No."

"Why not? You can afford it," Geffen continued. "What, are they
going to bury your money with you someday?"

Soon Spielberg, whose walls had been lined with vintage movie posters, bought his first painting, a René Magritte picture of a big green apple in an empty, mauve-colored hotel room. The seller: David Geffen. Spielberg became an art collector and credited Geffen with getting him started.

"David must like you," Jerry Breslauer told Spielberg, telling him that he had gotten the painting at a bargain price. "He really undercut himself."

"Why did you make such a bad deal for yourself?" Spielberg later asked Geffen.

"It's a *good* deal," Geffen insisted. "You are going to become a fanatic as an art collector. And I'm going to be able to sit on the sidelines and enjoy watching you build your collection."

Spielberg did not see that Geffen had other things in mind for the future and that a good deed now might entitle him to a favor later. In fact, one came up quickly. Geffen was beginning to develop a movie version of his hit play *Little Shop of Horrors,* and he wanted Spielberg to serve as co-producer. Spielberg signed on, and the news was rushed out to Army Archerd, who dutifully reported it in *Daily Variety.* Geffen delighted in telling people he was in business with the hottest director in town.

Not long after *Risky Business* wrapped, Paul Brickman screened his cut of it for Geffen, who loved it—up until the final few minutes. It had a bitter ending in which Joel Goodsen lost Lana, cracked his parents' crystal egg, and learned that Princeton has rejected his application.

Geffen could not believe the picture did not have a happy ending. He telephoned Brickman and exploded, demanding that he reshoot the final scenes so that Joel got accepted by Princeton.

"I am not going to let you turn this movie into a loser for me," Geffen yelled, so loudly that Brickman thought he would blow out his ears. "I already had a loser with *Personal Best,* and I am not going to take any chance of failure, and there is no chance that this movie will succeed if you don't change the ending!"

Brickman reminded Geffen of the promises he had made to let him make the picture the way he wanted. "To have Joel get into Princeton will just give the audience a false and artificial lift," Brickman explained. "This isn't about the hero winning. My picture is about the lessons of capitalism and what it teaches you and how hard it can be for some people."

"That was never the movie you wanted to make!" Geffen railed. The two engaged in a screaming match in which Geffen asserted, and Brickman denied, that the original script Geffen read had Joel being accepted into the Ivy League school. "All I'm asking you to do is to give me the ending of the film I bought in the first place!" Geffen shrieked. Geffen put Eric Eisner on Brickman, and Eisner began assaulting him, Jon Avnet, and Steve Tisch with daily phone calls insisting that Brickman film a new ending.

Brickman ignored Geffen's orders. A screening had been scheduled to test the movie with an audience, and Brickman crossed his fingers that the reaction would prove Geffen wrong. The screening, held at the Writers Guild Theater on Doheny Drive in Beverly Hills, was viewed by a crowd of teenagers recruited at a mall.

Just before the screening began, a staffer from the National Research Group, Hollywood's big audience-polling firm, asked the teenagers to stay in their seats at the end of the film to fill out cards describing their reactions to it.

The opening credits of *Risky Business* came on the screen, and the crowd quieted as soon as Tom Cruise as Joel began the intriguing narration. The audience was captivated. They cheered at the scene where Cruise danced in his underwear. They screamed when Joel accidentally allowed his father's forty-thousand-dollar Porsche, which he had been forbidden to drive, to slide down a hill and into Lake Michigan.

As the end of the movie neared, Brickman, Geffen, and the other executives were on the edges of their seats. As it turned out, the crowd was rendered mute when it realized Joel's dreams would not come true. Brickman got up from his seat and went to the lobby, feeling vindicated. He was delighted and convinced that they had gotten his movie's message.

They might have gotten the message, but they did not give the picture very high marks. The teenagers' response cards, detailing their reaction to the picture, did not suggest Warner Bros. had a hit on its hands. Only 38 percent of the audience indicated they "would recommend" the picture; the average positive response at the time was 44 percent.

Eric Eisner could not wait to begin gloating. He cornered Brickman in the lobby. "See, David and I are right. It doesn't work," he said. "You're going to have to reshoot the ending!" Brickman, who was overly sensitive, had grown to despise Eisner and was stunned that his first comment after the conclusion of the movie's first screening was a complaint.

As Geffen joined the discussion, Brickman looked at Geffen but pointed at Eisner. "Call off the dogs!" he said, his voice rising.

But Geffen shared Eisner's view. "He's gotta get into Princeton, he's gotta have that victory!" he screamed. "I want him to win!" Steve Tisch and Jon Avnet heard the argument from across the room and came running to Brickman's defense.

"The movie's not about winning," Brickman said, repeating his now-familiar argument. "I don't care what you say. I am not going to change the end. I am not going to wreck this movie."

Avnet implored Geffen to consider the possibility that the test scores were low for a reason other than the melancholy ending. "The movie is too sexy," Avnet said, explaining that it was a highly explicit scene in which Joel and Lana have sex on a Chicago El train that needed to be reshot and toned down. "It is too *new,* and the kids in the audience were embarrassed about how excited they were."

Geffen encouraged Brickman and his partners to reshoot whatever scenes they felt needed fine-tuning—but the ending had to be among them. The next day, Geffen arranged to meet Brickman, Avnet, and Tisch at Warner Bros. for a meeting with Bob Daly and Terry Semel, the studio's two top executives. There, Daly and Semel joined the chorus of those saying that the movie needed a new finale.

Geffen had calmed down since the night before and now presented his argument another way: "Look, why don't you go shoot the ending I want, and then we'll show both versions to an audience and see which they like better." Geffen even envisioned the new ending's dialogue, suggesting that Joel and Lana walk off arm in arm as she asks, "So, Joel, how many guys are there at Princeton?" Geffen thought it would set up the movie perfectly for a sequel.

Brickman was horrified by Geffen's suggestion. Determined to maintain the picture's integrity, he decided to reshoot the scenes he wanted to redo but not the ending Geffen demanded. "Let's just finish the movie we intended to make," he told Avnet.

Steven Antin was a nineteen-year-old actor when he met thirty-nine-year-old David Geffen at a party at his house on Angelo Drive. Antin, who had played roles in such forgettable movies as *Sweet 16* and *The Last American Virgin,* was blond and pretty, but he was also spoiled, vain, and arrogant. He thought of himself as the next James Dean.

At the party, Antin and his friends pointed fingers and made fun of the other young gay men in attendance. During his first conversation with Geffen, Antin made disparaging comments about the canary-yellow furniture Marlo Thomas had left behind. Geffen did not like him.

Antin left his sunglasses at Geffen's house, and when he returned a few days later to pick them up, Geffen met him at the front door. Now that Antin was not surrounded by his friends, Geffen found him to be charming, and he soon fell for him as hard as he had for Cher and Marlo.

Steve Antin was the kind of boyfriend Geffen could integrate into his life and introduce to his friends. He was also the first boyfriend Geffen introduced to his mother. One friend said Geffen had entered a phase in which "he was out of the closet to everyone but the world."

In no time, Geffen invited Antin to move in with him. He began lavishing him with gifts and took him—as well as Eric Eisner and his new girlfriend, Susannah Melvoin—on the Concorde for a first-class vacation to Europe. In Paris, Geffen and Antin stayed in the Coco Chanel suite at the Ritz, where Geffen, Joni Mitchell, and Robbie Robertson had stayed ten years earlier.

When Antin admired a Jeep Wrangler on the street, Geffen bought him one and left it in the driveway for him to discover the next morning. When Antin told Geffen he wanted a dog, Geffen put Linda Loddengaard on the case to find a golden retriever from a respected breeder. Steve named the dog Sara, after the Fleetwood Mac song of the same name. They traveled on the Warner corporate jet to New York, where Geffen took Antin to see *Cats* and *Dreamgirls*. Geffen soon told Antin that he loved him.

From the beginning, however, their relationship was tumultuous, and their twenty-year age difference was a problem. Antin was immature and difficult, and Geffen was frustrated that Antin was not equipped to participate in the emotionally intimate relationship he craved.

For a time, Antin's youthful good looks were enough to compensate for his eccentric behavior. He was irresponsible with his new dog, and Geffen freaked out when the clumsy animal knocked over expensive vases and defecated in the house. Geffen reeled when Antin was late for dates and exhibited obnoxious behavior in public.

"You are so inappropriate," he yelled at him once. "That is *not* OK behavior. You need to be in therapy and work these things out." Geffen attempted to get Antin to go to an est course, but Antin stubbornly refused. He was able to convince Antin to begin seeing a therapist; the one Antin found, Beatriz Foster, later became Geffen's therapist as well.

Antin adapted quickly to life as the lover of a millionaire. Even though Geffen was out of bed and working the phones each day before

6:00 A.M., Antin kept a more leisurely schedule and typically slept until nine or ten. If he was awakened before he desired, Antin displayed a surly side that frightened even Geffen. As a result, Geffen tiptoed out of the bedroom and went downstairs to make his phone calls. He implored his cook, Alice, and other members of the household staff to keep the noise level to a minimum until Antin awoke.

One morning Antin came downstairs and was surprised to see Geffen having breakfast with his mother. Batya was enormously proud of David and delighted to spend time with him, but when they got together, they typically fell into familiar old arguments.

"Mom, go buy yourself some decent clothes," David told her.

"I don't want to spend your money," she said.

Unlike Antin, Batya, the ever-frugal immigrant, had difficulty adjusting to her son's wealth. Antin looked on in amazement as they next began bickering about a renovation David had ordered for her house.

"The contractors are stealing from you," a suspicious Batya said. "I've seen them. They're taking extra wood home."

David found the accusations ludicrous and the conversation exasperating. "Who cares? Let them take it!" he fumed. "Don't worry about it, Ma. They're going to make the house beautiful."

When David looked up and saw Antin standing in the doorway, still sleepy and longing for his morning coffee, he jumped up to proudly make the introduction. "Ma, I want you to meet Steve," David said. "Steve, this is my mother." Antin smiled at Batya and took a seat at the table.

Batya raised her eyebrows, looked Antin over, and finally turned to David with a disapproving look. "He's not Jewish," she said, speaking with the authority of a gemologist spotting a fake diamond.

"Yes, he is," David said.

Batya got up from her chair and walked around to Antin to get a closer look. "You are *not* Jewish!"

"I'm Jewish," Antin told Batya, incredulous that she was accusing him of lying. "I promise you, I'm Jewish."

B usiness at Geffen Records continued to be lackluster through the end of 1982. The Donna Summer album produced by Quincy Jones failed to break out, as did Elton John's second album for Geffen, entitled *Jump Up!* It was clear now that Clive Davis spoke the truth: The John and Summer deals were tremendous money losers. They were in fact among the worst deals David Geffen ever made.

PolyGram, which had acquired Summer's previous label, Casablanca, was, in the meantime, relentless in arguing that Summer still owed them two albums under her old contract. Geffen was tired of bickering with them and helped broker a settlement in which they got her next record.

Just after the settlement, Geffen and Summer went to the Grammy Awards together and celebrated afterward at a crowded industry bash at Chasen's. As Summer stood in a line for the ladies' room, she was entranced by the sight of the downtrodden washroom attendant. The attendant was a hunched-over woman who pocketed small tips for turning on the water faucets and handing out paper towels, all the while attempting to dodge squirts of perfume and hair spray. "Boy," Summer said aloud, "*she* works hard for the money."

Suddenly Summer realized she had hit upon a winning lyric. After fruitlessly rifling through her purse in search of a scrap of paper, she began scribbling on a long stream of toilet paper. She asked the woman her name and vowed to use it, Onetta, in the song's opening line.

Summer did not sleep that night, obsessed with the lyric. The next morning, she went to the house of Michael Omartian, a producer friend, and the two finished the song. PolyGram released the record through its Mercury label, and "She Works Hard for the Money" became the most lucrative single Donna Summer ever recorded.

Geffen had tried every trick he knew to inspire the former disco diva to reach new heights. But now a competitor was reaping the rewards. Summer felt terrible about it but could not rightly sit on the album and deliver a stiff to PolyGram. Geffen did not think that Summer was purposefully harming him, but it was painful for him to watch the Poly-Gram record race up the charts, and the incident did affect the tenor of their relationship.

Even more distressing than the Summer debacle was the fact that Joni Mitchell and Neil Young delivered albums that did not sell. He lost money on Joni Mitchell's *Wild Things Run Fast* but continued to maintain that her presence would help lure other, more commercial artists. Neil Young's *Trans* was another financial catastrophe.

Geffen was plagued by more bad luck. He overruled his A&R man John Kalodner, who wanted to sign Genesis drummer Phil Collins, and instead led the company's effort to sign ex-Genesis lead singer Peter Gabriel. Gabriel's first Geffen album had a hit single, "Shock the Monkey," and he had other hits in the future, but they came nowhere near the megasuccess Collins had over the coming decade.

Geffen Records' only slam-dunk hit in 1982 was an album by Asia, who had been signed by Kalodner. The record, fueled by a hit single called "Heat of the Moment," charted Geffen Records' first double-platinum album. Its success, though, did not come close to offsetting the huge losses incurred by the many other duds. Geffen Records was in the red.

Geffen was impatient and desperately wanted the label to become an industry powerhouse. He soon came up with a bold plan he thought would leapfrog the label out of its rocky launch period. He began plotting to take over Elektra/Asylum Records. Geffen had long disregarded the Elektra portion of the label and often referred to the company as "his," even though he had sold the portion that he had created more than ten years earlier.

Under the leadership of Joe Smith, Elektra/Asylum was now struggling, thanks in part to the fact that the Eagles had broken up. Geffen heard that Steve Ross was unhappy with Smith and was planning to dump him soon anyway.

Geffen contacted Ross and quietly made a preposterous proposal: He offered to swap his 50 percent stake in Geffen Records for a 50 percent stake in Elektra/Asylum. Geffen and Eric Eisner went to see David Horowitz, Ross's lieutenant who oversaw the music group, and made a presentation in which they valued Geffen Records *more* than Elektra/Asylum. The move was vintage Geffen: When he was under pressure and business was poor, his plans became increasingly audacious. Sitting with a pair of deuces, Geffen often behaved as though he had a full house.

He harassed Horowitz in a series of telephone conversations that left Horowitz sweaty. But Horowitz, a rather proper man trained as a lawyer, could see at once that Geffen's proposal was absurd. For one thing, Geffen Records was a struggling three-year-old company with no significant assets or library. Elektra/Asylum Records, on the other hand, was thirty years old and had a valuable catalog, even if it was not doing well currently.

"David is trying to steal Elektra," Horowitz told Ross, informing him that he had rejected the proposal. Ross agreed with Horowitz, who continued his hunt for a new chief for the label. But Geffen continued to badger Horowitz. He also tried, in an odd twist, to drum up corporate interest for his proposal through Ted Ashley, who was now serving as Ross's vice chairman.

Horowitz, with the help and advice of Mo Ostin, finally hit upon the executive to revive Elektra/Asylum: Robert Krasnow, a vice president at Warner Bros. Records. Steve Ross approved the choice but soon began fearing Geffen's reaction. He told Ted Ashley that he thought they ought to reconsider Geffen's proposal. But in a sign of just how much Ross disliked confrontation, he did not tell David Horowitz this.

The negotiations to bring Krasnow to Elektra/Asylum dragged on for a couple of months before an agreement was made final. One Saturday in January 1983, just two days before a press conference was called to announce the hiring of Krasnow, Horowitz received a call from Ted Ashley. Ashley and Horowitz chatted about six or seven matters before Ashley dropped the bomb: "By the way," he said, "I now remember that Steve said something to me, maybe a month ago, that I should tell you that he had figured out a way to do a deal with Geffen on Elektra/Asylum. He wanted me to talk to you about it." For Ashley, making David Geffen happy was clearly not a priority.

Horowitz was shocked. Ross's office was right down the hall from his, and Ross had not said anything to him about this. "Ted, we're going to announce on Monday that Bob Krasnow is the new head of Elektra/Asylum," Horowitz responded. "We've signed a five-year contract with him. There's no way we're changing course. This ship has sailed. Everything's there but the bottle of champagne." Ashley did not protest, and the two men concluded their conversation.

Horowitz flew to Los Angeles the next day to prepare for the Monday-morning press conference. Coincidentally, he had scheduled a lunch meeting with Geffen that Monday to discuss routine business issues concerning Geffen Records. First thing Monday morning, Horowitz telephoned Geffen and the company's other label heads to tell them the news about Bob Krasnow. The top brass had successfully kept the appointment secret, but Horowitz wanted to let the division's top executives in on the news prior to the press briefing. Geffen was so surprised that he was rendered speechless. "I'll see you at lunch," Horowitz said, then went off to the press conference.

When Horowitz arrived at Le Dome, a glitzy Hollywood eatery on Sunset Boulevard where Geffen often lunched, he was surprised to see that Geffen was not at his usual table just inside the front door. "Mr. Geffen is sitting in the back today," the maître d' explained, then escorted Horowitz there.

Geffen stood up as Horowitz approached the table. Horowitz could not even get out the two-syllable *hello* before Geffen unleashed a blistering public attack. "That's *my* company!" he shouted. "That's *my* company! You've taken *my* company away from me!"

Diners fell quiet and watched as Geffen continued his tirade, spewing profanities at Horowitz and deriding the choice of Krasnow. Eric Eisner, who had presumably come along for the show, remained motionless and silent at the table.

"Well, I guess we're not having lunch today," Horowitz said calmly to Geffen. He turned and left the restaurant.

Back at his hotel, Horowitz telephoned Steve Ross in New York and told him about Geffen's outburst. "I have never been talked to that way by anyone in my life, I assure you," he told Ross.

Geffen never spoke to Horowitz again.

In March 1983, one month after he turned forty, Geffen took Cher as his date to the Los Angeles opening of *Dreamgirls.* He also got tickets for his mother, who went dressed in a long red gown and a fur coat.

"That's David's mother," one of Geffen's friends told a reporter at the party afterward, pointing to where Batya was sitting, wearing her trademark determined look. "We call her 'The Explanation.' "

John Kalodner was also at the opening, where he was struck by a brainstorm: Cher, he thought, could be a pop star once again. Since breaking up with Geffen, Cher had married and divorced Gregg All-man and burned through a series of other boyfriends, including Gene Simmons of Kiss. Her acting career had been legitimized following her Broadway debut in *Come Back to the 5 & Dime Jimmy Dean, Jimmy Dean,* which led to her playing Meryl Streep's friend in the film *Silkwood,* for which she received an Oscar nomination as best supporting actress. But her career as a music star had stalled; the title song of her last album, *Take Me Home,* had been a top-ten single in 1979, but she had not made a record since.

At the party, Kalodner took Geffen aside and told him his idea.

"You don't want to do this," Geffen told him firmly. "She is the most ungrateful person who ever lived. She will break your heart." But Kalodner continued to press Geffen, who finally introduced him to Cher.

"John wants me to sign you," Geffen told Cher. "He thinks that you could have a huge record again."

Cher was flattered but said that she was booked with a handful of movie commitments and had no time. Later, however, she did team with Kalodner and once again achieved major success as a recording star, becoming a key part of the Geffen Records success story.

The Tony Awards were held in New York at the newly christened Gershwin Theater on June 5, 1983. With eleven nominations, including one for Best Musical, *Cats* was the favorite to sweep. Geffen, once again sporting a beard, was excited to attend the awards with Steve Antin. After Antin demanded they buy new tuxedos, the two went shopping and purchased Giorgio Armani formal wear. Geffen and Antin went to the show with Calvin Klein and Bianca Jagger, as well as Bernie and Betty Jacobs.

It was a good sign early in the evening when Trevor Nunn won for Outstanding Direction of a Musical for *Cats*. Two actors from the show nominated for Outstanding Featured Actor lost out to Charles "Honi" Coles for *My One and Only*. The *Cats* tally increased, though, when Betty Buckley won the award for Outstanding Featured Actress.

At the commercial breaks, organizers of the telecast came out onto the stage and directed various people in the audience to quickly change seats so that the nominees of the next awards would be sitting in aisle seats, close to the stage. Geffen and Antin stayed in their seats in the middle of the tenth row until near the end of the program.

There was a standing ovation when Jessica Tandy won the Tony for Outstanding Performance by an Actress in a Play for her role in *Foxfire*. In the break just before the Best Musical award was to be given out, at which point *Cats* had already snagged six Tonys, a producer stepped out onto the stage with directions for the latest round of musical chairs. "Please listen carefully and as I call out your name, please get up, move to the aisle, and an usher will direct you to your new seats," the producer said. "Mr. and Mrs. David Geffen!" Steve Antin panicked and fixed a frozen stare on Geffen.

"You have to get up—now!" Geffen whispered.

"I can't!" he replied.

Geffen pulled Antin up from his seat, and the two moved out to the aisle. Antin, concerned about his fledgling acting career, was mortified. He could hear snickers and felt that everyone in the audience was looking at him as he found his new seat.

"Here to present the award for Best Musical," the announcer intoned, "is Miss Pamela Sousa, who plays Cassie in *A Chorus Line* at the

Shubert Theatre." Sousa listed off the nominees: *Blues in the Night, Cats, Merlin,* and *My One and Only.*

"And the winner is," Sousa said, opening the envelope, "*Cats!*"

Geffen took to the stage with Cameron Mackintosh and Bernie Jacobs to accept their statuettes. The former ten-year-old ticket scalper and show-tune-record scamster had conquered Broadway. He had a Tony Award, the highest award bestowed in the American theater, to prove it.

CHAPTER 24

"MUSICALLY UNCHARACTERISTIC"

‖

P aul Brickman continued to refuse to reshoot the ending of *Risky Business*. After reshooting the scenes he chose to perfect, Brickman went to Berlin to begin the chore of scoring the film with Tangerine Dream, a German synthesizer band.

Geffen seethed as the producers reported Brickman's intransigence. The animosity between the two camps worsened to the point that Geffen refused to even hear the compliments of people who had enjoyed the movie at the test screening.

"You have made a wonderful movie," effused Pat Kingsley, a public-relations whiz Geffen had hired for the film. "This is *The Graduate*."

"This is *not The Graduate*," Geffen bellowed, "and Paul Brickman is *no* Mike Nichols!"

Brickman did not personally hear that slam, but he heard Geffen's next demand loud and clear. With Brickman in Berlin, Geffen rousted Jon Avnet from a sound sleep at two-thirty in the morning to deliver an ultimatum.

"Either he shoots the new ending or I'm going to fire him," he said. "I've already started looking at some TV directors who will shoot the final scenes over."

When Geffen then broke down and began crying on the phone, Avnet was not certain he was serious and decided to call his bluff. "OK, fire him," Avnet told Geffen. "I think this is stupid. I disagree with you, but you know, just do it. You're torturing yourself, and you're torturing everyone else, too."

Avnet told Brickman about the conversation and helped Brickman weigh his options. Brickman did not want to get fired; the final dub of the movie's soundtrack had not been completed, and he feared that a TV director would ruin the entire picture, not just the ending.

"If you stay, you can protect the bulk of the film," Avnet told him. "If you leave, you will give up all control, and who knows what will happen." He suggested that Brickman cave in.

Under tremendous pressure, Brickman told Geffen he would write and shoot Geffen's ending, but only on the condition that he keep his word that a decision would not be made until after the two endings were tested against each other.

The actors and crew reassembled in June 1983 to reshoot the new scenes. In an effort to make the reshoots as inexpensive as possible, the filmmakers did not return to Chicago but instead found locations in Los Angeles that sufficed.

In Geffen's version, gone altogether was one of Brickman's favorite scenes, the one that in his mind captured the essence of the movie. As he had written and shot it, Joel and Lana said good-bye while standing on the observation deck at the top of the John Hancock Building at dawn. The morning commuters could be seen crawling up Lake Shore Drive in the distance as Joel looked ruefully at Lana, comforting her as he realizes the difficult life she is going to lead.

Brickman was depressed over the fate of his film and he struggled to find the energy to direct the new scenes. Avnet's temper rose as Eric Eisner hovered over the camera and attempted to influence the actors' performances.

Geffen and Jeffrey Katzenberg, Hollywood's
"golden retriever," the thirty-three-year-old production chief
at Paramount Pictures. (Peter Borsari)

"I have some ideas for this scene I want to share with Paul," Eisner said.

"Don't talk to Paul, you unbearable prick!" Avnet screamed. "*I'll* talk to Paul." A Golden Gloves amateur boxer from Philadelphia, Avnet barely managed to suppress the urge to break Eisner's nose. After all of the reshoots, the budget had crept up to $7.2 million.

Brickman and Geffen took the two versions of the movie to San Diego for screenings to test one against the other. At the end of the screenings, audience members were asked to evaluate the picture. Within a half hour, the results had been tabulated: The version with the happy ending received substantially higher marks, with 70 percent of the audience indicating that they would recommend the movie. Brickman and Avnet said that Brickman's version scored about "five to ten" points below the score charted by Geffen's version.

Geffen announced instantly that the movie would be released with Joel getting into Princeton. Geffen thought the movie had been improved immeasurably; Brickman thought it had been wrecked. On some level, they were both right, but the two men had different goals. Geffen's objective was for the picture to make money, and, in winning this standoff, he had brilliantly set up the film to do just that.

Despite the encouraging test results, Warners' enthusiasm for *Risky Business* remained lukewarm. The studio gave the picture a release date in August but determined that *Cujo,* the other movie it planned to open that month, deserved the bulk of the studio's attention and marketing resources.

At a meeting at Warners, Geffen was dismayed when the marketing staff showed him rough concepts for the movie's promotional poster. They focused on the party aspect of the picture and overflowed with scantily clad hookers servicing Joel and his friends.

"This is not just another summer, tits 'n' ass, teenage boys, testosterone laugh riot," Geffen fumed to Sandy Reisenbach, the studio's marketing chief. "This is a very smart, sophisticated, and original movie. If this is how you want to sell the picture I am happy to write you a check here and now for nine million to buy the picture back. I know I can find another distributor who understands and appreciates this movie!"

Reisenbach and his team agreed to develop alternate posters. Eric Eisner, focusing on one of the film's strongest images, suggested that the poster simply be a shot of Tom Cruise wearing the Ray-Ban sunglasses he wore in the movie. Geffen liked the idea, passed the suggestion along to Warner Bros., and told them he also wanted the poster to show the Porsche.

Paul Brickman, meanwhile, would not give up his fight for the ending in which he believed. He approached Geffen one final time, begging him to let him reinstate the scene at the top of the Hancock Building.

"David, let's compromise," Brickman started. "You got your big cheer when he gets into Princeton. Let me have this little moment at the end. It's what the film is all about. It's about what he learns. It's not about winning."

"No," Geffen said flatly. "No compromise."

What Brickman did not realize at the time was that Geffen was simply molding *Risky Business* in his own image. Geffen the millionaire had been a pure capitalist for most of his life, and for him capitalism was about winning. With the new ending, *Risky Business* became a mirror of Geffen's own story: If you maneuver enough, you can get away with anything, and winning is easy. It does not matter if you tell the truth, cheat on a test, or step on people on your way to the top. It only matters if you win.

On opening day, the picture received mostly the kinds of mixed reviews Warner Bros. had been expecting all along. *New York Times* critic Janet Maslin called it "both promising and exasperating," and Pauline Kael, writing in *The New Yorker,* termed it "vacuous." Some critics, including *New York* magazine's David Denby, said the movie was "confused" but did not point specifically to the happy ending as the problem. There were a number of positive notices, but only one critic, *Newsweek*'s David Ansen, had the foresight to see what the studio truly had on its hands. He called it "this summer's one genuine sleeper."

In its first weekend, *Risky Business* took in $4.2 million, an impressive third-place debut, given that Warner Bros. had booked it into only 670 theaters. The word of mouth on the picture was exceptional; the second weekend, *Risky Business* posted a 7 percent increase in box-office receipts. On the third weekend, it was again up, this time by 15 percent, showing a cumulative total of more than $20 million. It was a major hit.

But even in success, Paul Brickman and Jon Avnet felt ripped off. When they received their first profit statements from Warner Bros., they went nuts when they saw that they were being penalized financially because of the reshoots. The nine hundred thousand dollars of reshoots, including the new ending that Geffen had demanded, were itemized as "unapproved overages," and the filmmakers' profits were reduced because of them.

Brickman and Avnet cried foul, remembering that Geffen had approved all the additional shooting. Avnet was surprised when Geffen, who seemed to never shy away from confrontation, sidestepped the issue.

"It's not up to me. It's up to the contract," Geffen told Avnet, adding, "none of this is of any interest to me." Avnet and Brickman hired a lawyer and instructed him to draw up a possible claim.

The movie, meanwhile, went on to gross $63.5 million. Because of its low budget, it provided Geffen and Warner Bros., as well as Brickman and his producing partners, with enormous profits (Geffen Pictures pocketed $7 million). David Geffen finally had a big motion-picture hit, one that finally established him as a legitimate power player in the movie business.

Elton John's next record, *Too Low for Zero,* was the most successful album he made for Geffen Records. Although it contained "I Guess That's Why They Call It the Blues," a hit single that peaked at number four on the pop charts, the album's sales still fell far short of the megasales John had had at MCA. Geffen continued to lose money on the deal.

So Geffen once again looked to his past to find a star he believed could put Geffen Records on top. Now that the Eagles had broken up, Don Henley was pursuing a career as a solo artist. Because the Eagles still owed Elektra/Asylum Records a number of albums under an existing contract, Henley was forced to give the label his solo albums to make them whole. His first record, called *I Can't Stand Still,* did generate buzz, but sales were not impressive. For that, Henley blamed Elektra/Asylum chief Bob Krasnow. Krasnow had alienated the star when he had refused to pay for the services of independent promotion men to work the album. Henley wanted to leave Elektra/Asylum, but Krasnow refused to release him from his contract.

When Geffen learned about the brouhaha, he thought that perhaps he could woo the star. It was startling that Geffen was interested in working again with Henley, who had battled so viciously with him in the 1970s. But although Geffen did think Henley was a prima donna, he also had respect for his songwriting and singing abilities. Above all, Geffen was pragmatic: With his label suffering, the notion that Henley might be able to help it won out.

Geffen finagled permission from Steve Ross to contact Henley and offer to move his contract to Geffen Records. Ross again did not want to say no to Geffen and bought his argument that Henley, a litigious and stubborn fellow, might make trouble for the corporation if it did not resolve the drama. If Henley moved to Geffen Records, Geffen pointed out, the profits from his records would at least stay in the Warner Communications family.

Geffen contacted Henley and made his pitch, promising to do everything in his power to make his solo career a smash. The fact that they both distrusted Bob Krasnow gave them a premise on which to revive their old bond. "I'll kill for you," Geffen vowed.

Henley did not like Geffen, but he disliked Krasnow even more. He determined that Geffen was the lesser of two evils and signed to Geffen

Records. In the years to come, Henley made Geffen a fortune. But, as he had in the 1970s, Henley found fault with Geffen's business practices, and this time their relationship was to deteriorate into open warfare.

Geffen faced a more immediate showdown with another artist, one that became the most embarrassing chapter in the history of Geffen Records. Following his dud *Trans,* Neil Young began work on a country-music album that was to be called *Old Ways.* He envisioned the record as the final installment in a trilogy that also included 1972's *Harvest* and 1978's *Comes a Time.* But when Geffen heard the new album he hated it, and demanded that Young make a rock-'n'-roll album.

Young did not understand Geffen's problems with the record, but he relented and instead produced a rockabilly album called *Everybody's Rockin'.* Young donned the persona of an Elvis Presley–like character, slicked his hair back, and put together a backup band called the Shocking Pinks. Like *Trans,* however, the album was another commercial failure.

Geffen flipped out, convinced that Young had lost his mind and was deliberately making records that would not sell. In truth, Neil Young was increasingly drifting toward musical experimentation and was taking every step of his sometimes strange creative journey seriously. He had broken up with Crosby, Stills, and Nash mostly because the music they made together was far too mainstream for his sensibility. Young was the real thing, an artist who later became the stepfather of grunge. But there was nothing that was more antithetical to the sensibilities of David Geffen, the guy who wanted a happy ending at all times.

Neil Young's albums were rarely major sellers but his talent was revered. But Geffen could see Young only as a friend who had betrayed him. Geffen believed that Young was his label's secret weapon with untapped powers and that he had the unique ability to unleash them. Thus, when stellar sales did not materialize, Geffen popped, devastated by the amount of money he was losing.

The truth was that the economics of Young's deal made it difficult for Geffen Records to make money, and Geffen was unrealistic in thinking that Young could be his meal ticket. With the rare exception of a whopper such as *Harvest,* Young's albums typically sold only between 600,000 and 700,000 units domestically, far less than the three, four, or five million a label hoped to sell when shelling out million-dollar advances.

Geffen perhaps did not realize—and was remarkably insensitive to—the stressful trials Young was battling in his personal life. He was preoccupied with the welfare of his young son, Ben, who had been diagnosed with cerebral palsy. Neil and his wife, Pegi, were traumatized by Ben's illness and set out on a cross-country mission to find doctors and explore experimental therapies that might help him. Young was so torn up by the ordeal, as well as by a financial crunch he faced as a result of an income-tax investigation, that he may have adopted unusual musical guises in order to escape the mundane pressures at home.

Geffen did not care. He was so frustrated that he instructed Eric Eisner to stop authorizing payment of studio rent and other costs Young was incurring. Young learned of the decision when a session he had booked in New York to record a song called "Don't Take Your Love Away from Me" was canceled. It was the first time in his career that he had ever gone to a studio only to find the doors locked.

"What the hell is going on?" Elliot Roberts asked Geffen.

"You guys are fucking me," Geffen hollered. "You're just fucking me around."

Geffen told Roberts that Geffen Records would not release another penny until Young hired a producer for his next album who was either selected or approved by Geffen. He also demanded the right to approve the musical selections and arrangements.

Roberts thought Geffen, not Young, had lost his mind. Roberts and Young refused to submit to Geffen's demands and began spending their own money to cover recording costs.

When it became clear that Young had no intention of giving in, Geffen decided in a moment of abject senselessness that he would sue him. Filed on November 4, 1983, Geffen's suit charged Young with fraud and deceit, alleging that Young broke promises to deliver commercial albums. Geffen complained that *Trans* and *Everybody's Rockin'* were "musically uncharacteristic of Young's previous recordings" and that he had been damaged in excess of three million dollars because of it. It was apparent to nearly everyone except Geffen and his lawyers that the suit had no merit.

Roberts could not believe it. "You're everything we used to fight," he yelled at Geffen. "What do you mean we're making 'uncommercial' records? We've never made a *commercial* record!"

The lawsuit shocked Neil Young, who at first did not want to believe that Geffen was behind it. He eventually ceased all communication with Geffen, and grew even more upset when he began getting phone calls from people like Eddie Rosenblatt and John Kalodner issuing orders about his albums: At Warner Bros./Reprise, he had always had direct contact only with Mo Ostin.

Roberts's relationship with Young, meanwhile, also began to deteriorate as a result. "If you are such a great friend of David's, how come you can't make him see what a fool he's being?" Young asked. "How come you can't resolve this?"

News of the suit damaged Geffen's reputation in the music community. The two parties did not communicate, except in court documents, for more than a year. Young's hatred for Geffen escalated; he could not wait to get off of Geffen Records. He returned to Nashville to work on *Old Ways* and determined that he would sit on any surefire hits he composed.

"There's no fucking way I'm going to deliver the mother lode to these guys," Young thought to himself.

Geffen took Steve Antin to New York, where they saw *A Chorus Line*. Steve Ross lent Geffen his lavish home in East Hampton for several days, and Geffen wanted to show off the Hamptons to Antin. Michael Bennett was also going to be in East Hampton during their stay, and the three planned to meet for lunch.

Geffen himself had a home in East Hampton, but despite a renovation by Charles Gwathmey, he rarely used it and had recently decided to sell it. He did not want to pass up the opportunity to use Ross's much larger estate. At lunch at the Ross manse, Bennett told Geffen about his new musical, *Scandal* (which ultimately went unproduced), and added that he was having difficulty finding a composer with whom to collaborate. Geffen suggested Jimmy Webb and soon brokered a deal for the two men to work together.

After lunch, Geffen and Antin took Bennett to see Geffen's house. Called the Doctor Joiner House, it was located in town and situated on a beautiful pond.

"Oh, I love this house," Bennett exclaimed.

"Really? I'm going to sell it," Geffen responded.

"I want to buy it," Bennett told him. On the spot, Geffen agreed to sell the house, which he had bought for $800,000, to Bennett for a whopping $3.2 million.

But Geffen's relationship with Antin was proving to be not so carefree a transaction. Although they were both inexperienced at relationships, Geffen clearly had an intelligence and sophistication that Antin lacked, and it frustrated Geffen.

It reached the point where they could not even enjoy movies together. When they watched the new Shirley MacLaine film, *Terms of Endearment,* at the house on Angelo Drive, Geffen broke down and sobbed. Antin, still a belligerent kid, was dismayed that a grown man could react to a movie in such a manner.

The other issue, which actually proved to be more of a problem in Geffen's future relationships with boyfriends, was the gigantic financial imbalance between him and Antin. While Geffen was generous with Antin and in no way expected him to cover expenses, the fact that Geffen was rich and Antin was not naturally was a strain. Geffen time and again gave Rolex watches and other extravagant gifts to boyfriends, but his generosity sometimes caused other problems. It was a simple fact that Geffen could not easily sustain a relationship with someone who lived in a hovel in Hollywood or drove a beat-up car.

The ever-widening gulf between the two led to a separation in which Antin lived at Geffen's beach house in Malibu. Shortly, however, they reunited at the house on Angelo Drive to give the relationship another chance. The same problems resurfaced. The partnership's days became numbered when Antin learned that Geffen had not been monogamous. When Geffen later overheard Antin talking on the phone about an affair he planned to have, Geffen himself was hurt and confronted Antin. After an angry yelling match, the two decided to call it quits, bringing to an end their yearlong relationship. Antin moved to a small apartment in Hollywood.

The breakup was so ugly that when the Jeep that Geffen had given Antin disappeared, rumors swirled that Geffen had sent his henchmen to strip and torch the vehicle as retribution. Later, Antin and Geffen laughed about the rumors—Antin said it was stolen after he foolishly parked it in front of his house without an alarm or steering lock.

The breakup left Geffen depressed and lonely. Back in New York for the funeral of Walter Yetnikoff's mother, Geffen saw many old friends he had not seen for years. "You know, David," one chum told him after the service, "of all of us you're the one who became the most successful."

"Yeah, but it doesn't mean anything when you're dead," Geffen said sadly. "I have nothing really. I have no relationships, no family."

Following the success of *Risky Business,* Geffen and Eric Eisner put together an ambitious slate of movies to produce. They agreed to make *Lost in America,* a comedy directed by Geffen's old friend Albert Brooks, and *After Hours,* a disturbing black comedy directed by Martin Scorsese.

Geffen soon had a bold idea for a movie that he believed would set him apart from all the other producers in Hollywood. In a piece of good timing, Geffen had a year or so earlier forged a relationship with pop superstar Michael Jackson and offered to create a big-budget movie musical around him. Now Jackson's new album, *Thriller,* was breaking all sales records, and Geffen was better positioned than everyone else in Hollywood who wanted to work with him.

Geffen believed Jackson was tailor-made for the movies and predicted that he would be a huge star on the silver screen. Several years earlier, Jackson had played a supporting role in *The Wiz*, but Geffen believed that *Thriller* had set him up perfectly to play starring roles. Jackson was shy and fragile, but he responded to Geffen's brand of honest criticism and even found his brash style refreshing.

Jackson had a long-term recording contract with Columbia Records and was not free to move to another label, but that did not matter to Geffen. With the film pact, Geffen was suddenly one of the most influential voices in the life of one of the biggest stars the music business had known. And although he could not win Jackson's recording contract, Geffen would get what looked to be a can't-miss soundtrack—it would feature the first Michael Jackson tunes following *Thriller*—to distribute through Geffen Records.

Geffen next tried to repair his relationship with Paul Brickman. Geffen felt bad about the divide between them and offered a lucrative deal to lure Brickman back to his camp. In the wake of *Risky Business,* Brickman had become a hot commodity, and every studio in town was attempting to make a deal with him. Geffen worried about the hit his reputation would take if Brickman deserted him to make films elsewhere.

Geffen's biggest competitor for Brickman, he only eventually realized, was his friend Jeffrey Katzenberg, now the thirty-three-year-old production chief at Paramount Pictures. Katzenberg had become one of Geffen's closest friends, and he and his wife, Marilyn, spent time at Geffen's beach house—Geffen even reluctantly allowed the Katzenbergs' diapered twins to wade in his pool. Katzenberg, who like Geffen had a poor relationship with his only sibling, had grown to regard Geffen as a brother.

Katzenberg recruited Geffen as his mentor and called him often for advice. Having proved himself as Diller's assistant, Katzenberg had emerged as a gifted production executive whose legendary pursuits of actors, directors, and writers were so earnest that he came to be known as "the golden retriever." Whenever his new boss, Michael Eisner, assigned him to get a script or sign a writer, Katzenberg succeeded nine times out of ten.

Geffen went wild when he realized Katzenberg was the one driving up the price for Brickman. He grew more furious still when he caught him in a lie after confronting him about the matter. Geffen telephoned Katzenberg one morning at six-thirty and let him have it.

"You have really hurt me," he seethed. "You have put our friendship in jeopardy over this. Is that what you want to do? Life is not just about winning."

Geffen discharged a long diatribe about friendship and loyalty, charging that Katzenberg had crossed a line. Given the way in which he himself had conducted business with people he considered friends, Geffen would have been wise to follow the advice himself. It did not take a cynic to conclude that Geffen attacked Katzenberg simply because he feared he might otherwise lose Brickman. The only way, fair or not, that Geffen knew to knock Katzenberg out of the running was to threaten to become one nasty enemy if he was not allowed to win.

Geffen's harangue masterfully left Katzenberg on the brink of tears. Katzenberg hung up the phone, dropped his pursuit of Brickman, and pledged his future allegiance to David Geffen. In his mind, it was a watershed moment in which Geffen taught him a lesson he was never to forget. It was, he felt, that conversation that bound them together forever as friends.

Unbelievably, Paul Brickman signed a deal to direct future pictures for David Geffen. But he did so in part because it was the only way Geffen would give him and Avnet the profits they claimed they had been owed relating to the "unapproved overages" on *Risky Business.* Brickman's other condition was that Geffen guarantee him final-cut approval. Never again would David Geffen be able to coerce him into changing anything in a movie.

THE
RENEGOTIATION

|||

I t was the end of 1984, and Geffen Records was in deeper trouble than ever. Losing money on Elton John, Donna Summer, Joni Mitchell, and Neil Young, the label was in the red and posting a deficit substantial enough to be only barely offset by the advantageous foreign deal Geffen had made with CBS. After four years, the label had yet to show a profit.

But Geffen saw opportunity. His joint-venture deal with Warner Bros. Records was about to expire; the time to negotiate a new long-term contract had arrived. It was to be the most important negotiation of Geffen's life, and he successfully extracted an extraordinary deal that within a few years helped make him one of the wealthiest men in the country.

In pulling off the deal, he showed himself to be a shrewd, remarkably focused strategist. He had an uncanny ability to understand people, recognize their weaknesses, and capitalize on them. The negotiation also showed once again that Geffen had that rare ability to envision success: He clearly understood his power and knew how to get what he wanted.

But the negotiation also showed David Geffen at his worst, as a man willing to implode any business or personal relationship to attain his goal. Geffen's technique was preposterous, duplicitous, and downright awful. Despite his vocal denials to the contrary, Geffen in this critical moment looked quite a bit like Sammy Glick.

Geffen eventually fixed his eyes on one prize in the negotiation: He wanted Warner Bros. Records, at the end of a new five-year deal, to give to him the 50 percent equity stake it controlled in Geffen Records, giving him complete ownership of the label. It was an outrageous request, and Geffen knew it. Why would Warner Bros. agree to relinquish its equity stake in a company for which it had put up all the money and covered all the losses?

Geffen concluded that Mo Ostin, a tough and responsible deal-maker, was unlikely to grant him his request. Geffen thought that he could get what he wanted if he negotiated the contract directly with Steve Ross, who disliked confrontation and was so kindly disposed toward Geffen. "Don't leave me in the room alone with David Geffen," Ross once told Roger Smith, an executive vice president. "I tend to *give* him things."

Geffen figured it was an ideal time to squeeze Ross for all he was worth. Warner Communications had been facing the threat of a hostile takeover from Rupert Murdoch, the Australian publishing magnate, and Ross had asked Geffen, Barbra Streisand, and other friends to go to the press and state their loyalty. Geffen enthusiastically told *The New York Times* and *The Wall Street Journal* that he would sever his connection to Warner Communications if Murdoch took over. Ross solved the Murdoch threat by allowing Herbert Siegel's Chris-Craft Industries to acquire a 19 percent stake in Warner Communications, becoming the company's "white knight."

While Ross greatly appreciated Geffen's very public vote of confidence, he was also mindful that Geffen could be just as noisy if he suddenly became unhappy. Thus, when Geffen approached him regarding the renegotiation, Ross decided to give him just about anything he wanted.

Warner Bros. Records chief Mo Ostin. "If I have to deal with Mo," Geffen asserted, "we will fail." So he went after Ostin's wife. (Peter Borsari)

Geffen explained to Eddie Rosenblatt why he felt it was imperative to go around Mo Ostin and negotiate directly with Ross.

"If I have to deal with Mo, we will fail," Geffen told Rosenblatt flatly. But then Geffen shocked Rosenblatt by outlining a jaw-dropping premeditated plan to get Ostin out of the way. "I'm going to pick a fight with Mo so that I can refuse to speak to him. Then I can only deal with Steve."

It did not take long before Geffen found his fight. The rock group Van Halen, which was signed to Warner Bros. Records, wanted Geffen Records solo artist Sammy Hagar to replace David Lee Roth as their lead singer. Hagar wanted to do it, but Geffen made a huge stink, carping loudly that Ostin was stealing one of his few star acts. Hagar's latest album, *VOA,* had just been a platinum seller, and he owed the label several more records.

Geffen dragged the drama out for several months and tried to alienate Ostin with screaming assaults in which he demanded a large percentage of Van Halen's profits in exchange for Hagar's release. A deal was eventually struck, but Geffen had succeeded in dealing a serious blow to his friendship with Ostin. Because he thought Geffen was blowing the situation out of proportion, Ostin, while offended, was mostly perplexed.

What Ostin did not know was that the Van Halen skirmish was just the prelude in Geffen's plan to destroy their friendship. Now Geffen was girding for the kill shot.

"I'm going to take [Ostin's wife] Evelyn to lunch and say something really shitty to her," Geffen told Rosenblatt. Rosenblatt could not speak. He had, of course, witnessed firsthand Geffen's bullying tactics but did not believe he would intentionally hurt someone they both loved to get what he wanted.

"This is *essential,*" Geffen said. "If I don't have a fight with Mo, I will fail. The company will fail. And I'd rather *die* than fail."

Geffen took Evelyn Ostin to the Ivy, an expensive restaurant on Robertson Boulevard where celebrities were often spotted. Within Hollywood's daggers-out empire, Evelyn Ostin was the rare person who had virtually no enemies. She was a delightful woman, a sensitive soul whose eyes lit up when any opportunity came her way to help another person.

Evelyn knew that Mo and David had been having problems. But she had long had a friendship with David that was separate from her husband's working relationship with him, and they met from time to time to lunch and gossip about mutual friends.

Geffen wasted no time in his bid to provoke Evelyn. Just moments after they sat down, he said, "You know, Mo really doesn't care about you that much."

"David, this is the man I've been married to for thirty-four years!" Evelyn managed.

Geffen continued with his scripted comments, focusing on a serious illness Evelyn had had just a few years earlier. "When you got sick and he saw that everybody really loved you, that's when he started loving you," he said.

Evelyn blanched. "David!" she said. "How can you say that to me?"

Geffen, feeling that Evelyn had been weakened, began ranting about Mo and Evelyn's children, including one son who was battling some personal problems. Evelyn was so much taken by surprise that she hardly knew how to respond.

"David, I have to go now," she said quietly, rising from her seat before finishing her lunch. Dazed, she walked out.

When Geffen returned to the office after lunch, Linda Loddengaard grew incensed when he told her how he had behaved. "Call her up and apologize now!" she demanded. Geffen called, but he did not offer a genuine apology. Instead, he continued his campaign.

After Evelyn shared the news of her lunch with Mo, his exasperation toward Geffen was immense. "This time he's gone too far," he told her. The Ostins did not know that Geffen was using them to accomplish his goals; they simply thought he wanted to hurt them.

For Geffen, it was mission accomplished. He did not speak to the Ostins for the next year and a half.

S teve Ross knew about the feud between Geffen and Ostin, but it did not occur to him that it had anything to do with Geffen's objectives in his pending renegotiation. "Mo and I are not talking," Geffen told Ross. "He's all bent out of shape about this Sammy Hagar/Van Halen situation. But my deal is up. You're going to have to renegotiate it with me."

Geffen went to meet with Ross and, unloading the first shot in a two-pronged strategy, made the audacious demand that he wanted a five-year deal awarding him a five-million-dollar advance against future profits. Ross balked at the request, given that Warner had already flushed so much cash on a venture that was unquestionably a loser.

His first request rejected, Geffen then told Ross he would sign a new deal only if Ross agreed to give him, at the end of the new contract, the half of Geffen Records that Warner controlled. "If you don't do this, I'm leaving," Geffen threatened.

Steve Ross had done David Geffen the favor of setting him up in business with very handsome terms at a time when the industry had branded him a failure. Now Geffen was repaying him by demanding ownership of the venture into which Ross had sunk millions. Geffen would then be free to sell the label without having to give Warner a dime.

Frightened that Geffen might cause a public stink if both of his demands were vetoed, Ross, as Geffen had predicted, agreed to relinquish the equity stake. The truth was that Ross, in an unusual moment of shortsightedness, did not believe that Geffen Records was valuable, especially since Geffen already had absolute control of manufacturing and distribution. Ross figured that giving up the equity would be painless and a more prudent move than fronting a multimillion-dollar advance. This proved to be a disastrous mistake.

Ross delegated the task of working out the fine points of the negotiation to Elliot Goldman, the corporate executive who now oversaw the music group. Goldman agreed with Ross that Geffen's demand was a significant concession. Ross had long told Geffen that he would some-day buy his label, and Goldman simply could not see Geffen selling it to anyone else. But he also did not think Geffen was bluffing when he threatened to walk, and he did not want to be the one responsible for Geffen leaving the company.

As a condition to the new agreement, Goldman insisted that Geffen return the label's foreign-distribution rights to Warner Communications. The three-year deal Geffen had made with Walter Yetnikoff at CBS Records was still in effect, but Geffen and Yetnikoff, despite the failure of the deal, remained friendly enough to negotiate an early set-tlement. Yetnikoff was eager to be rid of it.

The new Geffen Records contract was drawn up and signed by both sides. Mo Ostin, rendered a non-player in the renegotiation, was flab-bergasted when he heard about the deal.

"Now is the time to *buy* Geffen Records," Ostin told Ross. "It's not the time to give it up for nothing!"

G effen and Neil Young had not spoken for more than a year. Their only communication was through lawsuits and countersuits. Gef-fen finally realized he had filed a lawsuit he could never win. His friendship with Elliot Roberts in tatters, Geffen instructed Eric Eisner to settle the dispute.

But the damage had been done, and Young wanted nothing more to do with Geffen. He decided to return to Reprise Records as soon as he met certain agreed-upon obligations to Geffen Records. A few years later, after Roberts spotted a magazine article in which Geffen candidly regretted suing Young, the three finally made amends.

As 1984 turned into 1985, Geffen Records finally had a hit album. Don Henley proved to be the star to give Geffen's label the big hit it needed. Henley's first solo record for the label, *Building the Perfect Beast,* contained a handful of hit singles, including "All She Wants to Do Is

Dance" and "The Boys of Summer." The record eventually went triple platinum, and Henley was honored with the Grammy Award for Best Rock Vocal Performance.

But the good times at Geffen Records were short-lived. As the sales of Henley's album peaked, a wicked cold spell set in. With his label faltering again, Geffen decided to shake up the staff and find new A&R executives to bring in fresh bands. In a stroke of brilliance, Geffen decided to have the company's A&R effort led by three talent scouts, each with different musical tastes. The idea of three A&R czars, not two, was inspired, as it nearly guaranteed that a fierce rivalry would ensue: who would perform the best, who would produce the most, and as a result, who would become the most famous. Geffen gave each of the three broad power to hire staff and select the bands they wanted to sign.

Of the people he already employed, it was clear that only John Kalodner could fill one of the three roles. Kalodner's recent track record with new acts had not been great, although he had recently signed the faded 1970s rock group Aerosmith and made the prediction that they would once again rise to glory. To his credit, a movie soundtrack he put together had just come out and was racing up the charts. The soundtrack to *Vision Quest,* a lame picture about high-school wrestlers, featured "Crazy for You," a number-one hit single by Madonna. The album gave Geffen an excuse to forge a friendship with the superstar.

For the other two A&R jobs, Geffen asked Kalodner who he believed the brightest newcomers in the industry were.

"Gary Gersh and Tom Zutaut," Kalodner said assuredly. "They are the best." Geffen hired both.

Gary Gersh was a polished twenty-nine-year-old who had built a name for himself at EMI Records with his work on David Bowie and John Waite albums. Gersh had collected records as a kid and, as a teenager, had written a letter to Geffen offering to sweep the floors at Asylum Records for free.

Tom Zutaut was a thick twenty-five-year-old with a round, cherubic face who while at Elektra Records had discovered Mötley Crüe, a hard-rock band from Los Angeles that was just taking off. Born in a southern suburb of Chicago, Zutaut was starstruck when he met Geffen and eager to work for him.

Unlike other label chiefs, Geffen refused to allow his A&R executives to take royalties on the albums on which they worked. Instead, in ways formal and informal, he promised them and a handful of other top executives small equity stakes in Geffen Records. His pitch was that if the label did well they would one day participate in a big score when the company was sold.

G effen's recent contract renegotiation had set up great future success for him, but he was impatient that the good times had not yet materialized. In the early 1970s, he had sold Asylum Records after only a year; his new venture was five years old. The second cash windfall he dreamed of seemed far off.

He soon had a brainstorm. Warner Communications had talked to Philips Electronics about a purchase of its PolyGram music unit, a deal that would have greatly increased Warner's global music operations. But the Federal Trade Commission had nixed the deal on the grounds that a merger would be anti-competitive. When Warner's deal fell apart, Geffen himself plotted to buy PolyGram.

Geffen struck up a friendship with PolyGram chief Jan Timmer, and the two discussed a proposal in which Geffen would buy 80 percent of PolyGram's U.S. operations and half of its foreign branch for just fifty million dollars. The deal would even include ownership of the plants where PolyGram manufactured compact discs, the music format that was catching on in America. It was the single best financial opportunity that had ever come Geffen's way. He figured he could flip the company in a couple of years and reap a fortune.

To make the PolyGram acquisition, Geffen would have to extricate himself from Warner Communications, since the FTC would surely oppose the deal on the same grounds that it had opposed the Warner transaction. Geffen went to Steve Ross and boldly requested that he let him leave the company. One thing was certain: David Geffen had nerve.

Although Steve Ross was a pushover for Geffen, he was no fool. Ross informed him that under no circumstances would he allow him to leave, especially in light of their new five-year deal. Geffen's talks with PolyGram soon fell apart, and he cursed Ross.

Meanwhile, Alan Hirschfield, who had left his job as chief executive at Twentieth Century Fox, had put together his own investor group to make a run at PolyGram. When Jan Timmer told him that PolyGram had also talked to Geffen, Hirschfield called Geffen with an idea. His thought was to buy PolyGram himself but bring Geffen in as co-owner and chief executive as soon as he was able to leave Warner.

Hirschfield arrived at Geffen's Sunset Boulevard office to offer him what he thought was a hot deal. But Geffen was interested in something else: settling an old score. Hirschfield shared his proposal with Geffen. "We're going to steal this company, David," he said. "It's a great opportunity and between the two of us—"

Geffen cut him off and began screaming. He was still angry that Hirschfield had not come to his rescue three years earlier when he begged him to have Fox distribute *Personal Best.* Geffen calculated that he had been a good friend to Hirschfield, supporting him through his battles at Columbia Pictures in the late 1970s, but that Hirschfield had not been a good friend to him.

"I have no intention of pursuing anything with you for the rest of my life!" Geffen unloaded. Hirschfield did not know what had hit him. Geffen became so blinded by his rage that he, for one of the first times in his life, missed out on a phenomenal business deal. One of his greatest strengths had been to envision success, to be able to see the endgame. But in this instant, as this incredible asset was being undersold, he allowed himself to lose track of the big prize.

In the end neither Geffen nor Hirschfield was able to make the acquisition. PolyGram finally took itself off the market and decided to turn its record operations around on its own. Thirteen years later, Universal Studios acquired the company for ten billion dollars.

Although he was battling one headache after another at work, Geffen suddenly had something to cheer about in his personal life. At age forty-two, he had met a dark-haired twenty-three-year-old named Robert Brassel and had fallen in love. Brassel lived in New York, where he worked in the merchandising department of Liz Claiborne. He stood six foot one and was so handsome that some people remarked that he looked as though he had stepped out of a Calvin Klein ad.

Brassel had more than beauty going for him. He was very quick and terrifically bright, and Geffen soon discovered that he enjoyed conversing with him as much as sharing his bed. Geffen had nearly given up on the notion that he could ever find a man who was both good-looking and smart, but Brassel met all of Geffen's criteria and then some. He was as fierce and intense as Geffen, and he offered him the kind of stimulating interaction he craved. Brassel soon left his job and moved to California, beginning a tumultuous relationship with Geffen that was to last a few years. Geffen's friends called Brassel the love of his life.

One of the things that Geffen liked about Bob Brassel was that he knew how to have a good time; drugs and alcohol were regularly a part of his recipe for fun. Use of cocaine and other drugs seemed to be at an all-time high among Hollywood people, and Geffen was part of a crowd that did its fair share. But shortly after they began dating, Geffen realized that Brassel's drug habit went beyond the recreational.

Strangely enough, for a time this made him even more appealing to Geffen. His codependent streak flared up just as it had during his relationships with Cher and others, and he got lost in Brassel's problems, coming on strong in a bid to save him.

Thanks to the connection he had made with Madonna through the *Vision Quest* soundtrack, Geffen snagged an invitation to the singer's wedding to Sean Penn, and he brought along Brassel as his date. There,

Geffen pulled aside his friend Carrie Fisher, who herself had recently sworn off drugs and gotten clean and sober.

"Can you help me?" he asked her. "I think we need to do an intervention," an exercise in which friends and family join forces to confront a loved one about his or her drug addiction.

Fisher had become one of Hollywood's most celebrated interventionists and she welcomed the opportunity to help Geffen and Brassel. She and Geffen forced Brassel to check into a drug-rehabilitation center. The process worked, for the time being.

Before long, Geffen and Brassel exchanged gold rings that they wore on their left ring fingers. They were supportive of each other's issues, and Geffen even attended Alcoholics Anonymous meetings with Brassel. In AA, Brassel picked up a phrase that had a big impact on Geffen: "You're as sick as your secrets." Geffen adopted it as his own mantra. "I totally believe that," he said. "I believe that a healthy person is a person who doesn't have to hide anything."

Dreamgirls closed on Broadway on August 4, 1985, after 1,522 performances over three and a half years. The show earned back its initial investment, but the prohibitive weekly operating costs, as well as a money-losing national tour, meant that the show provided Geffen and the other producers with only a modest profit.

Although the *Dreamgirls* cast album had been a winner for Geffen Records, the experience left Geffen feeling dissatisfied, mainly because his friendship with Michael Bennett had somehow derailed. Shortly after buying Geffen's house in East Hampton, Bennett had stopped returning Geffen's phone calls. Geffen could not figure out what he had done or what he had said to offend him.

Geffen's next Broadway venture looked to most people like a favor for Marlo Thomas. Geffen and the Shubert Organization agreed to produce a farce called *Social Security*. Although the critics hated the play and decimated Thomas ("She seems to be laboring under the misimpression she's appearing in 'Hedda Gabler,' " Frank Rich wrote in *The New York Times*), the show managed to run for eleven months.

At the Winter Garden Theatre just around the corner, *Cats* was well into its fourth year, delivering Geffen six million dollars a year in profits. But he began to stew after taking a hard look at the show's balance sheet: After a few years of capacity business, *Cats* had begun to show a slight dip in attendance, and the profit participants' income was immediately and negatively impacted. Geffen grew irate when he realized that his co-producer, the Shubert Organization, which as owner of the Winter Garden was also the show's landlord, charged the show the same rent it had charged when the show was playing to sellout crowds.

Geffen thought the deal was patently unfair. He was providing the landlord with an unusually stable tenant and thought it only fair that the rent be lowered. Geffen flipped out when Bernie Jacobs refused to adjust the deal, saying that the company's roles as producer and landlord were separate.

Geffen's friendship with Jacobs was soon dealt a fatal blow when Geffen learned that Jacobs had been the culprit in freezing his friendship with Michael Bennett. Jacobs had told Bennett that Geffen had ripped him off when he sold him his house in East Hampton. Geffen confronted Bennett and proved to Bennett's satisfaction that the terms had been fair. Geffen was able to repair the friendship just in time. Soon, Michael Bennett was dead, one of the countless friends Geffen lost to AIDS.

Frank Oz (center) on the set of the Little Shop of Horrors *movie with his stars, Ellen Greene and Rick Moranis. "It's a disaster! It's a disaster!" Geffen muttered. It wasn't, but it was a disappointment.* (Shooting Star)

TITANIC

‖

G effen Pictures was not doing much better than Geffen Records. Neither *Lost in America* nor *After Hours* was a significant hit, although each was made at a modest cost, and Geffen said he made one million dollars on each.

Ever since the *Personal Best* battle he had waged with Michael Ovitz, Geffen despised Ovitz. But Ovitz's power as the head of Creative Artists Agency was on the upswing, and Geffen believed he needed him to achieve his own success in the movie business. CAA was becoming a hot packager of movies, and Geffen wanted Ovitz to hand him a blockbuster on a silver platter. Geffen crafted a strategy: He would become one of Ovitz's most vocal fans and steer as many clients to him as possible, thereby instilling in Ovitz a sense of indebtedness.

Convinced he had played a major role in getting Madonna to sign with CAA, Geffen began harping on Ovitz to steer big stars and their movies to him. He grew angry when Ovitz did not instantly bestow upon him the preferential treatment he felt he deserved.

Plans for Geffen's Michael Jackson movie floundered amid a host of problems, including Geffen's inability to find the right script. Geffen Pictures developed "Streetdandy," a screenplay by *Flashdance* cowriter Tom Hedley, but Geffen was unable to get the increasingly reclusive pop star to commit to it. The deal soon expired, and the Gloved One again was a free agent.

Geffen turned his attention to the movie adaptation of *Little Shop of Horrors,* which continued to play to sold-out houses Off-Broadway. Geffen believed it could be twice as big as *Risky Business.*

But the deal Geffen had made to co-produce the movie with Steven Spielberg fell apart almost as soon as Army Archerd had announced it in *Daily Variety.* Geffen became angry with Spielberg after just a couple of meetings, and the two had a control fight. Geffen decided to produce the movie on his own.

He then went on a tirade, bad-mouthing Spielberg to anyone who would listen. "He's selfish, self-centered, egomaniacal, and worst of all—greedy," he told Julia Phillips, who had co-produced *Close Encounters of the Third Kind.*

Geffen soon found the director he had been looking for: Frank Oz, the voice of Muppets Fozzie Bear and Miss Piggy, who a year earlier had directed *The Muppets Take Manhattan.* Geffen told Oz he wanted the movie made for nine million dollars, but Oz told him that he did not see how it could be done for less than fifteen million.

After casting Rick Moranis and stage actress Ellen Greene in the lead roles of Seymour and Audrey, Geffen began hunting for big stars to spice up the movie with cameo appearances. Finally, Michael Ovitz came through with a favor that pleased Geffen: He arranged for his client Bill Murray, the star of *Ghostbusters,* to appear as a patient of a sadistic dentist played by Steve Martin.

Before sending Frank Oz and writer Howard Ashman off to London to begin production, Geffen gave them one piece of advice: Don't kill the two lead characters at the end of the film. At the end of the play, the gigantic flytrap named Audrey II overtook the flower shop and gobbled up Seymour and Audrey.

"At the end of the play, the cast comes out and takes a bow, and it's not realistic," Geffen said. "But it will be completely real in the movie. You do what you want, but trust me: If you kill them, you'll be in trouble."

Ashman and Oz looked at Geffen as though he had two heads. "You can't be serious," Ashman said. "I am not going to put a silly Hollywood ending on my story." Oz said that he, too, wanted to be true to the play. They told Geffen the movie would end just like the play.

N ineteen eighty-five had been Geffen Records' worst year yet. Aside from the *Vision Quest* soundtrack, the label did not release a single hit record. The year's losers included flops by such acts as the Style Council and Eric Carmen. For Geffen, whose name was above the front door of the label's headquarters, it was a very public failure.

Geffen took his frustration out on everyone, but he rode Eddie Rosenblatt especially hard. Scrambling for some kind of turnaround plan, Rosenblatt said that the label was misfiring in part because of weak promotion by Warner Bros. Relations with the label had suffered in the wake of Geffen's feud with Mo Ostin.

"We need our own promotion man," Rosenblatt said. "We're going to die if we don't get our own guy."

They settled on Al Coury, a promotion man who had spent a lifetime running the departments at RSO and Capitol Records. Geffen offered Coury, who was in semi-retirement, managing Irene Cara and playing golf on Fridays, a lucrative compensation package as well as a small equity stake in the company. He accepted, and Geffen directed him to begin working the network of independent promotion men known as "indies."

Coury arrived in time to oversee the release of Aerosmith's album *Done with Mirrors*. The group's drug problems were huge, however, and as a result the band had not done its best work. Coury tirelessly worked the indies, but *Done with Mirrors* fared worse than their previous album, *Rock in a Hard Place*.

Geffen watched as Coury struggled with the indies and soon decided that the label needed a full staff to support him. At the company's Christmas party, held at Chasen's, Geffen let Coury in on his plan. Coury agreed that having the label's own representatives in major markets working behind the indies would strengthen Geffen Records exponentially. It would be an expensive undertaking but one that would almost guarantee that its albums would get fair shots.

Geffen escaped to Hawaii for a New Year's vacation to unwind and recharge for another year. But more bad news found its way to him at the Kahala Hilton on Oahu. Patrick Goldstein, who wrote the "Pop Eye" column in the *Los Angeles Times,* published his annual music-label report card, and Geffen Records was panned.

"You know it was a bad year when an industry expert updates the old joke and says that the only difference between Geffen and the *Titanic* was that the ship had a better band," Goldstein wrote. Geffen took this as a personal attack and telephoned Goldstein to excoriate him.

In a repeat of Paul Brickman's situation on *Risky Business,* Frank Oz fell behind schedule shortly after filming started on *Little Shop of Horrors.* But his budget was more than twice that of *Risky Business,* and Geffen's anxiety level showed a commensurate rise. The movie, Oz timidly told Geffen in a call from the set in London, would cost far more than the already revised estimate of fifteen million dollars.

One issue was that the man-eating plant, the movie's central prop, was an enormous contraption made of foam rubber that looked realistic only when the sixty puppeteers working it hit their many complicated cues in concert. "Feed Me," a musical number in which Rick Moranis attempted to sate the insatiable appetite of the plant, took five weeks to shoot. The end of the movie, a special effects–laden sequence in which the plant took over the world, also proved to be more costly and time-consuming than Oz had guessed.

A not-insignificant problem was that Oz was an inexperienced director who found himself in over his head. Besides *The Muppets Take*

Manhattan, the only other picture on his résumé was a co-directing credit with Jim Henson for *The Dark Crystal,* a movie he admitted had been carried by Henson. *Little Shop of Horrors* represented the first time Oz had directed a picture with humans as its stars. The only "puppet" involved was larger and more complicated than any Muppet that Oz had ever encountered.

Geffen worried as the budget ballooned to thirty million dollars and in transatlantic phone calls begged Oz to watch every nickel. Geffen felt personally responsible for the cost overruns, but Bob Daly and Terry Semel, the studio's top executives, trusted that Geffen would pull it off. Nevertheless, with production of the movie behind schedule, the studio pulled it from its planned summer lineup and moved it to its roster of Christmastime offerings.

But even as the costs spiraled out of control, Geffen remained upbeat about the movie's prospects, convinced that it would be a box-office blockbuster. He had the dailies transferred to videotape and showed them to countless people in Hollywood. Oz was nervous as sources reported back to him that Geffen was showing off the footage; Oz had ordered that the set be closed and had been attempting to tightly guard the fact that John Candy and Jim Belushi and others were filming cameo appearances.

At one point, Geffen began to lose his patience with Oz. "I'd really like to reshoot the scene we did today," Oz told Geffen one day. "It's just not perfect."

"Frank, I'm not paying for perfect," Geffen told him firmly. "We're not reshooting this scene so you can say you have a perfect movie. It's merely *terrific,* and it'll have to stay that way."

Geffen's friendship with Mo Ostin was restored after he offered a simple apology that Ostin deemed genuine. Geffen never told him that he had manipulated the falling-out as part of his renegotiation. Evelyn also forgave Geffen, and their friendship was renewed. It was solidified when Geffen, making the ultimate Hollywood sacrifice, relinquished one of his weekly sessions with his latest therapist, Milton Wexler, and gave it to her.

On the other hand, Geffen's relationships with some of his key artists remained troubled. After Elton John's latest record, *Leather Jackets,* proved to be another flop, the star began to think that his old label, MCA, was not all that bad. He was tired of Geffen's reviews of his work. He blamed Geffen Records for botching the marketing of his albums.

When Geffen refused to allow Elton to put "Tonight," a song that had appeared originally on his 1976 *Blue Moves* album, on his new *Live in Australia* record, the two had a horrendous fight. More than ten years later, John still seethed over the issue. "Geffen wouldn't let us put this on the record," he told concert audiences when introducing the song. "Up yours, David!"

But the worst pain Geffen suffered related to Donna Summer. After giving the hit "She Works Hard for the Money" to PolyGram, Summer returned to Geffen Records with two more dud albums, *Cats Without Claws* and *All Systems Go.* The relationship took a nosedive after Summer, playing a concert, allegedly made a thoughtless and career-halting antihomosexual slur. "AIDS is God's revenge on gays," she was reported to have said.

Geffen went berserk. "This is going to cause you a tremendous amount of trouble," he said to her on the phone the next day. "You should disown this immediately." Geffen said that Summer told him she would not retract the comment; Summer, for her part, claimed she had never made it.

Geffen was right: The quote appeared in newspapers and magazines all over the world and succeeded in alienating the gay community, Summer's core constituency. Her Geffen Records contract up, she left the label.

Uncertain where to turn, Geffen decided to revisit an old plan that had failed. He again began pestering Steve Ross to sell him Elektra/Asylum Records. Bob Krasnow, who had now been head of Elektra/Asylum for nearly three years, was having little success in his bid to turn the label around. Geffen was relentless in his pursuit of his plan and used every opportunity to bad-mouth Krasnow to Ross.

There was certainly no love lost between Geffen and Krasnow, who had raised Geffen's ire to an all-time high by trimming the name of the label to just Elektra, tossing Geffen's Asylum moniker in the trash.

Ross had grown weary of Geffen's abuse and told his deputies that they should reopen the issue. "David has approached me again, he wants to buy Elektra," he told Elliot Goldman. "This is silly, he should have gotten it in the first place." When reports circulated that Ross was considering firing Krasnow, executives at the company pointed at Geffen as the instigator.

Within a couple of months, however, Elektra took off, scoring big with such acts as Metallica and Anita Baker. Krasnow became one of the most successful music executives ever to work for a Warner music label. Geffen finally gave up his pursuit of Elektra and even grudgingly gave Krasnow the respect he deserved.

Hungry for cash, Geffen went to plan B. Despite having renegotiated his contract just a little more than a year earlier, he went to Steve Ross with an offer. "You always said you would buy my company," Geffen said. "Why don't you buy it now? You can have it for fifty million." Ross passed.

The kind of turnaround that energized Elektra did not seem imminent at Geffen Records. Business was so bad that Geffen ordered every single expense scrutinized. Linda Loddengaard began issuing cost-cutting directives. In her usual brusque fashion, she even canceled subscriptions to *Billboard* and other trade magazines.

In the summer of 1986, Geffen Records finally released a hit record. Peter Gabriel gave Geffen the biggest solo album of his career, *So.* Propelled by a number-one single, "Sledgehammer," the album stayed on the album charts for ninety-three weeks, peaking at number two.

John Kalodner steadfastly believed that there were big hits to be culled from Aerosmith and went back into the studio with them to make their second Geffen album. He also saw promise in Whitesnake, a British heavy-metal band led by former Deep Purple vocalist David

Coverdale. Kalodner had signed the group a few years earlier, and their first album had charted decent sales. Kalodner was now at work on their follow-up record, certain that the group was ready for the big time.

Tom Zutaut found and signed Tesla, a blue-collar rock band from Sacramento. Zutaut liked their song "Modern Day Cowboy" and thought they had a heartland-rock sound that might just appeal to kids in the Midwest. He sent them out to make a debut album.

With disco dead and pop-music sales on the wane, a major shift was quietly and slowly under way in the music business; both Kalodner and Zutaut were on top of it. The next wave of successful bands would be hard rockers, a movement that was signaled in June 1986 when Cinderella, a band on Mercury Records, released a blockbuster album called *Night Songs.* Bon Jovi, a quintet that was also on Mercury, solidified the trend three months later with a number-one album called *Slippery When Wet.* The rock groups that Kalodner and Zutaut shepherded were soon to make Geffen Records the undisputed leader of the hard-rock ascendancy.

Gary Gersh did not relate to the musical genre that was taking shape; as a result, he got off to a painfully slow start in his new job. One of the few acts he wanted to sign was Robbie Robertson, who had been the last act Gersh signed at EMI before leaving for Geffen. Robertson and Geffen had spoken only a couple of times since their falling-out in 1974. But Gersh arranged a dinner in which the two put aside their differences and decided that a partnership again made sense. The connection to Robertson helped solidify Gersh's bond with Geffen, but it did not go far toward accomplishing his goal of finding sizzling new acts.

*L*ittle Shop of Horrors, millions of dollars over budget and three months behind schedule, finally wrapped in June 1986. Two months later, Geffen and Frank Oz, as well as Bob Daly and Terry Semel, boarded the Warner corporate jet and headed north to San Jose for a test screening.

Arriving at Syufy's Century 22 theaters, Geffen and the others were confident they had a winner on their hands. As the lights dimmed,

Frank Oz took a seat toward the back of the auditorium, a few rows behind Geffen, Daly, and Semel. It was the second of only three pictures his company made on which Geffen himself took a credit as producer, and he was proud as his name came on the screen.

It was clear the audience liked the picture from the first frame. Their laughter was so loud following some jokes that they missed other zingers. They cheered for Rick Moranis and applauded at the end of Steve Martin's hilarious turn.

Daly turned to Semel and patted him on the back. "We have a big hit here!" Daly said.

But fifteen minutes before the end of the picture, the executives could feel the temperature in the room drop when Audrey, the movie's heroine, collapsed outside the store and died. A few moments later, when the Venus flytrap gobbled up Rick Moranis, the room went downright cold. The audience began booing. They threw programs and popcorn buckets at the screen.

Even though he had early on predicted that killing the lead characters would be trouble, Geffen was stunned at the angry response. He loved the movie the way Frank Oz had made it and had hoped that his own prediction would be proved wrong. Geffen's stomach churned as kids in the audience, in response to questions posed by the specialists from National Research Group, decimated the picture.

Feeling nauseated, Geffen could stay in the theater for only a few minutes as the audience members talked even more precisely about what they liked and did not like about the movie. Geffen grew so queasy that he ran out of the theater and into the men's room. Pushing open the door to one of the stalls, he fell to his knees and vomited.

In the theater, the NRG staffers collected cards from each audience member that, among other things, asked if they would recommend the movie to a friend. The spirits of the Warner executives sank as they discovered that only 13 percent said they would advise someone else to go see it.

"It's a disaster! It's a disaster!" Geffen repeated quietly over and over on the plane back to Los Angeles. Employing a common studio tactic when faced with a troubled picture, the executives made a pact that they would lie and tell people the screening went well. If word leaked out about the ending, they agreed to say simply that the movie needed a little fine-tuning.

The next day, Frank Oz went to the studio to meet with Geffen, Daly, and Semel. Geffen told Oz he had to film a new happy ending in which the plant loses and the stars live. If he refused, Oz inferred, Geffen would either find another director to shoot a new ending or abandon the picture altogether. It seemed like the *Risky Business* drama all over again, only Oz could see that Geffen was right. The special effects–laden end sequence that had taken him so long to shoot—and caused the budget to get out of hand—would have to be scrapped.

Howard Ashman reluctantly went about writing a new scene to end the picture. Like Paul Brickman before him, Ashman grew sick as he put his pen to paper to concoct a predictable Hollywood finale. Now the plant would be blown up into a zillion pieces. Seymour and Audrey would marry and walk off into a sunset.

At the end of September, Oz returned to London to shoot the new ending. Oz and Ashman decided to bring back three chorus girls—who appeared throughout the picture—to sing an upbeat ditty at the very end. Since one of the three was unavailable, Oz had to cast a new actress for the reshoot. In order to avoid showing the new singer's face, Oz cleverly staged an entrance for the girls in which he panned down quickly after the original two actresses danced into the frame, catching only the torso and legs of the stand-in.

Reports soon leaked out that the test screening had gone poorly. Geffen and others went into damage-control mode: "The response at the sneak was the best in the history of Warners," Geffen told *New York* magazine. Barry Reardon, distribution chief at Warners, gave similar comments to *The Hollywood Reporter*. "The screening was a great success," he said. When pressed with reports about the ending, Geffen said that it was done so there could be a sequel, which he claimed was already at the "dealmaking" stage. "You can't do a sequel if you kill off the hero at the end," Geffen told the press.

Tom Zutaut was ecstatic about a group he discovered one Monday night at the Troubadour, the same club where Geffen had discovered so many acts fifteen years earlier. The group was called Guns N' Roses and was led by a singer named Axl Rose.

Zutaut was hooked after hearing just two songs, "Nightrain" and "Welcome to the Jungle." He could not exactly articulate why he believed this group had what it took to break out. All he knew was that his internal hot-act radar, which had proved infallible so many times before, was beeping wildly and telling him to sign the act.

Though it was difficult to contain his excitement, he nonchalantly left the club. The Troubadour was filled with A&R executives from other labels that night, and all of them seemed to be monitoring the others' reactions. Zutaut was eager to sign the band, but he wanted his competitors to think he was uninterested.

The next day, Zutaut met with Axl Rose and offered the band a contract. A couple of other record-label types had approached Rose after his set the night before, but Rose liked Zutaut and made just one request.

"If you can get us a check for seventy-five thousand dollars by Friday night at six P.M., we'll sign with you," Rose told him. "Otherwise, we're going to meet with some other people."

Zutaut, more effusive about an act than he had been since joining the company a year and a half earlier, went to Eddie Rosenblatt with the news. "This is gonna be the biggest rock-'n'-roll band in the world," he said, explaining his need for the check by Friday.

"Tom, the wheels just don't move that fast here," Rosenblatt responded.

"Well, we have to defeat the system," Zutaut countered. "Once the band goes into play, we're never gonna get them."

Rosenblatt rolled his eyes. "You know they say that, but they won't really do that."

Zutaut looked him dead in the eyes. "No, this guy is *nuts*. If he says it, he'll do it."

Zutaut took his case to Geffen, who also chuckled when he predicted how successful Guns N' Roses was going to be. "So, really," Geffen said, "the *biggest* rock-and-roll band in the world? You're serious?"

"David, I swear to God," Zutaut continued. "I have no doubt about it, and you have to make this happen. I have to have this check for seventy-five thousand by Friday at six."

Geffen paused for only a moment and then nodded his head. He called the business-affairs department at Warner Bros. Records, leapfrogged the usual bureaucracy, and insisted that a check be delivered to Geffen Records by Friday afternoon.

On Thursday, Zutaut went into a panic when Axl Rose called him with a warning. "I did something really stupid so I have to go back on my word," Rose said. "I had a meeting with Susan Collins at Chrysalis Records. I told her that we would sign with her if she walks naked from her office at ninety-two fifty-five Sunset down to Tower Records before six o'clock on Friday night."

The request might have seemed completely absurd to everyone else, but Zutaut was convinced that Collins and other competitors shared his belief that Guns N' Roses was destined for greatness; he actually worried that Collins might disrobe and streak to Tower just to sign the group.

"Axl, I already went to David Geffen," Zutaut huffed. "We're making the deal here. You can't do this."

Chrysalis was across the street from Geffen Records. On Friday afternoon, Zutaut, whose office faced Sunset, opened the blinds and watched nervously. He sweated as the hours passed by. At 6 P.M., Collins had not done the stunt. Zutaut breathed a giant sigh of relief. Later that night, Axl Rose and his compatriots showed up at Zutaut's office and signed a contract to record for Geffen Records.

Zutaut's prediction about his new signing's success proved to be a bit exaggerated but not much. The group charted phenomenal sales over the next few years, and arguably made David Geffen's record label the very valuable asset he hoped to create.

In the fall of 1986, the Walt Disney Company, now headed by former Paramount Pictures president Michael Eisner, began exploring the possibility of acquiring CBS Records. Jeffrey Katzenberg, Eisner's protégé at Paramount, joined his boss at Disney and was now chairman of the Walt Disney Studios unit.

Katzenberg, who was Geffen's most passionate acolyte, told Eisner they ought to hire Geffen as an adviser in the pursuit of CBS. Eisner and Frank Wells, now Eisner's number two, thought it was an unwise idea. Eisner was having conversations with CBS chairman Laurence Tisch and did not feel that he needed Geffen's help. He was close to an agreement with Tisch, but the two were unable to agree on a price. Tisch wanted $1.2 billion, but Eisner, a notorious bottom-fisher, was unwilling to go higher than $750 million.

Katzenberg insisted that Geffen could make an invaluable contribution. He convinced Eisner to allow Geffen to ride with them on the company plane to New York; on the ride, Geffen enthusiastically offered his services. By the time the plane landed in New York, Eisner felt it would be prudent to hire Geffen if only to neutralize him.

But Eisner and Wells grew apoplectic when they got reports that Geffen had leaked details of their bid to Walter Yetnikoff, who was trying to put together his own bid to acquire his division in a leveraged buyout. In the end, Tisch soon announced that CBS Records was not for sale.

The list of David Geffen's enemies was growing yet again. But within the story lay a silver lining that was not lost on Geffen. CBS Records was an extremely valuable asset and its sale discussions portended a remarkable escalation in the value of record companies over the next few years.

The trend was confirmed just a few weeks later when Bertelsmann AG, the West German publishing and entertainment conglomerate, paid three hundred million dollars for the 75 percent stake in RCA Records it did not already own. David Geffen had picked a good time to reenter the music business.

David and Mitchell with Deena (left) and a
sickly Batya, on Batya's final Mother's Day, 1987.
(Courtesy Deena Volovskaya)

BATYA

|||

G effen's relationship with Bob Brassel was rocky, and at various turns it seemed that it would implode. But soon they found a wonder cure that helped to breathe new life into their partnership. The odd potion was called Lifespring.

Lifespring was the est of the 1980s, a personal-growth course that attracted about a quarter of a million Americans. Lifespringers, as graduates of the course called themselves, believed the five-day, thirty-eight-hour course showed them the path to success and happiness. It had striking similarities to est; in fact, Lifespring founder John Haney had once worked with est wizard Werner Erhard at a company called Mind Dynamics.

Like est, Lifespring was a rule-laden experience set within a large-group format, in which people showed an amazing willingness to divulge their feelings in front of strangers. Through various exercises, some found themselves wailing like babies and tightly embracing strangers. The first course, known as "the basic," cost four hundred dollars.

Geffen and Brassel soon experienced "breakthrough," the ultimate prize in Lifespring. In est-style jargon, Lifespring teachers told participants that their breakthrough would come through "action" and "taking responsibility for your life."

Just as Geffen had become a proselytizer for est more than ten years earlier, now he and Brassel became zealous advocates of Lifespring. For them, the course delivered on the promise of "an enormous step toward freedom," and they eagerly pledged to spread the gospel.

Their relationship newly rejuvenated, Geffen and Brassel hosted Saturday lunches at the beach house in Malibu. Madonna, Carrie Fisher, Barry Diller, and Sandy Gallin were among the regulars. It was here that Brassel got the idea that he wanted to work in the film industry.

Geffen, now forty-three, helped him get a job at the Warner Bros. movie studio. His friend Mark Canton, the studio's president of production, agreed to take Brassel on as an executive assistant. On his first day, Geffen sent Canton an enormous bouquet of flowers to thank him.

Unfortunately, word spread quickly through the studio that Brassel was Geffen's boyfriend. Brassel, however, surprised everyone at the company with his intelligence and wit. Within just a few years, he won promotions that catapulted him to the top of the studio's production ranks. He was credited with helping to save some of the studio's biggest-budget movies.

A December 19 release date was set for *Little Shop of Horrors,* smack in the middle of a holiday movie season that included such films as the Eddie Murphy vehicle *The Golden Child* and *Star Trek IV: The Voyage Home.* With the new ending in place, Geffen thought he had an enormous hit on his hands. "This is the best thing I have ever been involved with," he told friends.

Geffen almost single-handedly created an enormous and positive buzz around the movie. He was the picture's biggest cheerleader, as he talked it up to everyone. The Warners publicity team eagerly got in on the action, having planned and hosted a Come Dressed as Your Favorite Plant contest in front of Mann's Chinese Theater in Hollywood the day of the film's opening.

Geffen's infectious enthusiasm wore off on such friends as Jeffrey Katzenberg. Geffen talked up Howard Ashman ceaselessly; he convinced Katzenberg to make a multi-picture deal with the lyricist. Katzenberg was seeking to revive Disney's moribund animated-movie franchise, and Geffen predicted that Ashman was the talent he needed. In the years to come, Ashman's clever lyrics inspired such blockbusters as *The Little Mermaid* and *Beauty and the Beast.* The movies in turn reenergized Disney and propelled its earnings to unprecedented heights.

Unfortunately for Geffen, *Little Shop of Horrors* was not destined to reap such good fortune. The picture opened to mediocre reviews, and audiences showed little interest in the live-action musical. Rick Moranis and Ellen Greene lacked the star appeal of the season's other movie offerings, and its box-office tally stalled out at $38.7 million. Geffen did not make a penny.

The failure of the picture left him devastated. The experience was so painful that he resolved to never again become so personally invested in a movie project. He determined to leave all but the most important moviemaking decisions to Eric Eisner. The company's next movie, a quirky comedy about a ghost called *Beetlejuice,* was to be Geffen's most successful movie to date, but he distanced himself from the project and in the end had very little to do with it.

With Geffen Records' own promotion department now in place, Geffen decided that he needed his own publicity and international operations, as well as his own CFO. For the international job, Eddie Rosenblatt believed the best candidate was Mel Posner, Geffen's deputy at Elektra/Asylum Records. But Posner had not forgotten the pain Geffen had caused him when he fired him in 1975.

"I'll do it as long as I don't have to deal with David every day," he said.

"You won't have to deal with David every day," Rosenblatt assured him. But Posner refused to sign the kind of long-term contract the label's other top executives had signed. So Geffen then asked him to lunch. He did not have any negative feelings about Posner, and he wanted the best man for the job.

Geffen took Posner to the Ivy, where he had destroyed Evelyn Ostin a few years earlier. Posner hoped the lunch would be short. Although he greatly admired Geffen's talents and thought of him as one of the best executives in the business, he found interactions with Geffen to be uncomfortable.

"David, I have to tell you, you're the only human being that intimidates me," Posner said.

"Mel, that's your problem," Geffen replied. "I don't do anything to intimidate you."

By the end of the meal, Geffen's famous salesmanship had won Posner over. He agreed to sign the contract.

In April 1987, Geffen Records released the blockbuster record that finally signaled the beginning of a turnaround. It was the label's second album by Whitesnake, the heavy-metal band John Kalodner had signed four years earlier.

Relieved and ecstatic, Geffen made the one-block walk from his office down to the Hornburg luxury-car dealership and purchased a Range Rover for Kalodner as a thank-you gift. He went back to Kalodner's office and presented him with the keys.

For once, the label did not simply have a single hit album in a vacuum. Two other records also sold a million units each. Tesla scored a major success with their first record, *Mechanical Resonance*. The other hit was the original Broadway cast recording of the musical *Les Misérables*.

Geffen once again went to Steve Ross and told him he would sell him his company right then and there. But now that the label was showing signs of life, Geffen had upped the price to seventy-five million dollars. Ross once again politely declined.

With a few hit records in the stores, Geffen decided to take Bob Brassel and Eric Eisner, who several months earlier had married a woman named Lisa Norris, to Mexico for a vacation. At Steve Ross's direction, Warner Communications had purchased an elegant house in Acapulco and made it available to Warner executives for the purpose of socializing with actors, singers, and other business partners. Called Villa Eden, it had tennis courts, a screening room, and a world-class cook. This was David Geffen's kind of perk, and he took full advantage of it.

It was Lisa Eisner's thirtieth birthday, and Geffen wanted to play host to an extravagant celebration. He had grown terrifically close to Eric and trusted him more than anyone else in the world. Geffen also liked Lisa, a stylish woman who was an editor at *Vogue.* For the party, Geffen invited her to bring some of her friends along on the Warner jet.

Bob Brassel had been in his new job at Warner Bros. just a few months, but it suited him famously. He proudly wore a Warners baseball cap nearly every day of the trip. Within a few months, he was promoted to production executive. In Mexico, he and Geffen relaxed and read books on chaise longues by a kidney-shaped pool. Geffen seemed, at last, to be content.

But when he returned to Los Angeles, Geffen discovered that his mother, who was a month shy of turning eighty, was very ill. Batya had had cancer for many years, but she had not told anyone, including her husband, Sam. She had been treated for breast cancer in 1972 but somehow managed to get through the operation without telling David or Mitchell. A woman with many secrets, Batya kept the documentation of her illness hidden in a locked closet in her home. But by the early 1980s, Batya's cancer had returned. This time it was slowly but surely crippling her.

She continued to refuse to admit she was sick or to discuss her illness with anyone except her doctor. But anyone who looked at her could tell that she was not well. Before she was sick, the four-foot-ten woman weighed 110 pounds. As she began to lose weight, her skin hung lifelessly on her tiny frame. The inexpensive wigs she had worn for years looked even more ill-fitting than before. She lost her appetite and her

*Geffen and boyfriend Bob Brassel (right, shirtless) throw a party
in Acapulco celebrating the thirtieth birthday of Lisa Eisner
(standing, extreme left). Lisa's husband, Eric Eisner, the president
of the David Geffen Company, stands third from the left.*

energy. She had trouble walking. Her strong will to live, passed along to both her sons, was beginning to fade.

David and Mitchell could tell that she was close to dying. The gulf between the brothers had only widened in recent years, and they had spent very little time together. Mitchell had stewed for years that David had not shown up at the bat mitzvah of Mitchell's younger daughter, Elaine. David had been financially generous with Mitchell, his wife, and their two daughters, but he did not care to spend time with them. David's riches seemed to cause Mitchell to feel jealous as well as indebted to his brother, making reconciliation unlikely. It also had not been lost on Mitchell that his mother still considered David her favorite child.

But in May 1987, the men put aside their differences and met at Mitchell's house on High Valley Road in Encino for a Mother's Day celebration they feared might be the last. David was uncomfortable attending family get-togethers, so he brought along a friend, movie producer Howard Rosenman, to help get through the day. The brothers soon after had another get-together at David's beach house. This time, Renee Geffen took a photograph of David, Bob Brassel, and Mitchell with their arms around Batya.

The positive change in David Geffen as a result of Lifespring and its calls for healthy relationships proved to be short-lived. He and Clive Davis, for example, remained alienated, and their relationship got much worse.

After Davis's negative comments in 1982 about some of Geffen's deals, Geffen stopped talking to him, and began an anti-Clive campaign in which he trashed him at every turn. "I'm not a fan of Clive Davis's. I don't speak to him. I haven't spoken to him for many years. He's an egomaniac, is what he is," he told Fredric Dannen, a journalist then doing research for a book on the music business. "He's such an arrogant fuck that he's of no interest to me."

The long-standing friendship between Geffen and Ahmet Ertegun, meanwhile, had somewhat amazingly survived Geffen's continual and persistent bad-mouthing. Things had been helped somewhat when Geffen apologized to him for spreading those damaging rumors that Ertegun was an anti-Semite. But the two were destined for more turbulent times in 1987 when Crosby, Stills, Nash & Young, the group that had brought them together, planned a onetime reunion album on Atlantic Records. Ertegun contacted Geffen because Neil Young was, for a few more months, under contract to Geffen Records.

Given that he had three of the four players under contract at Atlantic Records, Ertegun was dismayed when Geffen demanded that Geffen Records get 50 percent of the album's proceeds. "Listen, Ahmet," Geffen ranted. "Crosby, Stills, and Nash are *old fat farts*! The only one with any *talent* is Neil Young!" After much haggling, the two men finally worked out a deal, the terms of which were not disclosed, and CSNY the next year released *American Dream* on Atlantic.

Besides this kind of occasional dealmaking with artists with whom he had long relationships, Geffen now played virtually no role in the A&R activities at his label, leaving nearly all the decision-making to his troika of talent scouts. If the label was involved in a heated pursuit of a band, Geffen was sometimes called upon to lend his celebrity to help close a deal.

Geffen's three scouts disliked and distrusted one another, a fact that Geffen liked and even promoted. There was intense rumormongering and backstabbing among them. Zutaut and Kalodner told people that Gersh was the most audacious liar of all time. Gersh and Zutaut made fun of Kalodner and his geeky idea to revive Cher's singing career. Gersh and Kalodner complained that Zutaut was a petulant child who received preferential treatment.

Although his talent scouts knew that Geffen preferred Wagner to Whitesnake, from time to time they did seek his opinion on an act. Tom Zutaut, sensing he had found an act that Geffen himself might listen to, sent him the demo tapes for Edie Brickell and New Bohemians.

"I think this girl will sell a lot of records," Zutaut told Geffen, handing him the tape. "I think she's really special, and I think her song is a hit."

After listening to the songs, Geffen called Zutaut into his office. "You asked me for my opinion so I'm going to give it to you," Geffen said. "I think it's crap. I wouldn't sign her."

"I'm going to sign her anyway," he replied. Geffen, as usual, deferred to the creative wishes of his A&R team. Within a couple of years, Brickell married Geffen's former friend Paul Simon.

Similarly, John Kalodner kept in contact with Geffen about his plans to make an album with Cher. Geffen continued to warn him about her, but Kalodner pressed on. Since meeting Kalodner, Cher's star as an actress had continued to rise with roles in such films as *The Witches of Eastwick* and *Mask*. Kalodner was nervous when Cher, the biggest star he had ever worked with, came to meet him for the first time at his office. He again made his pitch that she could be a major pop star once again. She agreed to make a record.

In the fall of 1986, she telephoned Kalodner and said she could record the following June, just after completing two movies, *Moonstruck* and *Suspect*. Kalodner spent the next nine months pleading with the hottest songwriters to give Cher their best new songs. It was a hard sell; she had not had a hit album since 1979 and was not the first singer songwriters thought of when they shopped their best songs.

In the spring of 1987, Cher called Kalodner to confirm the plan. "You have me for four weeks, from June first to June twenty-ninth," Cher told him, explaining that she planned to spend the rest of the summer in Europe. "You find all the songs, all the producers, have everything ready, and I'll come in and sing."

Cher showed up and sang the songs Kalodner had selected, including "I Found Someone," cowritten by Michael Bolton, a singer who was trying to make a career as a solo artist. Cher loved the tune and proceeded to make a music video to promote it. She wanted to direct the video herself. For support and assistance, she hired Vilmos Zsigmond, an accomplished director of photography, and Harald Ortenburger, the camera operator from *Moonstruck*. But the day before the video was scheduled to be shot, Geffen called Cher and told her he was pulling the plug on the project. He told her he did not think she was competent enough to direct the video herself. He was also upset that Cher, now forty-one, had cast her twenty-two-year-old boyfriend, Robert Camiletti, in a key role in the video.

"You're not doing it, sweetheart! Not with that guy, not with you in control," Geffen shrieked. "Forget it!"

"Dave, fuck you!" Cher bellowed. She thought Geffen was jealous of her handsome boyfriend. Moreover, she was hurt that he thought she was incapable of directing a three-minute-and-forty-second music video, especially given that she would do it with some of the talented crew members who had just finished *Moonstruck.*

Geffen called her four times to vent his anger, but Cher hung up on him each time. She was determined to make the video. She decided that if Geffen would not pay for it, she would find another backer who would. That night, she persuaded Bally's Health & Tennis, the fitness chain for which she had done some commercials, to pick up the tab. The shoot began as scheduled the next day.

G uns N' Roses had been signed to Geffen Records for a year and a half before Tom Zutaut pulled a debut record out of the band. The record, which they named *Appetite for Destruction,* was released in August 1987. In the weeks prior to its release, Geffen paid little attention to the group and did not even know what its members looked like. One day he stormed into the lobby where the band was waiting for Zutaut and began screaming that someone was parked in his reserved parking space. The guitarist Slash had used his space, but he got up and moved his car.

When Geffen heard *Appetite for Destruction,* he found it unpleasant. But Tom Zutaut was convinced it was a winner. He worked with the band's managers to book a months-long tour. Zutaut's plan was to get the band's message out the old-fashioned way, going town to town and playing music to whomever showed up.

Zutaut hounded the promotion department, telling Al Coury and his staff that the record was going to be huge. But Coury bombed out: Despite their best efforts, the Geffen promotion team could not get radio stations to play the album's first single, "Welcome to the Jungle." They faced even more resistance from MTV, which opted not to play the band's videos. MTV had been a driving force behind the success of what industry types called heavy-metal "hair" bands, but now they were cutting back on the playtime allotted to such bands, believing that the trend had peaked. "They're certainly never gonna play this one in church," Coury sniped, commenting on the song's raunchy lyrics.

In September, Geffen Records had a big hit, and once again Geffen had John Kalodner to thank. Tim Collins, Aerosmith's manager, had helped get that band sober; Kalodner as a result was able to team them with a producer whom they would listen to, and together they made a huge record. The album, *Permanent Vacation,* was an instant winner, shocking industry wags who had dismissed the idea that the aging rockers led by Steven Tyler could replicate their 1970s success.

When it came time to make a music video for the hit "Dude (Looks Like a Lady)," Tyler cast Kalodner in a small part. Kalodner, with his long brown beard, appeared decked out in a wedding dress. While the song peaked at number fourteen on the pop charts, the album's next single, "Angel," did even better, rising to number three. *Permanent Vacation* eventually sold five million copies.

Kalodner's other faded star act was also positioned to stage a comeback. Cher's self-titled album was, in a bit of smart timing, released in December, the same month MGM released *Moonstruck.* Her fans went wild for the movie and the album, which included her first top-ten single since 1979. "I Found Someone" went to number ten on the charts. The video Geffen did not want to pay for helped to propel her back to star status in the music world. The next single, "We All Sleep Alone," went to number fourteen. The album was certified gold. Cher and Kalodner immediately made plans to make another record.

G effen did not become seriously involved with *Beetlejuice* until the movie was wrapped and the marketing was being prepared. Warner Bros. did research suggesting that the movie would fare better if it was titled "House Ghosts." Tim Burton, the movie's director, could not believe that Warners thought that title was superior.

"Why don't you just call it 'Scared Sheetless'?" Burton mocked. He was upset that Geffen agreed that the studio's idea merited consideration. Geffen and Warner Bros. later concluded, however, that Burton's title was better.

Geffen was preoccupied with thoughts of his ailing mother. For a few months, Sam secretly shuttled Batya to the doctor for weekly chemotherapy treatments, stopping each time at the apartment of her sister, Deena. Deena could tell that Batya was in serious trouble, even though she refused to discuss the illness she was battling. Each week, Deena prepared a feast in the hopes that Batya would eat. But she rarely took more than a nibble. She wanted only to sit on the couch and talk to her sister about their childhood back in the Ukraine.

In September 1987, Batya had a minor stroke and instructed Sam to drive her to the emergency room at Cedars-Sinai Medical Center. She regained her strength the same day but soon after was admitted to UCLA Medical Center, where Deena and Sam kept vigil over her in room 1010. David visited her there frequently, but Linda Loddengaard tracked him down, and he conducted business from her bedside. She was released shortly after the beginning of 1988, insisting that she was fine. She told Mitchell to go away on a planned skiing vacation. "I am going to live to be one hundred," she told him.

But she soon relapsed, and on March 6 she was admitted to Cedars-Sinai, where David had determined she would likely get better care. But Batya still refused to say the word *cancer*—even to her sister. Her cover was finally blown one day when a doctor came into her room while Deena was reading the newspaper. "What bothers us, Mrs. Sandler, is the tumor in your colon," the doctor said. Batya began shouting at the doctor, who backed out of the room. Embarrassed that her sister had heard the news, Batya pulled a blanket up over her head. Deena hid behind her newspaper, pretended that she had not heard the doctor, and cried quietly. Deena attempted to persuade Batya to talk, but she could sense that Batya was uninterested in doing so. The two never discussed it.

David sat at her bedside and engaged his mother in light conversation. Looking at her favorite son, she beamed as proudly at him as she had when he was only a child. Then it occurred to her to ask him a question.

"How much money do you have?" It was the first time she had ever asked.

David told her he had hundreds of millions of dollars.

Batya thought the response was deliciously funny, and she broke into a fit of loud and uncontrolled laughter. She was delighted at her son's success, an accomplishment she could not fathom. David laughed with her, but he feared her excessive laughter might induce a fatal heart attack. Batya told David that she wanted him to promise her that he would take care of Mitchell. David told her he would.

Her latest stroke had affected her ability to speak and to maneuver her right hand, but she was determined to regain her full capacities. Unbelievably, she succeeded at both.

"Mom, to what do you attribute this miracle?" David asked.

"I have no envy. I have no jealousy. And I have no hate," she said solemnly.

It was the last conversation the two ever had.

At 12:59 P.M. on March 10, 1988, Batya died. Although she had fibbed about her age throughout her entire life, in death at least her true age could be told: She was eighty.

Other secrets that Batya had held inside could also be told. The next day, Deena told David and Mitchell the tragic story of how her and Batya's parents and siblings had perished in the Holocaust. Suddenly, the horrible breakdown that led Batya to be institutionalized in the late 1940s began to make sense. David was horrified as he processed the details of how his relatives had been brutally murdered. He was stunned as he contemplated the pain his mother suffered from having kept the secret for so long.

David and Mitchell set about making plans for a small funeral. But David's friends responded to the news of Batya's death with a huge outpouring of sympathy, many telling Linda Loddengaard that they wanted to attend the funeral. The service, held at the Stephen S. Wise Temple off Mulholland Drive, drew such mourners as Warren Beatty, Allen Grubman, Sandy Gallin, and Barry Diller.

At the funeral, Geffen drew aside Sue Mengers, who like him was a combative figure who had made many enemies during her tenure as an agent.

"I want to tell you what my mother told me just before she died," he said. "She said, 'I have no envy. I have no jealousy. And I have no hate.' "

"Well, they'll never be able to say that about us," Mengers responded.

The group went to Mount Sinai Memorial Park, next to Forest Lawn, for an emotional graveside service. Bob Brassel was especially helpful to Mitchell, who broke down there. The group went back to Mitchell's house in Encino to sit shiva, the Jewish custom of receiving mourners and recalling the dead for seven days following a funeral.

At day's end, David went home to Malibu with Sandy Gallin and another friend, Joel Schumacher, the director of such films as *St. Elmo's Fire* and *The Lost Boys*. He took a shower, donned a white terry-cloth robe, and walked outside. The three men sat quietly on the steps looking out at the Pacific Ocean. Schumacher put his arm around Geffen, who began sobbing.

Geffen returned to Broadway to co-produce *M. Butterfly,* a play about a French diplomat's romance with a Chinese diva who turns out to be a man. The play, however, opened only ten days after Batya died, and a grieving David opted not to make the trip to New York for the opening.

Steve Ross invited him to spend the Easter holiday with him and his wife, Courtney. Geffen accepted. They sailed from Saint Bart's to Grenada. Mo and Evelyn Ostin, as well as Lorne Michaels and Quincy Jones, were also along for the trip. Geffen hoped that time away with old friends might help shake him out of his depression.

Good news reached Geffen on the boat. *Beetlejuice* had opened over the holiday weekend, and surprisingly the quirky picture had charted the biggest Easter opening ever. The movie went on to gross $73.3 million, $10 million more than the sizable tally charted by *Risky Business*. Geffen Pictures made about $10 million on the film; for several years it was Geffen's most successful movie.

When he returned to Los Angeles, he and Mitchell tended to their stepfather, Sam, and sought to assure him that they wanted him to stay in the house on Gilcrest Drive. David went to see Deena, who was now seventy-one. He wanted to provide for her in the way he had for his mother, encouraging her to move to Beverly Hills and share the Gilcrest house with Sam. She accepted his invitation.

When Batya's will was probated, her attorney informed David and Mitchell that she had a secret safe-deposit box at her bank on Wilshire Boulevard. "What could she possibly have that was so valuable to be under lock and key?" David asked his brother. He guessed that it might be money or jewelry.

Batya had hidden the key so well that they could not find it. Mitchell and David went to the bank, where an officer drilled the box open. Inside the box was another small box, which was wrapped in Saran Wrap. Inside that box was an envelope. When they opened the envelope, they found yet another envelope. Finally, they opened the second envelope to find the items Batya had treasured more than anything else: Her and Abe's American citizenship papers.

Batya, who had grown up in a family and in a country in which she had no voice, believed that there was nothing more valuable than being an American. David gulped hard as he realized how far she had come in her life. He took the papers, had them framed, and displayed them prominently in his screening room. They remained there as a constant reminder of the things, taken for granted by so many, that had been most important in his mother's life.

Geffen was troubled by the use of the word "faggot"
in a song by Guns N' Roses (lead singer Axl Rose is at center)
and concerned that the controversy might prompt scrutiny
of his private life. (Lyn McAfee/Shooting Star)

CHAPTER 28

TIME WARNER
SURPRISE

|||

In May 1988, sales of Guns N' Roses' debut album, *Appetite for Destruction,* tapered off at about two hundred thousand copies. It was a decent start for a new band, especially considering that there had been virtually no radio airplay. But Tom Zutaut was disappointed. He continued to hound the promotion department, begging them to push radio stations to play the record.

Finally, Eddie Rosenblatt told Zutaut it was time to give up the fight, but Zutaut refused. "No way. This record's just beginning," he told Rosenblatt. "We haven't even scratched the surface yet. There's a number-one single that is buried on the second side of the album. The promotion people have not even listened to it!" Zutaut told Rosenblatt that the winner was called "Sweet Child O' Mine," a song inspired by Axl Rose's then girlfriend, Erin Everly, daughter of Don Everly of the Everly Brothers.

Zutaut then took his case directly to Geffen.

"What is the one thing that I could do to help you?" Geffen asked.

"It would help," Zutaut said, "if you could get the 'Welcome to the

Jungle' video played on MTV." Zutaut predicted that the video would become one of the network's most requested, and would also help in breaking out the band.

Geffen agreed to grant Zutaut's wish and called MTV chief executive Tom Freston. Zutaut did not tell Geffen about MTV's policy not to air any more videos by "hair" bands such as Guns N' Roses. As a result, Geffen was taken off guard when Freston told him about the rule.

Freston, still grateful for Geffen's support in the early days of MTV, agreed to make an exception to the edict. But MTV would play it only once, at 3:00 A.M. on the East Coast, midnight on the West Coast.

Moments after the video was aired, the phones began to light up at MTV. The network's switchboard was inundated with calls from viewers demanding to see the video again. As Zutaut had predicted, it became one of the most-requested videos ever played on MTV. Almost overnight, sales of the album jumped to five hundred thousand units.

Al Coury and his promotion team began pitching "Sweet Child O' Mine." Thanks to the MTV exposure, stations eagerly put the tune into their rotation. "Sweet Child O' Mine" shot up the pop-music charts and on September 10 was named the number-one song in America, where it stayed for two weeks.

Appetite for Destruction, which had been on store shelves for ten months, went to number one on the album charts and remained there for five weeks. It was to be on the charts for nearly three years.

Geffen was thrilled, but he went out of his way to tell people that Tom Zutaut was responsible for the band's success. Geffen smartly empowered and enfranchised his executives by making sure they got the credit they deserved. As insurance against them leaving, he also saw that his executives were paid well. He knew how to keep the men happy: He soon went back to the Hornburg dealership to buy another Range Rover, this one for Zutaut.

Geffen's record company, movie and Broadway ventures, and real-estate investments were providing him with enormous profits. His house in Malibu, which he had expanded a few years earlier by acquiring the property to the south, grew once again as he purchased the lot to the north. It added up to a modest compound: A pool and a gym to the south and a screening room to the north flanked the main house. He sold the mansion on Angelo Drive and soon thereafter acquired a two-acre vacant lot in Beverly Hills. In yet another shrewd deal, he bought the entire block of offices that housed his record label along Sunset Boulevard. The executive offices were now housed in the westernmost building, at 9130 Sunset.

Unlike some people with money who preferred to enjoy their wealth privately, Geffen wanted everyone to know about his success. The optimum venue for such an announcement, in his eyes, was a listing in the Forbes 400, the magazine's annual report of the wealthiest Americans. In a display of his unmistakable chutzpah, Geffen personally called *Forbes*'s editors, lobbying to be included. He made his debut on the list in October 1988, when his net worth was reported at $240 million. It was an extraordinary leap, considering he said he had started the decade with just $30 million.

Geffen then and subsequently complained that the magazine underestimated his wealth. In any event, the fact remained that he was now in the really big money. He soon struck up a friendship with Richard Rainwater, the Texas money-man who had helped the Bass family make their billions. Rainwater invited Geffen to join an investor group that was taking a 4 percent equity position in Honeywell. Geffen would be a behind-the-scenes player in a proxy fight that forced the company's management to eliminate a "poison pill" from the corporate by-laws. After realizing a 30 percent gain, the group sold its shares.

But Geffen hungered for even more money. Following Bertelsmann's acquisition of RCA Records, in 1988 Sony stunned the entertainment world with its two-billion-dollar purchase of CBS Records.

Allen Grubman dubbed the day the deal was announced "the day the record business was 'bar mitzvahed.' " Geffen was in the right business, and his timing, as usual, was impeccable.

After a year in release, Guns N' Roses' *Appetite for Destruction* had sold nine million copies, giving Geffen Records profits of about thirteen million dollars, before taxes. The label soon hit with another big winner. Edie Brickell and New Bohemians, whom Geffen had opposed signing, had a giant debut record that went to number four and sold over a million copies.

Based on revenues, David Geffen had built the hottest independent record label in music-business history. It was an astounding turnaround, given the diminished circumstances Geffen Records had been in just two years earlier. Geffen had identified the right players to pick and signed what proved to be the most popular acts of the day, leaving them alone to do their jobs. The profits were so immense that Geffen soon acquired even more trappings of the super-rich, including a full-time chauffeur.

Of the three A&R czars at Geffen Records, Gary Gersh was faring the worst. In his three years, he had brought in few bands; the records he was overseeing mostly lost money. Even his winners, such as albums by Robbie Robertson and Pat Metheny, did not post sales anywhere near the stellar ones of the acts John Kalodner and Tom Zutaut had signed.

In June 1988, Gersh married Maria Mancuso, the daughter of Paramount Pictures chairman Frank Mancuso. After Gersh returned from his honeymoon, Geffen called him into his office and ripped into him. "Tom and John are delivering multiplatinum albums. . . . What are you doing?" he bellowed. "You're not focused here! You're lazy!"

In tears, Gersh went home to his bride. But the talking-to slapped him awake and illustrated a key part of Geffen's successful management style: He was direct and honest in his approach, knowing just how to inspire his employees, whether they were faring poorly or performing above expectations.

Gersh was now ready to kick into gear. He had been collecting music that kids in the percolating "postpunk" underground listened to and decided to make this genre his niche. One of the groups was a New York–based band called Sonic Youth. They had been around since 1981 but did not have a deal with a major label; Gersh masterminded a plan to quickly change that. The grunge scene was being born, and it soon became the second major musical movement that Geffen Records owned. The third piston in Geffen's A&R troika was beginning to fire.

In the meantime, Geffen was focusing on the big picture. With record-company values at an all-time high, he was busy calculating how best to maximize the value of the company he had created. For a moment, he was unsure whether he should sell the label as it was or build it through an acquisition. Despite the staggering prices labels were commanding, Geffen believed there were still some bargains to be had on a couple of independent labels; he began thinking about a purchase.

One was Chrysalis Records, the London-based label whose U.S. offices were just across the street from Geffen Records. With a small roster of acts, including Pat Benatar and Huey Lewis and the News, Chrysalis had had a disappointing year. Its problems had been exacerbated by reports that a planned Billy Idol album would be delayed.

Geffen mulled over the opportunity with Allen Grubman (who also, strangely enough, represented Chrysalis) and decided that Geffen Records would purchase, for six million dollars, an 8.4 percent stake in Chrysalis. In London, the decision was met with disdain. Chrysalis chairman Chris Wright complained to the *Financial Times* that Geffen's purchase was an unfriendly overture. Geffen told *The New York Times* that he had told Wright his purchase was for investment purposes only.

The second Guns N' Roses album, *G N' R Lies,* contained a song that left Geffen deeply troubled. Called "One in a Million," it featured homophobic lyrics including startling use of the word "faggot." Before it was released, Geffen warned Axl Rose that the song would provoke a controversy and cause him trouble. But Rose was insistent that the track remain on the album; Geffen demurred to the wishes of his hottest-selling act. He convinced himself that Rose was not homophobic and that the thoughts expressed in his song were feelings the rocker had once had but had long since come to terms with. *G N' R Lies* was another colossal hit, peaking at number two on the album charts.

Geffen was concerned that the song might prompt scrutiny of him as well. The spread of AIDS had spawned the creation of a gay-activist press that beseeched famous but closeted homosexuals to come out. Leaders of the movement argued that such admissions would prompt the government to do more to combat AIDS.

While Geffen had so far been spared the activists' spotlight, keeping his sexual orientation out of print became an increasingly time-consuming job. His fury was unleashed when he read a bootleg manuscript of a book about the record business called *Hit Men,* written by former *Institutional Investor* reporter Fredric Dannen. The unedited manuscript mentioned Geffen's homosexuality and included a footnote that said Geffen had been married in a gay wedding. Although it did not name names, the footnote apparently referred to a rumored commitment ceremony between Geffen and Bob Brassel. The book also said that Geffen's archenemy, Irving Azoff, referred to Geffen as "Mrs. Geffen."

Geffen was infuriated and began devising a strategy to have the references excised from the book. He first called Owen Laster, his old friend from the William Morris Agency who was now head of the agency's literary department. Geffen asked him if he had any influence with Random House, whose Times Books imprint was the publisher of *Hit Men,* and if he would call them on his behalf and complain.

"David, look, I'm a writer's agent," Laster said, shocked at Geffen's request and surprised about how agitated he was. "I make my living defending writers. I'm usually on the other end of these fights."

"But this isn't true!" Geffen screamed.

Laster reluctantly agreed to call Joni Evans, then the publisher of Random House. When Laster reported back that Evans refused to get involved, Geffen called Bert Fields, his hotshot Hollywood litigator, and instructed him to draft a threatening letter to Random House.

Fields wrote that Geffen had never been through any kind of wedding ceremony, including a homosexual one. He also asserted that Dannen had twisted Irving Azoff's use of the phrase "Mrs. Geffen." Fields said that Azoff's reference had nothing to do with homosexuality but was instead shorthand for Geffen's fastidiousness concerning his house and its contents.

Fields noted his disappointment that a reputable company like Random House would consider publishing sensational gossip. He insisted that a lawsuit would be forthcoming if the lines were not deleted. The publisher backed down and cut the passages.

Although he had decided against making a movie for Geffen Pictures, Michael Jackson continued to seek and value Geffen's advice. He asked him to become part of a three-man board of advisers who counseled him on career and financial matters. Shortly after taking the job, Geffen became the most influential voice in Jackson's life.

Geffen was soon handed the task of finding Jackson a new manager. Sandy Gallin, whose firm represented mostly such aging acts as Mac Davis and Dolly Parton, immediately began lobbying for the job. He wanted to reinvigorate his image by winning the contract to manage one of the hottest stars in the business.

But Geffen doubted Gallin was up to the steep challenge of handling Jackson. He also felt that he had already done too many favors for Gallin and questioned what Gallin had done for him in return. He had not forgotten how, in the wake of Geffen's painful breakup with Cher in 1975, Gallin had pursued and signed the singer against his wishes.

The friendship had survived that breach, but it was dealt other setbacks in the following years, and at various turns Geffen wanted to sever it permanently. But at such times some crisis would occur and one friend would come to the other's rescue. In 1985, for example,

Gallin had been diagnosed with metastasized melanoma, and Geffen had rushed to his bedside. It was at these moments that the tortured partnership showed its true value, allowing the relationship to stumble along until the next drama arose.

Geffen knew that Gallin's hot desire for Michael Jackson was not such a crisis, so he set about looking for a candidate he felt was better qualified. One of the first people he thought of was Howard Kaufman, who was running Irving Azoff's Front Line Management.

Azoff was now head of MCA Records, but, as Geffen had in the early 1970s, he had somehow finagled a shady arrangement in which he maintained ownership of his management company. Geffen hypocritically blasted Azoff in the press for the dual ownership: "You cannot be in the record business and manage artists on your own label—it's a conflict of interest," he told the *Los Angeles Times*. "How can a manager get the best deal he can for his client if the manager also works for the record company? It's very disturbing. If it's legal, it shouldn't be."

Geffen offered the Michael Jackson job to Kaufman apparently on the condition that he leave Front Line and drop all of Azoff's other clients, including Geffen Records superstar Don Henley. Kaufman reported Geffen's offer to Azoff but turned it down. Azoff blew up, convinced that Geffen was luring Kaufman only because it would destroy Front Line. Geffen called the charge ridiculous, saying he simply thought Kaufman was the best man for the job. But Azoff did not see it that way, and he rededicated himself to killing David Geffen.

Time—the magazine, pay-TV, and cable giant—and Warner Communications had for two years discussed the possibility of a joint venture or merger, but various issues had gotten in the way. Secret talks, however, began again in earnest in the spring of 1988.

Only a handful of people at each company was aware of the plan. In addition to Steve Ross, other Warner executives who knew about the merger included Bob Daly and Terry Semel. Steve Ross decided not to tell David Geffen.

On the night of Thursday, March 2, 1989, the boards of the companies approved a plan to combine to create an entertainment behemoth with a stock-market value of more than $15 billion, with annual revenues exceeding $10 billion. Ross and Time chairman J. Richard Munro vowed to hold the news secret until a press conference on Sunday, March 5. They knew a leak might lead to insider trading or other embarrassing problems that might compromise or even undo the transaction.

But on Friday afternoon, despite the executives' best efforts, the news started to leak. As his vast network of sources began reporting that something major was about to go down, Geffen's rage began to boil. He thought of himself as the most wired executive in Hollywood. Here he felt humiliated, not even knowing what was going on in his own backyard. He began to question his friendship with Ross. How could Ross be involved in such an important transaction without consulting or confiding in him?

Geffen flooded Ross's office in New York with phone calls, demanding to speak to the chairman. He also placed countless calls to other executives at the company, including his friend Terry Semel.

Ross refused to return Geffen's calls, wary of violating securities laws. But Semel, who was more of a peer to Geffen than Ross was, grew nervous when he saw all the messages from him. Reluctantly, he decided to call him.

"What is going on?" Geffen screamed, growing more irate by the moment. "Something big is obviously going on, and I want to know about it! I have made a very big contribution to this company, and I demand to know!"

"I can't talk about it, David," Semel stammered. "But I will call Steve and ask him to call you."

From his office in Burbank, Semel called Ross. "I've had many phone calls from David, and I know you have, too," Semel told Ross. "I did not tell him anything, but he is *very* agitated. You really have to call him. This is important."

"That's absolutely out of the question," Ross replied firmly. "We cannot discuss this with anybody. Sunday morning David will be right at the top of a list of a few people who I personally will call with the news."

"If you wait to call David on Sunday, you're going to have a big problem on your hands," Semel warned. "He is a member of the family, and he's not going to accept being informed along with the general public."

Ross would not be moved. "Ignore and avoid all these phone calls," he said. "Get off the phone. Don't talk to anybody. Just get into the weekend, and then we'll be fine."

Geffen awoke early Saturday morning and became even more livid when he saw the *Los Angeles Times*. TIME, WARNER REPORTEDLY ON VERGE OF MERGER read the newsbreaking headline on a story written by *Times* reporter Kathryn Harris. When reports of Geffen's anger filtered back to Ross, he became incensed with him, irritated that he was behaving like a petulant child. He decided not to make the call he had originally planned to make.

Geffen did not care about securities laws. All he could see was that Steve Ross had betrayed him. He was mortified that such a huge merger had taken place and that he had not been advised. Mo Ostin and Ahmet Ertegun also had not known, but Geffen believed his relationship with Ross entitled him to special privileges.

The situation only worsened. When the terms of the transaction became public, Geffen was outraged to discover that Ross did not reward him with the rich stock-option packages that he had bestowed upon such friends as Steven Spielberg and Barbra Streisand. Ross was flabbergasted when Geffen moaned that he had gotten nothing. "I gave you [the other] fifty percent of your company!" he said.

As if the slight by Ross had not been painful enough, two other people in Geffen's inner circle soon disappointed him. The first was his lawyer, Allen Grubman, who suddenly found himself in a difficult position when another of his clients, Chrysalis Records, asked him to represent them in a sale of a 50 percent stake to Thorn EMI. Chrysalis chairman Chris Wright, unnerved by Geffen's acquisition of a minority stake just two months earlier, told Grubman he wanted to move quickly and quietly with the transaction. As part of the deal, Chrysalis planned to buy back, at a substantial premium, Geffen's minority stake.

When Grubman called Geffen to announce that Chrysalis had made a deal with Thorn EMI, Geffen erupted, incensed that Grubman had not leaked the news to him. That Grubman represented both Geffen and Chrysalis was a reflection of the wackiness of the music business. Grubman, grateful for what Geffen had done for him, began to spin. He tried to explain that he had been sworn to secrecy. "As an attorney, I was in an impossible situation, David," Grubman said. "I just could not tell you."

But Geffen had no use for the promises Grubman had made to Chrysalis. "You should have told me!" Geffen railed. In a near repeat of the falling-out he had had with Gil Segel, Geffen believed he was entitled to preferential treatment because he had steered so many clients to Grubman.

"You're fired!" Geffen bellowed, hanging up.

The next month was the worst month of Allen Grubman's life. He was well aware of Geffen's power to destroy people, and he feared that he would attempt to ruin him. He called their mutual friends and obsessed about the situation. He was desperate to figure out a way to get back into Geffen's good graces.

His idea of a Chrysalis acquisition foiled, Geffen began plotting to sell his own label outright. His distribution pact with Warner Bros. Records was to expire at the end of 1990, at which point he would be able to sell it to whomever he wished.

Steve Ross had always said he would buy Geffen Records when Geffen was ready to sell. But because Ross had not told Geffen about the company's merger with Time, Geffen would now demand even tougher terms if Ross wanted to remain in business with him. There would be no inside price.

If Geffen could find anything positive about the Time Warner merger, it was that it showed yet again the extravagant values of music companies. He was delighted to realize that Geffen Records could fetch hundreds of millions of dollars in this overblown marketplace. The mistake he had made in 1972 when he had sold Asylum for cheap would not be repeated.

But as he dreamed of the big numbers his company might draw, he wanted to have complete control of the label. He was its majority shareholder, but he wanted to make a clean deal, with no one balking at his choice of a buyer. He decided to try to buy back the small equity stakes he had promised to such people as Eddie Rosenblatt, Linda Loddengaard, and his three A&R men. For Rosenblatt and the A&R executives, the buyouts would amount to whopping paydays of about five to six million dollars. Like the Range Rovers and other gifts he had doled out so generously before, the buyout packages would be consonant with his longtime generous treatment of his employees.

Knowing that any buyer would demand assurances that Geffen and his team would stay with the company after a purchase, Geffen decided to offer to buy out the stakeholders if and only if they agreed to sign new five-year employment contracts. Geffen called in henchman Eric Eisner, whom he had also promised an equity stake, and bestowed upon him the job of retrieving the stakes Geffen had promised employees. Geffen apparently told Eisner that if anyone asked why, he was to tell them simply that it was important at this time for Geffen to control 100 percent of the company.

Some of them, however, saw it differently. These people charged that Geffen, knowing that the company's value was near an all-time high, had grown greedy and wanted to keep the riches to himself. It was obvious that record companies were hot assets; anyone who read the papers knew that Geffen Records was one of the last major independent labels. The stakes, these people figured, were worth more than Geffen had valued them, and now he was intent on chaining them to the company before the market had placed a firm value on the label.

Linda Loddengaard was the first to balk. In her view, the request was unfair. She had been promised a percentage stake in the company, and she did not want to give it up. She had dedicated her life to Geffen and had served faithfully for seventeen years. She was essentially the general manager of Geffen's company and of his personal life. Some had dubbed her the Alexander Haig of Geffen Records, an aggressive assistant who took charge whenever Geffen was away.

The bond between the two broke abruptly during the last week of March 1989 when Loddengaard announced that she would not give up her stake. Furthermore, she demanded an audit of Geffen Records and informed Geffen that she had enlisted the services of a lawyer to investigate the matter. In a move that proved she had picked up a few tricks in the years she had worked for Geffen, she knew exactly which attorney to call: Geffen's longtime sparring partner David Braun.

Geffen fired Loddengaard on the spot. He was not about to negotiate the sale of his company with a dissident shareholder sitting right outside his office. As Loddengaard left the building at 9130 Sunset Boulevard for the last time, Geffen ordered that the locks on all the doors be changed instantly. The two never spoke to each other again. Within a year, however, Loddengaard received a settlement that more than compensated her for the contribution she had made to David Geffen's life.

Within a month, Geffen's relationships with three critically important allies had been severely damaged or destroyed: Steve Ross, the father figure who had been so generous; Linda Loddengaard, the mother hen who had protected his lifestyle so fiercely; and Allen Grubman, the flashy lawyer who had helped him weasel out of improvident deals and had made him a fortune on other ones.

Luckily for Eric Eisner, Loddengaard's refusal to relinquish her stake in Geffen Records did not seem to portend a companywide boycott. Eddie Rosenblatt, John Kalodner, and Tom Zutaut each freely agreed to the buyout. But Eisner encountered trouble when he got to Gary Gersh, still the least successful member of the A&R troika. Like

Loddengaard, Gersh thought that Geffen's request was both wrong and immoral. One reason why he had taken a job at Geffen Records was the contractual promise of an equity stake.

"Forget it," Gersh snapped at Eisner. "I'm not going to do it."

"You don't understand, this is what has to happen," Eisner told Gersh.

"You can't make me do it," Gersh responded. Gersh asked his father-in-law, Paramount Pictures chief Frank Mancuso, to examine his contract. Mancuso advised him not to return his stake. It is obviously valuable, Mancuso said, otherwise Geffen would not want it back.

"Every night I go home and I talk to my father-in-law about this," Gersh told Eisner. "I want you to know that I'm going to hire his attorneys, and I'm talking to him openly about everything you say to me."

Geffen was so irritated with Gersh that he stopped speaking to him. The battle dragged on for a couple of months before they reached a compromise. Gersh agreed to sell a portion of the stake he had been promised, but he insisted on retaining the remainder. The stake he refused to sell proved to be a bit more valuable than the portion he sold.

Geffen's friendship with Gersh survived, but another executive was soon to engage in a nasty battle with Geffen over the issue of a promised equity stake. Meanwhile, at home there was an equal amount of drama. An agonizing split was about to take place there as well.

CHAPTER 29

THE SALE

|||

Geffen's romance with Bob Brassel was an on-again, off-again affair, and they soon stopped wearing the rings they had exchanged. Geffen told friends that the relationship was fizzling because of Brassel's drug addictions. His problem was indeed a serious issue that was well known, even to most people at Warner Bros., where sometimes he disappeared from work for weeks at a time.

Despite these bad spells, Brassel was rising through the ranks at Warner Bros. Before long, he was named a vice president. Geffen was still in love with him and employed the assistance of such friends and reformed drug abusers as Carrie Fisher, Joel Schumacher, and Howard Rosenman to help him with rescue missions.

Once, Fisher and Geffen spent a night with Brassel at his house in West Hollywood (they maintained separate residences during most of their relationship) in order to ensure that he checked into a rehabilitation center the next morning. But when they awoke, Brassel had run away. "It was like massing on the borders of Cambodia, or trying to overtake some small government," Fisher said in describing the difficulty of the job.

Brassel's personal problems were clearly not the only reason for the relationship's demise, however. Among the many complications was the huge financial disparity between them, a problem that Geffen had faced before. He told a journalist that his complete dedication to work also made it difficult for him to find a place in his life for the relationship. As he schemed to sell his company, he was becoming focused solely on making the big score, losing sight of other matters.

Still, Geffen was saddened and depressed in the wake of the breakup. He was not a quitter, but he was forced to admit his inability to make the relationship work.

"Being gay is very different from being straight in the area of relationships," he said in a magazine interview. "Of course, there are gay people who've had a long-term relationship for fifty years, but they're not the rule. There's a disparity in heterosexual relationships that doesn't work in homosexual relationships."

There was a profound sadness of another kind in Geffen's life as well. By the start of 1989, AIDS had claimed the lives of more than forty-five thousand Americans, most of them gay men. Since the death of choreographer Michael Bennett in 1987, Geffen had lost many other friends and acquaintances to the disease.

David Bombyk, who had brought *Beetlejuice* to the company, had tried to keep secret the fact that he was dying of AIDS. It was not until he collapsed, ending up at Century City Hospital, that he told Geffen. Geffen arranged for him to be moved to Cedars-Sinai Medical Center, where Geffen knew a doctor he believed to be at the leading edge of AIDS therapies. Bombyk died a couple of weeks later, age thirty-six.

The death that affected Geffen the most was that of Steve Rubell, his pal and partying companion at Studio 54. Since having been released from prison in 1981, Rubell and Ian Schrager had conquered New York nightlife again with a club called the Palladium. But as he and Schrager launched a plan to open luxury hotels, Rubell fell ill. He died at Beth Israel Hospital in New York in late July 1989. He was forty-five.

A number of acquaintances who were dying of AIDS asked Geffen for money to help pay medical bills and other expenses. He did not turn

Onstage and offstage talent: a photo op for
John Kalodner, Geffen, Aerosmith's Joe Perry and
Steven Tyler, and Eddie Rosenblatt.

anyone down. Again showing his enormous capacity for kindness in the face of crisis, he wrote out checks to individuals and charities that were helping people with AIDS. In a benevolent gesture from which he had nothing to gain directly, Geffen played a key role in helping to bring together separate New York– and California-based organizations to form amfAR, the American Foundation for AIDS Research.

Geffen was desperate to find a movie to produce that would give him the credibility of his idol Sam Spiegel. To this end, he worked at cultivating a relationship with Michael Ovitz, who was more powerful than ever. He even helped engineer a vacation in which he and Bob Brassel, now just a close friend, went to Europe with Ovitz and his wife and a few other couples. The group, which included Ovitz's partner, Ron Meyer, Terry Semel, and *Rocky* co-producer Irwin Winkler, sailed for a week down the coast of Italy aboard Henry Ford's yacht.

But Geffen was running out of patience. He again started badgering Ovitz to give him one of the top-tier projects the agency was packaging. When Ovitz masterfully created a buzz around Bill Murray's next movie, *Quick Change,* Geffen telephoned Ovitz and told him it was payback time. Thanks to *Ghostbusters,* Murray was an enormous star, and he was believed to be box-office gold. His new comedy, which he planned to co-direct, was a farce about a bank robbery.

"I have been very good to you," Geffen ranted at Ovitz, rattling off each and every client he had helped steer to the agency. "But you have done nothing for me!"

Ovitz reminded Geffen that he had done him the favor of convincing Murray to play a role in *Little Shop of Horrors.* But Geffen, who had at the time appreciated the gesture, now insisted the favor did not count because the role had been a cameo. According to him, Ovitz still had a debt to pay.

In some ways, Ovitz had asked for it. He *had* promised Geffen help in landing winning movie projects. But he had also made similar promises to many other producers in Hollywood. As an agent, his job was to represent the best interests of his clients. Some people believed it was impossible for him to do so with so many conflicting debts.

"Why don't you have these expectations from Ronnie?" Ovitz asked Geffen, referring to Ron Meyer, the president of CAA. "He has as much to do with this company as I do." The reason was that Meyer, who unlike Ovitz had a strong friendship with Geffen, had wisely never made the promises Ovitz had.

Because of his recent successes, Bill Murray was in a position to score a major payday with *Quick Change*. Some agents would simply have set up an auction and given the project to the highest bidder. Ovitz did arrange meetings between Murray and other studios, but feeling the heat, he steered the project to Geffen.

Geffen got the movie he had wanted so badly. But, shortly, Murray instructed Ovitz to get him out of the deal, saying he was "uncomfortable with David's aura." Geffen grew incensed as Ovitz explained that they were changing their minds.

Even though the movie would turn out to be a flop for Warner Bros., Geffen recommitted himself to making Ovitz's life a nightmare. Some of Geffen's friends thought it fitting that he counted *Faust* among his favorite works of literature: If you accepted a favor from Geffen, it often meant that one day you might have to grant the one wish he decided would even the score.

In the meantime, *Risky Business* director Paul Brickman began work on his second film, a movie about a recently widowed woman called *Men Don't Leave*. Mindful not to repeat the disastrous experience of their last partnership, Geffen went out of his way to be supportive of Brickman and producer Jon Avnet. Geffen hated the film's title and voiced his opposition, but he did keep his promise to not interfere.

Following the huge success of his solo album *Building the Perfect Beast*, Don Henley insisted on renegotiating the seven-year contract he had signed with Geffen Records in 1984. Geffen agreed and in 1988 signed Henley to a new deal. Henley went about making his second solo album for the label. Making the record took far longer than he had originally expected, and his old anger toward Geffen resurfaced as Geffen rather uncharacteristically nagged him to finish. When he was finally done, the two clashed again. The dispute erupted when Eric Eisner attempted to force Henley to comply with a company policy limiting the number of "J-card" panels, on which song lyrics were usually printed, he could have for the cassette-tape packaging.

"They're nickel-and-diming me," Henley complained. He soon began calling the company "Nickel-and-Dime Records."

When the album, *The End of the Innocence,* was released in July 1989, it was an instant smash. Fueled by hit singles such as "The Heart of the Matter" and "New York Minute," as well as the title track, it sold more than five million copies and became the most successful solo effort of any former member of the Eagles. Its success further fueled Henley's ire because he believed Geffen was not giving him star treatment.

On the heels of Henley's winner, the company put out its second Cher album, *Heart of Stone,* a top-ten record that included the hit "If I Could Turn Back Time." Cher, who a year earlier had won the Best Actress Oscar for *Moonstruck,* had the biggest album of her career. Geffen Records seemed unstoppable. In addition, Aerosmith released its third album for the label, entitled *Pump;* it rocketed up the charts to number five, selling seven million records.

With projected 1989 revenues of $175 million, Geffen Records was no longer a small company. In three years, the staff had tripled to 110 employees. Geffen purchased a parcel of prime Beverly Hills real estate, and he hired Charles Gwathmey to design a much larger and more modern headquarters for the label there. In a bid to further increase the size of his entertainment empire, Geffen also set into motion plans to establish a small second record label.

Meanwhile, the buying spree in the music industry had reached a fever pitch. At the start of August, PolyGram agreed to buy Island Records, a rap and reggae specialist, for about $300 million. The next month, PolyGram bought A&M Records for $450 million.

These transactions left Geffen Records as the only major privately owned record label in the United States. Geffen realized the ally he needed most at that moment was Allen Grubman, who had had a hand in many of the recent sales. He was, Geffen figured, the best in the business. Geffen would have frozen him out of his life permanently, but Grubman had a unique skill and Geffen needed him. He called Grubman and rehired him.

"I don't want this to ever happen again," Geffen said, referring to the Chrysalis fiasco.

"David, I'm a lawyer," Grubman began.

"You understand what I'm saying?" Geffen interrupted. "I don't want this ever to happen again."

In the fall of 1989, Geffen invited Grubman to join him on a vacation at Villa Eden, the Warner retreat in Acapulco. It was on such trips that Geffen conducted business in every room of the house. Geffen also invited Tim Burton, whose follow-up to *Beetlejuice* had been that summer's blockbuster, *Batman*.

Before dawn one morning, Geffen knocked on Grubman's bedroom door. "Allen, it's me," he whispered. "We gotta talk."

Grubman invited Geffen in, and Geffen sat on the edge of the bed.

"It's time," Geffen said. "It's time to sell Geffen Records."

O ver the next several weeks, Geffen and Grubman talked about the most likely suitors and hypothesized that Geffen Records could, given the market, fetch several hundred million dollars. The label was finishing its best year yet, controlling 8 percent of the music business, according to *Billboard*. Only Columbia, with 10.62 percent, and Atlantic, with 9.33 percent, fared better. It was time to strike.

Besides Time Warner, Geffen and Grubman saw Disney, Paramount Communications, and Thorn EMI as potential bidders. MCA, home of Universal Pictures and the Universal Studios theme park, seemed a natural suitor, too, but there was a major obstacle: Irving Azoff, Geffen's longtime foe, was still in charge of MCA Records.

Like investment bankers analyzing merger candidates, Geffen and

Grubman analyzed each company and crafted a strategy. Geffen said he would contact Paramount Communications chairman Martin Davis. He also would handle Disney, knowing that Jeffrey Katzenberg, his most enthusiastic cheerleader, could talk up the proposal to Michael Eisner. Since Grubman had brokered Thorn EMI's acquisition of Chrysalis, he took charge of exploring that company's interest.

Geffen soon heard that Azoff was unhappy at MCA. Eager to have him leave MCA, Geffen cozied up to him. Azoff was still furious with Geffen for having tried to poach Howard Kaufman, but Geffen managed to renew their turbulent relationship, in which they sometimes claimed to be friends.

"This thing is really silly," Geffen said. "I don't want to hurt you anymore, and I'm too powerful for you to hurt. I forgive you for all the times you've fucked me in the past and for all the times you're going to fuck me in the future."

Geffen helped broker a deal in which Time Warner set Azoff up with an independent record deal, and soon he announced his resignation from MCA. An important chess piece had been moved.

Even though Steve Ross knew that Geffen planned to talk to other companies regarding an acquisition of his label, he did not believe that Geffen would seriously consider selling to anyone other than Time Warner. Near the end of 1989, Ross told his top advisers, Robert Morgado and Oded "Ed" Aboodi, to put together an offer.

On some level, Geffen did want to make the deal with Steve Ross. Despite the ill will he felt toward Ross in the wake of the Time Warner merger, Geffen still felt a strong emotional pull to the company. He liked film chiefs Bob Daly and Terry Semel. He had complicated but strong ties to both Ahmet Ertegun and Mo Ostin.

Geffen told Morgado and Aboodi he hoped they could work something out. "At the end of the day," he told them, "it's not just about money." Geffen assigned Eric Eisner and Lee Phillips—his lifelong attorney in Los Angeles who had seen his workload fall since Grubman had joined Geffen's stable of lawyers—to represent him in the Time Warner negotiations.

But for Steve Ross, the timing of Geffen's sale could not have been worse. Warner Communications' merger with Time had laden the company with debt, and Ross felt it would not be possible to buy the label outright for cash. He instructed Morgado and Aboodi to convince Geffen to defer his sale and simply sign a new seven-year distribution agreement. He told them to tell Geffen that he fully intended to one day make good on his longtime promise.

Geffen was bitterly disappointed with the offer. He was in no mood to accept another promise from Ross.

The other feelers Geffen and Grubman had put out did not produce instant offers either. At Disney, Michael Eisner and Frank Wells were not eager to be in business with David Geffen. Wells had never recovered from Geffen's behavior at the Warner Bros. movie studio in 1976. Additionally, both he and Eisner were irked about the aggressive lack of help they felt Geffen had offered them during their bid for CBS Records a few years earlier.

As for Paramount Communications, Martin Davis thought Geffen Records was an interesting play. But as part of any possible deal he insisted that Geffen report to Frank Mancuso. Geffen refused. MCA also expressed some interest, though it was unwilling to buy the whole company. Geffen felt that an acquisition by MCA was a long shot, even with Azoff gone. A stock deal equal to the terms Geffen was seeking would likely make him a larger shareholder than MCA's seventy-seven-year-old chairman, Lew Wasserman, the godfather of Hollywood.

With both Paramount and Disney, Geffen masterfully kept the acquisition talks in play. He did everything he could to keep the companies from delivering firm rejections. He wanted to keep the perception alive that there was a hot bidding war for Geffen Records.

In early January 1990, he finally got the bite for which he had been praying. Thorn EMI said it was interested in making a deal. The company offered to acquire Geffen Records for $350 million in cash, as well as equity in a new combined music operation that Geffen would co-manage with Thorn's music chief, James Fifield.

The Wall Street Journal soon published an article headlined GEFFEN RECORDS IS SAID TO DRAW SEVERAL SUITORS. The article, written by Richard Turner, named all the buyers Geffen and Grubman were in contact with and said that some had made offers "in excess of $800 million." Of all the potential acquirers, Paramount was said to be the most interested.

The only person quoted in the story was Geffen, who offered a seriously disingenuous comment: "While several parties have expressed interest in buying the company, I'm not shopping it, I haven't sold it and I'm not about to sell it." His only other comment was that he was renegotiating his contract with Time Warner.

Shortly after talks between Thorn and Geffen began, Thorn chairman Colin Southgate told James Fifield that he was concerned about putting too much of the company in Geffen's hands. But Fifield, who was friendly with Geffen, convinced Southgate that Geffen would be a good partner. With Thorn showing real interest, an insulted Geffen rejected Steve Ross's simple distribution extension as wholly unacceptable. Thorn and Geffen agreed for the moment to negotiate exclusively.

In February, Geffen went to the premiere of Paul Brickman's *Men Don't Leave.* Geffen had gotten his hands on the earliest reviews, and he showed them to Brickman and Avnet at the post-screening party. "We got killed in *Newsweek,*" Geffen said, deflating the celebratory mood. The picture proved to be a bust, grossing just $6.1 million. Many later agreed that the title, which Geffen had opposed, had hurt it at the box office.

Meanwhile, the exclusive negotiating period with Thorn EMI expired and no firm offer was on the table. Allen Grubman had been talking to the company for weeks, but the talks had lumbered along at a painfully slow pace. The issues that Thorn EMI had initially tagged as potential sticking points had now turned into full-blown problems.

As Thorn EMI began to question whether to do the deal, Geffen himself had concerns about the possible marriage. He liked Jim Fifield, but there was no chemistry with Colin Southgate. Indeed, some people could not envision Geffen selling to Thorn, given the disparaging remarks he had made about it in the past.

When Steve Ross learned that Geffen's exclusive negotiating period with Thorn EMI had lapsed, he decided to make another bid. He telephoned Bob Morgado, who was in Morocco at a conference of the music division's international managers, and told him to leave the meeting immediately and return to the United States.

"I have it all figured out," Ross told Morgado. "Ed Aboodi and I have been talking about an alternate proposal. I talked to David, and he's open to hearing it. I need you to come back and present it to him right away."

Eric Eisner and Lee Phillips flew to New York and met with Morgado and Aboodi, who described the new offer. Time Warner was now offering to pay $75 million for an option to purchase Geffen Records in four years. That, Ross figured, would buy him some time. Again, Geffen angrily rejected the offer. He wanted Ross to buy the company outright.

Allen Grubman continued to negotiate with Thorn EMI, but the discussions were now bogged down with tax complications. Grubman suddenly began to feel that the deal was doomed. "They say when a cough never goes away, you die from it," he said. "When a deal takes too long, it goes away."

With significant issues yet unresolved between Thorn and Geffen, on Monday, March 5, *The Wall Street Journal* published a story reporting that Geffen Records had agreed to be acquired by Thorn for seven hundred million dollars in cash and stock. The story attributed the news to an unidentified person "close to the negotiations." The article raised immediate speculation from those involved in the talks that an anxious

Geffen had leaked the story in an attempt to force Colin Southgate's hand, light a fire under Steve Ross, or prompt interest from an eleventh-hour bidder.

If in fact Geffen had leaked the story to the *Journal,* the strategy worked. Upon learning that Geffen had not yet signed a definitive agreement, Steve Ross went back to Ed Aboodi one final time and instructed him to draft yet another offer in which Time Warner would acquire all of Geffen's company. He put Aboodi and Morgado on an airplane to Los Angeles. They checked in to the Beverly Hills Hotel, where they had been told Geffen was meeting with the negotiating team representing Thorn EMI.

Geffen went back and forth between the two pink bungalows housing what seemed to be his two best prospects. In one bungalow, Morgado and Aboodi explained Time Warner's latest offer. Like many of the deals Ross and Aboodi had structured together, it was rather convoluted: The company would agree to buy Geffen Records and compensate Geffen with a new issue of preferred stock, which would be convertible at the above-market price of $250 a share. The stock would not pay a dividend, he added. Also, Aboodi said, Geffen would have to sign a seven-year deal.

Geffen listened but said little. He told the Time Warner executives that he would call them by the end of the day with an answer. Back at his office, he conferred with Allen Grubman, Eric Eisner, and Lee Phillips. They were in agreement that Time Warner's offer was lame. He then called Morgado and weighed in with his blistering review.

"I'm not going to fucking take this 'funny money' shit!" Geffen screamed. "You guys are wasting my time!"

Morgado shuddered as he picked up the phone to relay the news to Steve Ross in New York.

"You guys blew it!" Ross admonished Morgado and Aboodi, telling them that they had not sold the offer properly. "This is a great deal. David just didn't understand it! You fucked it up!"

Then the real magic took place. On Wednesday, March 7, Sidney Sheinberg, the president and chief operating officer of MCA, telephoned Geffen and asked if he was still entertaining offers. Since January, when Sheinberg had said MCA did not want to buy the company outright, Sheinberg had grown worried about the company's weak music unit. MCA had sat on the sidelines during the recent spate of music-industry mergers; now there was not much left to acquire. It was clear that Geffen Records' strength in pop, rock, and heavy metal would complement MCA's catalog of country and jazz. An acquisition would double MCA's market share to 15 percent.

Geffen told Sheinberg that he was still taking bids and left him with a tip: "These people at EMI and Warners have just driven me crazy," he said, telling Sheinberg that their complicated offers had left him nauseated.

"I'll get right back to you," Sheinberg said. Working the numbers in his office at the top of MCA's mirrored headquarters known as the Black Tower, Sheinberg walked the short distance down to Chairman Lew Wasserman's office and asked for his blessing to make Geffen an offer.

"This is a great opportunity," Sheinberg told Wasserman. "We need Geffen Records to stay competitive in the music business." Sheinberg told Wasserman that the stock deal would make Geffen a larger shareholder than even him, but he added that they could put certain voting restrictions on his position. Wasserman gave Sheinberg the green light.

"We're going to make you the biggest offer this company has ever made," Sheinberg told Geffen on the phone a few minutes later. "And I'm going to send it to you by messenger right now."

"It's 1990," Geffen blurted out. "Send me a fax."

In minutes, Geffen had Sheinberg's two-paragraph fax outlining an offer to buy Geffen Records in exchange for stock valued at about $545 million. It was substantially less than the $700 million he had discussed with Thorn, but it was *real;* it was also a clean, straightforward stock deal. What's more, Geffen felt more comfortable with the MCA management team than he did with the people at Thorn. "The devil sometimes arrives with the biggest check," he remembered his mother once said.

Geffen suddenly was convinced that MCA was the best possible company to acquire his label. A significant reason was that Wasserman was getting old. In the not-too-distant future, he might sell MCA. Geffen, ever looking to increase his stature in Hollywood, believed he might be able to gain control of MCA within five years.

He picked up the phone, dialed Sheinberg back, and told him he would like to meet with him at once.

When they got together, Geffen gently inquired about negotiating the purchase price. "Will you pay more?" he asked meekly.

"No," Sheinberg responded.

"Fine," Geffen said. "I'll take it."

GOOD FORTUNE

|||

Four days later, after a Sunday morning spent playing records at the Holmby Hills mansion of movie producer Ray Stark, Geffen went to the Beverly Hills office of MCA's attorneys. Geffen listened as Lew Wasserman listed a series of terms. Eager to reach an agreement that day, Geffen simply said yes to each one.

As part of the deal, Geffen got one million shares of a new class of convertible preferred stock that were to pay nearly seven million dollars a year in dividends. If and when he sold, the shares would immediately convert into ten million common shares. His 12 percent stake made him the company's biggest shareholder but with restricted voting rights. Geffen agreed to a five-year contract in which he would be paid an annual six-hundred-thousand-dollar salary. MCA would get Geffen Records, but Geffen's movie company and Broadway ventures were not part of the deal.

The bombshell that an eleventh-hour bidder had won the race was passed on to the Thorn EMI and Time Warner negotiating teams. After nearly twenty years as an integral part of the Warner entertainment family, David Geffen was breaking his complicated ties with Steve Ross, the man who arguably had had the most powerful impact on his life and career. To many it seemed Ross had been the father Geffen did not have but wanted so desperately. He had not respected his own father, but he did revere Ross. He even emulated him as he watched Ross, who also came from humble beginnings, transform his parking-lot and funeral-home businesses through clever dealmaking into the world's largest entertainment company.

But the good times were over: The son was now leaving home. Ross was hurt and disappointed. Although he had grown tired of Geffen's temper tantrums, he continued to have unwavering respect for Geffen's business prowess and did not want him to leave. But he felt that MCA was overpaying. He disputed the validity of the revenue and profit figures that Geffen had fed the press (Geffen said the label earned about $40 million on sales of $225 million). In preparing a statement for later release to the media, Ross elected to take the high road: "David made a great business deal and I wish him the best."

On Tuesday, March 13, spokespeople at MCA Records and Geffen Records began calling music-industry reporters to alert them that an important announcement would be forthcoming that afternoon. But as the day drew to a close, a few issues were still being finalized, and the spokespeople told the journalists that the announcement would be delayed until the next day. Still, Jube Shiver, Jr., and Michael Cieply of the *Los Angeles Times* latched onto the news and began drafting a story.

When Geffen learned that the *Times* was planning to scoop the announcement, he called his top executives. He did not want his staff to read the news in the paper. One by one, the executives made their way to Geffen's office: They knew that he had something of seismic proportions to announce.

Geffen walked in and looked about the room at the people who had helped him build the decade's most successful independent record company. Looking back at him were his record-company president, Eddie Rosenblatt; Eric Eisner, the president of the David Geffen Company; his A&R team, John Kalodner, Tom Zutaut, and Gary Gersh; Mel

MCA's chairman, Lew Wasserman, and president, Sidney Sheinberg,
make the winning bid to acquire Geffen Records. (Peter Borsari)

Posner, the international chief; Bryn Bridenthal, the publicity chair; Al Coury, the promotion man; Jim Walker, the CFO; Eddie Gilreath, the head of sales; and a couple of others.

"I have very exciting news," Geffen started, barely able to contain his enthusiasm. "I have agreed to sell the company . . . to MCA."

Everyone was shocked. No one knew Geffen had been negotiating with MCA, and most had expected him to say he had concluded a deal with Thorn EMI or Time Warner. In the music business, MCA had a reputation as a has-been, with wags dubbing it "Music Cemetery of America," a fact not lost on Geffen's team. Instead of breaking into applause, the executives were quiet.

"I will continue to be chairman. We will continue to do the same great job we have been doing," Geffen said. "This is going to be a very good thing for Geffen Records."

Finally, the silence was broken when Gary Gersh approached Geffen, shook his hand, and gave him a big hug. But tension still permeated the room. Mel Posner, believing that Geffen had made another decision based on what was good for him and not necessarily good for anyone else, raised his hand to ask a question.

"How is this going to affect the international department?" Posner asked without a smile, trying to keep his anger under control.

Geffen said he expected Geffen Records' international staff to stay intact and work in concert with MCA's global team.

Posner then asked another question about the ramifications the acquisition would have on his department. Geffen answered gamely.

Eddie Gilreath, who was sitting on the couch next to Posner, began to grumble about the deal.

"What's wrong?" Posner whispered.

"MCA has the worst fucking distribution in the world!" Gilreath replied.

"Tell David."

"No, no, no," Gilreath said, with an air of resignation.

Posner raised his hand again.

"Mel, is this another question about international?" Geffen asked, exasperated.

"No," Posner said calmly. "David, MCA has the worst distribution in the world. Are you going to be there for us?"

Geffen quickly adjourned the meeting. The other executives were surprised at Posner's nerve, even though some, including Zutaut and Bridenthal, shared his reservations.

Later that night, Posner decided to telephone Geffen and tell him there had been a misunderstanding.

"How could you piss on my parade?" Geffen screamed.

The next day, the *Los Angeles Times* broke the news. MCA and Geffen Records put out the press release, and other newspaper reporters went to work on their stories. On Wednesday, *The New York Times* ran the story on the front page, along with a photograph of Geffen. POP IMPRESARIO STRIKES GOLD IN $550 MILLION SALE TO MCA, the headline read.

The stock market, however, agreed with Steve Ross's evaluation that MCA had overpaid for Geffen Records. News of the acquisition sent MCA's stock down 1.875 to 54.50.

Although Geffen told the press that he owned 100 percent of Geffen Records, in fact there were at least two other equity holders at the time of the sale: Eric Eisner and Gary Gersh. But Gersh did not pocket any MCA stock as a result of the transaction. Instead, Geffen computed the value of the stake Gersh had refused to relinquish and gave him the sum in cash. Together with the buyout package he had received a year earlier Gersh's total was about ten million dollars.

The news of Gersh's cash windfall drew cries of outrage from Eddie Rosenblatt, John Kalodner, and Tom Zutaut, each of whom had received bonuses a year earlier of only about five to six million dollars. Kalodner and Zutaut were especially furious that the least successful member of the A&R troika had been given the most money.

Geffen refused to hear the complaints of Kalodner and Zutaut, but he was sympathetic to Rosenblatt's charge. More than anyone, Rosenblatt had led the company's day-to-day activities and held it together since the beginning. Geffen agreed to increase Rosenblatt's take to equal Gersh's.

He next wrote several much smaller checks to other executives, expressing his appreciation for their role in the company's success. Perhaps inevitably, however, a number of the people were left unhappy. Al Coury and Mel Posner, for example, charged Eric Eisner with deceit and claimed that he and Geffen had broken promises to "take care of them" when a sale materialized. Executives at the label surmised that Geffen was punishing Posner.

The attorney David Braun, meanwhile, apparently told Geffen that his new client, Linda Loddengaard, was prepared to file a lawsuit against him if an agreeable settlement could not be reached. Geffen agreed to pay Loddengaard the princely sum of five million dollars with one condition: That she agree never to disclose the details of Geffen's professional and personal affairs. Geffen's worst nightmare, it seemed, was that Loddengaard would one day write a book. She signed the agreement and retired to Santa Barbara.

His battle with Loddengaard was over at last, but another, much more unexpected personnel drama was brewing, and this one would floor everyone at the company, no one more than Geffen. Eric Eisner, it turns out, was upset about *his* take from the sale. He charged that Geffen had cheated him out of millions of dollars he had promised him. Eisner had gotten more than anyone except Geffen—his take was several million dollars higher than Gersh's and Rosenblatt's—but he believed that Geffen had promised him even more based on certain business targets he said he had met. He hired an attorney to examine the matter.

Ann Warner, the widow of Warner Bros. cofounder Jack L. Warner, died in late March at the age of eighty-two. Vulture-like, Beverly Hills real-estate brokers salivated when reports circulated that the storied twelve-acre estate the Warner family had called home since the 1930s would soon go on the market.

Geffen had long been fascinated with the Warner mansion. It was not far from the house he had bought from Marlo Thomas, and he had dreamed of living there. He telephoned Sandy Gallin and asked him to ride with him over to the house.

From the moment the two men arrived at the site, Geffen was captivated. There was nothing to see from the street, but once they passed through the gates, they followed a 300-foot-long, 200-foot-wide entry lined with trees, a waterfall, and an esplanade of statues, fountains, and greenery. The main house, designed by a modernist architect named Roland Coate, was a stately Georgian mansion with towering Greek Revival columns. The 13,600-square-foot house included eight bedrooms, a card room, a screening room, and a fifty-foot domed bar; Geffen particularly liked Jack Warner's office, which had been left intact. Outside, there was a pool, a tennis court, a nine-hole pitch-and-putt golf course, and a separate, smaller house with several bedrooms for the staff.

Geffen and Gallin were informed that a developer had already offered to buy and subdivide the property. Geffen was horrified that someone would consider breaking up this magnificent piece of land. Suddenly, he felt protective, even though just a month earlier he had made a painful split from the company that Jack Warner had founded with his three brothers from Ohio decades earlier. Still, Geffen had strong feelings about Warner Bros. He was enthralled with the life Jack Warner had created, and he very much wanted to live in his house.

"I'll buy it," Geffen offered. "I want everything." He told the Warners' daughters that he would buy it within ten days for $47.5 million if they agreed not to list it with a broker. They accepted the offer, which became the highest sum ever paid for a single-family home in America. Geffen got the house and everything in it, including Warner's Oscars and a library full of leather-bound scripts.

Joel Silver, the producer of *Die Hard,* who had convinced Geffen to co-produce with him a new action film with Bruce Willis to be called *The Last Boy Scout,* was excited about Geffen's new purchase. He was a

Hollywood history buff, and he told Geffen a slew of things he had read about the Warner estate, including a report that the dining room was wallpapered in a fabric that had come directly from the former imperial palace in Beijing's Forbidden City. Silver also told Geffen that the furniture in the Chippendale room was priceless.

Geffen was astounded that he might have actually gotten a bargain. Silver, armed with his books, went through the house and pointed out the treasures inside. After the tour, Geffen determined that the furniture alone was worth anywhere from fifty to seventy million dollars. Geffen repeated the stories to everyone and appeared to be even rather embarrassed at what a bargain he had gotten.

He contacted Rose Tarlow, whose Melrose Place antique shop was the most sought-out antiques source west of the Mississippi, and asked her to appraise the house's furnishings. Geffen drove Tarlow to the house and left her there, saying he would return in two hours. Tarlow made her way through the rambling mansion and began estimating the value of the furniture. She knew in minutes that most of the furnishings were ordinary nineteenth-century pieces, not the seventeenth-century treasures that Joel Silver thought they were.

There were a couple of antique mirrors as well as one or two chairs and a table that Tarlow considered valuable. The rest looked like stock furniture that perhaps was built by studio carpenters on the Warner Bros. back lot. In the dining room, Tarlow looked skeptically at the wallpaper. There was no way, she thought to herself, that this paper had hung in a Chinese palace hundreds of years ago.

When Geffen returned, Tarlow met him at the door. A petite woman, she was nervous about his reaction. But she was confident that she had made a proper assessment.

"David, I'm hard-pressed to say the things here are worth three million," Tarlow told him. "There are five good pieces. The rest is garbage."

Geffen was momentarily rendered speechless. But then he found something to say. "You don't know what the hell you're talking about!" he yelled. "You're crazy!"

Enraged, Geffen called Christie's and Sotheby's, ordering both auction houses to send their top appraisers to come make a valuation. After visiting the estate, the auction houses submitted independent appraisals that matched Tarlow's. One suggested that the items had a total value of $2.8 million; the other said the furnishings were worth just over $3 million. Joel Silver's books turned out to be fiction, filled with exaggerations fed to the writers by Jack Warner and the decorators who had helped fashion both the home and Warner's image.

Geffen was mortified but soon called Tarlow, begged her forgiveness, and began a campaign to tell everyone that she was a genius. He blamed Joel Silver for making him out to be a fool. But he quickly found the humor in the story, and it became one of his favorite dinnertime anecdotes.

He even convinced a reluctant Tarlow to take on the job of designing and decorating the house. It was not a task she wanted; she had been singularly unimpressed and dismayed by the mansion's amalgam of styles. "Every molding looks like it came off a birthday cake," she told Geffen. But she was intrigued by the idea of working with Geffen and on an unlimited budget.

Geffen remained convinced that he had paid a fair price. He recouped three million dollars by selling the Oscars and scripts to Warner Bros. He kept some of the furniture but gave some pieces away and sold many others at auction.

Soon he made another eye-popping purchase, buying for twenty million dollars a Gulfstream IV jet, perhaps the ultimate status symbol for any billionaire. He enlisted Tarlow's help to design its interior; soon, it was lushly carpeted and equipped with a state-of-the-art satellite-communications system and hundreds of movies. With a grand new house and a private jet, one thing did not change: Geffen still wore blue jeans and sneakers. He liked to tell reporters that he shopped at the Gap.

But Geffen also put some of the money to work for the good of others. He formed a charitable foundation, began donating his entire salary to it, and oversaw the selection of various charities as beneficiaries. In addition to giving money to amfAR, he also contributed significantly to AIDS Project Los Angeles (APLA), a service organization that had recently named him to its board of governors.

The publicity Geffen garnered as a result of his newfound wealth made him a target for Michelangelo Signorile, a radical columnist at the gay magazine *OutWeek*. A leading figure in ACT UP (AIDS Coalition to Unleash Power), Signorile had begun publishing in his columns the names of celebrities he claimed were gay or lesbian.

In one column, he issued an ultimatum to "closeted queers" in New York and Hollywood that seemed squarely aimed at Geffen and some of his friends: "Either you join us or we will begin immediately tearing down every wall, exposing your hypocrisies. . . . It's your decision which way you want to go. But don't think too long. Time is running out."

Geffen was not prepared to make the public acknowledgment that Signorile sought, but he nonetheless was ready for a fight. When the Gay Men's Health Crisis (GMHC), the country's largest AIDS organization, announced plans for a benefit concert themed "A Rock and a Hard Place," Geffen boldly offered up Guns N' Roses to play. Given the controversy sparked over "One in a Million," some people thought that Geffen's offer was brazen. GMHC felt pressure from the critics and declined Geffen's offer.

Geffen lashed out at GMHC. "I don't care what their [Guns N' Roses] record is," he told *Entertainment Weekly*. "If you need a blood donor and the only person who can give you a transfusion is Hitler, you take the blood."

Michael Musto, a columnist for *The Village Voice* and a friend of Signorile, called Geffen for further comment. "Guns N' Roses volunteered to do the benefit," Geffen told Musto. "GMHC are a bunch of assholes for dropping them."

In his next column, Musto attacked Geffen, writing that the coffers at Geffen Records were filled with "blood money" that had been made by Guns N' Roses. "David, the way to fight AIDS is to extinguish stupidity, not excuse it," Musto wrote. "Stop hiding behind checkbooks and hurt feelings and do something that will really help the fight. My friends are dying. We don't have time for this bullshit."

Signorile's next column in *OutWeek* was even angrier. "Geffen, you pig," he wrote, "we demand that you immediately stand up for yourself and this community and denounce and drop Guns N' Roses. We demand an apology for their gross, violence-inciting statements—both from you for not saying anything as they spewed such venom and from them for their ignorance.

"I don't care how much blood money you've given to fight AIDS. You slit our throats with one hand and help deaden the pain with the other. You, David Geffen, are the most horrifying kind of nightmare."

Signorile also printed the telephone number of Geffen Records and urged *OutWeek*'s readers to flood the company with calls of protest. Some even plastered the building at 9130 Sunset Boulevard with angry signs criticizing Geffen's handling of the matter.

G effen convinced Michael Jackson to supply a song for the soundtrack of the new Tom Cruise movie, *Days of Thunder*, which Geffen Records had been contracted to produce. But Geffen hit the ceiling when Walter Yetnikoff at CBS Records, Jackson's label, refused to allow Jackson to give Geffen the song, an outtake from the singer's *Bad* album. Yetnikoff telephoned Eric Eisner to scream about the matter, charging that Geffen's tactic was covert and devious. Yetnikoff escalated the war when he asked Eisner to pass along word that he would like Geffen to give his new girlfriend lessons in fellatio.

Geffen resolved to destroy Yetnikoff and perhaps even lure Michael Jackson to Geffen Records. He began bad-mouthing Yetnikoff to Jackson and argued that he had taken advantage of him on such ventures as the "Moonwalker" video.

Geffen's attorney Bert Fields soon informed him that he would be ill-advised to try to sign Jackson to Geffen Records. Jackson owed CBS Records four more albums under his contract. Under a California statute, Jackson could break the agreement, but any label that signed him could be sued for the estimated combined earnings of those albums—"a sum," *Hit Men* author Fredric Dannen quipped, "greater than the gross national product of Uganda."

When an article in *The Wall Street Journal* said that Yetnikoff would be gradually phased out of his job amid souring relationships with Jackson and Bruce Springsteen, music-industry executives speculated that Geffen had been the source. Although the article reported that Yetnikoff had signed a new contract, it said that Tommy Mottola, Yetnikoff's number-two and a friend of Geffen, had signed a longer one and was the "most logical successor." Yetnikoff was made an instant lame duck. Within a few months, Yetnikoff's fifteen-year reign as head of CBS Records came to a close. Geffen telephoned Irving Azoff, with whom he was friendly again, when he heard the news. "Ding-dong, the witch is dead!" he crowed.

Yetnikoff was convinced Geffen was the source behind the *Journal* story, though Geffen insisted he had nothing to do with it. "Methinks the lady doth protest too much," Yetnikoff said.

"Walter, your problem is you think money is the root of all evil," Geffen said during one call.

"Me, David?" Yetnikoff responded. "I'm Jewish. . . . The root of all evil, David, is fear. And what can I tell you? You're a frightened guy."

Geffen also turned on John Branca, Michael Jackson's lawyer, who had become Jackson's de facto manager since he'd fired Frank Dileo. Branca was close to Yetnikoff, and Geffen wanted him out, too. Influenced by Geffen's reports that Branca was getting too large a share of the singer's income, Jackson soon told Branca he was letting him go.

In addition, Geffen went on a rampage to ruin Branca, working the early-morning telephone and instructing many other people to fire him as well. Some, like Geffen's old friend Prince Rupert Loewenstein, the manager of the Rolling Stones, thought Geffen's request was wholly improper. When Loewenstein refused to heed Geffen's call, Geffen turned on him, too. Their friendship, dating to 1969, was finished.

Meanwhile, Geffen had not been able to find a manager to take on the job of handling Jackson. When Jon Landau, who managed Bruce

Springsteen, became the latest to turn down the position, Geffen did not know where to turn. Finally, with Sandy Gallin continuing to hound him, Geffen reluctantly brokered the marriage. Sandy Gallin got the prized assignment, but his friendship with David Geffen was to be compromised once again.

CAA's Michael Ovitz was no longer content to be Hollywood's top talent agent. A year earlier, he had stepped onto a much bigger stage, serving as an adviser, and pocketing a hefty fee, on Sony's five-billion-dollar acquisition of Columbia Pictures.

Now Ovitz surveyed the landscape and looked for another big corporate marriage to broker. Japanese companies were snapping up American assets almost daily, and Ovitz believed the next natural acquirer was Osaka-based Matsushita Electric Industrial, the world's largest producer of TV sets. Like Sony, Matsushita wanted to have a hand in the creation of entertainment programming, not just the VCRs and TVs that showcase it. Ovitz contacted the company and convinced them it was the right time to buy an American movie studio.

Fortunately for David Geffen, Ovitz told Matsushita that the studio they should acquire was MCA, of which Geffen was now the majority shareholder. Lew Wasserman bought Ovitz's pitch that it was time to sell. MCA's stock, suffering along with other entertainment stocks, was trading in the mid-thirty-dollar range. Wasserman gave Ovitz his blessing to initiate talks.

Unlike the Time Warner merger, from which Geffen had been left out, he was kept apprised of these talks. He spoke daily with Herbert Allen, the powerful head of the investment bank Allen & Company, Sid Sheinberg, and others.

Geffen sensed that his life was about to take another extraordinary turn. On the last Saturday of the summer, he was in New York and planning to be in SoHo for lunch with Allen Grubman. But en route to the restaurant in Grubman's car, Geffen suggested they go to Brooklyn and visit their childhood stomping grounds.

"I want to show you where I was born," Geffen told Grubman. First they went to Borough Park and stopped at the small shop on Thirteenth Avenue that had been headquarters to David's mother's corset business. Then they traveled two blocks to the brick apartment building at 5609 Fifteenth Avenue where Geffen had grown up. They went to Coney Island and walked to the end of the boardwalk. They exchanged stories for almost four hours.

"You know, Allen," Geffen said on the phone later that day, "I'm never going to be the same again. Today we remembered where we came from. All the struggles. We have a tendency to forget."

Ten days later, executives with knowledge of the acquisition talks leaked the news to Laura Landro, a reporter at *The Wall Street Journal.* On September 25, Landro and her *Journal* colleague Richard Turner reported that Matsushita was exploring a possible acquisition of MCA for $80 to $90 a share, or a total of $6.7 billion to $7.5 billion, easily surpassing the Sony-Columbia deal. The paper did not name its sources, but some people in Hollywood immediately began speculating that Landro's source had been David Geffen, who would clearly benefit from a run-up in the price. Others guessed Michael Ovitz had been the source, but many dismissed the theory, convinced that Ovitz appreciated the fact that publicity would make his conservative Japanese client uncomfortable.

Matsushita executives were indeed put off balance when the *Journal*'s story hit the newsstands. They had yet to meet face-to-face with Wasserman or Sheinberg. The day the article ran, MCA's stock soared to 54.25 a share, up from 34.50 a day earlier. The value of David Geffen's stake had increased by $197 million.

Because of the leak, reports soon surfaced that Sheinberg decided to take Geffen out of the loop until the deal was consummated. To the Matsushita team, the cast at MCA was a strange breed, none more so than David Geffen, who they had read had tangled so publicly with his previous boss. To help assuage Matsushita's fears about Geffen, Michael Ovitz arranged to take Masahiko Hirata, a Matsushita executive vice president, to meet with Geffen at his Sunset Boulevard offices.

"He's my friend," Ovitz told Hirata. "He's a good guy. He's going to make this work."

The cash deal was completed the Sunday following Thanksgiving, two months after the negotiating teams first met in person, with Matsushita agreeing to buy MCA for about $6.59 billion, or about sixty-six dollars a share. Geffen's ten million MCA shares, worth about $550 million in March when he had sold his record label, were now worth $660 million in cash. David Geffen emerged as the single biggest benefactor of a Japanese acquisition of a U.S. company in history.

Michael Ovitz pocketed a fee that totaled about forty million dollars. But he took away something from the deal on which a price could not be placed: His power in Hollywood, already monstrous, became even more formidable. *The Wall Street Journal* confirmed Ovitz as the new Wasserman, long the industry's éminence grise. "By precipitating the MCA/Matsushita agreement, Mr. Ovitz becomes a mover of corporate mountains, not merely somebody who puts pretty faces on the screen."

Geffen and Ovitz were seen lunching at Le Dome a week after the acquisition, but Geffen did not seem grateful for Ovitz's precipitation of his gigantic windfall. Instead, Geffen seemed to be jealous that the deal had put Ovitz center stage instead of him. Despite reports calling him the richest man in Hollywood, Geffen was apparently peeved when entertainment magazines still listed Ovitz as the most powerful in Hollywood. In the years to come, Geffen became an increasingly vocal critic of Mike Ovitz.

Word soon spread through Hollywood that Time Warner chairman Steve Ross had fallen terribly ill. At the end of November, Ross put out a brief news release explaining that he was beginning chemotherapy for prostate cancer. Although he assured his colleagues and Time Warner's shareholders that his physicians were optimistic and that he was maintaining a normal work schedule, the truth was that Ross's doctors predicted that he had only between six months and a year to live. His wife, Courtney, rushed home from a trip to Hong Kong and began to search for the best possible medical attention for her husband.

Geffen, meanwhile, was in heaven as the nation's media dueled it out, eager to interview the richest man in Hollywood. He bragged that in one week *Newsweek, GQ,* and *Forbes* all chased him with proposals to appear on their covers.

He accepted the offer from *Forbes* but was insistent that the magazine not out him. The reporters and editors were taken aback by the request; for years, Geffen had never hidden his sexuality. The in-depth profile cried out for some acknowledgment of his personal-life preference. Following a paragraph in which they described his newfound wealth, the editors rather awkwardly added, "And he's a bachelor to boot."

Geffen decided that the magazine had given him the ideal platform from which to crucify Steve Ross once and for all. Although he had lunched with Ross at his home in East Hampton shortly after selling his label to MCA, Geffen remained furious with him. He unleashed a string of vitriolic comments, blasting Ross for having failed to reward him with stock options and for not acquiring his record label. "His biggest get-off is when he can sit there after a deal is made and say how he took someone to the cleaners," he said.

Geffen had succeeded in achieving his dream of becoming one of the richest people in America, but he still could not manage to be magnanimous. He continued to take petty and vindictive potshots at the people who for decades had been his allies.

Ross was hurt deeply by Geffen's comments but refused to engage in a war of words. Courtney Ross, for her part, was apoplectic. She found it inconceivable that Geffen could make such horrible remarks, especially now, when her husband was battling a life-threatening illness. Others in the Warner family, including Steven Spielberg, Mo Ostin, and Ahmet Ertegun, were equally stunned by Geffen's outburst. Trashing Ross had become his favorite pastime, and he delighted in using every opportunity to say that Ross had "gotten the best" of him in every deal.

There were many who felt that Geffen had it backward.

CALVIN

‖

Matsushita's acquisition of MCA and the commensurate rise in David Geffen's net worth pushed Eric Eisner over the edge. He continued to believe that Geffen had cheated him out of millions of dollars from the sale of Geffen Records. The buzz was that while Geffen gave Eisner 5 percent of the purchase price, Eisner insisted he had been promised twice that. He threatened to sue Geffen unless he came up with the additional money.

The charges shocked and appalled Geffen. He thought the amount of money he had given Eisner was fair. Further, he believed his contribution to Eisner's *life* was more than generous. He had plucked him out of music-lawyer obscurity and had turned him into a Hollywood power player. He had stood by as Eisner's ego swelled in tandem with the Geffen entertainment empire. But now Geffen was dumbfounded as he realized that Eisner had convinced himself that his contribution was on a par with his own.

Eisner was a smart lawyer who had made a significant contribution to the company's success. Fulfilling the job Geffen had hired him to do in 1981, Eisner had become the bad cop who swooped in fiercely to negotiate the fine points of Geffen's deals and contracts. For example, he had obtained lucrative terms in Geffen Records' agreement to release the cast albums to such Broadway musicals as *Les Misérables* and *Miss Saigon.*

But Eisner was not the one who had signed John Lennon. He was not the one who landed the company the opportunity to invest in *Cats* or *Dreamgirls.* He was not the one who had convinced Steve Ross to give up Warner's half of Geffen Records.

Geffen saw Eisner's power play as the ultimate betrayal, and all the more painful because he had, in a way, taken on Eric and his wife, Lisa, as his family. The Eisners were a gay-friendly couple in whose home Geffen was always welcome. Indeed, he had shown them his gratitude and repaid them handsomely. Just two years previously, Geffen had charitably picked up the tab for a high-six-figure, three-bedroom addition to their house on Stone Canyon Road in Bel-Air. He had even given them some furniture from the Jack Warner estate. And Lisa, thanks to a Geffen recommendation, had picked up a valuable contract to offer image-consulting services to Michael Jackson.

Eisner was appreciative of Geffen's friendship; to him, the dispute was a business issue and nothing more. To be sure, Eisner was unhappy about other matters for which he had only himself to blame: Shortly before Matsushita's interest in acquiring MCA became public, Eisner sold, against Geffen's advice, his shares in MCA.

Wanting to avoid the publicity of a suit, Geffen instructed his attorneys to negotiate a settlement. Eisner would leave the company with about thirty-two million dollars. It was not the 10 percent that he felt he was owed, but it was slightly more than the 5 percent Geffen wanted to give him. He never spoke to the Eisners again.

The newly christened richest man in Hollywood celebrated his forty-eighth birthday with a star-studded extravaganza at Sandy Gallin's Malibu beach house. The celebrities Geffen advised now, in-

Calvin Klein revels in two Designer of the Year awards in the company of two of his closest friends, David Geffen and Fran Lebowitz. (AP/Wide World Photos)

cluding Michael Jackson and Madonna, as well as those he had counseled years ago, including Joni Mitchell and Jackson Browne, were on hand. So were his friends Elizabeth Taylor, Warren Beatty, and Carrie Fisher. The town's top moguls were also in attendance, including Barry Diller, Jeffrey Katzenberg, and Michael Eisner, as well as on-again, off-again archenemy Michael Ovitz.

Marianne Williamson, the new-age guru whose "Course in Miracles" lectures had taken Hollywood by storm, was a close friend of Geffen's and was also at Gallin's fete. After having met Williamson a few years earlier, Geffen had donated about one hundred thousand dollars to her nonprofit centers, which provided free services to people with AIDS. He became a zealous advocate of her spiritual sermons. "Money, sex, power," she preached in her teachings, uttering a message that seemed directed squarely at Geffen, "they're just temporary relief for minor existential pain."

At the party, the guests formed a circle, held hands, and bowed their heads as Williamson offered a blessing. She prayed for Geffen, asking that his financial success be accompanied by an equal degree of happiness and inner peace. Then she prayed for the other guests: "May we all be as rich as David in our souls," she beseeched.

Geffen bragged that he was about to pay the taxes that would make him America's biggest taxpayer. But the thrill of the Matsushita deal, and its effect in raising Geffen's net worth to nearly a billion dollars, proved to be short-lived. In a near repeat of the emotions he had struggled with in the wake of his sale of Asylum Records in 1972, Geffen was unhappy and bored.

With his second record company sold and four years remaining on his employment contract, Geffen felt that he had lost his purpose. He had little motivation to take his record company to another level. His movie company, which was operating under a new contract with Warner Bros., was not turning out the Sam Spiegel–like hits he had long craved. Most recently, *Defending Your Life,* a comedy with Meryl Streep and Albert Brooks, had been another underachiever.

He was restless and depressed because he did not have a platform from which to operate. To pass the time, he began to explore opportunities in which he could play with his money beyond the confines of Hollywood. Now he and Richard Rainwater made a bid for the failed Executive Life Insurance Company. They were outbid, but Geffen had sent a message to those who thought that Hollywood was his sole venue.

He became a player in the contemporary art world. Since acquiring the Picasso in 1970, he had collected many artworks. But in the early 1990s, with his purchase of David Hockney's *Double Portrait,* Geffen began a buying spree that soon made the art world take note. He built a collection of modern masterpieces that, for the artists and the periods he favored, was unparalleled, including many of the most valuable works by Jackson Pollock and Jasper Johns. For a time, he would be energized by his search, much as he had been when chasing hot music acts earlier in his career. Because he had no room for them, many of the new paintings went directly into storage. He planned to showcase his art in the Jack Warner mansion as soon as the massive construction, renovation, and decoration project was completed.

In its first survey since Matsushita's purchase of MCA, in October 1991 *Forbes* reported Geffen's net worth at $880 million, up from 1990's $515 million. "You guys get it wrong every year," Geffen told *Forbes,* claiming that he was worth well over $1 billion.

Six years after having joined Geffen Records, Gary Gersh at last delivered the megahit that put his contributions on a par with those of Tom Zutaut and John Kalodner. His act Sonic Youth directed him toward Nirvana, the Seattle-based band that was to galvanize the music world and define the new grunge movement. Led by a troubled twenty-three-year-old singer-songwriter named Kurt Cobain, Nirvana shook a generation of young music buyers awake with songs that lamented their pain and dissatisfaction with life.

The band's debut album for Geffen, *Nevermind,* was promoted with a provocative cover on which a naked baby boy floated in a pool with his arms outstretched toward a dollar bill attached like bait on a fishhook. The album made Geffen feel old. When he first heard it, he could not understand the lyrics Kurt Cobain was screaming. But young people got the message loud and clear, and the album went to the top of the album charts and sold over two million copies. Geffen established friendships with Cobain and his wife, Courtney Love, who had her own band called Hole.

The Guns N' Roses success story also continued with two albums, separate volumes of a record called *Use Your Illusion,* that were released simultaneously. But Geffen's relationship with Axl Rose disintegrated after he refused to allow the singer to sing with the Rolling Stones on their next album for Columbia. Madonna, who was not on Geffen Records, also stopped speaking to him when, after attending the Off-Broadway spoof *The Real Live Brady Bunch,* Geffen hired away her chauffeur, Philip Singer.

The money and dealmaking did not resolve Geffen's problems of isolation and loneliness. Three or four nights a week he was alone at the Malibu house watching movies in his screening room. He second-guessed the wisdom of buying the Jack Warner house, told people he now never planned to move into it, and only half jokingly asked if anyone knew an Arab sheik who would take it off his hands.

He once again yearned for a family of his own. With such a gigantic bank account, he contemplated a host of legacy issues and wondered to whom he would leave his fortune. He began thinking about his female friends and considered engineering a pregnancy whereby he would sire an heir. Marianne Williamson, apparently, was one woman who wanted to carry his child, but she and Geffen did not reach an agreement as to how such a transaction could be managed. Shortly thereafter, they had an argument over unrelated business matters, and their friendship collapsed. In the meantime, Geffen had bought a pet parrot, which he named Archie, to keep him company.

Everyone in Hollywood knew that Geffen was gay, but he was not yet prepared to make the public acknowledgment of his homosexuality that gay-rights activists continued to demand. He was drawing closer to a full admission, as evidenced by a feature in *Vanity Fair* in which he said, "I date men and I date women."

Not everyone believed him, though, and some writers were preparing to pounce. John Mendelssohn, who had written a book about the Kinks, secured a twenty-five-thousand-dollar advance from Birch Lane Press and set out to write a Geffen biography. Geffen, who told a journalist he wanted Pulitzer Prize winner Robert Caro to write his biography, was unhappy because he felt that Mendelssohn was a lightweight.

Mendelssohn became frustrated when Geffen, who asked his friends and associates not to talk to the writer, did not respond to his requests for an interview. Finally, Mendelssohn made it simple for Geffen to quash the book when he began to write him threatening letters that could be used to suggest malice in a libel suit.

"Stubborn, aincha?" Mendelssohn wrote to Geffen in one letter. "Time is running out . . . we have only a few weeks for you to help me acquire sufficient material about your good works to make it unnecessary for me to (pardon the expression) flesh out my accounts of your wanton wild-oats sowing."

Geffen put his attorney Bert Fields onto Birch Lane Press, a small publisher of unauthorized celebrity books. The publisher caved, apologized to Geffen, and asked Mendelssohn to return the advance.

G effen and Calvin Klein spoke on the telephone every day. They vacationed together and seemed to share their most intimate secrets with each other. Every year, Geffen and Barry Diller and Fran Lebowitz traveled to Klein's showroom on West Thirty-ninth Street in New York, cheering from front-row seats as models walked down the runway, displaying their friend's newest collections. In 1986, Geffen had gone to Rome when Klein, then forty-three, had married Kelly

Rector. He also helped Klein's daughter, Marci, land a job at *Saturday Night Live*. Geffen even purchased Klein's old vacation home in the gay community of Fire Island Pines, New York.

But in 1991, there was one thing Calvin Klein did not tell Geffen: His privately held fashion empire was on the brink of bankruptcy. Geffen learned about the drama when he read about it in *The Wall Street Journal*. The front-page article, headlined CALVIN KLEIN IS FACING A BIND AS MAGIC TOUCH APPEARS TO BE SLIPPING, presented a compelling argument that Klein's company was doomed. Not only was his core sportswear business struggling, but the company was also facing huge payments on junk-bond debt it was in no position to pay. It was an unfortunate time to stumble: The country was gripped in a recession, and even many financially fit U.S. firms were having a rough time making ends meet.

Geffen called Klein, who was devastated by the article, and gently asked him about the issues that had been raised in it. "How much money do you have?"

"I really don't know," Klein answered despondently. "I'm not sure."

"Well, it's your company, you have a right to know," Geffen told him. "Call your CFO. You should get on this right away."

Geffen offered to come to New York, look at Klein's books, and advise him about his options. Klein was surprised by the offer. It had not occurred to him that Geffen had the skills to evaluate an ailing fashion company. He soon learned that Geffen's management talents were translatable to businesses outside the music industry.

Geffen met with Klein and Barry Schwartz, his childhood pal and longtime business partner, along with other Klein deputies, at Klein's nineteenth-century beachfront house in East Hampton. It was a stormy session in which the panicked Calvin Klein team hollered at one another, some of them attempting to avoid being blamed for the company's troubles.

Geffen quickly saw the problem. In 1983, Klein and Schwartz had made an ill-fated decision to buy Puritan Fashions, the independent manufacturer of Calvin Klein jeans, for $65.8 million. Shortly after the purchase, the market for the jeans dropped sharply, and the company took on junk-bond debt to meet loan payments.

Geffen surmised that the company should be transformed from a manufacturing firm to a design, marketing, and licensing company. "You guys stink at manufacturing," he said. "You need to get out of that business."

Instead, Geffen continued, the company needed to focus on what it really knew: how to design and market the Calvin Klein brand name. "Calvin, you should only be focusing on the aesthetics," Geffen said. "You should just be designing the clothes and overseeing the marketing and advertising."

Geffen reprimanded Klein and Schwartz for excesses they could not afford. Among other things, he told them to sell their company jet, which cost them $2.5 million a year to maintain. He also told Klein to fire his chief financial officer and helped him hire Richard Martin, a top executive at Price Waterhouse, the accounting firm he himself used. Here was the "fixer" in action: David Geffen was now involved in the kind of problem solving that energized him more than anything else.

He then made an extraordinary offer to purchase all the company's outstanding junk-bond debt, which had a face value of sixty-two million dollars. The company did not even have enough money to cover its next payment of fifteen million, but Geffen said he would cover the entire bill so that it would have some breathing room.

Klein was stunned. He did not want to accept Geffen's offer, as he was fearful of exposing him to the risks and problems associated with his company. But he did not have a choice; it was made painfully clear to him that either Geffen bought the bonds or the company would have to file for bankruptcy.

Geffen knew Leon Black, the former architect of raids at Drexel Burnham Lambert and now a dealmaker backed by Credit Lyonnais, which controlled the bonds. Geffen asked Black to give him a good deal. "I'm not in this to make a profit," he said. "Calvin is one of my best friends, and I'm trying to help him out. It would mean a lot if you would me let me buy the bonds." Black believed Klein would turn his business around, but he wanted to maintain a good relationship with Geffen, so he agreed to sell the bonds to him at a bargain price. Geffen had masterfully cut the debt in a way that Klein or Schwartz could never have managed.

When the deal was announced, Geffen was careful to downplay the significance of the transaction. He emphasized that he had bought the bonds out of friendship, further stating that he had waived repayment of the principal for several years. He also told reporters that he had no plans to convert the debt into equity at a later date and that he did not intend to take an active role in the management of the company.

It was a charitable position that saved face for both Klein and Schwartz. But the truth was that Geffen, at Klein's invitation, did take a major role at the company. He began to strategize about how to transform Calvin Klein into a licensing and marketing company. He started looking for companies to purchase the licenses to manufacture the company's underwear and jeans.

Geffen even offered some key creative decisions: After spotting Mark Wahlberg, the sexy young star of the new rap group Marky Mark and the Funky Bunch, Geffen suggested that Klein dress him in his briefs and make him his new spokesmodel. Klein embraced the idea, and Geffen signed Wahlberg to star in an ad campaign for just one hundred thousand dollars.

As he sat at home and watched TV coverage of the Republican National Convention in August 1992, Geffen discovered another outlet for his money and power. The convention marked President George Bush's clinching of his party's nomination, but it was the speeches given by Pat Buchanan and the Reverend Pat Robertson that made Geffen steam. The two talked about an America that was white, Christian, heterosexual, and male. "There are people who just don't fit into that category," Geffen thought. He deplored what he called the political right's exclusionary politics.

Geffen contacted Mickey Kantor, a Los Angeles lawyer who was heading the Democratic campaign to elect Arkansas governor Bill Clinton. Geffen fumed to Kantor about the importance of stopping the right and offered to donate money to the Clinton campaign.

Rahm Emanuel, Clinton's brash thirty-two-year-old campaign finance director, wisely saw that Geffen was a man the Democrats needed on their side. The Clinton campaign, though bolstered by having won the Democratic nomination a month earlier, was plagued by cash-flow problems and faced a deficit of about one million dollars. It was a troubling position given that President Bush had $7.6 million in the bank, and Ross Perot, an independent candidate, had millions more. Geffen wrote a check to the Democratic National Committee for one hundred thousand dollars.

Emanuel engineered a meeting between Clinton and Geffen, inviting the show-business mogul to attend an intimate lunch at Doe's Eat Place, one of the governor's favorite steak houses in Little Rock. Emanuel sat Geffen next to Clinton, who talked to him and about ten other campaign donors about his liberal agenda. Clinton was directly courting the gay vote, promising to lift the ban on homosexuals in the military. This was a man Geffen wanted to see succeed.

Clinton and Geffen were perfectly positioned to help each other meet their goals; while Clinton was enamored of Hollywood and eager to use his position to meet stars, Geffen was fascinated with Washington and interested in extending his influence beyond the entertainment industry.

"Are you prepared to raise taxes?" Geffen asked Clinton. "Because I know that unless you're willing to raise taxes you aren't going to cure these problems."

Clinton was hoarse and cleared his throat uncomfortably as he outlined his objectives. Rahm Emanuel, who was sitting across from Geffen, signaled him to help the candidate out.

"Pour him some tea," Emanuel said quietly to Geffen. Geffen picked up a pitcher of iced tea and filled Clinton's glass.

Clinton and Geffen made a genuine connection over lunch, sowing the seeds of a friendship that was more intimate than the bonds Clinton forged with most other major campaign contributors. He soon counted Geffen among his circle of friends. Geffen was there for Clinton and his wife, Hillary, in good times and bad, offering money and emotional support when it was needed.

After the election, Geffen's relationship with the president introduced him into an entirely different power arena. Leading figures of business and industry such as Steve Ross were no longer at the center of his radar screen. His nameplate now could read, "David Geffen—Friend of the President."

In addition to politics, Geffen continued to give generously to AIDS-related causes. He gave the largest single gift ever for AIDS services when he donated one million dollars each to APLA and GMHC. After making the gift to APLA, the huge nonprofit service organization renamed their headquarters in Hollywood the David Geffen Center. They also decided to honor him, along with Barbra Streisand, at their sixth annual "Commitment to Life" benefit in November 1992. "Commitment to Life" had become an enormously successful fund-raiser at which APLA staged a star-studded concert at the Universal Amphitheater in Hollywood.

Geffen's friend Steve Tisch, chairman of APLA's board of directors, and Jeffrey Katzenberg together contacted Geffen, convincing him to accept the honor. He was reluctant to accept and nervous about making a speech. For all of his bravado, Geffen showed an unusual vulnerability about speaking before a large audience.

The crowd at the APLA benefit, which promised to fill all 6,251 seats, would certainly be the biggest live audience of his life. The speech he delivered made national news and changed his life forever.

COMING OUT

In the years following his mother's death, Geffen had chosen to have little communication with his family. He did not have much of a relationship with his brother, Mitchell, and only occasionally did he telephone his stepfather, Sam, and his aunt, Deena, who were now roommates in the house on Gilcrest Drive in Beverly Hills. With AIDS Project Los Angeles set to honor him, it did not occur to him to invite them to share in the happy occasion.

But the daughter of Geffen's cousin, Sonya Eichler, organized members of the family to attend. Mim Eichler Rivas spotted an ad for the benefit, contacted Mitchell's daughter Vivian, and told her about the event. "Why don't you call David's office and find out if David wants to have any of his family there?" Mim asked.

Vivian phoned David's secretary and secured six tickets. Mim's mother, Sonya, who had not seen David since 1957, planned to attend, along with Mitchell, Vivian, Mim, Deena, and Sam.

As the organizers of "Commitment to Life" put together a program of performances by such stars as Elton John, Billy Joel, and Liza Minnelli, Geffen obsessed about his acceptance speech. He asked Bryn Bridenthal, the publicity chief at Geffen Records, to try her hand at writing it. Bridenthal hired the best speechwriters she knew and wrote one draft herself.

But Geffen rejected the suggested speeches in favor of a more personal message that he himself had crafted.

On Wednesday, November 18, 1992, the day of the benefit, Geffen was terrified. He attended a noontime rehearsal and practiced reading his speech off of the TelePrompTer. That afternoon, he called Bridenthal and invited her to ride over to the benefit with him in his chauffeur-driven Lincoln Town Car. Bridenthal ran home to shower and change. But when she returned to the office twenty minutes before their departure time, Geffen's secretary told her that, antsy and nervous, he had left early.

At the amphitheater, Bridenthal caught up with Geffen, who had dressed up his blue jeans by wearing a navy jacket, white shirt, and red tie. Bridenthal escorted him down the red carpet and past the gauntlet of TV cameras and reporters who were on hand to film the hordes of arriving celebrities.

"We'll raise four million dollars tonight, which will feed and take care of and clothe a great many people who are in great need," Geffen told one interviewer. "It really is a wonderful night. And it speaks extraordinarily well of this community."

Inside the amphitheater, Geffen did not see his family until he sat down in an aisle seat just as the lights dimmed. Although he did not exchange more than a few words with any of his relatives that night, he looked down the row and smiled at his brother, his aunt, his stepfather, and the others.

Geffen's family was wowed as a congratulatory telegram sent from Bill Clinton, elected president only a couple of weeks earlier, was read. The liberal Hollywood crowd roared. Then Warren Beatty walked onstage to introduce Geffen and present him with the "Commitment to Life" award.

"The analogy of David and Goliath is hard for me to ignore," Beatty started. "As David's societal contribution mounts, and business, political,

Geffen on the night he was honored with the
AIDS Project Los Angeles "Commitment to Life" award.

(Russ Einhorn/Shooting Star)

and religious Goliaths blink in the aim of his slingshot, his intelligence focuses and his anger mobilizes," he continued. "And a mobilized David Geffen is something that you want working *for* you, not *against* you."

As Beatty finished his introduction, the audience leapt to its feet and cheered. Geffen walked toward the podium and tightly embraced Beatty. When the audience sat down, Geffen looked into the TelePrompTer, took a deep breath, touched his hand to his heart, and began his speech.

"Thank you," he said. "Thank you, Warren." He opened his remarks by thanking APLA and reciting daunting statistics about the number of people who had died from AIDS.

> We are in a health crisis that is overwhelming whole populations of people across the planet and yet we are still giving awards to people who simply do what they can to help. I'm greatly honored by this award. Honored by the people at APLA who have given it. And I'm honored most of all to be here with you tonight. This is a very special crowd. So many of you have given money and, more than money, so many of you have given love and passion and fear and humor and rage and time to stay with those you love and care about those you don't even know.
>
> So far we've proven so many people wrong. We've shown America that we are no longer afraid of ourselves or ashamed of ourselves. We've had the courage in the face of an unprecedented onslaught to reach out to each other and show the country the true meaning of "family values." Our president-elect is fond of saying "I still believe in a place called hope" and if there's any-where in America it is surely here. Hope that through this fight we will defeat not only AIDS but the bigotry and prejudice that surrounds it. Hope that we will do justice to all the courage and passion of those who have already fallen.

Next, he read a letter that Bill Miller, a friend who had died in 1986 at age thirty-one, had written to be read aloud at his own funeral. "AIDS makes your responsibility more urgent to be positive about our lifestyles and nurture and protect young gays who look up to us for hope that they too can lead a life uninhibited by fear and guilt and shame," Geffen read.

Then, David Geffen dropped the bombshell. It was a single line that in one moment ended a charade he had been playing for decades.

"As a gay man, I've come a long way to be here tonight," he said.

Geffen expected to be able to continue immediately with the next line of his speech, but the crowd burst into a sustained round of applause and whistles. He looked nervously out at the audience and smiled.

For years, David Geffen had resisted making such a statement, clinging to a strong belief that his sexual orientation was a private matter. But now he realized that by virtue of his success, he had become a public figure. What's more, he felt he could not justify standing before that particular audience, filled as it was with so many people who were infected with HIV and dealing with the serious issue of AIDS, and not acknowledge that he was gay.

The cheering finally subsided, and Geffen was able to finish his speech. "And in different places and by different paths we've all come a long way. And yet there is an equally long way to go. If I have learned anything I have learned this, that we must walk this path together. Thank you for this award and thank you most of all for what you have yet to do. Good night."

The event produced an avalanche of publicity, mostly because of the record amount that had been raised for AIDS causes and the numerous celebrities who had gathered to perform. But nearly all the reports, including stories aired on *CBS This Morning* and *NBC News at Sunrise,* contained the clip of David Geffen announcing that he was gay.

David Crosby was at home watching TV when he caught the news. Even in the late 1960s when he was booking Crosby, Stills, Nash & Young to play at Woodstock, it had been no secret Geffen was gay. But it was also not a matter that Geffen or his clients talked about much. Crosby had for decades watched Geffen struggle with his sexual identity.

The next morning, Crosby telephoned Geffen Records and left a message for Geffen to call him. Geffen, known for returning phone calls quickly, dialed Crosby back ten minutes later.

"I've always been so ready to jump into your shit when you were wrong," Crosby began. "I thought that when you did something right, I should let you know. I watched you on TV last night, and I was really proud of you. I thought that was a real stand-up move."

The speech transformed David Geffen into a spokesman on gay issues. He also became a role model, a position to which he never aspired. Even Michelangelo Signorile soon anointed Geffen a hero. *The Advocate,* a gay magazine, named him man of the year and put his photograph on the cover.

I n late October 1992, Steve Ross traveled to Los Angeles to undergo radical surgery, but the operation failed to halt the cancer and led to only more suffering. In mid-December, as Ross lay on his deathbed, Geffen flew to Little Rock to participate in an economic summit called by President-elect Clinton. He was one of only a few titans of the entertainment industry to have been invited to the summit. There, he met with the heads of companies such as Coca-Cola, Xerox, and American Airlines, as well as with various people who were accepting positions in Clinton's cabinet. Geffen bonded with Thomas F. McLarty 3rd, an Arkansas businessman and longtime Clinton friend who had been appointed chief of staff. An indication of just how much Geffen's circle had changed was that he met renowned investor Warren Buffett and said he felt the same thrill upon shaking his hand as he did when he first saw Bob Dylan perform in the 1960s.

One week later, on December 20, 1992, Steve Ross died. His body was flown back to New York. Courtney Ross arranged a funeral to be held at Guild Hall, near their home in East Hampton, that Wednesday, two days before Christmas. She invited a couple hundred friends and colleagues, including Steven Spielberg, Beverly Sills, and Quincy Jones. Paul Simon and Barbra Streisand sang. When the funeral was over, the tearful brigade made its way to the Springs, a cemetery in East Hampton, for a graveside burial ceremony.

Courtney Ross had not invited David Geffen. She was angry with him and felt that he had behaved miserably toward her husband. Others were also upset with Geffen. More than anyone outside the immediate family, Steven Spielberg had been at Ross's side during his final decline, and he empathized with Courtney. At one time, Spielberg and Geffen had been Ross's two most enthusiastic disciples, and as such, from time to time they had been thrown together at social occasions. Several years earlier, they had both been guests at the Rosses' home in East Hampton when Spielberg used his own video camera to shoot a mock version of *Jaws 5* in the pool.

But those idyllic memories were now far in the past, and Spielberg was disappointed that Geffen had chosen to vilify Ross in the media even as he was dying. Spielberg had spent the last months of Ross's life sitting with him in his backyard in East Hampton, reading books together and sharing stories about the past. David Geffen was nowhere in evidence.

After the funeral, Courtney Ross made plans for a much larger memorial service to be held at Carnegie Hall the following February. She compiled a guest list of several thousand and mailed out invitations. Once again, she very specifically omitted David Geffen's name.

Geffen was devastated. He remained firm in his belief that Ross had wronged him, but he nonetheless wanted to attend the memorial service, pay his respects, and achieve some measure of closure for himself. He telephoned Terry Semel, who had been invited to both services, and told him he wanted to go.

"You should go," Semel told Geffen. "He was your friend. You adored him. Go for Steve *and* for you." He added: "No one's going to throw you out." Armed with this encouragement, Geffen attended the memorial service. There, he mourned his longtime mentor and brought some finality to one of the most important relationships he had ever had.

In the future, Geffen revised history to convince himself that Steve

Ross had not valued their friendship. Many people in the Warner family found Geffen's assertion ludicrous. They argued that Ross had not only loved Geffen but had also constantly showed it by making deals that were favorable to Geffen and much to the company's detriment.

But that was not the way Geffen chose to see it. "Ours was really a business relationship. I had more of an illusion of a friendship than there really was," he said. "Steve never took a fatherly interest. I was an asset of his."

G effen eagerly answered the call when President Clinton asked him for feedback on his proposal to end the ban on homosexuals in the military. Even before being sworn in, Clinton had come under intense pressure from military officials, including General Colin Powell, the chairman of the Joint Chiefs of Staff, who said that removing the ban would be bad for discipline.

Geffen told Clinton that a broad-based, grassroots effort would be essential to turn the tide. The issue, which was quickly turning into a debacle of epic proportions, paired Clinton, a political neophyte criticized often for his arrogance, with Geffen, equally green and nearly as presumptuous.

After monitoring the developments on CNN, Geffen essentially offered to head the effort. Through Bob Burkett, a political operative he had hired to be his representative in Washington, Geffen organized the first meeting of groups that supported overturning the ban, including People for the American Way and the American Civil Liberties Union. With Geffen helping provide the seed money, the group hired a staff and came up with the slogan "Live and Let Serve."

The group also organized meetings between representatives and military leaders who were in favor of lifting the ban. Geffen also put the art department at Geffen Records on the job of creating newspaper ads advocating the overturning of the ban. One of the ads, which ran in *The New York Times,* was headlined NO ONE SIGNS UP FOR BOOT CAMP TO GET A DATE. The ads were paid for by the David Geffen Foundation.

Geffen, who had escaped service in Vietnam by meekly admitting he was homosexual, could not understand why anyone would want to serve in the military. "But if people who happen to be gay want to serve their country they should have the right to do so," he said.

The issue turned out to be one of the nastiest political quagmires of the Clinton presidency. In trying to pay back campaign benefactors such as Geffen, the president had wildly underestimated the controversy that would ensue, galvanizing conservatives and moving many centrists to the right. The soccer moms and African Americans who had elected Clinton had no passion for the subject. When the months-long battle finally ended, and with little else having thus been accomplished at the start of his presidency, Clinton had to settle for a no-win "don't ask, don't tell" compromise. Geffen, for his part, quickly backed away from the issue and advised Clinton that insisting on an out-and-out overturn was not worth political suicide.

At the time, some speculated that Geffen might abandon his record label, move to Washington, and take a job there. "No one's asked me," he told *The New York Times.* "If somebody felt there was a job I could actually do I would consider it—not out of any ambition to be in Washington, but I do want to rise to the occasion of serving there if warranted."

Joni Mitchell and Don Henley did not fail to notice that Geffen was far richer and more in the spotlight than they were. Two decades earlier, they had hired *him* to make *them* wealthy stars. Mitchell and Henley were as difficult and ego driven as Geffen was, and both now charged him with being greedy, petty, and cheap.

Henley was angry with himself for once again buying Geffen's pitch—the same one he had made to Asylum artists in the early 1970s—that Geffen Records would be a small family-oriented company where he would protect the artists. Henley realized that Geffen once again had built up a company so he could sell it and reap another enormous profit for himself. It had been an almost exact repeat of

Asylum Records, with one exception: Instead of making seven million dollars, this time David Geffen had made almost seven hundred million.

"Fuck you!" Henley screamed at Geffen, informing him that he was terminating his contract. "I'm outta here!" Even though his contract stated that he owed Geffen Records more albums, Henley put the inevitable Irving Azoff on the case to find an attorney to extricate him from the label. Now armed with a fax machine, Henley began drowning Geffen in scathing faxes. He was ready to fight all over again.

The argument his lawyer came up with was a claim that a "seven-year statute" allowed Henley to leave the label. Henley had renegotiated his Geffen Records contract in 1988 but now argued that the statute applied to his original 1984 contract. Henley also said he was terminating the contract because he believed that Geffen was no longer actively involved in running the company—he had a clause that said if Geffen left the company, so could Henley.

Geffen went crazy, convinced that Henley and Azoff were conspiring to cheat him. But he knew that the contract Henley had signed in 1988 had obligated him for an additional seven years. Under the contract, Geffen said, Henley owed the company two more studio albums and a greatest-hits collection. Geffen wasted no time in filing a thirty-million-dollar breach-of-contract suit against Henley. "This time, I'll never settle," Geffen told him.

Henley soon countersued, offering up the claim that a conspiracy existed among the six major record labels to ensure that if a performer such as Henley chose to leave one label, no one else would sign him. Geffen dismissed the allegation as nonsense. The reason other record companies didn't want Henley, Geffen said, was because he was old and "thoroughly unpleasant."

Henley fumed that Geffen did not give credit where credit was due. "He was seminal in our career," he said. "The difference between me and David is that I'm willing to admit he was very important in our career, where he in turn is not willing to admit that we are in large part responsible for putting him where he is today."

Joni Mitchell, whose relationship with Geffen had been erratic for years, was now turning increasingly hostile toward her former housemate. With her career on the decline and radio stations showing scant interest in her recent albums, Mitchell alleged that Geffen had pocketed revenue due her from her music-publishing company, which had been administered by Geffen Records. Geffen, for his part, denied the allegation. Mitchell's charge was never proved, and she did not file any legal action to arbitrate her claims.

"I don't make much money," she said. "I haven't seen a royalty check in twenty years." On that point, Mitchell was right, but that was not Geffen's fault: He had given her such a rich deal that none of her albums had been successful enough to recoup the one-million-dollar advances her contract guaranteed her.

The truth was that Mitchell was upset and bitter that the music industry had passed her by. In addition to Geffen, she also blamed record promoters for dismissing her as old news and critics for not understanding her divergent creative directions. But her lack of success came down to the records themselves: Even her most ardent fans found the records to be disappointing, compared with such earlier works as *Blue* and *Court and Spark.*

Eddie Rosenblatt was in Geffen's office when Mitchell stopped by to complain about the money she felt was owed her. She would not listen to Geffen's explanation, and a battle of wills soon erupted. Rosenblatt excused himself as they entered into screaming tirades in which each cited chapter and verse of every betrayal each felt the other had committed since the late 1960s.

"Let me go!" Mitchell said, demanding that Geffen release her from her contract.

"Joan, you're not gonna find a better deal out there than this, and I'll keep you here forever," Geffen said. "I'll never drop you."

"Slavery with tenure is not attractive to me!" she cried. When her contract soon came up, she accepted an invitation from Mo Ostin, whose Reprise label had released her first four albums beginning in 1968, to return to the Warner family.

G effen's childhood dream of winning an Academy Award seemed ever more elusive. His films had produced only a handful of modest commercial successes, no blockbusters, and zero Oscar nominations for Best Picture.

Despite its financial success, he was embarrassed by his company's most recent motion picture, *The Last Boy Scout,* and resolved never again to put his name on such a violent film. He was desperate to produce a motion picture that would bring him artistic recognition and legitimacy. One film on his development slate that he thought might win him such acclaim was *M. Butterfly,* a movie version of the play he had co-produced on Broadway. He hired David Cronenberg, the director of such offbeat films as *Naked Lunch* and *The Fly,* and vowed to stay far away during the creative process. Geffen's initial casting concerns that the audience would not buy John Lone as a man masquerading as a woman were apparently rendered moot when he viewed the director's cut.

"Terry, I'm over the moon. I just saw *M. Butterfly.* I mean . . . Academy Award," he told Terry Semel on a phone call from his plane en route to Los Angeles from New York. "It's great. And I can't believe we made it for seventeen million."

The other project Geffen thought might have Academy Award potential was a movie version of Anne Rice's novel *Interview with the Vampire,* which he had been trying to make for nearly four years. Geffen blew a fuse, however, when Julia Phillips, who was slated to co-produce the movie with him, published a memoir in which she portrayed Geffen as an egomaniac who had stolen her best ideas. Geffen said the book, *You'll Never Eat Lunch in This Town Again,* was "completely inaccurate." As a result, he fired her from the project.

Geffen forged ahead in his attempt to produce a winning script for the movie. He hired a number of writers, but none was able to come up with a script that pleased him. Finally, he asked the eccentric Rice herself to have a go at it. When her script came in, Geffen determined that it was the best version he had read yet. It needed work, but it could be used if he could find a director who could rewrite portions of it.

Anne Rice could be as stubborn as Geffen: Anyone could see that fireworks might explode between them at any moment. In the beginning, Geffen included her in the process and tried to accommodate her wishes. But he refused to consider Rutger Hauer, Rice's first choice for the lead role of Lestat, arguing that he was too old and lacked the star wattage that the picture needed. But he said he would pursue Daniel Day-Lewis, the star of *My Left Foot,* whom Rice also found acceptable for the role.

What Geffen did not tell Rice was that he had in the back of his mind another actor to play Lestat. Ever since their pairing on *Risky Business,* Geffen had looked for another opportunity to reteam with Tom Cruise, who had just finished shooting the movie based on John Grisham's novel *The Firm.*

In November 1992, Geffen contacted Cruise, who was in Australia vacationing with his wife, Nicole Kidman, and floated the idea. Geffen told Cruise that playing the villainous Lestat, the first bad guy Cruise would ever play, would complement his recent bold acting choices such as *Born on the Fourth of July.* Cruise was intrigued and promised to consider the offer.

Cruise's ideal costar, Geffen believed, was Brad Pitt, the young blond who had grabbed Geffen's attention in a steamy role in *Thelma and Louise.* The pairing of Cruise and Pitt, who was now appearing in *A River Runs Through It,* would make for box-office gold, Geffen figured. He invited Pitt to his Malibu beach house, where he did his usual winning sales job, convincing him that playing the part of Louis would make him a star.

Geffen also looked for a director and offered the job to the two people Anne Rice most wanted to see in charge, Ridley Scott and David Cronenberg. When both turned him down, Geffen became enamored of Neil Jordan, whose movie *The Crying Game* had just begun to play in U.S. theaters and was slowly captivating moviegoers.

Geffen persuaded Jordan to consider directing the movie. He sent him the screenplay Rice had written, as well as a copy of the novel. Jordan liked the book, but what really convinced him to sign on was his first meeting with Geffen. At Geffen's offices, Jordan told Geffen he was hesitant about making a big-budget Hollywood movie, having been accustomed to making low-budget movies overseas with unknown actors.

"Why don't you just make this movie as if it's an independent film?" Geffen told Jordan, attempting to soothe his nerves. Geffen won him over and offered him a sense of security he had not felt from any of the many other movie tycoons who were chasing him. Whereas Jordan found most Hollywood types cagey and noncommittal, Geffen was refreshingly direct and forthright.

Stephen Woolley, Jordan's producing partner, was shocked when he realized Geffen's directness extended beyond business. As he had done with so many other virtual strangers, Geffen trotted out intimate details of his private life with Woolley and Jordan. He told them the story of being with John Lennon hours before his assassination and bragged about the male prostitute he had been having sex with when he got the phone call that Lennon had been shot.

At their next meeting, Geffen told Jordan that he already had some fairly solid ideas regarding casting. "Here is my sense," he told them. "I want to cast Daniel Day-Lewis as Lestat and Brad Pitt as Louis." Jordan liked the choices and arranged to meet both actors.

FIFTY

|||

J effrey and Marilyn Katzenberg hosted a dinner party at their home in Beverly Hills to celebrate Geffen's fiftieth birthday on February 21, 1993. In youth-obsessed Hollywood, Geffen was seemingly unfazed by his advancing age. "I'm, like, delighted to be fifty," he told the *Los Angeles Times*. "It's not a bummer, you know? It's nothing."

He had much to celebrate, not the least of which was that the record company that bore his name continued its extraordinary winning streak. Its latest hit was *Get a Grip,* a chart-topping album by Aerosmith that sold more than seven million copies. Although he had long since given up discovering music acts for the label, Geffen was still in tune with pop culture. The morning after MTV aired the first episode of an animated series called *The Beavis and Butt-head Show,* Geffen telephoned Tom Freston, the chairman of MTV, predicted enormous success for the show, and made a deal to make a feature film based on the characters.

The Katzenbergs invited Barry Diller, Sandy Gallin, Calvin Klein, Ray Stark, and Carrie Fisher, among others, to the party and filled their dining room with silver and gold balloons. A cake featuring a swimsuit-clad Geffen talking, of course, on the telephone was wheeled out after dinner. The group then retired to the Katzenbergs' projection room, where they were treated to a performance by magicians Penn & Teller, the highlight of which was a trick wherein the two levitated Klein's wife, Kelly.

Geffen brought as his date his ex-boyfriend Bob Brassel. Since their breakup four years earlier, they had become tight friends as well as business partners. Brassel had risen to senior vice president of production at Warner Bros. and was the executive assigned to oversee all films made by Geffen Pictures.

Brassel worked with Geffen in securing a deal for Brad Pitt to play Louis in *Interview with the Vampire*. Neil Jordan, meanwhile, arranged to meet Daniel Day-Lewis in Dublin, where the actor was filming a drama called *In the Name of the Father*. Day-Lewis told Jordan that he was so immersed in the picture that he could not break even to read *Interview with the Vampire*. "If you wait until I'm done, then I'll read the script," Day-Lewis told Jordan.

The director-hunting and casting process had taken more time than Geffen had planned, but he was unperturbed when he realized his option on the film would expire at the beginning of May, technically forcing him to pay Anne Rice another one million dollars to extend the rights. Instead, he took out two-page ads in the Hollywood trade papers announcing that the film would begin shooting in April.

Geffen did not believe Rice would force him to renew the option, especially given that it was clear that production, after so many false starts, would definitely begin within a few months. "Anne is one of my friends," he told Bonni Lee, an executive at his film company. "She knows I'm going to make this movie. She's not going to stick me for that one million."

In New Orleans, however, Anne Rice was determined to hold firm on the agreement. In her opinion, Hollywood had messed around with her and her book for so long that even now, with a director under contract and offers out to actors, she remained skeptical. Claudia Eller, who

Geffen celebrates his fiftieth birthday with (from left)

Bob Brassel, Howard Rosenman, Jane Semel, and Ray Stark.

(Alan Berliner/Alan Berliner Studio)

wrote the "Dish" column in *Daily Variety,* called Rice and found out that she was unwilling to cut Geffen a break. If the picture did not go before the cameras by the end of April, Rice told Eller, the rights would "revert back to me in the first week of May."

Geffen became enraged when Eller contacted him for comment. "If you print this, I will never speak to you again!" he yelled. When Eller said she was going ahead with the story, Geffen disputed that the rights would revert to Rice in May but told her that it was not going to be an issue anyway: "We're going to shoot a week in April with Brad Pitt and pick up with Daniel Day-Lewis, as Lestat, in August," he said.

But the truth was that Geffen did not have a deal with Daniel Day-Lewis. After the actor finally read the script, he told Jordan he was not interested. Geffen then revisited his first notion of dream casting: Tom Cruise as the Vampire Lestat.

But the contract negotiations to bring Cruise on board stumbled along, and when Geffen's rights expired in early May and shooting had not begun, Anne Rice's attorney requested one million dollars for renewal. Geffen contacted Rice directly and convinced her to extend the rights deal without saddling him with the additional payment.

Finally, a deal with Tom Cruise was completed, although he was not able to begin filming until October. In the middle of July, as reports of the casting began to leak, Geffen worked up a new set of two-page ads for the trade papers in which he announced that Cruise would play Lestat and that shooting would begin October 18. As far as Geffen was concerned, he had secured the perfect cast, headed by the hottest movie star in the world.

To Anne Rice and her loyal fans, however, Geffen's casting choices were nightmares. Rice turned on Geffen and took to the media in order to blast the casting selections. She became the production's number-one enemy, despite the fact that her name was on the screenplay.

"It's like casting Huck Finn and Tom Sawyer in the movie," Rice told the *Los Angeles Times,* speaking of Cruise and Pitt. "Cruise is no more my Vampire Lestat than Edward G. Robinson is Rhett Butler. I'm not sure he knows what he's getting into. Cruise should do himself and everyone else a service and withdraw." Rice made a host of other disparaging comments, including jabs that Cruise was too short and had too high a voice to play Lestat.

Geffen pitched a fit when the *Times* called for comment. He could not believe that Rice would trash the picture, especially since she had been paid two million dollars and would have her name on it as screenwriter. He cut off all communication with her.

"To his credit, Tom wants to play a broad range of characters, just as Jack Nicholson, Paul Newman and Al Pacino did before him," Geffen told the *Times*. "Cruise, I predict, will get a Best Actor nomination and *Interview* will be nominated for a Best Picture Oscar of 1994."

The *Times*'s story also raised the first of what became a seemingly endless stream of rumors declaring dissension between Cruise and Pitt. "The rumors that Pitt is upset with the selection of Cruise are totally untrue—made up by agents trying to get their own clients cast," Geffen said. "I spoke to Brad this morning and he's thrilled."

Tom Cruise was deeply hurt by Rice's attack. But Geffen ministered to him, convincing him that Rice was simply a woman gone mad.

The film version of *M. Butterfly,* starring Jeremy Irons, was a financial bust, grossing less than two million dollars. A number of movie critics, echoing Geffen's original fears, said the film was ruined by the hard-to-believe performance of John Lone in the role of the man who masquerades as a female opera star. "His five o'clock shadow gives him away," Richard Corliss wrote in *Time* magazine.

Geffen turned to *Interview with the Vampire* and told Neil Jordan and Stephen Woolley that he planned to be intimately involved with the day-to-day production of the picture. But shortly after arriving on the set in Louisiana, Geffen became bored. Nervous and impatient, he was not well suited to the slow, methodical, and often tedious nature of moviemaking. He had never spent more than a few days on the sets of his previous films, and it quickly became clear that he was out of his element.

To be sure, Geffen had already contributed mightily to the production. He had had the instincts and contacts to hire major stars and an on-the-rise director. But the minutiae of a line producer's chores on location are somewhat akin to those of a baby-sitter; such tasks were not a good use of David Geffen's time. With Woolley on hand to ask Tom Cruise to shorten his contractual breaks between days of filming, for example, there was not much for Geffen to do. In fact, he was such an imposing presence that he himself became another star who had to be baby-sat.

After a day or so, Geffen's mind wandered to trivial matters, and it suddenly struck him that he was the only member of the senior production team who did not have a personal trailer. Tom Cruise, Brad Pitt, Neil Jordan, and Stephen Woolley all had enormous and lavishly outfitted trailers. Geffen blew up at Woolley and demanded to have his own trailer. Woolley was surprised, having previously asked Geffen what arrangements he required. Geffen at that time had responded that he would need only a fax machine in his hotel room and a car to shuttle him around.

Woolley put in a rush order for another trailer, which was delivered to the set the same day. Unfortunately, while the trailer gave Geffen a place to pace, it did not give him something to do. Within a couple of days, he grew exhausted, in part because the shooting was being done in the middle of the night. He then ditched his plan and flew home to Los Angeles.

On Halloween, just two weeks after filming began, the production of *Interview with the Vampire* was dealt an emotionally shattering blow. River Phoenix, the twenty-three-year-old actor who had been cast in the pivotal role of the interviewer, died shortly after collapsing outside the Viper Room, a nightclub just off Sunset Boulevard in West Hollywood. The Los Angeles County coroner said the death was caused by an overdose of cocaine and morphine. The filmmakers regrouped, and arrangements were made for Christian Slater to play the part.

Before long, various secrets and embarrassing details about the production were beginning to leak to the press. For instance, it was rumored that Cruise had demanded that his costumer manufacture special boots to make him appear taller than Pitt. Jordan and Woolley attempted to guard the set closely, but it proved to be an impossible task, especially with Anne Rice's besotted fans clamoring for details.

To Jordan and Woolley, the leaks and reports were maddening. It seemed to them as though someone with intimate knowledge of the production was leaking the information. Many times the details were wrong, but they always seemed to contain an element of truth. For example, it was true that Tom Cruise wore special elevator shoes to make him taller. But there was no truth to the constant rumors that Cruise and Pitt were fighting.

At first, Woolley suspected that Geffen was the source, since he had been so loose-lipped and indiscreet about his own life the first time they had met. What's more, on a couple of occasions, the news reports had appeared not long after Jordan and Woolley had discussed problems and issues with Geffen.

Woolley soon learned that Geffen was not the source. The culprit, though, was someone right inside his house. His projectionist, it turned out, had eavesdropped on their conversations as they watched dailies. Geffen promptly fired her, and the leaks stopped.

David Geffen had become the most effective AIDS fund-raiser in America, drawing money both from friends who shared his beliefs and from some who simply wanted to avoid getting on his bad side. The bully was at work again, only this time it was for the good of others—not the good of David Geffen.

When his friends Hillary Rodham Clinton and Jeffrey Katzenberg were themselves honored at the 1993 APLA "Commitment to Life" benefit, Geffen served as chairman of the event. He got on the telephone, boldly asking entertainment heavyweights for specific contributions. When they did not give as much as he asked for, he complained until they did. He grew particularly irked when Michael Eisner, Katzenberg's boss, initially suggested a donation smaller than those of some other entertainment-company CEOs. He telephoned Frank Wells, Eisner's number-two man, and griped that Eisner was being a cheapskate.

"Frank, this is kind of shameful," Geffen started. "Sid Sheinberg and Lew Wasserman, and people who are your corporate enemies are giving a hundred thousand, and Michael wants to give twenty-five thousand and spread that out over four years!"

"Let me take care of it," Wells said. Eisner eventually agreed to donate one hundred thousand dollars. With David Geffen as chairman, "Commitment to Life" that year raised $4.3 million, the largest amount in the benefit's history.

Millions of dollars, meanwhile, were continuing to pour into Geffen's private coffers as Geffen Records continued to dominate the industry. Its latest successes included another blockbuster by Nirvana and a giant album by a new group called Counting Crows, a band that had also been discovered by Gary Gersh. The alternative music wave was in full bloom and, like the hard rock and metal movements just before it, Geffen Records was leading the charge.

But with a year left on his MCA employment contract as chairman of Geffen Records, Geffen was still bored. Increasingly, he was tuning out the daily goings-on and told people he was leaning toward not renewing his contract at MCA.

He was vacationing in Barbados when he saw a report on CNN that the latest Guns N' Roses album contained a song, "Look at Your Game Girl," which had been written by mass murderer Charles Manson. The song prompted a cry of outrage from the public as well as from some of Geffen's oldest friends, who thought he had lost his mind.

Jimmy Webb, who had been close to Geffen at the time of the Manson murders, wrote him an angry letter, criticizing him for making Manson a star. Sharon Tate had been a friend of Webb's; another victim, hairstylist Jay Sebring, had been his barber. Enraged by Webb's letter, Geffen called Webb and castigated him for laying the blame at his feet.

In fact, Geffen was horrified that the song had come out on his label. He went to the band and explained how and why they had touched a nerve and argued strenuously that they ought to issue an apology. He finally succeeded in convincing Axl Rose that the money earned from the song should go to the child of one of the people killed in the Manson murder spree.

The economy was improving, and so was Calvin Klein's business. Lower interest rates enabled Klein to secure a fifty-eight-million-dollar loan from Citibank to buy back his junk-bond debt from Geffen. The transformation of Calvin Klein was nearly complete when Geffen negotiated a sale, for sixty-four million dollars, of the company's underwear business to Warnaco, a New York–based apparel manufacturer. Under the terms of the sale, Warnaco was to produce the underwear, paying Calvin Klein a royalty of about 5 percent annually. The company used the proceeds from the sale to pay off the Citibank loan; it forecast a profitable 1994.

Just as the drama in Klein's life was ending, another of Geffen's friends found himself in the midst of a crisis. This emergency energized Geffen and once again brought him to the front lines of battle. And in this instance, his rescue operation also led to a dramatic change in his own life.

All Hollywood was thrown into mourning when Frank Wells, the president of Walt Disney, died in a helicopter accident while on a ski trip in Nevada in April 1994. The balance of power in Hollywood abruptly shifted in many ways, beginning at Disney. In the wake of the tragedy, Jeffrey Katzenberg, who was chairman of the Disney Studios unit, insisted to Michael Eisner that he should be promoted into Wells's job. Katzenberg claimed that Eisner had promised to give him the job if Wells ever left.

But Eisner did not want to give Katzenberg the job. He thought he had taken too much credit for the success of *The Lion King* and other hit animated movies and that he was disrespectful toward Roy Disney, the company's vice chairman. Eisner claimed he had never promised the presidency to Katzenberg.

Geffen blanched as Katzenberg told him he planned to decline to exercise an option that would ensure that he remain as chairman of Walt Disney Studios until 1996. Katzenberg was thus giving up an estimated one hundred million dollars. He wanted to prove to Michael Eisner that he was serious about being promoted.

"Take the money and stay," Geffen told Katzenberg. "Don't worry. It'll all work out."

Only five days after Frank Wells died, Kurt Cobain, the twenty-seven-year-old star of Nirvana, was found dead of a self-inflicted shotgun wound to the head at his home in Seattle. While the suicide stunned both the music world and Cobain's fans, signs of his desperation abounded in his lyrics.

Throughout Nirvana's success, Cobain had struggled with addictions to both heroin and alcohol and had squabbled with his band mates over royalties. His marriage to Courtney Love was also strained. The two struggled to regain custody of their daughter from a relative after a damaging *Vanity Fair* profile was published.

Geffen's interaction with Cobain had been limited, although the rock star had visited Geffen in Malibu. Geffen had advised the Cobains to ignore the brouhaha created by the *Vanity Fair* article and not to engage in a war of words with its author, Lynn Hirschberg. After Cobain's death, Geffen contacted Love to express his sympathy, telling her he would always be available to help.

His relationship with Love illustrated his new role: He left executive decision making to Eddie Rosenblatt and acted as more of an adviser to the label and its stable of stars. For Love, whose own band was about to become a hit on his label, Geffen soon helped get another, far more flattering profile in *Vanity Fair,* one written by Kevin Sessums, a journalist who was a friend of his.

Then, an act from Geffen's past returned to offer him further riches and glory. Word swept through the industry that the Eagles were planning a reunion, a collaboration that Don Henley had once said would occur "when hell freezes over."

Henley and Glenn Frey were not friends. They had seen each other on only a couple of occasions since the Eagles had broken up in 1980. But Irving Azoff, the band's former manager who was now running his own Giant Records label, was desperate to orchestrate an Eagles reunion. He oversaw the creation of a tribute album on which such big country-music stars as Clint Black, Trisha Yearwood, and Vince Gill recorded the Eagles' old hits. In the first sign of a reconciliation, Azoff convinced Henley and Frey to appear together in a video for the cover of "Take It Easy."

When the tribute album, *Common Thread: The Songs of the Eagles,* was certified gold in early 1994, Azoff lured Henley and Frey, as well as Joe Walsh, to lunch with him in Aspen. Azoff used the success of the record as the linchpin of his campaign to convince the singers that America was hungering for an Eagles reunion.

In May 1994, the Eagles gave their first show together in fourteen years. The session, taped for broadcast on MTV, was an enormous success, and the band as a result agreed to go out on the road again.

Geffen was in the right place at the right time. He was still pursuing his lawsuit against Don Henley when the band's plans to reunite became public. Geffen offered to settle the suit in exchange for the new album and the right to release a "greatest hits" record of Henley's solos. More than twenty years after first teaming up, the Eagles were back on David Geffen's label. The album, from which the tour took its name, was called *Hell Freezes Over.*

*Geffen with Hillary Rodham Clinton, moments
before the president emerged from the White House for a
surprise forty-eighth birthday party.*

THE NEW STUDIO

|||

G effen had grown increasingly close to President Clinton and the First Lady, having firmly emerged as their go-to guy in Hollywood. In August 1994, Mrs. Clinton telephoned Geffen and asked him to help her pull off a surprise party for the president's forty-eighth birthday. Crosby, Stills & Nash was Clinton's favorite band, but he had never seen them perform live. She hoped Geffen could arrange to bring the trio to the White House for a command performance. Geffen said he would be delighted to help and eagerly accepted her invitation to attend the party himself.

Barbara Walters, meanwhile, had long flattered Geffen by telling him that she wanted to profile him on her Friday-night ABC News program, *20/20.* The problem, Walters knew, was that Geffen, despite being a celebrity in Hollywood, was largely unknown to television audiences. She knew she would have difficulty convincing the show's top brass that a report on David Geffen would translate into blockbuster ratings.

If any element of Geffen's career ever offered a news hook that might make him a viable subject on *20/20,* it was his newfound position as the richest man in Hollywood. Walters figured she could further popularize the piece by focusing on his role as producer of Tom Cruise's latest movie. She could then spice it up with testimonial interviews with Cruise and perhaps other famous friends such as Cher or Warren Beatty. Geffen invited Walters and her camera crew to sit in on a dubbing session in which he and Neil Jordan reviewed scenes from *Interview with the Vampire.*

In the meantime, Geffen's personal life suddenly became a little more interesting. Geffen had first noticed Todd Mulzet, a thirty-year-old sales manager at AT&T, at the so-called Military Party on Fire Island over the Fourth of July weekend. Since breaking up with Bob Brassel, Geffen had had a couple of relationships with younger men, but none had had the makings of a long-term partnership.

Born in Bethlehem, Pennsylvania, Mulzet had attended the University of Pittsburgh on a diving scholarship and studied math theory. He dreamed of diving in the Olympics and, even though he now had a full-time job, continued to train and take part in competitions around the country. It was clear to Geffen's friends that the relationship would not last. Unlike the needy, father figure–seeking young men to whom Geffen was most often attracted, Mulzet was headstrong and independent.

Still, winning Mulzet was a challenge Geffen relished. He left three messages on Mulzet's answering machine before finally convincing him to go to dinner. For their first date, Geffen took Mulzet to a restaurant in New York where he was to meet Barry Diller, Fran Lebowitz, Sandy Gallin, and Martin Peretz. At dinner, Mulzet became involved in a good-natured argument with Diller, now CEO of the West Chester, Pennsylvania–based QVC Network, over tax differences between Philadelphia and New Jersey.

Geffen was smitten with Mulzet and began calling him every day. He took him to the Broadway play *An Inspector Calls* and to one of Calvin Klein's fashion shows, and later to dinner with the Kleins. Using the script that had worked on most of his conquests, Geffen told Mulzet that Joni Mitchell had written "Free Man in Paris" about him. Geffen was surprised that Mulzet did not have any of Mitchell's records and directed his driver, Phil Singer, to put on "Free Man in Paris." Geffen sang along.

When Mulzet told Geffen he was heading to Moultrie, Georgia, to compete in a national diving competition, Geffen announced he would be in the stands to cheer him on. Geffen's secretary, Priscila Giraldo, who had succeeded Linda Loddengaard as his right hand, went about making the arrangements to land Geffen's Gulfstream IV jet at the tiny landing strip a few miles outside of town.

"Are there any five-star hotels in Moultrie?" Giraldo asked Mulzet.

"Priscila, Moultrie doesn't even have an airport," Mulzet explained, hoping that she could help him temper Geffen's expectations.

Geffen was falling fast for Mulzet. The day before he left for Georgia, he called him and asked him to join him at the party he was orchestrating for the president's birthday.

"Hillary wants us to come to Bill Clinton's surprise forty-eighth birthday party," he said.

"What do you mean she wants *us* to come?" Mulzet asked suspiciously.

"Hillary invited both of us," Geffen explained.

"When is it?"

"It's the day after your event," he said. "We would fly up to New York and pick up Crosby, Stills, and Nash and fly down to D.C."

Mulzet finished twentieth in the diving competition, distracted by Geffen's attendance and overwhelmed by the impending trip to the White House. As they landed in New York to rendezvous with the band, Geffen and Mulzet were met by the producers of *20/20,* who wanted to get some footage of Geffen boarding his jet. Mulzet appeared in the footage, trailing Geffen and looking less like a boyfriend than a well-groomed bodyguard.

On the plane, David Crosby, Stephen Stills, and Graham Nash had their first opportunity in years to catch up and reminisce about the old days with their former manager. Despite the fact that only a few years earlier he had berated them as "old fat farts," Geffen now joked with the guys, making their feuds seem all but forgotten. The three musicians, whose power and wealth was now far eclipsed by Geffen's, were excited and proud that Geffen had snared them another prime booking.

At the White House, they were directed to the South Lawn to set up their instruments. Geffen and Mulzet were met by Hillary Clinton, who embraced Geffen and explained the schedule for the celebration. Geffen proudly introduced Mulzet to the First Lady. Hillary Clinton disappeared into the White House to get her husband.

The White House staff, a few hundred people, had assembled on the lawn but was kept in a restricted area behind a rope in front of the stage. As Crosby, Stills & Nash broke into "Happy Birthday to You," the Clintons emerged from the White House. The president was truly surprised to realize his favorite band was leading the tune. As he approached the stage, Clinton then saw Geffen, also a surprise guest. When he motioned to Geffen to join him, Geffen grabbed Mulzet's hand and pulled him along. On the stage stood the president and First Lady, the vice president and his wife, David Geffen, and Todd Mulzet.

"I have to talk to you after this," Clinton whispered to Geffen as Crosby, Stills & Nash finished singing. "Don't leave here."

When the ceremony was over and Clinton and his wife finished greeting staff members, Clinton drew Geffen aside and asked him to come with him to the Oval Office. When Geffen motioned for Mulzet to join them, Clinton looked confused.

"Is that a fuckin' reporter?" Clinton snapped.

"No, that's Todd," Geffen said. "He's with me. Bill, I'd like you to meet Todd Mulzet."

"Oh, I'm sorry," Clinton said to Mulzet. "I thought you were a fuckin' reporter."

In the Oval Office, Clinton gestured for Geffen and Mulzet to make themselves comfortable. Making time for one of his top donors, Clinton relaxed with Geffen and told him he wanted some advice. He was angry at the news coverage his policies had gotten and frustrated at his failure to spin the media. Any time there was good news, he charged, it was relegated to the back page.

In the Oval Office, Todd Mulzet looks on as Geffen

gives President Clinton tips on how to spin the press.

(Courtesy Graham Nash)

Geffen launched into a forty-five-minute lecture on how to spin the press. This was Geffen's forte, and he had much advice to offer Clinton. The president listened intently and even nodded politely as Todd Mulzet chimed in with a comment about the politics of right-wing commentator Rush Limbaugh. Geffen advised Clinton that he should spend more time securing the support of some of the more liberal members of the Democratic Party.

A secretary stepped into the Oval Office every ten minutes to give a hand signal to the president that seemed to allow him an excuse if he wanted to end the meeting. After a few of these interruptions, Clinton turned to the aide and raised his hand. "Look, I don't want to be disturbed," he said. "I'll let you know."

Crosby, Nash, and Stills, meanwhile, had been waiting for their cue to enter the Oval Office for a photo opportunity. Geffen was just finishing up his press-spinning lesson when the singers were ushered in. Graham Nash snapped a picture of Geffen in action, with the president and Todd Mulzet listening to him.

Moments after Geffen and Mulzet said good-bye to the president, they got into a waiting car that was to take them to the airport. Geffen turned to Mulzet and grinned.

"How was I?" he asked.

"What do you mean?" Mulzet replied, a bit puzzled. "You were great."

"I did that for *you*," Geffen explained. "Imagine," he continued, after a pause. "*Me* . . . giving the president advice!"

"It's a little scary actually," Mulzet deadpanned. "As a citizen of the United States, it's not something I wanted to see."

Four days later, on Tuesday, August 23, Walt Disney chairman Michael Eisner stunned Jeffrey Katzenberg by calling him into his office and handing him a copy of a news release announcing Katzenberg's resignation. Their seventeen-year partnership, at Paramount

Pictures and through the revival they had overseen at Disney, had come to an end.

In July, Eisner had undergone a quadruple-bypass operation, which again prompted Katzenberg to pressure Eisner to name him president. But Eisner had again rebuffed Katzenberg's ploys for a promotion.

Word of Katzenberg's dismissal spread quickly. Hours after Eisner handed him his walking papers, Katzenberg received a telephone call from Steven Spielberg, a longtime friend, who was vacationing with his family in Jamaica at the home of *Back to the Future* director Robert Zemeckis.

"Why don't you guys do something together?" Zemeckis shouted in the background as Spielberg predicted future career successes for Katzenberg.

As he listened to Spielberg, Katzenberg was struck by the idea that a partnership with him would turn Hollywood upside down. In 1988, the two had teamed up to produce Disney's *Who Framed Roger Rabbit?* And just last year, they had gone into partnership and opened a family restaurant in Los Angeles. Fashioned after a submarine, it was called Dive!

"Jeff, let me quote you from *Back to the Future*," Spielberg said. "I'll quote Christopher Lloyd's last line in the movie, 'Where you're going you don't need roads.' "

"What do you mean *you*? I'm talking *we*," Katzenberg said. Spielberg did not think Katzenberg's pitch was altogether serious and did not respond to it.

Katzenberg's friends came to his defense, and none was more vocal than David Geffen. "Michael built Hollywood Records and Euro Disney," Geffen said, naming Disney's two big failures. "Jeffrey's responsible for everything else."

To the press, he was even more pointed: "Michael is a liar," he told *Los Angeles* magazine. "And anyone who has dealt with him—genuinely dealt with him—knows he is a liar." Geffen moved Eisner close to the top of his list of foes, launching an assault that lasted for the next several years.

Katzenberg's bitterness grew as corporate flunkies pressured him to vacate his office. There were no thank-yous from company directors. He had to sneak to clandestine parties for him held off the studio lot, one of which was given by five hundred Disney employees who paid for the party themselves. Elton John had to cancel a London party planned in Katzenberg's honor when Disney made it clear that Katzenberg would not be attending the U.K. premiere of *The Lion King.*

Katzenberg told Geffen he never wanted to work for anyone ever again.

"Well, good. Start a company. Do whatever you want," Geffen told him. "You can do it."

Katzenberg again called Spielberg, saying he had not been kidding when he had floated the idea of a partnership. "What do you think about starting a studio from scratch?" he asked.

"The idea of working with you in a creative way to make movies and TV is thrilling," Spielberg answered. "But I have no reason to leave MCA. That would be very hard." Sidney Sheinberg, MCA's president, had given Spielberg his first directing job when he was only twenty years old; he had served as a lifelong mentor. Spielberg knew that his departure would be a huge blow to MCA, which had reaped hundreds of millions of dollars from his films.

G effen loved the way *Interview with the Vampire* had turned out. He could not imagine that Anne Rice would not like it, too, if she would only sit down, watch it, and give it a chance. Recognizing that Rice could be the film's most powerful advocate, Geffen sensed that the moment to try to get her back on board had arrived. A test screening had been scheduled for Labor Day weekend. Geffen invited Rice, telling her that Tom Cruise and the entire cast would be on hand to register the audience's reaction. Unfortunately, Rice soon sent back word that she was unable to attend.

The weekend following their visit to the White House, Geffen and Todd Mulzet returned to Fire Island. There, they attended the Morning Party, a fund-raiser sponsored by GMHC. They left the party early and went back to Geffen's house, where Geffen made an emotional admission. "I love you," he told Mulzet, who said that he felt the same way.

Geffen invited Mulzet to come to Los Angeles for Labor Day weekend and the screening of *Interview with the Vampire*. Geffen entertained other houseguests that weekend, including Rahm Emanuel, now a senior White House aide, and his wife. While the Emanuels stayed in Malibu, Geffen and Mulzet took day trips to Las Vegas and San Francisco.

"You are the most stable person I know," Geffen said.

"*That's* frightening," Mulzet responded wryly..

"Why don't you think about moving out to Los Angeles?" Geffen asked.

Having known Geffen for only a few weeks, Mulzet was surprised at the invitation. But he enjoyed the time he was spending with him, and while he did not know precisely where the relationship was headed, he decided to take a chance and accept the offer. His seven years at AT&T entitled him to a two-year leave of absence, and so he decided to sublet his apartment and give life in Los Angeles a whirl.

The interest surrounding *Interview with the Vampire,* meanwhile, was so intense that the site of the test screening was kept a secret from even the stars and director. Only when Geffen and Mulzet met the cast and crew at the airport did they learn that they were heading for San Diego.

There was such an entourage that it took both Geffen's plane and the Warner Bros. corporate jet to accommodate all the participants. For the hour-long flight, Geffen's plane carried all the high-voltage talent, including Tom Cruise, Nicole Kidman, Brad Pitt, and Christian Slater. The other jet carried the top brass at Warner Bros., including Bob Daly and Terry Semel, as well as Bob Brassel and many others.

At the San Diego airport, the group was whisked away to the movie theater. After pulling into a parking garage, they took a back elevator into the theater. Unbeknownst to most of the audience, the group filed into the back rows as the lights dimmed. Unlike the heart-wrenching screenings of *Risky Business* and *Little Shop of Horrors,* this one was an unqualified winner.

Just before the lights came up, the stars and Warner Bros. executives headed back to Los Angeles. On the plane, Neil Jordan and his cast toasted the encouraging prospects. Geffen went to sit between Brad Pitt and his manager, Cynthia Pett.

"You know what this movie's going to do?" he said to Pitt. "It's going to take you from getting three million a picture to ten million a picture!"

Geffen was more convinced than ever that it was imperative to show the movie to Anne Rice. He decided to mail a videocassette of the film to her in New Orleans. It was a risky move; if Rice did not like the film, she was likely to broadcast her displeasure to the world in detail.

When the package arrived, Rice held the tape in her hand with trepidation. She had not heard from David Geffen in a year and a half. Although the movie had been filmed in her hometown, she had not visited the set once. Neither had she seen any clips from the film. She feared the worst.

From the very first frame, however, Rice was entranced. She was deeply moved by all the performances, including Cruise's, who she could not believe had totally embodied her Vampire Lestat. Perhaps embarrassed by the commotion she had caused earlier, she decided to take out a two-page ad in *Daily Variety* to apologize and offer a ringing endorsement of the picture. She also called Geffen, raved about Cruise and the picture, and told him about her plans for the ad.

Geffen immediately telephoned Tom Cruise. "You won't believe it," Geffen told his star. "Anne Rice just saw the movie, and she likes you, she loves it, you know. She really loves it!"

"You showed her the movie, and you didn't tell any of us?" a stunned Cruise asked.

"Yes, yes," Geffen said. "Don't worry about that now. But she loves it! She loves it!"

"You have the luck of the Irish, David Geffen," Cruise said.

Despite his earlier demurral, Steven Spielberg could not shake Jeffrey Katzenberg's proposal to form a new entertainment company, finding the possibilities alternately wondrous and frightening. But his wife, actress Kate Capshaw, was not thrilled. Spielberg and Capshaw had adopted five children, and Capshaw was concerned that the enterprise would take even more of his time away from their family. But as she witnessed how excited her husband had become, even Capshaw could not argue with it.

Spielberg began to consider Katzenberg's proposal more seriously after he learned that Sidney Sheinberg was unhappy and considering leaving MCA. Since selling MCA to Matsushita, Sheinberg and Lew Wasserman had bristled under their new owner's tight controls. Sheinberg and Wasserman now planned a bold effort to confront their Japanese owner and threaten to quit unless they were given more control and sufficient capital to fund acquisitions and expansion. The strained relations between the MCA managers and Matsushita had served to sour Spielberg on Hollywood's corporate culture and cause him to yearn for an entrepreneurial situation like what Katzenberg was pitching.

As Spielberg's enthusiasm grew, Katzenberg convinced him that they should bring in a third partner. The type of partner he had in mind was an executive who was schooled in the music business but who was also a financial wizard with outstanding creative instincts. Katzenberg's candidate was David Geffen.

The idea of Geffen joining Katzenberg and Spielberg seemed a bit odd. For one thing, Geffen was Hollywood's greatest entrepreneur and nearly all of his successes were ones in which he alone had made the decisions. His one major professional stumble had been at the Warner Bros. studio in 1976, when he had had to share decision-making responsibilities with others. "I'm not good unless my deciding to do it is the last decision that has to be made," he had told *The New York Times* in 1985. "If I have to sit and convince somebody why I'm enthusiastic about something, I'm already depressed." The idea of himself as a partner was a strange one for David Geffen.

What's more, while Geffen and Katzenberg were close friends, Geffen and Spielberg had a history of butting heads. Although both possessed outsize Hollywood egos, Spielberg, as exemplified by *Schindler's List,* was directed by a strong moral conscience; Geffen had his own ideas of what was right and what was wrong.

But Spielberg was able to see beyond Geffen's sometimes difficult personality and realize that he had much to offer the team. He was also apparently able to forgive him for the way he had treated Steve Ross near the end of his life. Katzenberg called Geffen with the invitation.

"No, I don't want to do that," Geffen responded. "What, are you crazy?"

"Well, would you at least talk to us?"

"I don't want to talk to you about *that,*" Geffen said. "I mean I'll *talk* to you."

"Why don't you just meet us at Steven's house tomorrow?" Katzenberg said. "Come over at twelve o'clock, we'll schmooze, and maybe we can just pick your brain."

"OK," Geffen responded warily, "but I'm not interested in this, Jeffrey."

Geffen knew he was not working to his capacity and was not certain he wanted to. Since the sale of Geffen Records in 1990, he was content to count his money and let others work on Hollywood's front line. Geffen now enjoyed his quiet life at the beach, reviewing daily reports of his investment portfolio and breezily contemplating the possibility of buying such baubles as the swanky Hotel Bel-Air. Although he claimed that his net worth had reached one billion dollars three years earlier, *Forbes* estimated that the fortune had just hit that mark. Now out of the junk-bond market, Geffen had become heavily invested in investment-grade bonds, where he made a killing on such companies as Time Warner, Boston Chicken, and Safeway. He claimed to have a 25 percent annualized return on his investments.

"Why do you need me?" Geffen asked Spielberg and Katzenberg shortly after arriving at Spielberg's posh home in the Los Angeles neighborhood of Pacific Palisades. "You guys cover all the bases."

After four hours of talking with Spielberg and Katzenberg—both of whom were espousing blue-sky dreams of what the three could accomplish if they combined their talents—Geffen was hooked. Spielberg and Katzenberg envisioned creating an entertainment company that reinvented the business in the trailblazing manner in which Douglas Fairbanks, D. W. Griffith, Charlie Chaplin, and Mary Pickford had founded United Artists in 1919.

At fifty-one, Geffen realized that his inner machinery demanded a bigger challenge than simply watching Geffen Records grow bigger and better. Taking Geffen Records from five hundred million in revenue to even one billion dollars would not involve the level of risk he felt he needed. The idea of being at the edge of potential failure again provided him with stimulation. Having founded two successful record labels, Geffen was charged once again to start from scratch.

Geffen now had the motivation to return to work. Money—the chance to make buckets of it—had motivated him in all his previous enterprises. But money was no longer a sound motivator. Geffen needed alternate inspiration, and Katzenberg and Spielberg succeeded in convincing him that he could be inspired simply by their shared desire to do good work.

The three made plans to meet again to discuss the idea but also made a pact to keep the talks a secret. All negotiations would be conducted in private, with no calendar notations and no secretaries involved. Spielberg did not even tell his mother.

Over the next couple of weeks, as the partners met and talked about their plans, Geffen kept pushing to keep things spontaneous. When Katzenberg characteristically came to one meeting armed with a business plan, Geffen made him throw it out. Geffen thought they could make it up as they went along and suggested they keep the enterprise free of a huge infrastructure and overhead. In this manner, he figured, the three could build a new business the way Louis Mayer, Samuel

Goldwyn, and Darryl Zanuck had built theirs, with pluck and instinct. "We're smart guys," Geffen kept saying to his partners, who, like him, were college dropouts.

The trio agreed that the company would focus on five major areas: movie production, TV production, animation, music, and multimedia. They brainstormed grand ideas to change how Hollywood operated. They wanted to devise new ways of structuring business relationships with artists and distributors. They talked about breaking new ground by letting artists participate in revenues. Katzenberg suggested ideas for new ways to structure the troubled relations between TV producers and networks.

Geffen, Katzenberg, and Spielberg all had busy schedules in September 1994, and they were never in Los Angeles at the same time. When they discovered that they had each been invited to attend a White House state dinner for Boris Yeltsin on September 28, they decided to huddle after the dinner. Geffen cannily asked Barbara Walters to be his date. A film clip of the two making their entrance at the affair was included prominently in her *20/20* profile.

The dinner marked the first time Geffen accepted President Clinton's invitation to spend the night in the Lincoln Bedroom. When the affair was over, Geffen said good night to Barbara Walters and prepared to leave the White House to join Spielberg and Katzenberg across the street at the Hay-Adams Hotel, where they were staying.

But Clinton pulled Geffen aside and asked him to hang out with him and Hillary in the residential quarters.

"I'm sure I'll talk to him for half an hour, then they'll go to bed, then I'll come over to the hotel and meet up with you guys," Geffen told Spielberg and Katzenberg.

At the Hay-Adams, Katzenberg and Spielberg ordered hamburgers from room service. They grew concerned when it became one o'clock in the morning and they had not heard from Geffen.

Geffen had ended up spending an hour and a half with the Clintons, talking in the solarium on the third floor of the residential quarters. He finally said good night and went to the Lincoln Bedroom on the second floor, just down the hall from the president's bedroom. He picked up the phone and called his future business partners.

"OK, I just finished," Geffen said hurriedly. "But it's one o'clock in the morning!"

"I don't care!" Katzenberg bellowed, concerned that this was the moment to strike the deal and worried that the three might not be in the same city together for some time. "Get over here now!"

Ten minutes later, Geffen called back. "I can't get over there," he said.

"What do you mean you can't get over here?" Katzenberg asked.

"There's no one around."

"David, you pick up the phone, you dial operator, and you say 'I gotta go over to the Hay-Adams. I need a ride.' "

Two minutes later, Geffen called again. "There's no car around," he said.

"Call a taxi! Or walk!" Katzenberg screamed. *"Get over here!"*

"All right, all right," Geffen said, hanging up the phone. He then called back the White House operator, who had, it turned out, arranged to get a car for Geffen but apparently failed to call him back to let him know. However, a Secret Service agent patrolling the hallway suggested that leaving the White House at that hour was not recommended.

Geffen called Katzenberg once again. "They won't let me out," he said.

"What do you mean, they won't let you out," Katzenberg asked.

"When the president goes to sleep, they lock up the wing, you can't get in or out."

"You're kidding me."

"No, they said to me, 'You can't leave, Mr. Geffen.' "

"So are you telling me you're a hostage?" Katzenberg asked.

"Yes, I'm telling you I'm a hostage."

"Well, then, we're doing this thing first thing in the morning!"

Geffen went to bed but awoke early and made his way to Spielberg's suite at the Hay-Adams by six-thirty. As Geffen walked in the room, the three men looked at one another and decided that the moment had arrived to commit. Spielberg told the two others that he was ready to sign on to the new venture, subject only to securing the endorsement of his mentors, Sid Sheinberg and Lew Wasserman. Sheinberg and Wasserman, Geffen and Katzenberg figured, would not likely stand in the way of their dream.

THE ANNOUNCEMENT

|||

S id Sheinberg was not certain what Steven Spielberg stood to gain from the new enterprise with Geffen and Katzenberg. "Why do you need this?" a skeptical Sheinberg asked. "How does this benefit you?"

Spielberg explained that he was ready to be the father, or at least a co-father, of his own business. "It benefits me because the idea of building something from the ground up, where I could actually be a co-owner, where I don't rent, I don't lease, I don't option but actually own—that appeals to me."

Convinced of Spielberg's worthy motivations, Sheinberg then offered his blessing. Spielberg told him that his new company would need to have a distribution contract with a major studio and said they would make the lucrative deal with MCA if Sheinberg was at the helm. Whichever studio landed the deal would handle distribution of the team's movies, home videos, records, and TV shows.

Spielberg, Geffen, and Katzenberg spent the next two weeks hammering out the details of their new company. They agreed that, at least initially, they would finance the venture and split the equity evenly. Though the initial capitalization would be relatively small, they expected to eventually take on some outside investors. The capitalization would also be increased by borrowings as well as "output deals," where others would provide up-front funding in anticipation of future rights.

Geffen was far and away the richest of the three Hollywood heavyweights. Spielberg was worth an estimated six hundred million. Katzenberg's fortune, on the other hand, was a fraction of that, and he was concerned about finding the money to cover his stake. To further complicate matters, Katzenberg had become embroiled in a dispute with Disney over the size of his departure settlement. Michael Eisner disputed Katzenberg's claims that he was owed a huge sum, compensating him for the future earnings of projects that he had put into production during his ten-year tenure.

The trio agreed that any one of them would be able to commit the company to a creative project even if the other two were not enthusiastic about it. Indicating that he did not want to commit himself 100 percent to the new enterprise, Spielberg insisted on retaining the right to make films for other studios.

With the company ready to go, the three partners next sought the blessing of eighty-one-year-old MCA chairman Lew Wasserman, the sole remaining founder and builder of a major studio. More than anyone, Wasserman was the link to the Hollywood of the past, the Hollywood that the three men were trying to revive. Wasserman, the industry's elder statesman, agreed to meet with the three at his home in Beverly Hills on the morning of Monday, October 10.

At the meeting, Wasserman spun stories about the history of Hollywood and showed them artifacts such as a color rendering of Mickey Mouse drawn by Walt Disney. Wasserman listened as the three men described their plan to create a studio designed from the perspective of filmmakers. He told them he believed in their plans and that MCA would provide support in any way needed.

After they left Wasserman, they traveled a few short blocks to Katzenberg's house to sign agreements spelling out their commitments

Steven Spielberg, Jeffrey Katzenberg, and Geffen field questions at the press conference to announce their new movie studio.

(Jean-Marc Giboux/Liaison Agency)

to one another and to the new enterprise. The moguls arranged to announce their as-yet-unnamed new venture at a press conference at the Peninsula Hotel in Beverly Hills two days later, on Wednesday, October 12, 1994. Katzenberg was obsessed about keeping the news secret until the press conference and fantasized about the manner in which it would be unveiled. "I have an announcement to make," he planned to say, standing alone at a microphone. "But I need to introduce you to two other people who play a major role in my plans." At that point, Geffen and Spielberg would come out from behind a curtain and join Katzenberg to deliver the big news.

The night before the press conference, the three partners, as well as Michael Ovitz and Bruce Ramer, Steven Spielberg's agent and lawyer respectively, met again at Katzenberg's house to make the final arrangements. They pored over a two-page press release, careful to make certain that it succinctly captured the essence of their new venture. As the partners debated minor changes in the release, Harry Clein, a Hollywood P.R. veteran the group had hired to represent them, phoned in the revisions to a writer back at his office.

As the trio rehearsed their remarks for the press conference, they became disheartened when they discovered that the news had leaked and would appear in some of the morning papers. Having alerted the press at 5:30 P.M. about the 8:30 A.M. conference, they had, in fact, invited reporters to start digging. Spielberg began to fret that the turnout at the press conference would be thin since the secret would be out.

The next morning, the front-page scoop in the *Los Angeles Times* destroyed Katzenberg's plan to emerge solo at the press conference and surprise the crowd by introducing Geffen and Spielberg. But the story, which Katzenberg and Geffen became convinced Michael Ovitz had leaked, only helped establish the announcement's importance.

Within minutes of the paper hitting the streets, the calls started coming in to the partners. Michael Eisner telephoned to congratulate them. Katzenberg was still hurt by Eisner's treatment of him but felt that his warm regards were genuine. Tom Hanks called Steven Spielberg and offered a moniker for the new company. "I think you should call it

'Dive! The Studio,' " he said, referring to Spielberg and Katzenberg's restaurant.

Some of the early-morning calls also brought hefty offers to invest in the new enterprise. Although they believed that their combined star power would afford them a warm welcome on Wall Street, the three were surprised to field investment offers that valued the company at two billion dollars.

By 8:00 A.M., the circular driveway in front of the Peninsula Hotel was jammed with satellite trucks from nearly every news-media organization in the nation. Spielberg and Katzenberg and their wives met Geffen in a small room just off the main ballroom to await their cue. Before the announcement, Geffen, sick to his stomach with anxiety, sipped ginger ale. "I haven't had this much adrenaline in twenty years," he told Spielberg.

The Verandah ballroom had filled to capacity, mostly with reporters and banks of TV cameras, the likes of which were normally reserved for presidential press conferences. The room was also packed by an uncharacteristically large collection of industry powerbrokers seeking to watch Hollywood history in the making.

As they made their entrance, Spielberg, Katzenberg, and Geffen were blinded by the glare of television lights and camera flashes. They took seats at a long table at the front of the room, with Katzenberg in the middle, flanked by Spielberg on his right and Geffen on his left. All three wore khaki pants. Katzenberg added a deep-blue dress shirt, a red tie with big yellow dots, and a blazer. Spielberg, his beard and mustache trimmed neatly, had donned a navy flannel shirt. Geffen appeared in a casual light-blue shirt and a cream-colored vest that remained unbuttoned.

His plan for a surprise opening bamboozled, Katzenberg instead opened the press conference with a joke. "There's a pretty giant misunderstanding here, it's a little embarrassing," he started. "The reason that we wanted to have this press conference this morning is to announce that the next Dive! restaurant opening will be in Las Vegas on April 15."

The news conference established that Katzenberg, freshly unem-

ployed, was to be the new company's top operations man. He began by
thanking Geffen and Spielberg for joining him in the new enterprise
and rattled off the five main entertainment areas in which the company
would operate, telling the crowd that they did not yet have a name for
the studio.

"I look at the three of us, and I figure this has gotta be the Dream
Team," Katzenberg said. "Certainly it's my Dream Team."

Spielberg then read a brief prepared statement. "Hollywood movie
studios were at their zenith when they were driven by point of view and
personalities," he said. "Together with Jeffrey and David, I want to create a place driven by ideas and the people who have them." Spielberg
said their plan was to create an unthreatening home for filmmakers to
explore and share "substantially" in every success.

Geffen then made an even briefer opening comment, noting that he
had more enthusiasm for this venture than he had ever felt in his life.
"I've always been on my own, and this is a great opportunity for me to
work with partners and start something new and get excited about
working once again," he said.

The new studio's founding partners were then assaulted by reporters' shouted questions. When one journalist asked how they would
split up managerial duties, Katzenberg replied that all three would be
involved in every aspect.

"I'm going to direct *Jurassic Park Two*," Geffen quipped. The laughter
from the joke died down, and he turned serious. "The truth of the matter is that hard as it is for people to believe, it's not motivated by any desire to make more since we all have far too much already," he said. "It's
to do good work. We really want to do good work and hope to do better work in the future."

The publicity on the evening news and in the papers the next day
was extraordinary, with many reports asserting that the three men were
the most powerful executives to combine forces behind a new entertainment company since the founding of United Artists. With no name
for their enterprise, the press picked up on Katzenberg's reference and
began calling the enterprise the Dream Team.

The rumor mill was churning with a report that Geffen had secretly married Keanu Reeves, the hunky star of *Speed*. The *Daily Mirror* in London reported that the two were "painting the town red at parties and going on wild shopping sprees." The story said they were seen at Barneys New York in Beverly Hills, "giggling like schoolboys as they tried on mounds of $500 shirts."

But the rumors were unfounded; neither had even met the other. The report, however, took on a life of its own; before long, American newspapers were printing the story. Geffen even ran into a man whose trainer swore he had attended the wedding.

The rumor probably was started because Todd Mulzet looked a little bit like Reeves, although the diver was shorter and stockier than the actor. A week after the press conference unveiling the new studio, Mulzet moved to Los Angeles and into Geffen's Malibu beach house. When he walked into the house, Geffen tossed him the keys to a BMW.

"Here's a car for you to use," he said.

Busy with the launch of his new company, Geffen rose sometimes as early as 4:00 A.M., beginning phone calls to the East Coast. At 7:00 A.M., he was so eager for company that he went back into the bedroom and flipped a switch that propelled the blinds open automatically, causing a torrent of sunlight to flood the room and reveal a view of the Pacific Ocean.

"So, what, are you going to work while you're out here or what?" Geffen asked Mulzet after a week.

Mulzet was a bit surprised. "I've been here a week. Yeah, I was thinking about working," he said. "But I also have never not worked since I was eleven, it might be nice to take a week or two off. I have no bills. You're feeding me. I have a place to stay."

"Why don't you go in and talk to Eddie Rosenblatt?" Geffen offered.

"David, I don't know if I want to work at your record company," Mulzet said. "That's a little, like, close to home."

"No, no, no," Geffen insisted. "Just go in and talk to him. Just talk to

Geffen is flanked by Tom Cruise and Neil Jordan at the premiere of Interview with the Vampire. *Also on hand (from left): Bob Daly, Terry Semel, Stan Winston, Christian Slater, Kirsten Dunst, Antonio Banderas, Brad Pitt, and Stephen Woolley.*

(Alan Berliner/Liaison Agency)

him. Bob Brassel can take you into Warner Brothers. Let him take you around."

"All right," Mulzet said. "When?"

Geffen was already on the phone calling Rosenblatt. "Eddie, I'm going to send somebody in to see you tomorrow about a job," he said and hung up. "You're going in tomorrow." Less than a week later, Mulzet started work at Geffen Records. He was given a job as an assistant in the international department, reporting to Mel Posner.

The November lineup of releases at Geffen Records seemed to have the makings of its best month ever. It appeared that Geffen even had a shot at replicating the smashing achievement of March 1974, when Elektra/Asylum Records had the top three albums on the *Billboard* chart. On deck were much-anticipated records by the Eagles, Aerosmith, and Nirvana—the last album the band made before Kurt Cobain's death.

The Nirvana album, *MTV Unplugged in New York,* debuted at number one on the chart. The Aerosmith record, *Big Ones,* was released the same day, landing at the lofty position of number six.

With the record company in top form, Geffen prepared for what became the best single month in the history of his movie company as well. Anne Rice attended the premiere of *Interview with the Vampire* in Los Angeles on November 9, satisfying her fans by signing plastic rats. More than two thousand screaming admirers were on hand to catch a glimpse of Tom Cruise and Brad Pitt.

The premiere was attended by Hollywood's A list, who filled both the Bruin and Village theaters in Westwood. On the red carpet, Geffen stopped to gamely offer interviews to the throngs of TV journalists. "It's the *Lawrence of Arabia* of vampire movies," Geffen told one reporter.

Warner Bros. arranged to block off two streets for the event and contracted to have the postpremiere party on the roof of a nearby parking structure. There was a seventy-five-thousand-square-foot burgundy tent outfitted in late-eighteenth-century New Orleans style. A twenty-one-piece orchestra in period costume entertained the attendees.

The movie opened on Friday, November 11; before the end of the afternoon, box-office reports from the matinees on the East Coast confirmed that Warner Bros. had a major hit on its hands. That night, ABC ran its profile of Geffen on *20/20,* calling it "The Geffen Touch." Barbara Walters crafted an enormously positive portrait of her friend, offering a healthy pitch for his new movie. She steered clear of any sensitive topics such as his ice-cold relationship with his brother. And although she credited him with having discovered the Eagles, she did not mention the ugly legal battle he had recently concluded with Don Henley.

When Walters asked Geffen about how John Lennon's death had affected him, Geffen showed a side of himself he rarely let the public see. He acknowledged that there was some force bigger than himself in the world. Whether or not he actually had a moral compass, he showed that at the very least he had an idea that it was critical to have one.

"I realized that the future is just an illusion," Geffen said. "You talk about your plans, but the fact of the matter is that you can only live right now, this very minute. I always think there's your plan, and there's God's plan, and your plan doesn't matter."

"I'm not perfect, and I make lots of mistakes," Geffen admitted. "And I hope I learn from them. And I hope I don't make the same mistake twice. But I'm very, very optimistic about what people can do who have the courage to try, and the willingness to fail. Because without failure, there is no success."

On Sunday, as the news came in that *Interview with the Vampire* had charted a whopping opening-weekend gross of $36.3 million, qualifying it as the biggest non-summer opening in history, Geffen celebrated with Todd Mulzet and Bob Brassel. The picture went on to gross $105 million in the United States, the first film from Geffen's company to cross the magic $100 million mark. As with all his movie profits since Geffen sold his record company in 1990, the money went into his charitable foundation.

But the film was not the critical triumph Geffen had desired. While *The New York Times* and *USA Today* were mostly positive, many other critics, including *Chicago Sun-Times* reviewer Roger Ebert, said it was boring and uninvolving.

Nevertheless, the success story of Geffen's entertainment empire seemingly had no end. The next day, Geffen Records released *Hell Freezes Over,* the Eagles' first new album in fourteen years, and it, too, debuted in the number-one position, knocking the new Nirvana record to number two. The Eagles' tour, which had started in May and was scheduled to last seven months, lasted more than two years and outgrossed all other competing concert acts, taking in more than seventy-five million dollars. The album sold more than seven million copies and stayed on *Billboard*'s chart for more than two years.

At the end of the week, Geffen took out ads in the entertainment-industry trade papers to crow about his number-one movie and number-one record. "It's been a hell of a week," the copy read, in a tongue-in-cheek reference to the demonic themes of the projects.

Jeffrey Katzenberg called Bob Iger, the president of Capital Cities/ABC, and floated a proposal in which the Dream Team would partner with ABC to create a new joint-venture TV studio. It was a novel concept: The Dream Team and ABC would make TV shows not just for ABC but also for its rivals. In an unprecedented arrangement, the plan also included a provision for the Dream Team to share in advertising revenues generated by its shows. The joint-venture studio seemed to usher in a new era in which the major TV networks challenged Hollywood studios as the primary sources of TV programming. The Dream Team–Cap Cities alliance seemed to fulfill the nascent studio's promise to do things differently.

Geffen had long professed ignorance about the TV business, but he went along with Spielberg and Katzenberg to make the deal at Cap Cities' headquarters on Manhattan's Upper West Side. As Spielberg and Katzenberg finalized the terms with Bob Iger, Geffen bonded with

Tom Murphy, Cap Cities' sixty-nine-year-old chairman and chief executive, clearing the way for the deal's approval from the very top. Once again, news of the deal landed the Dream Team on the front pages of newspapers everywhere.

There was more of the same hoopla when the team struck a partnership to develop interactive and multimedia products with Microsoft, unveiling the news at another press conference in which the three partners sat on a stage next to Bill Gates. Finally, the team announced a name for its venture, DreamWorks SKG, with an initial for each of the founding partners. Its blue-and-white logo featured a child holding a fishing line and perched on a crescent moon.

DreamWorks' blueprint for business was the brainchild of David Geffen, and it was to make him the most important person on the team. In his previous businesses, Geffen had proven to be a risk-averse executive, masterful at limiting overhead. But with such capital-intensive plans as building an animation company from the ground up, Geffen realized that staggering overhead would be unavoidable for Dream-Works. Thus, he brilliantly employed another tactic that had worked so well for him in the past: Use other people's money.

Geffen masterminded a deal in which the partners agreed to sell a one-third equity interest to outside investors for nine hundred million dollars. Eyebrows were raised on Wall Street when it was learned the partners were contributing a total of just one hundred million in exchange for a two-thirds equity interest. (Geffen's $33.3 million investment did not make a dent in his bank account.) If the company bled red ink, at least it would not be theirs.

Geffen romanced Paul Allen, the billionaire co-founder of Microsoft, and made a deal in which Allen invested five hundred million dollars, becoming DreamWorks' majority outside investor. Allen, whom Geffen quickly grew to like, gave Geffen three brightly colored shirts that he then seemed to wear nonstop. Geffen also was key in the discussions as DreamWorks arranged for one billion dollars in bank debt from Chemical Bank. When advances from a domestic pay-TV deal with Home Box Office and other worldwide output deals for home video and other services were set, the start-up had capital totaling about five billion dollars. The huge capitalization gave the team enough money to protect the company under the assumption, made by Geffen, that every single movie, record, TV show, and interactive game created in the first five years would fail.

As Geffen was immersed in DreamWorks' financing deals, Todd Mulzet, meanwhile, felt that Geffen was beginning to push him away. After vacationing on the private Caribbean island of Barbuda over the Thanksgiving holiday with Geffen, Barry Diller, Sandy Gallin, Calvin Klein, and a few others, Mulzet began to feel the chill. Geffen had designated a room in the as-yet-uncompleted Jack Warner mansion as Mulzet's, but, having succeeded in his pursuit of the young diver, he was losing interest. The relationship lacked passion, and the two began functioning not as lovers but as friendly roommates. The realities of a relationship had become far less interesting to Geffen than the chase. He soon suggested that Mulzet leave the Malibu house and move into the vacant guest house on the Warner estate.

Geffen had a convenient excuse for his lack of interest. For the first time in a number of years, he was now preoccupied with work. "You can't possibly be happy," he told Mulzet. "I'm not even *here.*" Within a couple of months, Mulzet returned the BMW and moved out of the guest house and into his own apartment.

G effen and his two famous partners were on the cover of *Time* magazine in the last week in March 1995, when Geffen Records hosted a going-away party for Geffen. Eddie Rosenblatt, whom Geffen had chosen to succeed him as chairman, rented out Chasen's, site of the company's annual Christmas parties. Invitations were sent to a handful of Geffen alumni, including the three A&R czars, all of whom had left in the previous year or two: John Kalodner was now in a senior A&R post at Sony Music; Tom Zutaut headed his own label, Enclave Records; and Gary Gersh had been named president of Capitol Records. Not invited to the affair were the two people who, besides

Eddie Rosenblatt, had been Geffen's closest confidants during the company's rise: Linda Loddengaard and Eric Eisner.

Geffen showed up in a white T-shirt, blue jeans, and a sport jacket. He mingled with the staff, which now totaled about 150 employees. When the dinner was over, a dozen or so Geffen executives took turns at the microphone to honor the label's founder.

Early in the lineup of speakers was Mel Posner. "David, you've inspired me to be better, and I hope I never disappoint you," Posner said diplomatically. "I wish you only continued success and the best of fortunes in the future."

Business-affairs chief David Berman, who as head of Capitol Records had been by sued by Geffen before he joined Geffen Records four years earlier, joked that he was uneasy about Geffen's departure. "I met David in 1970 and, if memory serves me right, the first time I met David he yelled at me," Berman started. "Then as a lawyer, at Warner Brothers, and at Capitol, I frequently dealt with David, and very frequently he yelled at me. Then in 1991 I had the pleasure of starting to work for David. And in the last four years, David's never yelled at me. I'm sorry to see him go, but I'm afraid he's going to start yelling at me again."

Jim Walker, the label's staid CFO, said he was experiencing emotions he had not expected. "I really love you," he said. Tom Zutaut thanked Geffen for being a good friend when his marriage collapsed. Bryn Bridenthal praised Geffen's media savvy and rattled off her six favorite Geffen quotes (including "I don't give a shit that some people don't like the idea").

John Kalodner expressed his gratitude, too: "Whether I'm making records for Sony or doing bikini waxing and gardening in Arizona, I'll always work for you in my heart," he said. "And you'll always be number one on my chart."

Eddie Rosenblatt was the last to speak. While he allowed that Geffen's "incessant questioning and prodding . . . has often driven us mere mortals slightly crazy," Rosenblatt said, "he's always brought us to a place we never saw or knew existed." This was his moment to gush:

"I've learned that he is truly an artist, a visionary who creates magic and who sees his dream as an ever-evolving path."

Rosenblatt then lifted his glass. "On behalf of all of us, David, at *your* record company, we wish you continued success and happiness. Now come up here. We'll give you a gold watch."

Geffen rose and walked to the front of the room as the crowd cheered. Rosenblatt presented him with a "yearbook" containing photographs of everyone on the staff and short personal notes from them. He then motioned for a staffer to bring a large gift-wrapped box to the podium.

"It's a *big* watch!" Geffen quipped, prompting laughter. Knowing Geffen's appreciation for art, the staff had purchased a small sculpture for him. After Geffen opened his gifts, Rosenblatt returned to his seat and Geffen began his farewell address.

"Normally I'm a nervous wreck getting up in front of people," he started. "But it's very easy for me to get up here and thank everybody for the incredible contribution everyone has made to my life."

He told the oft-repeated story of how Eddie Rosenblatt had called him in 1980, asking to be his partner. He was painfully gracious to Rosenblatt, who he acknowledged had done an admirable job working for a difficult boss. "Were the truth on the label, it would have been 'Geffen and Rosenblatt,' " Geffen said. "There have been good days and there have been bad days . . . and there were days when Eddie and I would sit around and say 'I'm going to kill Gary Gersh!' " The crowd broke into laughter.

> It makes me incredibly sad every day thinking that in two weeks [Geffen Records] will be there but I won't be there. That never occurred to me actually. The fact that it's coming up, there's a big part of me that could just break down and start crying about it. But there's another part of me that is full of joy about being at the edge of potential failure again.
>
> And starting from scratch again and doing it for all the right reasons, which are that it's fun to do this. That's what makes it

worthwhile. Because I can tell you that the money certainly doesn't make it worthwhile. Certainly I will never have played with, looked at, touched, or felt ninety-nine percent of it. It's just numbers on a financial statement. They don't mean shit. You die, you leave it to other people.

Eddie and I, even though we've fought with each other, and we have had *many* disagreements in these fifteen years as any two people do, we've never distrusted each other. Never. And that's a big accomplishment I think. It *is* in my life anyway and in my life experience.

People ask me, "Will your new record company be better than Geffen Records?" and I always say this: "I can't imagine how anything could be better than Geffen Records." And I can't imagine that anything else in the future will be better than this. It'll be different. And it'll be a challenge. I can only tell you that [Dream-Works Records] won't have Eddie and that will make it a lot harder. Because having Eddie has been a great thing. And I envy you all that you still have Eddie. But I can call.

It was a kind thing to say. But the future would show that Rosenblatt did not have the magic touch needed to keep the fire burning at Geffen Records.

CHAPTER 36

LUNCH WITH
MICHAEL OVITZ

|||

The midterm elections in November 1994 had been a staggering defeat for the Democrats. Surveying the carnage brought on by the angry electorate, some political strategists felt that President Clinton might be challenged for the nomination in 1996 or even forced to step aside and let someone else run.

Clinton was facing a new majority in the House and a hostile new speaker in Georgia representative Newt Gingrich. There was also a new majority in the Senate, where Republicans were hoping that their new power might give them a platform to mount additional investigations of the president on such controversial matters as his Whitewater real-estate investments and his family's personal finances.

David Geffen remained an unabashed fan—and the top Democratic fund-raisers knew it. The Democratic National Committee rushed to him and requested his assistance in helping to rebuild the party's coffers. This was not a time to give up the fight.

Taking up the cause, Geffen called Barbra Streisand, Whoopi Goldberg, Rob Reiner, and many other celebrities and asked them to pony up checks of fifty thousand dollars each; he succeeded in raising two million dollars. Geffen also chaired an event, hosted at Steven Spielberg's estate, at which Hollywood contributors partied with the president and his wife as Robin Williams and k. d. lang provided entertainment. Geffen himself wrote out another check to the DNC for one hundred thousand dollars. Some contributors had donated more, but no one had personally gotten on the telephone and raised as much money for the president as David Geffen.

He continued to do the same job with AIDS-related fund-raising, although on that front he not only raised huge sums but also became the cause's single largest private donor in the nation. In the summer of 1995, he gave $2.5 million to GMHC and $1.5 million to God's Love We Deliver, a nonprofit group that delivered meals to homebound people with AIDS. Each gift easily broke Geffen's own one-million-dollar record.

G effen, Spielberg, and Katzenberg wanted to make a distribution pact with MCA, but there was a big catch: They wanted Lew Wasserman and Sid Sheinberg to be happy. The two had failed to buy MCA back from Matsushita, which instead opted to sell 80 percent of MCA to Seagram, the Canadian spirits maker. Edgar Bronfman, Jr., the thirty-nine-year-old head of the company, had long been fascinated with Hollywood and wanted to own a studio. After purchasing MCA, Bronfman changed its name, opting to call it Universal Studios, the longtime moniker of its movie and theme-park units.

When Geffen and his partners saw how well Bronfman treated Wasserman and Sheinberg, they were ready to cut a deal with Universal. Of the three, Geffen had the closest relationship with Bronfman, having been introduced to him in the early 1970s by Barry Diller.

Despite the Dream Team's approval of Bronfman, Wall Street gave Seagram's plan to purchase Universal for $5.7 billion a far chillier reception. To finance the transaction, the liquor giant sold its 24.2 percent stake in Du Pont, which had provided for more than 70 percent of Seagram earnings, back to the chemical giant for $8.8 billion. Seagram

At an industry function, Carrie Fisher runs interference
between her friend David and his perennial nemesis
Michael Ovitz. (Peter Borsari)

stock lost as much as 10 percent of its value in the two days following the news that the Du Pont–Universal transaction was in the works.

Desperate to give Wall Street some good news, Bronfman attempted to finalize a distribution accord with the Dream Team quickly. Jeffrey Katzenberg, who had taken the lead in establishing many of the new company's business deals, submitted a proposal to Bronfman and Sid Sheinberg, who had agreed to stay on until new management was hired. Bronfman blanched as he looked over the deal and saw the impossibly tough terms that Katzenberg proposed.

The three DreamWorks partners met with Bronfman and Sheinberg one Sunday morning at Katzenberg's house in Beverly Hills to discuss the proposal. Bronfman opened the meeting by telling the Dream Team that the deal, as proposed by Katzenberg, was unacceptable.

Geffen railed at Bronfman for balking. "I have one job in the world now and that's to make him happy!" he ranted, pointing at Spielberg. "And you're putting me in a position where I cannot make him happy!" Geffen, slipping into a familiar role, had begun acting as Spielberg's de facto agent.

"David, stop screaming," Sid Sheinberg said calmly.

"I'm not screaming!" Geffen yelled.

"You're screaming, David," Sheinberg said.

Finally, Steven Spielberg piped up. "David, you know what would make me happy?" he asked.

"What?" Geffen asked angrily.

"Stop screaming," Spielberg said.

"David, do you *know* what the deal is?" Bronfman asked.

"Yes."

"How can you say the deal is fair if you know what the deal is?" Bronfman asked.

"Well, what's the deal?" Geffen asked, revealing that he had *not* read the agreement.

Bronfman explained how the deal was a clear money loser for Seagram. The profit margins were so thin that the liquor giant would not make a significant profit even if all of DreamWorks' movies were block-busters.

"That's not fair," Geffen said calmly, turning to Katzenberg and then to Bronfman. "We're not going to get anywhere here today," he said. "Let's just table this for now."

"I'm taking this over," Geffen told Bronfman, walking him to the front door. "I will make this deal with you. But we're going to wait until you get your management team in place."

Geffen thought Edgar Bronfman's first choice of an executive to head Universal stunk: Michael Ovitz, who was a friend of Bronfman and had been key in the transaction bringing MCA to Seagram. Even though he distrusted Ovitz, Geffen liked Bronfman and remained interested in making a distribution deal with him.

As the talks between Bronfman and Ovitz got under way, Geffen, obsessed with the situation, kept in constant communication with Bronfman. As the talks dragged on, Bronfman became impatient and uncomfortable with the terms and conditions Ovitz was seeking. Bronfman soon told Geffen that it appeared unlikely that he and Ovitz would come to terms.

"Edgar, this is ridiculous," Geffen said. "Of course he's going to make the deal."

"David, just trust me," Bronfman said. "This is not a done deal. I don't think it's going to happen."

"Nonsense," Geffen said. "He will never walk away from this deal. The moment you walk away, he'll come crawling back."

At the end of the first week of June 1995, negotiations between lawyers for both sides ended after a night of discussions that continued until nearly 2:00 A.M. The next morning, Bronfman and Ovitz walked away from the negotiating table.

While Bronfman was somewhat relieved that it did not work out, he still needed to find some good news to pump the stock up. He tracked down Geffen, who was at the Mayo Clinic in Rochester, Minnesota, along with his friend Ray Stark, where they were getting their annual physical examinations. Bronfman told him the Ovitz deal had died.

"You're kidding me, right?" Geffen said, shocked. "It'll get put back together."

"David, I promise you it will not get put back together," Bronfman explained. "But I want to make a distribution deal with you guys. Can we sit down and talk about this?"

Geffen agreed and made an appointment to meet with Bronfman a few days later. The day of the meeting, Bronfman drove to Malibu. During the forty-five-minute drive from Universal City, Bronfman fretted that he did not have a negotiating strategy, though he was en route to meet face-to-face with Hollywood's shrewdest dealmaker.

He decided his strategy would be simple: He would play to Geffen's sense of equity. "David, you are a fair person," Bronfman started. "I don't want this to be a protracted, difficult, unfriendly negotiation. Let me tell you exactly what's going to happen. You're going to tell me what the deal is, and I'm going to say yes."

"That's not fair!" Geffen said.

"It's the only way this will work," Bronfman replied.

Geffen and Bronfman soon worked out the major terms of a distribution deal in which Universal would collect a small fee for distributing DreamWorks' movies internationally as well as its records and TV shows worldwide. The deal gave Universal zero risk but only a small amount of upside. By four o'clock in the afternoon, Bronfman and Geffen shook hands on a wide-ranging ten-year distribution alliance.

The next day, with no definitive agreement signed, Geffen and Bronfman prepared to announce the deal. Reporters from a handful of newspapers were invited up to the fifteenth floor of Universal's Black Tower for short interviews with the two executives.

"Watch what happens to your stock," Geffen told Bronfman as they prepared to begin the interviews. Seagram stock, which had fallen below 30 in the wake of the failed Ovitz talks, jumped to 31 and within a few days headed up to 34.

The next day, Michael Ovitz telephoned Bronfman and criticized the deal, arguing that Bronfman had agreed to improvident terms and blasting him for giving up Universal's interest in Amblimation, the animation company that Spielberg had created but that Universal owned.

"You made a huge mistake by giving them Amblimation," Ovitz told Bronfman. "You didn't need to give that up."

Bronfman told Ovitz he disagreed; Amblimation had only one project in development—a cartoon version of *Cats,* as it happened—and had been troubled for years anyway. Bronfman was happy to give up the company and the overhead expense that went with it.

Bronfman telephoned Geffen and told him that Ovitz had called and pissed all over the deal. "You should know that Michael called and said this," Bronfman told Geffen.

"I can't believe it," Geffen replied. "Michael just called me and told me that he had called you and *congratulated* you on a great deal."

G effen's final major job in setting up the new studio was to launch its record company. When he learned that George Michael, the sinewy rock star and former member of the duo Wham!, was eager to leave Sony's record unit, he approached the singer with an offer to be the first artist signed to his new label. It was the same strategy Geffen had used in launching Geffen Records in 1980, when he had snagged Donna Summer.

But that strategy had failed. Some wondered if the signing of George Michael, who had scored in the late 1980s with "I Want Your Sex" and "Freedom," would prove any more successful than the Summer signing had. Michael's albums on Sony's Columbia label had been smash hits, but the singer had not had an original album in a number of years; some thought that his fame and appeal had peaked. What's more, Michael was embroiled in a long-running legal battle with Sony, which meant that any label that signed him would most likely have to pay big bucks to settle his litigation.

Geffen was so hot to get George Michael that DreamWorks did exactly that: The company agreed to pay about six million dollars to help extricate the artist from his Sony contract. The signing cost Dream-Works Records dearly, but it garnered the headlines Geffen wanted, establishing the new label as a contender.

Geffen next turned his attention toward finding an executive to run DreamWorks Records. He had no interest in running that business himself but wanted a first-class executive team to ensure its success. His first choice was Mo Ostin. Geffen went into signing mode and flooded Ostin with phone calls. He did everything he could to convince him to join DreamWorks.

Geffen's timing was fortuitous: After thirty-one years of service, Ostin had been ousted from Warner Bros. less than a year earlier, following a power struggle with Bob Morgado, who had been promoted to chairman of the Warner Music Group. The firing led to a year of turmoil at what had been the industry's most stable record company. At the end of the year, Bob Morgado himself was fired.

The availability of Ostin, a legend in the record business, set off a frenzy during which nearly every entertainment company attempted to sign him. Michael Eisner tried to get him to come to Disney, while Michael Fuchs, Morgado's successor at Time Warner, attempted to woo Ostin back.

Ostin sat down with his son Michael and with Lenny Waronker, his longtime friend and current president of Warner Bros. Records, and convinced them to leave Warner Bros. as well, joining him at a new company. They drew up a list of pros and cons of each company's offer.

Considering what Mo Ostin had been through with Geffen in the 1980s—the vicious and personal attack on his wife, Evelyn, for example—it seemed that Geffen did not stand a chance. But Ostin decided that the DreamWorks offer was truly the best. He did not want to return to Time Warner. Now sixty-eight, he also was not interested in signing on at Disney and enduring the pressures of working at a publicly traded company.

Ostin was drawn to DreamWorks' charter as a company that was independent, driven by quality, and sensitive to artists' needs. But the biggest plus in Ostin's mind, it turns out, was David Geffen. Despite all the stunts of the past, Ostin retained warm feelings for Geffen. It was important to Ostin to ally himself with a winner, and on that score, nobody could top Geffen.

By August 1995, Geffen had reached an agreement with the Ostins and Waronker to come to DreamWorks. It was indeed quite a reversal for Mo Ostin to be working for David Geffen. The situation, however, actually paralleled many others in Geffen's life: People he tangled with returned time and again for more. Alternately exasperating and exhilarating, some people found Geffen to be like an intoxicating drug. The high was indescribable, despite the fact that it would likely be followed by a wicked hangover.

W ith DreamWorks' financing set and an executive team in place, Geffen pulled back and gladly allowed Katzenberg and Spielberg to run the company. Katzenberg went into overdrive to establish DreamWorks' animation division, settling on a biblical script about Moses called *The Prince of Egypt* for its debut film.

Geffen was also uninterested in the latest project that had taken Spielberg's fancy, a plan to build a giant studio lot at a site known as Playa Vista, near Los Angeles International Airport. With much fanfare, the three moguls staged still another press conference, announcing that they would be the anchor tenants of a six-billion-dollar master-planned community, complete with an enormous technology and entertainment "campus" that would create thousands of jobs. But Geffen had a negative feeling about the project from the start and feared that the undertaking would distract from DreamWorks' business of making movies and records.

Since the planned new studio—whose site was the old airplane hangar where Howard Hughes had built the Spruce Goose—would take a couple of years to build, offices were built for Geffen and Katzenberg at Spielberg's Amblin Entertainment compound on the Universal Studios lot.

Geffen rarely went to his new office, however, and seemed detached, even somewhat ambivalent, about playing an active role in the company. Instead, he stayed at his home in Malibu, monitored the phones, and watched CNBC. Certainly, Geffen continued to schmooze Paul Allen, the company's biggest single investor. He spoke to Katzenberg numerous times every day. He spoke to Spielberg far less often, although their relationship nonetheless intensified. Spielberg was beginning to count on Geffen for advice on career matters, sometimes even sending him scripts and soliciting his opinion.

But Geffen did not invest himself in the enterprise in the same energetic way he had in his two record labels. It seemed almost as though he was doing the job as a kind of lark or perhaps as a favor to Katzenberg, who needed a job. Geffen did share Katzenberg's hatred of Michael Eisner, and beating Disney had seemed like an entertaining prospect. Working with Steven Spielberg, the most successful film director of all time, had also been a draw.

But now, as it came down to putting into action plans for making the enterprise fly, Geffen took a backseat, making himself available to help solve problems as they arose. His indifference—combined with Spielberg's lack of total commitment (his next movie, a sequel to *Jurassic Park,* was for Universal, not DreamWorks) and Katzenberg's singular focus on building an animation company to rival Disney—created the impression early on that DreamWorks was not operating as a cohesive company. It seemed as though nothing had changed: Spielberg continued to run his Amblin film company; Geffen was tangentially involved with operations at a record label staffed by a number of people with whom he had worked before; and Katzenberg was running a feature-animation department staffed by many loyalists he had raided from Disney.

Geffen disagreed with those who challenged his commitment to the venture. Disputing a *Newsweek* article that reported that the relationship between Spielberg and Katzenberg was headed for danger, Geffen insisted that the three titans got along just fine. "It's a mark of my maturity that I am happily comfortable being a partner with two other guys," he said. "We haven't had a disagreeable second since we've gone into business and that's the truth. I could not have done that twenty years ago."

G effen nearly doubled his net worth to almost two billion dollars in just a couple of years. Having made a fortune in bonds, he switched a sizable chunk of his money into the stock market and rode the wave of the biggest run-up in the history of Wall Street. In 1995, the Forbes 400 put Geffen's worth at $1.3 billion. The following year it clocked in at $1.9 billion.

Geffen's philanthropy continued to be a boon to the causes he already believed in, as well as to some new ones. He made five-million-dollar contributions to both the Westwood Playhouse and the Museum of Contemporary Art in downtown Los Angeles.

While many wealthy individuals made gifts anonymously, David Geffen always insisted on, or agreed to, having his name celebrated openly. Creating a legacy, Geffen soon had "children" around town that were instantly recognizable: In addition to the David Geffen Center of the AIDS Project Los Angeles headquarters, the Museum of Contemporary Art, in the midst of a makeover, changed the name of the Temporary Contemporary to the Geffen Contemporary. The Westwood Playhouse became the Geffen Playhouse. In New York, God's Love We Deliver renamed its SoHo kitchen the David Geffen Building, and GMHC created the David Geffen Center for HIV Prevention and Health Education. There was even a plaque placed out front of the modest Jewish educational center along a dirty stretch of Santa Monica Boulevard in West Hollywood that Geffen had purchased to honor his mother.

Andy Spahn, who ran Geffen's charitable foundation, said that it was the organizations themselves that insisted on using Geffen's name. They argued that doing so would provide them with an invaluable endorsement, which would in turn lead to contributions by other wealthy benefactors.

DreamWorks' innovative TV programming alliance with ABC was dealt a staggering blow when in August Disney made a whopping deal to acquire Capital Cities/ABC for nineteen billion dollars. With Geffen and Katzenberg locked in an ugly battle with Michael Eisner over Katzenberg's settlement agreement, it seemed impossible that the men could ever work together as partners. Katzenberg had retained the services of two high-powered law firms and was preparing to file a suit against Disney.

Two weeks after announcing the Cap Cities acquisition, Eisner hired Michael Ovitz, a friend with whom he had often vacationed, to be president of Disney. For Eisner, the move quieted Wall Street, which had called for him to hire a strong deputy to help run the company. For Ovitz, the deal provided a critical exit strategy from Creative Artists Agency. In the wake of the failed Universal talks, which were widely known, others at CAA had grown to distrust him. They did not believe Ovitz when he later insisted that he was committed to the agency and had no plans to leave it.

For his first act as president of Disney, Ovitz tried to broker a settlement between Eisner and Katzenberg. He hoped that in so doing he might be able to win some goodwill with Geffen and perhaps even get him off his back once and for all.

"I see no strategic benefit to you being in a litigation with an ex-employee who actually did a good job," Ovitz told Eisner, warning him of the horrendous publicity that would certainly follow if Katzenberg actually filed a lawsuit. "More important, why unleash David, who hates me and who hates you, on all this stuff?"

Eisner tentatively agreed with Ovitz. Ovitz called Katzenberg to tell him that Disney was at last open to settlement negotiations. He succeeded in getting Katzenberg to delay his suit, promising to broker a settlement acceptable to both parties. To avoid being seen by the media, Katzenberg suggested that he and Ovitz meet in the emergency room at

Saint Joseph's Hospital in Burbank, directly across the street from Disney headquarters.

Ovitz met with Katzenberg, but soon after, Eisner changed his mind about settling, convinced that Disney did not contractually owe Katzenberg the $250 million or so he was claiming. Ovitz was deeply embarrassed, and Geffen characteristically blasted him for reneging on his promise to solve the problem.

Frustrated, Geffen then called Eisner directly. At Geffen's request, Eisner dropped by his beach house to discuss the issue one afternoon. But the talk led nowhere and, in April 1996, Katzenberg filed suit against Disney.

It was for Michael Ovitz, however, that Geffen reserved his most vitriolic attacks. Geffen spent the next few months bad-mouthing him full-time. He especially delighted in talking to Ovitz's other enemies. When NBC West Coast president Don Ohlmeyer called Ovitz the "Antichrist" in *Newsweek,* Geffen jumped on the bandwagon. "Apparently Don Ohlmeyer thinks more highly of Michael Ovitz than I do," he told reporters.

Ovitz was hurt by Geffen's new round of carping, which took on an even more evil slant than before. Gossipy rumors about one of Ovitz's children and his alleged school-yard pranks were making the rounds in Hollywood, and Ovitz was convinced Geffen was the source behind them. He contacted Barry Diller, looking for sympathy. "Now I hear he's going around town saying terrible things about my children," Ovitz told him. "How can I make this guy stop?"

Seeking to end the ugly dispute, Ovitz bravely telephoned Geffen and sought to set up a meeting. Geffen agreed to meet and invited him to lunch at the Amblin offices in Universal City. Once again, Ovitz contacted Diller, looking for advice about how to deal with Geffen. "I just do not know what to say to him anymore," he said.

Diller was tired of hearing Ovitz and Geffen complain to him about each other. While he was not particularly interested in getting in the middle of their quarrel, he had a vested interest in seeing it end. "Well,

Mike, I don't know," Diller started, only half listening. "If I had that problem with somebody, and I wanted them to stop, I would say, 'Well, if you do it ever again I'm going to beat you up!' "

"*What!*" Ovitz exclaimed.

"If you've tried everything else, tell him if he keeps spreading rumors that you'll hit him!" Diller hung up and thought nothing more of the conversation, exasperated at the juvenile feud between his two friends.

Ovitz took Diller's advice literally. He even rehearsed the line in the event Geffen unleashed an insulting tirade, though he hoped it would not be necessary. He had long tried to find a common denominator in his relationship with Geffen. He had thought that perhaps their shared interest in art would be the key. Both men owned blue-chip collections of postwar masterpieces; Ovitz was even on the board of directors of the Museum of Modern Art. But Geffen was not interested in such conversations.

Just after their lunch meeting began, Geffen started in, ranting about past wrongs, rattling off everything he believed Ovitz had done to him, dating back to the *Personal Best* saga, fifteen years previously.

Ovitz was aghast as he watched Geffen's explosion, pausing for a moment to marvel at his inability to let even a single bygone be bygone. Having come armed with an olive branch in one hand and a sledgehammer in the other, Ovitz was not quite sure which to extend.

"You're so smart, so bright, so aggressive. . . . I wish to God you could take all your venom and turn it into something positive," Ovitz said. "Your whole life is so negative." He continued, "It's not enough for you to win. You have to have everyone else do poorly around you. They have to do badly. I don't get that."

Frustrated, Ovitz unleashed the line Diller had prepared for him. "David, if you keep saying bad things about me, I am going to beat you up!"

Geffen could not believe his ears. "Are you threatening me?" he screamed. "If you so much as touch me I'll have you arrested!"

Geffen left Ovitz in the dining room and raced back to his office. He worked the phones as he never had before, spreading the news that Mike Ovitz had threatened to beat him up. The word quickly got back to Diller, who was so stunned that he decided not to confess that he had been the instigator. "David was so insane over the moon that he frightened me!" Diller said.

The next night, Diller told a friend that he had provided Ovitz with the line that had prompted the eruption. "What's wrong with that?" Diller asked. "If David really has said these things and Mike has tried everything else, why shouldn't he just hit him?"

"Because it's illegal," the friend responded.

"It is *not* illegal!" Diller insisted. "That's ridiculous! People hit each other all the time!"

"You fool," the friend said. "It's called *battery*. If you hit someone, they can call the police and haul you away!"

At that point, Diller decided he would suck it up and tell Geffen the truth. "David, I know this is going to make you crazy, but I want you to know I'm the one who told Mike that he should threaten to beat you up," he said. "I didn't really mean it, I thought maybe it would help matters."

"*You!*" Geffen said in disbelief.

"Yes, I did it," Diller said. "I'm not saying you're right or wrong, I'm saying it's immaterial. He wants you to stop. You won't stop. What else is he going to say?"

Geffen and Sandy Gallin. Geffen's freeze-out shocked their makeshift family. (Peter Borsari)

THE LEATHER CHAIR

|||

D reamWorks was off to a slow start. Nearly two years after its formation, journalists began weighing in with articles claiming that
there were too many dreams and not enough works at the company. The
studio produced two TV shows in its first year, one of which, ABC's
Champs, was canceled quickly. The other, an hour-long drama called
High Incident, was barely picked up for a second season. The company
began work on two other star-driven sitcoms on which it pinned great
hopes: *Spin City,* starring Michael J. Fox, and *Ink,* with Ted Danson.

At the end of May 1996, production of DreamWorks' first movie, an
espionage drama called *The Peacemaker,* finally got under way. Hollywood snickered as it realized that the fancy trio, which had promised to
go about business differently, had a debut picture that looked to be a
rather formulaic action picture with TV actor George Clooney in the
lead role. Meanwhile, Steven Spielberg went to work filming his first
movie for DreamWorks, a historical saga about slavery called *Amistad.*

As expected, Geffen's biggest creative contributions to the company
were at its record unit. He was the key to DreamWorks snagging the

cast-album rights to the Broadway hit *Rent,* successfully fending off a rival bid from Ahmet Ertegun at Atlantic Records. Geffen also sat in on some meetings to help with the marketing of George Michael's debut DreamWorks album, *Older.* The record fell short of the platinum-selling status of Michael's earlier albums, however, and the rock star was soon blasting DreamWorks for mishandling its release.

The studio was six months ahead of schedule in its expenditures, spending its capital at a clip of $400 million a year, making it the costliest start-up in entertainment history. *Business Week* reported that profits were five years away at best.

The stories annoyed Geffen and motivated him to prove the skeptics wrong. "This is a marathon, not a sprint," he told *Business Week.* "Watch where we are at the end of the race."

G effen and Bob Brassel had not been lovers for many years, yet they remained close friends and supported each other as they dated other people. There was nothing Geffen would not do for Brassel, including giving him a job at his new company. Shortly after operations began, Geffen arranged for Brassel to leave Warner Bros. and join the film-production ranks at DreamWorks.

In the summer of 1996, Geffen encouraged Brassel to move to Malibu so the two could be neighbors. Geffen had found a house down the beach from his own and offered to buy it as a gift, but Brassel refused. He agreed to move there if Geffen rented it to him at market value. Excited that Brassel would be close by, Geffen enlisted the help of a local real-estate expert to set the rent. He asked Rose Tarlow, who continued to oversee the massive decorating project at the Jack Warner estate, to spruce up the place in preparation for Brassel's arrival.

A major drama ensued a week or so before the Fourth of July when Geffen had Brassel, Joel Schumacher, and Sandy Gallin to his beach house for lunch. When the meal was finished, Brassel offered to show his new house to Gallin.

"No, no, no," Geffen said. "The house isn't ready. Rose is having a leather chair made."

"I don't need a leather chair," Brassel responded, already embarrassed by Geffen's generosity.

Brassel cheerfully gave Gallin a tour and told him how excited he was about his impending move to Malibu. But when they had completed their walk-through, Gallin turned to Brassel with raised eyebrows.

"*How* much are you paying?" he asked.

"Seventy-five hundred," Brassel replied.

"*Take the leather chair,*" Gallin said, rolling his eyes, clearly insinuating that Geffen was overcharging him. After the two men parted, Brassel returned to Geffen's house and told him what Gallin had said.

Geffen dialed Gallin. "You told one of my best friends that I am taking advantage of him and charging him too much money for the house?" he screamed.

"That's not true," Gallin said. "I will never talk to Bob Brassel ever again."

"Don't you call Bob Brassel," Geffen warned Gallin. "I don't want him to have any stress or anxiety over this."

Geffen ticked off a list of betrayals he believed Gallin had committed against him throughout their twenty-five-year-plus friendship. Gallin's most recent comment was simply the thing that sent him over the edge.

Gallin could sense that Geffen was still furious when he did not hear from him over the next several days. The men were like brothers, having spoken to each other on average five times a day, every day—barring other spats—since the late 1960s.

Gallin went to New York, where he was planning to spend the Fourth of July at Calvin Klein's beach house in East Hampton. He decided to call Geffen and attempt a reconciliation. But the call only fueled Geffen's furor.

"I'm finished with you! You have hurt my feelings more than anybody has ever hurt my feelings!" he yelled. "Don't call me anymore. I don't ever want to talk to you again."

The circle of friends that Geffen and Sandy Gallin had shared for years was shocked as the months wore on and Geffen refused to make up with Gallin. The makeshift family—including Calvin Klein, Barry Diller, and Carole Bayer Sager, now the wife of Warner Bros. co-chairman Bob Daly—balanced phone calls from a heartbroken Gallin and an irate Geffen. The friends all attempted to broker a rapprochement, especially Diller, who did not believe the standoff would last. Geffen had had feuds with nearly everyone in the "family," including a number of whoppers with Diller, but none had gone this far.

The incident showed once again that, for all his bluster, Geffen was a fragile and frightened soul. The same emotional machinery that gave him his strength of conviction and purpose and had won him great fortune and accomplishment was a clear obstacle when it came to issues such as friendship. When Geffen was hurt, the pain was so great that the only way for him to feel safe again was to throw a fit, instantaneously creating a protective distance between himself and others. Once the negative energy was out of his system and the people around him had ducked for cover, Geffen could then consider whether he was unendangered and unscathed. The people around him, meanwhile, were so shaken and distracted by his screaming tirades that no one could see the frightened boy he still was. "The liabilities are the assets," Diller said. "He's gone through a lot, and goes through a lot, for what he gets."

Sandy Gallin became extremely disturbed as Geffen's freeze-out stretched into months. Geffen did not care what Gallin thought, believing only that he was envious of his money and success. "How important can that be to Sandy, who you've been friends with since the 1960s?" Sager asked him. She worried about what might happen if she invited both to celebrate Yom Kippur at her home.

Sager pressed Geffen to patch up his relationship with Gallin, but he was not interested. "Carole, I don't want to make up with him," he said. "I'm happier now that Sandy is out of my life. How come it's OK for you when two people get divorced? When friends of yours get divorced

I'm sure you're not on the phone calling them up and telling them to get back together."

Just as Geffen froze one friend out of his life, he came on strong as a saint to an old friend from whom he had been estranged. Sue Mengers, who had compiled her own long list of enemies during her reign as the most powerful agent in Hollywood, had known Geffen for nearly thirty years. As Michael Ovitz and his partners at CAA ascended to power, Mengers's star dimmed, and she retired to spend time with her husband. After a brief comeback attempt in the late 1980s, Mengers retreated behind the giant wooden doors of her home a block off Sunset Boulevard.

Like so many of Geffen's other friends, Mengers had had a tumultuous relationship with him and carried the battle scars to show for it. She had been outraged by his behavior toward her years earlier. Additionally, her husband, a film director named Jean-Claude Tramont, did not like him. For all these reasons, Mengers had spent little time with Geffen in recent years.

But after Geffen learned that Tramont was very ill, he called Mengers and vowed to do whatever he could to help. When she told him that Tramont was heading to Paris for a few days, Geffen insisted she go away with him to his home on Fire Island for a break from her stressful situation. He instructed Mengers, who at sixty was seven years older than he was, to pack a bag and meet him at the Santa Monica airport.

Of all of the people she knew in Hollywood, David Geffen was about the last person who Mengers would have guessed would rescue her in times of trouble. But on Fire Island, she and Geffen discussed their past differences and were able to piece together their friendship.

The last Geffen Pictures films that Geffen had greenlit before forming DreamWorks were now hitting theaters. But the movies were not all that interesting to him. *Joe's Apartment,* a film about cockroaches that had been inspired by a short film on MTV, was a box-office dud. Geffen saw big success with *Beavis and Butt-head Do America,* which he co-produced with Paramount. The film grossed sixty-three million dollars.

Even though *Michael Collins,* a movie about an Irish Republican Army revolutionary that continued Geffen's affiliation with director Neil Jordan, grossed only thirty-five million, Geffen was proud of the film. He had become Jordan's leading patron and soon agreed to back an original but very uncommercial picture of his called *The Butcher Boy,* about an Irish boy who acts out murderous fantasies. In contrast to the contentious relationships he had had with directors at the start of his producing career, Geffen's relationship with Jordan indicated an attitude of maturity and showed that, at least in this instance, he did not consider it worthwhile to expend his energy fighting. Perhaps more strikingly, *The Butcher Boy* showed that Geffen was willing to back his filmmaker, even with a picture that seemed to be a certain financial loser.

G effen's friendship with President Clinton was closer than ever. In the summer of 1996, Geffen offered once again to lend his formidable fund-raising talents to help the president win reelection that fall. Having agreed to co-chair a star-studded benefit in September, Geffen also signed on to host two intimate dinners at his Malibu home, at which his wealthiest friends would be able to share a few hours with the president. The guest lists for the dinners included such business titans as Lew Wasserman, Steve Jobs, August Busch IV, Paul Allen, Dirk Ziff, Ted Field, Peter Morton, Steve Tisch, and Susie Buffett, wife of Geffen's new idol, Warren Buffett. At one of the gatherings, Clinton showed up wearing blue jeans and cowboy boots and playfully admonished Martin Peretz about a tough story his *New Republic* magazine had published that week about the First Lady.

Although the guests were overwhelmed by Clinton's charm, they were also struck by the manner in which Geffen interacted with the president. He was notably deft as the emcee, personally introducing each of them to Clinton upon their arrival. A large rectangular table had been set up in Geffen's screening room for the meal, and he positioned himself across from Clinton at the dinner. He also moderated the discussion, demonstrating a certain amount of knowledge about every topic and skillfully making certain that everyone had a chance to say something.

At the end of one dinner, Geffen instructed his projectionist to lower the lights and roll a print of *The Birdcage,* a comedy starring Robin Williams. Clinton's aides expected him to duck out of the room once the movie began; they were surprised when he did not. The commander in chief stayed and watched the movie until the end.

In the weeks following the dinners, Geffen called the participants and asked them to write checks to support Clinton's reelection effort. From the twenty-four people who had attended the two dinners, Geffen raised two million dollars. He himself contributed another one hundred thousand to the Democratic National Committee; he was now Hollywood's leading contributor to the Democrats, having donated more than $575,000 over the past five years.

Geffen also asked those who attended the dinners, as well as many others, to buy tickets to an elaborate fund-raiser he was co-chairing, along with supermarket magnate Ron Burkle, to benefit the DNC. The benefit, called the Los Angeles National Presidential Gala, was to be held at Green Acres, the former Beverly Hills estate of silent-screen star Harold Lloyd. Geffen used his connections to line up the entertainment for the evening. In addition to Clinton favorite Barbra Streisand, Geffen also arranged to have the Neville Brothers perform and Maya Angelou read poetry. There was also another Clinton favorite with which Geffen had unique ties: the Eagles. Although Don Henley hated David Geffen, they did share a common belief in the president, and so he accepted Geffen's offer to perform at the event.

Emcee Tom Hanks welcomed the crowd and then brought Geffen to the stage to introduce the First Lady. Geffen's customary discomfort in speaking before a crowd grew when he discovered that the TelePrompTer did not have the latest version of his speech. Despite his anxiety, he stumbled his way through and shared with the attendees the moving story of how he and his brother had found their parents' citizenship papers in a safe-deposit box after their mother's death in 1988.

"To be able to live and work in the United States is a privilege," Geffen said. "My mother believed that there was nothing more valuable than being an American, and in this regard I am truly my mother's son."

Hillary Rodham Clinton then introduced her husband, who began his speech by acknowledging Geffen's contributions to his life and to his campaign. "Thank you, David Geffen, for living the dream of your parents," he said, adroitly referring back to Geffen's speech. "You are a great citizen, an honest and true friend who always tells me exactly what you think."

The sound of crickets filled the chilly nighttime air as Clinton roused the crowd with campaign rhetoric and thanked them for their donations. At the end of the evening, the DNC was $3.5 million richer.

Geffen's modern-art collection had grown so formidable that Kirk Varnedoe, the chief curator in the Department of Painting and Sculpture at the Museum of Modern Art, began to court him. Varnedoe watched in amazement as Geffen sometimes paid astonishing prices in order to wrest control of masterpieces from such collectors as S. I. Newhouse and Leo Castelli. He was astounded as Geffen cleverly launched an exceedingly complex plan to acquire *Woman III,* a masterwork by Willem de Kooning that had previously been owned by the shah of Iran. Many people had tried unsuccessfully to get the painting out of Tehran, but only Geffen had the brilliance to learn that the Iranians wanted something more valuable than money. He figured out that the Iranians, who regarded the shah's art collection as trash and a symbol of Western decadence, highly valued the *Shanama,* an ancient Persian manuscript owned by the Houghton family of Europe. Utilizing a worldwide network of art experts, Geffen arranged to buy an important fragment of the *Shanama* from the Houghtons and trade it to the Iranians for the de Kooning.

For Varnedoe, the friendship with Geffen paid off as the billionaire in 1995 donated an Andy Warhol painting to the museum (tellingly, the work was *Before and After,* which showed a woman's profile before and after a nose job). The connection proved even more valuable as the museum began making plans for a Jasper Johns exhibition. Geffen generously agreed to lend several paintings for the show, including such important works as *False Start, Out the Window,* and *Weeping Women.*

But he was unwilling to part with the work Varnedoe most wanted: *Target with Plaster Casts,* a seminal work in Johns's career and one of the most valuable paintings in Geffen's collection. In creating this work in 1955, Johns had used elements of a wax process and collage to paint a simple black and yellow archery target against a red background. Along the top of the painting sat a row of small wooden boxes, complete with hinged doors, each containing a colorful plaster cast of a body part, such as a hand, an ear, a foot, and a penis. It was the first and most famous of a number of target pictures Johns had painted. MoMA's show would be the most significant retrospective of the artist's work ever organized, and Varnedoe could not imagine it opening without the painting that David Geffen owned.

Geffen was steadfast in his refusal, and with good reason. *Target with Plaster Casts* was a fragile picture that had sustained some damage in storage, and Geffen worried whether it could withstand another cross-country trip. The timing of Varnedoe's request was also poor: The renovation of the Warner mansion in Beverly Hills was nearly complete. Geffen would soon, for the first time since buying the painting, be able to hang it in his home.

Varnedoe offered to send a conservator from the museum to Los Angeles and arrange for an extensive restoration of the work. He wrote three-page letters to Geffen, telling him about the importance of the exhibition and begging him to reconsider. He called mutual friends and asked them to intervene on his behalf.

Defensive and cantankerous, Geffen told Varnedoe to stop bothering him. "I don't want to hear about this anymore," Geffen finally complained. "If you press me on this one more time, I'm not lending the *rest* of the pictures."

Varnedoe was crushed. He was grateful for Geffen's other contributions and did not want to lose them. But he refused to give up, deciding to alter his pitch. He sent Geffen an unbound copy of the catalog that would accompany the show. It was an impressive-looking book, and he hoped that Geffen might see for himself how the show would not be complete without *Target with Plaster Casts*.

Ten days before the show's opening, Geffen was in New York and contacted Varnedoe, asking if he could tour the installation. Varnedoe was delighted and shrewdly elected to leave the opening wall vacant, planning to make one final pitch. If Geffen again said no, Varnedoe planned to put another *Target* painting from MoMA's own collection, *Target with Four Faces,* there.

When Geffen entered the museum, on Fifty-third Street just west of Fifth Avenue, he immediately asked Varnedoe about the empty wall. "What's going here?" he asked.

"Uh, *Target,*" Varnedoe answered.

"Oh, *your Target,*" David said.

"We'd still love to get your *Target,*" Varnedoe meekly allowed.

"No, no," Geffen said. "I'm not lending that painting. It's too fragile. Don't bother me about it."

Varnedoe led Geffen on a tour of the entire installation. Stopping back at the place where they had begun, Varnedoe decided to press Geffen one final time. "David, I know we can get the piece here safely," Varnedoe pleaded.

"How would you do it?" Geffen said, thawing for the first time.

Varnedoe quickly outlined a meticulous plan in which the painting's safety, not the cost of transport or any other issue, would be the paramount concern.

Geffen looked at the wall and then back at Varnedoe.

"OK," he said. "Come get it."

Two days after Christmas 1996, Sue Mengers's husband died at the age of sixty-six. Mengers was devastated, and Geffen was there to help, arranging for his driver to pick her up and bring her to his Malibu beach house for several weekends.

There were many people who called Mengers and offered condolences in the weeks immediately following Tramont's death, but Geffen soon showed that he was in it for the long haul. He turned down invitations to leave Los Angeles and go away on weekends, preferring instead to stay at his house and console Mengers.

Many people liked being around Sue Mengers because of her sarcastic wit. But now she was not in a mood to be funny. Geffen allowed her to mourn and mope around in a bathrobe if that was what she wanted to do. He let her grieve, but at times he also tried to cheer her up. He was a good friend.

Geffen himself was becoming something of a recluse. He rarely ventured outside, dreading having to make public appearances and looking for excuses to avoid such important company events as premieres. He was comfortable in the confines of his Malibu beach house and enjoyed the companionship that Mengers offered him. The two shared a love of watching television and eating food. They were glued to the TV coverage of the ongoing O. J. Simpson trial, at times making the ultimate sacrifice of refusing to take telephone calls.

Mengers's troubles were to intensify in the months to come, yet Geffen continued to respond in a compassionate way that Mengers found astonishing. His friends said that his devotion to and assistance of her was the most admirable thing he had ever done in his life.

Designer Rose Tarlow supervises
the top-to-bottom renovation of Geffen's prize acquisition,
the Jack Warner mansion in Beverly Hills. With an unlimited
budget, she turned it from a hodgepodge into a
state-of-the-art showplace. (Antoine Bootz)

CHAPTER 38

ANALYSIS
(AGAIN)

|||

G effen had become such an important Clinton friend that the First Lady left Washington in the middle of the January 1997 inauguration-week festivities to fly to New York and introduce him at an AIDS benefit. No one on Hillary Clinton's staff would have advocated an appearance at a major gay event a couple of days after the inauguration, especially given the president's miscalculation in having begun his first term with the gays-in-the-military issue. But she did not care; Geffen was an influential friend, and she shared his belief in the cause.

Geffen and his friend Joan Tisch had been tagged to be honored at Carnegie Hall by GMHC. Called "You Gotta Have Friends," the gala featured such presenters as Steve Martin, Rosie O'Donnell, and Michael Douglas and musical performances by Celine Dion, Reba McEntire, and Luther Vandross.

Barbara Walters opened the program and reflected on Geffen's oft-repeated mantra—"you're as sick as your secrets"—which he had mentioned during her *20/20* interview. "The only thing David seems to hide is his generosity," Walters said. "Of the thirty-five million plus his foundation has donated over the past five years, a sizable chunk has been slated for AIDS. Joan Tisch tells this Geffen story: After Joan asked David to increase his previous fifty-thousand-dollar gift to GMHC, he named his own sum: one million, the largest gift ever given to an AIDS service organization. And the check arrived unannounced in an envelope with a twenty-nine-cent stamp."

Steve Martin did a comedy routine in which he described what each letter in David Geffen's name stood for. *V*, for example, was for *vampire*. "People tried to talk Geffen out of casting Tom Cruise in the movie, but David insisted, 'How else am I going to meet him?' " The audience roared.

"*I*," he said, was "for *iconoclast*, a tasty rum drink that makes you say nasty things about Mike Ovitz." The *ff* in *Geffen*, Martin quipped, stood for "French franc, a guy David went out with." *E* was for *eyelash curl*. "Oops, that's for my Liza tribute!" Again, the crowd howled.

Hillary Clinton opened her remarks by thanking Geffen for sponsoring the trips of some of the people who had attended the first White House conference on HIV and AIDS. "As the president said in his inaugural address on Monday, each of us has a stake in the endurance of this democracy," she said. "Through their work, Joan and David exemplify the noblest qualities of citizenship and of humanity. They not only make financial contributions to the causes they believe in, they give of themselves, and they give unconditionally, never expecting anything in return."

Clinton then told the story about Geffen's mother's citizenship papers. "There is no doubt that David is keeping his mother's dream of the American dream alive by making it possible for others to pursue their own hopes and dreams," she said.

Although he was embarrassed by the honor and nervous once again about making a speech, Geffen was moved by the First Lady's comments and thrilled to have played a role in the evening's fund-raising. Indeed, the role he had played was huge, for the event raised as much money as had ever been raised for AIDS. GMHC's ambitious target had initially been $2.5 million, but Andy Spahn, the head of the David

Geffen Foundation, had called all of Geffen's wealthy friends and told them Geffen was being honored. The evening netted $4.3 million.

Felix Cavaliere, a member of the 1960s quartet the Rascals, telephoned Geffen in early April 1997 and broke the news to him that Laura Nyro had died of ovarian cancer. She was only forty-nine. In the years since their split, Nyro had released many albums on Columbia, but none of them approached the success she had achieved when David Geffen had been her manager. Geffen and Nyro had not spoken for years; he had not even known that she was sick.

The fragility of life became a central issue for Geffen as another close friend grew old and yet another faced a life-threatening illness. Ray Stark, the maverick movie producer, had long been one of Geffen's role models. Since meeting in the 1970s, Stark developed an extraordinary affection for Geffen and at one point even joked that the two should go into business together as DaveStar, a twist on Rastar, the name of Stark's production company. But now Stark was in his eighties, and his health was beginning to fail. Geffen's friendship with him intensified.

It soon became known that a friend of both Geffen and Stark was seriously ill. Dawn Steel was a gregarious executive who, when she was named president of Columbia Pictures in 1987, had been the first woman to head a major studio. In the 1970s, she had met and become friends with Geffen as she learned the movie business at Paramount from Barry Diller and Jeffrey Katzenberg. As with Stark, Geffen saw much of himself in Steel. She was a New Yorker with a raw brand of brash self-confidence. She also had towering charisma and seemed to be fearless.

Suddenly, Steel, just fifty years old, was diagnosed with a brain tumor. Stunned by the illness that had so randomly crippled his friend, Geffen offered to help her in any way. Together with Ray Stark, Geffen paid for an expensive experimental surgery to try to prolong Steel's life. Geffen kept in contact with Chuck Roven, Steel's husband, as Roven reported the mostly discouraging news on his wife's progress. She died on December 20, 1997.

The deaths of Laura Nyro and Dawn Steel once again prompted Geffen to examine his own life. It was not lost on him that both women had been younger than he was. He knew that at the very least both had had family to care for them. In the case of Nyro, he read that she had found a longtime companion, a woman named Maria Desiderio. He knew firsthand that Chuck Roven had rarely left Steel's side throughout her illness. But Geffen essentially had no family: He had not spoken to his brother for a couple of years and was largely out of touch with his aunt and stepfather.

Meanwhile, Sue Mengers, now Geffen's closest friend, was also in trouble. Having weathered the brutal illness and death of her husband just a few months earlier, Mengers was now diagnosed with a host of her own health problems. Before long, she underwent quadruple-bypass surgery. Again, Geffen was there for her, committing enormous amounts of time to her and doing everything he could to make certain she was comfortable. His actions surprised some of his other friends, who did not realize he was capable of such a great and selfless act of kindness.

Even more so than when he had saved Calvin Klein from the brink of bankruptcy, at this moment Geffen truly behaved admirably. His harshest critics, who claimed his love was always conditional, were forced to acknowledge that Geffen was in this case demonstrating unconditional dedication. After all, Mengers had long since retired from the entertainment business; there was nothing she could give Geffen to help either his career or his bank account.

Mengers shuttled back and forth between doctors' offices and Geffen's house. It was a far cry from her glamorous heyday in the 1970s when she introduced such dignitaries as Princess Margaret to the entertainment elite. She loved telling the story of how Geffen had horrified her by showing up in blue jeans and approaching the princess with a casual "Hiya!" To many, the new image of Geffen and Mengers, aging industry veterans ensconced in Geffen's house, seemed more like an image out of *Sunset Boulevard*.

Geffen realized that had it not been for him, Mengers might have fought her battles alone. His actions bespoke a person who was frightened and uncertain as to whether he was ready to die. It all raised a rather troubling question: Who would take care of David Geffen?

On June 19, 1997, *Cats* had its 6,138th performance, passing *A Chorus Line* to become the longest-running show on Broadway. A giant celebration was held, but Geffen did not attend. He also did not care to attend the Rock 'n' Roll Hall of Fame ceremonies during which Joni Mitchell, Crosby, Stills & Nash, and the Eagles were inducted. Geffen lived in the future, not in the past, and he was now concerned only with his new venture and with Sue Mengers.

Ironically, Geffen was not all that content with the present either. His fortune now stretched to nearly two billion dollars, but he was not in a serious relationship. He wanted more out of life.

While Geffen was in this somewhat contemplative mood, a friend was raving to him about his analyst. Geffen telephoned the doctor and arranged for a session. Soon, Geffen was again in five-day-a-week analysis, searching for ways to improve himself as a man and to find the meaning of life.

"I've been working on myself, and my demons and my nonsense and my fucked-up-ness for a long, long time," he had once told *Rolling Stone* magazine. "Which is not to say that I'm still not a little fucked up. I think you get better and better in tiny increments, and you die unhealed."

As it approached its third anniversary, DreamWorks continued to fight the perception that it was a disappointment. Although *Spin City* had become something of a hit for ABC, CBS's *Ink* was an expensive flop. DreamWorks' first feature film, *The Peacemaker,* barely broke even and was brutally attacked by the critics. *Amistad,* Steven Spielberg's first directorial effort for the company, was a disappointment. *The Mouse Hunt* did not turn out to be the runaway family Christmas hit the partners had hoped it would be. What's more, the company's plan to build its studio at Playa Vista was dealt a serious blow as the site's developer, Maguire Thomas Partners, encountered financial difficulties.

Although uninterested in Playa Vista, Geffen had slowly but surely grown more energized by the company's creative projects. He had earned the reputation as DreamWorks' fireman, always on hand to solve the latest crisis. When Jeffrey Katzenberg became involved in a nasty dispute with NBC over the ownership of TV pilots, Geffen stepped in. He gave himself a quick lesson in the economics of the TV business, and, acting almost as a disinterested mediator, offered a solution that made both parties happy.

He was also the key to DreamWorks obtaining a share of some big movies that Spielberg wanted to direct for other studios. One was *Saving Private Ryan,* a World War II script that was owned by Paramount Pictures. It looked like a can't-miss: Spielberg wanted to cast Tom Hanks as the leader of a squad sent to save a soldier whose three brothers were killed in action within days of one another.

Geffen went to see Jonathan Dolgen, head of the Viacom Entertainment Group, the parent company of Paramount, and informed him that Spielberg would not direct unless DreamWorks received 50 percent of the profits, as well as half the distribution rights. (As part of the deal, DreamWorks also agreed to split profits with Paramount on *Deep Impact,* a disaster picture developed by DreamWorks that Spielberg was co-producing; that picture, it turned out, would be the second-highest-grossing film the studio would release in its first five years in business.)

Katzenberg remained the studio's top operations man, while Geffen was rarely seen at the office. When the company's costly new animation facilities were completed, Katzenberg had to beg Geffen to come to Glendale for a tour. The animators, busy at work on *The Prince of Egypt,* were so stunned to see him that some asked for autographs.

In January 1998, Rose Tarlow put the finishing touches on the Jack Warner house. Surprising many of his friends who did not believe he would ever move in, Geffen did just that, nearly eight years after having purchased the sprawling estate. While the Warner house was a remarkable place for entertaining, Geffen's far smaller beach house was more a reflection of his blue-jeans personality. He began by spending weeknights at the house and returning to Malibu for the weekends.

The house represented something of a new beginning for Geffen, and he attempted to use it to stretch himself and become more sociable. He loved showing it off and bragging about Tarlow. He began hosting dinner parties there and used it as a venue to entice some of his estranged friends to conciliatory dinners. One night, Joni Mitchell visited. Another night, Geffen persuaded Steve Ross's widow, Courtney, in town from New York on a visit, to join him for a meal.

The month Geffen moved in, Sandy Gallin bravely called to offer an apology, even though he believed he had not done anything wrong. In a carefully rehearsed speech, he told Geffen he was sorry for the remark he had made to Bob Brassel about the rent Geffen was charging him. Gallin was desperate to be back in Geffen's good graces: The two men had not spoken for a year and a half.

Geffen was tired of feuding with Gallin and accepted his apology. The next day, the two old friends went to Nate 'n Al, the delicatessen in Beverly Hills where they had breakfasted many times before.

Barry Diller thought that perhaps Geffen might now even be amenable to shelving his feud with Michael Ovitz. Having arranged to have dinner with Ovitz one night at Locanda Veneta, Diller casually invited Geffen to come along, mentioning who his dinner companion was.

Ovitz was in his car and on his way to the restaurant when Diller reached him with the news that Geffen would be joining them. Mindful of their last luncheon, Ovitz was terrified. But, realizing Diller was once again trying to help, he stoically went to the restaurant. Since their last meeting, Ovitz had left Disney following a disastrous sixteen-month tenure in which he had clashed with longtime friend Michael Eisner.

To Ovitz's surprise, there were no fireworks at the dinner that night, only cordial conversation. But despite the apparent truce, Geffen had no intention of halting his feud with Ovitz. He continued his vendetta against him.

Back at DreamWorks, Geffen's crisis-management skills proved valuable again after George Michael was arrested in a small park across from the Beverly Hills Hotel. A plainclothes police officer monitoring the men's restroom, a site where gay men were known to meet for sex, busted Michael when the star began performing a "lewd act" in front of the cop. When he was booked, the singer first gave his real name, Georgios Kyriacos Panayiotou, and supplied his stage name only when asked if he used any other names.

Michael asked Geffen for guidance, even though he was unhappy with DreamWorks' handling of his last album. The next day, the tabloids had a field day; the *New York Post,* for example, put Michael's photograph on the front page along with the headline DOWN AND OUTED IN BEVERLY HILLS; three pages of coverage inside were headlined ZIP ME UP BEFORE YOU GO GO. Recognizing the futility in continuing to try to conceal his homosexuality, Michael decided to go on the offensive and make a national TV appearance to reveal the truth. Geffen called Maria Shriver and arranged for Michael to appear on her newsmagazine program *Dateline NBC* a few days later. But when the singer's representatives heard that the British tabloid press had obtained the embarrassingly detailed police report, Michael wanted to make a preemptive strike. He dumped the *Dateline NBC* plan and opted to make his announcement immediately on CNN.

Although DreamWorks was spending money extravagantly, Geffen told *Business Week* that even a modestly successful crop of movies, TV shows, and compact discs was expected to yield three hundred million dollars in positive cash flow by the end of 1999. He claimed that this figure was about what the partners had expected from the beginning.

"We would all rather die than fail," Geffen told *The New Yorker.* "I can't imagine failing. I cannot imagine that. There is no scenario in my head that I can conjure up. I know that I will succeed, because I am committing all the energy, intelligence, passion, and belief that I can muster up to make me do so. And that's true of my partners. My life can't be a failure, right? My life is a success: I'm a happy guy."

In the summer of 1998, the company's movie unit finally had a bona-fide home run. Spielberg's *Saving Private Ryan* was an instant smash, garnering phenomenal critical reviews and charting a worldwide box-office gross of $479 million, the company's biggest hit yet. Although there were still six months left in the year, Oscar handicappers were saying it would win the Academy Award for Best Picture.

Paul Allen now agreed to kick in another $160 million, acquiring more than half of a departing South Korean shareholder's stake and thereby becoming the studio's largest shareholder. While his stake had grown to 24 percent, each of the three founding partners' stakes remained at about 22 percent.

A lmost four years after Geffen left, Geffen Records was stumbling badly, despite a couple of hit records, including one by Courtney Love's band, Hole. Eddie Rosenblatt had failed to attract a new crop of winning acts; business fell into a deep slump.

After Seagram, which owned Geffen Records, acquired music giant PolyGram, the company went through a major consolidation, with Geffen Records becoming one of the casualties. MCA had paid $545 million for Geffen Records only eight years earlier, but now it was reduced to a skeleton operation with a few A&R executives. Such functions as marketing and promotion were taken over by Seagram's Interscope Records, a healthier full-service label.

In January 1999, 110 people lost their jobs at Geffen Records. Eddie Rosenblatt announced his retirement, and several other Geffen executives, including Mel Posner and Jim Walker, joined Geffen's team at DreamWorks Records.

"It's very sad for me," Geffen told the *Los Angeles Times.* "It's a painful thing to watch."

*"Tonight the spotlight is on you": Geffen gives
a warm buss to his mentor Ahmet Ertegun at a dinner
honoring Ertegun's fifty years in the music business.*
(Rita Black/Shooting Star)

CELEBRATION
CHAIRMAN

|||

The Prince of Egypt opened in December 1998 to mixed reviews and did not approach the megasuccess of Jeffrey Katzenberg's *Lion King* triumph at Disney. Nevertheless, a costly marketing campaign managed to propel it to just over one hundred million dollars at the U.S. box office. DreamWorks' other animated film, *Antz,* which featured Woody Allen voicing a neurotic insect, did almost as well.

Steven Spielberg, meanwhile, found yet another script developed by an outside studio that he wanted to direct, frustrating his two partners and again raising questions about his level of commitment to Dream-Works. The picture was *Minority Report,* a science-fiction epic that had been developed at Twentieth Century Fox. The film, set in the criminal-justice system of the future, tells of a time in which killers are arrested and convicted before they commit their crimes.

Minority Report became a problem when Spielberg, the most expensive director in the business, expressed interest in the project, and Tom Cruise, Hollywood's most expensive star, wanted the leading role. The salary demands of the two, combined with the already exor-

bitant budget of the picture, made it difficult for Fox and Dream-
Works to envision turning a profit on the picture, even if it set box-
office records.

To further complicate matters, Bill Mechanic, the chairman of Fox,
was still feeling burned by *Titanic,* a picture Fox had developed but on
which Paramount had been brought in as a co-producer. To Fox's dismay, Paramount wound up snagging domestic box-office and bragging
rights for the hugely successful picture. Now, only a short while later,
Fox was being asked to make a similar arrangement with *Minority Report.* Mechanic was naturally reluctant. Mechanic agreed to take on
DreamWorks as a partner on the project, but only on the condition that
it give Fox half of another Spielberg-directed film in the future.

But even with the Fox-DreamWorks partnership resolved, there was
still the issue of the budget. Geffen stepped in and ran the numbers
with Mechanic, but the two concluded that the deal just did not make
sense unless Spielberg and Cruise agreed to take less money. When neither party agreed to budge, Geffen called Mechanic and told him they
should let the picture die. "It's the right signal for us to send to Hollywood," Geffen said.

David Geffen was perhaps the only person who could speak to Spielberg as an equal and make the situation clear to him. With the project
dead, Geffen told Spielberg that the only way the film would get made
was if he and Cruise agreed to reconsider their salary demands. Spielberg was serious about wanting to make the movie and finally relented.
He called Cruise and got him to similarly cut his fee. Geffen then went
back to Mechanic and structured a complex deal in which the two studios would split many of the worldwide ancillary distribution rights.
The film was scheduled to begin shooting in February 2000 and tar-
geted to be released at the end of that year.

Meanwhile, Miramax Films' *Shakespeare in Love* had become a sur-
prise hit and now presented a major Oscar threat to *Saving Private Ryan.*
But although the Miramax movie had a certain momentum to it, many
Academy pundits still believed *Saving Private Ryan* would take home the
Best Picture prize.

On Oscar night, a tuxedo-clad Geffen attended the ceremonies with Sherry Lansing, chairman of Paramount Pictures, DreamWorks' co-producer of the film. The evening had its fair share of surprises, such as when the hyperactive Italian character actor Roberto Begnini won the Oscar for Best Actor in *Life Is Beautiful*, a film he also directed.

The DreamWorks team was relieved when Spielberg was awarded the Oscar for Best Director—so far, so good. But the mood turned deadly when Harrison Ford opened the envelope after reading the nominees for Best Picture. "And the Oscar goes to . . . ," began Ford, "*Shakespeare in Love.*"

The DreamWorks entourage applauded politely as Harvey Weinstein, the heavyset, blustery chairman of Miramax Films, jumped up and raced to the stage to accept his Oscar. At Barnaby's, a Los Angeles restaurant that DreamWorks and Paramount had rented for what they hoped would be a celebration, the mood of the crowd, which had been watching the show on TV screens, sank. As planned, Spielberg, Geffen, and Katzenberg, as well as Tom Hanks and many other stars, showed up when the program was over, but the tone of the evening was more like a wake than a party.

As American Express erected an enormous billboard featuring Geffen ("Cardmember since 1969") on the side of the Hyatt hotel on Sunset Boulevard in West Hollywood, Geffen was at home riveted to the televised Senate impeachment trial of President Bill Clinton. Geffen had been back to the White House a number of times, spending the night there again after a state dinner honoring Chinese president Jiang Zemin.

Geffen had consoled both the president and the First Lady in the aftermath of the disclosure that Clinton had lied about his sexual contact with White House intern Monica Lewinsky. On a swing through California, Clinton visited Geffen at the Warner house and asked him for advice on the speech he planned to deliver to the country acknowledging his indiscretion and deception.

As the drama played out, Geffen was in especially close touch with the First Lady, talking with her on the phone the day before the House of Representatives voted to impeach her husband. "I'm sure it's been a very difficult time for her," he told *The New York Times*. "I believe he didn't have the courage to tell her, and I suppose we're all in denial about the people we love."

Geffen grew incensed at Jim Rogan, the California Republican who was one of the House managers during the heated impeachment trial, and decided he would do everything in his power to defeat Rogan in the next election. In June 1999, he hosted a fund-raiser at Dream-Works' animation headquarters to support Adam Schiff, the Democrat and California state senator who planned to oppose Rogan in the fall of 2000. It was unusual indeed for an unknown House candidate to be feted at an event that raised one hundred thousand dollars, one and a half years prior to the election. Rogan's own fund-raising material warned that his campaign needed to fight off the "radical left wing movie mogul David Geffen."

As though the *Saving Private Ryan* Oscar loss were not dispiriting enough to the company, Jeffrey Katzenberg's lawsuit against Disney distracted many people at DreamWorks, causing business there to slow substantially. The lawsuit, now in its third year, was an ugly affair, especially once the trial began. On the stand one day, Disney chairman Michael Eisner was forced to admit he had probably said of Katzenberg, "I hate the little midget."

Complicating the studio's problems in 1999 was a cash crunch. The studio had not properly planned enough movie releases for the year. As a result, there was little money coming in, prompting the partners to issue cautionary directives about expenditures. The studio explained that business was expected to improve in 2000, when a complete slate of pictures would be released over the course of the year. Operational costs and overhead, including salary expenses for a staff that now ran to sixteen hundred employees, were far higher than those at any of David Geffen's previous businesses.

Before long, DreamWorks was rocked by another major setback. After nearly four years of haggling, the company announced that it had abandoned plans to build its much-hyped film studio at Playa Vista. The project had languished for years because of personal and business differences between the studio and Playa Vista's owners. The differences had seemed to be resolved, however, and in April 1999 Dream-Works completed its purchase of forty-seven acres at Playa Vista for twenty million dollars. But then the studio was unable to raise conventional bank financing to fund construction. DreamWorks backed out of the project, officially citing rising construction costs and a changing real-estate market.

Geffen, Spielberg, Katzenberg, and Paul Allen were to have put up a collective forty million dollars of the projected costs on Playa Vista themselves. They could have solved the financing problems by putting up millions more themselves, but they decided against contributing more of their own money. In announcing that it had killed the deal, DreamWorks said it planned to examine other opportunities, including possibly expanding the site of its animation facilities in Glendale.

The end of the Playa Vista talks fired a new round of speculation that DreamWorks might merge with or acquire Seagram's Universal studio. The deal made sense for both parties; following the PolyGram acquisition, Edgar Bronfman had transformed Universal into a giant music company, sold off most of Universal's TV operations to Barry Diller, and had yet to find a winning movie-production strategy. For Dream-Works, buying Universal's back lot and film library would give it the soundstages it needed, while allowing Spielberg to stay in his familiar Amblin headquarters. Geffen and his colleagues, however, issued strong denials that any acquisition or merger plan was in the works, maintaining the oft-repeated strategy that DreamWorks planned to grow from the inside.

Katzenberg's lawsuit with Disney, meanwhile, was nearing a de-

nouement. Geffen, who had tried numerous times to broker a settlement directly with Michael Eisner, finally made some headway in June
1999. He and Stanley Gold, a longtime Disney board member who was
close to Eisner, began having discussions. The two had many conversations and finally, on July 5, at Geffen's beach house, reached an agreement. "It's the perfect definition of a settlement," Geffen told reporters.
"Both parties felt they didn't get what they wanted. Disney paid more
than it wanted, and Jeffrey got less than he wanted."

With the lawsuit behind them, DreamWorks was able to once again
focus its energy on creating and building its business. As the company
celebrated its fifth anniversary, the company was still only a modest
business proposition and hardly a viable one at that. Although the
closely held enterprise's financial results were not made public, anyone
could see that far more money was going out the door than was coming
in. In 1999, it did not look as though DreamWorks was going to achieve
the three-hundred-million-dollar positive cash flow that Geffen had
projected a year earlier.

One major problem the company was slow to address was its
painfully low level of output in its core movie unit. Following the disappointing Oscar loss of *Saving Private Ryan,* Spielberg promised to devise a plan to ramp up production to compete with other studios, which
release between fifteen and twenty pictures a year. In 1999, Dream-
Works had only six live-action pictures on its roster, far less than the
level needed to cover the operating costs of its domestic-distribution
apparatus. With such small films as *The Love Letter,* starring Kate Capshaw, and the Jan de Bont horror picture *The Haunting,* the studio was
not a major competitor during the critical summer-movie season. In
the fall, the studio finally had another critical and box-office winner in
American Beauty, a black comedy starring Kevin Spacey and Annette
Bening.

DreamWorks' TV unit and its record company were also underper-
formers. The music unit, for its part, had posted weak results, with critically acclaimed but only marginally selling records by new acts such as

Rufus Wainwright, Elliott Smith, and a group called Buckcherry. There were some interesting albums in the pipeline, though, and supporters reminded the naysayers that even Geffen Records had not been profitable until its seventh year.

As he approached his fifty-seventh birthday, Geffen was living the life of the movie moguls he had read about more than three decades earlier in Bosley Crowther's *Hollywood Rajah*. He even lived in one of their homes. But apart from his servants and a secretary, Geffen was usually alone in the Jack Warner house, surrounded by his breathtaking modern-art collection. Edgar Bronfman noted that for someone who said money was not important, Geffen certainly talked about it a lot.

But other friends questioned whether his focus on money had distracted him from the things that were really important in life. "What's the difference if you have one billion or two billion?" Sue Mengers asked. "The next thing is really learning how to let go and enjoy this. It's like Brando. After all that acclamation, what else do you do?"

Pessimistic about the stock market, Geffen moved much of his fortune, now estimated by *Forbes* at $2.7 billion, back into bonds. He continued to financially support his brother, Mitchell, even though they had not spoken or seen each other for nearly five years. He also paid to move his stepfather and aunt into comfortable retirement homes, but he did not have much of a relationship with them either. He rarely turned down cousins he did not know when they asked for money; he even paid for one cousin's son to attend medical school.

He continued to pursue men who were half his age and, like his other gay friends, presided over parties that seem to have been stocked with decorative young men. He hosted a thirtieth-birthday celebration for Scott Fowler, a dancer who had played on Broadway in the ill-fated musical *The Red Shoes*.

Friends surmised that Geffen was perhaps envious of the bond between Barry Diller and Diane von Furstenberg. As unconventional as the relationship was, Diller and von Furstenberg nonetheless had an enduring and committed companionship. Geffen had tried to forge such a bond with Marlo Thomas and had for a time successfully made such a connection with Bob Brassel. But now, shortly after the leather-chair debacle, even that friendship had disintegrated. There was no longer a "significant other" in Geffen's life.

Invitations to Geffen's dinner parties were coveted. During these evenings, he gathered information on his enemies and displayed an un-usual interest in their doings. On one occasion, Geffen, ever vitriolic on the subject of Michael Ovitz, went into a tirade in front of his guests, one of whom was Sean Connery, a friend of Ovitz's.

Ovitz surfaced again in Hollywood when he launched a new personal-management enterprise called Artists Management Group (AMG). Geffen made no secret of his desire to see Ovitz fail and told the well-liked manager Rick Yorn, who represented Leonardo di Caprio, to beware of any dealmaking with Ovitz. Yorn disregarded Geffen's advice, made a deal with Ovitz, and became the young star of AMG.

Geffen also continued to be hateful about Don Henley and Joni Mitchell. But his venom was still most forcefully directed against Robert Towne. Towne said that, seventeen years after *Personal Best,* he was only beginning to recover from the battle he had waged with Gef-fen. When *Premiere* magazine called Geffen seeking a quote for a Towne profile it was preparing in advance of Towne's 1998 film *Without Limits,* Geffen delighted in taking off the gloves and blasting him once again. (The film was a box-office dud.)

Even the people who considered Geffen a friend had to be willing to accept some of his brutal honesty. Cher, for example, remained friendly with Geffen, sometimes going to his house for dinner and watching a movie with him. "He tells me how stupid I am, how my life is going nowhere, and that I have less money than he thinks I should have," she said.

Geffen vacationed with his friends and especially enjoyed trips with Diller on his yacht. Like his father, Abe, who had found solace in his tiny boat out on Lake George, it seemed that one of Geffen's favorite leisure-time activities was to just sit on a boat and watch the water.

He continued to hunt for a great movie to produce and held out hope that Neil Jordan might be the one to make it for him. Geffen had produced the *Crying Game* director's last three films and had lured him to DreamWorks, encouraging him to direct a big-budget, star-driven thriller called *In Dreams*. The film, starring Annette Bening and Robert Downey, Jr., was a critical and box-office bust. Geffen also contemplated a return to Broadway, telling Mel Brooks he would like to produce a musical version of his old movie *The Producers*.

His extraordinary philanthropy continued. He accepted the post of "celebration chairman" for an enormous benefit honoring Ahmet Ertegun on the occasion of his fiftieth anniversary in the music business. Geffen was, of course, Ertegun's most successful and most famous protégé, and it only made sense that Geffen hold the honorary position.

Ertegun and Geffen had sustained a love-hate relationship that spanned three decades. Now seventy-five, Ertegun was still working at Atlantic Records as co-chairman and co-CEO, although a younger executive, Val Azzoli, was in charge. The UJA Federation of New York rented out Pier Sixty on the Hudson River for the occasion.

Geffen hated these kinds of overblown industry tributes. He fidgeted in the nearly empty ballroom as cocktails were served next door in a smaller room packed with hundreds of people in black tie. Geffen finally braved the cocktail hour but stayed for only a few moments, until he discovered that Barry Diller's new yacht was docked just outside.

Geffen, dressed in a black tuxedo, eagerly left the party and ambled onto Diller's boat, where he found his friend dressed in blue jeans. They hung out together until Andy Spahn told Geffen the dinner was about to begin. Geffen said adieu to Diller and made his way through the crowded ballroom to his place at the head table, where Ertegun and his wife, Mica, were already seated.

Joe Smith, who often served as emcee of such company events, was in charge of the microphone. After dinner, the crowd awaited speeches by such notables as Henry Kissinger and performances by such Atlantic recording stars as Anita Baker. But the first tribute was to come from David Geffen.

Geffen walked to the stage amid thunderous applause, then looked down at Ahmet and Mica at the head table. He began with an old anecdote he had told countless times before. "I once asked Ahmet how to make it in the music business. He said, 'Well, you walk very slow like this.'"

Demonstrating the technique Ertegun had shown him back in 1968, Geffen bent over and walked several steps away from the microphone. The crowd howled with laughter.

"I said, 'Huh?' 'Walk very slow like this,' he repeated." Geffen stooped over once again and took several big steps, swaying far to the right and left. Again, the crowd burst into laughter.

"I said, 'What?' And he said, 'You walk very slow, and maybe by chance you'll bump into a genius, and he'll make you rich!'"

The crowd erupted once again.

Geffen began his more serious remarks with a description he might have wished was written about himself. "The long and amazing list of talent you discovered, nurtured, and with whom you often collaborated has entertained generations, while you have remained mostly in the background," Geffen said. "Tonight the spotlight is on you. No one is more deserving, and never have a group of friends, partners, and peers been happier to pay tribute to anyone than we are tonight. I am grateful to call you a mentor and even prouder to call you a friend."

His speech finished, Geffen returned to his seat at the head table. It was the perfect opening to what was to be a star-studded event. The evening was, truly, the pinnacle of Ertegun's career, if not, in fact, his life—a moment long awaited and richly deserved. The significance of his life's work and its effect on the entire industry was obvious to everyone there that night.

Yet the considerable importance of the moment seemed to have little impact on the one person who perhaps had the most to be grateful for—a man Ertegun had groomed, advised, encouraged, and helped to build, and whose own success was but another testament to his mentor's influence.

As Sony music chief Tommy Mottola was introduced following him, Geffen rose quickly from his seat, kissed Ertegun on the cheek, dashed out the door, and did not return.

ACKNOWLEDGMENTS

This book would be a far lesser work than it is but for the contributions of Kevin Salwen, an editor at *The Wall Street Journal* who has been my most selfless and discerning mentor and critic since I joined the paper in 1986. My sister, who married Kevin in 1987, may disagree, but I would say that I was the one who benefited most when they met at a Chicago Cubs game in 1979.

I knew virtually from the moment I met her that Ann Godoff, the president and editor in chief of Random House, was the person to edit my book. With tremendous skill and grace, Ann handed me the road map that kept me on track. I am exceptionally fortunate to have had my first book in her most capable hands.

Many other people at Random House made significant contributions to *The Operator,* especially Benjamin Dreyer, Timothy Mennel, Mary Bahr, Andy Carpenter, J. K. Lambert, Lesley Oelsner, Lauren Field, Carol Schneider, Kate Niedzwiecki, and Sarah D'Imperio. Michelle Abbrecht left Random House two years ago, but she nonetheless continued to make her sage advice and friendship available to me throughout the publishing process.

I owe a tremendous debt to my friend A. Scott Berg, the author of my favorite biography, *Max Perkins: Editor of Genius.* Scott was one of the first people I called after getting the idea to write this book, and he did much to help me get it off the ground. One of the most wonderful things Scott did was introduce me to Joy Harris, who became my agent and who watched over me every step of the way.

Many people at *The Wall Street Journal* contributed in various ways to this project. Managing editor Paul Steiger supported my idea to write this book from the very beginning and never flinched as I requested extensions to my leave-of-absence agreement.

As only an expert can do, Laura Landro showed me the ropes of reporting in Hollywood, and Joanne Lipman relentlessly pushed me to aim higher. I do not know why these two women chose me to be their pupil, but I am lucky that they did.

A number of other people in the *Journal* family deserve my acknowledgment, especially Steve Sansweet, Amy Stevens, David Jefferson, David Sanford, and Robin Haynes. I am also appreciative of the help of Richard Turner, a former *Journal* colleague who is now an editor at *Newsweek;* the title of this book was his happy inspiration.

I am indebted to all the people who agreed to be interviewed for this book, but three merit special mention. David Geffen's brother, Mitchell, never refused a question and tirelessly helped me piece together the story of how his parents met in Palestine, made their way to America, and began their life in New York. Deena Volovskaya, David Geffen's aunt, a woman who embarked on an utterly new life at an age when most people are thinking about letting the clock run out, is the most courageous person I have ever known; I am thankful for the many hours she spent with me. Sonya Eichler, one of Geffen's cousins, found and shared decades-old family letters that were the foundation for my understanding of the Geffen family and David's upbringing.

I happily thank DreamWorks marketing chief Terry Press, who offered lifesaving guidance at various critical turns. Bryn Bridenthal, who ran the publicity department at Geffen Records and now does the same at Dream-Works Records, proved to be an invaluable resource, as was her associate Roy Hamm.

Priscila Giraldo, Geffen's executive assistant, proved indispensable in helping me locate many of the people I interviewed; it was always a pleasure speaking with her. Andy Spahn, who runs Geffen's charitable foundation and oversees corporate communications at DreamWorks, was similarly obliging.

For various roles played behind the scenes, I am most appreciative of Susan Sayre Batton, Susan Patricco, John Berkson, Megan Ginsberg, Robert Wollman, Stephen Paley, Joel Bernstein, Patrick Goldstein, Dave Zimmer, Maja Thomas, Baker Bloodworth, Casey Wojciechowski, Stefanie Napoli, Cheryl Boone Isaacs, Stanley Isaacs, Jeff Bennett, Larry Bloustein, and Jane Ross.

For welcoming me into their homes while I was on the road researching this book, I am thankful to Glenn Finn, Patrick Campion, and Tom Harrison. I am especially indebted to Jeffrey Seller and Joshua Lehrer, who made me feel that their home in New York was mine, and who even served up meals to help me stay in The Zone.

I also wish to thank my grandmother, Esther King, who encouraged me to dream big dreams and showed me that with hard work anything is possible.

Finally, I wish to reiterate my thanks to the people acknowledged on this book's dedication page. I could not have pulled this off without the love of my parents, Don and June King, my brother, Bob, and my sister, Joan. For that, I will forever be grateful.

NOTES AND SOURCES

Most of the information in this book is based on interviews I conducted with David Geffen and people who know him. Unless otherwise noted, all corporate stock prices given in the text were obtained from the Daily Stock Price Record as published by Standard and Poor's, a division of McGraw-Hill, New York. In addition, the chart performances of music singles are according to the pop-music charts in *Billboard* magazine, as compiled in *Joel Whitburn's Billboard Top Pop Albums 1955–1996* (Menomonee Falls, Wisc.: Record Research, 1996).

CHAPTER 1: MADAM MISCHA

3 Abraham Geffen did not scrap: Mitchell Geffen interview, November 6, 1996.

3 He stumbled into a restaurant: Deena Volovskaya interview, December 14, 1996.

5 They set sail for America: Certificate of Arrival, Batia [*sic*] Geffen, November 12, 1931, SS *Ile de France,* issued December 27, 1932, U.S. Department of Labor, Bureau of Naturalization.

5 Batya Volovskaya was born: Deena Volovskaya interview, November 23, 1996.

6 "Mother can't eat": Ibid., December 14, 1996.

6 Military conscripts on an anti-Semitic rampage: Sonya Eichler interview, January 2, 1997; David Henry Geffen (David Geffen's first cousin) interview, January 17, 1997.

7 They boarded the *Statendam:* Manifest of *Statendam,* Holland-America Line, on record at the National Archives and Records Administration, New York, N.Y. Document processed on March 22, 1906.

7 Minnie gave birth: State of Illinois, Cook County, Report of Birth, "Baby Giffin" [*sic*], July 6, 1908, 519 W. Taylor Street, Chicago.

7 Crowded by the boarders: Fourteenth Census of the United States, 1920, Department of Commerce, Bureau of the Census, January 12, 1920, on file at the National Archives and Records Administration, New York, N.Y.

7 Elias had a weakness: David Henry Geffen interview, January 7, 1997; Sonya Eichler interview, January 7, 1996.

7 Abe confided to Isidore: Mitchell Geffen interview, January 7, 1996.

8 Isidore changed his name: David Henry Geffen interview, January 17, 1997; Sonya Eichler interview, January 7, 1996.

8 Drawn to Christian Science: Felix Mendelsohn, *Mental Healing in Judaism: Its Relationship to Christian Science and Psychoanalysis* (Chicago: Jewish Gift Shop Publishers, 1936).

8 Elias and Minnie became enraged: Sonya Eichler interview, January 14, 1997.

9 Died in his mother's arms: Department of Health, City of New York, Bureau of Records, Certificate of Death, February 1, 1926.

9 Batya was a proud woman: David Geffen interview, January 16, 1997.

9 A neighbor, knowing of Batya's talent: Mitchell Geffen interview, November 6, 1996.

10 Batya fibbed and said: Petition for Citizenship, U.S. Department of Labor, Naturalization Service, U.S. District Court, Southern District, New York, N.Y., April 28, 1933; Deena Volovskaya interview, July 12, 1997.

10 She returned to the courthouse: Oath of Allegiance, U.S. Department of Labor, Naturalization Service, U.S. District Court, Southern District, New York, N.Y., August 31, 1933.

11 The force of a hurricane: Mitchell Geffen interview, November 6, 1996; Sonya Eichler interview, February 22, 1997.

11 "One in a million!": Sonya Eichler interview, January 4, 1997.

12 Young Mischa's otherwise difficult childhood: Mitchell Geffen interview, November 6, 1996.

12 "Momma had a boy": Ibid.

14 Never stifled his rambunctious behavior: Mitchell Geffen interview, November 6, 1996; Sonya Eichler interview, April 29, 1998.

14 "If you pay attention": Rose Slutsky interview, February 4, 1997.

14 "God bless you, David": Sonya Eichler interview, April 29, 1998.

14 Mount Airy, North Carolina: Mitchell Geffen interview, January 7, 1997.

15 A telegram from one of Batya's younger sisters: Deena Volovskaya interview, November 23, 1996.

CHAPTER 2: LIKE MOTHER, LIKE SON

18 "Joani is dancing": Rose Slutsky interview, February 4, 1997.

18 "This fabric has spells": Mitchell Geffen interview, February 11, 1997.

18 At a candy store: David Geffen interview, January 16, 1997.

18 "Mom's crazy": Mitchell Geffen interview, February 11, 1997.

20 But Abe bribed: Ibid., November 6, 1996.

20 Overwhelming challenge for Minnie: David Geffen interview, January 16, 1997.

20 Wearing out his teachers: Department of Health, City of New York, School Medical Record, P.S. 180, February 1950, February 1951.

21 Holiday card she had received: Rose Slutsky interview, February 4, 1997.

21 First relationship with a psychiatrist: David Geffen interview, January 16, 1997.

22 How not to get hustled: Lisa Gubernick and Peter Newcomb, "The Richest Man in Hollywood," *Forbes,* December 24, 1990.

23 *My Fair Lady*: David Geffen interview, January 16, 1997.

23 Ordering tickets to the opening: Ibid.

23 Bribed schoolteachers with show tickets: Mitchell Geffen interview, November 6, 1996.

23 Joining the CBS Record Club: David Geffen interview, January 16, 1997; Mitchell Geffen interview, November 6, 1996.

24 She called the police: Barbara Walters, "The Geffen Touch," *20/20* (ABC), November 11, 1994.

24 She put a lock: Joan Slutsky Cutler interview, February 4, 1997.

24 "We don't want David": Mitchell Geffen interview, November 6, 1996.

24 His bar mitzvah: David Geffen interview, January 16, 1997.

26 "I want to earn": Walters, "Geffen Touch."

26 "He's enterprising, thinks": Sonya Eichler, letter to Igor and Julia Geffen, September 1957.

26 "Well, Abe, he's no": David Geffen interview, January 16, 1997.

26　"You may not be very": Sonya Eichler interview, January 4, 1997.

26　Fell into the water: David Geffen interview, January 16, 1997.

26　Batya ordered her husband: Sonya Eichler, letter to Igor and Julia Geffen, September 1957.

27　So neither did they: David Geffen interview, January 16, 1997; Mitchell Geffen interview, November 6, 1996.

27　Immature and "need[ed] improvement": Board of Education, City of New York, Pupil Personnel Record in Junior H.S., P.S. 227, Shallow Junior High, September 1954, September 1955, September 1956, February 1957.

27　David secretly forged their signatures: David Geffen interview, January 16, 1997.

29　David's marks in Hebrew: Board of Education, City of New York, Pupil Personnel Records in H.S., New Utrecht High School, January 1958, June 1958.

29　DeWild did not like David: Susan DeWild Horowitz interview, April 7, 1997.

30　Call Mitchell in Texas: Mitchell Geffen interview, November 6, 1996.

30　Healthy suspicions that their father: David Geffen interview, January 16, 1997; Mitchell Geffen interview, November 6, 1996.

31　Sue was cutting class: Susan DeWild Horowitz interview, April 7, 1997.

31　Branded a liar: A. S. Appel, teacher at New Utrecht High School, in note placed in David's permanent file, November 20, 1959.

32　"Rather talkative, self-centered": Mr. Cherniss, teacher at New Utrecht High School, in "character card" placed in David's permanent file, June 22, 1959.

32　Abe went to Saint Louis: Julia Geffen, letter to Mitchell Geffen, May 7, 1960.

32　"Your dad seems": Ibid.

32　Grade average of 73.59: Board of Education, City of New York, New Utrecht High School.

34　Arriving in Hollywood: David Geffen interview, January 16, 1997.

35　She telephoned Igor: Igor Geffen, letter to Sonya Eichler, August 2, 1960.

35　He began telling people he was enrolled: David Geffen, letter to Igor and Julia Geffen, n.d. but presumed to be late 1960.

35　Santa Monica City College: David Geffen interview, January 16, 1997.

36　"David, go downstairs": Ibid.

36 "Fuck you": Ibid.

36 "You know, Mitch": Ibid.; Mitchell Geffen interview, November 4, 1996.

CHAPTER 3: RUN, SAMMY, RUN

37 David stole a Social Security death-benefit check: David Geffen interview, January 16, 1997; Mitchell Geffen interview, July 23, 1998.

38 He applied to UCLA: David Geffen interview, January 16, 1997.

38 Mitchell encouraged him to come back: Mitchell Geffen interview, November 6, 1996.

38 Mitchell learned that marrying: Mitchell Geffen letter to Batya Geffen, February 1963.

40 "You're going to be a failure": Gubernick and Newcomb, "The Richest Man in Hollywood."

40 "They're all mine": Mark Ribowsky, *He's a Rebel: The Truth About Phil Spector—Rock and Roll's Legendary Madman* (New York: E. P. Dutton, 1989), 140.

41 He met Sonny Bono: David Geffen interview, April 15, 1999.

43 "Would you like to": Ibid., January 16, 1997.

43 Crying at the ceremony: Mitchell Geffen interview, May 18, 1998.

44 Do something about his nose: David Geffen interview, February 22, 1997.

44 "Well, folks, the show": Ibid., January 16, 1997; Grover Lewis, *Academy All the Way* (San Francisco: Straight Arrow Books, 1974), 242.

45 "You should be an agent": Alixe Gordin interview, November 20, 1996.

45 "My God, this wouldn't": Lewis, *Academy All the Way,* 243.

46 "I am Phil Spector's cousin": Howard Portnoy interview, October 30, 1996.

46 "Get out of here": Dennis Paget interview, October 9, 1996.

46 Portnoy sensed his story: Howard Portnoy interview, October 30, 1996.

47 His first day would be: Employee records at the William Morris Agency, Beverly Hills, Calif.

47 Paralyzed with fear: Lewis, *Academy All the Way,* 243.

47 Mitchell agreed and drafted: Mitchell Geffen interview, November 4, 1996.

49 Smoked marijuana, he did too: David Krebs interview, July 24, 1997.

49 Geffen plotted their careers: Ibid.

50 A rather odd duck: Barry Diller interview, September 24, 1997.

50 Told Gart his plan: Herb Gart interview, October 28, 1996.

51 "Who?" Litke asked: Ibid.

51 Romancing Nat Lefkowitz: Sally Lefkowitz interview, September 30, 1996.

51 "Moral instincts with ethical imperatives": *Daily Variety,* September 7, 1983.

52 Lied on his employment application: Scott Shukat interview, October 3, 1996.

53 "I saw this actor": Ibid.

53 Claimed to be Jerry Rubin: John Hartmann interview, November 6, 1996.

54 Peddling marijuana in the mailroom: Jeff Wald interview, October 22, 1996.

54 Larry Kurzon was initially: Larry Kurzon interview, October 1, 1997.

54 "David, no one's there": Elliot Roberts interview, November 11, 1996.

55 "David, put that away": Larry Kurzon interview, October 1, 1997.

55 "If you wake me": Scott Shukat interview, October 3, 1996.

56 "Look, if you just give": Ben Griefer interview, October 7, 1996.

57 His mother had breast cancer: Mitchell Geffen interview, November 4, 1996; David Geffen maintains he did not say this.

57 Griefer was irate: Sally Lefkowitz interview, September 30, 1996.

CHAPTER 4: ROCK 'N' ROLL

59 Amazed and amused by Geffen's: Owen Laster interview, October 10, 1996.

60 Signed Jordan Christopher: David Geffen interview, October 25, 1996.

60 Signed Carmen Mathews: Marty Litke interview, October 28, 1996.

61 A hippie named Lorne Michaels: Lorne Michaels interview, October 24, 1997.

62 "You know, I'm homosexual": John Hartmann interview, November 6, 1996.

62 "Oh, David, you don't": Larry Kurzon interview, October 1, 1997.

63 Told him to simply check "yes": David Geffen interview, February 27, 1997.

63 Jerry Brandt was not: Jerry Brandt interview, October 9, 1996.

63 He had been fired: Frank Rose, *The Agency: William Morris and the Hidden History of Show Business* (New York: HarperCollins, 1995), 268–70.

64 "Listen, jerk, you're twenty-two": Jerry Brandt interview, October 9, 1996.

64 "Animals? William Morris doesn't": Jeff Wald interview, October 22, 1996.

64 It was a miracle: Rose, *Agency,* 280.

65 Hundred-dollar-a-week raise: Owen Laster interview, October 10, 1996.

66 Meledandri was an elegant shop: Chris Meledandri interview, August 10, 1998.

66 Geffen began to weep: Elliot Roberts interview, November 11, 1996.

67 Meeting with Paul Simon: Scott Shukat interview, August 24, 1998.

67 Geffen signed the Association: Owen Laster interview, October 10, 1996; David Geffen interview, October 11, 1996.

67 A hot stock tip: Scott Shukat interview, August 24, 1998; Steve Leber interview, October 2, 1996.

68 On July 28, Klein: "Two New York Men Buy 56% Interest of Cameo-Parkway," *The Wall Street Journal,* July 31, 1967.

68 "I can't believe that": Barry Diller interview, September 24, 1997.

68 *The Carol Burnett Show:* Kenny Solms interview, May 5, 1997.

68 Awed by Geffen's meteoric rise: Joel Dean interview, January 21, 1998.

69 "Well, what do you think": Elliot Roberts interview, November 11, 1996.

72 Binder invited Geffen to dinner: Steve Binder interview, October 18, 1996.

73 Mogull could not relate: Artie Mogull interview, October 25, 1996.

73 Nothing short of a disaster: William Kloman, "Laura Nyro: She's the Hippest—and Maybe the Hottest?" *The New York Times,* October 6, 1968.

73 "What did you think?": Artie Mogull interview, October 25, 1996.

CHAPTER 5: TUNA FISH MUSIC

76 She had been mistreated: David Geffen interview, February 27, 1997.

76 Lighting an empty tampon: Steve Binder interview, October 18, 1996.

78 But the publishing arrangement: Steve Leber interview, October 2, 1996.

78 Decked out in black velvet: Michael Thomas, "Laura Nyro: A Bronx Ophelia in Black Velvet, a Mysterious Songwriter, She Is the Suavest and Fiercest New Singer in Pop Music," *Eye,* May 1969.

78 Loaned her money: Robert Windeler, "Laura Nyro: New Queen of Pop Music," *Entertainment World,* December 19, 1969.

79 He also arranged for his accountant: Stephen Paley interview, December 4, 1996.

79 "Don't be such a *chazzer*": Ibid.

79 He first experimented with acid: David Geffen interview, February 27, 1997.

80 Barovick fired off a telegram: Telegram to Celestial Music Corp. from Barovick, Konecky, and Bomser, September 6, 1967.

80 Went to see Jerry Schoenbaum: David Geffen interview, February 27, 1997.

80 Davis had been to the Monterey Pop: Clive Davis interview, December 6, 1996.

81 "I've seen the kind": Clive Davis, *Clive: Inside the Record Business* (New York: William Morrow, 1975), 97–98.

81 Paley snapped comical shots: Stephen Paley interview, December 20, 1996.

83 Leber seriously considered Geffen's offer: Steve Leber interview, October 2, 1996.

83 "Like my chair": Charlie Calello interview, January 9, 1997.

84 "There are two songs": Bones Howe interview, March 11, 1997.

86 Never in his long career: Clive Davis interview, December 6, 1996.

87 Slick, bouncy covers: *Up-Up and Away: The Fifth Dimension—The Definitive Collection,* liner notes (Arista Records, 1997).

87 One thousand dollars a week: Lewis, *Academy All the Way,* 244.

88 Ashley went to work: Ted Ashley interview, December 12, 1996.

88 Ashley sold his agency: Connie Bruck, *Master of the Game: Steve Ross and the Creation of Time Warner* (New York: Simon and Schuster, 1994), 48.

90 "If the bird ain't happy": Fred Goodman, *The Mansion on the Hill: Dylan, Young, Geffen, Springsteen, and the Head-on Collision of Rock and Commerce* (New York: Times Books, 1997), 84.

91 But the real clincher: Todd Schiffman interview, July 30, 1998.

91 "I don't give a shit": Ibid.

92 "We're going to get you": Ibid.
93 Begged him to take her home: Sandy Gallin interview, October 6, 1997.
94 "I think I'm going to": Bones Howe interview, March 11, 1997.
94 "I really understand what every": Ellen Sander interview, May 25, 1997.
94 "I have never had sex": David Geffen interview, May 22, 1997.
94 "I'm afraid that I'm gay": Ellen Sander interview, May 25, 1997.
96 The two did wind up having intercourse: Ibid.; David Geffen interview, May 22, 1997.

CHAPTER 6: MAGIC IN LAUREL CANYON

97 He and Todd Schiffman signed the Doors: Todd Schiffman interview, July 30, 1998.
98 "I really like it here": Sandy Gallin interview, October 6, 1997.
98 Davis showed some interest: David Geffen interview, January 16, 1997.
100 Crosby and Stephen Stills were harmonizing: David Crosby interview, March 16, 1998; Stephen Stills interview, June 7, 1997; Graham Nash interview, February 11, 1997.
100 "Sing that again": Dave Zimmer and Henry Diltz, *Crosby, Stills & Nash: The Authorized Biography* (New York: St. Martin's Press, 1984), 72–75.
101 Roberts did not know how: Elliot Roberts interview, November 11, 1996.
102 "You're fired!": David Geffen interview, February 27, 1997.
103 "We're in a shark pool": David Crosby interview, March 16, 1998.
104 "I don't think I": John Gibson, "David Geffen: It's the Artist, Not the Company," *Record World*, September 2, 1972.
104 "Is this what you listen": Lee Houskeeper interview, September 2, 1998.
104 Geffen ran to the phone: Ibid.
105 *Cashbox*, a music-industry trade: Alan Rindi, "Ashley's Geffen Opens Disk, Mgmt Complex," *Cashbox*, February 8, 1969.
107 "Get the fuck outta here!": Jerry Wexler interview, February 2, 1997.
107 "My God, they're animals": Lewis, *Academy All the Way*, 245.
107 Ahmet Ertegun was born in Turkey: Justine Picardie and Dorothy Wade, *Atlantic and the Godfathers of Rock and Roll* (London: Fourth Estate, 1993), 13–19.

108 "Well, you walk very slow": Lewis, *Academy All the Way,* 251.

109 Ertegun laid out a new plan: Ahmet Ertegun interview, December 12, 1996.

109 "Absolutely no": Lewis, *Academy All the Way,* 246.

110 "They're going to be huge!": David Geffen interview, March 3, 1997.

111 "I don't understand": Walters, "Geffen Touch."

111 There was a blinding blizzard: Lee Houskeeper interview, September 2, 1998.

112 "Say that you just told Laura": Ibid.

113 The sessions went smoothly: Zimmer and Diltz, *Crosby, Stills & Nash,* 81–84.

CHAPTER 7: MOGUL IN TRAINING

115 *Billboard* put the story: Mike Gross, "Geffen to Bow Label; Acts to Share in Profit," *Billboard,* May 24, 1969.

116 Swimming in the pool: Wayne Weisbart interview, January 23, 1998.

118 "We ought to add Neil": Zimmer and Diltz, *Crosby, Stills & Nash,* 92–93.

118 Roberts refused to be the one: Elliot Roberts interview, November 12, 1996.

119 "Kind of like a family/love thing": Lewis, *Academy All the Way,* 246.

120 A frightened Melcher and Bergen: David Geffen interview, March 19, 1997.

121 Geffen was anxious as he read: Barnard L. Collier, "300,000 at Folk-Rock Fair Camp Out in a Sea of Mud," *The New York Times,* August 17, 1969.

122 "Thank you": Zimmer and Diltz, *Crosby, Stills & Nash,* 100.

122 Something of a modern miracle: Ibid., 101–2.

123 Stills continued to tinker: Ibid., 111.

125 "There will never be a moment": David Geffen interview, February 27, 1997.

126 Davis and Geffen shook hands: Lewis, *Academy All the Way,* 247–48; Davis, *Clive,* 100.

126 Rivers agreed to sell him his house: Johnny Rivers interview, October 31, 1997.

127 The office directly adjacent to Fields's: Jeff Berg interview, August 14, 1998.

128 "Control it from both ends": Lewis, *Academy All the Way,* 247.

128 "You're really interested in a *career?*": Jimmy Webb interview, September 18, 1997.

129 "You know, what I admire": Sandy Gallin interview, October 6, 1997.

129 "One of the worst music agents": Joel Dean interview, January 21, 1998.

130 "David, read the note": Dodie Smith interview, November 1, 1996.

CHAPTER 8: SEEKING ASYLUM

131 "He's an agent": Jackson Browne interview, January 15, 1997.

132 "OK, I'll manage you": Ibid.

134 A concert in Denver: Zimmer and Diltz, *Crosby, Stills & Nash,* 125–27.

135 "Obnoxious, loud, demanding": David Crosby and Carl Gottlieb, *Long Time Gone: The Autobiography of David Crosby* (New York: Doubleday, 1988), 146.

135 "It's taking so long": Lewis, *Academy All the Way,* 248.

136 A meeting with Streisand: Richard Perry interview, May 9, 1997.

136 Geffen told Nyro to tell Streisand: Ellen Sander interview, May 25, 1997.

137 "It's terribly unfair": Lewis, *Academy All the Way,* 248.

138 Bought a Rolls-Royce Corniche: George W. S. Trow, Jr., "Eclectic, Reminiscent, Amused, Fickle, Perverse—A Profile of Ahmet Ertegun," *The New Yorker,* May 29, 1978.

138 "You should buy a painting": Ahmet Ertegun interview, December 12, 1996.

140 In Davis's office: Jackson Browne interview, January 15, 1997.

141 "Ahmet, look, I'm trying": David Geffen interview, March 19, 1997.

141 "You know what, David": Ahmet Ertegun interview, December 12, 1996.

141 Geffen's first thought: David Geffen interview, March 19, 1997.

142 He thought the deal: Alan Cohen interview, April 8, 1997.

142 "Asking me to come work here": Sandy Gallin interview, October 6, 1997.

143 The label was chintzy: David Krebs interview, July 24, 1997.

143 The venture was too risky: Dick Asher interview, August 29, 1997.

143 The real advantage: David Geffen interview, March 19, 1997.

144 "Gee, I don't know": Crosby and Gottlieb, *Long Time Gone,* 145.

145   An East Coast blonde: Leslie Morris interview, March 4, 1997.

145   Curt and chilly: Gary Gersh interview, October 22, 1997.

145   Loddengaard's softer side: Harlan Goodman interview, November 19, 1996.

145   Chocolate-colored shag carpet: Lewis, *Academy All the Way*, 239–40.

146   "There's no winning": David Geffen interview, March 19, 1997.

146   By the time Browne's first album: Lewis, *Academy All the Way*, 251.

147   "Direction" rather than "management": Gibson, "David Geffen."

147   Ample supply of marijuana: Elliot Roberts interview, November 12, 1996.

148   "I got it": Ibid., November 11, 1996.

149   "David, I have some terrible": Lewis, *Academy All the Way*, 248–49; Davis, *Clive*, 101.

150   Nyro's contract with Columbia was "over": Tony Lawrence, "New Asylum Label Readies First Product: Laura Nyro and Joni Mitchell Signed, Reveals Manager–Turned–Label Chief Geffen," *Record World*, July 31, 1971.

CHAPTER 9: HEARTBREAK

152   Geffen told him that Cat Stevens: Prince Rupert Loewenstein interview, August 14, 1997.

152   Geffen suggested that: Stephen Stills interview, June 7, 1997.

152   "Their last tour": Trow, "Eclectic, Reminiscent, Amused, Fickle, Perverse."

152   "You're not quite sure": Prince Rupert Loewenstein interview, August 14, 1997.

152   "What is it that you": Lewis, *Academy All the Way*, 254–55.

155   Though Ertegun still admired him: Trow, "Eclectic, Reminiscent, Amused, Fickle, Perverse."

155   Clive Davis was furious: Davis, *Clive*, 102.

155   He was in Los Angeles: Lee Houskeeper interview, September 2, 1998.

155   Geffen flew into a rage: Richard Chiaro interview, February 19, 1997.

155   Davis reasoned: Davis, *Clive*, 102.

155   Caught in the middle: Richard Chiaro interview, February 19, 1997.

156   "I want to stay": Lewis, *Academy All the Way*, 249.

157   Agreed to settle with Mogull: Artie Mogull interview, October 25, 1996.

157 He began to sob: David Geffen interview, February 27, 1997; Elliot Roberts interview, November 21, 1996.

158 "David Crosby is in a band": Goodman, *Mansion on the Hill,* 230.

159 A performance at Disneyland: Marc Eliot, *To the Limit: The Untold Story of the Eagles* (New York: Little, Brown, 1998), 60.

160 Geffen offered to pay: David Geffen interview, March 19, 1997; Eliot, *To the Limit,* 68.

160 Sent them to his dentist: Goodman, *Mansion on the Hill,* 233.

160 "I want to keep Asylum Records": Irving Azoff interview, April 21, 1998.

161 "I heard the tape": Ibid.

162 Pelted Geffen with eggs: John Gibson, "The Coast," *Record World,* July 1, 1972.

162 Geffen had a tussle: Jerry Heller interview, March 12, 1998.

162 "I don't have the burden": Lewis, *Academy All the Way,* 258.

163 Twelve million records: Ibid., 239.

163 "Not going to listen": Ibid., 253–54.

163 "Not going to carry dope": Crosby and Gottlieb, *Long Time Gone,* 227–28.

164 Wanted to get married: Lewis, *Academy All the Way,* 257.

164 *The Dating Game:* David Geffen interview, February 27, 1997.

165 "I don't think I'll": Ned Doheny interview, March 17, 1997.

165 Dined at Por Favor: Todd Schiffman interview, July 30, 1998. David Geffen said on December 18, 1996, that he had discovered the painting stolen when he returned home from the concert.

166 "Where can I get in touch": Ibid.

166 "Not only do I": Ahmet Ertegun interview, December 12, 1996.

CHAPTER 10: BIG DEAL

167 Ertegun hosted a party: "Atlantic Hosts Asylum Fete," *Record World,* March 11, 1972.

167 "We're going to be partners": Ahmet Ertegun interview, December 12, 1996.

167 "My favorite restaurant": Jerry Greenberg interview, January 30, 1997.

168 "Neil's next album is called *Harvest*": Ibid.

168 "I don't *know* Carole King": Jackson Browne interview, January 15, 1997.

170 "That's cool. Is it done?": Ibid.

171 Netting three million dollars: Julie Baumgold, "The Winning of Cher—And Some Other Major Achievements of David Geffen," *Esquire,* February 1975.

171 Eagles off to London: Eliot, *To the Limit,* 75–76.

172 "Number one in six weeks": John Gibson, "The Coast," *Record World,* May 6, 1972.

173 "Very close mouthed last week": Ibid., September 30, 1972.

173 Promise of an equity stake: John Hartmann interview, November 6, 1996.

174 "It's easy in music": Goodman, *Mansion on the Hill,* 232.

174 Warren Beatty and his girlfriend: Warren Beatty interview, July 7, 1997.

175 Police arrested Christopher Cornett: "Stolen $36,000 Picasso Recovered," *Los Angeles Times,* August 24, 1972.

175 "Take the picture back": Ahmet Ertegun interview, December 12, 1996.

176 Terrified that the band: David Geffen interview, March 19, 1997.

177 Robert Hilburn weighed in: Robert Hilburn, "A Rise from Mailroom to Record Asylum," *Los Angeles Times,* September 5, 1972.

177 *Record World,* in a story: Gibson, "It's the Artist, Not the Company."

177 Geffen reached for a cigarette: Jay Emmett interview, July 15, 1997.

177 "You can have it": David Geffen interview, March 19, 1997.

177 A conflict of interest: Goodman, *Mansion on the Hill,* 241.

178 Never again have to worry: David Geffen interview, March 19, 1997.

178 *Newsweek* weighed in: "Golden Boy," *Newsweek,* November 20, 1972.

179 "This is a huge mistake": Elliot Roberts interview, November 12, 1996.

179 Loudest complaints came from the Eagles: Irving Azoff interview, April 21, 1998.

181 Linda Ronstadt and others: Peter Asher interview, April 9, 1997.

181 "Nothing is going to change": Elliot Roberts interview, November 12, 1996.

181 Put the corset shop: Mitchell Geffen interview, August 3, 1998.

181 Sam helped Batya pack: Sam Sandler interview, July 12, 1997.

182 Within a few years: Deena Volovskaya interview, December 14, 1996.

CHAPTER 11: VACATION IN FRANCE

183   Net worth was about twelve million: David Sheff, "Playboy Interview: David Geffen," *Playboy,* September 1994.

183   Wearing Italian loafers: Lewis, *Academy All the Way,* 239–40.

184   The properties he purchased: David Geffen interview, May 22, 1997.

184   He was in London: Sheff, "Playboy Interview."

184   Rattled a pair of balls: Lewis, *Academy All the Way,* 249.

184   "I'm not happy": Sheff, "Playboy Interview."

184   Warren Beatty grew concerned: David Geffen interview, May 22, 1997; Warren Beatty interview, July 7, 1997.

184   Five-day-a-week analysis: Baumgold, "The Winning of Cher."

184   His relationship with his mother: Cher interview, April 17, 1997.

186   "The one thing I despise": Lewis, *Academy All the Way,* 256–57.

186   Decided he wanted to be straight: Sheff, "Playboy Interview."

186   "It's something I'm working on": Lewis, *Academy All the Way,* 257.

186   "My emotion is spent": Davis, *Clive,* 102.

186   Dispute with Doug Weston: David Geffen interview, March 19, 1997; Elliot Roberts interview, November 11, 1996.

187   A fresh coat: Lewis, *Academy All the Way,* 239.

187   Geffen continued to play: Irving Azoff interview, April 21, 1998.

187   Breaking under the strain: Elliot Roberts interview, November 12, 1996.

188   "Let me tell you": Harlan Goodman interview, November 19, 1996.

188   Anger the Eagles felt: Eliot, *To the Limit,* 92.

188   *Desperado,* was a commercial failure: Irving Azoff interview, April 21, 1998.

189   On a trip: Robbie Robertson interview, October 24, 1997.

190   Browne broke it off: David Crosby interview, March 16, 1998.

192   Robertson and the Band: Robbie Robertson interview, October 24, 1997.

194   Interested in learning French: David Geffen interview, May 22, 1997.

195   "Let me just put": Robbie Robertson interview, October 24, 1997.

195   Geffen whined about the stock: Alan Cohen interview, April 8, 1997.

196   Raise his salary to one million: David Geffen interview, April 24, 1997.

197 Loddengaard packed up: Steven Baker interview, March 24, 1997.

197 It was a promise: Jac Holzman interview, April 23, 1997.

198 The artists' best interests: Elliot Roberts interview, November 12, 1996.

198 The situation was complicated: Goodman, *Mansion on the Hill*, 241–42.

198 "Yeah, OK": John Hartmann interview, November 6, 1996.

198 "If you go with him": Goodman, *Mansion on the Hill*, 242.

198 Irving Azoff, meanwhile: Irving Azoff interview, April 21, 1998.

198 Poco had just fired: John Hartmann interview, November 19, 1996.

199 "This guy is going": David Geffen interview, March 19, 1997.

CHAPTER 12: "I GOT YOU BABE"

201 "I made more enemies": Robert Hilburn, "Roxy: Pop-Rock Takes a Step Uptown," *Los Angeles Times*, September 22, 1973.

202 Geffen, with the Dylans: Robbie Robertson interview, October 24, 1997.

203 "How can he live": Cher interview, April 17, 1997.

204 Blowup at the Flamingo: Sonny Bono, *And the Beat Goes On* (New York: Pocket Books, 1991), 197–201.

204 Cher's only escape: Cher interview, April 17, 1997.

206 "This is very interesting": Robbie Robertson interview, October 24, 1997.

206 Despite her attraction to him: Cher interview, April 17, 1997.

206 "I fucked her countless times": David Geffen interview, May 22, 1997.

206 "I was the first": Cher interview, April 17, 1997.

206 Having an affair: Bono, *And the Beat Goes On*, 207.

207 Knew which gas stations: Steven Baker interview, March 25, 1997.

207 To help Cher cope: David Geffen interview, June 12, 1997.

207 Flew into a rage: Cher interview, April 17, 1997.

209 He knew Tony Fantozzi: David Geffen interview, June 12, 1997.

209 Ross put together: Joe Smith interview, March 27, 1997.

211 Geffen turned his fury: David Horowitz interview, April 9, 1997.

212 Clive Davis had been fired: Fredric Dannen, *Hit Men* (New York: Times Books, 1990), 104, 107, 118.

212 "Columbia doesn't appreciate you ... contract for only one album": David Braun interview, May 7, 1997.

213 Geffen had won the headlines: "Dylan Forms Label; Elektra/Asylum to Distribute," *Record World*, December 15, 1973.

214 Geffen's ego swelled: Jerry Wexler interview, February 2, 1997.

215 "We can't have this!": Joe Smith interview, March 27, 1997.

216 "Tell Glenn he doesn't get": Eliot, *To the Limit,* 101.

217 Geffen had grown nervous: Ibid., 106.

217 "I'm not going to": Irving Azoff interview, April 21, 1998.

218 Rehearsals were painful: Bono, *And the Beat Goes On,* 210–12.

219 Divorce papers charging: *Cher Bono v. Salvatore "Sonny" Bono,* Case WEC32438, filed February 20, 1974, in Superior Court of the State of California, County of Los Angeles.

219 Bono next dropped a thirteen-million-dollar lawsuit: *Salvatore "Sonny" Bono v. David Geffen,* Case WEC32438, Cross-Complaint for Inducing Breach of and Interference with Contractual and Business Relations, filed March 8, 1974, in Superior Court of the State of California, County of Los Angeles.

219 Geffen was talking to CBS: David Geffen interview, June 12, 1997.

CHAPTER 13: "THE TIMES THEY ARE A-CHANGIN'"

221 "Will you stop jerking off": Sue Mengers interview, May 2, 1997.

221 Geffen wasted no time: David Geffen interview, April 15, 1999.

222 Cher and Geffen went to Aspen: Warren Beatty interview, July 7, 1997; Lou Adler interview, April 29, 1997.

222 "You know, I have": Charles Gwathmey interview, July 28, 1997.

224 Tried to clean her up: Gavin Dillard interview, January 25, 1999.

224 "I wish I had been born": Steve Tisch interview, June 11, 1997.

224 But one day: Cher interview, April 17, 1997.

225 She had suspected: Goldstein, "David Geffen: The *Rolling Stone* Interview," *Rolling Stone,* April 29, 1992.

225 Cher was eager: Cher interview, April 17, 1997.

225 "We want to thank": Robbie Robertson interview, October 24, 1997; Louie Kemp interview, June 6, 1997.

226 "I can't tell you": Robbie Robertson interview, October 24, 1997.

227 Mo Ostin, who was: Mo Ostin interview, September 12, 1997.

227 The room was decorated: Robert Hilburn, "Frosting on Geffen's Cake," *Los Angeles Times,* February 24, 1974.

227 The forecast was right: "Geffen's Golden Touch," *Time,* February 25, 1974.

228 Joni Mitchell's affection: Elliot Roberts interview, November 12, 1996.

228 A year earlier: Lewis, *Academy All the Way,* 258.

228 Other people were angry: Richard Perry interview, May 9, 1997.

228 One reason for Dylan's: David Braun interview, May 7, 1997.

229 Robertson felt a moral: Robbie Robertson interview, October 24, 1997.

229 Unbeknownst to Geffen: David Braun interview, May 7, 1997.

230 "David, we're not going": Ibid.; Mel Posner interview, March 31, 1997.

230 "You have to force": David Braun interview, May 7, 1997.

230 "OK, sweetheart": Cher interview, April 17, 1997.

231 "You can't change your mind": Robbie Robertson interview, October 24, 1997.

231 Braun told Geffen that he: David Braun interview, May 7, 1997.

232 He soon got the idea: Ahmet Ertegun interview, May 18, 1997.

233 News of the merger: "Atlantic, Elektra-Asylum Announce Merger of Firms; Ahmet Ertegun, David Geffen, Jerry Wexler to Key Posts," *Record World,* July 6, 1974.

233 "I'll take one in": Baumgold, "The Winning of Cher."

233 What Geffen did not realize: Jerry Wexler interview, February 2, 1997; Jerry Greenberg interview, January 30, 1997.

234 They did not like David Geffen: Ahmet Ertegun interview, May 18, 1997.

234 "How can you do": Ibid.

234 Cher missed living: Cher interview, April 17, 1997; Glenn Lovell, "Sonny and Cher's Desperate Tug-of-War for Their Daughter," *National Enquirer,* September 1974.

CHAPTER 14: HAMMER AND NAILS

237 Cher refused to deal: Bono, *And the Beat Goes On,* 215–16.

238 Batya read the tabloids: Deena Volovskaya provided the news clippings that Batya had saved.

238 Cher had been receiving: Lovell, "Sonny and Cher's Desperate Tug-of-War for Their Daughter."

239 Bringing armed guards into his studio: Ribowsky, *He's a Rebel,* 270–71.

239 Geffen told Cher he thought Spector was a lunatic: David Geffen interview, January 16, 1997; Cher interview, April 17, 1997.

239 "Like Cher was delivering": Mark Bego, *Cher!* (New York: Pocket Books, 1986), 81.

240 Spector grew so irritated: David Geffen interview, January 16, 1997; Cher interview, April 17, 1997.

240 Geffen met with Schlatter: George Schlatter interview, May 9, 1997.

241 With the custody battle: Cher interview, April 17, 1997.

241 The night before Cher: Alan Markfield, "Exclusive Interview with Cher: Sonny Begged Me to Return, but I Refused," *National Enquirer,* October 22, 1974.

241 She had been having an affair: Sheff, "Playboy Interview."

241 Throughout her four-week vacation: Cher interview, April 17, 1997.

242 The show, meanwhile: George Schlatter interview, May 9, 1997.

243 One who came to him: Anthony Haden-Guest, *The Last Party: Studio 54, Disco, and the Culture of the Night* (New York: William Morrow, 1997), 138–39.

244 It was not the last time: David Geffen interview, June 12, 1997.

244 "I want to read": Ted Ashley interview, December 13, 1996.

245 Like a spoiled child: Manny Gerard interview, July 23, 1997.

245 Mel Posner, Elektra/Asylum's: Mel Posner interview, March 31, 1997.

245 It soon became clear: George Schlatter interview, May 9, 1997.

246 Geffen and Cher were still: Digby Wolfe interview, May 28, 1997.

247 "You know what, Dave": Cher interview, April 17, 1997.

248 "I'll speak to you later": David Geffen interview, June 12, 1997.

248 "If you see me": Cher interview, April 17, 1997.

248 Geffen turned and flung: David Geffen interview, June 12, 1997.

248 "Come on, Tatum": Cher interview, April 17, 1997.

CHAPTER 15: GETTING "IT"

249 Geffen was so paralyzed: David Geffen interview, May 22, 1997.

249 "I think he's going": Mitchell Geffen interview, November 6, 1996.

249 "I've traded one short": Richard Schickel, "Cher—Cover Story," *Time,* March 17, 1975.

249 He sobbed to Warren Beatty: David Geffen interview, May 22, 1997.

250 When it seemed like: Ahmet Ertegun interview, December 12, 1996.

250 The story was headlined: Baumgold, "The Winning of Cher."

253 In early 1975: Barry Diller interview, September 24, 1997.

254 That summer, Geffen at: David Geffen interview, March 19, 1997.

254 By September 1975: Barry Diller interview, September 24, 1997.

254 At the airport: Jeffrey Katzenberg interview, September 17, 1997; Robert Sam Anson, "Geffen Ungloved," *Los Angeles,* July 1995.

254 When they reached Manhattan: Barry Diller interview, September 24, 1997.

255 Peter Guber, the production: David Geffen interview, May 22, 1997.

256 The first session: Richard Perry interview, May 9, 1997.

257 "Everything is fine": Cher interview, April 17, 1997.

257 Ross insisted that: Mel Posner interview, March 31, 1997.

258 He called Paula Weinstein: Paula Weinstein interview, June 4, 1997.

259 There was only one problem: Ibid.

259 Ashley and his girlfriend: Ted Ashley interview, December 13, 1996; Joyce Ashley interview, June 23, 1998.

259 Even the toughest: Terry Semel interview, June 27, 1997.

261 Frank Wells was relieved: Ibid.

261 Even as Geffen: David Geffen interview, March 29, 1997.

261 The movie studio: A. D. Murphy, "WB Reshuffles Executive Deck," *Daily Variety,* December 10, 1975.

CHAPTER 16: THE PICTURE BUSINESS

263 Marlo Thomas was living: Marlo Thomas interview, July 29, 1997.

267 Geffen reached back: Albert Brooks interview, April 22, 1997.

267 Meanwhile, Warren Beatty told: Warren Beatty interview, July 7, 1997; David Geffen interview, April 19, 1997; Paula Weinstein interview, June 4, 1997.

267 From the very beginning: Stephen Woolley interview, January 12, 1999.

268 But Geffen and everyone: Guy McElwaine interview, May 22, 1997.

269 "You didn't tell me": Paula Weinstein interview, June 4, 1997.

269 "How can you not": Marlo Thomas interview, July 29, 1997.

270 Despite the frustrations: David Geffen interview, May 3, 1997.

270 Called Steven Spielberg: Steven Spielberg interview, November 18, 1998.

271 The raid on Entebbe: Terry Semel interview, June 27, 1997; Guy McElwaine interview, May 22, 1997; Paula Weinstein interview, June 4, 1997.

271 Joyce Easton, Ashley's girlfriend: David Geffen interview, May 22, 1997; Terry Semel interview, June 27, 1997. Joyce Ashley, in inter-

view on June 23, 1998, said she does not recall this incident taking place.

271 Ashley began inviting John Calley: Paula Weinstein interview, June 4, 1997; Terry Semel interview, June 27, 1997.

272 "I want everyone": Guy McElwaine interview, May 22, 1997.

273 Geffen jumped onto the other: Terry Semel interview, June 27, 1997.

273 "I don't have to": Guy McElwaine interview, May 22, 1997. Ted Ashley, for his part, disputed that there was any such falling-out and said on December 13, 1996, "We've never had a harsh syllable."

CHAPTER 17: HEALTH SCARE

275 The morning after: Terry Semel interview, June 27, 1997.

275 Gossip reporter Rona Barrett: Paula Weinstein interview, June 4, 1997.

276 Albert Brooks had to: Albert Brooks interview, April 22, 1997.

276 Ashley and Frank Wells: Warren Beatty interview, July 7, 1997; Terry Semel interview, June 27, 1997.

277 Continued to pay Linda: David Geffen interview, August 11, 1997.

277 The lesson he had learned: Paul Simon interview, June 15, 1998.

278 Simon and David Braun: Ibid.

278 Geffen, who said he did not: Bill Holdship, "The Illusionist: David Geffen on the Mystique of Power, the Burden of Fame, and All Those Nasty Rumors," *BAM,* April 19, 1991.

278 Even while Geffen's professional: Marlo Thomas interview, July 29, 1997.

278 Geffen had a fling: Gavin Dillard interview, January 25, 1997.

279 By February: Marlo Thomas interview, July 29, 1997.

279 In the wake: Martin Peretz interview, August 4, 1997.

280 One of Geffen's favorites: Carrie Fisher interview, November 3, 1997.

280 "Don't ever let him": Irving Azoff interview, April 21, 1998.

280 Azoff filed suit: *Glen [sic] Frey, Randy Meisner, Bernie Leadon, Don Henley, and Don Felder v. Warner Bros. Inc., WB Music Corp., David Geffen, Companion Music, Benchmark Music, et al.,* Case C199570, filed September 8, 1977, in Superior Court of the State of California, County of Los Angeles.

281 It got worse: Gavin Dillard interview, January 25, 1997.

281 Geffen went to a urologist: David Geffen interview, May 22, 1997.

282 On his way to Cedars-Sinai: Sandy Gallin interview, March 11, 1998.

282 "The future is an illusion": David Geffen interview, May 22, 1997.

282 So-called transitional-cell carcinoma: Robert C. Wollman, M.D., interview, May 22, 1998. Wollman is not the Beverly Hills urologist referred to in the text.

282 The experience left him: David Geffen interview, May 22, 1997.

283 Even though the doctor: Paula Weinstein interview, June 13, 1997.

283 Then, seeking forgiveness: Guy McElwaine interview, May 22, 1997.

283 Warren Beatty and Robert Towne: Robert Towne interview, November 20, 1997.

283 Joni Mitchell did not: Mitchell Geffen interview, May 20, 1998.

283 "Let me out": Paula Weinstein interview, June 13, 1997.

283 Soon he was mad at: Ibid.

284 David Geffen's investments: John Duka, "The Ego and the Art of David Geffen," *The New York Times,* October 3, 1982.

284 He spent hour upon hour: Robert Towne interview, November 20, 1997; Ian Schrager interview, October 23, 1997.

285 At one such party: Curt Sanburn interview, August 15, 1997.

287 He invited a journalist: Paul Goldberger, "Architectural Approach: Inventive Spatial Solution for an Apartment in Manhattan," *Architectural Digest,* 1977.

287 Among his first guests: Alan Cohen interview, April 8, 1997.

288 Remaining eager to be distracted: David Geffen interview, August 11, 1997.

CHAPTER 18: THE MISTAKE

289 Klein had quickly achieved: Susan Cheever Cowley, "Soft and Sexy—Designer Calvin Klein," *Newsweek,* May 8, 1979.

289 Geffen's friend Ali MacGraw: Calvin Klein interview, October 2, 1996.

292 Geffen segued to a party: Donna Summer interview, December 19, 1997.

292 "Did you know Ahmet": Ahmet Ertegun interview, May 18, 1997.

292 Paging through *The New York Times:* David Geffen interview, August 11, 1997.

293 Even as he was deep: Ibid.

293 He periodically dated women: Carrie Fisher interview, October 13, 1997.

294 Students reported that Geffen was squiring: Curt Sanburn interview, August 15, 1997.

294 Vacations in Barbados together: David Geffen interview, May 22, 1997.

295 But soon Rubell's party: Haden-Guest, *Last Party,* 131–32.

295 He was shocked: David Geffen interview, May 22, 1997.

295 "I don't like the way": Ibid.; Sandy Gallin interview, March 11, 1998.

296 Geffen called Marlo Thomas: Marlo Thomas interview, July 29, 1997; David Geffen interview, May 22, 1997.

296 Some of Geffen's friends: Fran Lebowitz interview, December 12, 1997.

296 He admitted Geffen: David Geffen interview, May 22, 1997.

296 They were angry at the doctor: Marlo Thomas interview, July 29, 1997.

296 But their anger was likely misdirected: Robert C. Wollman, M.D., interview, May 22, 1998.

297 In the whisper circuit: Ahmet Ertegun interview, December 12, 1996.

297 "I never really felt": Sandy Gallin interview, March 11, 1998.

297 Geffen himself was not: David Geffen interview, May 22, 1997.

297 "We'd known": Goldstein "David Geffen."

298 To many people: Mo Ostin interview, September 12, 1997.

298 Hoping a vacation might help: Lorne Michaels interview, October 24, 1997; Paul Simon interview, June 15, 1998; Gubernick and Newcomb, "The Richest Man in Hollywood."

298 Soon, a proposal came: Alan Cohen interview, April 8, 1997.

299 Hirschfield and Geffen went: Alan Hirschfield interview, February 12, 1999.

299 "What do you think": David Braun interview, May 7, 1997.

299 Mo Ostin kept coming back: David Geffen interview, August 11, 1997; Mo Ostin interview, September 12, 1997.

CHAPTER 19: 1980: BACK TO WORK

301 Geffen was flattered: David Geffen interview, August 11, 1997.

302 Ostin offered Neil Young: Mo Ostin interview, September 12, 1997.

302 Geffen liked the proposal: David Geffen interview, August 11, 1997.

302 Marlo Thomas had introduced: Gerald Schoenfeld interview, August 1, 1997.

303 Gil Segel and Geffen's: Gil Segel interview, October 28, 1997; Lee Phillips interview, June 26, 1997.

303 Just when it looked: David Geffen interview, August 11, 1997.

303 Steve Ross signed off: Elliot Goldman interview, August 4, 1997.

304 Net worth had now grown: Gubernick and Newcomb, "The Richest Man in Hollywood."

304 The movie-production deal: Terry Semel interview, November 3, 1997; Bob Daly interview, September 5, 1997.

304 Even though Geffen was not: Mo Ostin interview, September 12, 1997.

304 At one such fete: Ahmet Ertegun interview, May 18, 1997.

305 40 James Lane: Dannen, *Hit Men,* 346.

305 In Los Angeles, the: David Geffen interview, August 11, 1997.

305 Shortly after the new label: Ibid.; Eddie Rosenblatt interview, June 2, 1997.

306 Ostin told him he: Mo Ostin interview, September 12, 1997.

306 The first A&R: David Geffen interview, August 11, 1997.

307 Geffen did not know what: Stan Cornyn interview, September 13, 1997.

307 Geffen did not like it: Calvin Klein interview, September 29, 1997.

308 He started by checking: David Geffen interview, August 11, 1997.

308 Tommy Mottola, a manager: Tommy Mottola interview, December 11, 1997; Allen Grubman interview, July 30, 1997.

309 Geffen then heard that: Donna Summer interview, December 19, 1997; John Mason interview, June 3, 1997.

309 He eagerly anted up: Duka, "The Ego and the Art of David Geffen."

309 News of the signing: Donna Summer interview, December 19, 1997; David Geffen interview, August 11, 1997.

309 Geffen continued to hound: Bob Daly interview, September 5, 1997; Terry Semel interview, November 3, 1997.

310 The movie had been developed: Robert Towne interview, November 20, 1997.

310 Warner Bros., for its part: Terry Semel interview, November 3, 1997.

310 Towne's new problem was: David Geffen interview, September 4, 1997.

311 Geffen stumbled upon another: Ibid., August 11, 1997.

311 Music-industry executives began banging: Yoko Ono interview, August 14, 1997.

CHAPTER 20: TRAGEDY OUTSIDE THE DAKOTA

313 Geffen was in New York: David Geffen, "A Reminiscence," *Rolling Stone,* January 22, 1981.

313 Ono, dressed in black: Yoko Ono interview, August 14, 1997.

313 She asked Geffen for a slew: Geffen, "A Reminiscence."

316 Geffen got the headlines: Adam Clymer, "Geffen, 3 Others Named as UC Regents," Los Angeles *Herald-Examiner,* September 19, 1980.

317 Donna Summer, for example: Donna Summer interview, December 19, 1997.

318 Geffen lashed out: Paul Grein, "A Slow Winter for Donna Summer," *Los Angeles Times,* January 3, 1981.

318 If Geffen was disappointed: David Geffen interview, August 11, 1997.

319 Critically, it received only: John Rockwell, "Leader of a Rock Group That Helped Define a Generation," *The New York Times,* December 9, 1980.

319 Allen Grubman kept the Hall: Allen Grubman interview, July 30, 1997.

320 Geffen was back in New York: Geffen, "A Reminiscence."

321 Lying next to him: Geffen told this story to Stephen Woolley, producer of *Interview with the Vampire.* Stephen Woolley interview, January 12, 1999.

321 A little after 11:00: Eddie Rosenblatt interview, July 1, 1997; Geffen, "A Reminiscence."

322 Lennon and Ono had left: Les Ledbetter, "John Lennon of Beatles Is Killed; Suspect Held in Shooting at Dakota," *The New York Times,* December 9, 1980.

322 Crowds of fans: Geffen, "A Reminiscence."

323 She complained of weak knees: Yoko Ono interview, August 14, 1997.

323 Wary of appearing exploitative: Kurt Loder, "Lennon Update," *Rolling Stone,* February 5, 1981.

324 Taking his cue from Ono: Steve Pond, "Geffen Boycotts 'Billboard,' " *Rolling Stone,* March 5, 1981.

324 Threatened to ruin him: David Geffen interview, September 4, 1997.

324 Diller changed his mind: Barry Diller interview, September 24, 1997.

324 He next phoned: Alan Hirschfield interview, February 12, 1999.

Sherry Lansing, in an interview on September 27, 1999, said it is "inconceivable " that she said what Hirschfield claims she said.

324 Two days before Christmas: Todd McCarthy, "Towne Resuming 'Personal' after Geffen Shutdown," *Daily Variety,* March 23, 1981; Aljean Harmetz, "$110 Million Suit over 'Personal Best,' " *The New York Times,* April 15, 1982.

324 Though he denied he used coke: Peter Biskind, *Easy Riders, Raging Bulls: How the Sex–Drugs–and–Rock 'N' Roll Generation Saved Holly-wood* (New York: Simon & Schuster, 1998), 396.

324 Towne was considered a notorious: David Geffen interview, September 4, 1996; Terry Semel interview, November 3, 1997.

325 The reality was that: Robert Towne interview, November 20, 1997.

326 Towne suspected that Geffen: Ibid.

326 Geffen moaned constantly: David Geffen interview, August 11, 1997.

327 He invited Eisner to spend time: Bill Gerber interview, August 18, 1997.

327 He needed to get a nose job: John Kalodner interview, August 29, 1997; Steve Antin interview, September 15, 1997.

328 "I'm just a boy": Paul Rosenfield, "David Is Goliath," *Vanity Fair,* March 1991.

328 Geffen became a proponent: Paul Simon interview, June 15, 1998.

CHAPTER 21: BIG DREAMS

329 Geffen's friend Michael Bennett: Bob Avian interview, July 24, 1997; Henry Krieger interview, July 1, 1999.

329 But *Big Dreams* sustained: Ken Mandelbaum, *"A Chorus Line" and the Musicals of Michael Bennett* (New York: St. Martin's Press, 1989), 215–16.

330 Right to turn the musical into a movie: Bob Avian interview, July 24, 1997.

332 Geffen was a hands-off: Ibid.

332 Some opinions he offered: Confidential source.

332 Geffen also offered one: David Geffen interview, July 24, 1997.

332 Weekly interest payments: *Robert Towne v. David Geffen, Geffen Films, Warner Bros., Warner Communications Inc., and Steven Ross,* C407184, filed April 13, 1982, in Supreme Court of California, County of Los Angeles.

332 The bankers at Boston Ventures: Jay Emmett interview, July 15, 1997.

333 Geffen began to tell people: David Geffen interview, September 4, 1997.

333 Geffen and Barry Diller: Barry Diller interview, September 24, 1997.

335 Geffen was panicked: Jay Emmett interview, July 15, 1997.

335 Ross instructed Bob Daly: Bob Daly interview, September 5, 1997; Terry Semel interview, November 3, 1997.

336 He was in the car: Eddie Rosenblatt interview, July 8, 1997.

337 International record-distribution company: David Geffen interview, August 11, 1997.

337 "Fifteen million to seventeen million": Ibid.

337 Grubman knew which of: Allen Grubman interview, July 30, 1997.

337 The deal irritated: David Horowitz interview, April 9, 1997.

338 Geffen fired Moroder: Donna Summer interview, December 19, 1997.

338 He saw clearly what: Tom Freston interview, July 28, 1997.

339 A David Hockney painting: Bob Avian interview, July 24, 1997.

339 "When Broadway history is": Frank Rich, " 'Dreamgirls,' Michael Bennett's New Musical, Opens," *The New York Times,* December 21, 1981.

340 Paul Simon said that CBS: Paul Simon interview, June 15, 1998.

CHAPTER 22: NOW AND FOREVER

343 Placement of the movie's credits: Robert Towne interview, November 20, 1997.

343 *Newsweek* called it "original": Jack Kroll, "Chariots of Desire," *Newsweek,* February 8, 1982.

343 "For what seems like": Joy Gould Boyum, "Gay Guys and Dull Dolls," *The Wall Street Journal,* February 12, 1982.

344 Two months after the movie's opening: *Robert Towne v. David Geffen, Geffen Films, Warner Bros., Warner Communications Inc., and Steven Ross,* C407184, filed April 13, 1982, in Supreme Court of California, County of Los Angeles.

344 "You just didn't love": Robert Towne interview, November 20, 1997.

345 Segel was cheating him: David Berman interview, July 7, 1997.

345 Segel insisted that his fee: Gil Segel interview, October 28, 1997.

345 Geffen said he fired: David Geffen interview, June 12, 1997.

345 But Segel, who had: Gil Segel interview, October 28, 1997.

345 He was never the same: Carole Bayer Sager interview, September 10, 1997.

346 Ironically enough, the script had: Steve Tisch interview, June 11, 1997.

347 He howled with laughter: David Geffen interview, September 4, 1997.

347 "I don't know if my": Steve Tisch interview, June 11, 1997.

347 From the start, Geffen seemed: Paul Brickman interview, July 11, 1997.

348 "I won't make the movie": David Geffen interview, September 4, 1997.

348 Nancy Klopper, the film's: Paul Brickman interview, July 11, 1997.

349 Everyone noticed Tom Cruise: Jon Avnet interview, August 26, 1997.

349 "Do you mind if": Tom Cruise interview, July 21, 1999.

349 Because the producers had already: Jon Avnet interview, August 26, 1997.

350 Geffen smartly recognized that: David Geffen interview, August 11, 1997.

351 This show, the most inexpensive: David Geffen interview, September 4, 1997; Cameron Mackintosh interview, November 19, 1997.

351 *Risky Business* began shooting: Jon Avnet interview, August 26, 1997.

353 Geffen was an extremely: Ibid.; Paul Brickman interview, July 11, 1997.

353 "It's your movie": Paul Brickman interview, July 11, 1997.

353 Before long, it became clear: David Geffen interview, August 11, 1997; Gerald Schoenfeld interview, August 1, 1997; Roger Smith interview, July 23, 1997.

354 Thanks to sales: Duka, "The Ego and the Art of David Geffen."

354 By the time *Cats:* Gerald Schoenfeld interview, August 1, 1997; Duka, "The Ego and the Art of David Geffen."

355 Geffen packaged up a Tiffany: Betty Jacobs interview, December 12, 1997.

355 He took Calvin Klein: Marci Klein interview, November 4, 1997.

355 "Whatever the other failings": Frank Rich, "Theater: Lloyd Webber's 'Cats,' " *The New York Times,* October 8, 1982.

355 The single best investment: David Geffen interview, August 11, 1997.

CHAPTER 23: THE ELEKTRA/ASYLUM FIASCO

357 "Gee, you've made a few": Steven Spielberg interview, November 18, 1998.

358 The news was rushed out: Army Archerd, "Just for Variety," *Daily Variety,* April 29, 1983.

358 Not long after *Risky:* David Geffen interview, September 4, 1997.

359 Brickman reminded Geffen: Paul Brickman interview, July 11, 1997.

359 "All I'm asking you": David Geffen interview, September 4, 1997.

359 Brickman ignored Geffen's orders: Paul Brickman interview, July 11, 1997.

360 Only 38 percent: Don Shewey, "On the Go with David Geffen," *The New York Times Magazine,* July 21, 1985.

360 Eric Eisner could not wait: Paul Brickman interview, July 11, 1997.

360 But Geffen shared Eisner's: David Geffen interview, September 4, 1997.

360 "The movie's not about winning": Paul Brickman interview, July 11, 1997.

360 Avnet implored Geffen: Jon Avnet interview, August 26, 1997.

360 Geffen encouraged Brickman: David Geffen interview, September 4, 1997.

361 Brickman was horrified: Paul Brickman interview, July 11, 1997.

361 Steven Antin was: Steve Antin interview, September 15, 1997.

361 He thought of himself: Steve Antin biography in publicity materials for *The Last American Virgin,* Academy of Motion Picture Arts and Sciences Library, Beverly Hills, California.

361 At the party: Steve Antin interview, September 15, 1997.

364 PolyGram, which had acquired: David Geffen interview, August 11, 1997.

364 Just after the settlement: Donna Summer interview, December 19, 1997.

365 Geffen was plagued by: John Kalodner interview, August 21, 1997.

365 He began plotting to take: David Horowitz interview, April 9, 1997.

368 Los Angeles opening of *Dreamgirls:* Shewey, "On the Go with David Geffen."

368 "You don't want to do": John Kalodner interview, August 29, 1997.

368 "John wants me to sign": Cher interview, April 17, 1997.

369 After Antin demanded they buy: Steve Antin interview, September 15, 1997.

CHAPTER 24: "MUSICALLY UNCHARACTERISTIC"

371 Paul Brickman continued to refuse: Paul Brickman interview, July 11, 1997.

371 "You have made a wonderful": Jon Avnet interview, August 26, 1997. David Geffen, in interview on September 4, 1997, said, "Trust me, I was never crying, never. *He* may have been crying, but I was not crying."

372 Under tremendous pressure: Paul Brickman, July 11, 1997.

374 "I have some ideas": Jon Avnet interview, August 26, 1997.

374 The version with the happy: Shewey, "On the Go with David Geffen."

374 Brickman and Avnet said: Jon Avnet interview, August 26, 1997; Paul Brickman interview, July 11, 1997.

374 Geffen announced instantly: David Geffen interview, September 4, 1997.

374 At a meeting at Warners: Steve Tisch interview, June 11, 1997.

375 Eric Eisner, focusing on one: Jon Avnet interview, August 26, 1997.

375 Paul Brickman, meanwhile, would: Paul Brickman interview, July 11, 1997.

375 *New York Times* critic: Janet Maslin, "Paul Brickman's 'Risky Business,' " *The New York Times,* August 5, 1983.

375 Pauline Kael, writing in: Pauline Kael, *The New Yorker,* September 5, 1983.

375 Some critics, including *New:* David Denby, "Supply-Side Hero," *New York,* August 22, 1983.

376 But even in success: Jon Avnet interview, August 26, 1997; Paul Brickman interview, July 11, 1997.

376 "It's not up to me": David Geffen interview, September 4, 1997.

376 Geffen Pictures pocketed: Lisa Gubernick, "For Me, This Is Tennis," *Forbes,* May 30, 1988.

377 Don Henley was pursuing: Irving Azoff interview, April 21, 1998.

378 Geffen faced a more immediate: Neil Young interview, February 5, 1998; Elliot Roberts interview, November 21, 1996.

379 When it became clear: *The David Geffen Company v. Neil Young,* C474373, filed November 4, 1983, in Superior Court of California, County of Los Angeles.

380 It was apparent to nearly everyone: Eddie Rosenblatt interview, June 2, 1997.

380 Roberts could not believe it: Elliot Roberts interview, November 21, 1996.

380   The lawsuit shocked Neil: Neil Young interview, February 5, 1998.
380   Geffen took Steve Antin: Steve Antin interview, September 15, 1997.
381   Geffen suggested Jimmy Webb: Jimmy Webb interview, September 18, 1997.
381   After lunch, Geffen and Antin: Steve Antin interview, September 15, 1997.
381   On the spot: Dannen, *Hit Men,* 362.
381   But Geffen's relationship with Antin: Steve Antin interview, August 11, 1998.
382   Back in New York: Gene Siskel, "David Geffen's Good Works," *Chicago Tribune,* February 8, 1987.
382   Geffen soon had a bold: Lynda Obst interview, June 30, 1997.
383   He and his wife, Marilyn: Marilyn Katzenberg interview, November 17, 1997.
383   Katzenberg recruited Geffen: Jeffrey Katzenberg interview, September 17, 1997.
384   But he did so: Paul Brickman interview, July 11, 1997; Jon Avnet interview, August 26, 1997.

CHAPTER 25: THE RENEGOTIATION

386   Geffen eventually fixed his eyes: David Geffen interview, August 11, 1997.
386   "Don't leave me": Roger Smith interview, July 23, 1997.
386   Geffen enthusiastically told: Bruck, *Master of the Game,* 204.
388   Geffen explained to Eddie: David Geffen interview, August 11, 1997.
388   Geffen dragged the drama out: Mo Ostin interview, September 12, 1997.
389   Evelyn knew that Mo and David: Evelyn Ostin interview, August 14, 1998.
389   Linda Loddengaard grew incensed: Ibid.
390   Steve Ross knew about: David Geffen interview, August 11, 1997.
390   Made the audacious demand: Gubernick and Newcomb, "The Richest Man in Hollywood."
390   Ross delegated the task: Elliot Goldman interview, August 4, 1997.
391   "Now is the time": Mo Ostin interview, September 12, 1997.
391   Geffen and Neil Young: Neil Young interview, February 5, 1998.
391   A few years later: Elliot Roberts interview, November 21, 1996.
392   For the other two: John Kalodner interview, August 21, 1997.

393 Unlike other label chiefs: Tom Zutaut interview, October 16, 1998; Gary Gersh interview, September 22, 1997.

393 He soon had a brainstorm: David Geffen interview, August 11, 1997.

394 Meanwhile, Alan Hirschfield: Alan Hirschfield interview, February 12, 1999.

395 Geffen suddenly had something: Carrie Fisher interview, October 13, 1997.

395 Geffen realized that Brassel's drug habit: David Geffen interview, October 2, 1997.

395 Geffen snagged an invitation: Howard Rosenman interview, September 17, 1997.

396 "Can you help me": Carrie Fisher interview, October 13, 1997.

396 Geffen and Brassel exchanged gold rings: Several photographs of the period show Geffen and/or Brassel wearing rings, including a *Chicago Tribune* photograph dated February 8, 1987, and other photographs in the author's collection.

396 Geffen even attended: David Geffen interview, August 11, 1997.

396 The critics hated the play: Frank Rich, " 'Social Security,' with Ron Silver and Marlo Thomas," *The New York Times,* April 18, 1986.

397 At the Winter Garden: Rosenfield, "David Is Goliath."

397 But he began to stew: Cameron Mackintosh interview, November 19, 1997.

397 Geffen's friendship with Jacobs: David Geffen interview, August 10, 1997.

CHAPTER 26: *TITANIC*

399 Geffen Pictures was not doing: Gubernick, "For Me, This Is Tennis."

399 He grew angry: Michael Ovitz interview, March 31, 1999.

399 Plans for Geffen's Michael Jackson: Lynda Obst interview, June 30, 1997.

400 He then went on a tirade: Julia Phillips, *You'll Never Eat Lunch in This Town Again* (New York: Random House, 1991), 528.

400 Made for nine million dollars: Frank Oz interview, August 20, 1997.

400 He arranged for his client: Michael Ovitz interview, March 31, 1999.

400 Before sending Frank Oz: David Geffen interview, September 4, 1997.

401   Ashman and Oz looked: Frank Oz interview, August 20, 1997.

401   Geffen took his frustration: John Kalodner interview, August 21, 1997.

401   Scrambling for some kind: Eddie Rosenblatt interview, July 1, 1997.

401   Geffen offered Coury, who was in: Al Coury interview, August 28, 1997.

402   "You know it was a bad": Patrick Goldstein, "Pop Eye: Labeling the Hits and Misses of 1985," *Los Angeles Times,* January 5, 1986.

402   In a repeat: Frank Oz interview, August 20, 1997.

403   Geffen's friendship with Mo Ostin: Mo Ostin interview, October 7, 1997.

404   Geffen's relationships with some: Elton John remarks, Fox Theater concert, Atlanta, February 23, 1999.

404   "AIDS is God's revenge": "Summer Not Saying She's Sorry in Song," *New York,* August 5, 1991; Jeffrey L. Newman, "Carry On," *Frontiers,* May 1, 1998.

404   Geffen went berserk: David Geffen interview, August 11, 1997.

404   Uncertain where to turn: Elliot Goldman interview, August 4, 1997.

405   No love lost: David Geffen interview, August 11, 1997.

405   Ross had grown weary: Elliot Goldman interview, August 4, 1997.

405   Hungry for cash: Gubernick and Newcomb, "The Richest Man in Hollywood."

405   Issuing cost-cutting directives: Tom Zutaut interview, October 16, 1998.

406   Robertson and Geffen had spoken: Robbie Robertson interview, October 24, 1997.

406   Two months later: David Geffen interview, September 4, 1997; Frank Oz interview, August 20, 1997.

407   "It's a disaster!": Frank Oz interview, August 20, 1997.

408   Reports soon leaked: "*Horrors* Reshooting Final Scene," *New York,* September 22, 1986; Martin A. Grove, *Hollywood Reporter,* August 11, 1986.

409   Tom Zutaut was ecstatic: Tom Zutaut interview, October 16, 1998.

411   In the fall of 1986: Jeffrey Katzenberg interview, September 17, 1997; confidential source.

CHAPTER 27: BATYA

413   Geffen's relationship with Bob Brassel: Howard Rosenman interview, September 17, 1997; Joel Schumacher interview, October 8, 1997.

414 Geffen, now forty-three: Bill Gerber interview, August 6, 1998.

414 "This is the best thing": David Geffen interview, September 4, 1997.

414 Geffen's infectious enthusiasm: Jeffrey Katzenberg interview, September 17, 1997.

415 The failure of the picture: David Geffen interview, September 4, 1997.

415 "I'll do it as long": Mel Posner interview, March 31, 1997.

416 Purchased a Range Rover: John Kalodner interview, August 21, 1997.

416 Seventy-five million dollars: Gubernick and Newcomb, "The Richest Man in Hollywood."

417 Geffen decided to take Bob Brassel: Howard Rosenman interview, October 10, 1997.

417 Batya had had cancer: Deena Volovskaya interview, March 17, 1999.

419 Mitchell had stewed: Mitchell Geffen interview, May 6, 1998.

419 "I'm not a fan": Dannen, *Hit Men,* 133–34.

420 Things had been helped somewhat: Ahmet Ertegun interview, May 18, 1997.

420 "Listen, Ahmet": Dannen, *Hit Men,* 134.

420 Zutaut and Kalodner told people: Tom Zutaut interview, October 16, 1998; John Kalodner interview, August 21, 1997.

420 Gersh and Zutaut made fun: John Kalodner interview, August 21, 1997.

420 Gersh and Kalodner complained: Ibid.; Gary Gersh interview, September 22, 1997.

420 Demo tapes for Edie Brickell: Tom Zutaut interview, October 16, 1998.

421 Similarly, John Kalodner: John Kalodner interview, August 21, 1997.

421 But the day before: Cher interview, April 17, 1997.

422 Geffen paid little attention: Tom Zutaut interview, October 16, 1998.

423 "They're certainly never gonna": Al Coury interview, August 28, 1997.

423 Tim Collins, Aerosmith's manager: John Kalodner interview, August 21, 1997.

423 Geffen did not become: Tim Burton interview, December 9, 1997.

424 Sam secretly shuttled Batya: Deena Volovskaya interview, March 17, 1999.

424 A planned skiing vacation: Mitchell Geffen interview, March 17, 1999.

424 But Batya still refused: Deena Volovskaya interview, March 17, 1999.

425 David sat at her bedside: Goldstein, "David Geffen."

425 Although she had fibbed: Deena Volovskaya interview, July 12, 1997.

425 David and Mitchell set about: Mitchell Geffen interview, March 18, 1999.

426 At the funeral: Goldstein, "David Geffen."

426 The group went to: Mitchell Geffen interview, March 18, 1999.

426 At day's end: Sandy Gallin interview, May 25, 1999; Joel Schumacher interview, October 8, 1997.

426 Steve Ross invited him: Mo Ostin interview, October 7, 1997.

427 Geffen Pictures made about: Gubernick, "For Me, This Is Tennis."

427 David went to see Deena: Deena Volovskaya interview, January 11, 1997.

427 When Batya's will was probated: David Geffen remarks, 1996 Los Angeles National Presidential Gala, Green Acres Estate, Beverly Hills, Calif., September 12, 1996, author's notes.

CHAPTER 28: TIME WARNER SURPRISE

429 In May 1988: Tom Zutaut interview, October 16, 1998.

430 Freston, still grateful: Tom Freston interview, July 28, 1997.

430 He soon went back: Tom Zutaut interview, October 16, 1998.

431 In a display of his unmistakable chutzpah: Confidential source.

431 He made his debut: "The Forbes Four Hundred," *Forbes,* October 24, 1988.

431 Richard Rainwater, the Texas money-man: Gubernick and Newcomb, "The Richest Man in Hollywood."

432 Sales of nine million copies: Ibid.

432 Returned from his honeymoon: Gary Gersh interview, September 22, 1997.

433 One was Chrysalis Records: Allen Grubman interview, July 30, 1997.

433 Geffen mulled over the opportunity: Andrea Adelson, "Producer of Pop Music Buys Stake in Chrysalis," *The New York Times,* January 6, 1989.

433 Geffen warned Axl Rose: Tom Zutaut interview, October 16, 1998.

434 His fury was unleashed: Owen Laster interview, October 10, 1996.

435 Fields wrote that Geffen: Bertram Fields, letter to Joni Evans, pub-

lisher, executive vice president, Random House, and to Fredric Dannen, in care of Random House, November 29, 1989.

435 Geffen was soon handed: Dannen, *Hit Men,* 339–40. (This material appears in the paperback edition, published in 1991.)

435 Sandy Gallin, whose firm: Sandy Gallin interview, August 1, 1998.

435 He had not forgotten: David Geffen interview, June 12, 1997.

436 Howard Kaufman, who was running: Irving Azoff interview, April 21, 1998.

436 Geffen hypocritically blasted Azoff: Wm. J. Knoedelseder, Jr., "MCA to Acquire 3 Companies Partly Owned by Azoff," *Los Angeles Times,* May 7, 1986.

436 Time—the magazine, pay-TV: Laura Landro, "Creating a Giant: Time-Warner Merger Will Help Fend Off Tough Global Rivals," *The Wall Street Journal,* March 6, 1989.

436 Only a handful of people: Terry Semel interview, March 24, 1997.

438 Geffen awoke early Saturday: Kathryn Harris, "Time, Warner Reportedly on Verge of Merger," *Los Angeles Times,* March 4, 1989.

438 When reports of Geffen's anger: Terry Semel interview, March 24, 1997.

438 Chrysalis chairman Chris Wright: Allen Grubman interview, July 30, 1997.

440 Geffen called in henchman Eric Eisner: Tom Zutaut interview, October 16, 1998; Al Coury interview, August 28, 1997.

440 Linda Loddengaard was the first: Gary Gersh interview, October 22, 1997.

441 Geffen ordered that the locks: Bryn Bridenthal interview, September 26, 1997.

441 But Eisner encountered trouble: Gary Gersh interview, September 22, 1997.

CHAPTER 29: THE SALE

443 His problem was indeed: David Geffen interview, October 2, 1997; Bill Gerber interview, August 18, 1997.

443 Geffen was still in love: Carrie Fisher interview, October 13, 1997; Howard Rosenman interview, October 9, 1997.

443 Fisher and Geffen spent: Carrie Fisher interview, October 13, 1997.

444 He told a journalist: Scheff, "Playboy Interview."

444 "Being gay is very different": Bernard Weinraub, "David Geffen: Still Hungry," *The New York Times Magazine,* May 2, 1993.

444 David Bombyk: Gloria Slate interview, August 19, 1997.

444 The death that affected Geffen: David Geffen interview, May 22, 1997.

446 Geffen played a key role: Howard Rosenman interview, September 17, 1997.

446 He again started badgering: Michael Ovitz interview, March 31, 1999.

446 In some ways: Confidential source.

447 "Why don't you have": Michael Ovitz interview, March 31, 1999.

447 Hated the film's title: Jon Avnet interview, August 26, 1997.

447 Don Henley insisted: Irving Azoff interview, April 21, 1998.

448 Projected 1989 revenues: Jeffrey Ressner, "Geffen's Coming of Age," *Rolling Stone,* July 27, 1989.

448 The buying spree: Richard L. Hudson and Laura Landro, "Unit of Philips Agrees to Buy Island Records," *The Wall Street Journal,* August 2, 1989; Kevin Goldman, "Philips's Polygram to Announce Pact to Acquire A&M," *The Wall Street Journal,* October 11, 1989.

449 "I don't want this": Allen Grubman interview, July 30, 1997.

449 It was on such trips: Tim Burton interview, December 9, 1997.

450 Geffen cozied up to him: Irving Azoff interview, April 21, 1998.

450 Even though Steve Ross: Elliot Goldman interview, August 4, 1997.

450 Geffen told Morgado and Aboodi: Bob Morgado interview, December 12, 1997.

451 Eisner and Frank Wells were not: Anson, "Geffen Ungloved."

451 Martin Davis thought: Martin Davis interview, June 22, 1998.

451 In early January: Richard Turner, "MCA Agrees to Buy Geffen Records," *The Wall Street Journal,* March 15, 1990.

452 *The Wall Street Journal:* Richard Turner, "Geffen Records Is Said to Draw Several Suitors," *The Wall Street Journal,* January 12, 1990.

452 Southgate told James Fifield: Turner, "MCA Agrees to Acquire Geffen Records."

452 Geffen had gotten his hands on: Paul Brickman interview, July 11, 1997.

452 Meanwhile, the exclusive negotiating: Allen Grubman interview, July 30, 1997.

453 When Steve Ross learned: Bob Morgado interview, December 12, 1997.

453 Allen Grubman continued: Allen Grubman interview, July 30, 1997.

453 With significant issues yet: Richard Turner, "Thorn to Buy Geffen

in Key Change for Record Industry," *The Wall Street Journal,* March 5, 1990.

454 Upon learning that Geffen: Bob Morgado interview, December 12, 1997.

454 Like many of the deals: Richard Turner, "Going Platinum: With All That Cash, and Famous Friends, What's a Guy to Do?" *The Wall Street Journal,* June 18, 1992.

454 Then the real magic: Sid Sheinberg interview, March 5, 1997; Lew Wasserman interview, March 12, 1997.

455 "We're going to make": Gubernick and Newcomb, "The Richest Man in Hollywood."

CHAPTER 30: GOOD FORTUNE

457 Four days later: Turner, "Going Platinum."

458 But the good times: Arthur Liman interview, December 9, 1996.

458 On Tuesday, March 13: Bryn Bridenthal interview, September 26, 1997; Gary Gersh interview, September 22, 1997.

460 "How is this going": Mel Posner interview, March 31, 1997.

461 The next day: Jube Shiver, Jr., and Michael Cieply, "Sources Say MCA to Announce Deal for Geffen Records," *Los Angeles Times,* March 14, 1990.

461 Although Geffen told the press: Gary Gersh interview, September 22, 1997.

461 The news of Gersh's: John Kalodner interview, August 21, 1997; Tom Zutaut interview, October 16, 1998.

462 He was sympathetic: Gary Gersh interview, September 22, 1997.

462 He next wrote several smaller: Bryn Bridenthal interview, September 26, 1997.

462 Al Coury and Mel Posner: Al Coury interview, August 28, 1997; Mel Posner interview, March 31, 1997.

462 Eric Eisner, it turns out: Gary Gersh interview, October 22, 1997.

463 Geffen had long been fascinated: Sandy Gallin interview, August 19, 1999.

463 Joel Silver, the producer: Joel Silver interview, October 2, 1997.

464 He contacted Rose Tarlow: Rose Tarlow interview, February 5, 1998.

465 He recouped three million: Weinraub, "David Geffen: Still Hungry."

466 The publicity Geffen garnered: Michelangelo Signorile interview, August 19, 1999; Michelangelo Signorile, *Queer in America* (New York: Random House, 1993), 301–3.

466 Ready for a fight: Ron Givens, "With a Little Help from Their Friends," *Entertainment Weekly,* April 1990.

466 Michael Musto, a columnist: Michael Musto, "La Dolce Musto," *The Village Voice,* May 1990.

467 Signorile's next column: Michelangelo Signorile, "Gossip Watch," *OutWeek,* May 16, 1990.

467 Geffen convinced Michael Jackson: Dannen, *Hit Men,* 337–38. (This material appears in the paperback edition, published in 1991.)

468 When an article: Laura Landro, "CBS Chief Ready to Phase Out Duties," *The Wall Street Journal,* August 17, 1990.

468 Yetnikoff was convinced: Rosenfield, "David Is Goliath."

468 Geffen also turned on John Branca: Dannen, *Hit Men,* 339. (This material appears in the paperback edition, published in 1991.)

468 Geffen went on a rampage: Prince Rupert Loewenstein interview, August 14, 1997.

468 Meanwhile, Geffen had not: Jon Landau interview, January 21, 1997.

469 Finally, with Sandy Gallin: Sandy Gallin interview, August 1, 1998.

469 On the last Saturday: Rosenfield, "David Is Goliath."

470 Ten days later: Laura Landro and Richard Turner, "Matsushita Explores Purchase of MCA," *The Wall Street Journal,* September 25, 1990.

470 Because of the leak: Peter J. Boyer, "Hollywood's King Cashes Out," *Vanity Fair,* February 1991.

471 To help assuage Matsushita's fears: Michael Ovitz interview, March 31, 1999.

471 Michael Ovitz pocketed: Richard Turner, Laura Landro, and Yumiko Ono, "Move Over, Sony: Matsushita Purchase of MCA Could Help Buyer Break Old Mold," *The Wall Street Journal,* November 26, 1990.

471 Word soon spread through: Bruck, *Master of the Game,* 301.

472 Geffen, meanwhile, was in heaven: Rosenfield, "David Is Goliath."

472 He accepted the offer: Confidential source.

472 Geffen decided that the magazine: Gubernick and Newcomb, "The Richest Man in Hollywood."

472 Although he had lunched: Goldstein, "David Geffen."

472 Courtney Ross, for her part: Steven Spielberg interview, November 18, 1998.

472 Ross had "gotten the best": Roger Smith interview, July 23, 1997.

CHAPTER 31: CALVIN

473　The buzz was that: Joel Silver interview, October 2, 1997.

473　He threatened to sue: David Geffen interview, April 19, 1997.

474　He had even given them: Andre Leon Talley, "L.A. Alfresco," *Vogue,* June 1991.

474　Eisner was unhappy: Joel Silver interview, October 2, 1997.

474　Eisner would leave the company: Goldstein, "David Geffen."

474　The newly christened richest: Sandy Gallin interview, May 25, 1999.

476　At the party: Carrie Fisher interview, November 3, 1997.

476　Geffen bragged: Goldstein, "David Geffen."

477　He became a player: Kirk Varnedoe interview, December 15, 1997.

477　In its first survey: "The Forbes Four Hundred," *Forbes,* October 21, 1991.

478　The album made Geffen feel old: Goldstein, "David Geffen."

478　But Geffen's relationship with Axl: Tom Zutaut interview, October 16, 1998.

478　Madonna, who was not: Guy Oseary interview, September 30, 1997.

478　He second-guessed the wisdom: Weinraub, "David Geffen: Still Hungry."

478　Considered engineering a pregnancy: Carrie Fisher interview, November 3, 1997.

479　He was drawing closer: Rosenfield, "David Is Goliath."

479　John Mendelssohn: Patrick Goldstein interview, May 6, 1997.

479　Finally, Mendelssohn made it simple: Cindy Adams, *New York Post,* November 13, 1991.

479　In 1986, Geffen had gone to Rome: Calvin Klein interview, September 29, 1997.

480　He also helped Klein: Marci Klein interview, November 4, 1997.

480　But in 1991: Calvin Klein interview, October 2, 1996.

480　Geffen learned about the drama: Teri Agins and Jeffrey A. Trachtenberg, "Designer Troubles: Calvin Klein Is Facing a Bind as Magic Touch Appears to Be Slipping," *The Wall Street Journal,* November 22, 1991.

480　Geffen called Klein, who was devastated: Calvin Klein interview, October 2, 1996.

480　Geffen met with Klein and Barry Schwartz: Barry Schwartz interview, June 18, 1998.

481　Helped him hire Richard Martin: Teri Agins, "Shaken by a Series of Business Setbacks, Calvin Klein Inc. Is Redesigning Itself," *The Wall Street Journal,* March 21, 1994.

481   Klein was stunned: Calvin Klein interview, October 2, 1996; Barry Schwartz interview, June 18, 1998.

481   Geffen knew Leon Black: Leon Black interview, June 23, 1998.

482   When the deal was announced: Teri Agins, "David Geffen Buys All Junk-Bond Debt of Calvin Klein Inc.," *The Wall Street Journal,* May 6, 1992.

482   He began to strategize: Barry Schwartz interview, June 18, 1998.

482   After spotting Mark Wahlberg: Weinraub, "David Geffen: Still Hungry."

482   As he sat at home: Ibid.

483   Rahm Emanuel, Clinton's brash: Rahm Emanuel interview, May 26, 1999.

483   "Are you prepared to": Goldstein, "David Geffen."

483   Clinton was hoarse: Rahm Emanuel interview, May 26, 1999.

484   He gave the largest: Steve Tisch interview, June 11, 1997; Jeffrey Katzenberg interview, September 17, 1997.

CHAPTER 32: COMING OUT

485   But the daughter: Sonya Eichler interview, October 6, 1997; Mim Eichler Rivas interview, December 18, 1996.

486   He asked Bryn Bridenthal: Bryn Bridenthal interview, October 10, 1997.

486   "We'll raise four": David Geffen comments, Prime 9 News at Eight, KCAL-TV, November 18, 1992; a spokesperson for AIDS Project Los Angeles said the event raised $3.6 million.

486   He looked down the row: Sonya Eichler interview, October 6, 1997.

486   "The analogy of David": Warren Beatty remarks, APLA Benefit, Universal Amphitheater, Universal City, Calif., November 18, 1992, author's notes.

488   "Thank you": David Geffen remarks, ibid.

489   David Crosby was at home: David Crosby interview, March 16, 1998.

490   Even Michelangelo Signorile: Signorile, *Queer in America,* 365.

490   *The Advocate,* a gay: Brendan Lemon, "David Geffen: Man of the Year," *The Advocate,* December 1992.

490   In late October 1992: Bruck, *Master of the Game,* 334.

490   In mid-December: Weinraub, "David Geffen: Still Hungry."

490   One week later: Bruck, *Master of the Game,* 340–41.

491 Courtney Ross had not invited: Terry Semel interview, March 24, 1999.

491 Others were also upset: Steven Spielberg interview, November 18, 1998.

491 After the funeral: Terry Semel interview, March 24, 1997.

492 "Ours was really a": Goldstein, "David Geffen."

492 "Steve never took": Weinraub, "David Geffen: Still Hungry."

492 Geffen eagerly answered: Alan Citron, "David Geffen Didn't Take the Money and Run," *Los Angeles Times,* March 7, 1993.

492 "No one's asked me": Weinraub, "David Geffen: Still Hungry."

493 Henley was angry: Irving Azoff interview, April 21, 1998; Robin Sloane interview, October 29, 1997.

494 "Fuck you": Eliot, *To the Limit,* 228.

494 Wasted no time in filing: *Geffen Records Inc. v. Don Henley,* Case #BC073696. Filed January 28, 1993, in Superior Court of California, County of Los Angeles.

494 "This time, I'll never": Eliot, *To the Limit,* 239.

494 The reason other record companies: Ibid., 240.

494 "He was seminal": Goodman, *Mansion on the Hill,* 359.

495 Joni Mitchell, whose relationship: Brantley Bardin, "Q&A: Joni Mitchell," *Details,* July 1996.

495 He had given her such: Joe Dolce, "Q&A: David Geffen," in ibid.

495 Eddie Rosenblatt was in Geffen's: Eddie Rosenblatt interview, July 8, 1997.

496 Might win him such acclaim: Weinraub, "David Geffen: Still Hungry."

497 In the beginning: Neil Jordan interview, May 26, 1999.

497 Geffen contacted Cruise: Tom Cruise interview, July 21, 1999; Jennet Conant, "Tom Cruise Bites Back—Vampire or Victim?" *Esquire,* March 1994.

497 Cruise's ideal costar: Neil Jordan interview, May 26, 1999; Bonni Lee interview, July 9, 1997.

498 "Why don't you just": Neil Jordan interview, May 26, 1999.

498 Stephen Woolley, Jordan's: Stephen Woolley interview, January 12, 1999.

CHAPTER 33: FIFTY

499 Geffen was seemingly unfazed: Citron, "David Geffen Didn't Take the Money and Run."

499 The morning after MTV: Tom Freston interview, July 28, 1997.

499 The Katzenbergs invited Barry: Marilyn Katzenberg interview, November 17, 1997.

500 Day-Lewis told Jordan: Stephen Woolley interview, January 12, 1999.

500 He was unperturbed: Bonni Lee interview, July 9, 1997.

500 In New Orleans: Claudia Eller interview, April 9, 1998; Claudia Eller, "Dish," *Daily Variety,* February 9, 1993.

500 But the truth: Claudia Eller, "Dish," *Daily Variety,* February 15, 1993.

502 But the contract negotiations: Bonni Lee interview, July 9, 1997.

502 "It's like casting Huck Finn": Elaine Dutka, *"Interview with the Vampire's* Picky Creator," *Los Angeles Times,* August 22, 1993.

503 Tom Cruise was deeply: Tom Cruise interview, July 21, 1999.

503 "His five o'clock shadow": Richard Corliss, "Betrayal in Beijing," *Time,* October 4, 1993.

503 Planned to be intimately involved: Stephen Woolley interview, January 12, 1999.

505 The culprit, though, was someone: Bonni Lee interview, July 9, 1997.

505 He grew particularly irked: Anson, "Geffen Ungloved."

506 With David Geffen as chairman: Figures supplied by AIDS Project Los Angeles.

506 Leaning toward not renewing: Alan Citron and Judy Brennan, "Is Geffen's Song Coming to an End?" *Los Angeles Times,* July 12, 1994.

506 He was vacationing in Barbados: Scheff, "Playboy Interview."

506 Jimmy Webb, who had: Jimmy Webb interview, September 18, 1997.

506 In fact, Geffen was horrified: Scheff, "Playboy Interview."

507 Lower interest rates: "Calvin Klein Inc.: Firm Buys Back $55 Million of Junk Debt from Geffen," *The Wall Street Journal,* June 17, 1993.

507 Geffen negotiated a sale: Linda Wachner interview, December 10, 1997; "Warnaco Group Is to Pay $64 Million for Rights to Calvin Klein Trademarks," *The Wall Street Journal,* January 19, 1994.

508 Geffen blanched as Katzenberg: Anson, "Geffen Ungloved."

508 Only five days after: Timothy Egan, "Kurt Cobain, Hesitant Poet of 'Grunge Rock,' Dead at 27," *The New York Times,* April 9, 1994.

508 The rock star had visited: Courtney Love interview, December 17, 1997.

509　When the tribute album: Eliot, *To the Limit,* 242.

509　Geffen was in the right: Irving Azoff interview, April 21, 1998.

CHAPTER 34: THE NEW STUDIO

511　Mrs. Clinton telephoned Geffen: Todd Mulzet interview, December 12, 1998.

512　Barbara Walters, meanwhile: Barbara Walters interview, August 4, 1997.

512　Geffen had first noticed Todd: Todd Mulzet interview, December 12, 1998.

513　On the plane: Stephen Stills interview, June 7, 1997.

514　At the White House: Todd Mulzet interview, December 12, 1998.

516　Crosby, Nash, and Stills: David Crosby interview, March 16, 1998.

516　Moments after Geffen: Todd Mulzet interview, December 12, 1998.

517　Word of Katzenberg's dismissal: Steven Spielberg interview, November 18, 1998; Bernard Weinraub and Geraldine Fabrikant, "A Hollywood Recipe: Vision, Wealth, Ego," *The New York Times,* October 16, 1994.

517　"Michael built Hollywood Records": Anson, "Geffen Ungloved."

518　Katzenberg told Geffen he never: David Geffen remarks, Geffen Records going-away party, March 29, 1995, transcript.

518　"What do you think": Weinraub and Fabrikant, "A Hollywood Recipe."

518　Returned to Fire Island: Todd Mulzet interview, December 12, 1998.

520　Geffen was more convinced: Tom Cruise interview, July 21, 1999.

520　When the package arrived: Anne Rice, advertisement purchased in *Daily Variety,* September 23, 1994.

520　Geffen immediately telephoned Tom Cruise: Tom Cruise interview, July 21, 1999.

521　Steven Spielberg could not: Weinraub and Fabrikant, "A Hollywood Recipe."

521　Spielberg began to consider: Richard Turner, "Three Moguls Send a Message to Corporate Hollywood," *The Wall Street Journal,* October 17, 1994.

521　"I'm not good unless": Shewey, "On the Go with David Geffen."

522　"No, I don't want to": David Geffen remarks, Geffen Records going-away party, March 29, 1995, transcript.

522　Swanky Hotel Bel-Air: Mitchell Pacelle and Pauline Yoshihashi,

"Japanese Owner of Hotel Bel-Air Loses Title; Resale Effort is Expected Soon," *The Wall Street Journal,* April 1, 1994.

522 *Forbes* estimated that the: "The Forbes Four Hundred," *Forbes,* October 17, 1994.

523 After four hours: David Geffen remarks, Geffen Records going-away party, March 29, 1995, transcript.

523 The three made plans: Turner, "Three Moguls Send a Message to Corporate Hollywood."

524 A White House state dinner: Jeffrey Katzenberg interview, June 18, 1999.

CHAPTER 35: THE ANNOUNCEMENT

527 Sid Sheinberg was not certain: Weinraub and Fabrikant, "A Hollywood Recipe."

528 The trio agreed: Turner, "Three Moguls Send a Message to Corporate Hollywood."

530 Katzenberg was obsessed: Harry Clein interview, June 3, 1999.

530 Convinced Michael Ovitz had leaked: Jeffrey Katzenberg interview, June 18, 1999.

530 Michael Eisner telephoned: Turner, "Three Moguls Send a Message to Corporate Hollywood."

531 "There's a pretty giant": Jeffrey Katzenberg remarks, Dream Team's press conference, Peninsula Hotel, Beverly Hills, California, October 12, 1994.

532 "Hollywood movie studios": Steven Spielberg remarks, ibid.

532 "I've always been": David Geffen remarks, ibid.

533 The rumor mill: "Careless Whispers: The Anatomy of a Hollywood Rumor," *Details,* February 1996.

533 Mulzet moved to Los Angeles: Todd Mulzet interview, December 12, 1998.

535 "It's the *Lawrence of Arabia*": Bill Higgins, "Creatures of the Night," *Los Angeles Times,* October 11, 1994.

536 ABC ran its profile: Walters, "Geffen Touch."

536 Geffen celebrated with Todd: Todd Mulzet interview, December 12, 1998.

537 The Eagles' tour: Eliot, *To the Limit,* 245.

538 DreamWorks' blueprint: Jeffrey Katzenberg interview, June 18, 1999.

538 Geffen masterminded a deal: Thomas R. King, "Paul Allen to Buy Stake in DreamWorks," *The Wall Street Journal,* March 20, 1995.

539   Todd Mulzet, meanwhile: Todd Mulzet interview, December 12, 1998.

539   Geffen and his two: Richard Corliss, "Hey, Let's Put on a Show! Start Our Own Multimedia Company! Get Investors to Give Us $2 Billion! Prove the Naysayers Wrong!: An Inside Look at the DreamWorks Saga—Act I," *Time,* March 27, 1995.

540   "David, you've inspired me": Mel Posner remarks, Geffen Records going-away party, March 29, 1995, transcript.

540   "I met David in 1970": David Berman remarks, ibid.

540   Jim Walker, the label's: Jim Walker remarks, ibid.

540   Tom Zutaut thanked Geffen: Tom Zutaut remarks, ibid.

540   "I don't give a shit": Bryn Bridenthal remarks, ibid.

540   "Whether I'm making records": John Kalodner remarks, ibid.

540   Eddie Rosenblatt was the last: Eddie Rosenblatt remarks, ibid.

541   "It's a *big* watch!": David Geffen remarks, ibid.

CHAPTER 36: LUNCH WITH MICHAEL OVITZ

544   Geffen himself wrote out: Center for Responsive Politics data, Washington, D.C.

544   Distribution pact with MCA: Thomas R. King, "MCA, Dream-Works Reach Wide-Ranging Distribution Accord," *The Wall Street Journal,* June 14, 1995.

544   Of the three: Edgar Bronfman interview, October 9, 1997.

548   He decided his strategy: Ibid.; Helene Hahn interview, February 10, 1998.

548   "David, you are a fair": Edgar Bronfman interview, October 9, 1997.

549   The company agreed to pay: "DreamWorks, Virgin Settle with Sony Corp. to Sign U.K. Pop Star," *The Wall Street Journal,* June 27, 1995.

550   Ostin sat down: Mo Ostin interview, September 12, 1997.

551   The anchor tenants: Thomas R. King, "DreamWorks to Build Its Dream Studio Amid $6 Billion Project in Los Angeles," *The Wall Street Journal,* December 14, 1995.

552   "It's a mark of my": David Geffen interview, May 22, 1997.

553   In 1995, the Forbes: "The Forbes Four Hundred," *Forbes,* October 16, 1995.

553   The following year: "The Forbes Four Hundred," *Forbes,* October 14, 1996.

553   Andy Spahn, who ran: Andy Spahn interview, April 3, 1997.

554   For his first act: Michael Ovitz interview, March 31, 1999.

554 Katzenberg suggested that he: Jeffrey Katzenberg interview, June 18, 1999.

555 Eisner changed his mind: Michael Ovitz interview, March 31, 1999.

555 Frustrated, Geffen then: Jeffrey Katzenberg interview, June 18, 1999.

555 But the talk led nowhere: Thomas R. King, "Home of 'Aladdin' and 'Lion King' Is Sued," *The Wall Street Journal,* April 10, 1996.

555 "Apparently Don Ohlmeyer thinks": James Warren, "Ovitz's Big-Time Image Cut Down to Size," *Chicago Tribune,* November 15, 1996.

555 Ovitz was hurt: Barry Diller interview, May 5, 1999.

556 Ovitz was aghast: Michael Ovitz interview, March 31, 1999.

556 "Are you threatening me": Barry Diller interview, May 5, 1999.

CHAPTER 37: THE LEATHER CHAIR

559 DreamWorks was off to a slow: Ron Grover, "Plenty of Dreams, Not Enough Works?" *BusinessWeek,* July 22, 1996.

560 He was the key: Jeffrey Seller interview, July 18, 1999.

560 In the summer of 1996: Sandy Gallin interview, May 25, 1999.

562 "How important can that": Carole Bayer Sager interview, September 10, 1997.

563 Strong as a saint: Fran Lebowitz interview, December 12, 1997.

563 Like so many of Geffen's: Sue Mengers interview, May 2, 1997.

564 Geffen's relationship with Jordan: Neil Jordan interview, May 26, 1999.

564 In the summer of 1996: Martin Peretz interview, August 4, 1997.

566 "To be able to live": David Geffen remarks, 1996 Los Angeles National Presidential Gala, Green Acres Estate, Beverly Hills, Calif., September 12, 1996, author's notes.

563 "Thank you, David Geffen": Bill Clinton remarks, ibid.

566 Geffen's modern-art collection: Kirk Varnedoe interview, December 15, 1997.

566 Geffen was there to help: Sue Mengers interview, May 2, 1997.

569 The most admirable thing: Fran Lebowitz interview, December 12, 1997.

CHAPTER 38: ANALYSIS (AGAIN)

571 "The only thing David seems": Barbara Walters remarks, GMHC Benefit, Carnegie Hall, New York, January 22, 1997, author's notes.

572 "People tried to talk Geffen": Steve Martin remarks, ibid.

572 Hillary Clinton opened her remarks: Hillary Clinton remarks, ibid.

572 GMHC's ambitious target: Andy Spahn interview, June 3, 1999.

573 Felix Cavaliere, a member: David Geffen interview, April 9, 1997.

573 Go into business together as DaveStar: Ray Stark interview, May 21, 1997.

574 She underwent quadruple-bypass: Liz Smith, *Los Angeles Times,* November 26, 1997.

574 She loved telling the story: Sue Mengers interview, May 2, 1997.

575 His fortune now stretched: "The Forbes Four Hundred," *Forbes,* October 1997.

575 While Geffen was in: Mo Ostin interview, October 7, 1997.

575 "I've been working on myself": Goldstein, "David Geffen."

575 What's more, the company's plan: Bruce Orwall, "Bad Dream: Spielberg & Co. Get Tangled in Woes of an L.A. Developer," *The Wall Street Journal,* March 10, 1997.

576 A nasty dispute with NBC: Jeffrey Katzenberg interview, June 18, 1999.

576 He was also the key: Steven Spielberg interview, November 18, 1998.

577 One night, Joni Mitchell: David Geffen interview, October 4, 1997.

577 Geffen persuaded Steve Ross's widow: Terry Semel interview, March 24, 1997.

577 The month Geffen moved: Sandy Gallin interview, May 25, 1999.

577 Having arranged to have dinner: Barry Diller interview, May 5, 1999.

578 Asked Geffen for guidance: Bryn Bridenthal interview, April 15, 1998.

578 Tabloids had a field day: Brendan Bourne, Robin Gregg, and Tracy Connor, " 'Lewd' George Busted in Boys' Room," *New York Post,* April 9, 1998.

578 Geffen called Maria Shriver: Bryn Bridenthal interview, April 15, 1998.

578 Even a modestly successful: Ron Grover, "Will This Be Dream-Works' Dream Summer?" *BusinessWeek,* July 13, 1998.

578 "We would all rather die": John Seabrook, "The Many Lives of David Geffen," *The New Yorker,* February 23 and March 2, 1998.

579 Paul Allen now agreed: Bruce Orwall, "Allen to Increase Stake in DreamWorks to Become Firm's Biggest Shareholder," *The Wall Street Journal,* July 8, 1998.

579 In January 1999: Robert Hilburn, Geoff Boucher, and Chuck Philips, "A&M Records Closes; Geffen Lays Off 110," *Los Angeles Times,* January 22, 1999.

CHAPTER 39: CELEBRATION CHAIRMAN

581 The salary demands: Bill Mechanic interview, July 1, 1999.

582 Spielberg was serious: Tom Cruise interview, July 21, 1999.

584 The day before the House: Joel Schumacher interview, December 18, 1998.

584 "I'm sure it's been": Melinda Henneberger, "Words of Commitment, Hints of Anger," *The New York Times,* August 19, 1998.

584 Complicating the studio's problems: Bruce Orwall, "DreamWorks Ends Its Plan to Build Playa Vista Studio," *The Wall Street Journal,* July 2, 1999.

586 "It's the perfect definition": Bruce Orwall, "Denouement in the Clash of Hollywood Titans," *The Wall Street Journal,* July 8, 1999.

587 Edgar Bronfman noted: Edgar Bronfman interview, October 9, 1997.

587 "What's the difference": Sue Mengers interview, May 2, 1997.

587 Pessimistic about the stock: "The Forbes Four Hundred," *Forbes,* October 12, 1998, and *Forbes,* October 11, 1999.

587 He continued to financially: Mitchell Geffen interview, May 6, 1998.

588 Geffen made no secret: Nikki Finke, "Agent Provocateur," *New York,* September 28, 1998.

588 When *Premiere* magazine called: David Geffen interview, October 2, 1997.

588 "He tells me how stupid": Cher interview, April 17, 1997.

590 "I once asked Ahmet": David Geffen remarks, UJA Federation Benefit Honoring Ahmet Ertegun, Pier 60, New York, October 15, 1998, author's notes.

INDEX

Page numbers in italics refer to illustrations.

ABOUT THE AUTHOR

TOM KING has been a reporter at *The Wall Street Journal* since 1989 and has reported on the entertainment industry from the paper's Los Angeles bureau since 1991.

ABOUT THE TYPE

This book was set in Bembo, a typeface based on an old-style Roman face that was used for Cardinal Bembo's tract *De Aetna* in 1495. Bembo was cut by Francisco Griffo in the early sixteenth century. The Lanston Monotype Company of Philadelphia brought the well-proportioned letterforms of Bembo to the United States in the 1930s.